Travelling the Turf

Artist: **Heather St Clair Davis DOWN TO THE START** *Courtesy of:* **Frost & Reed**

KENSINGTON WEST PRODUCTIONS

HEXHAM ENGLAND

Kensington West Productions Ltd,
5 Cattle Market, Hexham,
Northumberland NE46 1NJ
Tel: (01434) 609933 Fax: (01434) 600066/600422
e mail: kwp@kensingtonwest.demon.co.uk
web site: www.kensingtonwest.demon.co.uk
or visit: www.amazon.co.uk

Editor
Julian West

Assistant Editor
Barry Roxburgh

Consultant Editors
Helen Parker, Nicola Clements,
Mark Scandle

Design & Production
Diane Ridley

Cartography
Rosemary Coates

Origination
Pre Press,
Hong Kong

Printing
Liang Yu Printing Factory,
Hong Kong

With Special thanks to:
NR Design

Front cover
Artist: Peter Curling, FROSTY MORNING
Courtesy of: Rosenstiel's

Back cover
Artist: Peter Smith, CREE LODGE STRING
Courtesy of: Frost & Reed

Artist: Roy Miller, CAP & WHIP
Courtesy of: The Artist

Artist: Philip Toon, FRANKIE
Courtesy of: The Artist

Artist: **Terence Gilbert ROYAL ASCOT**
Courtesy of: **The Artist**

ROYAL ASCOT

First Day

OFFICIAL RACECARD £1.50

Acknowledgements

It is nigh on impossible to thank the many people who have helped with the production of Travelling the Turf. The idea for the book is now fifteen years old and it is difficult to believe that it has now reached its fourteenth edition. I would, however, like to mention a few people who have been particularly helpful.

I am grateful to the many racecourse managers and their staff for all their kindness and help. By and large, the management of racecourses has come on spectacularly and we offer all involved our sincere good wishes. We are especially grateful to those who have helped us from abroad by sending in information and details without whose help much of our research would have been impossible. I would like to thank Betty O'Connell and all the Irish Horseracing Board who have helped us to improve the Irish section this year.

I would also like to thank Sir Michael Stoute for his kind Foreword. Michael is an outstanding ambassador for the sport and long may he continue to train with such brilliance.

There are many contributors to a book of this kind and I would warmly thank Rosemary Coates for her excellent maps. The exceptional array of fine art included in Travelling The Turf has become a hallmark of the title and I am very grateful to the many artists who have so kindly agreed to have their work reproduced. As ever the copyright is retained by the artist. Please contact us if you require any further information on the artists or indeed the art appearing in this edition and we will do our utmost to assist.

I am also indebted to numerous hoteliers for assisting us with the compilation of our local favourites. We wish them every success. Long may they prosper!

I am also grateful to the British Horseracing Board for allowing us to use the racing calendar within the pages of Travelling the Turf. It is an invaluable document and of vital help to a book of this nature. They are well organised in their race planning and we are extremely grateful. I am also most grateful to John Paine of Racecourse Communications Ltd for permitting the use of the 'Under Starters Orders' article and to Tim Darby for his help with 'Owning a Racehorse'. Hopefully this section will be of both interest and assistance to those lucky enough to be contemplating a purchase.

I would like to thank the Tote and Wetherbys for their assistance in sponsoring the book. Both companies play significant roles in the industry and we wish them well as the millennium draws to its close. I am also grateful to Barry Roxburgh for his hard work in editing this years material.

I would also like to thank my fellow Directors and Shareholders for their support and acknowledge the hard work of my colleagues at Kensington West Productions.

Finally, I would like to thank my wife, Janet, and our family for their support. Without them Travelling The Turf would remain a non starter.

All that remains in this edition, is for me to wish you well, on and off the turf.

For Mowël McGraws, The Fry, The Slug and Boz

Contents

Artist: **Kristine Nason HEAD STUDIES OF ROYAL ATHLETE** *Courtesy of:* **The Artist**

*I*n *the exciting world of racing it's difficult going back 15 minutes never mind 15 years: jockeys, trainers, owners and punters always look forward hopefully to the next race after celebrating or commiserating over the result of the last. But here is Travelling The Turf still going strong after what most jockeys would regard as a lifetime's career.*

When American champion jockey Gary Stevens came to Britain this year he said it was because it was boring going left-handed around a flat oval in the States. Well, if nothing else, racing is not and never should be boring. We all like to search out new pastures for punting pleasure and this is the book that helps you do just that. Racing might have its serious concerns about finances and the quality of horses running, but let's not forget that above all it should be fun.

Whether it's Fontwell or Flemington Park, Worcester or Woodbine, wherever you go racing in the world you can count on Travelling the Turf to go the distance with up to date information that will help you maximise the pleasure of a day at the races. I look forward to reading it for the next fifteen years and I hope you will too.

John Francome

Artist: **Hubert De Watrigant** *ATTITUDES Courtesy of:* **Osborne Studio Gallery**

Over the past fifteen years Travelling the Turf has been privileged to have some of racing's most distinguished personalities contribute a Foreword to each edition. People such as Brough Scott, Lady Tavistock, Jonjo O'Neill, Peter Scudamore, Dick Hern, Cath Walwyn, Lester Piggott, Lord Zetland, Peter O'Sullevan, Robert Sangster, Frankie Dettori, Sir Michael Stoute and this year John Francome, are all passionate about racing and have expressed that passion through these pages.

For while racing will always be about horses and winning and losing, in Britain it's also about the fellowship that can be shared in the whole spangled variety of people and places and tracks unique to this bow-legged Isle.

Brough Scott 1987

Loving racing and everything to do with it as I do, the book is naturally a great joy to me, but even more important is that it transcends just us racing folk and is a really useful guide for everyone.

Lady Tavistock 1988

A non-drinking, ex-jockey I may not personally be able to recommend the Ruddles or the Tetley bitter, or even the Sancerre or Sauvignon, but no-one enjoys more the camaraderie and atmosphere of a good old English pub, restaurant or hotel.

Jonjo O'Neill 1989

I must admit that I only recently came across Travelling the Turf but already I have found it invaluable and wonder how I managed without it before.

Peter Scudamore 1990

Where else could you find out how to get to every meeting in the country, what it's like when you get there and where to have dinner and stay the night before, or afterwards?

Dick Hern 1991

The British racing public appreciate the good fortune of having racecourses that are so individual in character. Travelling the Turf reflects this and caters for those who genuinely like horses.

Cath Walwyn 1992

This book is beautifully compiled and produced, and makes a welcome addition to any racing library. I am sure it will have a wide appeal and could well encourage many to go racing for the first time.

Lester Piggott 1993

During the next few years the customer will once again become king on our racecourses. Families will be catered for in a more modern and welcoming way and many more people, particularly young people, will discover that a day at the races with added entertainment thrown in can be as fine a way of spending their time as any other.

Lord Zetland 1994

Hotels and restaurants are as subject to variance in form as any racehorse - a factor comprehensively reflected in this review of establishments local to the racecourses of Great Britain and Ireland. While a further feature is a detailed appraisal of the racecourses themselves. Several, happily, showing improved form.

Peter O'Sullevan 1995

The pleasure the sport brings is to be measured not only in the roar of the packed stands at Cheltenham and Ascot, but also in the more intimate surroundings of smaller courses such as Kelso and Fontwell.

Robert Sangster 1996

One of the outstanding features of British racing that keeps coming home to me during my travels around the world is that every single course in the country is so different in every way. Each track has its own atmosphere and all racing fans enjoy the different benefits to be found at each venue.

Frankie Dettori 1997

Travelling the Turf has become an integral part of the British racing scene. British racecourses have become much more 'customer friendly' recently and Travelling the Turf's annual appraisal is certainly a great incentive to their continuing improvement.

Sir Michael Stoute 1998

Fifteen years is within recent memory for most people and yet looking back to the very first edition of Travelling the Turf in 1985 it is really quite amazing how much has changed in the world of racing and racecourses since then. One simple and basic fact stands out - despite the late '80s boom turning to bust for the first half of the next decade, taking with it a huge slice of corporate sponsorship, all 59 of Britain's racecourses have managed not only to survive, but to positively thrive with new innovations and facilities for the punting public.

Artist: **Terence Gilbert RACING IMPRESSION**
Courtesy of: **The Artist**

During the same time we have heard constant tales of woe amongst those responsible for the management of horse racing, particularly on the financial front. Yet, when you think of how many high street shops and banks have closed during the same time, what other industry has managed to pull through with all of its plant intact? There have also been some incredible steps forward. Sunday racing was given no chance in the late 1980s due to various government legislation, now it is the norm. Sponsorship is prevalent with the Classics fully sponsored. People cringed when we heard of the Ever Ready Derby, but let's face it, if this had not won serious sponsorship then the race itself may have suffered more than it has - now, I am thankful to be able to say that it is on the way back. I do still feel that the event needs to be made into an even bigger spectacle, taking on the sporting events with which it will inevitably have to compete.

For many, however, it is not the high profile racecourses that count, but the smaller local track that they might attend from time to time. It's incredible how these racecourses have, in the main improved, but I still feel that many racecourses have missed a trick when it comes to local marketing initiatives and from my own experience it is categoric that few racecourses have a genuinely creative sales and marketing department in situ. Far worse, however, the industry itself has almost nothing to offer - a sport as huge as this should take a bigger lead in promoting itself nationally, not just locally. Tax-free betting, free entertainment for children and a cracking day out - who but the real enthusiast know that much fun is on offer not as the exception, but as the rule.

The bookies moan and groan about margins and profits, but go into any of the major chains high street shops and they bear little resemblance to those of a decade and a half ago. Sit down, watch the big screen and have a cup of coffee from the snack bar. If Britain moves any closer to the continent in attitude if not euro, soon you might be able to order a vin ordinaire and have it delivered to your table with your betting slip!

Some people say that British racing must look to the example of racecourses in other countries, and in some aspects of accessibility, price and comfort, they are right. But at the same time let us not forget that major racecourses in some of those same countries such as France and the United States have been forced to close during the past decade causing a permanent loss to racing's diversity there.

British Racecourses which get their formula right and offer an attractive package to the public have few problems today. In its own modest way, Travelling the Turf has spent the past 10 years encouraging excellence in racecourse management by presenting an award to the "Racecourse of the Year". In 1997 it was our great pleasure to present the award to York, which in the admirable and capable hands of John Smith has gone from strength to strength in offering some of the best value-for-money facilities around; in 1999 this shining example to all racecourses was rewarded with the largest crowd assembled on the Knavesmire since 1945 to witness Achilles beating Siege in a thrilling finish in the John Smith's Cup; formerly known as the Magnet Cup, it is the longest sponsored flat race in Britain. One day later the rewards of Sunday racing were brought home at Haydock when a near record 15,000 people turned out under bright sunshine for the Sir Alex Ferguson raceday. The fact that almost all the players of the three-cup winning champions Manchester United football team were there obviously helped, but well done Haydock for promoting and staging a family day out that many will remember. It's small wonder that Haydock was named Travelling the Turf's Racecourse of the Year for 1998 and became the first course to regain the award in the millennium year with its continued excellence after their impressive refurbishment programme.

Artist: **David Trundley WARREN HILL**
Courtesy of: **The Artist**

As ever, money is the root of many problems; or if you are an optimist, the seed of all opportunity. Looking ahead, British racing will get the opportunity of a lifetime in 2002 when the current contract of SIS to provide live pictures of race meetings to betting shops expires. Look at what has happened to other sports such as football, rugby and cricket in just the past few years and you don't need a crystal ball to foresee that major changes and prospects are in the offing.

The industry and the powers that be might squabble over the Levy Board's grant to racing, but this will pall into insignificance if racing manages to capitalise on just how much the television rights to its product are really worth. There are some smart people out there now who know this and are buying up racecourses - not to close down and sell them off for houses as was the threatened practice of the 80s housing boom - but who have determined that many racecourses with their valuable fixture lists will be worth much more money than people realise

Artist: **Klaus Philipp AFTER THE RACE**
Courtesy of: **The Artist**

for their ownership of sporting rights the value of which can be maximised through the sale of television airtime and live picture feeds. Channel 4 recently paid Cheltenham handsomely to cover its fixtures and this could just represent the beginning of a potentially profitable bidding war between Sky, Channel 4 and a newly sports-invigorated BBC that pledges to claw back many sports fixtures which it has lost under a seemingly indifferent previous administration. This is in addition to the rights that can soon be negotiated with SIS and the bookmakers. It is absolutely essential that the powers that be do not make a mess of this. Ownership of the product is absolutely key and rest assured the opportunity of the racecourses to be in a genuinely stronger position is not one that comes regularly. The punter now expects televised coverage in the betting shops, whereas five years ago, they did not. Live sport is now the norm, not the exception and this is the time to re-sell the racing product to the betting fraternity, re-negotiate a fair percentage for the product and then put together a formula which works for all. Take a higher percentage than is currently taken, and then when turnover exceeds a given amount, have a bonus float which is split equitably between all - you may just find that you get the industry working as one not as various, fragmented groupings.

Money and television rights apart, the fact is that racing represents much better value to those going racing than ever before. Looking back over the past 15 years, admission charges for all enclosures have gone up but patrons of all enclosures get a lot more for their money than ever before. York and Haydock are just two examples of the many courses that have made continuing improvements to their stands, catering and general facilities. Similarly you can't compare Newcastle, Hexham and Brighton to what they were like a decade and a half ago. Physical improvements have also been joined by a new attitude to the racegoer: a warm welcome and friendliness are the order of today's racing, not the exception. Visitors to Ascot will no doubt heartily agree!

A quick review of admission charges over the past fifteen years shows that annual membership and admission to all enclosures have just about doubled over the period, which represents less than the compounded rate of inflation since 1985. And when you consider what today's racegoer gets for his or her money, the value for money scale is way up. At Newcastle's Gosforth Park racecourse in 1999 it costs £14 for admission to the members, £9 for Tattersalls and £4 for the Silver Ring - all of which boast outstanding new facilities. In 1986, the same prices were £8, £5 and £2. When you consider that attending a Newcastle football match (if you can get a ticket) at St James Park now costs about £29 compared with £8 fifteen years ago or that the price of what some would claim is now inferior beer has doubled to £2, then the value for money argument seems obvious. Furthermore, if you happen to have children they are far more often than not allowed in free and there are very few sports that offer this. What's more, the facilities for families and children have improved tremendously.

Getting in to Ascot Heath for the Royal Meeting in 1986 for 50 pence was probably one of the bargains of the century, but at the same time today, you can still attend York's Ebor Meeting for a mere £3 in the Course Enclosure or the Cheltenham Festival for £10 in the Courage Enclosure. Some people may point to admission charges for racing in other countries and argue that British racing is overpriced and therefore inaccessible to many. But it you look more closely at courses in North America or France, for example, you will find that low

(or in some cases - no) admission charges alone do not pull in the crowds. Go to an ordinary fixture at Woodbine or Longchamp and you will find yourself rattling around great canyons of grandstands virtually alone. Giving away the product is more likely a sign of desperation rather than success. Most people don't mind paying for an exciting, well turned out product.

But the past and present are only prologue to the future. Where will racing be going in the next fifteen years? Clearly there are no easy answers to this monster of a question. Travelling the Turf conducted a survey of all 59 British racecourses to find out what the people on the front lines of running them think what they and the powers that be should be doing. We also asked some of the leading participants in the game - from scribes to trainers - what they thought as well.

As you might expect, a wide rang of opinion emerged, but some common themes came through pretty strongly. Prime among these were the two 'B's - Betting and Bureaucracy. Betting, if not the root of all evil to some, was certainly not contributing its fair share to maintaining the standard of the product. Bureaucracy, definitely the root of all evil to the majority, was clearly running rampant and making everyone's life a misery.

Artist: **Jay Kirkman JOCKEY IN GOLD**
Courtesy of: **Rosenstiel's**

The government's assistance was often invoked on the question of a return from betting, and its sanity when it came to bureaucracy. The trouble seems to be that amongst the management of racecourses, the BHB is not very popular at the moment: on the bureaucracy front it is seen as part of the problem, not the solution, and when it comes to betting, reasonably powerless. In managing the fixture list, it has actually caused a major and unacceptable divide in the sport.

On a more positive note, racecourses believe that they are getting the formula of presenting an attractive product to the public right at last and this should secure their future into the Millennium. The majority of courses that responded were justifiably proud of the improvements either planned or already made to their facilities. An unprecedented number of new stands have been built during the past few years, not the least of which will be the Newmarket complex when completed next year. Equally important though is the new 'customer friendly' approach to racegoers.

Artist: **Alison Wilson THE LIMEKILNS**
Courtesy of: **The Artist**

Some sample comments:

Good quality racing and family entertainment are the key things.

Considerable investment in improving and upgrading the facilities provides us with a brighter future than ever.

We strive to combine quality racing, a warm Yorkshire welcome, superb facilities and a great atmosphere.

We promote the sport to various target groups through themed meetings such as Newcomers Day, Ladies Day and Family Day.

We have achieved 100 per cent sponsorship of all races at the course.

We have moved from being a bit run down to becoming the best small racecourse in the UK with our new £1 million development.

We now play a vital role in Scotland's leisure industry.

We have invested extensively in terms of both finance and personnel and now have the basis on which to build a potentially useful business, from both a commercial and community viewpoint.

We care about all our patrons no matter which ring they attend and aim to give them a great day out.

Our valued team are keen to help provide a quality and efficient service with exceptional value for money.

We are constantly improving and upgrading the racecourse and our young, innovative and flexible team have lots of new ideas and total commitment.

We are Britain's finest country racecourse offering unrivalled customer service and competitive prices.

With a £4 million investment in the new stand we are setting the standard for the next Millennium.

Artist: **Jay Kirkman JOCKEY IN BLUE**
Courtesy of: **Rosenstiel's**

So, where they have the power to make a difference, racecourses feel that they are doing their bit. But what do other people in the industry think could be done to improve racing.

1. What do you feel has been the best change for the good of racing to have taken place in the last 15 years?

2. What in racing do you wish had been caried out differently over the last 15 years?

3. What would you most want to happen in the racing world in the next five years?

Sir Peter O'Sullevan

1. Awareness of the need to inhibit excessive use of the whip.
2. Implementation of guidelines in respect of whip abuse.
3. Sublimation of sectional interest in favour of the interests of the sport.

Mr Peter Jones

1. Big screens on racecourses.
2. SIS should have been developed/kept for the benefit of racing.
3. Payment for racing by the off course bookmakers to be linked to supply of pictures.

Mr Peter Savill

1. Sunday racing.
2. The SIS negotiation.
3. An additional £105 million to come into racing.

Artist: **John Atkins UPHILL WORK**
Courtesy of: **The Artist**

Mr David Nicholson

1. Making sure jockeys use the whip correctly.
2. To get rid of the bookmakers. Unfortunately this seems impossible!
3. Get the prize money right for National Hunt racing, i.e. more money for lower grade races with an emphasis on chases.

Mr Kim Bailey

1. Sponsorship and reclaiming VAT.
2. Race planning.
3. Vast improvement in prize money.

Mr John Dunlop

1. The increased influence of the TOTE.
2. The formation of the BHB
3. Agreement between racing's various factions.

Mr Josh Gifford

1. All the improvements as regards making it safer - the removal of concrete posts, plastic running rails and wings, better helmets and better medical cover.
2. I still wish that flu vaccination had not been made compulsory.
3. Anything that can improve enjoyment, safety and accessibility of racing and NO more racecourses to be closed.

Mr Jack Berry

1. The introduction of Syndicate and Corporate entertaining, I feel has been the best change for the good of racing.
2. I wish the relevant authorities had never abolished apprenticeships.
3. I hope that during the next five years, we have got better prize money in the lower class races, as in that particular department, it is worse than it was nine years ago. I also think it would be a better system for people to claim horses, out of claimers, before the race and not after it.

Mr Ian Balding

1. The formation of the BHB.
2. Racings relationship with the Bookmakers.
3. The Tote to be owned and run by RACING plc (or BHB).

Mr Tommy Stack

1. Plastic rails.
2. Stewards getting too severe on whip rules.
3. Raise prize money in lower class races.

Artist: **Alison Wilson CANTERING DOWN**
Courtesy of: **The Artist**

Mr David Roe

1. The dramatic improvement of facilities at certain racecourses.
2. The sport remaining a sport and not a money machine primarily for the benefit of gambling, too many poor quality races.
3. The money generated being more evenly spread throughout the whole industry - staff, owners, courses, training for all, equine charities, etc.

Mr Graham Rock

1. Establishment of BHB.
2. Racing should have set up/owned SIS.
3. Deregulation to allow pool betting (via Tote) in pubs and clubs.

Mr Richard Pitman

1. Introduction of daily racing televised on The Racing Channel, 7 hours per day, 7 days a week. The punter and pro have access now to visual form which tells so much more than written form.
2. Introduction of All Weather racing should have included a Grade One course to elevate the concept from its current level.
3. Current hurdles abolished in favour of Southwell's version which resemble small fences - horses adopt bad jumping habits from our current obstacles. Also, Haydock Park's open ditch in front of stands replaced with a plain fence to shorten the run in and make chases much more exciting!

Mr Marcus Armytage

1. The redevelopment of Cheltenham and Aintree resulting in .wonderful. 'festivals'. Improved ground-management, plastic rails.
2. (a) I wish bookmakers had been stood up to 15 years ago not just when P. Savill arrived.
   (b) The winners enclosure at Kempton! It's terrible.
   (c) Too much racing on occasions.
3. The 'Big' bookmakers to put more back into racing than they have done in the past, either through a big increase in sponsoring or through the levy.

Lord Oaksey

1. Various safety measures to benefit jockeys. Plastic rails now almost universal, much improved crash helmets, back pads. Stricter and longer suspensions after concussion.
2. I would like the Levy Board's ratio of prize money assistance as between flat and jumping at present 60-40 in favour of the flat - at least to be 50-50 and, better still, to be reversed! More top 3 year olds kept in training for one, better still, two seasons. Nijinsky vs. Mill Reef and Brigadier Gerrard?
3. A complete change in attitude to, and use of, the whip. Hitting a horse should be the very last resort - regarded as an unstylish, unfashionable and undesirable part of jockeyship.

Mr John Francome

1. Tighter controls on use of whip.
2. SIS wholly owned by racing and not 40% bookmakers.
3. BHB to take control of SIS in 2002 and restrict T.V. coverage of racing to Tote shops only.

Mr Frankie Dettori

1. Sponsorship.
2. For the Jockey Club to find "one" only leader. (Strong!)
3. To centralise racing more.

Mr Tony McCoy

1. The safety railing at all racecourses and the improved medical staff - excellent.
2. I'm very happy with the industry that has been so good to me.
3. Personally - to win a "Grand National".

Mr Richard Dunwoody

1. On-course medical facilities (ie. paramedics at all meetings) have improved enormously.
2. Jockey sponsorship - introduction of which has taken 10 years. The attitude of BHB and some owners to this has been incredibly dated!
3. To move forward with other successful sports racing will have to capitalise on its major events. In some way create a premier league.

*Artist: **Refna Hamey** RICHARD DUNWOODY*
*Courtesy of: **The Artist***

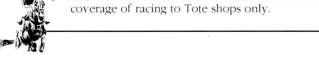

Mr Tony Dobbin

1. Doing away with All Weather jump racing,Jockeys sponsorship.
2. Fixture lists, especially for northern racing in early season and summer racing.
3. Improvement in prize money. Stable staff wage to be considerably raised.

Artist: **Roy Miller EARLY FROST**
Courtesy of: **The Artist**

Mr Edward Gillespie

1. Moving Derby Day to a Saturday, enabling the race to be re-invented on a day when most people are potential customers of one sort or another. It is now up to Management and the industry to market the race properly.
2. John Hughes died. He would have sorted out most of racing's petty in-fighting and given us all a lot more fun.
3. The emergence of a horse to win the Triple Crown, Champion Hurdle and Gold Cup in consecutive years. Not asking much!

Mr Douglas Erskine-Crum

1. Improved management of racecourses.
2. Formation of strong, centralised marketing focus.
3. A revised racing programme for both flat and National Hunt which creates a clear narrative rather than a number of disconnected events which are difficult to understand.

Racing and betting is changing rapidly with the advent of new technologies such as interactive television, the Internet and telephone accounts, as well as new types of punting such as spread betting. No longer are you confined to having your shilling on at the neighbourhood bookies, now you can roam the world for the best prices and the best non-taxable deal. There are no guarantees that any of this economic activity will actually find its way back to the racing industry that provides it with its raison d'etre.

However we are willing to predict that the lure of watching balls dropping from a drum will never replace

the thrill of actually being at the races as those thundering hooves pound down the stretch with your money riding on a close finish, or the celebration or commiseration of the aftermath.

Racing is and always has been much more than just betting on horses and this book has encouraged and helped many to find out just how enjoyable a day at the races can be. A good day out racing, a drink and dinner and then bed - Travelling the Turf is unique in maximising your racing pleasure.

We are proud of the fact that Travelling the Turf was Kensington West's very first book and the idea still seems as fresh today as it did in 1985. We hope it will prove to be just that in 2015. Have a great Millennium, both on and off the turf.

Artist: **Peter Smith DOWN THE BACKSTRAIGHT**
Courtesy of: **Frost & Reedt**

Racecourse of the Year 2000 - Introduction

It may appear somewhat obvious but Travelling the Turf's major objective is to encourage people to go racing. It is also to try to suggest some additional ideas so racegoers can enjoy a slightly extended trip - hopefully celebrating a famous win in a delightful hotel or boozer. In the fifteen years since we began publishing Travelling the Turf it is breathtaking to witness the improvements that have taken place. Racecourses to a greater or lesser degree have developed their buildings and Newmarket is shortly to open what we all hope will be a state of the art monument to one of the world's historic racing sites - the Rowley Mile. Other courses, Newbury and Ascot to name two, have plans afoot to refurbish and redesign major parts of their grandstands.

The major reason why this is so refreshing is that it is not just the larger racecourses that have progressed so well but also so many smaller racecourses. It is generally well known that most racecourses have become far more customer friendly - mind you it's fair to say that back in 1985 some courses were in some cases positively unfriendly. Ascot is the example most often quoted but there were many others. Amusingly, of the first three letters I sent to racecourses suggesting the idea for Travelling the Turf, two of them (from Newmarket and Ascot) said 'forget it'! I'm so glad we didn't - apart from anything else it has been tremendous fun compiling the book. One racecourse which, from the beginning, has always been positive about the book is Haydock Park - it's deeply ironic that so many of the very best racecourses have always been the most positive and welcoming. I remember vividly, in my various visits to Haydock Park, a generally high standard of facility and today they are as good as ever and the welcome remains supremely commendable. It is, however, the smaller details that count as well and, from the turn out of the paddock to the bars and loos, Haydock Park has excelled.

Catering remains a somewhat thorny issue at some racecourses and it is fair to say that service can be poor and food a little stodgy. The more serious claim however, could be levelled at the prices charged. For relatively unimaginative fayre fairly hefty sums are the norm at many courses. In most instances the catering is actually not in the hands of the racecourse but local or national caterers. However, to me it is essential that the Racecourse Executive keep a close eye on this - because it really is, other than having a bet, the main item on the agenda for most racegoers. If the food is poor or expensive or both or the service is slow it reflects directly on the racecourse, no matter whose logo happens to adorn the waiter or waitress's chest. Naturally, third parties need to make a decent return but it should not effect the reputation of the racecourse.

Next year we are going to add to our British racecourse award an international award - certainly there are some excellent courses out there in the big wide world, however, British racecourses remain varied and in most cases well run. Haydock Park is one of those that provides an exceptional feast for racegoers on and off the track.

Artist: **Graham Isom COOL DAWN**
Courtesy of: **Rosenstiel's**

Innovation, attention to detail and a strong marketing drive are just some of the reasons why we have awarded the Travelling the Turf Racecourse of the Year Award to Haydock Park for an unprecedented second time. Haydock first won the award in 1998 and although the course was thoroughly deserving then, in the intervening years it has not only redeveloped many of its facilities, it has remained supremely positive, thoroughly professional and probably above all very, very proud of what Haydock does best - providing excellent racing throughout the year and first class facilities for use on non-race days. To win the award

once demonstrates outstanding performance, but to do so twice we hope represents a small but poignant commendation that serious hard work and a positive approach still makes you stand out in a crowd.

We have always put as much stock in what racecourses do for the average racegoer and their families as what they offer to the well-heeled in the Members' or the corporate sponsors in their boxes. We are happy to report that Haydock passes this test with flying colours. The experience of going racing at Haydock is an excellent one in all enclosures. The fact that Haydock Park is also attracting more than its fair share of young racegoers is not only testament to its facilities and reputation but also to its initiative and marketing ability.

An excellent example of what Haydock has achieved was when the course hosted the Sir Alex Ferguson Testimonial Race Day on the 11th of July 1999. Absolutely perfect weather, an entertaining card of competitive racing, huge crowds brought out by the presence of one of football's men of the moment and his Manchester United team, held on a Sunday when families could enjoy the occasion and beamed live to millions of television viewers - surely a very satisfying outcome for effort put in by the Haydock management and staff.

Strong marketing and innovative ideas that bring the crowds contribute greatly to Haydock's success. Four Ladies Evening meetings, the Alex Ferguson race day on a Sunday and an open-air concert by rock music

legends Simply Red were the recipe for a successful summer flat season. Promotions continue into the winter jump racing months with special offers for parties and groups during the Christmas holiday season as well. Haydock also highlights another point probably not 'sung and danced' about by the central marketing team in racing. Recent research shows that racing is the most female friendly spectator sport - at Haydock Park initiatives are regularly carried out to encourage women to go racing.

The course has also been extremely successful in appealing to the corporate community, not only in sponsoring races and entertaining their guests on race days, but using the facilities for conferences, exhibitions and shows on non race days.

In 1999 Haydock added to its already excellent facilities with the opening of the new Centenary Grandstand, a complete make over of the old County Stand that had been built 100 years previously at the founding of the racecourse. The historic look of the ground floor area has been retained with its unique staircase and fireplace. The Lancaster Suite, traditionally used by owners and trainers has been extensively refurbished. The Sandon Bar has been re-designed and the Chasers Bar much improved, while a suite for annual badge holders has been introduced. The first floor has been re-aligned with the neighbouring Tommy Whittle stand. Space has been doubled and the Horseshoe and Champagne bars rebuilt. This has cemented a firm partnership with on-course caterers

Letheby & Christopher who provide hospitality services at 15 other British racecourses and now have the modern facilities to present excellent dining and refreshment to suit every requirement. It is also worth noting that for just about every race meeting some initiative is undertaken to make racing more fun and more friendly - yes, dare I say it - customer friendly. Indeed, whenever possible the Executive will try to ensure that all aspects that are difficult to comprehend for the first time or occasional racegoer are explained well, so the sport - the main event of the day - comes to life.

When we first researched Travelling the Turf, Haydock Park offered a supremely impressive list of fixtures which combined with an amazing list of free fixtures at other racecourses. This value for money is still offered to the Haydock Annual Members who have, in our view, one of the best deals in racing at home and away. Racing highlights in the calendar include the Peter Marsh Chase and the Greenalls Grand National trial in January and February, The Old Newton Cup and Lancashire Oaks in July, The Rose of Lancaster Stakes and Coral Cup in August, and the Stanley Leisure Sprint Cup in September. In November the Edward Hanmer Memorial Chase and the One Man Novices Chase take place.

Congratulations to Managing Director Richard Thomas and your team, on winning the Racecourse of the Year award for the second time - you've earned all your success.

most significant developments to have taken place at the racecourse in the last 15 years. Here are a few of his thoughts.

Artist: **Graham Isom AT THE START**
Courtesy of: **Rosenstiel's**

Cheltenham is a superb racecourse, but more than that it is surely one of the great amphitheatres of sport and in the National Hunt Festival it delivers three days of horse racing without compare.

We have published *Travelling the Turf* for some fifteen years now, and to mark this period we are creating a one off celebratory award. This goes to Cheltenham and all those that help make this racecourse such a success and who have not only fostered its development but positively enhanced it. The supremo at Cheltenham is Edward Gillespie but he would be the first to concede that this success could not have been achieved without the support of a strong board and management team and a really hard working team of full time staff and many others who work at the racecourse on racedays. There were times when Gillespie, rather like the captain of a ship, would almost single handedly try to stop the waves of Irish support from entering the winner's enclosure. I remember seeing him 'bobbing up' after Dawn Run had won the Gold Cup a considerable distance from the bridge of his ship amidst a crowd of eager supporters. Today the after race celebration is just one area that has been improved - small changes but it is these as much as the huge alterations to the grandstands that have marked the continued improvement of this racecourse.

J.W. - Anyone visiting the racecourse who had not been for ten years would see some magnificent changes, but what of the track itself - that crucial part of the course that racegoers may often forget but the professionals see as crucial?

E.G. - It has taken us a long time to convince ourselves and others that Cheltenham is a winter racecourse. For years we struggled to get the track right for the start of our season, 'traditionally' in the beginning of October. The course is set on heavy clay and given anything other than an extremely wet summer, it will not come right naturally for National Hunt racing by early October. During the last 15 years we experimented with the Park Course, concentrating irrigation on a less testing circuit - and combined that with the French style hurdles - to encourage National Hunt bred horses to compete. We extended the irrigation and changed our regime of watering earlier than before. Eventually it dawned on us that the only way of preventing criticism of 'too-fast' ground for disappointing fields in early October - and having a knock-on effect of over-irrigating in the autumn that could (and did) lead to softer-than-ideal ground in the winter and spring - was to start the season later - at the end of October.

Reducing our season to 6 months has considerably benefited the preparation of better grass and ground for the three day November meeting and for the winter.

Just like the owners and trainers we always have an eye on March when preparing ground for October - January but are nearer to providing 'the best possible ground for all meetings' than 15 years ago.

It is still possible for the going to come up really heavy - as it did in April 1998. Those who claim that this is no longer the case are wrong!

Artist: **Graham Isom IN THE PADDOCK**
Courtesy of: **Rosenstiel's**

The 1999 Festival was blessed with some glorious weather, it was similarly fair when I visited in June to discuss with Edward Gillespie what he felt were the

As for the configuration of the track, we have widened the course where possible, levelled and adjusted the landing area for the 3rd last on the Old Course - all of these changes have been made with safety in mind.

We continue to invest in localised drainage with the ultimate aim of allowing every horse to run up to his and her ability.

J.W. - I hear that huge investment has taken place at the racecourse in the last 15 years. What are the real sums that have been outlayed and what were your main hopes when making this expenditure?

E.G. - Since 1978, over £30 million has been spent on the redevelopment of the stands and paddock with 3 stages completed in the last 15 years. The greatest impact was achieved with the Tattersalls Stand (1997) which cost £10 million and provides a wide range of facilities for the Panoramic Restaurant to the Betting Hall. Our aim - as we continue to invest - is to provide every racegoer with top quality accommodation, regardless of their level of expenditure.

Artist: **Grabam Isom TURNING FOR HOME**
Courtesy of: **Rosenstiel's**

J.W. - You have a reputation for considering the small details as well as the big issues. What do you feel have been the most interesting innovations to have taken place recently?

E.G. - We are fortunate to be financially secure (quite rare for a racecourse until SIS came along) and can back our own judgement on how racegoers might respond. We're not always right, but if you try enough ideas some of them work. It's really down to being perceptive to what might appeal - Free Food Day is a good example. If I owned a racecourse, it would be Free Food Day every day. The actual risk of offering what amounts to an average of £3 per person is low risk compared with the return.

We like to entertain from the moment people arrive - with interviews, parades, the Hall of Fame, music, etc. Of course, some people don't like certain aspects but it helps people enjoy the day more.

J.W. - A number of new races have been introduced over the years presumably to enhance the day's entertainment; what has been your policy here?

E.G. - We have tried to reflect the entirety of National Hunt racing - extending the range to include the Bumper at the Festival and the Cross Country Steeplechases. Also small changes in conditions to help up with trends of horse-type - the influence of French Breds etc.

Getting the right mix - like a good meal - is essential, we therefore provide some high quality and some competitive Handicaps, as well as opportunities for up and coming stars. We do tend to stand up to the Race Planners. We listen to what they have to say and then do what we had in mind in the first place. Sometimes it works . . .

J.W. - Racing Days and occasions have often been at the forefront of our thinking . . . recommending a good ale house, or hotel as well as good racing is our raison d'être, what makes your calendar particularly appealing?

E.G. - The Festival is absolutely crucial to National Hunt racing. It is not the Cheltenham Festival. We just happen to host it. The National Hunt Festival is as much owned by the jockeys, stable staff and racegoers as it is by Cheltenham, whose responsibility it is to perpetuate the magic.

The Murphy's is going well - changing the name was an essential part of the success and it will continue to grow. The Tripleprint Meeting is as good a day's racing as you'll get anywhere - as is the January Saturday.

Equally, Hunter Chase Evening is a bit like Village Cricket Final day at Lords.

The mix is very important.

J.W. - What is your major hope for the next ten years?

E.G. - The anticipation for the Festival has become mega and that roar as the Supreme Novice Hurdle starts is like the celebration that the Festival is actually here - at last. People currently talk up the Festival and Cheltenham generally. That is important - that they understand the place and the event, know where to go, meet their friends and have a good time.

We have been incredibly lucky with the horses. 1983 was Michael Dickinson's Gold Cup. Then we had Dawn Run, Norton's Coin, Desert Orchid . . . and now Istabraq plus some fantastic 2 mile chasers.

If we can achieve anything like the magic moments of the last 15 years in the next 10, we'll keep the place warm for a few years to come!

Artist: **Grabam Isom   THE END OF THE RACE**
Courtesy of: **Rosenstiel's**

Any Event Limited

Incorporating
Edrich Lawson Entertaining

"Wherever we looked there seemed to be a constant flow of horses, walking, circling, galloping; snaking out from David Loder's yard, returning to Heath House Stables, snorting their way up Lang Hill. We counted over 500 horses in the 30 minutes that we stood beside the Moulton Road. As Henry Cecil's string of 25 passed us I saw the racing industry as a vast ocean liner and we were in the engine room. Below us, the wheels and pistons, watched by the stokers, went through their well oiled routines." *The thoughts of a race-goer after having spent a rewarding hour on the gallops at Newmarket.*

Whether it be Middleham Moor, the downs above Lambourn or on the gallops at Arundel Castle, spending the first hours of a day with a trainer, walking his horses straining their way towards you out of the mist is an unforgettable enhancement to a day's racing.

Any Event Ltd offer an unparalleled service to all those who race with them. Apart from their memorable training yard and stud visits prior to racing they promise to enhance your time at the racecourse. We have developed a special relationship with racecourses, trainers, the racing press and with many others allowing us now to advise and guide clients towards a successful and memorable day at the races.

A SPECIAL DAY AT THE RACES WITH ANY EVENT LTD

Any Event Ltd can offer you the chance to entertain your guests with a visit to a trainer's yard followed by a day at one of the leading racecourses in the UK. A luxury bus will meet your group and take you to the trainers yard for an exclusive insight into behind the scenes. On arrival you will be met by the trainer and entertained to a full English breakfast before being taken around the yard and introduced to his staff and jockeys. There may also be the chance of seeing the stable vet or blacksmith at work. You will also be taken up to the gallops where you will see his string in action.

Following this tour you will be taken to the racecourse, where a superb private facility will be waiting for you. You will be offered a glass or two of champagne before sitting down to an excellent five course lunch complemented by wines and liqueurs of your choice. The trainer will join you for a drink to answer any questions you might have forgotten to ask him at his yard. The day's racing starts at approximately 2 pm and can be watched from the superb viewing facilities of the Member's Grandstand. A representative of Any Event will be with you throughout the day and can arrange visits to the paddock, start or weighing room should any of your guests wish it. He will also run a small sweepstake competition. Afternoon tea will be served mid-afternoon and a complimentary bar will be open throughout the day.

As mentioned Any Event Ltd would be delighted to offer a number of 'Enhancements' to your day including:

- **Stud visit**
- **Trainer's yard visit**
- **Racing dinner the night before racing**
- **Guided tour of Tattersalls during the sales**
- **Visit to the Animal Health Trust**
- **Watching horses in the equine swimming pool**
- **Tour of the Jockey Club Rooms, The National Stud, or the Racing Museum in Newmarket or Lambourn**
- **Visit to the Weighing room**
- **Attend the start of a race at the stalls**
- **Racing celebrities and tipsters in your box**
- **Sweepstake competitions**
- **Guide to reading the form**

We have special arrangements at many different racecourses such as Newbury, Newmarket, Chester, Uttoxeter, Perth and Towcester.

Please contact Piers Lawson at their offices below:

Any Event Ltd, 32 Chapter St, London SW1P 4NX Tel: 0171 834 7585 Fax: 0171 834 7588 Mobile: 0860 617 914
Email: pierslawson@anyevent.co.uk or visit our website: www.anyevent.co.uk

Any Event Limited
Incorporating
Edrich Lawson Entertaining

Racing Tours Worldwide

France • Ireland • Dubai • Hong Kong • Japan • Australia • South Africa • USA

Ranging from Ireland to Victoria in Australia, Any Event Ltd are in a position to organise any level of racing tour abroad for groups of 10 or more. Racing at The Curragh can be combined with a tour of Coolmere Stud and golf at the K Club. Staying at the beautiful Mount Juliet near Thomastown, once home of the McCalmont family, you could sally forth onto their golf course after a morning at the Norelands Stud owned and run by Harry McCalmont.

Whether it be Deauville in August, Prix de l'Arc de Triomphe in October, Sha Tin in December or Dubai in March, Any Event Ltd can tailor make a tour to your requirements. We combine the excitement of racing with the pleasure of playing on some of the world's most fabulous golf courses. If wine-tasting, dune-driving or relaxing with a drink by the hotel pool is what you require, Any Event's racing tours will cater for your taste.

So give us a call, organise your group and we'll race the world.

Cricket • Badminton Horse Trials • Golf Days • Conferences • Cultural Tours •
Parties and Receptions • Team Building

Any Event Ltd is a company dedicated to tour and event management. As an experienced team of event managers we pride ourselves with our ability to co-ordinate innovative and imaginative tours and events. The contacts and knowledge of the business built up over 30 years of combined service, enable Any Event to design a refreshing and original selection of activities which are uniquely tailor made to our clients. The other divisions of our company are dedicated to corporate parties, conferences, receptions and team building events. The private groups division is specialised in tailor made tours and spouse programmes in both the UK and overseas. The sporting Division provides excellent packages for all major sporting events for both spectators and participators - from golf days to private tours of Badminton Horse Trials.

It would be a pleasure to discuss any ideas that you might have so please contct us and ask for a brochure

Piers Lawson at
Any Event Ltd,
32 Chapter Street,
London SW1P 4NX
Tel: 0171 834 7585
Fax: 0171 834 7588
Mobile: 0860 617 914
Email: pierslawson@anyevent.co.uk

Georgia Morris at
Any Event Ltd,
Top Floor, Heritage Court,
Lower Bridge Street, Chester, Cheshire CH1 1RD
Tel: 01244 345 310
Fax: 01244 311 829
Mobile: 0774 777 6980
Email: georgiamorris@anyevent.co.uk

visit our website: www.anyevent.co.uk

The SITWELL ARMS

Set in six acres of grounds adjoining Renishaw Park Golf Club and less than one mile from Junction 30 of the M1, the Hotel has excellent facilities, including 30 spacious en suite bedrooms with direct dial telephone, colour television, bedside radio/alarm, tea and coffee making facilities.

The oak beamed restaurant with its interesting decor is the ideal place for a relaxing meal. We offer an extensive and reasonably priced à la carte menu with imaginative dishes as well as a full range of traditional grills.

The Leger Room with its Oak Refectory tables is available for dinner parties and smaller functions up to 36 people.

The Sitwell Arms has for several years held a license approving Civil Wedding Ceremonies to be conducted on the premises.

With facilities flexible enough for groups from 6-200 the hotel caters for business meetings, conferences, presentations, exhibitions and banqueting functions.

Station Road, Renishaw,
Derbyshire S21 3WF
Tel: 01246 435226
Fax: 01246 433915

Artist: **Graham Isom TURNING FOR HOME**
Courtesy of: **Rosenstiel's**

Key to Symbols

Alongside the course map of each racecourse, you will see two or three Tote symbols. These signify what Tote facilities are available there.

(Tote)

The normal Tote pool betting points you will find on every racecourse in the country. Here you can bet race by race - Win, Place, Each Way, Dual Forecast - or try one of the Tote's special combination bets - Trifecta, Jackpot, Placepot or Quadpot.

(Tote Credit)

For members of the Tote Credit Club (holders of a Tote Credit account), there is an exclusive betting office on racecourses. In comfortable, carpeted surroundings you can enjoy a full range of Pool bets and SP bets with complete SIS and Tote odds betting displays.

(Tote Bookmakers)

At many racecourses you will also find a Tote Bookmakers shop in different enclosures. Here you can get the same SP betting service you'd expect to find in your local High Street shop. This includes special prices on the day's feature events, all kinds of multiple bets from doubles to yankees, and SIS coverage of other meetings.

Racing Calendar

Artist: **Peter Smith** *THE HEADS OF AYR* *Courtesy of:* ***Frost & Reed***

JANUARY

Date	Race Name	Racecourse
3rd	Unicoin Handicap Steeple Chase	Cheltenham
8th	Anthony Mildmay, Peter Cazalet Memorial Handicap Steeple Chase	Sandown Park
8th	Sun 'King of the Punters' Tolworth Novices' Hurdle	Sandown Park
13th	Towton Novices' Steeple Chase	Wetherby
15th	Victor Chandler Chase (Handicap)	Ascot
15th	Northern Echo Dipper Novices' Steeple Chase	Newcastle
16th	Tote Warwick National Handicap Chase	Warwick
21st	PML Lightning Novices' Steeple Chase	Ascot
22nd	Peter Marsh Steeple Chase (Handicap)	Haydock Park
22nd	Intercity Champion Hurdle Trial	Haydock Park
22nd	Tote Premier Long Distance Hurdle	Haydock Park
22nd	Tote Lanzarote Handicap Hurdle	Kempton Park
29th	Marchpole Cleeve Hurdle	Cheltenham
29th	Pillar Property Investment Steeple Chase	Cheltenham
29th	Wragge & Co Finesse Four Years Old Novices' Hurdle	Cheltenham
29th	Stakis Westgate Casino Great Yorkshire Chase (Hcap)	Doncaster
29th	River Don Novices' Hurdle	Doncaster

Artist: **Roy Miller** **WINTER WORK** *Courtesy of:* **The Artist**

JANUARY

2nd Sunday	Uttoxeter Exeter LINGFIELD PARK (AWT) Plumpton		**18th Tuesday**	Carlisle Folkestone WOLVERHAMPTON (AWT)
3rd Monday **(Bank Holiday)**	Ayr SOUTHWELL (AWT) Cheltenham Folkestone		**19th Wednesday**	Newcastle Huntingdon LINGFIELD PARK (AWT)
4th Tuesday	Musselburgh WOLVERHAMPTON (AWT)		**20th Thursday**	Ludlow Taunton WOLVERHAMPTON (AWT)
5th Wednesday	Catterick Bridge Leicester LINGFIELD PARK (AWT)		**21st Friday**	Kelso SOUTHWELL (AWT) Ascot
6th Thursday	Catterick Bridge Taunton WOLVERHAMPTON (AWT)		**22nd Saturday**	Catterick Bridge WOLVERHAMPTON (AWT) Kempton Park Haydock Park LINGFIELD PARK (AWT)
7th Friday	Ludlow SOUTHWELL (AWT) Towcester		**23rd Sunday**	
8th Saturday	Haydock Park LINGFIELD PARK (AWT) WOLVERHAMPTON (AWT) Sandown Park Warwick		**24th Monday**	Wetherby (R) SOUTHWELL (AWT)
9th Sunday			**25th Tuesday**	Leicester Fontwell park (R) WOLVERHAMPTON (AWT)
10th Monday	Fakenham Fontwell Park SOUTHWELL (AWT)		**26th Wednesday**	Sedgefield Southwell (R) LINGFIELD PARK (AWT)
11th Tuesday	Hereford (R) Leicester WOLVERHAMPTON (AWT)		**27th Thursday**	Huntingdon Wincanton WOLVERHAMPTON(AWT)
12th Wednesday	Sedgefield Kempton Park LINGFIELD PARK (AWT)		**28th Friday**	Doncaster SOUTHWELL (AWT) FOLKESTONE
13th Thursday	Wetherby WOLVERHAMPTON (AWT) Wincanton		**29th Saturday**	Ayr Cheltenham LINGFIELD PARK (AWT) Doncaster
14th Friday	Musselburgh SOUTHWELL (AWT) Folkestone		**30th Sunday**	
15th Saturday	Newcastle Warwick Ascot LINGFIELD PARK		**31st Monday**	SOUTHWELL (AWT) Plumpton Taunton
16th Sunday				
17th Monday	Doncaster SOUTHWELL (AWT) Plumpton		Capitals: Flat Racing Lower Case: National Hunt AWT (All Weather Track) †Evening Meeting	

FEBRUARY

Date	Race Name	Racecourse
5th	Tote Bookmakers Sandown Hurdle (Handicap)	Sandown Park
5th	Scilly Isles Novices' Steeple Chase	Sandown Park
5th	Agfa Diamond Steeple Chase (Limited Handicap)	Sandown Park
5th	Singer & Friedlander National Trial (Handicap Steeple Chase)	Uttoxeter
5th	Rossington Main Novices' Hurdle	Wetherby
9th	Persian War Premier Novices' Hurdle	Chepstow
9th	John Hughes Grand National Trial (Handicap Chase)	Chepstow
10th	Premier 'National Hunt' Auction Novices' Hurdle	Wincanton
12th	Gold Trophy (Handicap Hurdle)	Newbury
12th	Mitsubishi Shogun Game Spirit Steeple Chase	Newbury
19th	Mitsibushi Shogun Ascot Steeple Chase	Ascot
19th	Gerard Group Reynoldstown Novices' Chase	Ascot
19th	Tote Eider Handicap Steeple Chase	Newcastle
19th	Michael Page International Group Kingmaker Novices' Chase	Warwick
24th	Axminster 100 Kingwell Hurdle	Wincanton
24th	Jim Ford Challenge Cup (Steeple Chase)	Wincanton
26th	Greenalls Grand National Trial (Handicap Chase)	Haydock Park
26th	Racing Post Steeple Chase (Handicap)	Kempton Park
26th	Mitsubishi Shogun Pendil Novices' Steeple Chase	Kempton Park
26th	Money Store Rendalsham Hurdle (Limited Handicap)	Kempton Park
26th	Voice Newspaper Adonis Juvenile Novices' Hurdle	Kempton Park
26th	Weekender Dovecote Novices' Hurdle	Kempton Park

Artist: **Philip Toon** *DECEMBER MORNING* *Courtesy of:* **The Artist**

FEBRUARY

1st Tuesday	Musselburgh Kempton Park WOLVERHAMPTON (AWT)	**17th Thursday**	WOLVERHAMPTON (AWT) Sandown Park Taunton
2nd Wednesday	Newcastle Leicester LINGFIELD PARK (AWT)	**18th Friday**	Fakenham Sandown Park SOUTHWELL (AWT)
3rd Thursday	Kelso Towcester WOLVERHAMPTON (AWT)	**19th Saturday**	Newcastle Warwick Ascot WOLVERHAMPTON (AWT) LINGFIELD PARK (AWT)
4th Friday	Catterick Bridge SOUTHWELL (AWT) Folkestone	**20th Sunday**	
5th Saturday	Wetherby Uttoxeter LINGFIELD PARK (AWT) WOLVERHAMPTON (AWT) Sandown Park	**21st Monday**	Carlisle Fontwell Park SOUTHWELL (AWT)
6th Sunday		**22nd Tuesday**	Sedgefield Folkestone WOLVERHAMPTON (AWT)
7th Monday	Newcastle Fontwell Park SOUTHWELL (AWT)	**23rd Wednesday**	Doncaster Ludlow LINGFIELD PARK (AWT)
8th Tuesday	Carlisle Warwick WOLVERHAMPTON (AWT)	**24th Thursday**	Huntingdon Wincanton WOLVERHAMPTON (AWT)
9th Wednesday	Ludlow Chepstow LINGFIELD PARK (AWT)	**25th Friday**	Market Rasen Kempton Park SOUTHWELL (AWT)
10th Thursday	Huntingdon Wincanton WOLVERHAMPTON (AWT)	**26th Saturday**	Haydock Park Kempton Park Musselburgh LINGFIELD PARK (AWT)
11th Friday	Bangor-On-Dee Newbury SOUTHWELL (AWT)	**27th Sunday**	
12th Saturday	Ayr LINGFIELD PARK (AWT) Catterick Bridge Newbury Haydock Park	**28th Monday**	Newcastle SOUTHWELL (AWT) Plumpton
13th Sunday		**29th Tuesday**	Catterick Bridge Leicester WOLVERHAMPTON (AWT)
14th Monday	Hereford Plumpton SOUTHWELL (AWT)		
15th Tuesday	Sedgefield Folkestone WOLVERHAMPTON (AWT)		
16th Wednesday	Musselburgh Leicester LINGFIELD PARK (AWT)	Capitals: Flat Racing Lower Case: National Hunt AWT (All Weather Track) †Evening Meeting	

MARCH

Date	Race Name	Racecourse
1st	Prestige Novices' Hurdle	Chepstow
4th	Pertemps Grimthorpe Handicap Chase	Doncaster
4th	Mitsubishi Shogun Trophy Handicap Chase	Doncaster
7th	McEwan's Durham National (Handicap Chase)	Sedgefield
11th	European Breeders Fund 'National Hunt' Novices' Hurdle Final	Sandown Park
11th	Sunderlands Imperial Cup (Handicap Hurdle)	Sandown Park
11th	M & N Group Sir Peter O'Sullevan Novices' Hurdle	Chepstow
14th	Citroen Supreme Novices' Hurdle	Cheltenham
14th	Guinness Arkle Challenge Trophy Novices' Chase	Cheltenham
14th	Smurfit Champion Hurdle Challenge Trophy	Cheltenham
15th	Queen Mother Champion Steeple Chase	Cheltenham
15th	Royal & Sun Alliance Novices' Hurdle	Cheltenham
15th	Royal & Sun Alliance Novices' Steeple Chase	Cheltenham
15th	Coral Cup (Handicap Hurdle)	Cheltenham
15th	Weatherbys Champion Bumper	Cheltenham
16th	Tote Cheltenham Gold Cup Steeple Chase	Cheltenham
16th	Bonusprint Stayers' Hurdle	Uttoxeter
16th	Elite Racing Club Triumph Hurdle (Novices')	Doncaster
16th	Vincent O'Brien County Handicap Hurdle	Doncaster
18th	Marstons Pedigree Midlands Grand National (Handicap Steeple Chase)	Uttoxeter
23rd	Tote Handicap Stakes	Doncaster
23rd	Doncaster Mile	Doncaster
24th	Worthington Spring Mile (Handicap)	Doncaster
24th	Ashleybank Investments Scottish Borders National (Handicap Steeple Chase)	Kelso
25th	Worthington Lincoln Handicap	Doncaster
25th	Cammidge Trophy	Doncaster
25th	Panacur Guard EBF Mares' NH Final (Novices' Hurdle)	Newbury

Artist: **Peter Curling** ISTABRAQ *Courtesy of:* **Rosenstiel's**

MARCH

1st Wednesday	Wetherby Chepstow LINGFIELD PARK (AWT)	**17th Friday**	Fakenham Folkestone SOUTHWELL (AWT)
2nd Thursday	Ludlow Taunton WOLVERHAMPTON (AWT)	**18th Saturday**	Newcastle Market Rasen Lingfield Park (mixed AWT) Uttoxeter
3rd Friday	Doncaster Newbury Kelso	**19th Sunday**	
4th Saturday	Doncaster Huntingdon Newbury Warwick LINGFIELD PARK (AWT) †WOLVERHAMPTON (AWT)	**20th Monday**	SOUTHWELL (AWT) Folkestone
5th Sunday		**21st Tuesday**	Sedgefield Exeter Fontwell Park
6th Monday	Musselburgh SOUTHWELL (AWT) Fontwell	**22nd Wednesday**	Ludlow Chepstow Towcester
7th Tuesday	Sedgefield Leicester Exeter	**23rd Thursday**	DONCASTER Wincanton WOLVERHAMPTON (AWT)
8th Wednesday	Catterick Bridge Bangor-On-Dee LINGFIELD PARK (AWT)	**24th Friday**	DONCASTER Newbury Kelso
9th Thursday	Carlisle Wincanton Towcester	**25th Saturday**	DONCASTER Bangor-On-Dee Newbury †WOLVERHAMPTON (AWT) KEMPTON PARK
10th Friday	Ayr Hereford Sandown Park	**26th Sunday**	
11th Saturday	Ayr †WOLVERHAMPTON (AWT) (MIXED) Chepstow Sandown Park	**27th Monday**	SOUTHWELL (AWT) WINDSOR
12th Sunday		**28th Tuesday**	NEWCASTLE WOLVERHAMPTON (AWT) Sandown Park (mixed)
13th Monday	Stratford-On-Avon Plumpton Taunton	**29th Wednesday**	CATTERICK BRIDGE NOTTINGHAM LINGFIELD PARK (AWT)
14th Tuesday	Sedgefield Cheltenham SOUTHWELL (AWT)	**30th Thursday**	MUSSELBURGH LEICESTER Taunton
15th Wednesday	Cheltenham Newton Abbot Huntingdon	**31st Friday**	Carlisle SOUTHWELL Uttoxeter.
16th Thursday	Hexham Cheltenham WOLVERHAMPTON (AWT)	Capitals: Flat Racing Lower Case: National Hunt AWT (All Weather Track) †Evening Meeting	

APRIL

Date	Race Name	Racecourse
1st	Field Marshal Stakes	Haydock Park
5th	Grosvenor Casinos Long Distance Hurdle	Ascot
6th	Martell Cup Steeple Chase	Aintree
6th	Sandeman Maghull Novices' Steeple Chase	Aintree
6th	Glenlivet Anniversary Novices' Hurdle	Aintree
6th	Barton and Guestier Top Novices' Hurdle	Aintree
7th	Mumm Melling Steeple Chase	Aintree
7th	Mumm Mildmay Novices' Steeple Chase	Aintree
7th	Belle Epoque Sefton Novices' Hurdle	Aintree
7th	Martell Mersey Novices' Hurdle	Aintree
8th	Martell Grand National Steeple Chase (Handicap)	Aintree
8th	Martell Aintree Hurdle	Aintree
8th	Martell Red Rum Steeple Chase (Limited Handicap)	Aintree
8th	Martell Champion Standard Bumper	Aintree
18th	Shadwell Stud Nell Gwyn Stakes (fillies)	Newmarket
18th	NGK Spark Plugs European Free Handicap	Newmarket
19th	Faucets for Mira Rada Showers Novices' Hurdle	Cheltenham
19th	Weatherbys Earl Of Sefton Stakes	Newmarket
19th	Victor Chandler European Handicap	Newmarket
20th	Silver Trophy Steeple Chase	Cheltenham
20th	EBF/Doncaster Bloodstock Sales Mares' Only Bumper Final	Cheltenham
20th	City Index Craven Stakes (colts & geldings)	Newmarket
20th	Feilden Stakes	Newmarket
14th	Dubai Duty Free Fred Darling Stakes (fillies)	Newbury
15th	Stakis Casinos Scottish Grand National (Handicap Steeple Chase)	Ayr
15th	Scotsman Novices' Handicap Steeple Chase	Ayr
15th	Edinburgh Woollen Mill Future Champion Novices' Steeple Chase	Ayr
15th	Samsung Electronics Scottish Champion Hurdle (Handicap)	Ayr
15th	Lanes End Farm John Porter Stakes	Newbury
15th	Tripleprint Greenham Stakes (colts & geldings)	Newbury
15th	Thirsk Classic Trial	Thirsk
22nd	Milcars Easter Stakes (colts & geldings)	Kempton Park
22nd	Milcars Masaka Stakes (fillies)	Kempton Park
24th	Coral Rosebery Handicap Stakes	Kempton Park
24th	Magnolia Stakes	Kempton Park
28th	Credit Suisse Private Banking Mile	Sandown Park
28th	Whitbread Gold Cup (Handicap Steeple Chase)	Sandown Park
28th	Thresher Classic Trial	Sandown Park
28th	Marriott Hotels Gordon Richards Stakes	Sandown Park
28th	Peter Sandrovitch Leicestershire Stakes	Leicester

Artist: **John King** **THE WORK RIDERS** *Courtesy of:* **Osborne Studio Gallery**

APRIL

1st Saturday	HAYDOCK PARK(MIXED) Market Rasen Ascot Hexham	**18th Tuesday**	NEWMARKET Exeter FOLKESTONE
3rd Monday	Kelso WARWICK Plumpton	**19th Wednesday**	BEVERLEY Cheltenham NEWMARKET
4th Tuesday	Newcastle NOTTINGHAM Exeter	**20th Thursday**	RIPON Cheltenham NEWMARKET
5th Wednesday	RIPON Ludlow Ascot	**21st Friday**	
6th Thursday	Aintree LEICESTER Taunton	**22nd Saturday**	Carlisle Towcester KEMPTON PARK HAYDOCK PARK Newton Abbot
7th Friday	Aintree LINGFIELD PARK Sedgefield	**23rd Sunday**	
8th Saturday	Aintree Hereford HAMILTON PARK	**24th Monday (Bank Holiday)**	Carlise Fakenham Chepstow NEWCASTLE Hereford Market Rasen KEMPTON PARK Wetherby WARWICK Huntingdon Plumpton Wincanton. NOTTINGHAM Towcester Uttoxeter
9th Sunday		**25th Tuesday**	Wetherby SOUTHWELL (AWT) Uttoxeter
10th Monday	SOUTHWELL WINDSOR	**26th Wednesday**	CATTERICK BRIDGE EPSOM Perth
11th Tuesday	PONTEFRACT WOLVERHAMPTON (AWT)	**27th Thursday**	BEVERLEY Fontwell Park Perth
12th Wednesday	WARWICK Chepstow LINGFIELD PARK (AWT)	**28th Friday**	Perth SANDOWN PARK WOLVERHAMPTON (AWT)
13th Thursday	MUSSELBURGH Ludlow BRIGHTON	**29th Saturday**	RIPON LEICESTER SANDOWN PARK (MIXED) Sedgefield Market Rasen
14th Friday	Ayr NEWBURY THIRSK	**30th Sunday**	
15th Saturday	Ayr Bangor-On-Dee NEWBURY THIRSK Stratford-On-Avon †WOLVERHAMPTON (AWT)		
16th Sunday			
17th Monday	Hexham WINDSOR PONTEFRACT	Capitals: Flat Racing Lower Case: National Hunt AWT (All Weather Track) †Evening Meeting	

31

MAY

Date	Race Name	Racecourse
1st	Jubilee Handicap Stakes	Kempton Park
2nd	EBF Landsdown Fillies Stakes	Bath
3rd	Insulpak Sagaro Stakes	Ascot
3rd	Insulpak Victoria Cup (Handicap)	Ascot
3rd	Gardner Merchant Pavillion Stakes	Ascot
5th	Sagitta Jockey Club Stakes	Newmarket
5th	Dahlia Stakes (fillies)	Newmarket
5th	Green Ridge Stables Newmarket Stakes (colts)	Newmarket
6th	Crowther Homes Swinton Handicap Hurdle	Haydock Park
6th	Crowther Homes Spring Trophy HandicapTote Chester Cup (Handicap)	Haydock Park
6th	Sagitta 2000 Guineas Stakes (colts and fillies)	Newmarket
6th	Ladbrokes Handicap Stakes	Newmarket
6th	Palace House Stakes	Newmarket
7th	Sagitta 1000 Guineas Stakes (fillies)	Newmarket
7th	R.L. Davison Pretty Polly Stakes (fillies)	Newmarket
9th	Victor Chandler Chester Vase	Chester
10th	Tote Chester Cup (Handicap)	Chester
10th	Shadwell Stud Cheshire Oaks (fillies) Tattersalls Musidora Stakes (fillies)	Chester
11th	Ormonde Stakes	Chester
11th	Letheby & Christopher Dee Stakes	Chester
11th	Huxley Stakes	Chester
13th	Pertemps Derby Trial Stakes	Lingfield Park
13th	Tote Sprint Handicap Stakes	Lingfield Park
13th	Victor Chandler Oaks Trial Stakes	Lingfield Park
13th	MER Car Polish Chartwell Fillies Stakes	Lingfield Park
16th	Tattersalls Musidora Stakes (fillies)	York
16th	William Hill Stakes (Handicap)	York
16th	Shepherd Trophy Rated Stakes	York
17th	Grosvenor Casinos Dante Stakes	York
17th	Grosvenor Casinos Hambelton Rated Stakes	York
17th	Grosvenor Casinos Middleton Stakes (fillies)	York
18th	Merewood Homes Yorkshire Cup	York
18th	Duke Of York Victor Chandler Stakes	York
18th	Michael Seely Memorial Glasgow Stakes	York
19th	Sun Life of Canada Group of Companies Fillies' Trial Stakes	Newbury
20th	Juddmonte Lockinge Stakes	Newbury
20th	Aston Park Stakes	Newbury
20th	Coral Sprint Handicap Stakes	Newmarket
20th	Milcars King Charles II Stakes	Newmarket
20th	British Airways Charlotte Fillies' Stakes	Newmarket
23rd	Tote Trifecta Handicap Stakes	Goodwood
23rd	Compass UK Leisure Predominate Stakes	Goodwood
24th	ABN Amro Handicap Stakes	Goodwood
24th	Victor Chandler Lupe Stakes (fillies)	Goodwood
25th	BT Alex Brown Festival Stakes.	Goodwood
25th	EBF Conqueror Stakes (fillies)	Goodwood
27th	Ring & Brymer Achilles Stakes	Kempton Park
27th	Courage Best Leisure Stakes	Lingfield Park
27th	Tote Credit Club Silver Bowl (handicap)	Haydock Park
27th	Sandy Lane Rated Stakes	Haydock Park
27th	John Charcol Mortgage Advisers Heron Stakes	Kempton Park
29th	Zetland Gold Cup (Handicap)	Redcar
29th	Tripleprint Temple Stakes	Sandown Park
29th	Bonusprint Henry II Stakes	Sandown Park
30th	Brigadier Gerard Stakes	Sandown Park
30th	National Stakes	Sandown Park

MAY

1st Monday **(Bank Holiday)**	DONCASTER Ludlow Fontwell Park NEWCASTLE Towcester KEMPTON PARK WARWICK	**17th Wednesday**	†Perth †Huntingdon BRIGHTON York EXETER †Folkestone
2nd Tuesday	†Huntingdon BATH NOTTINGHAM †WINDSOR	**18th Thursday**	Perth SALISBURY YORK
3rd Wednesday	†Kelso †Cheltenham ASCOT PONTEFRACT EXETER	**19th Friday**	†Aintree NOTTINGHAM NEWBURY †HAMILTON PARK †Stratford-On-Avon THIRSK
4th Thursday	REDCAR BRIGHTON WOLVERHAMPTON (AWT)	**20th Saturday**	THIRSK Bangor-On-Dee NEWBURY †Hexham NOTTINGHAM †LINGFIELD PARK †WOLVERHAMPTON (AWT)
5th Friday	MUSSELBURGH †Bangor-On-Dee Folkestone †Sedgefield NEWMARKET	**21st Sunday**	
6th Saturday	HAYDOCK PARK (MIXED) Hereford THIRSK NEWMARKET Uttoxeter	**22nd Monday**	†MUSSELBURGH BATH SOUTHWELL (AWT) †WINDSOR
7th Sunday	HAMILTON PARK NEWMARKET SALISBURY	**23rd Tuesday**	BEVERLEY GOODWOOD
8th Monday	Newcastle SOUTHWELL (AWT) †WINDSOR Towcester	**24th Wednesday**	Kelso †Uttoxeter †BRIGHTON Worcester GOODWOOD
9th Tuesday	CHESTER BRIGHTON Exeter	**25th Thursday**	NEWCASTLE GOODWOOD Newton Abbot
10th Wednesday	†Wetherby CHESTER Chepstow Fakenham	**26th Friday**	SOUTHWELL (AWT) †BRIGHTON †PON- TEFRACT Towcester
11th Thursday	HAMILTON PARK CHESTER WOLVERHAMPTON (AWT)	**27th Saturday**	Cartmel †Market Rasen KEMPTON PARK DONCASTER †WARWICK †LINGFIELD PARK HAYDOCK PARK Hexham
12th Friday	CARLISLE NOTTINGHAM LINGFIELD PARK †Stratford-On-Avon †Wincanton	**28th Sunday**	
13th Saturday	BEVERLEY †Market Rasen LINGFIELD PARK Hexham †Warwick Worcester	**29th Monday** **(Bank Holiday)**	Cartmel Hereford CHEPSTOW Redcar Huntingdon Fontwell Park Wetherby LEICESTER SANDOWN PARK
14th Sunday		**30th Tuesday**	†Hexham LEICESTER †SANDOWN PARK REDCAR
15th Monday	REDCAR SOUTHWELL (AWT) WINDSOR †Towcester	**31st Wednesday**	Cartmel SOUTHWELL †NEWBURY †RIPON YARMOUTH
16th Tuesday	YORK Hereford	Capitals: Flat Racing Lower Case: National Hunt AWT (All Weather Track) †Evening Meeting	

JUNE

Date	Race Name	Racecourse
3rd	Horse And Hound Cup	Stratford-On-Avon
9th	Vodafone Oaks (fillies)	Epsom Downs
9th	Vodafone Coronation Cup	Epsom Downs
9th	Vodafone Victress Stakes	Epsom Downs
9th	Vodafone Woodcote Stakes	Epsom Downs
10th	Vodafone Derby (colts & fillies)	Epsom Downs
10th	Vodafone Handicap Stakes	Epsom Downs
10th	Vodafone Diomed Stakes	Epsom Downs
10th	Vodafone 'Dash' Rated Stakes	Epsom Downs
10th	Vodafone Surrey Stakes	Epsom Downs
10th	Joseph Holt Derby Brewery John Of Gaunt Stakes	Haydock Park
11th	Baileys Irish Cream Liqueur Fairway Stakes	Newmarket
15th	Ballymacoll Stud Stakes	Newbury
17th	William Hill Trophy (Handicap)	York
18th	Leicester Mercury 125 Stakes	Leicester
20th	St James's Palace Stakes (colts)	Royal Ascot
20th	Prince Of Wales's Stakes	Royal Ascot
20th	Queen Anne Stakes	Royal Ascot
20th	Coventry Stakes	Royal Ascot
21st	Coronation Stakes (fillies)	Royal Ascot
21st	Royal Hunt Cup (Handicap)	Royal Ascot
21st	Jersey Stakes	Royal Ascot
21st	Queen's Vase Stakes	Royal Ascot
21st	Queen Mary Stakes (fillies)	Royal Ascot
22nd	Gold Cup	Royal Ascot
22nd	Ribblesdale Stakes (fillies)	Royal Ascot
22nd	Cork And Orrery Stakes	Royal Ascot
22nd	Norfolk Stakes	Royal Ascot
22nd	Chesham Stakes	Royal Ascot
23rd	Hardwicke Stakes	Royal Ascot
23rd	King's Stand Stakes	Royal Ascot
23rd	King Edward VII Stakes (colts & geldings)	Royal Ascot
23rd	Wokingham Stakes (Handicap)	Royal Ascot
24th	Ladbroke Handicap	Ascot
24th	London Clubs Fern Hill Rated Stakes (fillies)	Ascot
24th	Milcars New Stakes	Ascot
28th	Crowther Homes Carlisle Bell Handicap Stakes	Carlisle
28th	Mowlem Gala Stakes	Kempton Park
29th	UCB Films Cumberland Plate (Handicap)	Carlisle

Artist: **Hubert de Watrigant WARREN HILL** *Courtesy of:* **Osborne Studio Gallery**

JUNE

1st Thursday	AYR GOODWOOD Newton Abbot	**17th Saturday**	Hexham NOTTINGHAM BATH YORK SANDOWN PARK
2nd Friday	AYR NOTTINGHAM BATH CATTERICK BRIDGE †BRIGHTON †Stratford-On-Avon †BATH	**18th Sunday**	CARLISLE LEICESTER SALISBURY
3rd Saturday	CATTERICK BRIDGE NEWMARKET LINGFIELD PARK MUSSELBURGH Stratford-On-Avon	**19th Monday**	MUSSELBURGH †WARWICK BRIGHTON †WINDSOR
4th Sunday	PONTEFRACT Fakenham WARWICK	**20th Tuesday**	THIRSK ASCOT
5th Monday	CARLISLE LEICESTER †WINDSOR †THIRSK	**21st Wednesday**	HAMILTON PARK ASCOT WOLVERHAMPTON (AWT) †RIPON †Worcester †KEMPTON PARK
6th Tuesday	Uttoxeter LINGFIELD PARK	**22nd Thursday**	RIPON SOUTHWELL (AWT) ASCOT
7th Wednesday	†BEVERLEY †CHESTER †Folkestone NEWCASTLE Market Rasen YARMOUTH	**23rd Friday**	AYR †NEWMARKET ASCOT Hexham †GOODWOOD REDCAR
8th Thursday	HAYDOCK PARK †Uttoxeter CHEPSTOW Perth †NEWBURY	**24th Saturday**	AYR Market Rasen ASCOT REDCAR Newton Abbot
9th Friday	CATTERICK BRIDGE †GOODWOOD SOUTHWELL (AWT) † Perth EPSOM DOWNS †HAYDOCK PARK	**25th Sunday**	Perth LINGFIELD PARK PONTEFRACT
10th Saturday	DONCASTER Worcester EPSOM DOWNS HAYDOCK PARK	**26th Monday**	MUSSELBURGH NOTTINGHAM †WINDSOR †YARMOUTH
11th Sunday	RIPON NEWMARKET Worcester	**27th Tuesday**	BEVERLEY LINGFIELD PARK
12th Monday	†PONTEFRACT NOTTINGHAM Newton Abbot †WINDSOR	**28th Wednesday**	CARLISLE †CHESTER †KEMPTON PARK WARWICK †HAMILTON PARK SALISBURY
13th Tuesday	REDCAR SALISBURY	**29th Thursday**	CARLISLE SALISBURY NEWCASTLE
14th Wednesday	BEVERLEY Hereford †KEMPTON PARK †HAMILTON PARK LINGFIELD PARK	**30th Friday**	†NEWCASTLE NEWMARKET FOLKESTONE SOUTHWELL (AWT) †GOOD WOOD †Stratford-On-Avon
15th Thursday	HAMILTON PARK †Uttoxeter †BRIGHTON YARMOUTH NEWBURY		
16th Friday	YORK SOUTHWELL (AWT) †CHEPSTOW †GOODWOOD †Newton Abbot SANDOWN PARK	Capitals: Flat Racing Lower Case: National Hunt AWT (All Weather Track) †Evening Meeting	

JULY

Date	Race Name	Racecourse
1st	Fosters Lager Northumberland Plate	Newcastle
1st	EBF/Kronenbourg 1664 Hoppings Stakes	Newcastle
1st	John Smith's Extra Smooth Chipchase Stakes	Newcastle
1st	Van Geest Criterion Stakes	Newmarket
1st	Fred Archer Stakes	Newmarket
1st	High Havens Empress Stakes (fillies)	Newmarket
2nd	'On The House' Stakes	Goodwood
7th	Hong Kong Jockey Club Trophy (handicap)	Sandown Park
7th	Sino Group Dragon Stakes	Sandown Park
8th	Letheby & Christopher Old Newton Cup (Handicap)	Haydock Park
8th	Payne And Gunter Lancashire Oaks Stakes (fillies)	Haydock Park
8th	Leith's July Trophy	Haydock Park
8th	Coral Eclipse Stakes	Sandown Park
8th	Porcelanosa Sprint Stakes	Sandown Park
11th	Princess of Wales' Greene King Stakes	Newmarket
11th	Charles Heidsieck Champagne Cherry Hinton Stakes	Newmarket
12th	Greene King Falmouth Stakes (fillies)	Newmarket
12th	TNT International Aviation July Stakes	Newmarket
12th	Bahrain Trophy	Newmarket
13th	Darley July Cup	Newmarket
13th	Ladbroke Bunbury Cup (Handicap)	Newmarket
13th	Weatherbys Superlative Stakes	Newmarket
14th	Stanley Racing Summer Stakes (fillies)	York
15th	Michael Page International Silver Trophy Stakes	Ascot
15th	Jani City Wall Stakes	Chester
15th	John Smith's Cup (Handicap)	York
15th	Foster's Silver Cup Rated Stakes	York
22nd	Weatherbys Super Sprint (auction race)	Newbury
22nd	Hamlet Cigars Steventon Stakes	Newbury
22nd	Ruinart Chanpagne Hackwood Stakes	Newbury
22nd	Rose Bowl Stakes	Newbury
22nd	Food Brokers Animal Health Trust Trophy (Handicap)	Newmarket
22nd	Food Brokers Aphrodite Stakes (fillies)	Newmarket
24th	Tennant Caledonian Breweries Scottish Classic	Ayr
27th	Milcars Star Stakes (fillies)	Sandown Park
28th	Fawley Stud Golden Daffodil Stakes (fillies)	Chepstow
29th	King George VI and The Queen Elizabeth Diamond Stakes	Ascot
29th	Princess Margaret Stakes (fillies)	Ascot
29th	Reed Print Beeswing Stakes	Newcastle

Artist: **Peter Smith** *GOING OUT TO THE GALLOPS* *Courtesy of:* **Frost & Reed**

JULY

1st Saturday	†DONCASTER NEWMARKET BATH NEWCASTLE Worcester †LINGFIELD PARK †Newton Abbot	**17th Monday**	AYR †Wolverhampton Newton Abbot WINDSOR
2nd Sunday	DONCASTER Uttoxeter GOODWOOD	**18th Tuesday**	BEVERLEY BRIGHTON
3rd Monday	†MUSSELBURGH SOUTHWELL (AWT) †WINDSOR PONTEFRACT	**19th Wednesday**	CATTERICK BRIDGE †Worcester †KEMPTON PARK† DONCASTER YARMOUTH LINGFIELD PARK
4th Tuesday	HAMILTON PARK YARMOUTH	**20th Thursday**	HAMILTON PARK LEICESTER BATH †Sedgefield †EPSOM DOWNS
5th Wednesday	CATTERICK BRIDGE †YARMOUTH BRIGHTON †EPSOM DOWNS	**21st Friday**	CARLISLE †NEWMARKET NEWBURY †HAMILTON PARK SOUTHWELL (AWT) †PONTEFRACT
6th Thursday	CATTERICK BRIDGE CHEPSTOW HAYDOCK PARK	**22nd Saturday**	RIPON Market Rasen NEWBURY NEWMARKET WARWICK
7th Friday	†BEVERLEY WARWICK †SALISBURY †HAYDOCK PARK Wolverhampton SANDOWN PARK	**23rd Sunday**	REDCAR Southwell KEMPTON PARK
8th Saturday	BEVERLEY LEICESTER CHEPSTOW HAYDOCK PARK SANDOWN PARK	**24th Monday**	AYR BRIGHTON †BEVERLEY †WINDSOR
9th Sunday	NEWCASTLE Market Rasen SANDOWN PARK	**25th Tuesday**	YARMOUTH BRIGHTON
10th Monday	MUSSELBURGH BATH †RIPON †WINDSOR	**26th Wednesday**	CATTERICK BRIDGE †LEICESTER †SANDOWN PARK Worcester
11th Tuesday	PONTEFRACT NEWMARKET	**27th Thursday**	Sedgefield BATH SANDOWN PARK
12th Wednesday	DONCASTER NEWMARKET †KEMPTON PARK †Worcester LINGFIELD PARK	**28th Friday**	THIRSK NEWMARKET ASCOT SOUTHWELL (AWT) †CHEPSTOW †SALISBURY
13th Thursday	DONCASTER NEWMARKET EPSOM DOWNS FOLKESTONE WOLVERHAMPTON (AWT)	**29th Saturday**	NEWCASTLE NOTTINGHAM ASCOT REDCAR Stratford-On-Avon
14th Friday	†HAMILTON PARK †CHEPSTOW YORK LINGFIELD PARK SOUTHWELL (AWT) †CHESTER	**30th Sunday**	RIPON NEWMARKET ASCOT
15th Saturday	YORK CHESTER ASCOT NOTTINGHAM SALISBURY	**31st Monday**	NEWCASTLE †YARMOUTH FOLKESTONE †WINDSOR
16th Sunday	HAYDOCK PARK NEWBURY Stratford-On-Avon	Capitals: Flat Racing Lower Case: National Hunt AWT (All Weather Track) †Evening Meeting	

AUGUST

Date	Race Name	Racecourse
1st	Marchpole Cup (Handicap)	Goodwood
1st	Peugeot Gordon Stakes	Goodwood
2nd	Champagne Lanson Sussex Stakes	Goodwood
2nd	Tote Gold Trophy	Goodwood
2nd	Richmond Stakes (colts & geldings)	Goodwood
3rd	William Hill Mile (Handicap)	Goodwood
3rd	Goodwood Cup	Goodwood
3rd	Lanson Champagne Vintage Stakes	Goodwood
3rd	Oak Tree Stakes (fillies)	Goodwood
4th	Volvo Contracts Globetrotter Stakes (Handicap)	Goodwood
4th	Theo Fennell Glorious Rated Stakes	Goodwood
4th	Jockey Club Of Kenya Molecomb Stakes	Goodwood
5th	Vodafone Stewards Cup (Handicap)	Goodwood
5th	Vodafone Nassau Stakes	Chester
5th	Vodafone Thoroughbred Stakes	Ascot
6th	Intercity Group Queensferry Stakes	Haydock Park
12th	Tote International handicap	Newmarket
12th	Petros Rose Of Lancaster Stakes	Newmarket
12th	Joe Jennings Bookmakers Handicap Stakes	Ascot
12th	Milcars Sweet Solera Stakes	Salisbury
13th	Bovis Homes Valiant Stakes	Newbury
16th	European Breeders Fund Upavon Stakes (fillies)	Newbury
18th	Hungerford Stakes	Newbury
18th	Washington Singer Stakes	Newbury
19th	Geoffrey Freer Stakes	Ripon
19th	Swettenham Stud St Hugh's Stakes	Wolverhampton
19th	William Hill Great St Wilfred Handicap Stakes	York
19th	Weatherbys Dash	York
19th	Solario Stakes	Sandown Park
19th	Ford Atlanta Stakes (fillies)	Sandown Park
20th	Chester Rated Stakes (Handicap)	Chester
20th	Flying Fillies' Stakes	Pontefract
22nd	Juddmonte International Stakes	York
22nd	Stakis Casinos Great Voltigeur Stakes (colts & geldings)	York
22nd	Weatherbys Insurance Lonsdale Stakes	York
22nd	Breckenbrough Racing Acomb Stakes	York
23rd	Aston Upthorpe Yorkshire Oaks (fillies)	York
23rd	Scottish Equitable Gimrack Stakes (colts & geldings)	York
23rd	Tote Ebor (Handicap)	York
23rd	Costcutter Roses Stakes (colts & geldings)	York
24th	Peugeot Lowther Stakes (fillies)	York
24th	Persimmon Homes Nunthorpe Stakes	York
24th	Bradford & Bingley Rated Stakes	York
24th	EBF Galtres Stakes (fillies)	York
24th	McArthurglen Designer Outlet City Of York Stakes	York
25th	Hopeful Stakes	Newmarket
26th	Celebration Mile	Goodwood
26th	Sport on 5 March Stakes	Goodwood
26th	Winter Hill Stakes	Windsor
27th	Link for the Right Mobile Phone Prestige Stakes (fillies)	Goodwood
28th	Hennessy Cognac Blaydon Race (Nursery Handicap)	Newcastle
28th	Chisholm Bookmakers Virginia Rated Stakes	Newcastle
28th	Ripon Champion Two Years Old Trophy	Ripon

AUGUST

1st Tuesday	BEVERLEY GOODWOOD	**17th Thursday**	EPSOM DOWNS SALISBURY BEVERLEY
2nd Wednesday	CARLISLE †LEICESTER GOOD WOOD †MUSSELBURGH †KEMPTON PARK Newton Abbot	**18th Friday**	†CATTERICK BRIDGE CHESTER FOLKESTONE †NEWMARKET NEWBURY †SANDOWN PARK
3rd Thursday	Sedgefield GOODWOOD	**19th Saturday**	Bangor-On-Dee †LINGFIELD PARK RIPON †HAYDOCK PARK †WOLVERHAMPTON (AWT) NEWBURY SANDOWN PARK
4th Friday	†AYR Bangor-On-Dee GOODWOOD THIRSK †NEWMARKET †NOTTINGHAM	**20th Sunday**	PONTEFRACT CHESTER BATH
5th Saturday	DONCASTER NEWMARKET GOODWOOD THIRSK Worcester	**21st Monday**	NOTTINGHAM BRIGHTON
6th Sunday	CHESTER NEWBURY Market Rasen	**22nd Tuesday**	HAMILTON PARK YORK
7th Monday	†CARLISLE Newton Abbot RIPON †WINDSOR	**23rd Wednesday**	CARLISLE B†RIGHTON †Perth LINGFIELD PARK YORK
8th Tuesday	CATTERICK BRIDGE BATH	**24th Thursday**	MUSSELBURGH FOLKESTONE YORK
9th Wednesday	NEWCASTLE †LEICESTER BRIGHTON PONTEFRACT †YARMOUTH †SANDOWN PARK	**25th Friday**	†NEWCASTLE NEWMARKET †BATH THIRSK †Uttoxeter Fontwell Park
10th Thursday	HAYDOCK PARK BRIGHTON CHEPSTOW	**26th Saturday**	BEVERLEY NEWMARKET GOODWOOD Cartmel †Worcester †WINDSOR †REDCAR
11th Friday	†HAYDOCK PARK †NEWMARKET LINGFIELD PARK WOLVERHAMPTON (AWT) SALISBURY †Worcester	**27th Sunday**	BEVERLEY YARMOUTH GOODWOOD
12th Saturday	HAYDOCK PARK NEWMARKET ASCOT REDCAR Stratford-On-Avon	**28th Monday (Bank Holiday)**	Cartmel Huntingdon CHEPSTOW NEWCASTLE Southwell EPSOM DOWNS RIPON WARWICK Fontwell Park Newton Abbot
13th Sunday	REDCAR LEICESTER ASCOT	**29th Tuesday**	RIPON Uttoxeter
14th Monday	†THIRSK Southwell †KEMPTON PARK WINDSOR	**30th Wednesday**	YORK BRIGHTON Newton Abbot
15th Tuesday	AYR Newton Abbot	**31st Thursday**	MUSSELBURGH LINGFIELD PARK SALISBURY
16th Wednesday	BEVERLEY YARMOUTH †EPSOM DOWNS †HAMILTON PARK SALISBURY	Capitals: Flat Racing Lower Case: National Hunt AWT (All Weather Track) †Evening Meeting	

SEPTEMBER

Date	Race Name	Racecourse
1st	Michael J Lonsdale Fortune Stakes	Epsom Downs
2nd	Victor Chandler September Stakes	Kempton Park
2nd	Stanley Leisure Sprint Cup	Haydock Park
3rd	Strensall Stakes	York
6th	£200,000 St Leger Yearling Stakes	Doncaster
8th	Constant Security Park Hill Stakes (fillies)	Doncaster
6th	Tote Trifecta Portland Handicap Stakes	Doncaster
6th	Sirenia Stakes	Epsom Downs
7th	Great North Eastern Railway Doncaster Cup	Doncaster
7th	Great North Eastern Railway Park Stakes	Doncaster
7th	May Hill Stakes (fillies)	Doncaster
7th	Kyoto Sceptre Stakes (fillies)	Doncaster
7th	Scarbrough Stakes	Doncaster
8th	Frigidaire Champagne Stakes (colts & geldings)	Doncaster
8th	Mallard Handicap Stakes	Doncaster
8th	0 & K Troy Stakes	Doncaster
8th	Bellway Homes Stardom Stakes	Goodwood
8th	DBS St Leger Stakes (colts & fillies)	Doncaster
9th	Polypipe Plc Flying Childers Stakes	Doncaster
9th	Rothmans Royals Handicap Stakes	Doncaster
9th	Rothmans Royals St Leger Stakes (colts & fillies)	Doncaster
9th	Caffrey's Select Stakes	Goodwood
12th	John Musker Stakes (fillies)	Great Yarmouth
14th	Ayrshire & Arran Harry Rosebery Trophy	Ayr
15th	Dubai Duty Free Cup	Newbury
15th	Dubai Airport World Trophy	Newbury
16th	Peugeot Doonside Cup	Ayr
16th	Ladbroke (Ayr) Gold Cup (Handicap)	Ayr
16th	Faucets First for Faucets Firth Of Clyde Stakes (fillies)	Ayr
16th	Dubai Arc Trial	Newbury
16th	Mill Reef Stakes	Newbury
16th	Courage Handicap Stakes	Newbury
20th	Caffrey's Ale Foundation Stakes	Goodwood
21st	Charlton Hunt Supreme Stakes	Goodwood
23rd	Queen Elizabeth II Stakes	Ascot
23rd	Meon Valley Stud Fillies Mile	Ascot
23rd	Scoop 6 Handicap	Ascot
23rd	John Hopkins Cumberland Lodge Stakes	Ascot
23rd	Gardner Merchant Rosemary Rated Stakes (fillies)	Ascot
24th	Ritz Club Handicap	Ascot
24th	Gardner Merchant Diadem Stakes	Ascot
24th	Serpentine Gallery Royal Lodge Stakes	Ascot
24th	Mail On Sunday Millennium Mile Final (Handicap)	Ascot
24th	Riggs Bank Harvest Stakes (fillies)	Ascot
25th	Tote Handicap Stakes	Hamilton Park
26th	£300,000 Tattersalls Houghton Sales Stakes	Newmarket
26th	Shadwell Stud Cheveley Park Stakes (fillies)	Newmarket
28th	Saudi Arabian Airlines Middle Park Stakes (colts)	Newmarket
28th	Joel Stakes	Newmarket
28th	JRA Nakayama Rous Stakes	Newmarket
29th	Fishpools Furnishings Godolphin Stakes	Newmarket
29tht	Somerville Tattersall Stakes (colts & geldings)	Newmarket
30th	Tote Cambridgeshire Handicap Stakes	Newmarket
30th	Sun Chariot Stakes (fillies)	Newmarket
30th	Jockey Club Cup	Newmarket
30th	Oh So Sharp Stakes (fillies)	Newmarket
30th	ntl Two-Year-Old Trophy	Redcar

SEPTEMBER

1st Friday	HAYDOCK PARK EPSOM DOWNS Sedgefield	**17th Sunday**	
2nd Saturday	HAYDOCK PARK Stratford-On-Avon KEMPTON PARK THIRSK †WOLVERHAMPTON (AWT)	**18th Monday**	LEICESTER KEMPTON PARK
3rd Sunday	HAMILTON PARK KEMPTON PARK YORK	**19th Tuesday**	BEVERLEY Fontwell Park
4th Monday	HAMILTON PARK BATH	**20th Wednesday**	Perth CHESTER GOODWOOD
5th Tuesday	LEICESTER LINGFIELD PARK	**21st Thursday**	Perth GOODWOOD PONTEFRACT
6th Wednesday	DONCASTER Hereford EPSOM DOWNS	**22nd Friday**	HAYDOCK PARK LINGFIELD PARK REDCAR
7th Thursday	DONCASTER CHEPSTOW Newton Abbot	**23rd Saturday**	HAYDOCK PARK Market Rasen ASCOT Plumpton
8th Friday	DONCASTER Worcester GOODWOOD	**24th Sunday**	MUSSELBURGH Huntingdon ASCOT BRIGHTON
9th Saturday	DONCASTER Bangor-On-Dee GOODWOOD Worcester	**25th Monday**	HAMILTON PARK BATH Exeter
10th Sunday		**26th Tuesday**	Sedgefield NEWMARKET SOUTHWELL (AWT)
11th Monday	WARWICK Plumpton	**27th Wednesday**	NEWCASTLE BRIGHTON SALISBURY
12th Tuesday	Sedgefield YARMOUTH	**28th Thursday**	Hereford NEWMARKET NOTTINGHAM
13th Wednesday	BEVERLEY YARMOUTH SANDOWN PARK	**29th Friday**	Hexham NEWMARKET LINGFIELD PARK
14th Thursday	AYR YARMOUTH PONTEFRACT	**30th Saturday**	REDCAR NEWMARKET Chepstow Uttoxeter SANDOWN PARK †WOLVERHAMPTON (AWT)
15th Friday	AYR NOTTINGHAM NEWBURY		
16th Saturday	AYR NEWMARKET NEWBURY CATTERICK BRIDGE †WOLVERHAMPTON (AWT)	Capitals: Flat Racing Lower Case: National Hunt AWT (All Weather Track) †Evening Meeting	

OCTOBER

Date	Race Name	Racecourse
7th	Princess Royal Stakes (fillies)	Ascot
7th	Willmott Dixon Cornwallis Stakes	Ascot
7th	Financial Dynamics October Stakes (fillies)	Ascot
7th	Tom McGee Autumn Stakes	Ascot
7th	Coral Sprint Trophy Handicap Stakes	York
7th	Coldstream Guards Rockingham Stakes	York
12th	Grangewood Severals Stakes (fillies)	Newmarket
13th	£100,000 Tattersalls Autumn Auction Stakes	Newmarket
13th	Z. T. Egerton Stud Darley Stakes	Newmarket
13th	Bedford Lodge Hotel Bentinck Stakes	Newmarket
14th	Dubai Champion Stakes	Newmarket
14th	Saudi Arabian Airlines Dewhurst Stakes (colts & fillies)	Newmarket
14th	Tote Cesarewitch (Handicap)	Newmarket
14th	Challenge Stakes	Newmarket
14th	Owen Brown Rockfel Stakes (fillies)	Newmarket
16th	Tote Silver Tankard	Pontefract
20th	DBS October Yearling Stakes	Doncaster
20th	Vodafone Horris Hill Stakes (colts & geldings)	Newbury
21st	Racing Post Trophy (colts & fillies)	Doncaster
21st	Doncaster Stakes	Doncaster
21st	Perpetual St Simon Stakes	Newbury
21st	Radley Stakes (fillies)	Newbury
22nd	Desert Orchid South Western Pattern Steeple Chase (Limited Handicap)	Wincanton
27th	NGK Spark Plugs Stubbs Rated Stakes	Newmarket
27th	James Seymour Stakes	Newmarket
28th	Ladbroke Autumn Handicap	Newmarket
28th	Marshall Stakes	Newmarket
28th	NGK Spark Plugs Zetland Stakes	Newmarket
28th	Peterhouse Group Charlie Hall Steeple Chase	Wetherby
28th	Tote West Yorkshire Hurdle	Wetherby
28th	Wensleydale Novices' Hurdle	Wetherby
31st	William Hill Haldon Gold Cup Chase (Limited Handicap)	Exeter

Artist: **John Atkins** *WET MORNING AT MIDDLEHAM Courtesy of:* **The Artist**

OCTOBER

1st Sunday	Kelso Market Rasen Fontwell Park		**17th Tuesday**	WOLVERHAMPTON (AWT) Exeter YARMOUTH
2nd Monday	PONTEFRACT Folkestone		**18th Wednesday**	NEWCASTLE NOTTINGHAM Chepstow
3rd Tuesday	CATTERICK BRIDGE Southwell WOLVERHAMPTON (AWT)		**19th Thursday**	Ludlow BATH BRIGHTON
4th Wednesday	Towcester Exeter LINGFIELD PARK		**20th Friday**	DONCASTER Fakenham NEWBURY
5th Thursday	YORK Ludlow Wincanton		**21st Saturday**	Carlisle Southwell NEWBURY DONCASTER Kempton Park
6th Friday	Carlisle Huntingdon YORK		**22nd Sunday**	Aintree Towcester Wincanton
7th Saturday	Hexham Bangor-On-Dee ASCOT YORK Southwell		**23rd Monday**	Bangor-On-Dee LINGFIELD PARK LEICESTER
8th Sunday			**24th Tuesday**	REDCAR Cheltenham NOTTINGHAM
9th Monday	AYR LEICESTER WINDSOR		**25th Wednesday**	Cheltenham Fontwell Park YARMOUTH
10th Tuesday	AYR LEICESTER Sedgefield		**26th Thursday**	Sedgefield Stratford-On-Avon WINDSOR
11th Wednesday	HAYDOCK PARK LINGFIELD PARK Wetherby		**27th Friday**	Wetherby NEWMARKET BRIGHTON Towcester
12th Thursday	REDCAR NEWMARKET Taunton		**28th Saturday**	Kelso NEWMARKET Ascot Wetherby †WOLVERHAMPTON (AWT)
13th Friday	REDCAR Hereford NEWMARKET		**29th Sunday**	
14th Saturday	CATTERICK BRIDGE Market Rasen NEWMARKET Kelso †WOLVERHAMPTON		**30th Monday**	REDCAR NOTTINGHAM Plumpton
15th Sunday			**31st Tuesday**	CATTERICK BRIDGE Warwick Exeter
16th Monday	PONTEFRACT SOUTHWELL (AWT) Plumpton		Capitals: Flat Racing Lower Case: National Hunt AWT (All Weather Track) †Evening Meeting	

43

NOVEMBER

Date	Race Name	Racecourse
3rd	Classic Novices Hurdle	Uttoxeter
4th	Tote Silver Trophy Hurdle (Handicap)	Chepstow
4th	Rising Stars Novices' Steeple Chase	Chepstow
4th	Tote November Handicap	Doncaster
4th	CIU Serlby Stakes	Doncaster
4th	Charles Sidney Mercedes Benz Wentworth Stakes	Doncaster
4th	Badger Beer Handicap Steeple Chase	Wincanton
4th	Tanglefoot Elite Hurdle	Wincanton
8th	Worcester Novices' Steeple Chase	Worcester
10th	Sporting Index Cross Country Steeple Chase	Cheltenham
11th	Murphy's Gold Cup Handicap Steeple Chase	Cheltenham
11th	Mackeson Novices' Hurdle	Cheltenham
11th	Edward Hanmer Memorial Handicap Steeple Chase	Haydock Park
12th	Murphy Draughtflow Handicap Hurdle	Cheltenham
12th	Greyhounds as Pets November Novices' Steeple Chase	Cheltenham
17th	Pricewaterhousecoopers Ascot Hurdle	Ascot
18th	Tote Becher Chase (Handicap)	Aintree
18th	First National Bank Gold Cup Chase (Handicap)	Ascot
18th	Independant Insurance Peterborough Steeple Chase	Huntingdon
18th	Wulfrun Stakes	Lingfield Park
18th	Ladbrokes Handicap Stakes	Lingfield Park
25th	Hennessy Cognac Gold Cup Handicap Steeple Chase	Newbury
25th	Ladbroke Handicap Hurdle	Newbury
25th	Equity Financial Collections Gerry Feilden Hurdle	Newbury
25th	Solaglas Long Distance Hurdle	Newbury
25th	"Fighting Fifth" Hurdle (Limited Handicap)	Newcastle

Artist: **John Atkins GOING UP TO LOW MOOR, MIDDLEHAM** *Courtesy of:* **The Artist**

NOVEMBER

1st Wednesday	MUSSELBURGH Kempton Park Newton Abbot	**17th Friday**	SOUTHWELL (AWT) Ascot Exeter
2nd Thursday	Haydock Park Towcester WINDSOR	**18th Saturday**	Catterick Bridge Huntingdon Ascot Aintree LINGFIELD PARK
3rd Friday	DONCASTER Uttoxeter Hexham	**19th Sunday**	
4th Saturday	DONCASTER Chepstow Sandown Park Wincanton	**20th Monday**	Newcastle Ludlow SOUTHWELL (AWT)
5th Sunday		**21st Tuesday**	Market Rasen WOLVERHAMPTON (AWT)
6th Monday	SOUTHWELL (AWT) Fontwell Park Carlisle	**22nd Wednesday**	Wetherby Chepstow LINGFIELD PARK (AWT)
7th Tuesday	Sedgefield Huntingdon LINGFIELD PARK (AWT)	**23rd Thursday**	Carlisle Uttoxeter Taunton
8th Wednesday	Kelso Folkestone Newbury	**24th Friday**	Bangor-On-Dee Newbury SOUTHWELL (AWT)
9th Thursday	Ludlow LINGFIELD PARK Taunton	**25th Saturday**	Haydock Park Warwick Newbury Newcastle †WOLVERHAMPTON (AWT)
10th Friday	Newcastle Cheltenham SOUTHWELL (AWT)	**26th Sunday**	
11th Saturday	Ayr Cheltenham Haydock Park Uttoxeter †WOLVERHAMPTON (AWT)	**27th Monday**	SOUTHWELL (AWT) Folkestone Kelso
12th Sunday	Ayr Cheltenham Wetherby	**28th Tuesday**	LINGFIELD PARK Newton Abbot Hereford
13th Monday	Leicester Plumpton SOUTHWELL (AWT)	**29th Wednesday**	Catterick Bridge Plumpton WOLVERHAMPTON (AWT)
14th Tuesday	Hereford Newton Abbot LINGFIELD PARK (AWT)	**30th Thursday**	Leicester Wincanton Market Rasen
15th Wednesday	Hexham Kempton Park WOLVERHAMPTON (AWT)		
16th Thursday	Sedgefield Warwick Wincanton	Capitals: Flat Racing Lower Case: National Hunt AWT (All Weather Track) †Evening Meeting	

DECEMBER

Date	Race Name	Racecourse
1st	Bovis Crowngap Winter Novices' Hurdle	Sandown Park
2nd	Corl Rehearsal Steeple Chase (Handicap)	Chepstow
2nd	Mitsubishi Shogun Tingle Creek Trophy Chase	Sandown Park
2nd	William Hill Handicap Hurdle	Sandown Park
2nd	Extraman Henry VIII Novices' Steeple Chase	Sandown Park
9th	Tripleprint Gold Cup (Handicap Steeple Chase)	Cheltenham
9th	Bonusprint Bula Hurdle	Cheltenham
9th	DoubleprintBristol Novices' Hurdle	Cheltenham
9th	Tommy Whittle Steeple Chase	Haydock Park
9th	Arena Leisure December Novices' Chase	Lingfield Park
9th	TJH Group Summit Novices' Hurdle	Lingfield Park
16th	Cantor Fitzgerald Long Walk Hurdle	Ascot
16th	Tote Silver Cup (Handicap Steeple Chase)	Ascot
16th	Noel Novices' Steeple Chase	Ascot
16th	Mitie Group Kennel Gate Novices' Hurdle	Ascot
26th	Pertemps King George VI Steeple Chase	Kempton Park
26th	Network Design International Feltham Novices' Chase	Kempton Park
26th	Castleford Steeple Chase	Wetherby
27th	Coral Welsh National (Handicap Steeple Chase)	Chepstow
27th	Finale Junior Novices' Hurdler	Chepstow
27th	Chepstow 'Championship' Standard Open Bumper	Chepstow
27th	Pertemps Christmas Hurdle	Kempton Park
27th	Rowland Meyrick Handicap Steeple Chase	Wetherby
29th	Challow Hurdle	Newbury
30th	Old Year Handicap Steeple Chase	Cheltenham
30th	Old Millennium Handicap Hurdle	Cheltenham

Information correct at time of going to press but dates are subject to possible alteration.

Artist: **Heather St Clair Davis IN STEP** *Courtesy of:* **Frost & Reed**

DECEMBER

1st Friday	Southwell Exeter Sandown Park	**17th Sunday**	
2nd Saturday	Wetherby Towcester Chepstow †WOLVERHAMPTON (AWT) Sandown Park	**18th Monday**	Kelso SOUTHWELL (AWT)
3rd Sunday		**19th Tuesday**	Folkestone WOLVERHAMPTON (AWT)
4th Monday	Ayr Fakenham SOUTHWELL (AWT)	**20th Wednesday**	Newcastle LINGFIELD PARK (AWT) Newbury
5th Tuesday	Sedgefield Fontwell Park WOLVERHAMPTON (AWT)	**21st Thursday**	Newcastle Ludlow SOUTHWELL (AWT)
6th Wednesday	Hexham Leicester LINGFIELD PARK (AWT)	**22nd Friday**	
7th Thursday	Huntingdon Taunton Ludlow	**23th Saturday**	
8th Friday	Doncaster Cheltenham SOUTHWELL (AWT)	**24th Sunday**	
9th Saturday	Doncaster Cheltenham Lingfield Park Haydock Park WOLVERHAMPTON (AWT)	**25th Monday**	
10th Sunday		**26th Tuesday (Bank Holiday)**	Ayr Hereford Kempton Park Sedgefield Huntingdon Newton Abbot Wetherby Market Rasen Wincanton WOLVERHAMPTON (AWT)
11th Monday	SOUTHWELL (AWT) Plumpton	**27th Wednesday**	Wetherby Leicester Chepstow Kempton Park
12th Tuesday	Musselburgh Hereford WOLVERHAMPTON (AWT)	**28th Thursday**	Haydock Park LINGFIELD PARK (AWT) Musselburgh Taunton
13th Wednesday	Catterick Bridge Bangor-On-Dee LINGFIELD PARK (AWT)	**29th Friday**	Carlisle Southwell Newbury Stratford-On-Avon
14th Thursday	Catterick Bridge Towcester Exeter	**30th Saturday**	Catterick Bridge Cheltenham Fontwell Park Warwick
15th Friday	SOUTHWELL (AWT) Folkestone Uttoxeter	**31st Sunday**	
16th Saturday	Uttoxeter Ascot Warwick LINGFIELD PARK (AWT)	Capitals: Flat Racing Lower Case: National Hunt AWT (All Weather Track) †Evening Meeting	

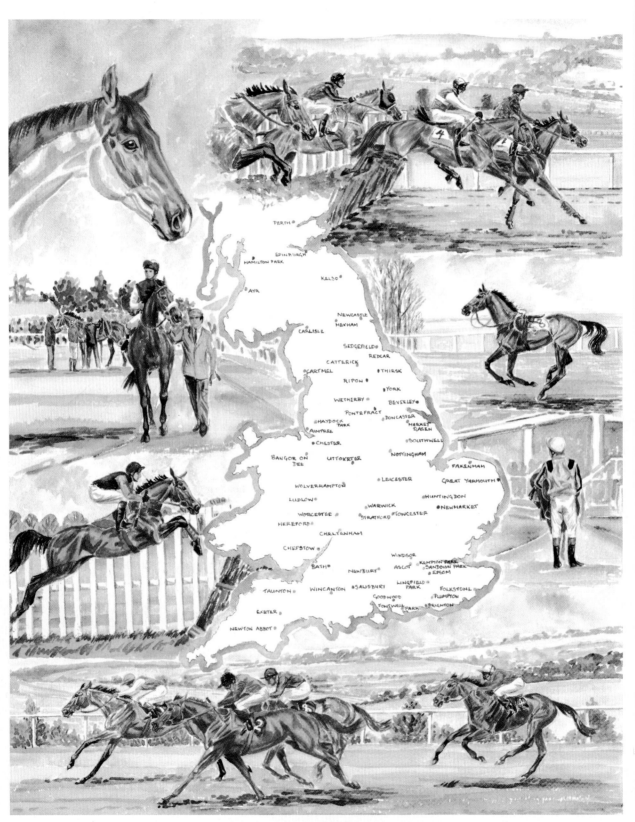

Artist: **Rosemary Coates** *THE RACECOURSES OF BRITAIN* Courtesy of: **The Artist**

British Racecourses

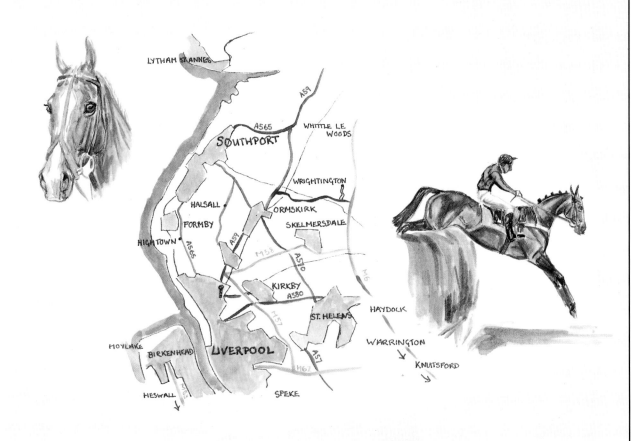

Artist: **Peter Smith HE'S DONE IT AGAIN!** *Courtesy of:* **Frost & Reed**

Aintree is in the capable and safe hands of **Charles Barnett**, who acts as the **Managing Director** and **Clerk of the Course**. **Ian Renton** is the **Assistant Clerk of the Course** and the **Operations Manager** is **Andrew Tulloch**. with **Dickon White** as **Marketing Manager**. If you wish to make enquiries with reference to the Grand National Festival, please write to **Aintree Racecourse Co Ltd, Aintree, Liverpool L9 5AS. Tel 0151 523 2600 Fax 0151 530 1512.**

The racecourse itself lies seven miles from the centre of Liverpool in the suburb of Aintree and approximately one mile from the end of the M58 and M57. Travellers coming up from London should expect a journey of some 213 miles. The M1/M6 double is the answer for these southerners, while visitors from north of Merseyside might care to use another motorway double—the M6 followed by the M58. Northbound travellers from Birmingham should use the M5 before joining the M6/M57. If you are a train traveller then the Euston line is the one to be on. From Liverpool Central take the Merseyrail to Aintree. The station is opposite the course entrance. The No 5 bus from Lime Street also stops next to the track. Car drivers should note that there are over 230 acres in which to park your car or coach—follow the signs for your chosen enclosure and arrive early to see the non-race entertainment and avoid the queues! Perhaps a better idea is to use the free 'park and ride' system which was successfully launched in 1998. Coach parking is no longer allowed in the central enclosure, giving much improved viewing on the Mildmay course. The Steeplechase enclosure has seated viewing for 600 and a total capacity of 25,000. The cost of parking varies from £5 to £25 on the Saturday. If you prefer to fly, (helicopters only please), do contact the course in advance. You will need written permission from Philip Pickford. Contact him on 0161 799 6967.

The Aintree Festival lasts three days, during which racing of the highest quality is guaranteed. Each day features pattern races, and champions and old favourites reappear every year, particularly in the National with many horses seeming to love the big day and being kept in reserve just for the occasion. Some come straight from the Cheltenham Festival, attempting to enhance or redeem reputations. As the shrewd punter knows, Cheltenham form can be well and truly reversed at Aintree. During the meeting, racing takes place over three different courses—the Grand National course, the Mildmay course and the Hurdle course. Thursday features the John Hughes Memorial Race over the National fences, whetting the appetite for the big day. You also have a sight of the Grand National fences on the Friday, during the Martell Foxhunters Chase, and prospective star hurdlers appear in the Glenlivet Hurdle.

Aintree has a members' scheme, the Grand National Club which offers a private room, choice of badge, four course lunch, champagne reception, and private parking. Costs are £275 single, £495 joint. For the Grand National meeting admission charges vary from £20-25 for the County enclosure on Thursday, rising to £65 for a place in the Aintree, Queen Mother or County stands on Grand National Day. Three day badges are also available and if you buy them before January 1st the price drops from £105 to £95 for the Aintree and Queen Mother stands with similar discounts for the County, Glenlivet stands and Tattersalls. But you don't have to spend this much to enjoy the wonders of Aintree on National Day as a mere £7 will get you into the Steeplechase enclosure and you can bring the kids for a modest £2 a head; excellent value considering you will be closer to the action than many others attending. The Steeplechase and Tattersalls Enclosures have bookmaking and Tote facilities, and an arcade of shops. Entry to these enclosures costs between £5 and £16, depending on the day. Transfer badges may be purchased daily subject to availability. Various discounts are available for parties of 25 or more if you contact the course well in advance.

One sensible addition to Aintree's facilities is the starvision screens, of which there are six on National Day, giving you a life size view of the action—essential for some if they are to see the racing, given the large crowds that attend. The November Becher's meeting is also a first class event, and the May evening meeting has also become a regular fixture, which is a pleasure to report. A new visitor attraction, opened in July 1999, which gives people the chance to experience the Grand National virtual reality ride!

Aintree is continually improving itself and the latest addition to the facilities is the new Princess Royal Stand which was opened on Martell Grand National Day in 1998. It includes a large ground floor Irish Bar, incorporating a betting shop and food and drink outlets for Tattersalls racegoers. There is seating for 1,000 people, plus standing room for a further 2,000, with access to the Mumm Champagne Bar. There are also 16 private rooms in the new stand, 10 of which overlook the racecourse. On the top floor is the magnificent Martell Suite which is a restaurant seating 350 with its own private viewing balcony for patrons and unrivalled views of the course. Other new facilities in Tattersalls include the Chair Pavilion which overlooks the Chair fence; this will bring extra coffee shop facilities to Tatts patrons in 2000. Course management also plans to improve the availability of coffee shop catering next year in the County Enclosure by adding double decker bus facilities.

Other restaurants at Aintree are the County Reserved Dining Room (advance bookings only) the Rendezvous (with wheelchair access) and the Courtyard (for County badge holders only) where you can expect to pay between £17 and £20 per head. Catering at all on-course eateries is by racecourse specialists Letheby & Christopher.

There is little doubt that the connection between racing, both flat and over the jumps, on both sides of the Irish Sea has grown stronger in recent years and nowhere has this been better highlighted than the emotional victory of the Irish trained Bobbyjo in the 1999 Grand National. Four horses, each with the great prize in their grasp, came to the last but it was Paul Carberry who pulled his mount out to save a couple of lengths at the elbow and went on to emulate the feat of his father, Tommy on L'Escargot in 1975. With Aidan O'Brien's Istabraq confirming his undisputed superiority over hurdles at the same meeting, it was a fantastic double for the Irish. With SIS bringing live coverage of racing from Ireland to British betting shops and the growing number of punters trekking across to attend popular racing festivals such as those at Punchestown and Galway to emulate the Irish invasion of Cheltenham and Aintree, the connection will surely grow in the coming years.

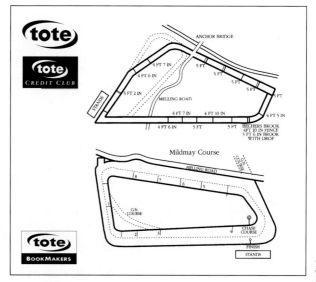

51

In Liverpool, the more luxurious hotels include the **Atlantic Tower Thistle** 0151 227 4444, which boasts two especially remarkable sights: the docklands of the river Mersey and a giant statue of one of Liverpool's best known sons, John Lennon. Other good smaller hotels include The **Park** 0151 525 7555 and **Devonshire House** 0151 260 2414. A good place for a pre-race celebration can be found at the **Trials Hotel** 0151 227 1021—an excellent atmosphere to savour here. The **Liverpool Moat House** 0151 471 9988 is also a good runner in this national field. A perfect restaurant for visiting racegoers is the well thought of **Becher's Brook** 0151 707 0005

From a mind-boggling selection of establishments one prominent example is the **Aachen House** 0151 709 3477. In Liverpool there are a number of restaurants to sample and an extremely popular bistro for lunch or dinner is **La Grande Bouffe** 0151 236 3375. Lovers of Italian cuisine might consider **Ristorante Del Secolo** 0131 236 4004. Finally, a marvellous pub to visit is the celebrated **Philharmonic**—a great place to assess the form on Grand National Eve.

The Lancashire coast yields some excellent golf courses: Royal Liverpool, Royal Birkdale and Royal Lytham St Annes. In Lytham, the **Clifton Arms** (01253) 739898 is a thoughtfully modernised Edwardian hotel. **Taps** (01253) 736226 should appeal to lovers of both sport and real ale. In Lytham St Anne's, the **Dalmeny Hotel** (01253) 712236 is well turned out and the restaurant, **C'est La Vie** is well thought of—well named for the racing fraternity. The **Grand** (01253) 721288 and The **Bedford** (01253) 724636 are also worthy candidates. Further south, in Southport with its gorgeous sands where Red Rum used to gallop, there are a number of good pubs and a hotel of note is the **Scarisbrick** (01704) 543000. The **New Bold** Hotel (01704) 532578 also merits a pre-race inspection and for a budget break, the **Ambassador** (01704) 543998

will almost certainly lead to a return visit. Two restaurants to consider include The **Warehouse Brasserie** (01704) 544602 and **Ho'Lee Chow's** (01704) 551167. Those coming from the south, wishing to break their journey prior to Aintree might consider either the **Jolly Thresher**, Broomedge or the **Spinner and Bergamot**, Comberbach or the **George and Dragon**, Great Budworth.

It may well be that our golfing supremo might have wished to visit Hoylake. If this was the case, then he might have been tempted to stay at the **Bowler Hat Hotel**, Birkenhead 0151 652 4931. The **Lord Daresbury Hotel** (01925) 267331, handily situated near to Warrington is also one to consider. Also near Warrington the **Park Royal International Hotel** (01925) 730706 does special racing breaks including racing papers and transport to and from the racecourse. If you are envisaging a particularly good day and don't mind a trip, **Paul Heathcote's Restaurant** (01772) 784969 is outstanding and can be found in Longridge near Preston.

For those who want to make a weekend of it, there are many places to visit slightly further afield. The **Inn at Whitewell**, (01200) 448222 in Whitewell to the north of Aintree is a splendid ancient inn, whilst at Knutsford, the **Cottons Hotel**, (01565) 650333 is well worth a look. Staying in Cheshire, the **Hartford Hall Hotel**, (01606) 75711 at Northwich offers 16th century charm along with 20th century comfort. **Nunsmere Hall** (01606) 889100 is a really excellent stayer where the Garden Room Restaurant is first class. What is more, the hotel is almost entirely surrounded by a lake—ideal for throwing oneself in if the big ante-post bet on the National falls at the first and brings down the wife's selection! At Woolton, The **Woolton Redbourne** 0151 421 1500 is a top notch hotel to start and end a great sporting weekend. Finally, if any more suggestions are needed, then turn to the Haydock Park section for inspiration.

Artist: **Peter Curling** **ALDANITI** *Courtesy of:* **Rosenstiel's**

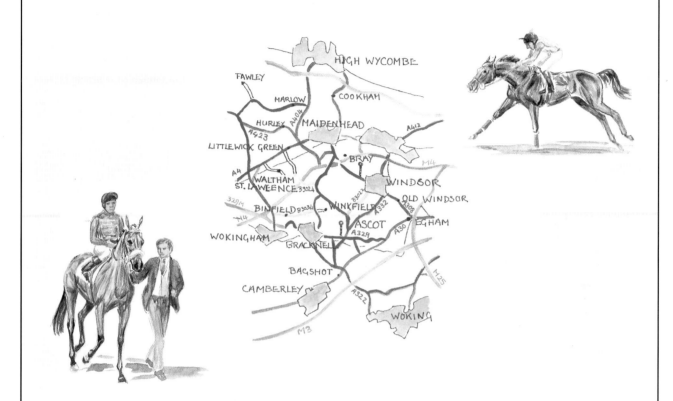

Artist: **Jacquie Jones   THE DESPERATE DRIVE**   _Courtesy of:_ **The Park Gallery**

Fredrick's Hotel and Restaurant

Fredrick's, a calm oasis with ultimate accessibility, is set in two and a half acres of attractive gardens in the heart of Berkshire. Privately owned and managed by The Lösel Family for 22 years, this hotel and its equally famous restaurant have become a byword for quality and excellence. Fredrick's is widely renowned for its distinctive style, luxurious comfort, good food and above all its exceptional personal service combined with a warm and friendly welcome.

From the moment you enter the immaculate reception of this luxury AA four red star hotel with its cascading waterfall, rich furnishings, antiques and abundant flower displays, a warm and friendly welcome awaits you. 'Putting people first' is the guiding philosophy behind the running of this sumptuously equipped hotel which is indicative of the style of service that guests can expect during their stay.

The hotel's thirty seven luxuriously furnished bedrooms, including five superb suites, a number of which have their own private patio or balcony, offer guests every degree of comfort and are tastefully decorated with individuality and style and provide useful features such as hairdryers, trouser presses and ironing facilities. All rooms are equipped with direct dial telephone, radio, colour TV with satellite, minibars plus ample towelling robes and slippers. On arrival, hotel guests are greeted with a choice of either champagne, white wine or sherry and a bowl of fresh fruit is placed in every room.

Through from the reception is the Wintergarden overlooking the delightful patio where guests can relax and enjoy the view of the gardens, beyond which lie the fairways and greens of Maidenhead Golf Club. In the hotel cocktail bar guests can enjoy an informal drink before sampling the culinary delights offered in Fredrick's Restaurant. Widely acknowledged and recognised by all the major guides as one of the finest restaurants in the south of England, Fredrick's offers truly outstanding cuisine. Guests are treated to the finest gourmet cooking prepared from the best of fresh and seasonal ingredients under the supervision of Executive Chef, Brian Cutler.

Open daily, Fredrick's offers an extensive à la carte and table d'hôte menu plus an excellent value Sunday lunch. This combination of culinary expertise, a comprehensive wine list together with thoughtful and attentive service in delightful surroundings, ensures that every meal at Fredrick's is a special occasion.

Fredrick's Hotel and Restaurant, close to Junction 8/9 on the M4 motorway and the centre of Maidenhead, provides a highly accessible location for visitors to the Thames Valley. With a reputation for offering the best of good food, comfort and hospitality, Fredrick's is an ideal base for playing Wentworth, Sunningdale, the Berkshire and Temple and is also perfect for those attending the races at Ascot and Windsor or Henley Regatta in July.

Fredrick's Hotel and Restaurant
Shoppenhangers Road Maidenhead
Tel: (01628) 581000
Fax: (01628) 771054
e mail: reservations@fredricks-hotel.co.uk
web site: www.fredricks-hotel.co.uk

Ascot is a really outstanding sporting venue. It used to suffer from a terribly stuffy image, but all that has gone now. Today, Ascot provides style and class but is most certainly not aloof. It is also interesting to note that the racecorse is endeavouring to use its brand logo - a relatively recent mark when compared with others to enhance star products - an interesting concept amongst a plethora of new ideas from a thoroughly progressive team who we wish well.

The management team includes **Douglas Erskine Crum, Chief Executive, Nicholas Cheyne**, the **Clerk of the Course** and **Danny Homan, Sales & Marketing Director. Her Majesty's Representative** is **Lord Hartington**. The authorities can be contacted at **Ascot Racecourse, Ascot, Berkshire. Tel (01344) 622211. Fax (01344) 628299**. There is a credit card hotline for all bookings on (01344) 876456 and car park details are dealt with on (01344) 20768.

The racecourse lies approximately midway between the M3 and the M4. Travellers from the west should use the M3, exiting at junction 3 or the M4, exiting at junction 10. The A329 is a possibility for people from the east. From London exit at junction 6 of the M4 and turn south through Windsor Great Park. The traffic for the big meetings is usually heavy so an early start is recommended. Indeed, so much so, that the train is often a sensible alternative. Although the station is a fairly stiff three furlongs uphill to the grandstand, one is generally rewarded by a smooth trip from Waterloo giving you plenty of time to peruse the form before the racing. Helicopters are permitted to land during major meetings through Hascombe Aviation Services: (01279) 814632.

The course hosts some 24 racedays and these range from high quality midweek jump meetings in winter to the summer heat of the King George VI and Queen Elizabeth Diamond Stakes, the Festival and Royal Ascot. The Royal Meeting is one of the social occasions of the year with the Royal Family parading down the centre of the course before the racing on all four days. The popularity of the event is staggering: picnics in the car park are always a feast and there is a constant popping of champagne corks before, and after the racing. As in 1999, the 2000 Festival of British Racing will be run over two days.

It should be emphasised that people who attend the royal event merely for the binge are really missing out. The four days of equine excellence are purely and simply the best in the racing year. Tickets to the Royal Enclosure are available provided you follow the proper formalities. All enquiries should be made in writing to Her Majesty's Representative, Ascot Office, St James's Palace, London SW1A 1BP. Visitors from abroad should apply to their embassies. Admission to other enclosures is less demanding and less formal, and racegoers can still enjoy the pomp of the occasion. As a spectacle of elegance, the meeting really takes some beating, and as a race meeting there is no match!

Apart from the Royal Meeting which is at its busiest on Thursday, Gold Cup Day, the Queen Elizabeth II Stakes at the Festival and Diamond Day in July, there are some excellent jump meetings. These include the Victor Chandler Steeplechase in January, the First National Bank Gold Cup in November and the Cantor Fitzgerald Day in December.

Whichever day you decide to go, there are definite advantages in becoming an Annual Member—special rooms and viewing areas are reserved for convenience, the Club dining room and Garden room are two examples. The Annual Membership is only £145 although it does not admit you to the Royal Meeting. Members may also purchase a guest's transferable badge which is priced at £115. Younger racing enthusiasts (17-25 year olds) should not mind the first rate junior membership price of £50. Everyone is welcome at Ascot and you can book in advance for the Royal Meeting for the Grandstand and Paddock from January 1st. In 1999 prices for the Members for Royal Ascot were £36 for Tuesday, Wednesday and Friday and £44 for the Thursday. Be sure to book well in advance. For the Festival meeting and Diamond Day, a charge of £25 was asked for the Members, while £15 allowed you into the Grandstand and £5 the Silver Ring, which is good value. On all other days throughout the year, the Silver Ring was £5, the Grandstand and Paddock £10 and the Members £15. Prices have yet to be confirmed for 2000.

All of Ascot's enclosures have good facilities and good viewing. The course has made some improvements during the past year and the first floor of the Grandstand has been fully refurbished, as have a number of public bars. The course offers reductions of up to 25 per cent on admission charges on certain days and there are a huge number of boxes at the course but—and here's the catch—there is a 35 year waiting list! However, they are often leased on a daily basis. Contact the racecourse to make general enquiries with regard to dates, availability, size etc (01344) 622211. There are numerous rooms, bars and snack outlets in which to indulge—most named after champions that have graced Ascot's turf. There is now a large area set aside for owners and trainers. The food ranges from four course, waitress served luncheons to hot snacks and sandwiches. Facilities for the disabled are very good and there is a playground for under 11s and free crèche for under 8s. A Barclays Bank is also open in the Grandstand, together with several shops.

It is great to hear of plans to redevelop the vast stands of Ascot. Let's hope the success of these developments is as profound as the atmosphere at the racecourse itself. The racecourse, owned by the crown, should also consider as well as nurturing its own young brand, an association similar to that found at Wimbledon with truly excellent trademarks. The Royal Family is being encouraged to fund itself more progressively and if done sensitively this will be a wonderful way of incorporating revenue without detracting from the style of this outstanding racecourse.

It was the King George VI and Queen Elizabeth Diamond Stakes that again produced one of the races of the season at Ascot in July. Daylami's amazing turn of foot ensured the older horse's victory over the three-year olds, including Derby winner Oath and second-placed Daliapour, and helped inject fresh interest into the Emirates World Series. Racing needs more hardy performers such as Daylami to maintain the public's interest and, hopefully, the success of the World Series at Ascot and other racecourses around the world will prove to be a huge success - time, as ever in racing, will tell.

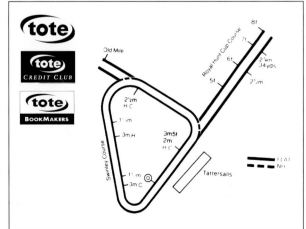

There are numerous excellent hostelries in Berkshire's leafy countryside making ideal ports of call for a pre or post-race chat. We start our Ascot recommendations with a pub and restaurant double, the **Winkfield** (01344) 883498 in Winkfield Row—there is fine bar food here and a cosy restaurant. Another good eating establishment located in Ascot is the **Thatched Tavern** (01344) 620874—a great atmosphere here as well with first rate beer. The **Rose and Crown** (01344) 882051 has some rooms and good food, its very handy for the racecourse.

Back in Winkfield, one finds the **Olde Hatchet** which is both handy and friendly and the small restaurant is well worth considering. Another pub with a restaurant is the **White Hart**—the bar snacks here are good. Further west, and in Waltham St Lawrence, the **Bell** is a pub restaurant with a beautifully relaxed atmosphere, ideal

Artist: **Susie Whitcombe STRAIGHT MILE START**
Courtesy of: **Osborne Studio Gallery**

for explaining the disastrous losses of the afternoons racing to one's better half! (but don't take the children)

Binfield has more than its fair share of good boozers—the **Stag and Hounds** and the **Victoria Arms** are two of several that should be sampled. Or if one happens to be heading to, or coming from, the south west perhaps you might try the **Crooked Billet** (01734) 780438 in Wokingham and there are numerous others in the surrounding villages of this pleasant part of England.

If Ascot is the throne of racing then a similar title might befit the renowned **Waterside Inn** at Bray (01628) 20691—booking here is absolutely essential—massively expensive, but renowned Michel Roux restaurant with some gorgeous rooms for those who really want to push the boat out. Also at Bray, the **Monkey Island Hotel** (01628) 623400, securely anchored on its own private island, is an idyllic retreat from the bustle of Ascot. The **Hinds Head** here is a popular pub to shortlist. Another jewel is the **Brickmakers Arms** (01276) 472267 - very good fayre here.

There are many people who will dash straight home after racing but for people wishing to stay locally, there

are a number of possibilities; the **Berystede Hotel** (01344) 623311 on the Bagshot Road in Ascot, in Bagshot itself, the **Pennyhill Park Hotel** (01276) 471774 a grand country mansion which also has a commendable restaurant, the **Latymer Room**, and its own 9 hole golf course. An alternative which is less pricey is the **Cricketers**, also in Bagshot (01276) 473196. A little further south one arrives in Camberley. Here, the **Frimley Hall Hotel** (01276) 28321 is not cheap but most comfortable. Other places that are well worth considering include a brace of hotels in Egham, in neighbouring Surrey. Neither is particularly cheap, but both are extremely comfortable. They are **Great Fosters** (01784) 433822, an outstandingly elegant former hunting lodge with good facilities, and the **Runnymede** (01784) 436171 where a Thames-side setting adds scenic splendour—a warm favourite for racegoers. A jolly restaurant in Egham should also be noted when visiting the races or bloodstock sales—The **Olive Grove** (01784) 439494, where Mediterranean cuisine is the order of the day. Maidenhead is also handy for the course and **Fredrick's Hotel** (01628) 635934 is well worth a visit (a superb restaurant here as well). Continuing northwards, one finds another stylish establishment, the **Bell Inn** (01296) 630252 at Aston Clinton. Both the restaurant and hotel are outstanding—a day at Ascot, followed by an evening at the Bell would, to put it mildly, be memorable. In Sonning, **The Great House** (01734) 692277 comes particularly well recommended for both service and value while in Hurley, **Ye Olde Bell** (01628) 825881 boasts a wealth of charming features and extremely comfortable bedrooms. Further out in Pingewood, the **Kirtons Hotel and Country Club** (01734) 500885, offers a spectacular lakeside situation, but is modern by comparison. Another modern and excellently equipped hotel is the Swiss styled **Coppid Beech** (01344) 303333—a good restaurant here as well.

In Ascot itself, the **Royal Berkshire Hotel** (01344) 623322, is a superb Queen Anne mansion with excellent restaurants and is worth noting when visiting this esteemed course. Ascot is synonymous with style and if one wishes to experience the real glamour of days gone by, then a visit to the singularly magnificent **Cliveden** (01628) 668561 is in order. Former home of the Astor family, the house is now a hotel of unrivalled elegance. Another handy local favourite is the **Stirrups Hotel** (01344) 882284 at Maidens Green near Bracknell a hotel and restaurant combination with prominent racing themes. A night spent in Ascot does not have to be extravagantly expensive. For affordable comfort try the **Highclere Hotel** (01344) 625220 at Sunninghill. The **Jade Fountain** (01344) 427070, in the High Street is also a good choice for those who enjoy Chinese cooking. Other ideas for the Ascot racegoer can be found in the Windsor, Sandown and Kempton sections of this book. Whatever happens at the racetrack there are numerous fine hostelries at which to celebrate or commiserate in and around Ascot—a thoroughbred racecourse.

Please note the illustrations are for guidance only. The printing process may vary colours slightly. Sizes are not to a uniform scale throughout the list.

Sizes quoted are for paper size unless otherwise stated.

All prints are limited editions unless otherwise stated.

WE THREE KINGS
by Susan Crawford   14" x 25" or 7" x 12"

THE SNOW TUNNEL by Roy Miller   19" × 14"

SUDDEN BLIZZARD
by Roy Miller   12 ½" × 13"

DESERT ORCHID
by Claire Burton   17" × 15"

EVERGREEN CHAMPIONS
by Roy Miller   17 ½" × 22"

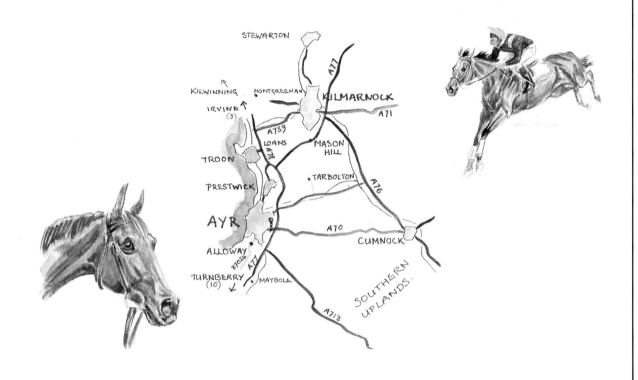

Artist: **Barry Linklater JOCKEYS UP** *Courtesy of:* **W H Patterson Gallery**

The **Clerk of the Course** and **General Manager** at Ayr can be contacted at **2 Whitletts Road, Ayr, KA8 0JE. Tel (01292) 264179. Fax (01292) 610140. E mail: info@ayr-racecourse.co.uk web site: www.ayr-racecourse.co.uk** On racedays there is an on-course office at the main Eglinton Stand entrance.

The track is situated just outside Ayr and is easily accessible via the dual carriageway which bypasses the town centre. The course is about 400 miles from London but the motorway network should see you through smoothly and the A713, the A70 and the A77 will carry you to Ayr from Glasgow on the latter stages of your journey to the large, free car parks. If the car journey sounds too much like hard work, then Prestwick Airport is located only 15 minutes away from the racecourse while Glasgow International Airport is only 45 minutes from Ayr. The airstrip in the centre of the course is suitable only for helicopters but please notify the racecourse of your intended arrival. Trains depart from London Euston and the station at Ayr is a mile from the course where a bus trip will complete your journey.

The management have been very successful in attracting sponsorship at Scotland's premier racecourse. There are several races to look out for, including the Stakis Casinos Scottish National in April, the Tennant Caledonian Brewery Scottish Classic in July and the popular Western Meeting in September which features the Ladbroke Ayr Gold Cup. This three day meeting provides excellent racing and the ideal excuse for a jaunt to the superb Ayrshire coast.

The daily admission rates vary from meeting to meeting. Daily entrance in 1999 to the Club Enclosure was priced from £14-£25, while entrance to the Grandstand and Paddock cost between £7 and £10. OAPs and students with the appropriate identification are welcomed to the racecourse at £4 for most meetings with children under 16 of course admitted free. Ayr have introduced some innovative ways to get people to "Come Racing!" including Family Newcomers Days when £7 admits you to all enclosures and a Ladies Evening in July where the same price admits the fairer sex to the Members. Two day badges cost £35 for the Members and £15 for the Grandstand for the Scottish National Meeting and £48 and £20 respectively for the Gold Cup meeting in September. For parties of ten or more there is a special offer of £13 to include admission to the Grandstand and lunch in the Eglinton Suite. If you wish to become an Annual Member, a double badge together with a complimentary parking pass in the Western House Car Park will cost around £200. A joining fee of £100 is also required. This will allow you to attend Ayr's 25 annual fixtures as well reciprocal meetings at other racecourses.

The on-course catering facilities, managed by Strachan Kerr, are comprehensive, ranging from a full tented village to the Western House which caters for parties of 60 to 200, and the Eglinton Rooms which can hold up to 400 guests. The Princess Royal Stand offers twelve private boxes for groups of up to 20 close to the winning post and two large sponsors' rooms which can hold up to 90 guests. Private rooms and private boxes are also available for daily hire in the recently refurbished Craigie Stand accomodating from 14 to 90 guests.. There are various restaurants and snack bars at Ayr including the club restaurant in the Western House, a champagne and seafood bar in the Members' and the Eglinton Restaurant in the Grandstand.

Facilities for the disabled include viewing ramps and lavatories in all enclosures and ground floor bars. There is a Ladbrokes betting shop in the Grandstand. Ayr is a fine racecourse boasting competitive racing and some spectacular betting events. All in all, this is an excellent racecourse.

Local Favourites

There are all manner of guesthouses in and around Ayr and the local tourist board will help with any enquiries. People wishing for hotel accommodation also have a good choice when visiting West Scotland and Ayr racecourse.

The **Turnberry Hotel** (01655) 331000 is an extremely stylish place to stay with an array of leisure facilities, including two world-famous golf courses, the Ailsa and the Arran. Ayr itself is a busy market town which overlooks the Firth of Clyde. The coastline reveals some charming sandy beaches and attractive fishing villages. The town has many restaurants, bars and hotels but two hotels which stand out particularly are **Fairfield House** (01292) 267461 and **Manor Park Hotel** (01292) 479365, recently refurbished and offering excellent cuisine. At Alloway, the **North Park Hotel** (01292) 442336 and the **Burns Monument** (01292) 442426 merit consideration. **Ladyburn** (01655) 740585 at Maybole lies within easy reach of Ayr and also many of the renowned local golf courses and is family run, welcoming and offers excellent food. Good fare can also be found in Ayr at **Fouters Bistro** (01292) 261391 and **The Stables** (01292) 283704—good Scottish cooking. **Highgrove House** (01292) 312511 is a good restaurant with rooms to note in Troon.

More golf is available in Prestwick and, as you might imagine, the town is also well placed for the nearby airport of the same name. **Fairways Hotel** (01292) 70396 is a convenient guesthouse. But if it's racing you are after, an ideal place to stay near the racecourse is the **Carlton Toby** (01292) 76811 on the Ayr road. The bedrooms are comfortable and the bars and restaurant should also be visited. Further north still, one arrives at yet another golfing delight, Troon. Three more hotels to note are the **Marine Highland** (01292) 314444 which overlooks the golf course and the Isle of Arran. This is a well equipped and comfortable hotel with a superb bistro. Secondly, visit **Piersland House** (01292) 314747 and **Lochgreen House** (01292) 313343 is also first class. A short way from Irvine in the Montgreenan Estate, near Kilwinning, lies the **Montgreenan Mansion House** (01294) 557733, former home of Lord Glasgow. Two miles from the village of Stewarton, amid the valleys and countryside, is the splendid **Chapeltoun House Hotel** (01560) 482696—quite tremendous. Our final thoughts are situated someway south of Ayr, **Knockinaam Lodge** (01776) 810471, Portpatrick, is an outstanding hotel with a first class restaurant—a real favourite. Alternatively for those on their way south **Farlam Hall** (016977) 46234, near Brampton is another good tip. A very warm welcome, outstanding food and comfortable bedrooms—a winning treble.

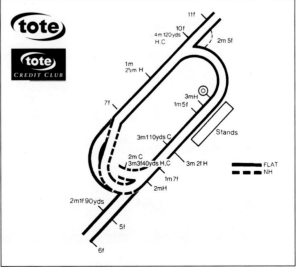

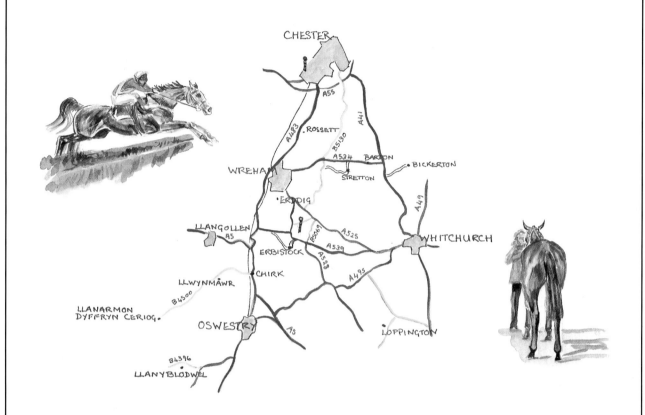

Artist: **Malcolm Coward GOING WELL** _Courtesy of:_ **Sally Mitchell Fine Arts**

The Secretary and Clerk of the Course is **Major Michael Webster**, who can be contacted by writing to **The Racecourse Office, Overton Road, Bangor-on-Dee, Wrexham LL13 0DA. Tel (01978) 780323 Fax (01978) 780985. E mail bangordee@aol.com**

The course is located in the Bryn y Pys estate near Bangor-on-Dee on the Welsh border. Chester is some 15 miles to the north and Shrewsbury some 25 miles south. London is a full 180 miles away. The major routes to the course are the A525 from Stoke and the M6. The A41 to Wolverhampton, and the M54 and A41 north towards Chester, can be used to link with the M56 network of the north west. The course itself lies on the A525, but to reach the course it is necessary to turn off the bypass, drive through the village and onto the B5069 for Overton-on-Dee. There are also a number of minor routes, the B5130 for instance, which can be taken in preference to the A roads to enjoy the border country-side. There is plenty of free parking at the course. The A5 from Llangollen will assist people travelling from inland Wales. Wrexham and its rail network is four miles away and is part of the Euston line, as are nearby Chester and Shrewsbury. A free bus services is provided by the racecourse, leaving Wrexham Station one and a half hours before the first race and returning after racing. If you wish to make a speedy entry/departure then your helicopter is welcomed, though please contact the Clerk of the Course.

Among the major racing highlights are the Wynnstay Hunt evening, the North Western Area point-to-point championship final in May, and the Countryside Charity Day in October. If you do make the excellent decision to embark on a day at Bangor-on-Dee, then you will not be too shocked by the entrance prices that await you: £10 for the Paddock and £5 for the Course Enclosure. If you are intent on making regular visits to the track then you ought to consider an Annual Members badge: £100 is the asking price and it is worth noting that the members' car park has one of the best vantage points from which to view the racing. In addition to the days at Bangor, there are 14 reciprocal meetings at some exceptional racecourses. If you are planning to take a party racing at Bangor, discounts of 25 per cent are available for groups of 12 or more and a free racecard and betting vouchers come with all advance bookings. A new building houses the impressive Owners, Trainers and Bangor Annual Members bar, and the Sponsors' suite. A new seafood and wine bar (Bookings 01676 535237) is also popular with Owners and Trainers. Larger parties should note that marquees are available. The course authorities have pointed out that they will accept sponsorship for as little as £250 but, quite naturally, would prefer to have at least £1000 per race but can, on occasions accommodate birthdays and other anniversary celebrations for a smaller amount. The sponsors' package includes a return of ten per cent of the sponsorship contribution in free badges and additional badges can be purchased at a reduced rate. There is a restaurant in the Paddock enclosure and the caterers are Hughes of Welshpool (01938) 553366 if you wish to make bookings. There are also snacks available at the bars, where you can munch roast beef sandwiches whilst watching the closed circuit television.

Children and wheelchair-bound racegoers are admitted free and the latter have the benefit of a wheelchair viewing stand. There is ample car parking overlooking the course where a reserved space may be booked by phoning the racecourse. There are public telephones and betting shops in the Paddock enclosure and a 'walk in' Tote betting office. The whole course delights with its country

setting and splendid atmosphere. If you are seeking a fun day out in 2000 at one of Britain's idyllic national hunt courses, make sure that Bangor is on the shortlist.

Local Favourites

This is an area rife with hotels and hostelries. A favourite establishment with the racing fraternity is the **Cross Foxes Inn** (01978) 780380. The **Carden Park Hotel** (01829) 731000 also comes highly recommended and is ideal for combining a day at the races with a spot of golf. A favourite local pub is the **Royal Oak** (01978) 780289 in Bangor.

Some of the best places to stay are in Llangollen, home of the Eisteddfod festival of song and dance for those who appreciate a fiesta as well as a flutter. The **Hand Hotel** (01978) 860303 affords an extremely comfortable stay, while in Bridge Street, the **Royal Hotel** (01978) 860202 enjoys a fine setting over the River Dee. The restaurant here is good and the bar's ideal for a leisurely chat before racing. **Rhydonnen Ucha Rhewl** (01978) 860153 is modestly priced and can also offer shooting and trout fishing. Three miles east, the **Bryn Howel Hotel** (01978) 860331 is another cosy place. One of the most strikingly pretty spots is the Horseshoe Pass where the **Britannia Inn** (01978) 860144 is a pleasant place to relax. If you are merely looking for a restaurant with views over the waters of the Dee, then **Caesars** (01978) 860133, where an imaginative menu makes good use of fresh local produce, is an excellent idea. If you prefer a wine bar, **Gales** (01978) 860089 is well thought of and ideal for an early lunch, though it has a few bedrooms too Another good performer is the **Cross Lanes** (01978) 780555—extremely convenient and increasingly popular with the racing fraternity, it offers special racing breaks.

In Llanarmon Dyffryn Ceiriog, the **West Arms** (01691) 600665 is over 400 years old and remains a charming place to stay. The **Hand** (01691) 600264 is also most welcoming, as is the **Golden Pheasant** (01978) 718281 in Llwynmawr. In Llanyblodwell, the **Horseshoe** is particularly recommended for people who might wish to take in some fishing, good bar food and good value accommodation. Another Shropshire selection is the **Blacksmiths Arms**, Loppington, some way south but worth the trip. Closer to hand and quite appropriately titled, the **Stableyard Country Restaurant** (01978) 780642 is another fine local performer. Also close at hand is the **Buck House Hotel** (01978) 780336, extremely handy for the racecourse for those of you who prefer not to travel too far to the races.

Further south in the quiet town of Oswestry, the **Wynnstay** (01691) 655261 is an appealing Georgian inn. And in Morda, a little south of Oswestry, the **Sweeney Hall Hotel** (01691) 652450 has a beautiful parkland setting and a good restaurant. Finally, **Dearnford Hall** (01948) 662319 is a first rate classy performer.

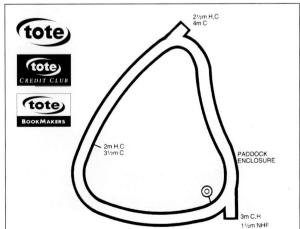

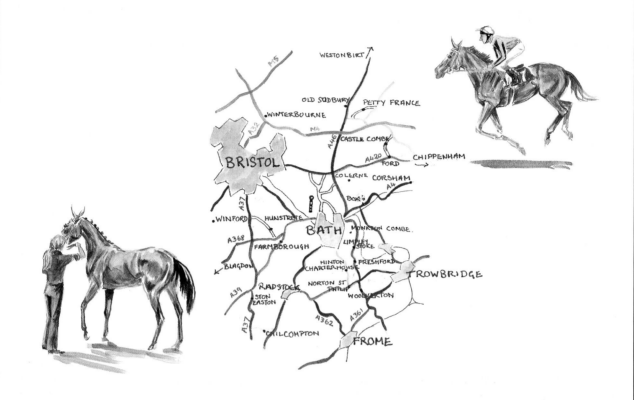

Artist: **Peter Smith THE LAST FURLONG** _Courtesy of:_ **Frost & Reed**

The **Secretary** of this beautiful track outside Bath is Sylvia **Wilcox**, who can be contacted at **The Bath Racecourse Co Ltd**, Lansdown, Bath BA1 9BU Tel (01225) 424609/(01295) 688030 Fax (01225) 444415/(01295) 688211 **Rodger Farrant** is **Clerk of the Course** and can be contacted on **(01291) 622260**.

In order to reach Bath racecourse several points should be noted: London is approximately 100 miles away, Bath three miles away and Bristol ten miles yonder. The M4 route is quick but rather boring while the A4 is more interesting but can be fairly congested. Junction 18 off the M4 is the appropriate exit point. The course is well signposted from here, nestling amidst the villages of Kelston, Charlcombe, Swainswick and North Stoke. For travellers from the north and west the M5/M4 is the better route while the A46 is an alternative if time is not so pressing. If, however, time is of the essence and you decide to take a helicopter, then please land at the north end of the coach park. Car parking areas abound and are free although if you wish to park in the centre of the course, a charge of £5 is levied—which admits the driver only. All additional occupants will also be charged. Members are entitled to reserved parking. The railway station in Bath is on the main Paddington-South Wales line and buses from the station go to the racecourse.

The 2000 fixture list is expected to follow a similar pattern to last year with 14 flat race meetings. The course's feature race remains the Somerset Stakes. Although crowds are always fairly good at Bath, the course is, not surprisingly, at its busiest during its weekend fixtures in June and July. The charge for a day's racing at Bath is £14 for a Daily Members badge, £10 if you prefer the Tattersalls and £5 or £2 if you have an inkling for the Silver Ring or the Course Enclosures. The Annual Members badge is priced at £94 whilst a double badge can be ordered for £188. Junior Members (21 and under) are asked to part with £20 which is good value. Annual Members also enjoy thirteen reciprocal race meetings. One final point worth noting is that if you want to organise a larger gathering a 20 per cent saving can be made on parties of 20 or more, but this applies only to the Tattersalls and Silver Ring enclosures.

There are a total of nine private boxes available for hire and betting vouchers in units of two or five can be pre-arranged in advance for guests. Should you wish to take a larger party, there are three rooms available for entertaining. Catering is organised by Letheby & Christopher, (01242) 523203. These facilities are well used so you are advised to book well in advance. If you would prefer a marquee then these can be erected—please contact the racecourse office for further details. You can also make bookings for lunch in the Members and Tattersalls Restaurant—indeed, this is sometimes advisable. One final point that should be noted is that there is access to the stand roof which makes for an interesting vantage point.

If you are disabled or taking a disabled friend racing, then do contact the course and they will make life as easy as possible for you. Telephones can be found at various points on the course and there is a betting shop serving Tatts and the Silver Ring.

Local Favourites

Bath is a beautiful city with many good hotels and restaurants among its attractions. An excellent hotel is the **Priory** (01225) 331922, where the French cuisine is superb and the Georgian mansion exudes luxury. The **Lansdown Grove** (01225) 315891 is also charming and slightly less expensive!

Bargain seekers will also find solace at the **Laura Place Hotel** (01225) 463815, **Orchard Lodge Hotel** (01225) 466115 and **Paradise House Hotel** (01225) 317723. If money is no object two for the shortlist are the **Bath Spa** (01225) 444424 and the majestic **Royal Crescent** (01225) 823333. Heading south out of town quickly brings you to the excellent **Combe Grove Manor** (01225) 834644 at Monkton Combe. There are some excellent leisure facilities here as well.

The hotel and fine restaurant of **Ston Easton Park** (01761) 241631 is one for the notebook—an outstanding pedigree well worth a detour if your funds are in plentiful supply. In Hinton Charterhouse, **Homewood Park** (01225) 723731 and **Green Lane House** (01225) 723631 are both good. The former is extremely grand, the latter far less so but most pleasant. In Hunstrete, the **Hunstrete House Hotel** (01761) 490490 boasts an outstanding restaurant in a distinguished Georgian manor house set in rolling parkland. Nearby Chelwood houses the first class **Chelwood House** (01761) 490730. **Lucknam Park** (01225) 742777 at Colerne near Bath is another Georgian manor house, quite unsurpassed in luxury and cuisine. There are all manner of restaurants to sample in Bath among the best are **Lettonie** (01225) 446676, the **Hole in the Wall** (01225) 425242 and **Clos du Roy** (01225) 444450.

Less pricey, but extremely comfortable accommodation can be discovered in Limpley Stoke, at the **Cliffe** (01225) 723226 which has a tremendous restaurant. In Beanacre, **Beechfield House** (01225) 703700 is outstanding. A similar summary could be applied to the **Old Bell** (01666) 822344 in Malmesbury which is a rapidly improving type and well worth considering. In Winterbourne, the **Jarvis Grange Hotel** at Northwoods (01454) 777333 is an elegant place to stay with good leisure facilities and in Dunkirk, the **Petty France** (01454) 238361 is also good. But people who are content with a bar snack or just a post-race pint may care to try any of the following gems. Stanton Wick offers the **Carpenter's Arms** (01761) 490202 a tremendous all rounder, good ales, excellent food, bar meals and restaurant, even some cosy bedrooms if required. The **George** (01373) 834224 at Norton St Philip is charming. **The Plaine** (01373) 834723 is a delightful place to stay near here. **The Inn** at Freshford and the **Red Lion** at Woolverton are appealing, and returning to Hinton Charterhouse, the **Stag** has style. The **Royal Oak**, Winsford, has a delightful country setting, and nearby in Ford, the **White Hart** (01249) 782213 is a welcoming pub with a pleasant restaurant and some bedrooms. Another splendid **White Hart** lies in the charming village of Castle Combe. Our final selection is the **Manor House** (01249) 782206 also at Castle Combe. Romance is in the air here and racegoers with a conscience should consider it a firm favourite for their less enthusiastic partners, particularly if they also enjoy golf!

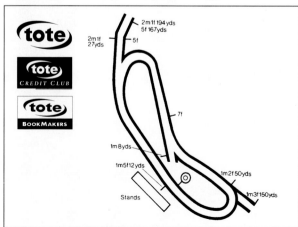

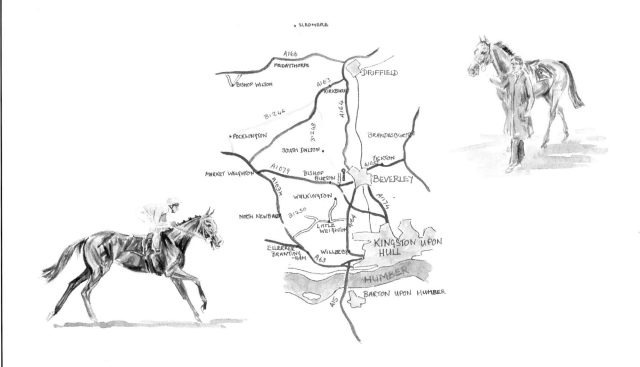

Artist: **Margaret Barrett CLASS AND COURAGE** *Courtesy of:* **The Artist**

The people to contact at this excellent track are headed by **John Cleverly**, who acts as **Manager. Mrs J Parry** is the **Secretary**, and **Mrs Jane Johnson** is in charge of sponsorship, marketing and other bookings. Contact them at: **The Racecourse, York Road, Beverley, HU17 8QZ. Tel (01482) 867488/882645. Fax (01482) 863892.**

Beverley itself is situated to the south east of York and north west of the Humber estuary. The southbound traveller should make best use of the A1, the A19 and the A1079. If one is travelling from the south or east make your way via the A1(M) to the M62, exit left through North Cave (junction 38) and from there pursue the B1230. From Lincolnshire, the A15 Humber Bridge followed by the A164 is probably a good each-way bet. There are a number of routes east of Beverley. Should one be venturing from that part of the country, the A1035 looks to be the obvious choice. When it comes to a train journey the best idea is to go to Beverley itself, although it may be prudent to journey via York or Doncaster and thus catch a faster train. An intermittent bus service runs from Beverley station when you reach that destination. For more speedy journeys, helicopters will come in handy. If you happen to have one available you are welcome to land it in the centre of the course. Parking for your helicopter is free, as it is for your car. There is a separate car park for Members at the course.

The 2000 fixture list will probably contain about the same number of fixtures as 1999—18 days—and there will again be a Sunday fixture in August. The first July meeting is a popular occasion—well worth attending. The feature races are now worth approximately £15,000 each and they are two of the well established ones: the Brian Yeardley Continental Two Year Old Trophy and the Hilary Needler Trophy.

For 2000, the daily fee will be £14 for admission to the Members Enclosure (£9 for 16-21 year olds), £9 for Tattersalls, £3 for the Silver Ring and £2 for the Course. Party rates are offered for all enclosures except the Club Enclosure, with groups of between 10 and 30 being offered admission to Tatts for £8 and groups of more than 30 for £7. Annual Members at Beverley pay £90 for a single badge. An Associate Membership (two people) is £140 and Junior Members can purchase discounted subscriptions of £50 per annum. Under 16s are admitted free of charge provided they are accompanied.

The main grandstand has been extended to include a larger club dining room with a suite of three entertaining boxes which may be taken as one to accommodate a large party. On the second floor there is a box suitable for parties of up to 50 in addition to the four original boxes. Prices are available on application to Mrs Johnson at the racecourse office. A recent addition to the facilities is a new weighing room with a Paddock Bar perched above it which offers wonderful views of the racecourse and the surrounding countryside. Bookings can be made for the restaurants and should you need to make any catering enquiries then Craven Gilpin, the racecourse caterers, 0113 287 6387, are the chaps to contact. If you really want to push the boat out, the racecourse staff will be happy to organise the erection of a marquee.

There are three telephones at the course—vital for placing those bets should you be out of cash as there is no bank here. There are however two betting shops, in Tattersalls and the Silver Ring should you wish to lighten your purse, or hopefully add to it.

Local Favourites
Beverley is a flourishing market town surrounded by outstanding countryside. To the north, the Wolds and the Yorkshire Moors. To the west, the Pennines and to the east, ragged coastline. The 17th century **Beverley Arms Hotel** (01482) 869241 is an extremely comfortable inn in which to stay and a good place from which to explore.

Aside from the Beverley Arms, the **White Horse** (01482) 868103 better known as Nellies, has a superbly traditional pub atmosphere. The **Kings Head** (01482) 868103 is also a good pub to put the racegoer in the right spirit before racing—or equally after the racing is over as the latter has some satisfactory bedrooms. **Lairgate** (01482) 882141 is also a worthy contender. **Cerutti 2** (01482) 866700 is a restaurant with good form. Nearby, a number of welcoming hotels include the **Tickton Grange Hotel** (01964) 543666 a superb Georgian country house two miles from Beverley. Slightly further afield in Driffield one finds the **Bell Hotel** (01377) 256661, a pleasant inn in the market place—ideal for a post-race bar snack or dinner in the restaurant.

Alternatives to the south of Beverley include **Rowley Manor** (01482) 848248 at Little Weighton—a splendid parkland setting with a particularly relaxing bar, ideal for studying overnight declarations in style. There is further comfort to be found with another manor, this time in Willerby, the **Willerby Manor** (01482) 652616, a mention here also for the **Grange Park Hotel** (01482) 656488, just to the south of Beverley—well-equipped and comfortable. If you are lured into Hull then an excellent restaurant in which to have a bite is **Ceruttis** (01482) 328501, a harbourside spot with first rate seafood.

In Brandesburton, the **Dacre Arms** (01964) 542392 appeals—note the Wensleydale Ploughmans, while in Bishop Burton, the **Altisidora** is a friendly pub with a delightful setting. The pub takes its name from the 1813 St Leger winner. In South Dalton, the **Pipe and Glass** (01430) 810246 has great character and serves good food while in Market Weighton, the **Londesborough Arms** (01430) 872214 also has bedrooms and is a very friendly place to stay. The **Triton** in Sledmere (01377) 236644 is very popular and ideally situated for **Sledmere House**—well worth a post-race inspection. Yorkshire Pudding lovers should note the **Half Moon** (01482) 843403 at Skidby. The **Manor House** (01482) 881645 at Walkington is very relaxing and the restaurant is first class. Our final recommendation for all 'foodies' is the **Winteringham Fields** (01724) 733096. Here the food is fantastic and there are some delightful bedrooms as well—one for the notebook for those of you considering a trip to Beverley races in 2000.

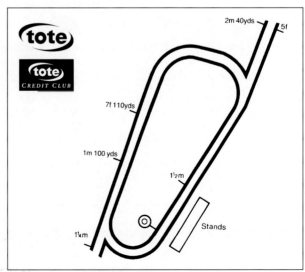

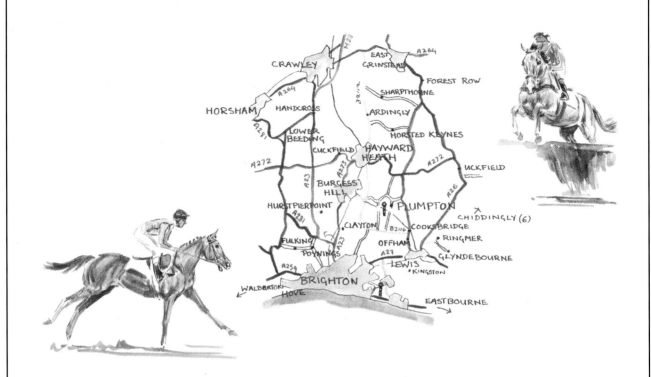

Artist: **Katy Sodeau** **LAST TO LOAD, BRIGHTON** _Courtesy of:_ **The Artist**

Anew team has taken over at Brighton recently, reflecting the partnership that now runs the course between Northern Racing Limited and Brighton and Hove Council. **Jeremy Martin** is **Racing Manager** and **Clerk of the Course**, **Phil Bell** is **Commercial Manager** and **Judy Welsh** is **Racecourse Secretary**. They can be contacted on **(01273) 603580** by **Fax (01273) 673267**. Should you wish to write, the address is **Brighton Racecourse Company Limited, Brighton Racecourse, Freshfield Road, Brighton, East Sussex, BN2 2XZ.**

The course is situated in one of Brighton's eastern suburbs, high up on White Hawk Hill and about a 60 mile journey from the capital. If you are coming from outside Brighton, head towards Sussex University on the A27 and take the exit for Woodingdean. In the centre of Woodingdean, turn right at the traffic lights and a mile down the road lies the racecourse. Alternatively, however, you can follow the signs to the racecourse through the town centre, which may take a little longer. The London-Brighton Victoria rail line is most efficient and there is a courtesy bus service from the station to the racecourse on racedays with two trips back after the last. The Brighton/Hove buses all stop near the course too. There is plenty of space for car parking which is provided free.

Under the leadership of Chairman, Stan Clarke, £13 million has been spent on new facilities, inluding a Member's Bar, Parade Ring and Winner's Enclosure, hospitality rooms and an Owners and Trainers Bar. Considerable investment is planned over the next few years to improve many more areas, particularly the public facilities in the Grandstand.

Prices are likely to remain the same as for the 1999 season with admission to the Members costing £12. The price for Tattersalls is £8 with £5 per car and £4 per occupant for the Silver Ring. Annual Membership was priced at £130 with a discount if purchased before New Year's day. This includes free car parking and reciprocal meetings at several other courses including Epsom, Sandown Park, Windsor, Folkestone and others as well as all meetings at Uttoxeter and Newcastle as an added bonus. If you are planning a group outing you will be entitled to a discount of 20 per cent for parties of 20 or more.

Parties of between 12 and 150 can be entertained in various places around the racecourse and private boxes can cater for up to 200 guests. There are also sites for marquees which can hold 200 guests comfortably. All inclusive hospitality packages are available at £60-£80 plus VAT per head. There are also numerous bars throughout the course as well as a more formal restaurant, bookings for which can be made by telephoning the racecourse. It is worth noting that all of these facilities are also available for use on non-racedays.

There are no banks on site, but there is a recently refurbished and much improved betting shop located in Tatts. Facilities for children are provided although only at summer meetings. We are pleased to say that course management is currently reviewing facilities for the disabled and some improvements may be forthcoming; currently there is access to all floors of the Grandstand by lift.

I am also pleased to say that a number of sponsorship and marketing opportunities are now available at Brighton. Race sponsors are offered a free box and admission tickets. The number of tickets you receive depends on the amount you give as sponsorship—amounts start from £500 and the more you pay the more you get.

Whether you are a prospective sponsor, a company looking for a venue for corporate hospitality or just a simple punter, Brighton is a fine course and well worth a visit.

Local Favourites

Perhaps it's the sea air that makes so many organisations choose Brighton for their annual conference. The best seafront hotels in Brighton are the **Grand** (01273) 321188 which is quite grand, the **Stakis Metropole** (01273) 775432 headquarters to many a political conference, the startlingly modern **Brighton Thistle** (01273) 206700, the **Stakis** (formerly the Bedford) (01273) 329744, and the **Old Ship** (01273) 329001. Highly recommended by the racecourse management are several restaurants in Brighton itself including **Al Duomo** (01273) 326741 and **Al Forno** (01273) 324905 for fans of Italian cuisine. and **Gars** for Chinese near the Town Hall (01273) 321321. Two restaurants also to note include **Langan's Bistro** (01273) 606933 and the unpretentious but good **Black Chapati** (01273) 699011. **Whytes** (01273) 776618 is also well worth considering.

The waters of Brighton stretch round the coast and meet with Hove. Here a number of good hotels can be found. One of the best is the **Sackville** (01273) 736292—a pleasant seafront hotel. The **Hungry Monk** (01323) 482178, Jevington, is a restaurant to delight you with a wonderful atmosphere and first rate food. Local recommendations also include **Otello** for Italian (01273) 729774. and for Indian, **Ganges Brasserie** (01273) 728292. Also not far away from Brighton in Kingston near Lewes you are encouraged to try **Juggs** (01273) 472523—a great 15th century pub with good real ales and excellent home made food. **Shelleys** (01273) 472361 is a noted hotel in the High Street.

If you are not content with the seaside offerings in Brighton, then Eastbourne is an elegant and slightly more tranquil alternative. Good value accommodation is plentiful. Examples include the **Bay Lodge Hotel** (01323) 732515 and **Hotel Mandalay** (01323) 729222. However, the star of the show is the impressive **De Vere Grand** (01323) 412345—great for families, expensive but very good. A busy pub to note for its tremendous views is the **Devil's Dyke** at Devil's Dyke on the downs above the town. For some really good food, the **Tottington Manor Hotel Restaurant** (01903) 815757 at Edburton is also worth a visit, as is the extremely comfortable **Stakis Avisford Park Hotel** (01243) 551215 at Walberton—well worth the extra journey for those who enjoy excellent food and sporting facilities.

A final selection that should not be overlooked includes **Amberley Castle** (01798) 831992—medieval style and 20th century comfort. We would also strongly recommend a hotel of real character, **Ockenden Manor** (01444) 416111—a _Travelling the Turf_ favourite. Further north at the delightfully named Pease Pottage, the **Cottesmore Golf & Country Club** (01293) 528256 comes highly recommended.

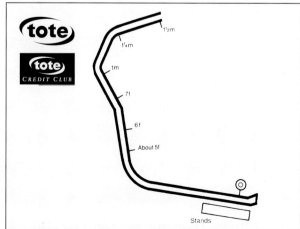

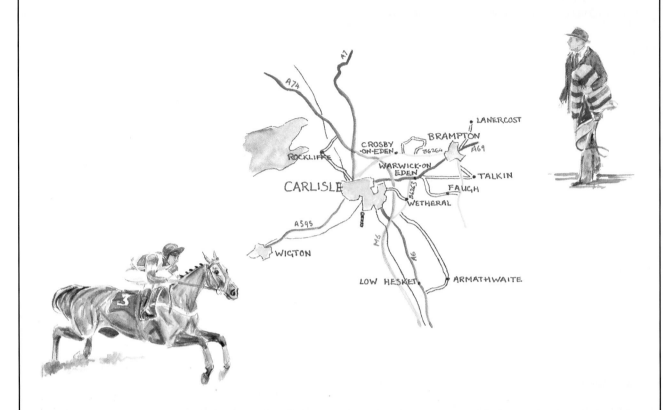

Artist: **Barrie Linklater** **_THE GREY IS COMING THROUGH NOW_** _Courtesy of:_ **W H Patterson Gallery**

At Carlisle, **Johnnie Fenwicke-Clennell** is the **Clerk of the Course** and **Racing Manager**, **Teddy Robinson** the **Executive Chairman** and **Mrs Ann Bliss** the **Administration Director and Secretary**. The course address is **The Grandstand Office, The Racecourse, Durdar Road, Carlisle, Cumbria, CA2 4TS. Tel (01228) 522973. Fax (01228) 591827.**

Carlisle is a good 300 miles from the capital. However, it is easy to reach for racegoers from all areas of the country. The M6 is the motorway to follow, exiting at junction 42 and then following the signs two miles to the course. The A69 Carlisle-Newcastle road is the best route from the north east whilst people from areas west of Carlisle should travel on the A595 or the A596. The racecourse is two miles south of the town and the No 66 bus from Carlisle will deposit you at the course. From London, Carlisle bound trains depart from Euston station or alternatively you can jump on a Kings Cross train and change at Newcastle upon Tyne. If you are making the trip by car you will find some 20 acres of grass on which to park your motor. Aviators please note that Carlisle airport is some eight miles away. Helicopters can land on the racecourse provided prior arrangements have been made.

The Cumberland Plate and the Carlisle Bell, two of the course's major races, are steeped in tradition and a delight to attend. Racing at Carlisle takes place every month of the year and a new irrigation system has recently been added to help the going. In 1999 the weekday admission charge to the Club enclosure was £12, while Saturdays, Bank Holidays and evenings are £14, with entry to Tattersalls set at £7. Pensioners and under 21s receive a £3 discount.

Annual Membership is £100, and an additional Lady's Club badge will cost £50. Fourteen reciprocal meetings are also laid on for the Carlisle Member. People under 21 will be glad to know that membership is priced at £50.

Party organisers will be pleased to hear that parties of 10 or more save 20 per cent per badge to the Tattersalls and Club enclosures, plus a free badge. This rises to a 25 per cent discount for groups larger than 45.

Facilities at Carlisle include the highly regarded Club restaurant (please book) and Tattersalls cafeteria as well as the enlarged and welcoming Red Rum Owners and Trainers room and coffee and wine bars. There is also a refurbished bar and restaurant in the old Tote building—the very first Tote in operation, beating Newmarket by 15 minutes! With regard to more private facilities, five rooms are available in which 20 to 100 guests can be entertained at a cost of £80 minimum. Marquees can also be organised and there is a large hall which seats between 250 and 300 people.

Enquiries with regard to on-course catering should be addressed to the secretary, Mrs Ann Bliss. Expect to pay between £18 and £15 for lunch in the restaurant. Romfords (01434) 688 864 also supply the catering for the cafeteria and snack bars. Children are admitted free of charge to the racecourse if accompanied by an adult and there is a free crèche provided for fixtures during the school holidays. Facilities for disabled racegoers are most considerate at Carlisle with two viewing ramps, specially equipped toilets and easily accessible bars. There is also a trackside car park and picnic area where a levy of £3 per car (£5 on Saturdays, bank holidays and evenings) is requested. There is a betting shop in the Paddock area but no banks are in operation on the course. This friendly racecourse is well positioned between Lakeland and the Borders and those of us seeking a day's racing while touring beautiful countryside will find Carlisle a welcoming port of call.

Local Favourites
In Carlisle itself, one finds a number of possible candidates for a quiet and comfortable night. Firstly, **Cumbria Park** (01228) 522887 is a distinct posibility. **Number Thirty One** (01228) 597080 is a small stylish Victorian town house worthy of note. A restaurant to consider is **No. 10** (01228) 524183. Another guest house of note is **Avondale** (01228) 523012 - excellent value. Secondly, visitors should note the **Cumbrian Hotel** (01228) 531951 in Court Square.

North of Carlisle lies Rockcliffe where a good pub for a snack is the **Crown and Thistle**. The village guards the mouth of the River Eden and is particularly convenient for the A74. Another riverside setting is provided by the extremely pleasant and welcoming **Crosby Lodge Hotel** (01228) 573618 in Crosby-on-Eden. This hotel enjoys a pastoral setting and also has a good restaurant. Returning to Warwick-on-Eden, the **Queen's Arms** (01228) 560699 is another inn of character. Here you will find a restaurant and some comfortable bedrooms. In Talkin, as well as a good golf course, one finds the **Hare and Hounds Inn** (016977) 3456. **Tarn End** at Talkin Tarn (016977) 2340 is a good restaurant which also provides homely accommodation. This is an ideal spot for an early evening stroll to work up a good appetite as the inn is surrounded by some beautiful fells. Another good thought is the **Blacksmiths Arms**— great for bar snacks and some rooms as well.

North of the A69 at Lanercost, the **Abbey Bridge Inn** (016977) 2224 is an unusual pub but a most appealing hostelry in which to savour a winner in the last. However, **Farlam Hall Hotel** (016977) 46234 is definitely the pick of the paddock, a splendid 17th century manor house in gorgeous grounds and a grand restaurant as well—a really classical performer in every way. A nearby hotel to note is the **Crown** (01228) 561888, a coaching inn with first rate facilities. Last, but certainly not least, for the younger punter planning a racing honeymoon to Carlisle (of which there are surely hundreds!) the **Greenlaw Guest House** (01461) 338361 at Gretna Green will provide the required accommodation. The surrounding hostelries and friendly people coupled with a well balanced calendar of sporting fixtures make a visit to Carlisle racecourse a priority for those of you who have not enjoyed the pleasure.

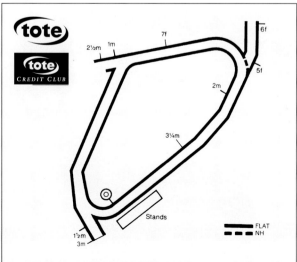

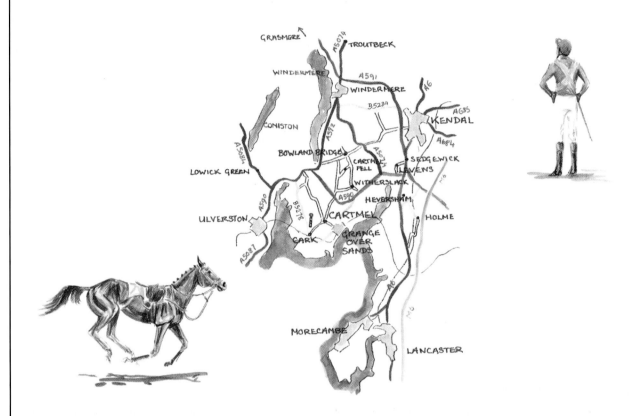

Artist: **Refna Hamey** *FRIENDS UNTIL THE LAST* Courtesy of: **The Artist**

Cartmel offers festival racing with a fun 'shirtsleeve' atmosphere which makes a welcome contrast to some of the country's more 'stiff upper lip' racecourses. It is immensely popular and a thoroughly successful part of Britain's racing scene. The **Clerk of the Course** is **Charles Barnett** and he and the **General Manager, Andrew Tulloch** can be contacted at **Cartmel Steeplechases Ltd, c/o Aintree Racecourse Co Ltd, Ormskirk Road, Aintree Liverpool L9 5AS. Tel 0151 523 2600 Fax 0151 530 1512**. On racedays contact them at the racecourse itself on **Tel (01539) 536340 Fax (01539) 536004.**

The road to the course meanders through the hills of the Lake District. The most direct routes into the area from the north and south are via the M6, exiting at junction 36 for the A590. From the north east, the A69 is a good bet, whereas the A590 will assist eastbound race-goers. A word of warning, leave plenty of time if travelling by car, especially on bank holidays when traffic can be horrific. By train, the Euston line which stops at Cark in Cartmel and Grange-over-Sands is your best bet. Parking facilities are separated into two categories: cars parked in the Paddock Parks are charged £5 while the Course Area is free. Helicopters can land here too but only by prior arrangement with the Clerk.

Until the early 1960s racing was held at Cartmel only once a year, on Spring Bank Holiday Monday. Since then it has grown to five days with the addition of an extra meeting in August. The mondays of the Spring Bank Holiday and the August Bank Holiday provide the main and the most popular meetings. Racegoers come from all over the country to enjoy the racing here. After all, what could be better than to spend a week at Cartmel in May with the non-racedays being spent in the surrounding countryside of the Lake District?

The subscription rate for Annual Membership is £90. This gives the member two badges (a single badge costs £50) and a car pass, plus access to a special viewing area. Demand is always high for these badges and as a result the Members' Enclosure has no Daily Members. The Paddock Enclosure is priced at £10 and the Course, £4, while accompanied children under 16 are admitted free. There are half price entrance charges to the Paddock and the Course for senior citizens. A 20 per cent discount on all admission prices is available for badges purchased 30 days before race meetings. There are continued improvements at the track—a back stairway enables Members to gain easier access to their own vantage point. The new press room can accommodate up to eleven journalists, and a coach park has been added. Despite the changes, including the encouragement of hacks, the Manager's ultimate policy is to foster the pleasant atmosphere and character of the racecourse.

The race meeting however, brings more than horses to this rural setting. A traditional funfair is in attendance and marquees can be provided for parties on request. Picnickers are positively encouraged here although there is a catering marquee in the Paddock. Enquiries with regard to on-course catering should be directed to Romfords, The Boundary, Langley, Haydon Bridge, Northumberland, Tel: (01434) 688864. Disabled racegoers have their own viewing area at Cartmel. Other public facilities include telephones (for those all-important bets) and a betting shop in the Paddock. Cartmel racecourse is a huge success with large crowds attending any race meeting held there, a real testimonial to good old fashioned country fair fun. Other racecourses are not so fortunate. A visit in 2000 could be a hot favourite.

Local Favourites

There is no shortage of hotels in this part of the world and a little guidance cannot go amiss. In Cartmel itself, **Aynsome Manor** (015395) 36653 is a super old manor house which makes a good base. The **King's Arms** holds an imposing position in the square and the **Cavendish Arms** (015395) 36240 is thoroughly recommended. **Uplands** (015395) 36248 is a really pleasing restaurant with rooms if you wish to push the boat out. In Cartmel Fell, one finds the absolutely terrific **Mason's Arms** (015395) 68486, always a friendly crowd and some excellent cooking—watch the foreign beers though, they bring on nasty hangovers when mixed with our own brews—just as well it also has bedrooms! In Heversham, the **Blue Bell** (015395) 62018 offers excellent value bar lunches and some accommodation. A little further west in Lowick Green, the **Farmer's Arms** is a pub with similar facilities and an excellent dining room.

Two packs of **Hounds** and a couple of **Hares**, one at Bowland Bridge (015395) 68333 and another at Levens, both with good value bar food. The **Swan** (015395) 31681 at Newby Bridge comes with an enviable reputation and is less than five miles from the racecourse. Two other pleasant establishments with accommodation are the outstanding **Queen's Head** (015394) 32174, Troutbeck, north of Windermere which also yields the **Mortal Man** (015394) 33193 with its particularly friendly welcome and first class cooking. Bowness-on-Windermere offers two appealing restaurants: the **Gilpin Lodge** (015394) 88818 which has a beautiful situation two miles out of the town—bedrooms here are first class; and **Linthwaite House** (015394) 88600 a hotel with fine cooking. In Windermere, there are some spectacular establishments: **Rogers** (015394) 44954 is a relaxing French restaurant—well worth trying. At the **Miller Howe** (015394) 42536 first class cuisine, breathtaking views and some really special accommodation make this a favourite in the most challenging of fields. Another good runner is **Holbeck Ghyll** (015394) 32375—outstanding menus can be enjoyed here. Further good hotels can be found in and around Underbarrow overlooking the Lyth Valley. In Crook, the **Wild Boar** (015394) 45225 is a comfortable place to stay. Another absolute pearl of an hotel is to be found in Grasmere—**Michael's Nook** (015394) 35496 is delightfully cosy and conjures up exceptional cooking. Grasmere also offers the **White Moss House Hotel** (015394) 35295—another gem. A similarly favourable critique can be made of the **Wordsworth Hotel** (015394) 35592. Cumbria has a whole host of outstanding hotels and what better excuse could one have for visiting than Cartmel Races?

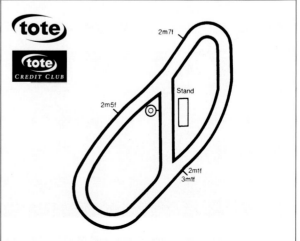

Artist: **Peter Smith COMING IN AFTER THE LAST RACE, EVENING** *Courtesy of:* **Frost & Reed**

The General Manager and Clerk of the Course for flat racing at Catterick is John Gundill, a well known figure in both British and international racing circles. The winter jumping programme is administered by Charles Enderby. The address for all correspondence is The Racecourse, Catterick Bridge, Richmond, North Yorkshire, DL10 7PE. Tel (01748) 811478 Fax (01748) 811082.

Catterick is very convenient for the north and southbound traveller. The A1 is the route to follow and Catterick lies a short distance from the junction of the A66 (Scotch Corner) on the east side of the Great North Road. Travellers from York should take the A59 west until they reach the A1 and then drive north. From another nearby racecourse town—Thirsk (south east), the A170 and the A61 lead to the A1. By rail the nearest station is at Darlington which is on the speedy line from London's Kings Cross. With regard to parking there are two options. The reserved car park costs £2 a car (or £30 for an annual pass) though on ground adjacent to the racecourse there is free parking for both cars and coaches.

Racing has been taking place at Catterick since 1783 and the course has a full calendar of 27 days from January 1st to December 31st, with a new flat fixture in November. A number of distinguished trainers have yards nearby and consequently many a fair nag has been sent up here in the past. Smaller country courses offer outstanding value for money in terms of sponsorship and promotion, sometimes attracting as much local media coverage as the big tracks. As we have already mentioned, Catterick is well situated and eager to attract commercial support, with Leeds, Bradford, York, Newcastle, Teeside and Manchester fairly close by. It is surprising that more local businessmen have not taken the opportunity to utilise Catterick as a medium for publicity. A quick glance at the Catterick fixture list will indicate that the course holds a good mixture of jump and flat racing with Wednesdays and Saturdays the two most popular days.

In 1999 a joint husband and wife Annual Members badge was good value at £140, while a single badge was £78. Annual Membership also includes eleven reciprocal racedays, as well as six cricket matches at Headingley, 4 at Scarborough and 1 at Harrogate. Juniors between the ages of 16 and 21 years were asked £37—excellent value. By comparison, £12 was asked for joining the Members for a single meeting. Tattersalls was slightly better value at £8, while the Course Enclosure was priced at £2.50. All children under 16 are admitted free when accompanied by an adult. These prices may increase in 2000.

If you want to organise parties then Catterick is quite definitely a place to do it. There is a £2 reduction for Tattersalls if as few as ten people get together and there is also one free pass for every tenth person.

In recent years, Catterick has benefitted from an extensive face lift, including refurbishment of the Parade Ring Bar, the Owners and Trainers Bar, Gods Solution Bar, Dining Room and many of the facilities for jockeys have been improved as well. The old 1926 Grandstand has been extended to provide three private hospitality suites, all with a magnificent view of the course. There are two private luncheon rooms, both of which are extremely comfortable, with space for between 20 and 60 guests to sit down or 80 people to enjoy a more simple buffet and these can be hired at very reasonable rates.

There are a number of experienced personalities involved with the running of the course and they have ambitious plans for the enhancement of racecourse facilities with continual upgrading and expansion projects in the pipeline. If you enjoy your racing in either the height of summer or the depths of winter, don't forget that, in racing parlance, Catterick is an improving type. Catterick has fondly christened itself 'the course with character'—I have no doubt that in this instance the character will show through extremely well. A visit in 2000 is a must.

Local Favourites

With the North Yorkshire moors so close by, Catterick is an ideal place to escape to when a major gamble has gone astray. Alternatively, the dales and fells offer an outstanding number of small hotels and pubs in which to celebrate.

In this area, Middleham stands out as prime racing country with some excellent local establishments. Most notably, the Millers House Hotel (01969) 622630 in Middleham which offers quality accommodation and a restaurant of note. Special racing breaks are also on offer here. Also note Waterford House (01969) 622090—small but most appealing. The Forester Arms at Carlton (01969) 640272 is a restaurant of note. The Bridge Inn (01325) 350106 in Stapleton is not residential, but has a good pub restaurant. The Black Swan (01969) 622221 in Middleham is another must for all racegoers. Another training area is Richmond and here the Castle Tavern (01748) 823187 should be noted, fine ales and some good home cooking. In East Layton nearby the Fox Hall Inn (01325) 718262 is a good value place to stay and the restaurant is also worth a visit. The Sandpiper at Leyburn is a good pub, as is the convenient Farmers Arms but you must remember these are only a small selection of some 400 public houses to be found in North Yorkshire. Moulton also reveals a really excellent port of call. The Black Bull Inn (01325) 377289 has particularly good fish and for loved ones, the carefully restored Brighton Belle Pullman Car is ideal for gruesome twosomes. In fact, if you are in the doghouse this establishment is a great place to visit. A short journey south reveals Northallerton and yet more good accommodation in the form of Porch House (01609) 779831.

Scotch Corner also provides a convenient hotel which is handy for a number of courses, the Scotch Corner Hotel (01748) 850900. An alternative is the Vintage Hotel (01748) 824424. Both are only minutes away from the A1. Much of this area is somewhat remote but that is part of its charm. What could be better than a day in the country of North Yorkshire and an evening beside the fire in one of its many friendly hostelries. Thirsk and Ripon may offer alternative suggestions. The Blue Lion at East Witton (01969) 624273 is a fine example—good ale and pleasant bedrooms.

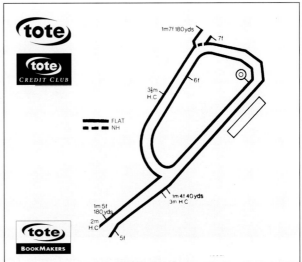

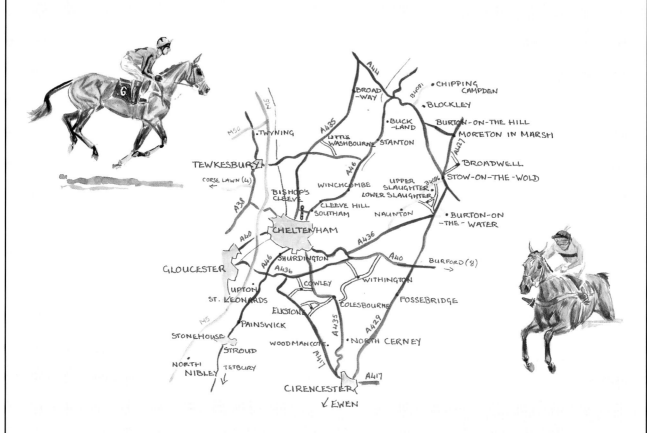

Artist: **Heather St Clair Davis** **DON'T LET UP** *Courtesy of:* **Frost & Reed**

The Cottage In The Wood

The award-winning Cottage in the Wood Hotel and Restaurant enjoys one of the finest settings of any hotel in England. Set high on the Malvern Hills, the views unfold below and stretch for 30 miles to the Cotswold Hills that form the horizon.

John and Sue Pattin who bought the hotel twelve years ago, saw one of the side benefits the close proximity of Cheltenham Racecourse—"Beats driving down from London" says John—a pilgrimage they used to make frequently.

Apart from Cheltenham which is about half an hour's drive away, within an hour there are a further five racecourses—Worcester, Hereford, Ludlow, Stratford and Warwick. Truly, this is racing country.

The Cottage in the Wood, an AA 3-star country house hotel, offers 20 bedrooms spread across three buildings, each with an individual character of its own. The main house is a late Georgian dower house, once part of the Blackmore Park Estate owned by the Duke of Gandolfi, which houses the elegant restaurant, lounge and bar together with eight guest bedrooms.

The building giving its name to the hotel is Beech Cottage, once "The Cottage" which now offers four cottagey bedrooms. Dating from around 1650 it has been in its time both a woodman's cottage and a scrumpy house for walkers on the hills. It's a quiet haven now!

A few yards further on brings you to the Coach House, once cover for the horses and carriages of the house. It must have been a challenge negotiating the drive with a coach and four! It now houses eight bedrooms which, although smaller, offer the finest views of all down the valley to Cheltenham and beyond to Gloucester.

The restaurant offers fine cuisine under the direction of Dominic Pattin (Maria, his eldest sister is General Manager, making it a real family run hotel). It is separately recommended by Egon Ronay and by the AA with the award of two rosettes.

Malvern makes a superb touring base to visit the cathedral cites of Worcester, Hereford and Gloucester. The Forest of Dean, Stratford and Shakespeare country, Cotswolds and the rural charm of timeless Herefordshire and the Welsh Marches all await.

Below the hotel lie the Worcestershire Golf Course and the Three Counties Showground, which has year round events.

The Cottage in the Wood offers inclusive bargain rates these are available for two nights or more, seven days of the week virtually year round.

The Cottage in the Wood Hotel and Restaurant
Holywell Road
Malvern Wells
Worcestershire
WR14 4LG
Tel: (01684) 575859
Fax: (01684) 560662

It is a joy to write about Cheltenham racecourse as there is so much to say that is positive. It may have some deficiencies - Andrew Lloyd Webber, a welcome recruit to racing's new owners courtesy of his wife's love of horses, slated the catering - but when it comes to racing and all round excellence of entertainment, Cheltenham has no peers. We wish them continued success in the new millennium.

Edward Gillespie and the **Clerk of the Course**, can be contacted at **Cheltenham Racecourse, Prestbury Park, Cheltenham GL50 4SH. Tel (01242) 513014. Fax (01242) 224227.** For advance bookings for the Festival, ring (01242) 226226. Credit cards are welcome.

If you are planning to visit these gorgeous Gloucestershire gallops then you are advised to take the train. The main line service leaves Paddington and arrives at Cheltenham Lansdown where a bus is available to take you to the racecourse. By car, London is 95 miles away and the course is a mile from Cheltenham's busy town centre. Traffic from the A40 is advised to turn right at the lights near Andoversford which is signposted for Stow on the Wold and aim for Winchcombe. People who prefer the motorway will use the M4 and the M5—the former should be exited at junction 15 and the latter at junction 4 to make the best ground towards Prestbury Park. If you are coming from the north, there are now big improvements which allow you to bypass Evesham. Whichever direction you approach from, you will find AA signs to guide you to the racecourse. If people wish to travel by helicopter, inform the course in advance and you will be welcomed. There is parking for 14,000 cars—all free except during the Festival, when a parking voucher will cost you £5. For members and coaches parking is free at all times.

Rates of admission vary quite substantially depending on the day, but for the 1999/2000 season prices will vary from £12 to £60 for the Club and £12 to £30 for Tattersalls. For the Courage Enclosure, entrance ranges from £5 to £10. Naturally prices are higher for the National Hunt Festival but you can save money by booking in advance. A Club badge for the Thursday costs £40 until January 1st, £45 until March 1 and £60 on the day. Badges for the Tuesday and Wednesday are £37.50 in advance and £50 up to March 3rd, Tattersalls costs £17 in advance for Tuesday and Wednesday, rising to £20 after March 3rd (£20 rising to £25 for Thursday). A three day badge at £125 is available from January 2nd until January 25th. You can also save in Tattersalls and Courage with advance group bookings. For groups of fifteen and over, booking before March 3rd will be charged at £15 for Tattersalls and £7 for Courage. Advance booking also ensures your admission, which is wise in view of the capacity crowds that attend the Festival. Because of these huge crowds, you are advised, when travelling by car, to arrive early and to listen to the traffic reports on the Festival radio (1584 KHz) a first class service. Above all, be patient!

The National Hunt Festival with its massive crowds reflects the interest in this superb sporting meeting. Gems in the crown include the Tote Cheltenham Gold Cup, the Queen Mother Champion Chase and the Smurfit Champion Hurdle. Cheltenham offers a feast of racing in an excellent atmosphere and amidst a perfect setting. Other meetings to note include the Murphy's Gold Cup in November, and in December the Tripleprint Gold Cup.

Annual Membership should definitely be considered here. £150 is the asking price plus a £100 enrolment fee for new Members. This includes entry to the National Hunt Festival. Membership excluding the Festival is £50 for enrolment and £75 for membership. Seniors (over 65

years) are charged an enrolment fee of £15 and membership at £60 whilst Juniors (under 25 years) are charged a membership fee of £90. Membership lasts for the season (Oct—May).

The course is always superbly well turned out. Facilities include over 100 boxes which are let on an annual basis. However, these can be obtained for a day at a cost of £250-£500 (except during the National Hunt Festival) accommodating between 12 and 24 persons. Several rooms are also available for private parties numbering between 40 and 200 people. The new Tattersalls Grandstand sports a betting hall, bars, buffets, 700 seats, boxes and a 300-seater tiered panoramic restaurant. There are sites for marquees if required and the ever-expanding metropolis of the tented village at the Festival is a pleasure to be a part of. For people who prefer their own catering, stick to the car parks and organise your own picnics—thoroughly recommended if the weather happens to be good—though this can be a bit of a long shot. There is a good restaurant, the Gold Cup Restaurant for which booking is advised. Tel: (01242) 523203. Other restaurants include the Mandarin and Sea Pigeon, plus a carvery and of course, Barry Copes' excellent seafood bar. The fish and chips in Tatts is a recommended outsider. A new addition to the stable is the L'Escargot Bar behind Tatts. This I imagine, is named after the great chaser rather than the well known French dish. All in all, there are over 90 food outlets during the Festival so you shouldn't go hungry. At smaller meetings there is less choice but the crowds are far smaller and the racecourse itself is more of a pleasure to visit.

Although children are admitted free (except for the Festival) there are no special facilities for them but I understand they are on the agenda for the Course Enclosure. Disabled racegoers are well looked after with special areas overlooking the parade ring and on the lawn in the Club.

At a recent meeting at Cheltenham, I was delighted to hear about initiatives to remarket racing to younger racegoers. At the time no firm plans were in place but rest assured the initiatives will be positive and thoroughly sensitive in taking a small step to further improve opportunities for racing at Cheltenham for this crucial market. Cheltenham is a magnificent venue, over the fifteen years since *Travelling the Turf* has been published it has always endeavoured to address any shortcomings and stride ahead with novel ideas. The award for fifteen years of excellence is testimony to this and is thoroughly deserved.

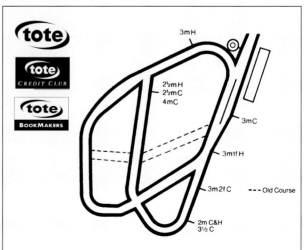

Cheltenham never stages a bad day's racing, though sometimes the weather can be quite extraordinarily bitter. However, this of course, is a natural hazard of the winter game and certainly at Cheltenham one has the blessing of some really first class accommodation and drinking haunts in which to shelter before or after (preferably both) a day at the races. But they do get busy so do try to book well in advance.

Cheltenham itself owes its growth to the discovery of a mineral spring in 1715. Today, the Pittville Pump Room dispenses the only drinkable alkaline water in Britain which may make a pleasant change from the numerous bottles of whisky, champagne and of course Guinness. The best known hotels in town are the **Queen's** (01242) 514724, scene of many a fine Irish celebration after racing, and the **Cheltenham Park Hotel** (01242) 222021 which is actually two miles out of Cheltenham, set in nine acres of gorgeous grounds. **On The Park** (01242) 518898 is a very civilised town house hotel which also houses a tremendous restaurant (01242) 227713. There are numerous other small hotels and guesthouses too—a quick phone call to the local tourist authority is always a good idea. A charming Georgian hotel is **Prestbury House** (01242) 529533. Some ideas for dinner after racing include **81 Restaurant** (01242) 222466 a good restaurant and also bistro of some distinction. **Le Champignon Sauvage** (01242) 573449 is excellent too. Neither establishment is cheap but both provide excellent excuses for a post-race celebration of major proportions. Less expensive dining and an appealing Chinese restaurant can be found at the **Mayflower** (01242) 522426. Also in the town itself, the **Golden Valley Thistle Hotel** (01242) 232691 is modern but most comfortable. For the Festival you must book well in advance. Some people stay as far away as Bath, Stratford or Hereford while others commute daily to the Festival. Naturally, it is easier to find accommodation outside the March extravaganza but plans should not be made at the last minute if you can possibly avoid it.

It should also be emphasised that although opulence and extravagance are not an uncommon feature of this neck of the woods, cost-conscious visitors are by no means forgotten and some excellent establishments are **Lypiatt House** (01242) 224994, **Prestbury House** (01242) 529533, **Charlton Kings** (01242) 231061 and **Butts Farm** (01242) 524982.

There are also some super restaurants in the better hotels clustered around Cheltenham. In Shurdington, the **Greenway** (01242) 862352 has a lovely rural setting and is a really first class hotel in which to stay. Elsewhere, in nearby Southam, the **Hotel de la Bere** (01242) 237771 is convenient for the racecourse and there are good leisure facilities here while in Bishops Cleeve, the **Cleeveway House** (01242) 672585 is a striking Cotswold building with an outstanding restaurant and some very reasonable accommodation too. Upton St Leonards brings us **Hatton Court** (01452) 617412, an elegant hotel in Cotswold stone with good views over the Severn Valley.

One option when racing at Cheltenham is to head off into the nearby Cotswolds. The Cotswolds are an ideal dumping ground in which to discard one's non-racing partners—a wealth of country houses, galleries and antique shops should keep them quiet. **Wesley House** (01242) 602366 is a delight and **Sudeley Castle** is also particularly good. Some places to catch an hour or two's kip are any one of three hotels located in Broadway. The **Lygon Arms** (01386) 852255 exudes charm and style and the Great Hall which acts as the restaurant is superb—expect a fairly large bill though. The **Dormy House**

(01386) 852711 is another excellent hotel/restaurant. The **Broadway Hotel** (01386) 852401 is a beautiful Tudor hotel, complete with minstrels gallery, and nearby **Collin House** (01386) 858354 is excellent—a good each way selection without a doubt. If you are looking for a superbly run pub with an excellent atmosphere try the **Crown and Trumpet** (01386) 853202—it's tremendous. There are also a number of smaller establishments including **Barn House** (01386) 858633, **Windrush House** (01386) 853577 and **The Old Rectory** at Willersey (01386) 853729 no restaurants but excellent accommodation. A perfect example of a Cotswold manor is the **Buckland Manor** (01386) 852626 in Buckland—once again luxurious rooms accompany an outstanding restaurant. In Upper Slaughter another elegant building, the **Lords of the Manor** (01451) 820243 can be found; superbly comfortable and a fine place for breakfast and dinner. Moreton-in-Marsh, riddled with antique shops, is also the home of the **Manor House Hotel** (01608) 650501—another for your shortlist. Another magnificent hotel is **Lower Slaughter Manor** (01451) 820456 in Lower Slaughter. Supreme comfort and excellent cuisine make this an outstanding favourite in any field. **The Lamb Inn** at Great Rissington (01451) 820388 is also well worth considering.

Although many are able to take in all three days of the Festival, some have to make do with a quick visit. Places to stop afterwards include a number of quaint villages which inevitably yield a selection of boozers. In Colesbourne, the **Colesbourne Inn** (01242)870376 is a good stop off point for a pre-race breakfast or dinner post racing - there's also some good value accomodation. The **Green Dragon** near Cowley is a super place for bar food. Filling bar snacks and some accommodation are also good at the popular **Mill Inn** (01242) 890204 in Withington, a town which also houses the charming **Halewell Close** (01242) 890238. This conveniently placed house is a pleasure in which to stay and an excellent base from which to visit Prestbury Park. A pleasant Whitbread house in Painswick is the **Royal Oak**, a good idea if you're heading for Tetbury. There are a number of worthy hotels to consider in this area. In Tetbury itself one finds the **Snooty Fox Hotel** (01666) 502436 which is a welcoming coaching inn and the **Close** (01666) 502272 in Tetbury is also extremely promising. A little way outside the town one finds one of the area's most outstanding hotel and restaurant, **Calcot Manor** (01666) 890391—tremendous.

Further afield in Malvern Wells, the **Cottage in the Wood** (01684) 575859 offers luxurious accommodation and excellent food and wines. For pub lovers the **Hare and Hounds** in Westonbirt (01666) 880233 is popular with Cheltenham racegoers. People bolting up the M5 may pause for thought as well as a swift one at Twyning where the **Village Inn** is a pleasant village pub. Travellers on the A46 should note the **Mount** at Stanton—more good value food and a fine collection of racing prints. For another place to enjoy good food and pub accommodation try the **Kings Head**, Bledington (01608) 658365 a first class stayer.

There are a number of other very fine hotels to consider. Some of the best include the outstanding **Corse Lawn House Hotel**, Corse Lawn (01452) 780479. This is tremendously well run but inevitably packed for Cheltenham—its restaurant is also excellent and well worth booking months in advance. Further away in Blockley, near Moreton-in-Marsh, **Lower Brook House** (01386) 700286 is a delightful Cotswold inn. Cirencester offers two inns of note; the **Fleece Hotel** (01285) 658507 and the 14th century **King's Head** (01285) 653322. **Stratton**

House Hotel (01285) 651761 on the Gloucester Road also has pre-race appeal. Crossing the county to the Forest of Dean and Coleford, try the **Speech House** (01594) 822607–intimately pleasing.

Outside Cirencester in Ewen, one finds the **Wild Duck Inn** (01285) 770310 a fine old inn. Another nearby roost in a welcoming market place hotel, the **Bull** (01285) 712535 can be found in Fairford.

Returning to the Cotswolds, that lovely part of England–various ideas for a recommended Cheltenham stayer include: the **Old Farmhouse Hotel** (01451) 830232 in Lower Swell and in Moreton-in-Marsh, the **Redesdale Arms** (01608) 650308. In Stonehouse, the **Stonehouse Court Hotel** (01453) 825155 is a fine manor house with an excellent reputation, while **Wyck Hill House Hotel** (01451) 31936 in busy Stow on the Wold also fits into the manorial category and the restaurant here is very good. A compliment should also be paid to the popular **Dial House** (01451) 22244 a most pleasant hotel in Bourton on the Water. Continuing our Cotswold tour, the Chipping Campden area is well worth a visit–preferably a long one. The superb **Cotswold House Hotel** (01386) 840330 is a beautiful Regency building where your stay will be both comfortable and relaxing. The restaurant, the **Garden Room** is also good. Two inns to note here include the **Kings Arms** (01386) 840256 and the pleasant **Noel Arms** (01386) 840317. For the lover of Italian food, **Caminetto** (01386) 840330 is a local favourite, whilst just outside Chipping Campden, **Charingworth Manor** (01386) 78555 at Charingworth is a hotel where no expense is spared in making the guests' stay a memorable one. The **Malt House** (01386) 840295 at Broad Campden is also first class.

Less vaunted, but more reasonably priced post-race stabling can be secured in a number of the pubs that riddle the villages of Gloucestershire. In North Nibley, the **Black Horse** (01453) 546841 is recommended–a friendly, beamed pub with some bedrooms available if you want to make a weekend of it. Blockley offers the **Crown** (01386) 700245 with an excellent array of real ales, bedrooms and good bar food. Some fair bar snacks can be tried in the **Slug and Lettuce** in Cirencester. The **New Inn** (01453) 543659 in Waterley Bottom is also highly recommended. In North Cerney, the **Bathurst Arms** (01285) 831281 offers good bed and breakfast besides being a welcoming and popular pub. In Naunton, the **Black Horse** (01451) 850378 is also charming:–excellent bar food and some accommodation here. The same can be said of the **George** in Winchcombe–a converted Whitbread establishment and also the **Bakers Arms** at Broad Campden (01386) 840515. People returning to London have a plethora of places to discover. If you wish to break the journey consider Eynsham–here one finds a whole clutch of boozers, the best of which is **Newlands** (01865) 881486 which also boasts a first class restaurant. Yet more pleasant village pubs abound, in Fossebridge, the **Fossebridge** (01285) 720721 is popular and in Ford, the **Plough** (01249) 782215 has two bedrooms and is a lively local.

There are literally hundreds of hostelries in which to reflect on the outcome of the race, and a few not to be missed are the the **Kilkeney** near Dowdeswell, the **Fox** at Lower Oddington and the **Apple Tree** in Woodmancote– local favourites for a first class racecourse.

Halewell Close

For racegoers visiting Cheltenham, Stratford or Warwick, Halewell Close could easily become a habit hard to break. Elizabeth Carey-Wilson opened her lovely Cotswold stone house to guests in the early 1980s, and welcomes all visitors as if they are friends. Imagine a private and luxurious house party, in an informal relaxed atmosphere and you can picture Halewell Close.

Situated on the edge of the pretty village of Withington and set in fifty acres of private grounds, Halewell Close has six large double or twin bedrooms, all with bathrooms en suite, colour television and things like coffee, tea, biscuits, even playing cards.

There are plenty of good pubs and restaurants in the area, breakfast time is flexible from 9am onwards. There is plenty of space in which to relax, including a quiet comfortable sitting room for guests' use.

A large garden with stone terraces leads to a swimming pool heated from the end of May till September. Natural springs feed a five acre trout lake and alongside there is a stretch of the river Coln where fishing is available.

The local countryside is ideal for walking and is dotted with most attractive villages and all the sights and activities of the Cotswolds. For a delightful change of pace and a truly individual experience, Halewell Close is absolutely perfect.

Halewell Close
Withington
Nr Cheltenham
Glos GL54 4BN
Tel: (01242) 890238
Fax: (01242) 890332

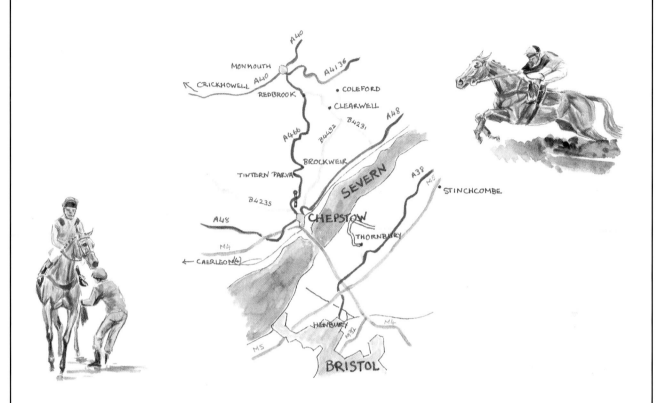

Artist: **John Atkins CHEPSTOW FINAL FURLONG** _Courtesy of:_ **The Artist**

The management at Chepstow is headed by **Managing Director George Francis**, with **Rodger Farrant** as **Clerk of the Course**, and Peter Horleston as Company Secretary. All enquiries should be made to **Chepstow Racecourse, Chepstow, Monmouthshire NP6 5YH. Tel (01291) 622260 Fax (01291) 627061 e mail: enquiries@chepstow-race course.co.uk web site: www.chepstow-racecourse.co.uk.**

Since the opening of the Severn Bridge, now some thirty odd years ago, Chepstow became much more accessible from the east and London via the M4. The recent opening of the second Severn Crossing now takes the M4 traffic away from Chepstow so there should be few delays on what the course now regards as its private bridge! From the east and south west on the M5 or M4 , follow the signs for Chepstow. On the M48, having crossed the 'old' bridge leave at Junction 2. From the west on the M4 again follow signs for Chepstow M48. Once at the course you will be delighted to hear that all parking is free. Chepstow has a rail station and the racecourse is a mile's canter from the town centre. Bristol Parkway station is a 25 minute drive away and this might be a good bet if you are travelling from London's Paddington station. There is a bus service (Chepstow to Monmouth) which will deposit you outside the course. If a helicopter is more your style then you may land in the middle of the track, opposite the stands. As yet light aircraft are not allowed.

Chepstow racecourse usually hosts a total of 23 days racing—14 meetings over the jumps and 9 on the flat course. Chepstow meetings are all one-day occasions. The year's racing begins in February and there are at least two meetings per month throughout the rest of the year. The course is perhaps best noted for its National Hunt racing, but we should also emphasise the beauty of the setting and the local countryside—an opportunity to visit Chepstow at any time should always be taken, especially when the spirit is somewhat waning. Feature events include the Coral Welsh National, the Rehearsal Chase, the Tote Silver Trophy over jumps and the Golden Daffodil Stakes on the flat.

Chepstow Membership in 1999 cost £155. This includes an amazing 27 away days at 16 other courses including Ascot, Ayr, Bangor, Bath Exeter, Goodwood, Ludlow, Newbury, Newton Abbot, Plumpton, Salisbury, Taunton, Uttoxeter,Wincanton,Windsor, and Wolverhampton—an impressive list. The Membership badge is not transferable but a second Member's badge can be transferred. A total of 50 days racing for £155 can't be bad value! A half year membership is also available at £90 and two badges can be purchased for a total of £180. 1999 daily charges were £15 in Members and £11 in Tatts. The Silver Ring and Centre Course prices were £6 each but are only used on Bank holiday meetings. It is important to note that prices for the Coral Welsh National are inevitably higher at £22 (Members) and £16 (Tattersalls) and that the two cheaper enclosures are open only on Easter Monday, the Whitsun Bank Holiday, the midsummer Sunday meeting and August Bank Holiday. If you are organising a party then a reduction of £1 per person will be made for parties of 20 or more booked seven days in advance for the Tattersalls or Members Enclosure and the organiser will receive a free ticket. Another generous concession relates to pensioners, with a £3 entrance charge to the course on public holidays and £5 to Tattersalls on other days. At the other end of the age scale a crèche is now available for children up to eleven at £3 per hour from midday onwards.

Chepstow is set in 370 acres of parkland and nestles in the slopes of the Wye Valley. Its facilities include 39 boxes, and nine hospitality suites which can be hired on racedays. £2 million has been spent on the provision of new private boxes and hospitality suites, which cater for 25 to 200 people. Marquees can be arranged for larger functions. The racecourse has three exhibition halls of varying sizes as well as the more exclusive Piercefield Suite. The caterers Letheby & Christopher have varying menus on offer. Enquiries with regard to catering should be made to them on (01242) 523203 (racedays (01291) 625189). The Paddock to the rear of the Grandstand is large and provides the racegoer with a good vantage point. The course also provides a reserved viewing area for wheelchair racegoers. The improvement programme has continued recently with a better crèche facility, a new extension to the Tattersalls' bar and new pass holders and members' entrances. Chepstow is a charming course in an equally charming setting and is definitely one for the notebook.

Local Favourites
Although not quite on the Welsh side of the border, a quite exceptional hotel is the **Thornbury Castle** (01454) 281182. It is an expensive establishment but has much charm and history as well as comforts that make it all the more appealing. People who wish to stay more locally should consider Chepstow itself where the **Castle View** (01291) 620349, may merit attention. Another to keep in mind is the **Beaufort Hotel** (01291) 624927 which comes recommended by the racecourse management as does the **Piercefield Inn** (01291) 622614, a good pub to note. The **George Hotel** (01291) 625363 adjoins the 16th century gate and town walls. This is another good spot for a pint and a snack. The **Bridge** has a lovely setting and is worth a visit. The best place to stay if you're a golfer as well as a racing enthusiast is the **Marriott St Pierre Hotel** (01291) 625261. The hotel also offers a whole string of other leisure facilities. Similarly good golf and accommodation can be found at **Celtic Manor** (01633) 413000 near Newport.

The Welsh border country is well known for its beauty. Some particularly good ideas include a visit to Crickhowell for a night at **Gliffaes** (01874) 730371, a friendly hotel, or a visit to the **Bear Hotel** (01873) 810408. Other thoughts include the **Crown** at Whitebrook (01600) 860254—a popular place to stay with an excellent restaurant. Be sure to consider the **Village Green Restaurant** (01600) 860119 in Trellech on your way to Monmouth—there are some good value rooms available here. The **Carpenters Arms** in Shirenewton is a pub of note. In Clearwell, a country inn with bedrooms and restaurant and friendly bars is the **Wyndham Arms** (01594) 833666. The **Clearwell Castle** (01594) 832320 is another popular suggestion—this 18th century edifice is an amazing place to stay especially for lovers of four posters. Remote but very welcoming **Llanwenarth House** (01873) 830289 is a hotel of merit for your consideration. Whilst finally, a well located inn for the Forest of Dean is **Speech House**, Coleford (01594) 822607—some more four posters for the romantic racegoer. Nearby Tintern also offers a few gems, **Parva Farmhouse** (01291) 68941 a restaurant with rooms is worthy of a pre race inspection.

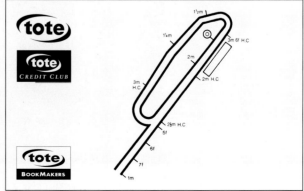

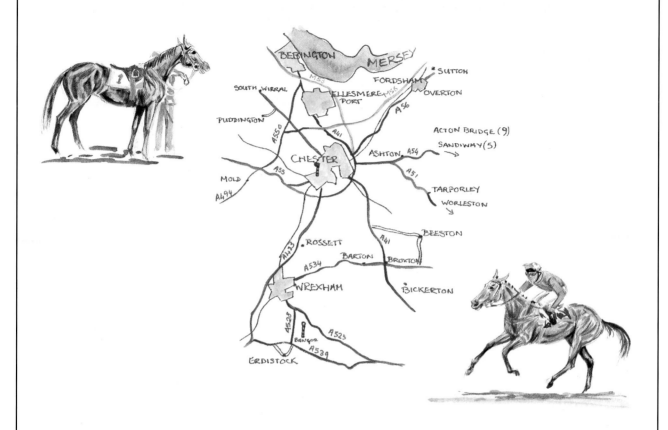

Artist: **Paul Hart** **ROUNDING THE TURN** _Courtesy of:_ **The Artist**

Artist: **Heather St Clair Davis WASHING DOWN** *Courtesy of:* **Frost & Reed**

The Park Royal International Hotel

The Park Royal International Hotel, Health and Leisure Spa is set in the heart of the Cheshire countryside yet only one minute from junction 10 of the M56 motorway, three minutes from the M6 and 12 minutes from Manchester airport.

Located midway between Aintree, Chester and Haydock racecourses the hotel provides fully air-conditioned conference and banqueting suites for up to 400 guests, 140 deluxe en suite bedrooms, the award-winning AA rosette Harlequin restaurant along with comfortable lounges and bars.

You can relax in the superb state of the art health and leisure spa, facilities include a 22m swimming pool, sauna, steam room, whirlpool bath, solarium, dance studio and gymnasium. Also available is the Retreat Beauty Centre, with 6 beauty suites and a hydrotherapy suite.

The Park Royal Hotel offers a standard of service and excellence which is unrivalled.

An ideal venue for a short break.

The Park Royal International Hotel, Health & Leisure Spa
Stretton Road, Stretton
Warrington, Cheshire WA4 4NS
Tel: (01925) 730706 Fax: (01925) 730740

82

Chester is one of the most appealing racecourses in Britain. This delightful course is managed by **Charles Barnett** who is both **Chief Executive** and **Clerk of the Course**. and Lucy Moreau is **Marketing Manager**. They can be contacted at: **The Racecourse, Chester, Cheshire, CH1 2LY. Tel (01244) 323170 Fax (01244) 344971**

The racecourse lies to the south east of the town. The M6/M56 motorways serve racegoers from the north and south of the country, exiting at junction 14. Eastbound travellers will find the M62/M6/M56 the clearest route into Chester while A roads abound in the area. The course itself is well signposted by AA and RAC signs and the Chester bypass avoids the busy city centre. Cars and coaches can be parked in the centre of the course and the respective prices are £2 and £5.

The Euston line goes directly to Chester General and there is a bus service from the station to the course on racedays. For those who travel by helicopter there is a landing pad available.

The pattern of racing in 2000 is likely to follow that of 1999. The principal event is the May Festival meeting and the feature races include the Chester Vase, the Capital Bank Dee Stakes, the Shadwell Stud Cheshire Oaks and the Tote Chester Cup. This mini-festival is a true delight for racing enthusiasts. Annual Membership at Chester costs £200. This includes free car parking and free Members entrance for a day at Bangor-on-Dee, Carlisle, Doncaster, Worcester, York, Goodwood and Uttoxeter. Another advantage for the Annual Member is the provision of a special marquee for the May meeting. A really first class idea. A three day badge for the May meeting costs £80 and the daily rate for Tuesday and Thursday is £27 There are limits to capacity for the May Festival meeting and for the County Stand. Advance booking is a necessity for the County Enclosure. Daily Junior badges for racegoers (aged 17 and under) cost £5. Reserved seats for the three days cost an additional £30. Tattersalls charges are £15, and the Dee Stands cost £5 per day. There is also a charge of £3 for spectators on the open course. Coaches and mini buses can be parked on course for £5 but booking is essential. For the remaining meetings, daily badges cost £17-20 in the County Stand, £11-12 in Tatts and the Paddock, and £4 in the Dee Stands.

Visitors to the County Stand can view the magnificent panorama of the Roodee, the wide sweep of the River Dee and the Welsh Hills beyond. Children are admitted free to all enclosures except the Members but there are no special facilities for them due to the restricted space. Disabled people have a small reserved stand in the Paddock with a raised level ramp, washroom and a private box facility by the winning post with CCTV. There are betting shops in Tattersalls and the Dee Stands. The racecourse has made a major investment in the new Paddock Pavilion, with new bars and entertainment areas and a new press stand. A new tented facility at every meeting, the Paddock Restaurant can be pre-booked by ringing the racecourse in advance. The Tatts stand has also been refurbished with steppings to the grandstand and a new betting hall with food and bar areas beneath. Chester is an outstanding racecourse in every way and its popularity grows year after year.

Local Favourites

A splendid place to stay is the **Chester Grosvenor** (01244) 324024—the restaurant is particularly well thought of. **Broxton Hall** (01829) 782321, and **Thornton Hall** 0151 336 3938 also come highly recommended. Back in Chester, there is an abundance of guesthouses and small hotels so the racegoer on a more limited budget should not worry. Names worth mentioning here are the **Chester Court** (01244) 320779, **Green Gables** (01244) 372243, the **Dene Hotel** (01244) 321165 and the **White Lion** (01928) 722949. Not the cheapest, but still an outstanding favourite, is **Crabwall Manor** (01244) 851666 two miles outside Chester.

Venturing some way north of Chester to the South Wirral and Puddington, one finds the **Craxton Wood Hotel** 0151 339 4717 with a small but selective and very stylish restaurant. People looking for a little luxury when visiting the city should consider one of several hotels. In St Johns Street, **Blossoms** (01244) 323186 is close to the city centre and its many amenities include a good restaurant and two friendly bars. The **Malt Shoppe** and the **Snooty Fox** are both well worth considering. A little farther afield, but still convenient for the city is a splendid country house hotel, the **Mollington Banastre Hotel** (01244) 851471. There are excellent facilities available here—together with two restaurants—and its own village pub. In Rowton lies another fine country house—the **Rowton Hall Hotel** (01244) 335262—the service here is good and if you don't want to be in the middle of Chester this may well be the answer. South of the city lies the excellent value and secluded **Pheasant Inn** (01829) 70434. A relative newcomer to the Chester field, is the **Chester International Hotel** (01244) 322330. Meanwhile, the **Wild Boar Inn** (01829) 260309 at Beeston has modern facilities and a pleasing setting. The **Park Royal International Hotel** (01925) 730706 does special racing breaks including transport to the racecourse.

In the countryside, there are some fine pubs to note. The **Bickerton Poacher** in Bickerton is an exceptionally busy pub but is good fun too. The **Cock O'Barton** at Barton is quieter. Further south in Whitchurch is **Dearnford Hall** (01948) 662319 providing top class accommodation. In Taporley, the **Swan** (01829) 733838 is a worthy Greenall's pub with a restaurant and some bedrooms if you require them. The **Rising Sun** is also a pub to note here. More of the same can be found in Sutton, north west of Chester at **Sutton Hall**. Finally, a very special hotel can be found at Mold, some twelve miles from Chester. Here, a warm welcome awaits you at **Soughton Hall** (01352) 840811, a stunning hotel in Italianate style with a fine à la carte restaurant. With outstanding hotels and a first class racecourse, a visit to Chester in 2000 simply must be organised.

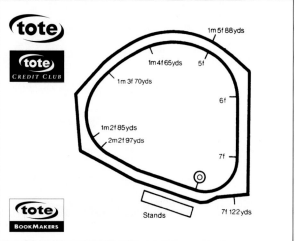

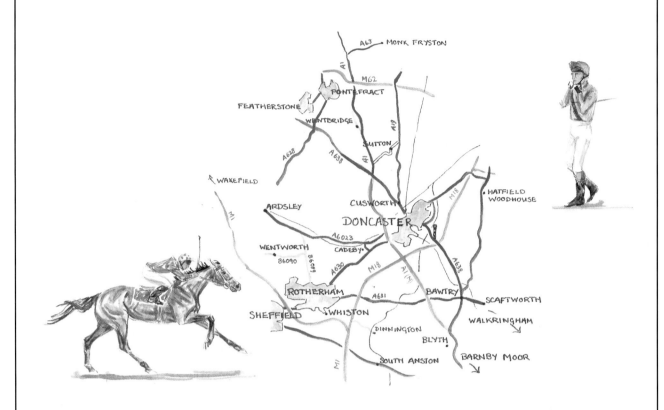

Artist: **Peter Smith** **TOO CLOSE TO CALL** Courtesy of: **Frost & Reed**

The racecourse, owned by Doncaster Metropolitan Borough Council, is managed by International Racecourse Management Ltd. Chief Executive. **John Sanderson** is **Clerk of the Course**, sales and marketing is run by **Tim Betteridge** with **Chris Oliver** as the **Office Manager**. Doncaster's exhibition and conference centre is open all year round and information can be obtained by writing to **The Grandstand, Leger Way, Doncaster. DN2 6BB. Tel (01302) 320066/7 Fax (01302) 323271.**

Doncaster racecourse is in South Yorkshire, one mile from the centre of the town itself. The course is within easy reach of motorways and there is a dual carriageway to the course car parks. The A1 and the M1/M18 are good routes from the south and signs now direct racegoers from all motorway approaches. If you are coming from the west then use the A57 and M18 and from the east the M18 and M180. Let the train take the strain from Kings Cross and your journey time will be 85 minutes with a bus from the town to complete the final leg of the journey. Buses from Doncaster (Nos 55, 170 and 171) will drop you 300 metres from the gates—perfect! Helicopters are permitted to land at Doncaster but only by special arrangement so if this is your desired mode of transport then please check with the Office Manager first. Car parking is easy here with space for 3000 cars—all free. There is also a reserved area for Members.

The season at Doncaster consists of 28 days racing, twenty flat and eight over the sticks. Principal meetings are the St Leger Festival in September and the Worthington Lincoln in March, the Racing Post Trophy in October and the Tote November Handicap. Doncaster has the honour of opening and closing the flat season—a worthy privilege for an excellent racecourse.

Rates of admission for 2000 vary from meeting to meeting and day to day. There is a standard charge of £15 for the Members Enclosure and £9 for the Tattersalls but these are higher on more prestigious racedays. £4 is the standard charge for the Family Enclosure and again this rises on principal days. For example, charges for St Leger day are £28, £16 and £6 respectively. Annual Membership at Doncaster costs £195. Included in this are 21 reciprocal meetings from Newbury through to Chester and entrance to Yorkshire Cricket Club matches on eleven days. This has to be good value. Dual Membership offers husband and wife a double badge for £295 and Junior Badges are £95. Party discounts are also available and you should contact the racecourse for full details if you are planning a large outing. When you are inviting guests, don't forget to tell them that the course runs a strict dress code of "Jacket and tie, and no jeans allowed" in the Members Enclosure. There's nothing more embarrassing than having a guest turned away because of their attire! Boxes, and there are a total of 70 now, are let on an annual basis. A tented village exists for the St Leger meeting. A £1 million refurbishment programme has recently been completed in the Family Enclosure.

There are numerous bars together with corporate facilities. The Lincoln Restaurant is situated in the Yorkshire Stand and tables are allocated on a first come first served basis. The Hospitality Club in the St Leger Banqueting Suite is designed to give racegoers a full day at the races in a corporate hospitality style without the need for large numbers (a minimum of two people). The caterers are Metro and can be contacted on (01302) 349740. Doncaster has taken a positive lead in promoting racing as family entertainment and raceday activities include a professionally staffed crèche, children's rides, craft stalls and a selection of raceday music. The Giant Screen is present on major racedays and the course has developed its own corporate entertainment department as well as catering for party bookings. Doncaster is a really friendly well run racecourse and one which in recent years has dramatically improved. There are a total of 59 racecourses in Britain. Doncaster is the most historic and is fast becoming one of the best. A visit in 2000 is highly recommended.

Local Favourites
The most historic of Yorkshire racecourses is to be found at Doncaster—perhaps not the most attractive of towns but an excellent racecourse nonetheless. In Doncaster, the **Grand St Leger** (01302) 364111 is extremely comfortable and its restaurant has an imaginative menu. The **Doncaster Moat House** (01302) 310331 is also very appealing. A little south of the town, in Bawtry, stands the **Crown Hotel** (01302) 710341, a pleasant inn in a quiet market square. The **Regent Hotel** (01302) 364180 and the **Mount Pleasant** (01302) 868696 are shortlisted by people in the know, and the **Rockingham Arms** (01302) 360980 also has a good reputation. Two other hotels to consider are the **Quality Danum Hotel** (01302) 342261 in the town centre—and the **Earl of Doncaster** (01302) 361371, a mere half mile from the racecourse. One final thought for lovers of Indian cooking is the **Aagrah** (01302) 728888, it's well worthwhile.

For people who may want a little more comfort and style there are two hotels that are warmly recommended north of Doncaster. In Wentbridge, the **Wentbridge House Hotel** (01977) 620444 has a pleasant location in the parkland scenery of the Went Valley. **Monk Fryston Hall Hotel** (01977) 682369 is found in the West Riding village of the same name. Pubs to note nearby include the excellent **Inn at Cadeby** and the **Green Tree** at Hatfield Woodhouse (01302) 840305—a few bedrooms here and good value bar food. An inside tip is the **Old Bell** at Barnby Moor (01717) 705212—very old world. Finally, a restaurant to note is the **Epworth Tap** in Epworth (01427) 873333, a relaxing place to dine.

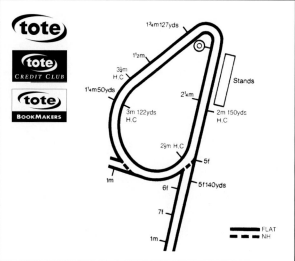

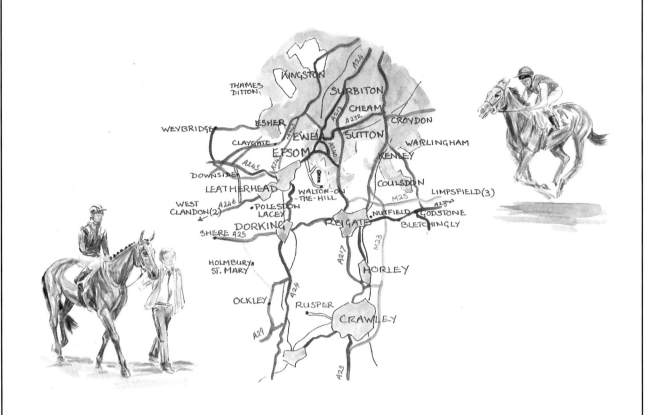

Artist: **Peter Smith** **TOP OF THE HILL** *Courtesy of:* **Frost & Reed**

The home of the Derby, Epsom holds a special place in British and world racing. While the accomplishments of jockeys, horses and trainers on other racecourses may fade from view with the passage of time, the connections of the Derby winner become part of history forever. Last year's edition was no exception and the names of Cecil, Fallon and Oath are now inscribed on the roll of honour - no matter what the future might hold!

Andrew Cooper is the **Clerk of the Course** and **Racing Manager** and **Stephen Wallis** is the **General Manager** at Epsom. **Mrs Sue Ellen** is the **Managing Director** and **Jo Dillon** is the **Membership Secretary** who also handles ticket sales. **Tim Darby** is the **Marketing and Sponsorship Manager** for United Racecourses and can be reached on (01372) 461253. The racecourse can be contacted directly on Tel (01372) 726311 Fax (01372) 748253 but all enquiries are dealt with at Sandown and should be addressed to **United Racecourses, Sandown Park Racecourse, Esher, Surrey KT10 9AJ. Tel (01372) 464348 Fax (01372) 470427** There is a ticket line **Tel (01372) 470047**.

Epsom itself stands on the Surrey Downs of the same name. The mode of transportation depends significantly on the meeting. Derby Day is enormously busy—even helicopters hover in line. However, on other days traffic is less congested. The racecourse is fairly close to the centre of London and people heading from that direction should pursue the A3 south, exiting at the Tolworth junction. Traffic from the west is advised to join the M25 and exit at junction 8 or 9 for the course. The M25, if it is flowing freely, also serves people from the east and the south of the country. The A217 is the best route to observe in order to complete your northbound journey. An excellent idea is to take the train. Lines from the London stations of Waterloo, Charing Cross and Victoria stretch to Epsom. The Downs can be reached from Victoria alone, while Tattenham Corner visitors should take trains from either London Bridge or Charing Cross. If you travel to Epsom by train, buses will take you to the course itself. However, passengers to Tattenham Corner station can enjoy a pleasant walk across the Downs before racing. Many people have picnics here and this seems as ideal a place as any to indulge in your nosebag. Other places in which to have a pre-race snack are the car parks, of which there are many. Charges vary according to your particular setting. Finally, if you are lucky enough to travel by helicopter, you can land here—it's quite a sight I assure you.

There is a range of charges for the various enclosures. Derby Day is unsurprisingly expensive. Admission to the Queens Stand on Derby Day is restricted to Annual Members. Admission to the Club Enclosure costs £40 on Derby Day. Reserved seats cost £18 in advance or £30 if you just show up on the day. Oaks Day will set you back £35 for Club admission. The more relaxed Lonsdale, Walton and Tattenham enclosures are priced at between £4 and £1, with the Grandstand at between £12 and £20. For both Derby Day and Oaks Day there are discounts for advance bookings. To get a comprehensive listing of the various charges contact the racecourse. Annual Membership in 1999 was priced at £130. A Junior Membership badge was priced at £60. The principal advantage of this membership is that it gives you admission to the Members Enclosure for the Derby—a real bonus. Finally, a number of rooms and private boxes are available. Please ring the racecourse for full details.

There is a restaurant in the Members Enclosure and you should book. A less busy alternative can be found in the Grandstand. The numerous snack bars serve sandwiches but these are fairly expensive. Disabled facilities have been radically improved at Epsom with ramps, lifts and toilets now provided. A bank can be found behind the Grandstand during Derby week should you blow all your cash early on in the Tote or Coral betting facilities. Also please note that children under 16 are admitted free to all enclosures except the Members on Derby Day. In one of several fairly fundamental changes at the course the Paddock has been relocated and is now behind the Grandstand. This has ensured that the action has been condensed somewhat, which has to be an improvement.

There has always been and probably always will be great debate about The Derby being the ultimate test for three year-olds and therefore the key pointer to later success at stud. Derby winners still go for very high prices when sold to stud, unfortunately now more likely to head for distant places such as Japan than stay at home to improve the domestic breed. The fairness of the descent to Tattenham Corner and the toll it takes on young legs is open to discussion, but there can be no doubt that a Derby winner will always need courage, grit and determination to go with outstanding ability and a turn of foot, attributes that will always be in demand amongst the best bloodstock.

The pedigree of the Derby speaks for itself and it is the challenge of the distinguished racing and business brains, as proprietors of Epsom, to ensure its development in future years.

In the coming years Epsom should continue to reap the rewards of moving Derby Day to a weekend; despite the howls of protest by the traditionalists, there are clearly no odds in moving the event back to a time when most people can't attend or watch. From a punter's perspective the new fixture list is firmly, and rightly, committed to weekend racing and the Derby weekend should be the annual highlight of this. In an increasingly busy world, there is always going to be competition for the public's attention - from going to the local DIY to other major sporting events on a Saturday. Can we fly a kite for holding both the Derby and the Oaks on a Sunday to produce the best day's flat racing of the whole year? The weekend action would then start on a Saturday evening with a great carnival party on the Downs with masses of large field handicaps and a super bet to challenge the punters, with lots of entertainment for the whole family and a grand fireworks finale to finish. This would firmly position Epsom and the Derby as the jewel in the crown of British flat racing.

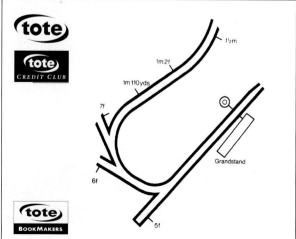

Artist: **Roy Miller CHECK UP** _Courtesy of:_ **The Artist**

People who are staying in this area (rather than in the capital) should note the **Burford Bridge Hotel** (01306) 884561, in Burford Bridge near Dorking—a welcoming hotel beside the A24 and well sited for Epsom Downs. The **White Horse Hotel**, (01306) 881138 also has great character, though less class. Both of these are ideal for the tourist as they date back centuries. **Partners and Sons** (01306) 882826 is a popular restaurant to sample. Epsom itself contains the **Epsom Downs Hotel** (01372) 740643, a good value and relaxing hotel. **Le Raj** (01739) 371371 will appeal to lovers of Indian cuisine. In Banstead, a convenient yet unpretentious stayer is the **Heathside** (01737) 353355. Further south in Rusper, an hotel for people who enjoy a little peace and quiet, **Ghyll Manor** (01293) 871571 is a comfortable old manor house.

Turning back towards the racecourse again, the busy town of Reigate is home to the **Cranleigh Hotel** (01737) 223417 and the **Bridge House** (01737) 246801, both unpretentious and good value. The **Whyte Harte** (01883) 743231 in Bletchingly is also a fine place to stay, as is the **Bell** (01883) 743133 in Godstone—ideal for a steak and a drink.

There are numerous pubs to be found in the area—some near, some far. The **Harrow** in Thames Ditton is most obliging as is the **Jolly Farmer** in Weybridge. In Kenley one finds the **Wattenden Arms**, an extremely popular pub with some distinguished bar food available. The **Plough** at Blackbrook is also very civilised and the **Plough** (01306) 711793 at Coldharbour offers good food, beer and some accommodation.

If you're contemplating dinner, a local favourite is **Partners West Street** (01306) 882826 in Dorking. In Surbiton, **Chez Max** 0181 399 2365 is also good—a small restaurant with an ambitious French menu.

An alternative nearby is to be found in Chipstead—the **Ramblers Rest** (01737) 552661 is not cheap but offers a really first class menu, friendly service and a distinguished wine list. Finally, in Hersham the **Dining Room** (01932) 231686 is reported to be excellent, where a friendly atmosphere accompanies bold English cooking

The **Old School House** (01306) 711224 in Ockley should be noted—the well priced menu is extremely appealing. Another pleasant pub to inspect near here is the **Punch Bowl** which has a lovely setting and serves some simple bar snacks as well as having a good dining room. Two other pubs to note while in this area of Surrey include another part of the kings anatomy, on this occasion the **Kings Head**, to be found in Holmbury St Mary, a really good atmosphere here. In Shere, the **White Horse** is also popular—rightly so—it is charming and offers some excellent home-made food. People who are fond of eating and enjoy the ambience of a good restaurant should try the **Onslow Arms** (01483) 222447 in West Clandon—a classic of its type. The **Bulls Head** is also good here as is the **Jarvis Thatchers Hotel** (01483) 284291, both comfortable and convenient.

The Derby attracts all sorts of people. Gypsies promise you luck but you will still lose your shirt. The Derby is one of the most colourful events of the year and if you want to end it in style visit the village of Nutfield. The hotel here is situated in the former local priory, **Nutfield Priory** (01737) 822066, the perfect place to count your winnings or lick your wounds after a day at the Derby.

Finally, if your appetite has not been whetted by any of these suggestions (unlikely!), then turn to the Kempton Park and Sandown recommendations where you will see more places to satisfy the Surrey racegoer.

Artist: **Roy Miller FRISKY 2 YEAR OLDS** _Courtesy of:_ **The Artist**

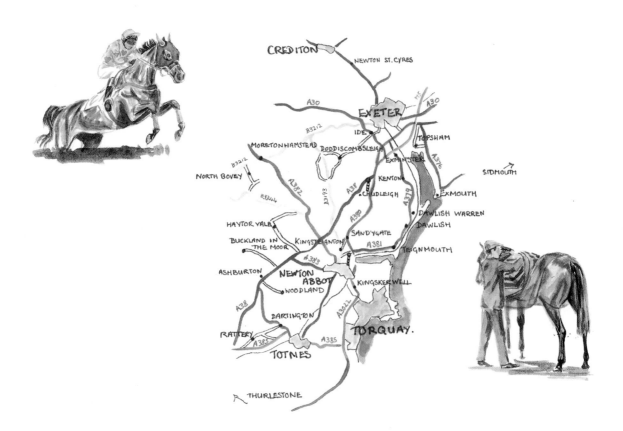

Artist: **Graham Isom** **COMING IN** *Courtesy of:* **Rosenstiel's**

If you are planning a visit to England's delightful West Country then stop off at Exeter racecourse. This pleasant track is in the capable hands of **Mr G Billson, General Manager, Mr B Soper** as **Raceday Manager** and **Secretary**, and **Mrs Charlotte Faulkner** as **Club Secretary**. The address is **Devon & Exeter Steeplechases Ltd, Exeter Racecourse, Kennford Nr Exeter, EX6 7XS. Tel (01392) 832599. Fax (01392) 833454.**

When travelling to the course it may be as well to stick to the motorways to ensure a speedy route—the M5 feeds from the M4 and the M6. The course is some 190 miles from London and seven miles south west of Exeter. The A38 is the best route to take having exhausted the motorway network and brings traffic eastbound from Plymouth. The course lies a mere stone's throw away from this A road. On arrival at the racecourse there is ample car parking to be found. Essentially this is free, though there is a £2 charge for a special position on the rails. The nearest train station is at Exeter, St Davids, which can be comfortably reached from Paddington. On racedays there is a free bus service to the course from the central bus station in Exeter City Centre

The programme at Exeter features 13 National Hunt meetings and two Flat meetings, the main race being Gold Cup Day at the end of October. However, racing spans the year here and lovers of the Devon sun should note the splendid Red Cross Day meeting in early October. Lovers of winter sport should sample the national hunt fixtures, which are seldom affected by seasonal weather. In order to become an Annual Member the sum of £105 is charged for a single badge. This also includes some 23 reciprocal days, although Exeter members certainly have to do some travelling to enjoy them! Daily rates are £11 for the Members and Tattersalls, Grandstand and Paddock and a really good value £5 for the Silver Ring. Party discounts are available for the Members and Tattersalls—please apply to the course for further details.

The course has hospitality rooms in the new Tote building which can hold up to 30 people each, while the old one has been converted to accommodate two function rooms for large parties. The Brockman Stand features a new betting hall and owners and trainers bar as well as three new hospitality rooms with spectacular views of the course. The new Paddock which incorporates the winners enclosure and provides much improved views of the pre-saddling enclosure, will be in place for the start of the 1999 winter season. There is also the Desert Orchid Restaurant, which is capable of seating up to 100 people. Booking details are available from Mrs Faulkner (01392) 832599. More elaborate catering can also be arranged through the Catering Division (01392) 832599 and there are facilities for marquees if you wish to have a really good party.

The only drawback to what must be considered to be one of Britain's favourite courses is the lack of facilities for under 16s, although there is a family room in the old Tote building, and accompanied chilren under 16 are admitted free to the Racecourse. Telephones at the racecourse are located in Tattersalls where there is also a betting shop. For the disabled there is a special viewing platform and toilet facilities. This is a wonderful part of the world and a thoroughly pleasant racecourse. A trip is strongly tipped, throughout the year.

Local Favourites
Three miles from the racecourse is the **Lord Haldon**

(01392) 832483, a highly commended country house hotel which organises special racing breaks for visitors to Exeter as well as to Newton Abbot. East of the course lies Exeter and here the **Royal Clarence** (01392) 319955 is the pick of the paddock. **Buckerell Lodge** (01392) 221111 and **St Olaves Court** (01392) 217736 also have considerable appeal—both have good restaurants. The **White Hart** (01392) 79897 wins approval from those seeking a characterful inn, **Southgate** (01392) 412812 is also a well thought of establishment.

One thought for golfers and holidaymakers alike is the **Thurlestone Hotel** (01548) 560382 in Thurlestone. A number of these hotels are much quieter in the off season and are therefore that much more appealing, so book up now and take a well earned break.

A good sporting break hotel is the **Manor House** (01647) 40355 at Moretonhampstead. **Woodhayes** (01404) 822237 in Whimple is a real favourite. Both the restaurant and accommodation here are first class. The **Old Mill** (01392) 259480 in Ide is a cosy and stylish restaurant with good fish. In Diddiscombsleigh, one pub that really should be noted is the welcoming (but somewhat oddly named) **Nobody Inn** (01647) 52394, with good value bedrooms if you like pub accommodation. The bar food and wine here here are good. Close by, the **Huntsman** is a grand alternative. A tremendous pub for a visit after racing is the **Coaching Inn**, Chudleigh—great character and food, whilst on the coast the **Bay Hotel** (01626) 774123 is a comforatale place to stay. Another place to eat is the **Thatch** in Haldon. In North Bovey, the **Ring of Bells** (01647) 40375 is a well known real ale pub with accommodation which is also good value. For those spreading their sightseeing net slightly wider, the **Cridford Inn** (01626) 853694 is also most appealing—an historic inn, offering good food and accommodation—ideal. **Combe House** (01404) 42756, Gittisham, is another outstanding hotel and restaurant, while **Bel Alp House** (01364) 661217 is an excellent country house hotel.

Heading further into Dartmoor there are some really first class hotels. In Chagford, the **Gidleigh Park Hotel** (01647) 432367 is isolated but beautiful and has a first class restaurant. The **Great Tree Hotel** (01647) 432491 is also extremely tranquil while the **Mill End** (01647) 432282 has yet another delightfully quiet setting in the Teign Valley. Finally, some twenty miles from Exeter is Ashburton, which houses the **Holne Chase Hotel** (01364) 631471, a lovely country house hotel where fishing is available and a warm welcome assured.

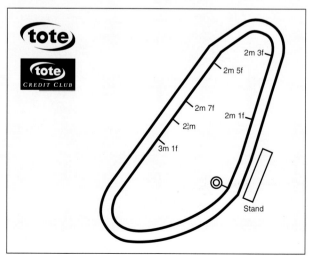

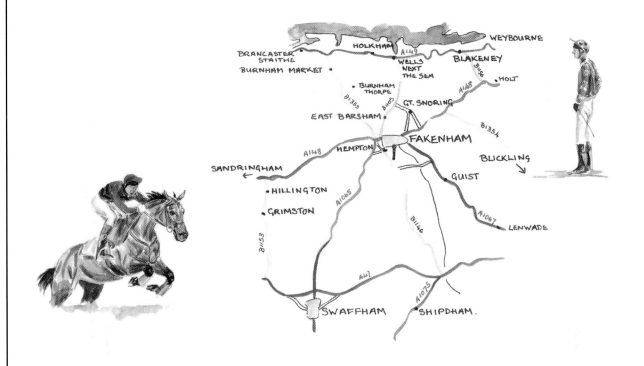

Artist: **Vic Granger** **RACING AT FAKENHAM** *Courtesy of:* **The Artist**

Artist: **Mark Churms** **THE FINISH** *Courtesy of:* **The Artist**

The Old Rectory

The Old Rectory at Great Snoring, a former manor house noted for its architectural history, stands in one and a half acres of walled garden and nestles contentedly beside the village church. The house, which dates back to 1500 is ideal, secluded and splendidly personal. All this within a ten minute drive of the racecourse at Fakenham.

Relaxed informality is assured, made possible by the size of the 'hotel'—there are just six bedrooms, each one different from the other. The dining room is fascinating, with stone mullion windows and heavy oak beams. It is a versatile room where guests enjoy delicious dinners and hearty breakfasts. Amongst the recommendations are Egon Ronay, The Good Hotel Guide, Which? Hotel Guide, The Best of Britain and The Charming Small Hotel Guide.

For those who relish in the idea of independence together with service, The Sheltons self-contained cottages provide the answer. They are serviced on a daily basis and have the trappings of the traditional hotel but allow the guests complete freedom and flexibility. The Sheltons have been sympathetically constructed in the grounds of The Old Rectory which, with the neighbouring Church, provide a majestic backdrop for this unique mews development.

The Old Rectory
Great Snoring
Fakenham
Norfolk NR21 0HP
Tel: (01328) 820597
Fax: (01328) 820048
e mail: greatsnoringoldrectory@compuserve.com

Fakenham

Now this is a racecourse which is well worth a visit. It has a tremendous atmosphere and is great fun. **David Hunter** is **Clerk of the Course** and **Racecourse Manager**, and **Vivien Pope** is the **Company Secretary**. All enquiries should be addressed to **The Racecourse, Fakenham, Norfolk NR21 7NY. Tel (01328) 862388. Fax (01328) 855908.** Fakenham is a great advertisement for racing at the lower end of the spectrum. By and large it appears good value for money and like several similar courses, it often provides a more enjoyable day's racing than its more illustrious competitors.

Fakenham is situated just off the A148 and the town is bypassed to the north making your journey somewhat less tricky. Although the course is well signposted from all directions, London is 125 miles away, King's Lynn 22 miles and Norwich 26 miles. From the north, the A1 and A17 combine to make the most direct route. From the south use the A1065, from the west the A148 and from the east the A1067. Parking facilities at the course are thankfully very good. The main railway station is some 22 miles away at King's Lynn (departing Liverpool Street and King's Cross). However, what the area lacks in the way of public transport it makes up for in terms of private facilities. Helicopters may land in the centre of the course.

Despite being a seven-meeting country course, Fakenham has some fairly worthwhile prizes and is well sponsored by local and national firms. Racing highlights are the Prince of Wales Cup, Queen's Cup, David Keith Memorial Chase, Graham Building Supplies Handicap Steeplechase and the Stephenson Smart Handicap Steeplechase. Easter Monday is the major raceday and much recommended. The May meeting is now held on a Sunday.

Badges cost £14 for the Members on Easter and May meetings and £12 on other days. Similarly, Tattersalls prices varied between £10 and £6 on different days. The Silver Ring costs £5 for the May Meeting, on bank holidays and evening meetings and £6 on other days. But please note that Tattersalls and the Silver Ring are combined as one enclosure except on bank holidays and for the May Meeting. If you're local or just keen on Fakenham then you should buy a £75 annual double badge—a worthwhile saving. Annual single badges can be ordered for £50 and a year's membership includes reciprocal days at Huntingdon, Market Rasen, Yarmouth, Southwell, Warwick and Bangor plus one car park badge. Daily badge holders must pay £6 or £7 on Easter Monday and in May to park in the Members'. If you're thinking of organising a party to go to Fakenham a 30 per cent discount is available for groups of 30 or more who book in advance, 20 per cent for groups of 20 to 29, and 10 per cent for groups of 10 to 19. If you want to make a real day and night of it, marquees can be hired and all the various trimmings laid on. The Paddock Buffet Restaurant serves good food (there is no need to book) and there is also a members restaurant. The caterers are Event Caterers (01603) 219991 Fax: (01603) 219992.

Facilities for the disabled are good here and include their own viewing stand and reserved parking. Children are welcome at Fakenham and are admitted free if under 16 and accompanied by an adult. A new creche is also available for a small charge. There is a Tote betting shop close to the paddock but no bank to replenish your wallet should you be unsuccessful. Fakenham also operates an upmarket caravan/camping site ideally situated for sampling Norfolk's delights, with the added benefit of free entry to race meetings. All in all, Fakenham is a small, rural and friendly racecourse, well run, well supported and recommended to all those who relish travelling the turf.

Local Favourites

Where better to dream of tomorrow's winners than in the serenely peaceful village of Great Snoring? Here, the secluded and personal **Old Rectory** (01328) 820597 is an impressive manor house dating back to 1500. Another outstanding place to stay and eat is to be found at Grimston here **Congham Hall** (01485) 600250 is a delightful country house. The **Fakenham Wine Bar** (01328) 862032 is also a popular haunt, and special mention must be made of the **Old Forge Restaurant** (01328) 878345 at Thursford, which specialises in seafood.. And now for a few inspired selections: **Yetmans Restaurant** in Holt (01263) 713320 is reputed to be very good and we are also informed that **Lenwade House Hotel** in Lenwade (01603) 872288 and **Grady's Country House Hotel** in Swaffham (01760) 723355 are delightful. Last, but most definitely not least, the quaintly named Barney houses the highly recommended **Old Brick Kilns** (01328) 878305.

If you decide that a little sea air is in order then the **Jolly Sailors** (01485) 210314 at Brancaster Staithe may be somewhere to visit after racing—a pleasant bar and a fine English menu in the restaurant. A little way from the coast, two locations should be considered. Firstly, in Burnham Market, **Fishes** (01328) 738588 where some superb fish can be enjoyed in an informal atmosphere, and secondly, in Burnham Thorpe, the **Lord Nelson**—an original pub with an excellent drop of Greene King.

In Fakenham, there is **Sculthorpe Mill** (01328) 856161 or the **Wensum Lodge Hotel** (01328) 862100, as well as the **Crown** (01328) 710209, a pleasant inn with a restaurant and some accommodation. Moving into Blakeney, you find the **Blakeney Hotel** (01263) 740797 a comfortable family run hotel, while the **Manor Hotel** (01263) 740376 has a marvellous quayside setting. Two pubs to note are the **Kings Arms** and the **White Horse** where excellent bar food is available—ideal for a weekend visit after racing. Just west of here, **Morston Hall**, (01263) 741041 has a good racing name and an excellent reputation. Some way off one finds the **Maltings Hotel** (01263) 588731 near the sea—most appealing. Similarly try the **Hoste Arms** in Burnham Market (01328) 738777, it's a superb inn. Three final places to consider are the **Old Bakehouse** (01328) 820454 in Little Walsingham which offers accommodation, food and a characterful bar. The **White Horse** (01328) 820645 is an inn to note. The **Buckinghamshire Arms** (01263) 732133 in Blickling is also well worth a visit. I am looking forward to my next visit already—one for the diary in 2000.

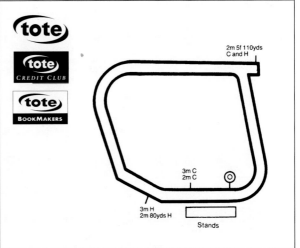

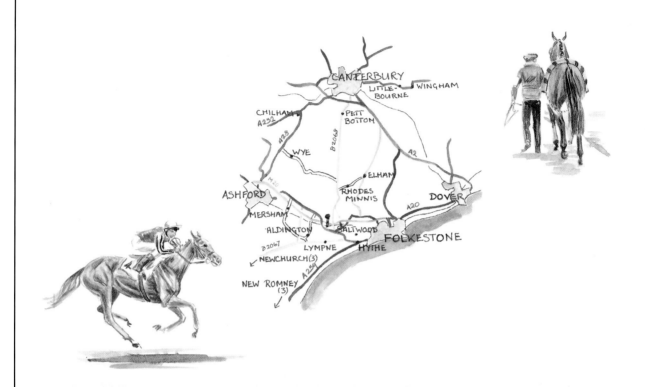

Artist: **Peter Smith** **EVENING MEET - GOING OUT** *Courtesy of:* **Frost & Reed**

The Director of Racing is Geoff Stickels and he can be contacted c/o Lingfield Park Racecourse, Racecourse Road, Lingfield, Surrey RH7 6PQ Tel (01342) 834800 Fax (01342) 832833. The **Chief Executive** here is **Graham Parr** and **Claudia Fisher** is the **Sales & Marketing Director**.

Located four miles west of Folkestone, Kent's only track is a mere 65 miles from London. Road users from London should leave the M20 at junction 11 where there is a sign directing you to the racecourse and take the A20 towards Lympne, Newingreen and Sellinge. The racecourse is only about one mile from the motorway. From Canterbury the best route is the B2068, the historic Roman 'Stone Street', picking up the AA signs as you go over junction 11. Train users are well catered for—special raceday services depart Charing Cross and Waterloo East (three minutes later) to Westenhanger. The station adjoins the course and is about 100 metres from the main entrance (telephone 0171 928 5100 for details). There is no bus service. Those with helicopters should call the racecourse the day before the meeting to make landing arrangements. Whatever your mode of transport, you will find ample free parking and for those who like to pack a hamper, you can picnic from a car park and watch the racing.

The racecourse has a mixed calendar with about 20 fixtures, the most popular invariably being the aptly named Garden of England Day which traditionally takes place in early September and is well worth a visit, as is the United Hunts, the May jumps meeting.

For the 1999/2000 season, Annual Membership is priced at £130. One of the particular benefits of your membership is that it includes ten reciprocal meetings at other tracks. This means that punters can enjoy a taste of flat racing and chasing and hurdling as well as show jumping—ideal for lovers of all manner of equestrian pursuits.

Daily rates are £10 for a combined Members and Grandstand admission and £4 per car and £4 per occupant in the Picnic Enclosure. People wishing to organise a party of 20 or more will receive a discount of 20 per cent per person. This should be organised through the racecourse management in advance of the meeting. Children under 16 are admitted free to all areas if accompanied by an adult.

If a picnic sounds like hard work then it may be an idea to sample one of the two restaurants, one of which overlooks the course. Bookings should be made through the racecourse caterers, Letheby & Christopher (01273) 814566. The course has twelve splendid boxes which can seat up to 16 guests and are available for hire on a daily basis. Corporate hospitality rates are from £35 per head. If you are inclined to go for a real bash, then the management will be happy to guide you on the various possibilities available here at Folkestone.

If you wish to place an off-track punt then Tattersalls is where you will find the necessary betting facilities. There is no bank yet at this course and other facilities, including those for disabled, are limited.

There are numerous plans afoot for the continued improvement of Folkestone racecourse. It's interesting to note that the course has only one basic admission charge which allows the punter to enter all areas. This is probably a move that many other courses could consider adopting and well done Folkstone for breaking down the mystery for the new racegoer of having to decide between something called the Silver Ring and Tattersalls!

Local Favourites

A hotel with a watery view is the **Clifton** (01303) 851231 in Folkestone. Reasonably priced accommodation can also be found at the **Belmonte Private Hotel** (01303) 254470. There are a number of restaurants to consider; **Pauls** (01303) 259697 in Bouverie Road is a fine place to spend an evening—the fish and shellfish here are particularly good. **La Tavernetta** (01303) 254953 is another long-standing favourite—Italian cuisine on this occasion. If you are in Hythe and are searching for a good place to stay then the **Hythe Imperial** (01303) 267441 should be the answer. This hotel is particularly comfortable and offers excellent leisure facilities including special golf packages, ideal for those of you who enjoy following the fairways as much as travelling the turf. **Stade Court** (01303) 268263 is less elaborate than its near neighbour but most accommodating and friendly. Sandgate a little west of Folkestone offers The **Sandgate Hotel** (01303) 220444, a fine hotel and restaurant.

Dover obviously contains a host of more modest guesthouses where the welcome is guaranteed to be greater than the bill. Potential gems include **Number One** (01304) 202007 and **Walletts Court** (01304) 852424 which is really outstanding. This is definitely one for those who enjoy good service and some style. An excellent restaurant as well. You'll find it at St Margaret's at Cliffe. In Wingham, the **Red Lion** (01227) 720217 offers a good restaurant and some satisfactory, well priced bedrooms.

One of the most appealing things about Kent is the many pubs one can find. In the delightfully named Petts Bottom, the **Duck** (01227) 830354 is a welcoming pub. The aptly named **Flying Horse** in Boughton Aluph (01233) 260914 is a pub to note—some accommodation here. Chilham, a most attractive little village, offers the **White Horse**, an old coaching inn and the **Woolpack** (01227) 730208 where some good accommodation is offered, making it an ideal base for preparing one's excursion to the racecourse. If you can't relax in this village you may as well call it a day! Another pub well worth a visit is the **Five Bells** at Brabourne (01303) 813334 - first class food. The star of the show, in terms of intimate dining, is to be found in Wye, the **Wife of Bath** (01233) 812540. Finally, **Eastwell Manor** (01233) 213000, situated in the gorgeous Eastwell Park, Ashford, is a delightful place with a first class dining room, a front runner in any field. Ideal if you've won a packet on the last at Folkestone.

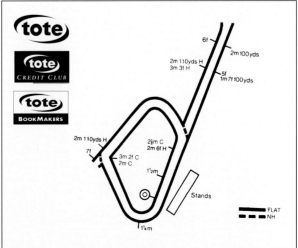

Holding court over sixty-two acres of private grounds in the midst of a three thousand acre estate Eastwell Manor Hotel offers a most appealing combination of luxurious surroundings, service second to none, and a cuisine that is the envy of the county. Quite simply it is the perfect setting in which to relax and enjoy yourself; to celebrate family occasions such as weddings and parties; or to rendezvous with friends and colleagues for those important business meetings, conferences, seminars or reunions.

Relaxing in the opulence of superb guest rooms and suites on a site whose history spans back almost a thousand years, you will soon come to understand how Eastwell has gained such a reputation for service and comfort. Whether your visit is in summer or winter there can be no doubting the rather special atmosphere that only a spacious country mansion can offer, making your stay an experience to remember.

On a sunny day there are terraces overlooking beautiful gardens, while in winter tranquil log fired lounges are temptingly cosy. For the energetic the estate grounds and surrounding countryside offer numerous walking, jogging and riding routes; or perhaps make new friends over a game of tennis in the grounds or a round of golf at the adjacent Ashford Golf Club. Better still, take the opportunity to develop new skills—archery, falconry, and clay-pigeon shooting can all be arranged. If that sounds a bit too energetic how about a leisurly swim in the outdoor heated swimming pool, a little croquet or pitch-and-putt, while in January 2000 Eastwell Pavilion will be opening (see Eastwell Mews for details).

After such a day surrender body and soul to a relaxing hot bath, and later, to a mouthwatering selection of traditional or contemporary cuisine, impeccably served and accompanied by a choice of aperitifs, wines and liqueurs, guaranteed to satisfy the most discerning palate.

Eastwell Manor prides itself on its experience and expertise in organising conference and corporate events of any kind. In addition to superb support facilities within secluded, richly panelled conference rooms, the hotel offers the finest cuisine served as you wish, from buffet to luncheon to private dining.

Eastwell Manor is conveniently located for that car journey to France by Le Shuttle or through the ferry ports at Folkestone and Dover. Ashford International station is only a couple of miles away to take you to Paris for lunch or tea or for that trip to L'Arc de Triomphe, or for a visit to one of France's major horse racing events.

Eastwell Manor
Eastwell Park
Boughton Lees, Ashford
Kent TN25 4HR
Tel: (01233) 213000
Fax: (01233) 635530

Eastwell Mews is a beautiful conversion of the Victorian stable block set in the 3,000 acre estate of Eastwell Park. The accommodation consists of 19 Courtyard Apartments or Country Cottages, which provide a choice of 1, 2 and 3 bedroom family units.

The cottages are all furnished in their own individual styles and they either have views over the elegant gardens of Eastwell Manor, over the Kent countryside or the peaceful courtyards. Some of the units have patio doors leading out to their own gardens, all of which have the magic of Eastwell with a history dating back nearly 1,000 years.

The cottages at Eastwell Mews are extremely comfortable and include en-suite facilities, fully fitted kitchen, colour television and satellite stations in all bedrooms and lounges. There is also a video recorder, direct dial telephones, along with a self service laundry. All linen and bedding are provided and baby sitting and maid service are available through prior arrangement. So whether you are visiting for business or pleasure, everything you could possibly need is available. January 2000 sees the opening of Eastwell Pavilion with a 20m indoor swimming pool, gymnasium, sauna, jacuzzi, steam room, large therapy pool and 10 treatment rooms offering a complete selection of therapeutic facilities, all of which are available to all guests.

Prices start from £350.00 for a short stay in the smaller cottage and depending on your length of stay and cottage required a rate can be obtained from the reception at Eastwell Manor along with a brochure and information pack.

Conveniently located for visiting the historic city of Canterbury and the charming and beautiful villages of Kent and Sussex and with easy access to the Channel ports, Le Shuttle and Eurostar. Eastwell Mews enables couples, families and business travellers alike the ideal venue in the 'Garden of England'. For the racegoer Eastwell Mews is ideally located for the courses at Folkestone, Plumpton and Brighton, with the track at Lingfield Park and London courses of Epsom, Kempton, Sandown, Ascot and Windsor a little further afield.

All of the facilities at the adjoining Eastwell Manor are available to residents including its award winning restaurant, bars, outdoor 20 metre heated swimming pool, heated spa pool, all weather tennis court, gardens and terraces.

Eastwell Mews
Eastwell Manor, Eastwell Park
Broughton Lees, Ashford
Kent TN25 4HR
Tel: (01233) 213000
Fax: (01233) 635530
Freephone: 0500 526735

Artist: **Claire Eva Burton** **BEECH ROAD** *Courtesy of:* **Rosenstiel's**

There is no more pleasant a course for a day's National Hunt racing than Fontwell Park where **Jonathan Garratt** is the **Chief Executive** and **David McHarg** is the **Clerk of the Course**. They can be contacted on **(01243) 543335**.

The racecourse is conveniently situated adjacent to the A27 and the A29 roundabout, midway between Arundel and Chichester. London is 60 miles using the M23 and the A29. The M23 adjoins the M25—that frustratingly one-paced track. The A3 is the best selection to make if one is keen to pursue a trunk road. The trains into this county run from Victoria and the nearest station is at Barnham. There are free buses from the station to the course on racedays so this may be an alternative mode of transport. There is ample car parking available which is provided free. Helicopters may be landed close to the track if you call ahead to make arrangements.

The racecourse staged seventeen National Hunt fixtures in 1999 and fixtures for 2000 are expected to follow a similar pattern. The bank holiday fixture in August which started a few years ago continues to provide some summer sport. The most popular annual event is usually the Spring Bank Holiday meeting in May. There are many Monday and Tuesday meetings at Fontwell Park and it may be a good idea to relax for a few days in West Sussex and take in one such meeting. The National Spirit Champion Hurdle Trial in the second half of February often provides a few Cheltenham Pointers.

Entrance to the racecourse is priced at £14 for daily admission to the Members, £10 for the Tattersalls Enclosure and £6 for the Silver Ring, while OAP's can gain entry for half price, at £3. Children under 16 enter free but there is a limit of two children per adult. There are very popular picnic car parks in the Silver Ring and in the centre of the course, if you want to make a real day out of it. An additional charge is made of £4 per car. The Annual Members badge, which includes eleven reciprocal meetings, was priced at £120 in 1999. If you are thinking of organising a party to go to Fontwell races then you can arrange discounted admission prices by booking in advance.

There are 15 private boxes at the course, all recently redecorated, and each can cater for up to 20 guests. There are also larger rooms for 70-90 people and these are also undergoing refurbishment; one will have a new balcony overlooking the paddock added to it. The racecourse management are happy to assist in organising parties and invite you to drop by anytime to see the facilities.

There is a club restaurant at Fontwell and bookings can be made through the racecourse office. The Kerman Stand provides bars, also being refurbished, Tote credit and additional boxes for entertaining. Snack bars can also be found throughout the enclosures and there is an off-course betting area in the Paddock although no banks. There are lavatories for disabled people positioned in the Silver Ring Enclosure and Tattersalls. If you are blessed with a clear crisp windless day's racing at Fontwell and a couple of fancied flutters oblige you will be pretty close to heaven. Even if they don't you can still anticipate a fine day's racing. A visit to this charming Sussex racecourse is always recommended.

Local Favourites

Where better to begin our gastronomic wander around this most pleasant of English counties than in Storrington where we find **Manleys** (01903) 742331—a very distinguished restaurant. It is extremely popular and bookings for both lunch and dinner are strongly advised. The **Old Forge** (01903) 743402 is also excellent. Also in Storrington,

one can find a really beautifully situated hotel, **Abingworth Hall** (01798) 813636. There is a warm welcome here and the food and wine list are also first class. However, perhaps even more delightful is the outstanding **Little Thakeham** (01903) 744416 with its Lutyens exterior and gardens in the style of Gertrude Jekyll. The hotel and the restaurant are both outstanding.

Another extremely peaceful and relaxing hotel and restaurant double is the **Roundabout Hotel** (01798) 813838 in West Chiltington. If one chooses to visit Arundel, perhaps to view the castle or to browse through some of the delightful antique shops, a particularly relaxing establishment is the **Norfolk Arms** (01903) 882101—a coaching inn for over 200 years and still welcoming today. There are numerous pubs in Arundel but one to note is the **Swan** (01903) 882314. In addition to bar snacks and a pleasant welcome there is some accommodation here too. A really excellent choice found in Climping is **Bailiffscourt** (01903) 723511—this is the form choice in a truly excellent field. Findon is a pleasing racing village where you will find **Findon Manor** (01903) 872733, a welcoming hotel, and the **Village House** (01903) 873350 where good food can be expected. In the alarmingly named Burpham, The **George and Dragon** (01903) 883131 offers fine fayre to keep the wind up. The **Royal Oak** at Walberton (01243) 552865 also offers good food.

Not everyone will be able to slumber in Sussex, but any visit should certainly be combined with one of the many splendid pubs that adorn the county. The **Fox** at Charlton is a convenient diversion and the **White Hart** at South Harting is especially handy for Goodwood and Fontwell visitors. Farther afield, the **Black Horse** (01798) 342424 in Byworth is also worth a visit—a comprehensive range of bar snacks and a really cosy restaurant, ideal for a quiet evening after racing. In Petworth, there are a number of places to note. The **Angel** (01798) 342153 in Angel Street offers good value food in a pleasant medieval inn—the bedrooms also have appeal. The **Welldiggers** also welcomes; good food and friendly atmosphere combine extremely well. The **White Horse** at Sutton (01798) 869221 is also pleasant. In Pulborough, the **Chequers Hotel** (01798) 872486 is a small Queen Anne building where lunch and dinner are both well priced. **Stane Street Hollow** (01798) 872819 is a charming restaurant. More expensive, but quite superb, is nearby **Amberley Castle** (01798) 831992 near Arundel. Its outer walls predate racing itself—a fine atmosphere in which to consider the heritage of this sport.

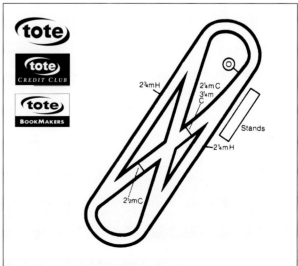

Artist: **Peter Smith JOCKEYS UP, PLEASE** _Courtesy of:_ **Frost & Reed**

A beautiful 'medieval' manor, Bailiffscourt, standing amid thirty two acres of tranquil Sussex farmland and just two hundred yards from a rare stretch of unspoilt coastline, is situated three miles south of the historic town of Arundel and only a twenty minute drive from Chichester, home of the famous Festival Theatre.

Portsmouth, Southampton and Eastbourne are all within easy driving distance and London is approximately an hour and a half away by car.

This rambling masterpiece and spectacular country house hotel affords individually priced and extravagantly furnished bedrooms—some featuring four poster beds and log fires—each with bathroom en suite, colour television, direct dial telephone and hairdryer.

The award-winning Tapestry restaurant offers fine cuisine and an excellent selection of wines. In the summer, lighter meals may be taken in the walled garden or rose-clad courtyard.

The relaxed and romantic atmosphere does not mean, however, that the corporate entertainer is neglected. Indeed, companies are welcome to this extra special setting for board meetings and conferences—welcome to take over the whole hotel for two or three days as their own country house!

Set in verdant parkland, Bailiffscourt boasts a swimming pool, tennis courts, croquet lawn, golf practice area and helicopter landing pad. You can hack along the beach or ride downland at Arundel, two miles away. Littlehampton provides first class golf courses and windsurfing. Many famous racing 'names' stay here.

Whether you're in pursuit of business or pleasure, Bailiffscourt awaits you.

Bailiffscourt
Climping
West Sussex BN17 5RW
Tel: (01903) 723511 Fax: (01903) 723107
e mail: bailiffscourt@hshotels.co.uk
website: www.hshotels.co.uk

Goodwood

Goodwood enjoys one of the most scenic settings in world racing. It also offers in Glorious Goodwood one of the racing and social events of the year. A visit to the course is thoroughly recommended.

The management team at Goodwood is headed by **Rod Fabricius**, who acts as **Clerk** and **General Manager, Emma Everest, Hospitality Sales Manager** and **John Thompson** who is Goodwood's **Racecourse Manager.** They can be contacted at **Goodwood Racecourse, Goodwood House, Chichester, West Sussex PO18 0PS** Tel (01243) 755022 Fax (01243) 755025.

The racecourse is a 66 mile journey from London. Chichester, the nearest large town, is some five miles away. Chichester railway station is on the Victoria line and there is an efficient bus service from the station to the course on racedays. If you do travel by car from London the journey time is likely to be an hour and a half. The A29 or the A3 doubled up with the A27 should produce a satisfactory result. The A27, which bypasses Chichester, also serves racegoers from the east and west and has recently been improved. Goodwood has ample parking and this is provided free or at £2 (£5 for the July Festival) depending on how far you are prepared to walk. Light aircraft can land at Goodwood Airfield, two miles from the course. Helicopters or taxis can be taken to the course from there. Goodwood racecourse provides a prospectus with some of the best information available so do telephone in advance so you can make your own individual arrangements.

Major races to note are the William Hill Mile at the Glorious Goodwood meeting, the Grosvenor Casinos Cup, the Goodwood Cup, the Vodafone Stewards Cup, the Richmond Stakes and the jewel of the year, the outstanding Sussex Stakes.

The annual membership subscription at Goodwood is £165, admitting the member to the Richmond Enclosure on all Goodwood racedays in the year. The cost however, does not include parking which is an extra £45 per annum. Free owners and trainers valet parking is available from the west entrance. Twenty-nine reciprocal events are arranged at twenty-one other venues. At the July meeting, daily badges are not on sale to the general public but Members may purchase them at £40 each after 1 June. Entry to the Gordon Enclosure for this meeting costs £17 before the 1st of June and £20 thereafter, while entry to the Public Enclosure costs £6 before June 1st and £7 after. At all other meetings, day badges for the Members are obtainable at £17, with £10 being the price for the Gordon Enclosure and £5 for the Public Enclosure. Members are advised to make reservations for seats for the July meeting. Junior Membership (5-25) can be purchased for £75. Parties of 20 or more are entitled to discounts in all enclosures except the Richmond Enclosure.

Tailored packages are available for all your entertainment requirements. Please contact Emma Everest for further details. There are many facilities at Goodwood to suit all tastes and budgets. Enquiries with regard to the catering should be made to Payne & Gunter (01243) 775350. They do a fine job of providing all the ingredients for a good day's racing. The ever-expanding tented village and the superb racing makes for massive crowds at the July fixture, so be warned. Try to arrive at the racecourse in plenty of time, Goodwood always provides a number of worthwhile additional attractions before racing commences.

The third Duke of Richmond organised the first Goodwood race meeting in 1801. It was a friendly competition between himself and other army officers. The event was such a success that in the following year the public was admitted. Thereafter the fame of the location and quality of racing has been so widely acclaimed that racing here has gone from strength to unbridled strength. But Goodwood is also an occasion in the sporting calendar to savour and has been referred to as 'a garden party with racing tacked on'.

Top racing it is too! In addition to this, Goodwood organises various events during the summer meetings which include barbecues, jazz and steel bands, over 65s days and family days—all of which are highly recommended. Other especially laudable points about the course are the excellent children's playground, the lifts and stands for the disabled and numerous betting facilities. There is a Gordon Enclosure crèche facility at Sunday/July/August meetings.

Goodwood has a tremendous setting on the South Downs and certainly the major rebuilding programmes of recent years have improved the course. Goodwood is constantly being improved and when coupled with the sport available it makes one of the most glorious amphitheatres in racing.

Goodwood has always had a stylish way of doing things and is not afraid to take on something new. This past year saw the course host a race meeting with a difference - an international event that featured teams of horses and jockeys representing various countries.. Although like any 'first' it was not without its sceptics, these are the kind of initiatives that racing must continue to try if it is to capture the wider public's imagination. Let's hope the powers that be go ahead and build on their first year's experience.

Goodwood looks forward to celebrating its 200th anniversary in 2002 and has great plans to bring in the double century in fine style. A complete makeover of the paddock area is on the cards and there will probably be further tie-ins between horse racing and the motor racing of the increasingly popular Goodwood Festival of Speed.

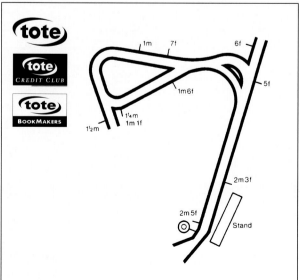

Marriott Goodwood Park Hotel & Country Club

Situated within the grounds of historical Goodwood House, ancestral home to the Dukes of Richmond, the Marriott Goodwood Park Hotel & Country Club is surrounded by 12,000 acres of Goodwood Park Estate.

Sympathetically developed, the first class accommodation that distinguishes Marriott hotels provides 94 bedrooms including an elegant four poster and executive rooms.

The award-winning Richmond Room restaurant serves the best of modern English cuisine, and the Goodwood Sports Café Bar is available for more informal meals. The conference facilities can entertain from 10 to 150 delegates and for a uniquely sumptuous setting for a banquet or reception, the State Rooms of Goodwood House itself can be booked for functions linked to your conference.

The leisure facilities offered by the hotel include an indoor, ozone treated swimming pool, spa bath, sauna, steam room, aerobic studio, tennis courts and a fully equipped fitness gym. There is also a health and beauty salon and a solarium.

The 18 hole golf course has for its backdrop beautiful Goodwood House. Clubs and buggies are available for hire and with a retail sports shop, practice ground and professional tuition the player's every need, both practical and aesthetic, is catered for.

Goodwood Racing Breaks are another popular feature of the hotel with the famous racecourse only one mile away and are offered on meetings in May, June, August, and September. The elegant Festival meeting is held each July.

Guests wishing a more peaceful holiday will enjoy exploring the rolling Sussex Downs and a visit to Chichester is not to be missed with its harbour, cathedral and theatre. Arundel Castle is well worth a visit as is the town of Brighton.

Whether you are wanting to improve your golf handicap, visit the races, explore the sights of the South of England or simply unwind from the stress of everyday life, the thoughtful and helpful staff at Marriott Goodwood Park Hotel are waiting to welcome you.

Marriott Goodwood Park Hotel & Country Club
Goodwood
Chichester
West Sussex PO18 0QB
Tel: (01243) 775537
Fax: (01243) 520120

There are all manner of good reasons for visiting Goodwood, not least because it is surrounded by some first rate hotels, but make sure you book early as the crowds are enormous. The **Marriott Goodwood Park Hotel** (01243) 775537 is a charming hotel with some delightful rooms, a pleasant restaurant and a friendly welcome that make for a thoroughly worthwhile place to stay. Lovers of golf should make a point of booking here. A visit to nearby Goodwood House should also be fitted in if at all possible. The **Royal Norfolk Hotel** (01243) 826222 in Bognor Regis offers special Goodwood weekly rates. Bognor was incidentally given the addition of Regis after George V recuperated there in 1929. If it was good enough for him, it's good enough for me. The part 16th century **Inglenook** (01243) 262495 is also a worthy consideration in this tricky field.

Goodwood is situated between Midhurst and Chichester. Both towns have a lot to offer. Near Midhurst in Bepton, the **Park House Hotel** (01730) 812880 is a great favourite—thoroughly relaxing and very welcoming. The **Spread Eagle** (01730) 816911 is a first class 18th century inn and certainly one of the best of its type. The accommodation is most comfortable and both lunch and dinner in the restaurant are good. There are a number of excellent pubs in and near to Midhurst and the civilized **Angel** (01730) 812421 offers good value bedrooms and an excellent restaurant, the Cowdray Room. Midhurst really is ideal for lovers of the post-race pub crawl. Restaurants are also in abundance—**Maxines** (01730) 816271 is well thought of. West of Midhurst is Pulborough, home of the **Chequers Hotel** (01798) 872486, an ideal base for some energetic exploration of the countryside, as is the majestic **Amberley Castle** (01798) 831992 which simply oozes history and class. A genuine favourite in any field. **Stane Street Hollow** (01798) 872819 is well worth a try, but make sure you book a table.

Travelling south on the A286 en route to Chichester, one finds the **Horse and Groom** in Singleton, a pleasant pub. However, in Chichester there are a number of other delights including **Comme Ça** (01243) 788724, a confident nap in any field. Meanwhile, lovers of traditional English food should sample the **Old Cottage Inn** (01243) 773294 in Tangmere. The **Bedford Hotel** (01243) 778000 is a satisfactory place to spend the night. The streets of Chichester are often extremely busy. There are some excellent shops—ideal if you don't wish to attend every day of Glorious Goodwood. At night, the streets have an excellent atmosphere and the cathedral and the Festival Theatre (01243) 781312 are worth a visit. Further west one arrives in Bosham, a delightful village which houses the **Millstream Hotel** (01243) 573234, an attractive small hotel which is a convenient place to stay, especially if you like the coast. In Chilgrove, the **White Horse Inn** (01243) 359219 is excellent—a superb pub and also a fine restaurant not to be missed, the wine list here is breathtaking. In case you take the wrong road out of Chichester and find yourself heading east, do not despair, but head instead for Rustington, where the **Kenmore Guest House** (01903) 784634 will ease the most furrowed brow. Finally, in Langrish, near Petersfield, **Langrish House** (01730) 266941 is a little farther

Artist: **John Atkins PULLING UP, GOODWOOD EVENING**
Courtesy of: **The Artist**

afield but is particularly enjoyable.

If, by chance, you anticipate owning or backing a winner, we strongly recommend that you book a table in **Fleur de Sel** (01428) 651462 in Haslemere, an outstanding French restaurant. Two pleasant pubs can be located by people trekking northwards. In Lickfold, the **Lickfold Inn** (01798) 861285 is a fine Tudor establishment which offers some good value bar snacks and some accommodation. The **Coach and Horses** at Compton (01705) 631228 is a friendly local to try as is the **Anglesey Arms** (01243) 773474 a particularly convenient local favourite. Meanwhile the **Three Horseshoes** lies just off the B2141 between Chichester and Petersfield and is recommended. The **Elsted Inn** (01730) 813662, Elsted, also offers some excellent pub grub and a similar accolade can be given to the first rate **Halfway Bridge** (01798) 861281 at. For people seeking more liquid refreshment, visit the Chilsdown vineyard. Near Chichester, the Fishbourne Roman Palace is worth a peep while the Weald and Downland Open Air Museum is also something to note. We are grateful to the Goodwood team for suggesting the following places to try: the **Fox Goes Free**, in Charlton, the **Hurdlemakers** in East Dean, and the **Trundle Inn** in West Dean. These are recommendations from the horse's mouth so to speak and should definitely be carefully considered when assessing the form. The **Stakis Avisford Park** (01243) 551215, comes with a strong recommendation from the racecourse executive. A great *Travelling the Turf* favourite is **South Lodge**, Lower Beeding (01403) 891711—a first class hotel and restaurant double and with excellent golf too.

If you have any energy left and the summer sun still shines, one place you should not miss near Plumpton is **Glyndebourne** (01273) 812321—the location of the Glyndebourne Festival (May to mid-August). If you can tie in racing with an evening's opera the contrast will be enormous, but the appeal no less great. **Horsted Place,** Uckfield (01825) 750581 provides a luxurious base, depending of course, on the state of the following day's betting fund! Golfers will find this hotel particularly appealing. The thought of a day or more at Goodwood fills the heart with joy. A night or two at Horsted Place is icing on a tremendous cake.

Amberley Castle

When Bishop Luffa of Chichester began the building of Amberley Castle in the early 1100s he can hardly have foreseen that 900 years later his country retreat would have survived the ravages of centuries as well as the destructive force of Oliver Cromwell's army. Yet today, Amberley Castle stands majestic as if determined to endure as long as the softly undulating Sussex downland landscape which is its setting.

For most of its long history, few were privileged enough to experience the peace that lies within the massive embrace of the ancient curtain wall. For Amberley Castle was a private residence, tenanted for the best part of half a millenium by wealthy and influential bishops.

Since 1989, however, the life of Amberley Castle is no longer an enigmatic secret. Owners Martin and Joy Cummings have hoisted the portcullis to welcome the world to share the splendour of their historic castle home. For Amberley Castle has been transformed by the Cummings into a country house hotel offering its guests an incomparable blend of luxury, cuisine and service in the matchless surroundings of this magical building.

Each room, individually designed and decorated with jacuzzi bath en suite, is named after a Sussex castle—and there are a few which have access by a stone spiral staircase to the battlements. Guests are never in doubt that this is a real castle.

The Queen's Restaurant, a handsome barrel-vaulted room, is so named for its 17th century mural depicting King Charles II and his queen, Catherine of Braganza, who visited Amberley Castle in the early 1680s. Now it is the perfect setting for Castle Cuisine, the prix fixé dinner menu which reflects historical recipes and local ingredients in a contemporary style. To complement the excellent food, the Castle's wine list is both extensive and interesting.

It is hard to believe that so much tranquillity and seclusion can be so easily accessible from London, but you can be in Amberley in little more than an hour by main line train from Victoria or by road from Heathrow. Gatwick is a mere forty minutes away.

Yet Amberley, decidedly one of the most picturesque of Sussex downland villages, is country—not suburb. With a wealth of breathtaking walks and an abundance of country pursuits on hand, it's perfect for blowing cobwebs away or unwinding city tensions.

Amberley Castle
Amberley, Nr Arundel
West Sussex BN18 9ND
Tel: (01798) 831992
Fax: (01798) 831998

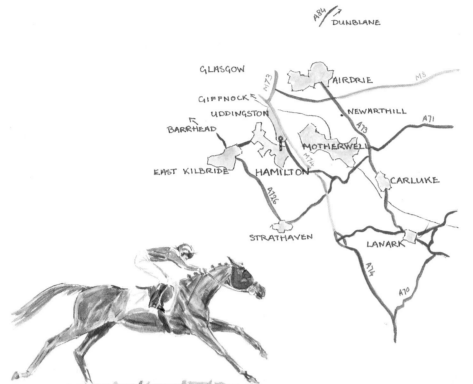

Artist: **Peter Smith WASHING DOWN, HAMILTON PARK** *Courtesy of:* **Frost & Reed**

The person in charge at Hamilton is **Clerk of the Course** and **Chief Executive, Hazel Dudgeon,** who can be contacted at **Hamilton Park Racecourse, Bothwell Road, Hamilton, Lanarkshire ML3 0DY. Tel (01698) 283806. Fax: (01698) 286621.**

The course is 10 miles south of Glasgow, in Hamilton, and the track is accessible from Glasgow via the M74, junction 5 or from Edinburgh via the M8, junction 6 and the A723, which runs near the course from east to west. The A776 from East Kilbride may prove an alternative route for eastbound travellers. For punters from the south, the A74 and the M74, junction 5 is an advisable route from Carlisle. Glasgow Central is the city's principal station and trains from London can be caught at Euston. There is a connecting line to Hamilton West which is the course's local station. Other public transport possibilities are the buses from Glasgow which pass the gates of the course. People with light aircraft and helicopters can't land at the course itself but a shuttle service between Heathrow and Glasgow as well as other major cities, could be of some use if you need to make a big plunge and wish to avoid paying tax!

In 1999 there were 17 days of flat racing at Hamilton Park with plenty of action between March and September, including a Family Night and a Ladies Night. Evening meetings are well worth considering here—ideal for unwinding after a hard day's work in Glasgow. The most popular meeting remains the Saints & Sinners Charity Meeting held in June. I imagine a number of both can be found at such events.

The Annual Membership rates are as follows: a single badge will cost £125 and a double badge (lady and gent) will cost £200. A more fleeting relationship with Hamilton will cost £12 for a Members badge or £7 for the Paddock with a reduced rate if you are a student or a pensioner. The reduced rate for 1999 is £4.

There are various points that should be noted when considering your trip to Hamilton Park. If you are planning a day out for more than ten people you will receive a discount and this applies to all enclosures. Full details can be obtained from the Secretary but there are private boxes of various sizes and a sponsors' room. Marquees are also available. The caterers at Hamilton are Peppermill Catering and they can be contacted on (01698) 429 310. There are various restaurants—Club dining room, snack bars and a string of drinks bars but, as one might expect, these are fairly busy areas. The Winning Post Bar is an exclusive facility for owners, trainers and Annual Members with a full bar and seafood menu.

The course is compact and the atmosphere is excellent. Those with children under 16 will be pleased to hear about their free admission and the playground. There are some facilities for disabled racegoers which include a snack bar but be warned, there are no banking facilities, although Tote cash and credit facilities are available. So if you intend to make use of the on-course betting shops bring your stake money with you.

There have been some major developments at Hamilton Park in recent years which include the extension of the Grandstand to accommodate additional boxes. Local people should note that the facilities can be used for conferences and receptions throughout the year. Hamilton Park may not be one of Britain's foremost racecourses but with a situation near to Glasgow the racecourse is extremely popular and to be a part of the throng when your fancy is coming through the field is a happy feeling indeed. Furthermore, it is fair to report that recent years have seen some excellent initiatives developed—may this continue in 2000 and for many years thereafter.

Local Favourites

Within one mile of the course, the **Cricklewood Hotel** (01698) 853 172 is a favourite for eating, drinking and a bed for the night. For the businessman, the **Marriott** 0141 226 5577 in Argyle Street offers pleasant cocktail bars and a wealth of leisure facilities. The **Glasgow Hilton** 0141 304 5555 is another high-rise hotel but is well run and comfortable with an excellent restaurant, while the **Stakis Grosvenor** 0141 339 8811 is a most impressive hotel with a delightful situation opposite the Botanical Gardens. The **Terrace Restaurant** is well worth visiting. Glasgow offers a variety of attractions and an exquisite Victorian hotel in which to stay is **One Devonshire Gardens** 0141 339 2001, home of a renowned restaurant. Finally, the **Malmasion** 0141 572 1000 is delightfully luxurious and will appeal to those who enjoy contemporary design.

Glasgow has become a veritable Mecca for lovers of fine cuisine with **Rogano** 0141 248 4055 one of its most celebrated. The **Buttery** 0141 221 8188 in Argyle Street, is convenient for the Holiday Inn and an excellent spot for lunch or dinner. Upstairs is expensive and correspondingly elegant while downstairs has a more relaxed air. **D'Arcy's** 0141 226 4309 is also good fun as is the outstanding **Puppet Theatre** 0141 339 8444. A Cantonese restaurant with an extensive menu can be found in Sauchiehall Street—it's called **Loon Fung** 0141 332 1240. **Chimms** (Chinese) and the **Grapevine** on Bothwell Road are also well thought of. **Amber Regent** 0141 331 1655 also provides Chinese cuisine of an award-winning standard. Just around the corner, the **Ubiquitous Chip** 0141 334 5007 is also fancied in a quite competitive field.

To the west of Glasgow stands **Gleddoch House** (01475) 540711, a distinguished hotel and restaurant. Built on the banks of the Clyde this impressive hotel is particularly charming and golfers will be delighted to hear that there is a nearby course. Golf courses, like pubs, are never far away in Glasgow and its surrounds. Those who like pubs and bars should try **Babbity Bowster** 0141 552 5055.

Returning south of the Clyde, East Kilbride. Two superbly Scottish names to note are the **Stakis** (01355) 236300 and secondly, the **Bruce Swallow** (013552) 29771. Both are modern, friendly and relatively convenient for the racecourse. The **Westpoint Hotel** (013552) 36300 is ideal for those who may be on business or who prefer hotels with extensive leisure facilities—the restaurant here is also good. Within a mile of the racecourse is the **Silvertrees Hotel** (01698) 852311. It is family run and well regarded by the local racing fraternity. Finally, seek out **Chapeltoun House** (01560) 482696, one for the notebook in 2000.

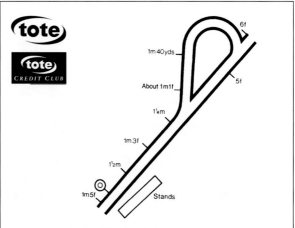

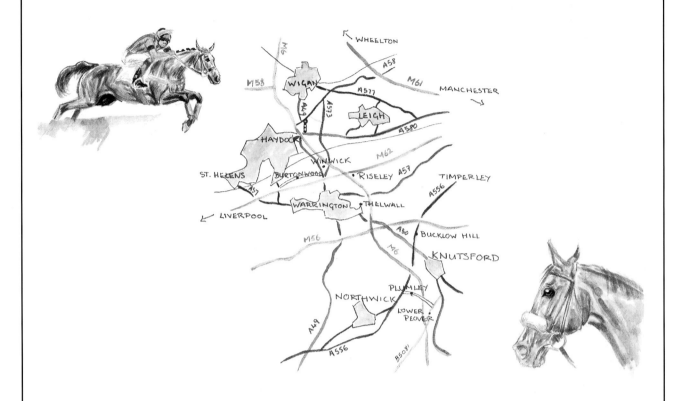

Artist: **Peter Smith CLEAR AT THE THIRD** *Courtesy of:* **Frost & Reed**

Haydock Park is the best all-round racecourse in the north of England, just one of the reasons why it was named Travelling the Turf's *Racecourse of the Year* in both 1998 and 2000. **Major P W F Arkwright** and **R G Thomas** act as **Clerk** and **General Manager** respectively, while **Richard Thomas** is **Managing Director** and **Stephen Mansfield** fills the role of **Operations Manager** with **Dean Martin** as the **Sales Manager.** They can be contacted at **Haydock Park Racecourse, Newton-le-Willows, Merseyside WA12 0HQ. Tel (01942) 725963 Fax (01942) 270879.** For further information on racing at Haydock call Talking Pages **0800 600 900** or visit their **web site: www.demon.co.uk/racenews/haydock.**

Access to the course is off the A49 close to Ashton. The course is superbly served by motorways and the M6 and the M62 converge close by. The new Thelwell viaduct on the M6 has already improved traffic conditions. An additional entrance has also been opened to provide easier access to the Owners and Trainers car park from the A580 end of the racecourse. In order to ensure entry through the western gate, M6 traffic from the north can leave at junction 24 and turn left, then right at the lights—the racecourse is a mile further, on the left. To arrive by train catch the Euston train to Warrington Bank Quay or take the local link to Newton-le-Willows, or catch the 320 bus from Liverpool which will deposit you at the gates. More speedy access can be obtained by using the landing strip or helipad.

The fixture list for 2000 at Haydock should follow that of 1999, which hosted 29 fixtures, with three Friday evening meetings during the summer, a new Saturday evening meeting in August and one Sunday fixture in July. Highlight of the flat season here is always the Old Newton Cup meeting held in early July. For admission to the County Enclosure in 2000 you will pay £17 (£20 on Saturdays and bank holidays). For Tattersalls the price will be £10 and £5 for the Newton Enclosure. On weekends the prices are £12 and £6 respectively. Haydock's Park Suite is a panoramic dining facility that will cost you £56 and a badge must be purchased in advance to confirm your booking. You will however receive a free racecard. Pensioners are admitted to Tattersalls and the Newton Enclosure at half price, while accompanied children under 16 and those confined to wheelchairs are free. An Annual Badge for the County Stand offers a definite saving. In 1999 a single badge for the year was priced at £190 and £65 for Juniors (under 21). This included a special car pass and twelve reciprocal days racing at twelve different courses. The racecourse also offers discounts in Tattersalls and the Newton Enclosure for parties of 25 or more.

Private facilities at Haydock Park are excellent—they include 32 boxes and six luncheon rooms. The boxes are sited on three floors of the Tommy Whittle Stand, and can accommodate up to 20 people. All boxes are let on a long term basis but a daily waiting list is maintained as several are made available for sub-let every raceday. There is also the Premier Suite from whose glass front you can observe the finishing post, opposite. For larger parties the luncheon rooms can be linked together. The Park Suite can seat 450 people but can be sectioned off to accommodate smaller parties. CCTV and Tote facilities are also provided. If you wish to use this restaurant, bookings for a table start three months prior to each raceday. A more fun way of catering for a larger party may be to organise a marquee. The Lancaster restaurant in the County Enclosure offers à la carte and tables can be booked in advance by telephoning the sales office.

Improvements continue to be made at this excellent course, with the building of the Centenary Stand which was opened in May 1999 and other renovations costing £3 million. The project provides additional capacity in the County Stand, extended catering facilities and improved parking. With attendance levels already running at a five-year high at Haydock, this will ensure even more racing fans will be able to enjoy its facilities in comfort in 2000.

Local Favourites

In Lower Peover, the **Bells of Peover** (01565) 722269 has a delightful setting and as well as super bar food the restaurant is recommended. North of the Bells, in Plumley, the **Smoker** (01565) 722338 which has an adjoining restaurant as well as serving excellent bar food can be recommended. The **Dog Inn** (01625) 861421 in Over Peover offers good food and some accommodation. **Ye Olde Parkgate Inn** (01625) 861455 is also good. In Mobberley, the **Bird In Hand** (01565) 873149 is one of the growing band of good food pubs. Other pubs in the area include the extremely welcoming **Fiddle i'th' Bag** at Burtonwood. The **Pickering Arms** at Thelwell is an attractive and friendly village local while in Risley, the **Noggin** is another popular food pub. However, perhaps the most convenient pub for the racecourse is the **Bay Horse** or even the relaxing **County Inn**. An enticing alternative is the **Bulls Head** (01942) 671621 in Newton-le-Willows where the food, beer and atmosphere are good and if you wish to make a really early start bedrooms can be organised. Another likely place for the early bird is the **Haydock Forte Posthouse** at Newton-le-Willows (01942) 717878 for it stands in parkland fringing the Haydock Park racecourse. For those expectant racegoers travelling from Liverpool on the A580, a **Travelodge** provides a convenient stopover. There is also the **Haydock Thistle** (01942) 272000 which lies near to the course. The **Park Royal International** Hotel (01925) 730706 at Stretten does special racing breaks including transport to the racecourse. Another first class post race retreat is the **Park Hall** Hotel (01257) 452090, well placed and welcoming.

Simply Heathcotes 0161 835 3536 is a good restaurant as is **Brasserie St Pierre** 0161 228 0231 and the **Royal Orchid** 0161 236 5183. Another polished hotel is the **Portland Thistle** Hotel 0161 228 3400, an elegant establishment which also boasts an extremely good leisure centre. The **Victoria and Albert** 0161 832 1188 in a converted 19th century warehouse is first class with a television themed interior The **Holiday Inn** 0161 236 3333 is also good. Manchester boasts an outstanding array of cosmopolitan cooking. **Yang Sing** 0161 236 2200 in Princess Street is an excellent Chinese restaurant. **Blinkers** 0161 228 2503 is an appropriately named French restaurant, while near the airport **Moss Nook** 0161 437 4778 is the most established restaurant in the area. Some rooms here as well for those wishing to stay.

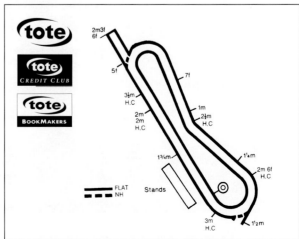

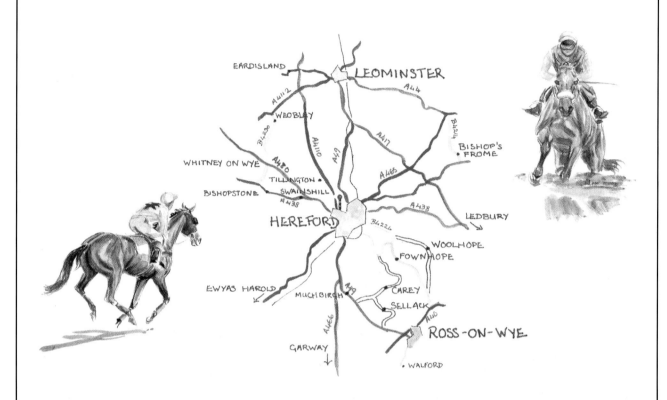

Artist: **Refna Hamey** **LOOSE TAILS AND TIDY TAIL** *Courtesy of:* **The Artist**

Britain, like France has a multitude of charming rustic racecourses and with so much of England being taken up by sprawling urbanisation it is a real pleasure to escape to the country. The shire of Hereford contains many such green fields and within its acres a welcoming picturesque racecourse, Hereford. The team in charge at Hereford are **Clerk of the Course** and **Secretary, John Williams** and **Manager** of the course, **Jason Loosemor**. They can be contacted at **The Racecourse, Roman Road, Hereford HR4 9QU** or **Shepherds Meadow, Lane Head, Eaton Bishop, Hereford HR2 9UA. Tel: (01981) 250436** or **Fax: (01981) 250192.**

Hereford racecourse is clearly signposted and there are good roads on the northern outskirts of the city. Indeed, the whole area is bordered by several major roads from the Midlands, South Wales and the south west. From the north, the racecourse can be reached via the A49 from Leominster and the A4110. The main southern approach roads are the A49 and the A495. The A438 through Hereford itself passes close to the racecourse and there's also an approach on the A4103 from Worcester. London is approximately 120 miles away and if you are travelling to Hereford by train then Paddington station is the one from which to make your departure. The station is a mile from the course and a taxi will be required from there unless you wish to take a short stroll. Should you be fairly busy and/or well off then subject to prior arrangement helicopters are welcome. If you decide to take the motor, two large free car parks await you, one of which is a picnic style car park with a complete view of all the racing. Please note however, that the entrance for the Course Enclosure is off the A49, whilst the Tattersalls entrance can be found off the A4103.

The racecourse held 15 National Hunt meetings in 1999. The bank holiday fixture in April is the most popular and there is also a splendid alternative to the Grand National. As the Clerk of the Course points out, most of the racing here is bread and butter stuff but there are often large fields and racing is competitive. The course also has a Boxing Day feature in addition to the existing three bank holiday meetings. Admission to the Members Enclosure is £13 and £10 for Tattersalls and the Course costs £5. There is no Annual Membership here. Discounts are available for Tattersalls for larger groups and you should contact the racecourse for further details.

Boxes are available to hire on a daily basis and differ in size catering for up to 40 guests. There is a larger room which will take up to 150 guests or marquees can be erected if you wish for an even bigger party. There is also a restaurant in the Course Enclosure where there is no need to book. Various packages are on offer here from the caterers, Hughes of Welshpool (01432) 353135. The usual snack bars are dotted around the course for those who only need a quick bite. If you wish to take your children racing and they are under 16 they are admitted free. Disabled racegoers will be pleased to note that access is easy from Tattersalls and there is also a special viewing area. There is a betting shop in Tattersalls as well as a new Owners and Trainers bar.

Hereford is one of those delightful out of the way county towns where the pace of life is slightly slower than average. The horses may also be of lesser speed than those seen at Ascot or Cheltenham but racing is still competitive here and should you wish for a peaceful day out, there are few finer courses at which to spend the day. There are few places in England which are truly away from it all. Hereford is one of those places—try to visit it in 2000.

Local Favourites

For those who wish to really soak up the racecourse atmosphere, a five minute walk from the aforementioned track brings one to the doorstep of the **Starting Gate Inn** which is attached to the extremely convenient **Travel Inn** (01432) 274853. The **Green Dragon** (01432) 272506 and the **Three Counties Hotel** (01432) 275114, dating from 1850, are also safe bets (always a dangerous claim to make). Pubs to try amidst the Malvern Hills include the splendid and highly recommended **Bunch of Carrots** (01432) 870237 at Hampton Bishop, a leading riverside pub about three miles from the course. The **Butchers Arms** (01432) 860281 at Woolhope, a half-timbered building which offers good bar food, a restaurant and some pleasing accommodation. Nearby, in Fownhope, the **Green Man** (01432) 860243 is a popular local fancy with excellent food and good pub accommodation. The **Ancient Camp Inn** (01981) 250449 in Ruckhall is a first rate stayer as is the **Olde Salutation** (01544) 318443 in Weobley. To the north through Leominster lies Kimbolton where you'll find the **Lower Bache** Guest House (01568) 750304 offering charming accommodation, first class food and wonderful views. In Ledbury the timbered **Feathers** (01531) 635266 is appealing. The **Hope End** (01531) 633616, at Hope End, is also peaceful with a fine restaurant. Another Ledbury thought is **Ye Olde Talbot** (01531) 632963 which has a beautiful exterior as well as a friendly interior. Northwest of Ledbury in Bishops Frome, you come across the **Green Dragon** (01885) 490607 whose good beer, filling bar food and traditional atmosphere make for a perfect post-race rendezvous.

The county of Herefordshire, characterised by brown and white faced cows, is stunning, with the countryside approaching the Welsh border of particular note. In this direction, the **Lord Nelson** (01981) 22208 at Bishopstone has a good restaurant and bar food. In Eardisland, the **White Swan** is a good stop-off point for people travelling north, while at Whitney-on-Wye, the **Rhydspence** (01497) 831262 offers superb bar meals and some accommodation—a must for a long weekend if booked well in advance. Venturing back towards England, one finds the **Broad Oak**, Eastway, an excellent place for a post-race supper. Where else? At Sellack, try the **Lough Pool** (no rooms here though). Our trip comes full circle at delightful Ross-on-Wye where some outstanding hotels can be found. The **Chase** (01989) 763161 is a charmingly personal Victorian hotel and **Pengethley Manor** (01989) 730211 a little outside the town, is also a marvellous hotel with a super restaurant. Finally, **Pheasants** (01989) 565751 is a restaurant with rooms to note. It provides another excuse for visiting this gorgeous area.

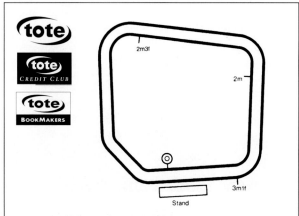

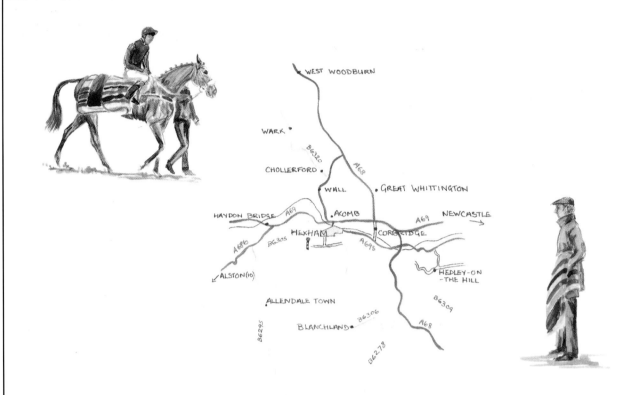

Artist: **Dennis C Kirtley** **EXPLORATION** *Courtesy of:* **The Artist**

Newbrough Park is set in its own delightful grounds and gardens with views over the picturesque Tyne Valley.

This south facing and elegant family run house has recently been completely refurbished with great attention paid to its impressive 18th century period detail. All the bedrooms have each been individually decorated.

On arrival guests may be assured that they will receive a warm and pleasant welcome from their hosts, June and Henry.

Original menus, fine wines and English breakfasts are par for the course at Newbrough Park.

With Hadrian's Wall literally a stone's throw away, it should be noted that Newbrough Park is the nearest Country House providing guest accommodation for those attending Hexham Racecourse and Vindolanda Fort, the house offers an ideal base for those visiting Newcastle Racecourse as well as enjoying an excellent situation just off the A69 for en-route journeys to Scotland or the South of England.

Newbrough Park
Newbrough
Nr Hexham
Northumberland NE47 5AR
Tel: (01434) 674545 Fax: (01434) 674544

Artist: **Jay Kirkman LINING UP** *Courtesy of:* **Jonathon Cooper, Park Walk Gallery**

Clerk of the Course, Secretary and Manager at this delightful course are all roles which are admirably carried out by **Charles Enderby**, who can be contacted at **The Racecourse Office, The Riding, Hexham, Northumberland. Tel (01434) 606881. Fax (01434) 605814.** and **Mrs Linda Clements** who handles all **Sponsorship** and would be delighted to show prospective clients around Tel (01434) 609643.

Hexham lies 20 miles from Newcastle, about 35 miles from Carlisle and some 300 miles from the bustle of Trafalgar Square. The course itself is a mile south of the market town of Hexham, sandwiched between the B6305 and the B6306. The road from Newcastle to Carlisle, the A69, is convenient for joining either of these two minor roads. The Newcastle western bypass should speed up your journey considerably if you are using the A1. If you are northbound on the A1 and have a little extra time in which to make your journey, leave the A1 at its junction with the A68 and follow the road through the Durham hills—stunning. The M6 and the A69 are the most direct routes for those travelling from Carlisle and the west of the country, although the A686 through the Gilderdale Forest is an appealing alternative. There are bus and train stations in Hexham. Newcastle is on the main Kings Cross—Edinburgh route and the journey time is swift. A connecting train can be caught from Newcastle to Hexham. There is a free bus from the train and bus stations to the racecourse on racedays. The majority of racegoers however, seem to drive to the course where there are acres of free parking and Members have a reserved area. There is also plenty of room in this charming, peaceful setting to land your noisy helicopter but please notify the course prior to your arrival.

To take advantage of the better weather, Hexham now stages a couple of summer jumping fixtures in June as part of its 14 fixture annual programme. The biggest day of the year is a local derby for point to pointers in the form of the Heart of All England Maiden Hunter Chase. In 2000 admission charges will be £10 for Members and £7 for Tattersalls. OAPs are allowed in to Tatts for only £5 and children 16 and under are free. If you wish to enroll as an Annual Member in the Hexham Race Club, the price will be £60 for a single and £100 for a double badge. This is excellent value as it includes car parking close to the stands at Hexham, as well as 17 reciprocal meetings at nearby Carlisle, Newcastle, and Kelso as well as Perth, Catterick, Bangor, Ripon, Hamilton, Ayr and Haydock. For people wishing to organise parties, there is a 20 per cent reduction for groups of 15 or more in both enclosures and a free bottle of whisky for the organisers of parties over 50.

The racecourse has just completed a major expansion programme which has seen the completion of the new Ramshaw Stand, which provides excellent facilities in the Members when the weather is less than kind. There is a new Members' Bar on the ground floor and you can enjoy the carvery and a drink in the Curlew Room on the first floor. The stand has a lift and therefore can accommodate the needs of disabled people. There are also three new private boxes on the top floor which can cater for up to 30 sponsor's or private guests. Larger parties can be accommodated by using a large adjoining room, or for parties of up to 180 people, the Henderson Room in the connecting stand may be used. The new stand has extensive Tote facilities and many television monitors. Recent improvements have also been carried out to provide a new Tote betting shop with a bar.

Prices and specifications for catering can be found out by contacting the excellent local caterers—Romfords (01434) 688864. Disabled people can enjoy a superb view of racing from their own special car park which can be entered next to owners/trainers gate at the west end of the stands.

This is one of the most scenic of England's National Hunt racecourses and has one of the finest views of any course in Britain. With its new stand, a watering system to ensure good going and a fixture list that takes advantage of the summer weather, Hexham is a sure bet for a visit in 2000.

Local Favourites
Hexham is a delightful market town and is ideally situated for touring the world heritage site of Hadrian's Wall and the Northumberland National Park with its hundreds of square miles of rugged beauty. A recently opened hotel is **Lauder Grange** (01434) 634646, it has good early reports.

Just north of Hexham at Chollerford the **George Hotel** (01434) 681611 is a famous hostelry that is right on the river North Tyne. Just to the south of Hexham is the **Lord Crewe Arms** (01434) 675251, hidden deep in the valley of the Derwent River in Blanchland, a delightful place whose setting has gone unchanged for centuries. Just a few miles down the river Tyne lies Corbridge, another picturesque village with some interesting shops. Here the **Black Bull** is a popular meeting place and the busy **Corbridge Tandoori** (01434) 633676 is a good bet for an evening meal. If you wish to stay in the village, the **Angel Inn** (01434) 632119 has pleasant bedrooms and good food.

Back in Hexham itself, the **Beaumont Hotel** (01434) 602331 overlooks the Abbey grounds and is a convenient place to stay for the racegoer. A pub of note is the **Tap & Spile** which has excellent real ales. Almost opposite, on the other side of the road from Hexham racecourse is **Danielle's Bistro** (01434) 601122. A good bet for Italian is **La Famiglia** (01434) 601700 tucked away on St Mary's Chare. For Indian cuisine don't pass by **Diwan-E-Am** (01434) 603191 on Hexham's main street. Just south of the racecourse the **Dipton Mill** pub is perfectly placed for a drink and lunch before racing. Excellent home-made food and real ale made in its own brewery.

In Wall, a few miles up the North Tyne, the **Hadrian Hotel** (01434) 681232 offers a reasonably priced bed for the night as well as some excellent food. Across the river at Newbrough, **Newbrough Lodge** (01434) 674545 is a fine country house with rooms, while in the village of Great Whittington the **Queens Head** can be highly recommended. Also not far away is **The Rat** at Anick, where you are sure to receive a warm welcome.

A final thought is **Slaley Hall** (01434) 673350 a five star hotel with excellent leisure facilities and a championship golf course. If you prefer a pleasant pub, the recently refurbished **Travellers Rest** on the same road is an ideal place to end your day after a visit to one of Britain's most picturesque racecourses.

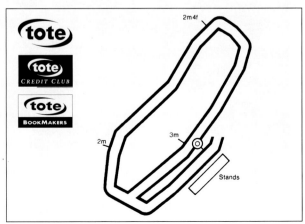

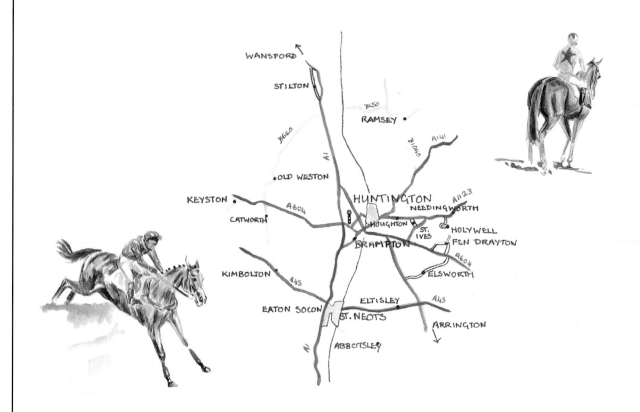

Artist: **Jonathan Trowell** **WINTER GAME** _Courtesy of:_ **The Artist**

The Haycock is set in the picturesque village of Wansford surrounded by unspoilt Cambridgeshire stone cottages. This 16th Century coaching inn has a remarkable and eventful past. Both Mary Queen of Scots and the young Queen Victoria have visited the hotel. It is even said that The Haycock once changed hands over a game of cards!

A warm, informal country welcome makes you feel at home instantly and each bedroom is individually furnished in traditional country-style fabrics. Ideal for meetings and seminars, The Haycock has a self contained business centre offering dedicated service and support for all of your business and corporate events. There are six fully equipped boardrooms or, for larger conferences, The Drayton Room and Ballroom have their own reception areas to welcome guests or delegates. Soaring oak beams and real log fires, as well as the private garden areas, make The Haycock the ideal location for weddings or other special occasions.

The hotel has 50 bedrooms and suites all of which have private bathrooms, colour televisions with satellite and teletext, direct dial telephone, trouser press, hair dryer, tea & coffee making facilities and, for a small extra fee, a special welcome pack can be organised including flowers, chocolates and champagne.

The restaurant offers a comprehensive à la carte menu of traditional but imaginative English dishes while the Orchard Brasserie is less formal but no less enjoyable. You may like to take a stroll through the grounds where you'll see pétanque courts and the village cricket pitch. Stop off at the hotel's bar and taste some of the many real ales on offer.

For the racegoer The Haycock is situated close to Huntingdon raceourse with Nottingham, Leicester and Newmarket slightly further afield. Situated adjacent to the A1 and A47 the hotel is easily accessible and a fine base for exploring the beautiful countryside in the area.

The Haycock
Wansford
Peterborough
Cambridgeshire
PE8 6JA
Tel: (01780) 782223
Fax: (01780) 783031

The **Clerk of the Course, Hugo Bevan** and the **Manager, Jim Allen**, can be contacted at the **Racecourse Office,** Brampton, Huntingdon, Cambridgeshire PE18 8NN. **Tel (01480) 453373. Fax (01480) 455275.**

The course lies just outside Brampton, conveniently positioned for travellers from the south (London is 60 miles away) and also from the north as it is a mile to the east of the A1, just off the A14, the A1/M11 road link, which takes you right past the course. The nearest railway station is just outside Huntingdon, two miles away. It's on the main 125 line and a very short journey from Kings Cross. There is no direct bus service from the station to the racecourse but there is a bus to Brampton, one and a quarter miles from Huntingdon, and taxis are easy to find.

They only race over the sticks at Huntingdon, but a full 18 day fixture list is on offer. The most popular tend to be Easter Monday and Boxing Day which always guarantee large crowds. Highlights include the Sidney Banks Memorial Hurdle and the Peterborough Chase, which carries a prize of £35,000 and often produces excellent fields.

Huntingdon Racecourse which is presided over by Hugo the Huntingdon Hound, a 7 foot high mascot, has free parking for cars and coaches, and if a picnic is the order of the day there is no charge for parking adjacent to the rails. The charge for Double Membership was £180 in 1999 whereas a single badge cost £95. Junior Membership (16-24) was available at £50. There was a £13 charge for a Daily Member's badge whilst the entrance charge for Tatts was £10 and the cost for the popular Course Enclosure picnic car park was £5, although these prices may increase in 2000. The management offer a 20 per cent discount for parties of 15 or more in Tattersalls. The Tattersall's bars have recently been refurbished with some new outlets for snacks added and Gifford's Bar now affords views of the course and the parade ring/winner's enclosure. Various boxes on the course provide for parties of all sizes, with prices ranging from £250 to £650 plus VAT. The course has six viewing boxes, which can accommodate between 12 and 24 people and have an unrivalled view of the track. The latest innovation, at prices starting from £500, are trackside chalets which can seat up to 75 people. The Centenary Rooms can seat up to 60, with an individual Tote point and bar and a large private viewing area. The Waterloo Room can hold up to 100 and is very popular with social clubs and works outings.

It is encouraging to note that the boxes are taken by companies from all over the country and not merely local concerns. Marquees can also be arranged for larger parties of 50 or more. The course management allows children under 16 to be admitted free of charge and on its bank holiday fixtures provides a variety of children's entertainments and crèche facilities.

The racegoer is able to lunch in either the Members or Tattersalls restaurants. Booking is advisable for the former. There is a new 170 seat members restaurant and now also have two large bar areas. The caterers are Letheby & Christopher and they can be contacted on (01638) 662750. A selection of snacks is available from the bars which are scattered through the Grandstand and in the Course Enclosure. There are public telephones on the course but there is no bank, which makes life frustrating if you spot a likely winner and you've blown all your cash! The course's off-track betting shop is, however, a retreat for the hardened punter who wants to keep in touch with racing around the country and escape the outrageous odds that some bookmakers lay when taking money for races elsewhere. This is a friendly unpretentious racetrack which offers competitive racing. Hunting-don is steadily being improved and is definitely worthy of a visit in 2000.

Local Favourites

The town's foremost hotel is the **Old Bridge** (01480) 452681, a popular meeting place where one can enjoy a drink, a quiet lunch, a more comprehensive dinner in the fine restaurant or if you have travelled some distance, a room for the night. You should be well satisfied on all counts. An alternative suggestion is the **George** (01480) 432444, another popular bar with satisfactory accommodation. The **Stukeleys Country Hotel** (01480) 456927 is five minutes from the course. The bar is always busy and the bar snack menu and restaurant offer a variety of meals.

In Fen Drayton, the **Three Tuns** (01954) 230242 is another pleasant drinking establishment—very popular with people in the know throughout Cambridgeshire. The **Lion Hotel** (01480) 810313 at Buckden, just off the A1 south of Huntingdon is a 15th century coaching house offering a friendly, personal welcome. In Arrington, the **Hardwicke Arms** (01223) 208802 is a super little pub with some excellent rooms. Another nearby hall which doubles as an hotel has a particularly appropriate name, **Slepe Hall** (01480) 463122 (pronounced as in a long snooze!) in St Ives. Needingworth near by has the **Pike and Eel** (01480) 463336—exceptionally cosy, offering comfortable accommodation and views of the River Ouse with boats mooring in front of the inn. The **Old Ferry Boat** at Holywell (01480) 463227 is also good. Fine food and accommodation to consider. A good pub restaurant is sheltered within the **Pheasant** (01832) 710241 at Keyston, and if you prefer a bar snack then you will not be disappointed. For people who are unable to sample these various offerings and need to journey home up the A1 a pint at the **Bell** (0733) 241066 at Stilton may be an idea—a splendid hotel with an excellent restaurant as well as a comfortable bar. Nearby, The **Loch Fyne Oyster Bar** in Elton (01832) 280298 is an informal seafood restaurant to consider. Those going south should perhaps try one of three pubs near to the A1. Firstly the **Leeds Arms** (01480) 880283 at Eltisley which is a particularly welcoming establishment offering some good food and accommodation. The **Eight Bells** in the pleasant village of Abbotsley is also worth a stop and finally, the **White Horse** (01480) 474453 at Eaton Socon is a part 13th century inn with a pleasant restaurant, good atmosphere and also some bedrooms. Two other first class pubs with restaurants to note are the **Three Horseshoes** in Madingley (01954) 210221 and the excellent **Anchor** at Sutton Gault (01353) 778537—first class food and some bedrooms. The perfect places to celebrate having plundered the bookies.

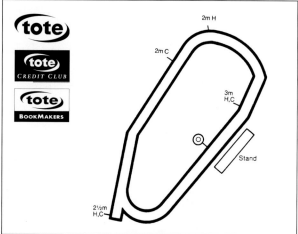

Built in 1882 by the famous architect Charles Barry, using stones from nearby Twizel Castle, Tillmouth typifies a more leisured age. A secluded mansion, set in fifteen acres of mature parkland and gardens, you'll feel yourself relax into it's atmosphere of a bygone age.

All of the fourteen en suite bedrooms are generous in size and individually furnished to the highest standard. The spacious public rooms are furnished with the same attention to detail and open log fires create a relaxing ambience.

Tillmouth Park is an ideal centre for country pursuits - fishing, shooting, riding and of course, golf. Spring fishing packages can be arranged on the river Tweed with all the fisherman's requirements catered for. There is also an abundance of excellent shooting in the Borders within 30 minutes drive of the hotel. Berwick-upon-Tweed and the Hirsel at Coldstream are just two excellent golf courses nearby. There are many stately homes to visit such as Floors Castle, Manderston and Paxton. Ruined abbeys, Flodden Field and Holy Island are all within easy reach. Kelso Racecourse is only 15 minutes drive away.

The Library Dining Room offers fresh local produce imaginatively prepared and presented by Head Chef David Jeffrreys. To match the award winning food there is an extensive wine list and comprehensive range of malt whiskies.

You can be assured of a warm welcome in the Borders when you visit Tillmouth Park.

Tillmouth Park Hotel
Cornhill-On-Tweed
Northumberland
TD12 4UU
Tel: (01890) 882255
Fax: (01890) 882540

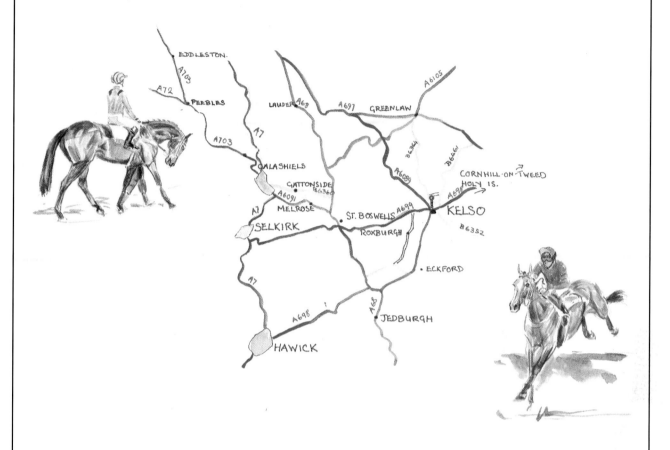

Artist: **Roy Miller** **AUTUMN MIST** *Courtesy of:* **The Artist**

This friendly course is exceptionally well administered by **Richard Landale** who is the **Manager** and **Secretary** and is the person to contact for further information at the following address: c/o **Sale & Partners, 18-20 Glendale Road, Wooler, Northumberland NE71 6DW. Tel (01668) 281611. Fax (01668) 281113.** The **Clerk of the Course** is **Jonnie Fenwicke-Clennell.**

Kelso is easy to find and the course lies to the north of the town itself, off the A6089 and the A699. The journey from London is 320 miles. The A1(M) is the best route to take and the A697 or the A698 both lead to spectacular routes through the Borders and Northumberland. From the west take the M6 to junction 44, from here the A7 and the A698 are the best roads to choose. From Edinburgh the A68 and the A698 is the combination to follow. Both the Edinburgh and Newcastle bypasses have now been completed and Kelso itself now has a new bypass road, so make sure you don't go whizzing by in haste.

There are other options for your journey, but the car has to be the best bet. The nearest railway station is in Berwick, 22 miles away on the Kings Cross line. There are no buses to the course from the station, but the racecourse can arrange transportation. Aviators are also diverted to nearby Winfield but helicopters are now welcomed. It seems fairly obvious then, that some form of motor transportation is in order and there is, after all, the incentive of free parking. What's more, there is no reserved area for Members—first come, first served. Special disabled parking can also be arranged in advance.

Kelso are extremely able at finding sponsorship for their races and with good prize money on offer competitive fields are almost always assured. Of course the going is all important and a new irrigation system should help ground conditions in the Spring and Autumn. With a Sunday fixture in September and two Saturday fixtures in October, Kelso should be able to maintain its outstanding record of attracting people to a course which has no large close centres to draw from. Basically, it's very well served by local people because it provides excellent value in a welcoming atmosphere.

Admission prices are in line with most country courses. £12 is the midweek price for admission to the Members (£15 on Saturdays) £7 for the Tattersalls Enclosure or £4 if you happen to be an OAP. Annual Membership, which includes a private bar/viewing room and 21 reciprocal days, costs £170 for a double badge, £90 for a single and £65 for OAPs. Generous discounts of up to 50% are available to pre-booked parties. As far as corporate hospitality is concerned, Kelso offers the new Younger Grandstand with five boxes, four to accommodate up to 25 people and one that will hold 45. There is also the Dukes Room (50 people), the Hamilton and Tweedie rooms (70 people), the Berrymoss Box (12 people), the Doody Room (20 people) and three viewing boxes. Please apply to the Secretary. Prices start from £100. Marquees can be erected and will hold up to 850 guests. The catering is provided by two local firms and a very high standard of home cooked delicious food is available at tremendous value—breakfast £2.50, lunch £7.50. Taking tea in the restaurant next to the parade ring is a particularly delightful way to pass the last race or two and a new bar, The Buchanan Room has opened in Tattersalls.

The course is well stocked with the standard items expected of a racecourse and children under 16 are admitted free. Although there is no bank, the Secretary will usually cash cheques and there is a betting shop in the Tattersalls Enclosure, together with a new Tote building in which to spend your money! There are WCs and viewing ramps for the disabled. More unusually there is a golf course in the middle of the course, and a Sunday market throughout the year.

Kelso is one of the most welcoming racecourses in the country and is also one of the best run and many others could learn from the management here. We wish all involved a successful 2000.

Local Favourites

We choose to start our journey at a real favourite, **Roxburghe Hotel and Golf Course** (01573) 450331—formerly Sunlaws House, a hotel of distinction. You will find this hotel just south of Kelso at Heiton. The hotel is beautifully furnished and the restaurant first rate. The hotel is a great favourite and a trip to Kelso followed by a visit here is about as good as it gets. If you enjoy Golf or Salmon fishing then this is the jewel for you. Further north, in Kelso itself an extremely pleasant market town, one finds the **Ednam House Hotel** (01573) 224168. The Tweedside setting has obvious appeal for anglers, but the hotel is also convenient for the racecourse. Another place to visit is the **Queens Head Hotel** (01573) 224636—the bar snacks here are good, as indeed they are at the **Cross Keys Hotel** (01573) 223303 in Kelso's town square. Kelso is a pleasant border town and there are a number of pleasant shops for non racing friends to visit.

Rain or shine, Melrose is a charming border town and Burts Hotel (01896) 822285 is the one to note—good bar meals and more formal meals as well as good accommodation. Dunfermline House (01896) 822148 is a splendid guesthouse close to Melrose Abbey. The George and Abbotsford Hotel (01896) 822308 is worth more than a little consideration. A little further south, in St Boswells, two hotels should also be noted. Firstly, the most hospitable Buccleuch Arms (01835) 822243 and the highly recommended Dryburgh Abbey (01835) 822261. The Collingwood Arms (01890) 882424 in Cornhill, The Besom Inn at Coldstream (01890) 882391 and the Tankerville Arms (01668) 281581 in Wooler also come highly recommended by those in the know.

Well warmed up, you may decide to brave the elements and visit Gattonside. Here, the **Hoebridge Inn** (01896) 823082 is appealing. Trekking north towards the uplands, one arrives in Lauder. Here, the **Black Bull** (01578) 712208 is a pleasant, modernised Georgian coaching inn. Eddleston offers the excellent **Horseshoe Inn**. Again a fair distance from Kelso, one finds Ettrickbridge. Here, **Ettrickshaws** (01750) 52229 is well worth the journey—good value hospitality and some extremely imaginative set menus. The **Phillipburn House Hotel** (01750) 20747 is also a pleasant place in which to stay. The **Wheatsheaf** (01890) 860257 in Swinton is also a good choice. Finally, the **Tillmouth Park Hotel** (01890) 882255 boasts nine miles of excellent salmon fishing on the river Tweed and also organises packages for racegoers—a cosy hospitable hotel ideal for anyone travelling from the south.

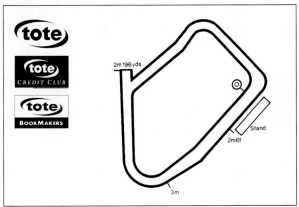

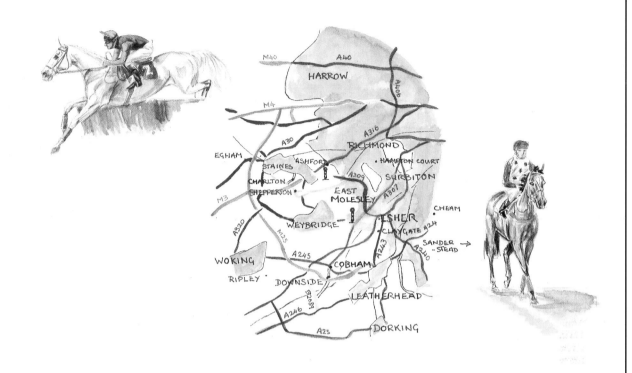

Artist: **Roy Miller** **COMING IN AT KEMPTON** _Courtesy of:_ **The Artist**

Kempton Park has come on leaps and bounds during the past few years and with the completion of its £9 million refurbishment of the main grandstand is poised to offer the racing public in London and the South East some of the best facilities in British racing.

The **General Manager, Julian Thick**, and the **Secretary, Jacky Birch** can be contacted at **Kempton Park Racecourse, Staines Road East, Sunbury-on-Thames TW16 5AQ. Tel (01932) 782292 Fax (01932) 782044.** Information on corporate hospitality is available from **Hector Nunns** and sponsorship enquiries are dealt with by **Tim Darby** at Sandown Park racecourse on **(01372) 461253.**

The racecourse is situated some 15 miles from central London and is well served by the motorway links. The M25 and the M3 make the trip in from the country especially good. For the popular evening meetings however, one should consider the rush hour build-up. The A316 and the A308 will take you over the Thames to within a stone's throw of the racecourse. The A308 via Hampton Court is the best road from the south. For train travellers, there is an excellent service direct to the course from Waterloo. For those travelling by bus, there is a bus stop outside the racecourse gates and buses can be taken from Staines and Kingston. The main car park lies adjacent to the Grandstand and costs £2, while free parking can be found in the Silver Ring car park and in the centre of the course. If you wish to arrive by helicopter, that's fine, but light aircraft are not welcomed. Helicopters are requested to land between the dovecote and the lake—but phone in advance and notify the course.

Kempton provides some superb racing throughout the year and the highlight is, without doubt, the Christmas Festival, including the Tripleprint King George VI Steeplechase on Boxing Day. The post-Christmas euphoria always makes for a jovial atmosphere. You can guarantee the King George will provide a memorable spectacle. June features the Gala Evening with bands, barbecues, a funfair and fireworks. Purists may argue that this is far from what racing is really all about, but Kempton is booming, the racing is of a very competitive standard and if you go along I will bet you a fiver straight you'll have a great time.

There was a total of 22 meetings here in 1999, with 13 on the flat and 9 over the jumps. This should also be largely the case in 2000. An excellent selection of races can be seen and the rates for Daily Membership last year were as follows. On Premium days, a charge of £16 was levied, which rose to £29 for Classic days such as the King George and dropped to £14 on Feature days. Junior Members (17-21 years) prices were £10 on Premium Days and £8 on Feature Days. No discounts are offered on Classic days. You could, however, save some money on badges if they were booked in advance, which took a fiver off a badge for big meetings. You would have to book at least a week in advance especially for Premier and Classic days. Entrance to the Paddock Enclosure in 1999 was priced at £12 (£14 on Boxing Day) while the Silver Ring cost you £5 (£10 on Boxing Day). Accompanied children under 16 are admitted free to all enclosures. Annual Membership in 1999 cost £170 for a full (both flat and jump meetings) single membership which included a free label for the Members' car park. For those 17-21 years old this dropped to £85. A single membership for National Hunt racing only stood at £95, while a similar arrangement for the flat was £105. Reciprocal arrangements were made for admission by members at Goodwood, Taunton, Lingfield, Newbury, Newton Abbot, Epsom and Sandown. A special rate of admission is offered to parties of 12 or more, and discounts are available on purchases of more than one member's badge at certain meetings.

The facilities at Kempton are excellent and boxes, suites and conference areas can all be organised. The private boxes are let annually, but they do become available on some days and there are usually one or two up for grabs and on quieter days they represent excellent value. They also have balconies overlooking the racecourse and its very attractive grounds. Certainly as far as venues for entertaining go these boxes take some beating. The boxes can seat twelve people for lunch or about 20 for a less formal buffet. Each box has closed circuit television, private bar facilities and a number of other perks. Prices for these rooms range from £550 to £650, the location being the deciding factor. The management generally know whether boxes are free two to three weeks in advance. This may not leave much time to organise a party, but for those who do not need to plan too far in advance it is a first class idea.

Lunch is available in the new Jubilee Restaurant from £69 per person. If you wish to have lunch before racing, contact Pam Lewis on (01372) 463072. More modest refreshments and nourishment can be found in numerous snack bars, particularly on the ground floor of the new Grandstand which is also home to the Sporting Index Sports Bar. Finally, one may enjoy a picnic in the course enclosure car parks, should this be your form of nourishment.

Facilities for children include a playground in the centre of the course and a crèche. Good amenities for disabled people including a viewing ramp can also be found. Owners are made particularly welcome with discounts on lunch and a very welcome bottle of bubbly for the successful owners.

It is the attention to detail of small things such as these that saw Kempton rewarded with the Travelling the Turf Racecourse of the Year award for 1999. Good quality racing is to be found here year-round and perhaps it is the proximity to London and its international access that have secured the presence of some notable jockeys such as Olivier Peslier, Gerald Mosse and Dominique Boeuf from France. When they take on Frankie Dettori and Kieren Fallon the excitement of watching the best riders in action certainly attracts the fans.

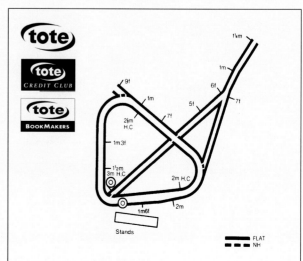

This luxurious hotel is conveniently situated in Weybridge, just a thirty minute train journey from London and within easy access of both Heathrow and Gatwick airports. Set in its own acres of parkland and surrounded by the beautiful Surrey countryside it is the perfect location for business and pleasure alike. Traditional style and charm are combined with modern luxuries to make your stay here a memorable one.

Many of the bedrooms enjoy delightful views over the extensive grounds and the Broadwater Lake. All rooms are tastefully designed to a high standard of comfort and decor and range from superior to the larger deluxe rooms and suites. All have direct dial telephone, tea and coffee making facilities, a trouser press and satellite televisions.

Dining in the elegant Broadwater Restaurant is a pleasure not to be missed. Guests are invited to choose from a creative à la carte menu which caters for all tastes and incorporates only the finest ingredients.

The Oatlands Park is the perfect venue for both board meetings and conferences, with the highly skilled management team ensuring that the whole event runs smoothly and efficiently.

Dinner dances can be arranged for up to 220 guests, or perhaps visitors would like to attend one of the themed evenings - whether the choice is a Henry VIII banquet or even a 'Night at the Races'.

For racegoers the hotel could not be more conveniently situated being close to many famous racecourses - Kempton Park, Sandown, Ascot and Epsom. The hotel can arrange many activities ranging from laser clay pigeon shooting to corporate golf days on its own 9 hole course.

For the less energetic a quiet stroll around the beautiful gardens is the perfect way to relax or perhaps you might enjoy a friendly game of croquet or boules.

Oatlands Park Hotel
Oatlands Drive
Weybridge
Surrey
KT13 9HB
Tel: (01932) 847242
Fax: (01932) 842252

Racing at either Sandown or Kempton offers a great variety of enticing possibilities for culinary refreshment. Those journeying back to the capital should also find that many of the following suggestions make convenient and relaxing stop-offs.

In Esher, **Good Earth** (01372) 462489 offers a good Chinese menu, while lovers of South East Asian fayre will enjoy **La Orient** (01372) 466628. In East Molesey, one finds an extremely popular French restaurant, **Le Chien Qui Fume** 0181-979 7150.

Pubs conveniently placed for Sandown include the **Albert Arms** and the **Cricketers**. Alternatively for Kempton try the **Kings Head** in Shepperton, or the **Three Horseshoes** in Laleham. If you are staying in the area, then there are a number of possibilities to consider. In Weybridge, the **Oatlands Park Hotel** (01932) 847242 is an ever improving favourite. A well appointed alternative is the **Ship Thistle Hotel** (01932) 848364, while **Casa Romana** (01932) 843470 is an exciting Italian affair. Alternatively, another place for your post-race nosebag is to be found in Woking, at the reasonably priced **Wheatsheaf** (014837) 73047. Leisure lovers and golfers should note the outstanding country house hotel, **Selsdon Park** 0181-657 8811 in Sanderstead, a thoroughly delightful establishment. A smaller but extremely refined establishment is the **Angel Hotel** (01483) 64555 in Guildford. Excellent cuisine combines well with all the comforts one could wish for—a real find.

In Cobham we might consider three options. The **Woodlands Park Hotel** (0137 284) 3933, at Stoke D'Abernon, **Il Giardino** (01932) 863973 a very favourable Italian restaurant or if one just wants a post-race pint, the **Cricketers**. In Ripley, south west of Cobham, another restaurant beckons, **Michels'** (01483) 224777—outstanding French cuisine. Finally, the **Hilton National** (01932) 864471 in Cobham is a large, well run concern from the internationally acclaimed stable of the same name.

Turning to London, there are a whole mass of outstanding restaurants, some cheap and cheerful, others cheerful until the bill comes! Outside the capital, however, a number of establishments might be thought of. In Richmond, one finds all manner of good eating places and pubs, and two good hotels as well. There are numerous boozers to sample on route but a little gem with excellent food is the **White Horse** off Sheen Lane in Richmond, ideal for post-

race fayre. The **Petersham** 0181 940 7471 is ideal and has a very good restaurant and the **Richmond Gate** 0181 940 0061 which is a worthwhile port of call and has been warmly recommended of late. Richmond itself has good shopping and a range of restaurants and pubs to suit all tastes and budgets. Down by the Thames, the appropriately named **River Terrace** 0181 332 2524 not only offers the 'Old Father' but also provides first rate cooking. In Egham one should note several establishments. The **Eclipse** is an ideal place for a drink (should be nearer Sandown, I suppose), the **Olive Grove** (01784) 439494 is a good restaurant to note, while **Great Fosters** (01784) 433822 is an interesting building which houses a good hotel—obviously better value than Central London offerings. The **Runnymede** (01784) 436171 is more modern but is a popular visiting spot for the many who travel this way. In Staines, the **Swan** is a fine public house as is the **Harrow** in Compton, south of Guildford—note the racing prints here. In Sunbury-on-Thames, the **Castle** (019327) 83647 is a pleasant French restaurant and Shepperton is also handy for the racecourse where the **Warren Lodge** (01932) 242972 is a good place to stay—its terrace overlooks the Thames. The **Anchor Hotel** (01932) 221618 is another worthy candidate—pleasant bars and bedrooms and not too pricey. One of the largest hotels in the area is the **Shepperton Moat House** (01932) 241404, less intimate than some by virtue of its size, but a worthy recommendation just the same. The **Thames Court** (01932) 221957 in Surbiton is another spot to note. This restaurant offers French cuisine while the bar has a variety of sandwiches and cold meats—excellent. Surbiton also offers the **Warwick Guesthouse** 0181 399 5837 for excellent value accommodation. Also note **Chez Max** 0181 399 2365, an enjoyable restaurant in which to dine. Alternatively, **Le Petit Max** 0181 977 0236 is a good place to visit after an evening at Kempton, or Sandown for that matter.

Racegoers who enjoy cricket should seek out the **Swan** in Claygate in summer as it doubles as the local cricket pavilion—excellent bar food as well.

If you are coming back through London, the following tips should cover most options. The **Kings Arms**, Hampton Court is a good pub for a pint either before or after racing and we also recommend the **Imperial Arms** 0171 736 9179 run by racing enthusiasts. It serves first class food and excellent wine and beer—a real favourite. An outstanding hotel offering style and comfort can be found on Wimbledon Common, **Cannizaro House** 0181 879 1464. This sumptuous Georgian mansion is an elegant but friendly hotel in which to stay. There are also a variety of pubs and restaurants in Wimbledon, all great fun. If you want to celebrate in style but don't wish to return to the better known West End eating haunts, try the popular **Riva** 0181 748 0434 in Barnes, the **Blue Elephant** 0171 386 7005 in Fulham Broadway—excellent Thai food—or the **River Café** 0171 381 6217, Hammersmith, for unbeatable new-wave Italian cuisine. **The Canteen** 0171 351 7330 in Chelsea Harbour is also superb.

Restaurants closer to the racecourse which are well thought of include **Sonny's** 0181 748 0393 in Barnes, **Crowthers** 0181 876 6372, and **Monsieur Max** 0181 979 5546.

Artist: **Klaus Philipp** THE FINISH *Courtesy of:* **The Artist**

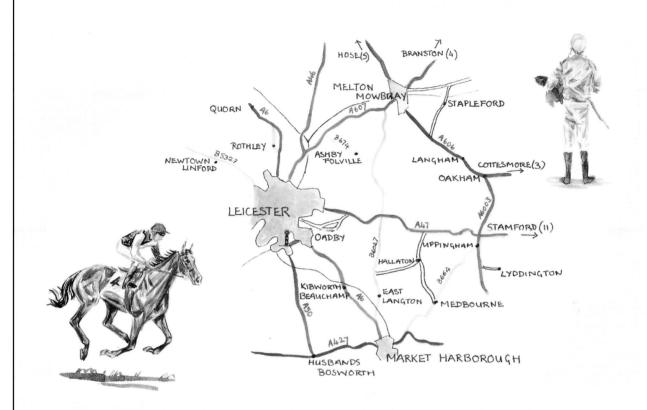

Artist: **Barrie Linklater PARADE RING POTENTIAL** *Courtesy of:* **Patterson Gallery**

Originally known as Charnwood House, the Quorn Country Hotel has an interesting history dating back to the Domesday Book. Throughout the following centuries, the property has changed hands several times until occupied by the Firr family, famed in hunting circles, who established the Quorn Hunt, the most renowned in England. Thus the name for the present day hotel was found.

Set in the heart of rural Leicestershire with four acres of landscaped gardens, the hotel has been awarded RAC awards for its restaurant, comfort and service, maintaining higher than average four star standards for ten consecutive years, as well as receiving two rosettes from the AA for fine cuisine.

All 23 bedrooms are en-suite with air conditioning, satellite television, 3 direct dial telephone lines, a working area, mini bar and secretarial facilities. Those visiting on business will find all their needs catered for - the hotel can offers rooms for whatever style of meeting you favour - from the increasingly popular breakfast meetings, to workshops, one to one meetings and formal and informal presentations. The hotel is also the ideal location for weddings and banquets.

Dining takes place either in the bright and airy Orangery Room or the cozy Shires Restaurant, the latter of which is divided into four sections with button back seats and alcoves. For less formal meals, there are bar snacks and for a real spot of relaxation drinks can be taken in the gardens which the River Soar runs through.

The hotel is situated just outside Loughborough quite close to the M1. Leicester racecourse is close by and racegoers can also visit the tracks at Huntingdon, Nottingham and Newmarket slightly further afield.

Quorn Country Hotel
Charnwood House
Quorn
Nr Loughborough
Leicestershire
LE12 8BB
Tel: (01509) 415050
Fax: (01509) 415557

The Clerk of the Course is Captain Nick Lees and Company Secretary and Manager, is R Parrott. They can be contacted at The Racecourse, Oadby, Leicester, LE2 4AL. Tel: (0116) 271 6515. Fax: (0116) 271 1746.

Leicester racecourse is in Oadby, two miles south east of Leicester on the A6 Market Harborough Road. Both the M1, exit junction 21, and the M69 might prove useful in reaching the track. From the west and Birmingham (40 miles away) take the M6 exiting at junction 2 and follow the M69 to the M1. Try to use the B5418 and avoid Leicester's one-way system at all costs. Southbound travellers will find the A46 and the M1 the best routes while the A6 and the M1 are possibilities for the northbound racegoer. People making the journey from Newmarket might wish to use the A47 turn off before Leicester, through Evington. The Southern District Distributor Road links the M1 (junction 21) with the A6 at the entrance to the course. Trains run from St Pancras to Leicester, a journey of about an hour and a half. A bus service runs from the station on racedays and there is a regular service from Leicester City to the track. The ample parking facilities are provided free of charge here and if you have a helicopter, you can land it in the centre of the course.

Leicester enjoys a full year of flat and National Hunt. There are no Annual Members but in 2000 Daily Members will pay £13 for a badge, and those in Tattersalls £10. Rates include a free card and parking. Discounts are offered on parties of 20 or more booked in advance into Tattersalls. £25 admits a car and four occupants to the Picnic Car Park.

Dramatic changes have taken place at Leicester during the past few years. The old Tattersalls and Silver Ring grandstands have been replaced by a new Tatts stand with a betting hall on the ground floor and a restaurant upstairs which is open for banqueting on non-racedays. At the top of the grandstand the Fernie Room has been refurbished and is available for daily lettings, as is the Barleythorpe Seafood restaurant. These complement the Belvoir Bar in the Club Enclosure where boxes can accommodate 12-14 for a sit-down meal or 20 for a buffet, and three double boxes that will take 30 to 40 people quite comfortably. The accommodation is equipped with closed circuit television and private Tote betting facilities. Marquees can be erected in the Paddock area if required.

In the new grandstand, the Conference Centre can accommodate anything from a theatre style meeting for up to 400 people down to a private party for 50. For bookings contact Mr Buckle on (0116) 271 9840

The caterers, Drewetts, can be contacted on (01788) 544171 and will be able to assist with menus. There is a playground for children, and viewing stands in the Members for disabled people. There are public telephones in all enclosures and a Ladbrokes betting shop in Tattersalls but there are no banks at the racecourse.

Leicester is a well situated racecourse and it is excellent to report the developments that have taken place—one to bear in mind when scanning the 2000 racing calendar!

Local Favourites

If you wish to stay in the city then one suggestion is that you plump for one of the larger hotels in the city centre. The **Holiday Inn** (0116) 2531161 is particularly modern but has swimming pools and that sort of thing to make up for the situation. Less modern, Victorian actually, is the **Jarvis Grand** (0116) 255 5599—note here a particularly good coffee shop and some welcoming bars. The **Stakis Leicester** (0116) 2630066 is another to be considered. Among the vast number of guesthouses and B&Bs in the area, **Leigh Court** (01886) 832275 and the **Scotia Hotel** (0116) 254 9200 stand out from the crowd.

In Rothley, the **Rothley Court** (0116) 237 4141 is a manor house with a super setting and restaurant. **The Limes** (0116) 2302531 also has a good local reputation. In Quorn itself, the **Quorn Country Hotel** (01509) 415050 blends together a combination of traditional hospitality and modern amenities. There are a number of appealing pubs to be found in and around Charnwood and one of them is the **Carrington Arms** (01664) 840228, Ashby Folville—good bar food here. A longer trip for a hotel of merit is the **Johnscliffe Hotel** in Newtown Linford (01530) 242228. South of the city in Whetstone, the **Old Vicarage** (0116) 277 1195 is a pleasant restaurant close to Leicester. The **Three Swans** (01858) 466644 at Market Harborough is another comfortable and highly recommended establishment. In Old Dalby, the **Crown Inn** (01664) 823134 dates from the 17th century and is a lovely place for a pint and a fireside chat—there's also a fairly handy restaurant. A hotel of note is the **Harboro Hotel** (01664) 60121. The restaurant here is also worth a visit. Alternative accommodation can be found in the **George** (01664) 62112, an extremely comfortable and well looked after inn which is strongly recommended. The **Rose and Crown** in Hose is a popular pub with tremendous character and some good food. In Braunston, as opposed to Branston, The **Old Plough** (01572) 722714 is also very welcoming while on the way to Oakham, the **Noel Arms** at Langham is also recommended—a good restaurant here (01572) 722931. Two supremely popular pubs are the **Bell** at East Langton (01858) 545567 and the **Berwicke Arms,** Hallaton, (01858) 89217, both renowned for really first rate food. Finally, the remotely set **Old Barn** (01858) 545215 offers good food in the evenings and some pleasant accommodation.

First class is a description one should also apply to the area's leading hotel, **Hambleton Hall** (01572) 756991. The grounds lead down to Rutland Water and the bedrooms are superb. The highlight of the house is the restaurant—outstanding. Less grand, but no less welcoming accommodation can be found in Oakham's market place—the **George**, a good place for a drink, as is the **Nevill Arms**, Medbourne (01858) 565288—some accommodation as well —and the **Marquess Of Exeter** at Lydington (01572) 822477. The adjoining hotel has a good restaurant and accommodation. A worthy addition to the well stocked Oakham stable is the **Whipper-In Hotel** (01572) 756971. The bedrooms here have great individual charm and the restaurant is excellent. A final thought for lovers of over-the-top quality, try **Stapleford Park** (01572) 787522—a really fine choice if you've got a winning jackpot ticket.

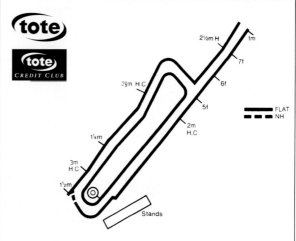

One of the most exclusive hotels in England, set in 135 acres of private parkland, Alexander House reflects a bygone era when English country house living was a most sought after ideal. In the ambience created by its stunning decor, tasteful furnishing and splendid works of art, Alexander House successfully combines tradition with all the modern-day comforts and facilities

The oldest part of the present house, facing the south lawn, was once a farmhouse, dating from the 17th century. A stone dated 1608 survives in the boundary wall and is thought to be a lintel from an earlier building on the site. Some of England's most important families have made Alexander House their home, including poet Percy Bysshe Shelley and William Campbell, Governor of the Bank of England.

Today Alexander House has 15 exclusive bedrooms and a wealth of public and meeting rooms. The hotel has a range of amenities for those who enjoy the outdoors including croquet, clock golf and tennis courts on site, as well as golf, fishing, clay pigeon shooting, archery, riding and off road driving further afield.

Superb table d'hôte and à la carte meals are served in Alexander's Restaurant which is renowned for its delicious classic English and French cuisine, rare wines and vintage ports. The menus emphasise the goodness of fresh natural foods carefully prepared and artistically presented.

Located close to Turners Hill and East Grinstead in the West Sussex countryside, there are a host of places of interest to visit including the Natural Trust properties at Wakefield, Hever Castle, Sir Winston Churchill's Chartwell, the operas at Glyndebourne and, for those travelling the turf, the course at Lingfield Park is close by with the courses at Goodwood, Fontwell Park, Brighton and Plumpton not too far away.

Alexander House
Turners Hill
West Sussex RH10 4QD
Tel: (01342) 714914
Fax: (01342) 717328
e mail: info@alexanderhouse.co.uk
web site: http://www.alexanderhouse.co.uk

Artist: **Kalus Philipp** **THEY'RE OFF** *Courtesy of:* **The Artist**

The Clerk of the Course is Fergus Cameron who can be contacted at Racecourse Road, Lingfield, Surrey RH7 6PQ. Tel (01342) 834800. Fax (01342) 832833. The Chief Executive here is Graham Parr and the Marketing Director is Claudia Fisher.

Lingfield is easily accessible from London which is only 21 miles away. The M25 and the A22 are the best routes to follow from the capital. The racecourse itself is on the B2029. The A22 is the best route for northbound travellers, exiting for the course at Newchapel. Westbound travellers should take the A264 while those heading east should pursue the M25 and the A22, exiting at junction 6. On arrival, there is a choice of car parks with parking for 7000 cars. The public car park is free.

The Members in the centre of the course is more convenient but a charge of £3 is levied if space is reserved in advance. If you don't want to take the car then a train from Victoria or London Bridge to Lingfield Station is a convenient option (with combined rail and race tickets available) and a short walk will see you to the racecourse gates. For more local requirements, the 429 bus from East Grinstead to Godstone will take you via the track. If speed is of the essence then helicopters are free to land in the centre of the course provided you make the arrangements in advance.

There are a staggering 72 meetings, offering both flat and jump racing on the grass track and all-weather course. These include some really worthwhile evening racing. The most popular event of the year is the excellent Classic trials meeting in May, featuring the Derby Trial, and the Oaks Trial. The Silver Trophy Meeting is also popular. The rates for entrance to Lingfield in 1999 were £15 for the Club and £10 for the Family enclosure. Children under 16 who are accompanied by an adult are admitted free but there is a maximum of two children per adult. Prices rise to £16 and £12 respectively on Stakes day and Silver Trophy day, and to £18 and £13 on Derby Trial day. Discounts are available for groups of 20 to 40, with further reductions for groups of over 40. Annual Members in 1999 were charged £160. This included reciprocal dates at Epsom, Folkestone, Brighton, Sandown, Windsor, Goodwood and Hickstead as well as social membership of the Lingfield Park golf club.

Lingfield Park is an excellent and popular place at which to entertain as the facilities are good. Boxes for 12-350 guests are available. Private boxes all have racecourse videos as does the Eclipse Suite. For people who want a far bigger function, the Garden Room in the Pavilion in the Members Enclosure can accommodate from 20 to 350 people. There are four restaurants—the Derby Restaurant in Tattersalls, the Trackside Carvery, the Brasserie in the Members & the new Champagne & Seafood Restaurant. You could also try the User Friendly bar in Tattersalls. Both the Members and Grandstand Enclosures have betting shops as well as Tote facilities. There is a play area for children and a crèche for 3 to 7 year olds. There are special viewing areas and lavatories for disabled people as well as car parks and it is good to see the course making an effort here. As yet there is no bank at the track—so come prepared if you like a flutter. The Ladbrokes betting shop is located in Tattersalls. All-weather racing is already beginning to show its merits in keeping the industry moving. Some may say that it fails to attract top racehorses—but what about the US? With the principal races in the Breeders Cup on dirt, it would be great if a really prestigious race could be held on Britain's all-weather to catch the imagination more in this country. With its new management in place we wish Lingfield good fortune for 2000.

Local Favourites

Lingfield Park is surrounded by good hostelries. Sampling a different one after each meeting of the year would not be impossible. Some notable examples are the Hare & Hounds (01342) 832351 in Lingfield and the Castle Inn (01892) 870247 in the delightful village of Chiddingstone. Other suggestions in the locality include the Crown (01892) 864742 at Groombridge—a pleasantly situated old inn with some fine ales, a restaurant and some bedrooms if needs be. The Bottle House (01892) 870306 and the Spotted Dog (01892) 870253 in Penhurst are also firm favourites, as is the Royal Oak at Dormansland—ideal for a pint or two. In Edenbridge. Honours Mill (01732) 866757 is a handy place to enjoy good food and wine—be sure to book and Haxted Mill (01732) 862914 is also worth investigating. Another one to try is Goldhill Mill (01732) 851626 a really outstanding B&B—no restaurant though. Another good restaurant to consider is the Old Lodge at Limpsfield (01883) 712996. This establishment is not cheap but it is extremely well thought of. Also note La Bonne Auberge (01342) 892318 in South Godstone where superb French cooking can be enjoyed in elegant surroundings.

If you are keen to stay nearby, then several ideas spring to mind. Firstly, the Copthorne (01342) 714971 in the village of Copthorne has much appeal, (good restaurant and leisure facilities), while in Tonbridge, the Rose and Crown (01732) 357966 in Tonbridge High Street is also a satisfactory port of call. To the south, in Royal Tunbridge Wells, the Royal Wells Inn (01892) 511188 is excellent value and a super place to stay—the restaurant is also worth a visit. On Mount Ephraim, the Spa Hotel (01892) 520331 boasts outstanding facilities and a commendable restaurant. Cheevers (01892) 545524 is also extremely good—English cooking here. One should also consider Thackerays House (01892) 511921, which not only boasts an outstanding menu but also has a divine wine list. What better place to end up after a successful day's sport? Well, Gravetye Manor (01342) 810567, is an outstanding hotel and restaurant double and Ashdown Park (01342) 824988 offers relaxation and excellent cuisine. Other less grand, but worthy recommendations in East Grinstead include the Jarvis Felbridge Hotel (01342) 326992, the Woodbury House (01342) 313657, and the Cranfield Lodge Hotel (01342) 321251, which are all well worth a visit. In a similar vein, nearby Hartfield offers Bolebrook Watermill (01892) 770425—exceptional value and very charming. Racegoers who thirst after sheer luxury will appreciate Alexander House (01342) 714914. Located at Turners Hall—not terribly close to the racecourse but well worth a detour. Finally a pub to note the excellent George & Dragon at Speldhurst—a fine friendly boozer to count ones ill-gotten gains.

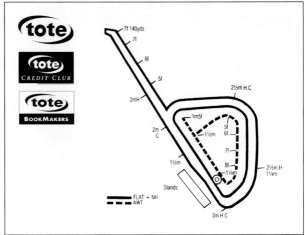

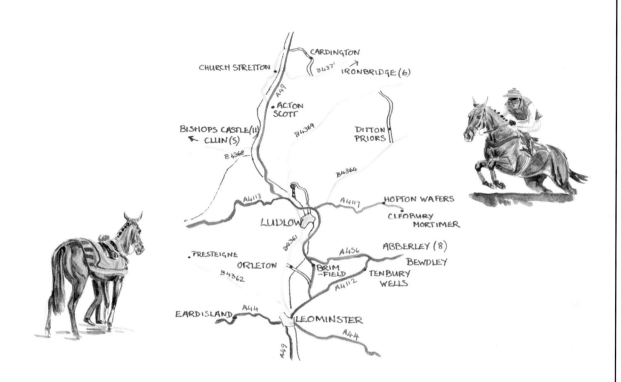

Artist: **Malcolm Coward LAST FLIGHT** Courtesy of: **Sally Mitchell Fine Arts**

The **Clerk of the Course** and **Secretary** at Ludlow is **Bob Davies**. He can be contacted at **Shepherds Meadow, Eaton Bishop, Lane Head, Hereford HR2 9UA. Tel (01981) 250052 Fax (01981) 250192**. Alternatively, on racedays **Tel (01584) 856221** or **Fax (01584) 856217**.

The racecourse is situated in beautiful Shropshire countryside yet the course is easily accessible from major routes. The track is two miles north-west of Ludlow. The favoured routes are the A49 via Shrewsbury from the north or through Hereford from the south. Racegoers from areas west of Ludlow should follow the A4113. Travellers from the east of the country should aim to reach the A44 from Worcester and then make the best use of the A49. Anyone wishing to circumnavigate the town should use the Ludlow bypass. There are both rail and bus stations in Ludlow and the Midland Red runs from Hereford to Shrewsbury on the A49. The railway station is small but the line can be joined from Newport which in turn is on a direct route from Paddington or from Euston, via Shrewsbury. There is ample free parking should you decide to drive. Cars can be parked alongside the course in the spring and autumn although this is restricted during the winter months. Helicopters can also land at Ludlow providing you ask permission first.

The racecourse now stages 15 meetings, all National Hunt, and the principal of these is the Charity Meeting in April—in 2000 this will be in aid of the Cancer Unit Trust at Royal Shrewsbury Hospital. Major races include the Forbra Gold Cup in March and the Prince of Wales Amateur Riders' Handicap Chase in December. All of the fixtures, bar one on May Bank Holiday, take place during the week—no doubt to the delight of the local farming community. However, the ordinary mortal should not be put off midweek racing—and certainly Ludlow is a pleasant and friendly racecourse to visit.

Annual Membership in 1999 was priced at £110 with 20 reciprocal meetings including Newton Abbot, Wolverhampton, Taunton, Uttoxeter, Chester, Stratford, Warwick, Chepstow, Exeter and Bangor. Juniors (under 21s) are entitled to a reduced rate which in 1999 was £75. Daily admission charges are £14 for the Members, £10 for Tatts and £5 for the Course Ring. Senior Citizens have the concession of a £2 refreshment voucher for use in Tattersalls and discounts are available for groups of 12 or more. Disabled people in wheelchairs are allowed into the Members at the same price as Tattersalls.

The Members building, the Clive Pavilion provides bar and restaurant facilities for Annual Members, owners and trainers. Non-raceday functions for up to 500 people can also be accommodated. There are two spacious rooms available for entertaining parties of between 25 and 35. Marquees can be arranged at the racecourse if you are planning a large party. The marquees can cater for groups from 30 to 350. The cost of an 'all-in' party is approximately £40 per person, including racecard, lunch and admission. The course caterers are Hughes of Welshpool who can be contacted on (01938) 553366. Hughes also deal with all functions on non-racedays. In addition to the new restaurant, snacks are available from Tattersalls and Members. A 3 year programme has just been completed with improvements being made to all the bends, and the fences, plus a reservoir and watering system has been installed. The Course bar was refurbished a few years ago and new Tote facilities were installed, as well as more seating.

Children are welcome here and they will be entertained by the free bouncy castle at late spring meetings. For those even younger there is now a mother and baby room for Course patrons. The disabled racegoer is provided with a viewing ramp and ground floor toilet facilities. Tote credit facilities are available in the Members. The racecourse betting shop is now run by the Tote and if you are a punter with a fancy at another course, then the licensed betting office in Tatts allows you to punt on that cert. Ludlow is to be applauded for its commitment to provide modern facilities in all areas. It benefits from its splendid scenic location and delights in a peace that is seldom found in Britain. A good reason for visiting Shropshire, and where better place to start than the racecourse.

Local Favourites
A number of fine establishments can be found in Ludlow. **Overton Grange** (01584) 873500 is an Edwardian manor offering excellent cuisine. The 16th century **Feathers Hotel** (01584) 875261 is extremely popular and offers a good restaurant. More moderately priced accommodation is found at **No 28** (01584) 876996 and **Cecil** (01584) 872442. Two pubs to note are the **Bull** and the **Church**, both providing a great atmosphere for a pre or post-race rendezvous. Another hotel in which to spoil yourself is **Dinham Hall** (01584) 876464 which has a first class restaurant and comfortable rooms. A restaurant for those who delight in excellent food is the **Merchant House** (01584) 875438—but do book. The **Unicorn** (01584) 873555 is a pub worthy of note here, with some accommodation too. Two other thoughts for good food are the well named **Oaks** (01584) 872325 and **The Courtyard** (01584) 878080.

Just over the border in Wales, the **Radnorshire Arms Hotel** (01544) 267406 at Presteigne is steeped in history—a favourite of Elizabeth I who lived here once. East of Ludlow at Abberley, along the A443, the **Elms Hotel** (01299) 896666 is another hotel with an impressive history and thoughtful service. To the south in Leominster, the racegoer will find a haven of peace and hospitality at **Withenfield Guest House** (01568) 612011. We also recommend the **Marsh Country Hotel** (01568) 613952—a delightful timbered house with a really fine restaurant—definitely one for the shortlist.

In the curiously named Hopton Wafers, the **Crown Inn** (01299) 270372 is a popular pub which provides an excellent bar menu and restaurant. In Clun, the **Sun Inn** (01588) 640277 is a 15th century listed building which also has good value accommodation and bar snacks. Thirteen miles south of Shrewsbury is Church Stretton, home of the **Denehurst Hotel** (01694) 722699 and in nearby All Stretton you'll find the **Stretton Hall Hotel** (01694) 723224—ideal if you want peace and quiet in a traditional style. Before leaving the area consider The **Roebuck** in Brimfield, whose **Poppies** restaurant (01584) 72230 is first class. Clearly, a visit to Ludlow is in order for national hunt enthusiasts. If you haven't been, try to go in 2000, it's a really pleasant course.

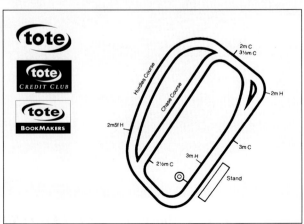

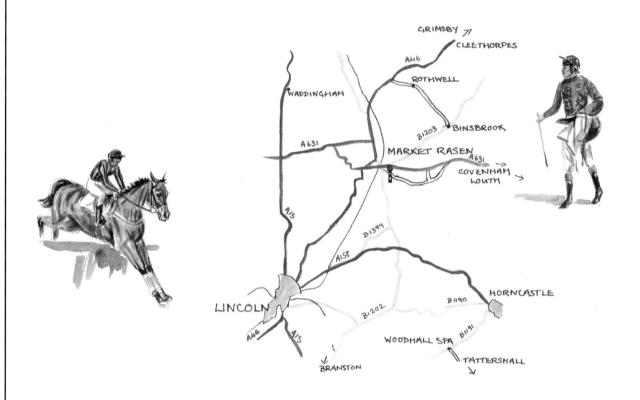

Artist: **Michael Robson** **_JUMPING AT MARKET RASEN_** _Courtesy of:_ **The Artist**

Major Charles Moore acts as **Clerk of the Course** and **Manager** and **Pip Adams** is the **Racecourse Manager** at this pleasant Lincolnshire course. **Stephen Bakin** is **Track Foreman** and **Victoria Nicholson** is the Sales/Marketing Assistant. All the members of this team can be contacted at: **The Racecourse, Legsby Road, Market Rasen, Lincs. LN8 3EA Tel (01673) 843434. Fax (01673) 844532. web site: www.marketrasenraces.co.uk e mail: marketrasen@rht.net**

The racecourse is some twelve miles north east of the county town of Lincoln, just off the A46, midway between Lincoln and Grimsby. The course is adjacent to the A631 on the eastern edge of the town approximately 150 miles from London. The A1 is the closest major road to the course and this, coupled with the A46, is the best route from the south. From the north, use a combination of the M62, M18 and M180 link to the A15, then the A631 at Caenby Corner. Those travelling by train should note that Market Rasen is on the Newark to Cleethorpes line. Change at Newark if you are coming from Kings Cross. The station is approximately ten minutes walk from the course. Should you travel by car you will find ample free parking. Market Rasen is also the place to take your helicopter. During the war the course was requisitioned and used as an anti-aircraft headquarters. Fear not, you are unlikely to be shot down.

The racing pattern in 1999 included 19 meetings plus two point-to-points and a day's Arab Racing. The course's most popular occasions are traditionally their Easter Monday and Boxing Day meetings, the most popular races being the Lincolnshire National held on Boxing Day, and the Handicap 'Chase and Hurdle staged at the summer meeting in June. The rates for admission in 1999 were £14, £10 and £5 for the Members', Tattersalls and Silver Ring respectively, although Tatts was only £6 for midweek afternoon fixtures. A Jubilee Club for pensioners gives reduced admission to Tatts and the Silver Ring. Prices may, however, be higher on Premium days. If you are planning on taking a party of people, special rates are available depending on the numbers—15 or more is the usual figure. Contact the Secretary for terms. Annual Members are charged £125 for a single subscription while £210 is the price for a husband and wife dual membership. This entitles members to exclusive facilities together with 18 reciprocal dates at other courses all over the country.

There are facilities for all sorts of parties and they vary in number, price and location. The Club Enclosure's private boxes have been increased to an impressive 17, eight on annual lets and nine corporate rooms let on a daily basis. The County Room can take parties of up to 100 people, or smaller groups if desired. and the Brocklesby Suite can cater for parties of up to 300. There is also a pay and play golf course which can be made available for corporate entertainment or as part of conference activities. Bookings should be made through the Commercial Manager and the price will be around £395. The caterers can be contacted through the racecourse and provide a selection of meals in a choice of bars and restaurants. Alternatively, you may wish to take a picnic and there are two designated picnic areas. In 1999 the charge for entrance to these areas is £3 per car and £5 per adult occupant. In addition improved facilities include a new winners enclosure.

If you are disabled there is a special viewing area and two specially adapted lavatories. At the Saturday and Bank Holiday meetings a fully supervised crèche is provided on the first floor of the Silver Ring Stand. For older children, there is a recently refurbished playground. All accompanied children under 16 are admitted free of charge. Annual and Daily Members can take advantage of the dining room in the Brocklesbury Suite which offers lunch and views of the course. There is also a recently renovated Members Bar and Champagne Bar. Bookings for the restaurant may be made direct with the caterers, Craven Gilpin 0113 287 6387.

Lincolnshire remains one of England's most unspoiled counties and if you are looking for a new racecourse to visit in 2000 Market Rasen would make a fine choice.

Local Favourites

Steeped in history,with narrow cobbled streets, Lincoln is filled with antique and craft shops. Lovers of history should visit the cathedral which holds one of the original copies of the Magna Carta. An appealing place to eat is the **Wig and Mitre** (01522) 537482 on the appropriately named Steep Hill. There are a large number of hotels to be found in the city. The **Forte Post House** (01522) 502341 is modern but has pleasant views and is comfortable. More convenient and with a city centre setting is the **White Hart Hotel** (01522) 526222 a particular pleasing establishment. **The Courtyard by Marriott** (01522) 544244 is also well worth noting. Extremely comfortable but less expensive accommodation can be found in the **Moor Lodge Hotel** (01522) 791366, Branston, a little way outside the city. Lincoln also offers the outstanding, particularly from a price point of view, **D'Isney Place Hotel** (01522) 538881. The **Jews House** (01522) 524851 is an inspired French restaurant. Those wishing to stay close to the racecourse should note the **Limes Hotel** (01673) 842357, Market Rasen, for good accommodation, food and service. The town also boasts a friendly and popular restaurant to consider, **Jossals** (01673) 843948. **Kenwick Park** (01507) 608806 in Louth is further afield but worth considering. In the opposite direction is the **Village** (01427) 788309 where the comfort and attention may make it your last stop! The convenient **Admiral Rodney** (01507) 523131 and the **Petwood House Hotel** (01526) 352411 offer special racing packages—check with the hotel for details. The **Washingborough Hall Hotel** (01522) 790340 is also one to note for those who like a little extra luxury.

Those merely looking for a pub for a pre-race pint, or post-race celebration are directed to the **White Swan** which is thoroughly recommended. To the revamped **Chase** or the excellent **Red Lion**. A more than comfortable bed for the night can be found at the **Waveney Guest House** (01673) 843236 and **Beechwood Guest House** (01673) 844043. The **Black Horse** (01507) 343646 at Donnington on Bain is a good all-round performer. Less convenient is Woodhall Spa, but this town should be visited not for racing but for some excellent golf. The **Golf Hotel** (01526) 53535 and the Edwardian **Dower House Hotel** (01526) 52588 are both good. Two pubs relatively near to the racecourse are the **Chicken** at Bingrook with good bar food, and the **Nickerson Arms** at Rothwell, also remote but worth finding just the same. One final thought, consider a trip to Stamford and a night at the **George** (01780) 55171. This really is one of our leading recommendations—a must for all lovers of fine hotels.

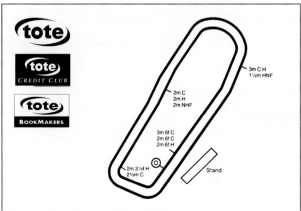

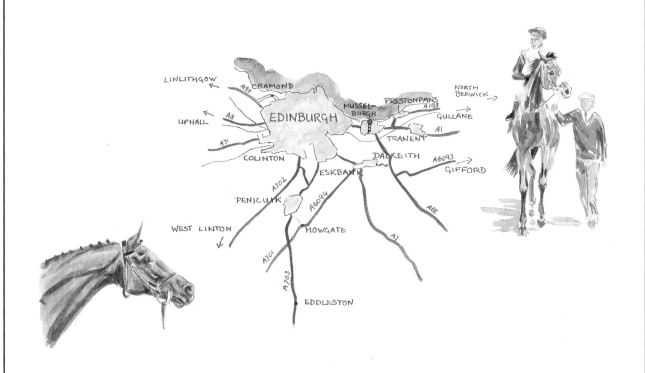

Artist: **Claire Eva Burton LEADING UP** *Courtesy of:* **The Artist**

The **Manager** and **Clerk of the Course** at Musselburgh can be reached on **0131 665 2859 Fax 0131 653 2083**. Bill Farnsworth, who is in charge of corporate hospitality is contactable on **0131 665 2859 Fax 0131 6532083**. E mail **info@musselburgh-racecourse.co.uk web site: www.musselburgh-racecourse.co.uk**.

The racecourse stands proudly around the historic golf course of Musselburgh links which in turn lies on the Firth of Forth. Its situation, six miles east of Scotland's capital city, is some 350 miles north of its English counterpart. The major routes to be considered are the M8 and the City bypass from the west and the A1 and A198 from the east. The A7, A68 and A702 should be used for people coming from the south. The Musselburgh bypass (A1) is now in operation and traffic for the racecourse is much improved as a result.

Edinburgh's main railway station, Waverley, is on the excellent Intercity 125 line and Kings Cross is little more than three and a half hours away. The nearest station to the course is Musselburgh East and on racedays a courtesy bus from here will take you to the course. Check with the racecourse to find out which trains it meets. If you decide to drive you will be pleased to hear there is an excellent choice of areas in which to park your car and these are all free. Coaches are also welcome. If you are an aviator and happen to be passing in your helicopter, approach the course from the north and land in an area adjacent to the car park.

There are two enclosures, the Members which costs £12 for a day badge and the Grandstand and Paddock where a fee of £7 was charged for entry unless you happened to be an OAP or unemployed–in which case there was a £4 levy. Accompanied children under 16 years are allowed in free and entertainment is provided for them at some meetings. £120 is charged for a years membership with £80 being asked for an additional badge, while National Hunt season membership is available at £50. Membership includes reserved parking and reciprocal meetings at ten other courses. The 1999 fixture list was spread throughout the year with fourteen days of flat racing and eight days over the jumps. There were two evening meetings during the summer, two Saturday fixtures and one on Sunday in September.

Sponsors' rooms are available for hire in the Queen's Stand, where you can entertain in style. Local companies can sponsor fences and hurdles as well as the races themselves. A hospitality complex opened a few years ago comprising 6 private boxes for groups of up to 24, a large ground floor room for parties of between 100 and 150 and a new lads canteen. The first floor Grandstand has been refurbished and there is now a Members Restaurant overlooking the racecourse. On the ground floor of the Grandstand, the Pinkie Bar has also been redone, with snacks available to patrons here.

There are a number of snack bars throughout the course and two restaurants, the Tote Club and the Paddock. If you are keen to know more with regard to the racecourse catering, your initial contact should be Bill Farnsworth on 0131 665 2859.

November 1999 sees the start of a £1 million development to include a new weigh-in room; owners, trainers and members entrance; on-course betting shop, public food and bar outlet, plus a Tote Credit facility.

As you would expect, there are public telephones, and viewing ramps, loos and some bars for the disabled racegoers. No banking facilities are available, but if you have a particular fancy then the Tote run an on-course shop. A pleasant racecourse which is well worth a visit when looking for a few winners in 2000.

Local Favourites

Outside Edinburgh, a simply outstanding hotel should be visited if at all possible. It has the class of a Derby winner and a history and character as rich as the Grand National–**Greywalls** (01620) 842144. Overlooking Muirfield, this superb hotel and restaurant is thoroughly recommended. Gullane also reveals an excellent restaurant **La Potinière** (01620) 843214–which is small, cosy, refined and enormously popular. You really must plan ahead and book if you want a table here, but it's well worth it. Golfing enthusiasts will vouch for the fact that guesthouses of ambience abound–the **Golfers Inn** (01620) 843259 is but one example. South of Gullane in Gifford, the **Tweeddale Arms** (01620) 810240 makes a good base–ideal for exploring the East Lothian coast. **Bonars** (01620) 810264 is a good restaurant to consider. Remaining outside the city, one finds Howgate and the **Old Howgate Inn** (01968) 674244, a splendid pub for food as is the **Horseshoes Inn** at Eddleston a little south of Howgate. Nearby the **Cringletie House Hotel** (01721) 730233 is an extremely welcoming hotel–comfortable too. The restaurant is also very good. Returning north to Penicuik, one finds another fine pub with a separate restaurant and some bedrooms, **Habbies Howe** (01968) 676969. In Haddington the **Waterside Bistro** (01620) 835674 comes highly recommended.

There is a whole host of restaurants outside Edinburgh. Pride of place goes to the **Champany Inn** (01506) 834532 in Linlithgow where the steaks are said to be among the finest in Britain. The **Lauriston Farm Restaurant** 0131 312 7071 is another where a slight detour will reap tasty dividends. Another within easy shooting distance is **The Cockatoo** on Old Craighill Road 0131 660 1211. A restaurant within a hotel can be found in Uphall–**Houstoun House** (01506) 853831 is a charming place in which to stay with a delightful restaurant. Finally, mention should be made of the **Cramond Inn** 0131 336 2035 at Cramond, a pleasant place to spend an evening.

In Edinburgh itself the **Caledonian Hotel** 0131 225 2433 is grand, superbly comfortable and the **Pompadour** restaurant is really something to cherish and the **George Hotel** 0131 225 1251 is first class. Less traditional is the **Sheraton Grand Hotel**, one of the racecourse's major sponsors, 0131 229 9131 which stands opposite the Usher Hall. As you will imagine there are a whole range of hotels in Edinburgh and it is a delightful city to visit. **Channings** 0131 315 2226 is a townhouse hotel to savour.

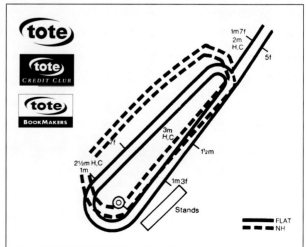

Artist: **Claire Eva Burton** **THE 1997 HENNESSY GOLD CUP** *Courtesy of:* **Rosenstiel's**

The **Managing Director** at Newbury is **Mark Kershaw** and he can be contacted at **The Racecourse, Newbury, Berkshire RG14 7NZ. Tel (01635) 40015. Fax (01635) 528354.** The **Hon David Sieff** is Newbury's Chairman.

Travellers from the east and London should use the M4 (junction 12) and complete their journey on the A4. Eastbound racegoers should also use the M4 (junction 13), while those from the south and north converge on the A34, causing chaos and terrible queues which must be circumvented if possible. However, the new bypass which is now open is helping to alleviate the situation. One good thing—there is plenty of excellent parking once you finally do arrive! It's entirely free except for the Strathmead car park at £2 and in the picnic car park where there is a £5 charge on Hennessy Day and £4 on all other days, plus £4 per adult.

A new and good idea for all meetings is to take advantage of the train. On production of your rail ticket you get £2 off entry to Members, except on Hennessy Day. Finally, if anybody wishes to jet in there is a landing strip at the racecourse, situated in the centre of the track. Please contact the Secretary for details.

With 28 days of racing both on the flat and over the jumps the Newbury racegoer is blessed with some outstanding fixtures. Races such as the Tote Gold Trophy, the Tripleprint Greenham Stakes, the Juddmonte Lockinge Stakes, the Geoffrey Freer Stakes, the Vodafone Horris Hill Stakes, the Perpetual St Simon Stakes, the Dubai Duty Free International Raceday and the Hennessy Gold Cup make racing at Newbury a delight. With so many top races on the flat and over the jumps, it's not surprising that the course is popular.

Despite the quality of racing, Double Membership was well priced at £380 in 1999 which included one non-transferable badge and one transferable badge. Single Members are charged £190. Junior Membership is £95 (18-25 years olds) and there is a joining fee of £25. A car park badge is also provided together with 23 reciprocal meetings at some excellent racecourses. In 1999 a National Hunt only membership was introduced available at a cost of £95, an excellent deal for fans of the jumping game. Daily admission to the Club Enclosure costs between £15-£26 depending on the meeting. Tattersalls will be priced at between £8 and £12 and the Silver Ring, Geoffrey Freer Stand and picnic car park at £4-£6. Parties are encouraged and 20 per cent discounts are offered to groups of twelve or more except in the Members. Seats can be reserved at a cost of £5 but bookings must be made in advance. Credit card bookings are also accepted.

The Newbury racegoer is able to enjoy an excellent view of the racecourse from most areas. The Members Restaurant can accommodate 220 people. In the Cafe Normandie steaks are the order of the day. The Moët et Chandon Champagne Bar has moved to the Hampshire Stand and offers a complete sports information service as part of the facilities. The Manton Club Room, on the top floor of the Hampshire Stand, offers a bar, restaurant, TV and betting facilities to Annual Members. If you do have any catering enquiries, telephone Mark Atkinson, the Catering Manager at Ring & Brymer (01635) 521081. Facilities for larger parties (up to 1,000) can also be arranged. Corporate entertaining facilities at Newbury are now first class and boxes and function rooms of various sizes can be reserved. Naturally, costs will vary dramatically but contact the racecourse and you are sure to be well taken care of. There are many other snack bars in all the enclosures and the restaurants and bars are open two hours before the first race. Children and under 18s are admitted free into all enclosures. Younger punters may wish to make use of

the Rocking Horse Nursery, which takes two to eight year olds. The fully staffed crèche is open on non-racedays as well as racedays. The idea of encouraging families to go racing is a good one and can only be of benefit for the track and hopefully the sport in general.

The racecourse provides good viewing facilities together with lavatories for the disabled. Telephones are available but surprisingly no bank has yet set up shop despite repeated requests from Newbury's management. Indeed, there have been many demands made on the Newbury Executive in recent years. By and large, they have down well and the racecourse is now one of the very best in the country. Some of the character may have been lost but this has been replaced by an amphitheatre for racing that exudes class. There are other smaller and more thoughtful examples of Newbury's efforts too. Each owner is invited for a drink and given a complimentary video should their horse win. This may seem almost trivial but owners put a lot into the sport and such little touches are appreciated.

In the years since *Travelling the Turf* has been published Newbury has achieved a great deal. It has responded to the many demands made upon it by the present day punter, offering good facilities and top class racing.

In spite of all this praise, however, there are still many areas that can be improved to make going racing the first class experience that everyone expects. Running a racecourse means operating a service business and management should pay heed to the fact that the paying public now expects and demands levels of service, and a customer-friendly approach, or it will take its leisure money elsewhere.

Newbury has always been an immensely popular racecourse and has in the past decade consistently improved its facilities and is continuing to do so in a thoroughly impressive way. Surprisingly, it lost its way in the racecourse friendliness stakes but hopefully this can be put down as a blip. It nestles in an area where racing has a strong following, is handy for London and racing's second 'city' Lambourn. It therefore need not worry as much as other courses about proposed changes to the fixture list which will jeopardise some key race nights and consequent gate receipts. Some degree of harmony has broken out with the racecourses and the BHB, as so called marketing cash has been offered - this is seen by some as compensation. It is also deeply ironic because in my experience the best racing marketing is found when a racecourse is full of atmosphere with people having a great time . . . and a place like Newbury on a Saturday evening would be one such great opportunity.

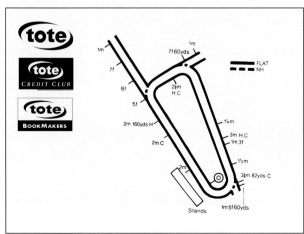

Newbury racecourse is ideally situated well away from the capital but conveniently placed for folk from Hampshire, Oxfordshire, Berkshire and other ritzy shires of the south. In Newbury itself the **Chequers Hotel** (01635) 38000 is most convenient while at Stroud Green, the **Plough on the Green** offers a superb garden, covered barbecue area and an excellent bar. Just 500 yards opposite the main car park entrance and five minutes walk across Stroud Green it is very popular on racedays with racegoers in the know.

Farther afield, a hotel certainly worth an inspection is **Jarvis Elcot Park Hotel & Country Club** (01488) 658100, a Georgian mansion set in 16 acres of parkland overlooking the Kennet Valley. The restaurant is good here and some attractive two-day breaks are available.

Slightly farther afield is Hungerford and within its compass are some first class places to visit. The **Jarvis Bear Hotel** (01488) 682512 is probably the best place to stay. It is a 13th century inn with an excellent welcome. If you are looking for something to eat then the set lunches are recommended while the evening menu is also good. An alternative eating place to the Bear is an extremely pleasant pub the **John O'Gaunt** (01488) 683535—a tremendous meeting place before and after racing. There are a number of bedrooms too. **Marshgate Cottage** (01488) 682307 also provides a more than comfortable bed for the night. Hungerford itself is riddled with antique shops and to many it may well be worth a visit on this score alone.

On to Pangbourne, and an old favourite, the **Copper Inn** (0118) 984 2244, which is thoroughly recommended. The **White Hart Inn** at Hampstead Marshall (01488) 658201 has also shown good form—good food and pleasant bedrooms. Another outstanding inn is located in Yattendon: the **Royal Oak** (01635) 201325. Once again, a splendid all-round performer—simple homely bars, a decent fire, cosy bedrooms and a really excellent restaurant. In Goring, the **John Barleycorn** and the **Miller of Mansfield** are fun pubs, ideal for a post-race celebration. Both offer simple accommodation and good bar food. The **Leatherne Bottle** (01491) 872667 offers a pleasant riverside setting in which to imbibe—a good restaurant as well. Across the Thames and into Streatley more lavish accommodation can be found at the **Swan Diplomat** (01491) 873737. An outstanding restaurant accompanies the hotel which also boasts fine leisure facilities.

Towards Wallingford, at Moulsford, lies the glorious Thames-side retreat, the **Beetle and Wedge** (01491) 651381. The restaurant here is outstanding. A real must. In Aldworth, the **Bell** is a really cosy pub in which to take shelter. Heading towards the rolling Berkshire Downs and the Ilsleys, a number of pubs can be found. In East Ilsley, the **Crown and Horns** (01635) 281205 deserves a particular mention—not least for its excellent collection of sporting prints and racing photographs, with accommodation available too. Racing enthusiasts will also enjoy the **Hare & Hounds** at Lambourn—a well trained landlord! The **Stag** is another decent pub, while in nearby West Ilsley the **Harrow** is pleasant and offers good home cooking. The **Sun in the Wood** (01635) 42377 also offers good food. Finally, for the real galloping gourmets, a trip to Great Milton will yield the majestic **Le Manoir aux Quat' Saisons** (01844) 278881. This is a restaurant with rooms of international acclaim. You will need a decent winner to meet the bill here but it is well worth it.

A pub with excellent food is the **Dundas Arms** (01488) 658263 at Kintbury. The restaurant has pride of place here but if you are looking for a place to stay this may be your solution. The bedrooms are located in a converted stable block. In Chieveley, the **Blue Boar** (01635) 248236 is handy for the M4, junction 13. In a secluded downs setting, its thatched exterior hides some splendid bar food and excellent ales. Accommodation is also available here. Another pub with an extremely popular restaurant and some comfortable bedrooms is the **Five Bells** at Wickham (01488) 38242. The answer has to be to take Friday off—go racing—eat a good lunch and in the evening nestle down in a quiet pub ready for racing on Saturday. If you do, note the **Winterbourne Arms** (01635) 248200—a pub with good food.

Other ideas? Well, in Stanford Dingley the **Old Boot** (01734) 744292 is worth a visit while the **Bull** (01734) 744409 here is a grand pub, a definite if you have won on the last. If you're travelling on the A4, as many people will, one place to pull over at is the **Rising Sun**, Woolhampton—really first class beer, good bar snacks and if you are feeling a little more peckish there is a separate restaurant. In Kingsclere, a particularly strong racing influence in the village and a rather good pub as well is the **Crown Inn** (01635) 298956.

If you get round even half of the above for goodness sake don't drive home! To that end, a few more excellent hotels. In Hurstbourne Tarrant, **Esseborne Manor** (01264) 736444 is outstanding—once again a tremendous restaurant, a warmly recommended all rounder. People heading south might wish to stay at Silchester. The **Romans Hotel** (01734) 700421 could be the answer—well priced and very comfortable.

Between Newbury and Ascot, in Shinfield one finds **L'Ortolan** (01734) 883783. The chef has an outstanding reputation and style, and high quality cuisine is quite categorically odds on. In Pingewood, the **Kirtons Hotel & Country Club** (01734) 500885 does a special racegoers package which offers good value. Nearer to Newbury, at Old Burghclere, the **Dew Pond** (01635) 278408 is well worth considering.

Newbury is one of the south's growth areas and new hotels to add to your list include **The Vineyard** (01635) 528770 in Stockcross, the **Hilton National** (01635) 529000 in the town itself and the recently refurbished **Queens Hotel** (01635) 44518 only 2 minutes from the racecourse. The Hilton is owned by Ladbrokes and will inevitably be developing weekend breaks to tie in with the racing at Newbury. The **Donnington Valley Hotel** (01635) 551199 is also one for your shortlist. The **Stakis Newbury** (01635) 247010 is also worth considering.

Outside the town, but within a decent stone's throw, one finds **Regency Park Hotel** (01635) 871555 another first class candidate for a visit, as is a hotel that has been warmly recommended by one of our readers—the **Hinds Head Hotel** (01734) 712194 in Aldermaston. It sounds tremendous and reminds me to ask readers to let us know of any good information they might have. As all punters know, it is useful to have a little inside knowledge!

One final thought before you depart from this immensely talented field of favourites is **Hollington House** (01635) 255100 which lies three miles south of Newbury. An Edwardian mansion of style, the house has been carefully restored and converted to provide a hotel of real class. Good food, fine wines and the superb gardens are good reasons to visit this delightful hotel.

We hope you plunder a bounty or two while racing at Newbury in 2000. Very few racecourses offer as much and these local favourites also make up a select field. Whether you are popping in for a pint or two before or after racing, or organising a weekend away from it all, Berkshire offers no end of distractions.

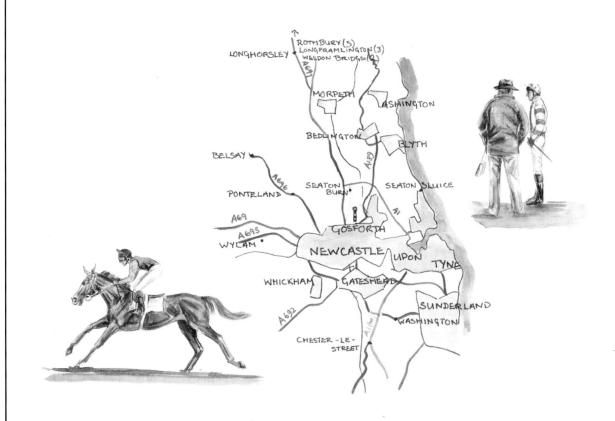

Artist: **Katy Sodeau** *AT THE FINISH* *Courtesy of:* **The Artist**

Major David McAllister is Clerk of the Course and he, together with the Chairman, Stan Clarke and the Commercial & Marketing Manager, Malcolm Winters can be contacted at Newcastle Racecourse, High Gosforth Park, Newcastle upon Tyne NE3 5HP. Tel 0191 236 2020. Fax 0191 236 7761.

Those who are making the trip to Newcastle from the south should remember that the city can be bypassed by following the A1. The racecourse is in High Gosforth Park, which can be accessed by taking the junction signposted Wideopen. The same applies to those travelling from the north. From the east, use the A19 and A1056. The Western bypass has cut about twenty minutes from the journey around the city. The journey from Newcastle's Tyneside to London's Thameside is a good 280 miles and one mode of transport to use is the electrified Great North Eastern Railway service from Kings Cross. The course is a further four miles or so from Newcastle's Central Station—a fifteen minute taxi journey. The Metro, Newcastle's underground, can be taken to South Gosforth, Regent Centre or Four Lane Ends, and on racedays a free bus service operates between these stations and the course, two hours prior to the first race and for one hour after the last. Quicker transportation can be found by using the nearby airport or, if prior notice is given, you may land a helicopter. There is ample parking, all free of charge, with areas for Annual Members and disabled guests.

There are now 28 flat and national hunt fixtures at Gosforth Park and the highlight of the season is the new three day Northumberland Plate Festival in late June which runs from Thursday to Saturday and includes a Friday evening meeting. Saturday sees the £125,000 Northumberland Plate, a handicap over two miles which always attracts large fields. Highlights of the National Hunt season are the Fighting Fifth Hurdle and the Eider Chase, one of the warm up races for the Grand National.

Members Club Enclosure badges cost £15 increasing to £25 at the Plate meeting. Good value are Tattersalls at £10 (£12 for Plate Day) or the Silver Ring at £5 at all times. There is a Club discount of £3 per person in the Club for parties of 15 or more, with a £2 discount in Tattersalls for similar sized groups. OAPs and disabled people receive a £2 discount in all enclosures. Annual Membership is £250 for a double badge and £165 for a single. These prices include a car park badge and a very generous 15 reciprocal meetings, as well as free admission to all Uttoxeter and Brighton races.

The facilities at the course include privately leased boxes and rooms for hire and areas for marquees should you have something a little more adventurous in mind. The Members' Enclosure comprises restaurants, a carvery, bars and a food take away counter, with a separate restaurant for owners and trainers. The Silver Ring and Tattersalls both have massive grandstand, long bars, toilets, betting shop, Tote, food take away counters and access to a Family Foodhall. Numerous snack bars are available for you while you sup the Newky Brown.

Annual and Daily Members have benefited from the many improvements at the course. The refurbished Members' Grandstand has twelve hospitality boxes, with an Annual Members restaurant/bar and a Daily Members' Bar and Carvery take away counter, also Tote and betting shops are available.

Children under 16, with an adult are admitted free to all enclosures. At weekend and Bank Holiday meetings entertainments are arranged for them—including Punch & Judy shows, fun fair rides, face painting etc.

Since Gosforth Park has been taken over, there has been a £4 million renovation programme to date. Moving the Winners Enclosure to the front of the stands has been a major benefit for all racegoers. The reinstatement of the first furlong on the picturesque Straight Mile—over which the Hennessy Cognac Blaydon Race is now run is also a plus for the course. The reintroduction of the Blaydon Races in August is an obvious and appealing marketing concept. Make no mistake, this is a racecourse on the up. One to visit in 2000.

Local Favourites

The busy city of Newcastle lies close to the racecourse, but at the same time, Scotland, the Lake District and North Yorkshire are all within striking distance. In the Tyne Valley a Country House to consider is Newbrough Lodge (01434) 674545. A pleasant place to stay in Longhorsley is the Linden Hall Hotel (01670) 516611—it has a delightful setting in 300 acres of parkland, with the added attraction of an 18 hole golf course. The Granby (01665) 570228 in Longframlington, further north, is an ideal pub for a weekend in the country. Also out of town is the Plough Inn (01661) 853555—a pub with a restaurant and Horton Grange (01661) 860686 located five miles from the course. The restaurant here is excellent.

Two comfortable hotels are the Holiday Inn in Seaton Burn 0191 236 5432 with good leisure facilities—ideal for business people—and the Swallow Gosforth Park Hotel 0191 236 4111. This is an excellent, modern hotel where the Brandling restaurant offers nouvelle cuisine. Both are convenient for the racecourse, the latter being right next door. In town The Copthorne 0191 222 0333 and the Vermont 0191 233 1010 are excellent.

Newcastle also has a variety of fabulous restaurants. The Fisherman's Lodge in Jesmond Dene 0191 281 3281 is a super restaurant while on the quayside Trattoria Uno 0191 261 5264 is very popular. Lovers of Chinese food are spoilt for choice on Stowell Street. Sample any of the following; the Mandarin 0191 261 7881, the King Neptune 0191 261 6657, the Royal Circle 0191 261 2300 and the Palace Garden 0191 232 3117 and for lovers of Indian cuisine, Sachins 0191 261 9035, serves up a tasty treat. Arguably Newcastle's finest restaurant is 21 Queen Street 0191 222 0755 on Princes Wharf virtually beneath the Tyne Bridge. Round the corner, Courtney's 0191 232 5537 is also very good.

Some great pubs of note include the Crown Posada, and Kinnears, part of the Theatre Royal on Grey Street. Also, the Shiremoor House Farm 0191 257 6302 pub and restaurant, which is noted for its beer range. Lovers of nightlife must check out the Quayside—for atmosphere it's hard to beat.

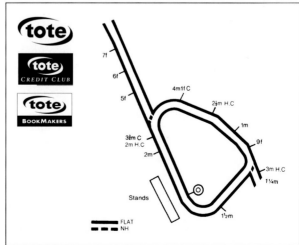

Overlooking Melford's magnificent green, the Countrymen has received wide acclaim for its superb food and splendid accommodation. Recognised by all major guides, the Countrymen is enjoyed by visitors and locals alike.

Classically influenced, mouthwatering dishes are freshly made to order by Stephen, who trained at the Dorchester in London. He uses fresh locally grown Suffolk produce seasoned with herbs cultivated in his own garden. The Countrymen offers a wide choice of fixed price menus and a full à la carte menu to stimulate your tastebuds. Just the thing after a hard day at the races.

The menu changes regularly to reflect seasonal dishes and Stephen's specialities. For a real treat why not try the gastronomic menu which boasts five fabulous courses accompanied by fine wines personally chosen by Janet. Putting her wine expertise to good use she is always happy to advise which bottle to select for that special occasion or simply a good glass to enjoy before dinner.

Adding another string to their bow proprietors Jan and Steve have now opened a delightful bistro and wine bar to accompany their well established restaurant, offering a selection of old and new world wines, in an informal and relaxed atmosphere.

After your meal retire to the comfort of the lounge or pass through the French windows into the walled courtyard garden beyond. Just the place to unwind after dinner or whilst studying the Racing Post after a hearty country breakfast. If you still have the energy then you will find walls lined with bookcases offering reading matter on every conceivable subject and games to while away the time on rainy days.

And so to bed. From this vantage point, there are panoramic views over Long Melford and you can be forgiven for thinking that you have stepped back in time a couple of centuries. Each of the bedrooms is individually furnished with country antiques whilst offering all modern amenities. All rooms have en suite bathrooms, colour televisions, direct dial telephones and generous hospitality trays. If you are lucky you could be sleeping in one of the two four poster beds or luxuriating in an antique brass bedstead or even a mahogany half tester in the bridal suite. Several of the rooms are suitable for families and well behaved children are very welcome. Dogs are accepted by appointment.

Long Melford is famous for quaint architecture and a wealth of antique shops. A stone's throw away are two 15th century manor houses. Kentwell Hall lovingly restored to its medieval splendour and National Trust Melford Hall, the family seat of the Hyde-Parkers, who are still in residence. Other places of interest nearby include the wool village of Lavenham, historic Bury St Edmunds, Sudbury, the birthplace of Thomas Gainsborough, the university city of Cambridge, Newmarket, the home of British racing, and Constable country.

A veritable home from home. You can be assured of a warm welcome at the Countrymen in Melford.

The Countrymen
The Green
Long Melford
Suffolk, CO10 9DN
Tel: (01787) 312356
Fax: (01787) 374557

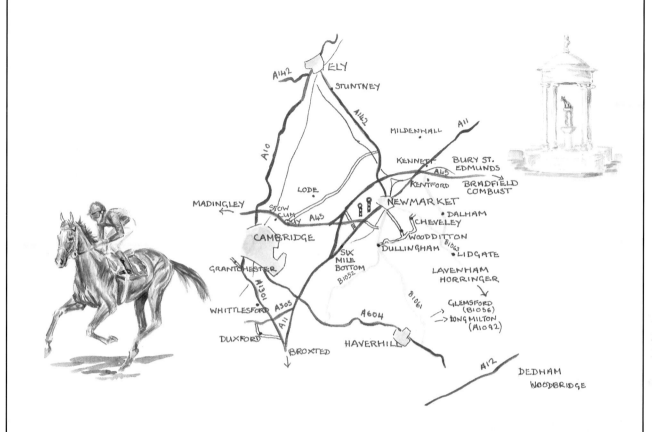

Artist: **Peter Smith HELL FOR LEATHER** _Courtesy of:_ **Frost & Reed**

Hintlesham Hall, originally built in the 1570s, with a stunning Georgian façade offers the best in country house elegance and charm. Gracious living, good food and wine, attentive service and tranquil relaxation greet every guest to the hotel.

The Hall is set in over 170 acres of rolling Suffolk countryside, some of which is devoted to a beautiful 18 hole championship, full length golf course, and has 33 luxurious bedrooms and suites of differing shapes and sizes, some with four poster beds. Thoughtful attention to detail pervades the hotel and this includes the restaurant. Head Chef, Alan Ford, believes good food starts with good produce. French truffles, Scottish salmon, Cornish scallops and Suffolk lobsters are just some of the enticements of the menu which changes seasonally. There is an award-winning 300 bin wine list which ranges the world from France to Australia.

All moods are reflected in Hintlesham's fine reception rooms—the intimate book-lined library, the tranquil, spacious Garden Room and the cool entrance arcade. The Hall is just 45 minutes drive from Newmarket and is an ideal base from which to explore East Anglia, be it the medieval wool villages of Lavenham and Kersey, Long Melford and Woodbridge with their wealth of antique shops or Dedham and Flatford Mill, famous for their Constable associations. The cathedral city of Norwich and the University colleges of Cambridge are close by.

However, perhaps most importantly, Hintlesham Hall is the perfect retreat for those who wish to go nowhere at all.

Hintlesham Hall
Hintlesham
Suffolk
IP8 3NS
Tel: (01473) 652268
Fax: (01473) 652463

The town of Newmarket seems to breathe racing and it is blessed with two of the finest courses in Britain. The Guineas meeting successfully staged at the July Course in 1999 will herald the opening of the new Millennium Stand which will provide state of the art facilities and we wish them well with this. The management team here is headed by **Nick Lees** the **Clerk of the Course** and **Director of Racing**, and by the new **Managing Director Kim Deshayes**. They are ably assisted by **Gaynor Haxby** as **Commercial Manager** and **Christian Mitchell** as **Operations Manager** who can be contacted at **Westfield House, Camridge Road, Newmarket, Suffolk CB8 0TG.** Tel (01638) 663482 Fax (01638) 663044 or at **The Racecourse, Rowley Mile.** Tel (01638) 662762. The **July Racecourse** telephone number is (01638) 662752. You can also visit Newmarket via the Internet at **www.newmarketracecourses.co.uk.**

Crowds flock to Newmarket for their many popular meetings, so an early start is recommended. From London it is a mere 60 mile sprint up the M11—exit junction 9 for the new dual carriageway A11, leaving it at Six Mile Bottom and thence to Newmarket. The A14 links Felixstowe with the M1 and M6, and the A1 will assist both northbound and southbound visitors. Racegoers on busy days should note the back exit via Exning onto the A14, thus avoiding the particularly heavy going. From Norwich and the east, the A11 is the obvious route, while from Bury St Edmunds the A45 can be useful. There are numerous car parks on the Heath for both cars and coaches and you may park in the car park for a mere of £2.

If travelling by train, start at Liverpool Street. Buses meet the trains in Cambridge and ensure prompt delivery to the races. A further innovation is the introduction of a separate free bus service to the course from the station and Newmarket High Street. The CAA have given their permission for use of the July landing strip when there is racing on the July course, although craft must not land or take off over the racecourse buildings. The Rowley Mile strip can also be used.

Major races include the two Classics, the Sagitta 1000 Guineas, and 2000 Guineas. Special entertainment is usually laid on including bands and special children's facilities and an enormous shopping mall—and of course, first class racing. Other highlights include the Cesarewitch, the Cambridgeshire, the Craven Stakes, the Cheveley Park Stakes, the Middle Park, and the Dewhurst.

The ambience of the two Newmarket courses—the Rowley Mile and in the July Racecourse—is totally different with the former featuring racing in spring and autumn in a highly professional manner and the latter creating an excellent atmosphere in beautiful surroundings for the more relaxed summer meetings. Attending one of the popular evening meetings on the July Course is a tremendous way to relax and forget your troubles.

In 2000, membership rates will be £250 for an Annual Members badge with a £50 joining fee which will include free admission and car parking at 33 meetings, and a reciprocal day's racing at Cheltenham. For Juniors (16-25), a badge is well priced at £100 with a £15 joining fee. Inaugural membership requires an additional fee of £35 for senior members and £10 for juniors. Daily prices vary. On the 1000 and 2000 Guineas days and the Dubai Champion Stakes Day Members Badges cost around £30. Other feature days are priced at £22 with all other days at the £18 mark. Admission to the Grandstand is £11 on ordinary days, rising to £13 on the four big days. The Silver Ring enclosure has a similar system—£5 and £3 being the respective asking prices. Parties of 10 or more are offered a 20 per cent discount if arranged in advance with the racecourse. Children under 16 years are admitted free and there is a creche which is open on all days on the July course and on some fixtures held on the Rowley mile. A fully equipped playground is available throughout the season. One of many recent developments at Newmarket is the introduction of a Triple Crown ticket that includes admission to the racecourse, the National Stud and the National Horseracing Museum which can be purchased from any of the three venues. In 1999 the 16-25 club and pensioners were admitted to the Grandstand and Paddock for £5.50 on normal days and £6.50 for the feature days in May and October. Similar discounts were offered to holders of Students Union cards

Of course during the building of the new stand on the Rowley Mile Course, the facilities for corporate entertaining were moved to the July Course. On the July Course, the oak panelled Queens Room and the Jockey Club Dining Room are also available for hire. As the entertainment facilities are so comprehensive it is advisable to contact the racecourse. The racecourse caterers Letheby & Christopher, (01638) 662750 are also happy to assist with any catering problems. The old thatched bar on the July Course has been replaced by the splendid Dante Bar and will soon be complemented by a refurbished and adjoining new Members Bar. The new Ocean Swell Bar has also been a great success.

Telephones are available as are banks as well as extra betting facilities. Disabled people have lavatories, escalators help the elderly and overall, everyone from junior to senior is well catered for. Newmarket offers two well run racecourses. They differ dramatically—the Rowley Mile exudes history while the July Course is one of the most picturesque in the country.

Newmarket is the capital of British Racing and a trip around the town to the gallops, museum, National Stud and all manner of friendly boozers will reveal this spirit. The racecourse needs to be a beacon of this excellence - after all this is where so many of the great tussles took place in those early days, on the Rowley Mile. It is also essential that Newmarket comes up with some really exciting new racing initiatives to demonstrate that it is not merely a place to go flat racing. Then the real challenge comes . . . and that is to ensure that like Cheltenham it is not only a place of racing pilgrimage but one of national sporting heritage . . . if the Executive can succeed in this furlong racing will be forever grateful. We wish them the best of British.

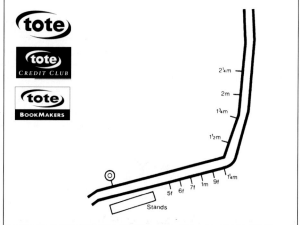

The Rowley Mile

I cannot recommend a visit to Newmarket more highly. If you want to stay in style and don't mind a short drive, **Swynford Paddocks** (01638) 570234 is ideal. This outstanding hotel located in Six Mile Bottom has elegant bedrooms and an excellent restaurant. Closer to home, the High Street of Newmarket offers a number of places to stay. The **Rutland Arms** (01638) 664251 and the **White Hart** (01638) 663051 opposite the Jockey Club are both comfortable and convenient, while on the Bury Road, the **Bedford Lodge** (01638) 663175 is a popular racing location. Bar snacks in all the above hotels are good and dining is also available. Lovers of Chinese food should earmark **The Fountain**—pricey but good. A less extravagant, although still highly recommended establishment is **Hill Farmhouse** (01638) 730253 which can be found to the south of the racecourse in Kirtling. A modern, but well located hotel is the **Heath Court** (01638) 667171—ideal for early morning gallops. There are many outstanding hotels in East Anglia. One thinks of **Le Maison Talbooth** (01206) 322367 in Dedham near Colchester (note the outstanding Talbooth restaurant—really first class). In Woodbridge, **Seckford Hall** (01394) 385678 is a supremely comfortable country house hotel, while closer to Newmarket in Bury St Edmunds, the **Angel** (01284) 753926 is a fine house with a first class restaurant. **Ravenwood Hall** (01359) 271542 at Rougham Green is also well placed for visiting racegoers and a warm welcome is assured. Further south in Broxted, the **Whitehall** (01279) 850603 is another appealing manor with a splendid restaurant. The **Great House** (01787) 247431 at Lavenham should not be forgotten either with delicious French and English cooking. Meanwhile at Hintlesham, one finds **Hintlesham Hall** (01473) 852334—a classic stayer with a golf course and some excellent cuisine.

Lovers of pub food will also be spoilt. In Dullingham, the **Kings Head** (01634) 842709 is a friendly, extremely busy racing pub with an excellent restaurant. In nearby Woodditton, another popular pub is the **Three Blackbirds** (01638) 730811, a mere five minute's drive from the Rowley Mile racecourse. Other excellent establishments include two **Red Lions** one at Icklingham (01638) 717802 and one at Hinxton (01799) 530601 good food at both. The **Star** at Lidgate is also a good choice and the racing fraternity are particularly keen on the **Old Plough** at Ashley.

Two Cambridge hotels often used for Newmarket meetings are the **University Arms** (01223) 351241 and the **Garden House** (01223) 259988. The one overlooks Parkers Piece and the other the River Cam—both are excellent. Cambridge is also the perfect town in which to leave the person who may find a day or a week at the races a trifle tedious. Two excellent restaurants to note in the city are **Midsummer House** (01223) 369299 on Midsummer Common or **22 Chesterton Road** (01223) 351880—ideal for pre-sales, or post-racing discussions.

Other restaurants to consider include **Bradfield House** (01284) 386301 at Bradfield Combust—excellent English cooking, but do note the restaurant closes for lunch on Saturday—some rooms here as well. The **Hole in the Wall** (01223) 812282 in Wilbraham is a fine restaurant, but please remember to book in advance. Also in Bury St Edmunds is the **Butterfly** (01284) 760884, with a modern, continental feel, and in nearby Ixworth **Theobalds Restaurant** (01359) 31707 is there for discovering, open fire and all. North of Newmarket one finds the superb cathedral at Ely. In the same town the **Lamb** (01353) 663574 is comfortable while the **Old Fire Engine** (01353) 662582 produces some outstanding food—well worth the trip. If Chinese cooking is

Swynford Paddocks Hotel & Restaurant

Swynford Paddocks is an elegant eighteenth century country house hotel nestling in idyllic countryside with racehorses grazing its pastures. Situated just outside Newmarket, and only six miles from the ancient university city of Cambridge, the hotel is reached easily from both the A11 and A14.

The hotel's 15 bedrooms, each with views of the surrounding countryside, are individually decorated to the highest standards. The intimate panelled restaurant is renowned for its first-class cuisine and features an imaginative menu which changes regularly to take advantage of fresh seasonal fayre.

The hotel's relaxing atmosphere, tranquil surroundings and ample parking make it an ideal venue for all forms of corporate entertainment. The extensive and attractive grounds form an ideal backdrop for any event, while a luxury marquee can accommodate up to 180 guests.

Swynford Paddocks Hotel & Restaurant,
Six Mile Bottom, Newmarket, Suffolk CB8 0UE
Tel: (01638) 570234 Fax: (01638) 570283
web site: www.swynfordpaddocks.com
e mail: sales@swynfordpaddocks.com

SWYNFORD PADDOCKS
HOTEL AND RESTAURANT

Swynford Paddocks Stud

Whether it's a racehorse enjoying a break before resuming its career, convalescence after surgery or a yearling or juvenile embarking on a pre-sales or pre-training regime, we cater for their every need.

A modern dedicated foaling unit allows us to take in expectant mares through to delivery, as well as mares scheduled to be covered. Stallion selection and mare compatibility, timings and budgets, the welfare of mares and foals - we can assist you in your quest for future winners.

For further information please contact the Stud Manager on (01638) 570232, or the hotel.

your style then try the **Peking Duck** (01353) 662063. Another good hotel near Ely is the aptly named **Fenlands Lodge** (01353) 667047, which is comfortable and the restaurant is also good. In Glemsford, a restaurant to short list is **Barretts** (01787) 281573—excellent sauces and a fine wine list. **Stocks Restaurant** (01223) 811202 in Botisham also comes warmly recommended by a man in the know.

In case you have time between racing and opening time, or whatever you happen to be awaiting in Newmarket, we would strongly recommend you visit the National Horseracing Museum, a well thought-out establishment which owes much to the support of Britain's best known owners. The High Street reveals all manner of interesting shops—saddlers, tailors, bookshops and galleries.

With the fabulous array of weekend meetings as well as midweek occasions we will endeavour to recommend some pleasant inns, or pubs with rooms nearby. In Kennett, north of Newmarket, the **Bell** (01638) 750286 is an idea, while to the south, in Kirtling, the **Queens Head** (01638) 731177 will not disappoint. Further afield in Lavenham, the **Swan** (01787) 247477 is a delightful 14th century inn which also boasts a first class restaurant A free house which is a delight to visit is the **Angel** at Lavenham (01787) 247388—good food and some accommodation—ideal. While in Long Melford, three establishments are worth considering: firstly, the excellent **Countrymen at Melford** (01787) 312356 is highly recommended and secondly, the **Bull** (01787) 378494. Finally, **Chimneys** (01787) 379806 is a restaurant with an excellent reputation. **Alfonso's** (01787) 280372 in Cavendish is a splendid Italian restaurant opposite the village green. Returning towards Newmarket, the **Bell** (01638) 717272 at Mildenhall is a fine

all-rounder and is pretty good value. Also consider the **Green Man** at Six Mile Bottom (01638) 570373 it is owned by a very keen racing man and by all accounts an evening here offers that happy combination of quality fayre and good company.

One final thought for the racing enthusiast who also enjoys golf and has a taste for style and elegance—try **Hanbury Manor** (01920) 487722. It is a fair distance from Newmarket but is outstanding in every way. A place to spoil your non-racing partner!

Racing at Newmarket is to be recommended. From the bustling betting shop to the early morning gallops, from a smoke filled boozer to wide open heath, this is quintessentially a racing town and if you are looking for a day or two away in 2000, Newmarket is a worthy favourite.

The July Course

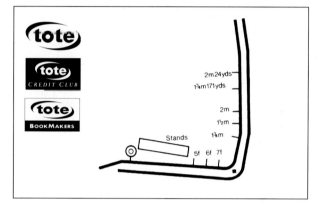

Situated in three acres of secluded gardens, Bedford Lodge Hotel is a striking combination of the classic and the new, possessing a character and ambience all of its own.

Originally built as a hunting lodge for the Duke of Bedford, it has a fascinating history and is charmingly decorated to reflect Newmarket's most famous pastime, horse racing. Recent developments, made in keeping with the existing style, have provided more accommodation, conference and banqueting facilities.

The racing theme is carried through to the hotel's fifty-six luxurious bedrooms all of which have en-suite facilities and are named after racecourses across Britain.

The hotel has an extensive and well equipped leisure complex, that includes pool, sauna, steam room, spa, beauty salon and gym. There are qualified fitness advisers on hand and the complex is available for use by all residents.

Ideally located for you to explore the beautiful local countryside and historic centre of Newmarket, Bedford Lodge has a warm and relaxing atmosphere and the food is magnificent and the service impeccable. The elegant Godolphin Restaurant provides both table d'hôte and à la carte menus daily along with an impressive wine selection.

Bedford Lodge is situated just one hour from London and boasts easy access to the main routes into the region.

Make the event special.

BEDFORD LODGE HOTEL

Bedford Lodge Hotel
Bury Road,
Newmarket,
Suffolk,
CB8 7BX
Tel: (01638) 663175
Fax: (01638) 667391

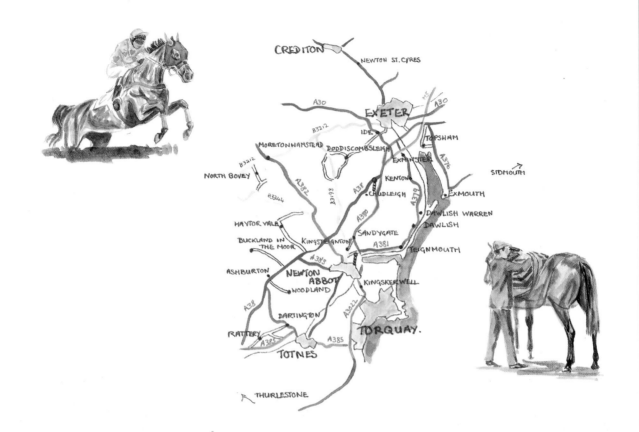

Artist: **Margaret Barrett MUDSLINGERS** *Courtesy of:* **The Artist**

The course is managed by **Pat Masterson** and he will be able to provide details of all the goings on at Newton Abbot. The **Clerk of the Course** is M J Trickey and all enquiries should be directed to **The Racecourse, Kingsteignton Road, Newton Abbot. Tel (01626) 353235, Fax (01626) 336972.**

The racecourse is easily accessible via the M5 joined by the M4 and M6. The course is located just off the A380 which joins the M5. If you are journeying from Cornwall then a number of A roads are convenient. The A38 from Plymouth and the A30 via Okehampton are two obvious selections. It is as well to try to time your journey well because the M5 can get ridiculously one-paced on occasions. Despite the rural setting, the public transport services are good. Trains depart from Paddington and a bus can then be taken from the local station to the racecourse. Helicopters are welcomed at the course and car parking is free unless you wish to park beside the course rails.

The feature races in a busy fixture list of National Hunt racing include the Claude Whitley Memorial Cup Steeplechase and William Hill Hurdle, both £8000 added races in November, along with the Langstone Cliff Hotel Steeplechase and Thurlestone Hotel Hurdle on Boxing Day. The course holds an abundance of meetings in August and the course has just added some summer jumping to its calendar.

Newton Abbot is one of the few racecourses for which there is no Members Enclosure. The two enclosures are the Paddock for which a charge of £11 applies and £5 for the Course Enclosure. Despite the absence of a Members Enclosure, a season ticket can be obtained for £120 which includes 33 reciprocal meetings. People who are holidaying in groups and local people should note the following discount rates. Essentially, if you get ten or more people together you will save £2 per head on admission into the Tattersalls Enclosure if you book in advance. The course has a good selection of sponsors and they generally make use of the private function rooms. Eleven private boxes are also available for hire, some by the day, The Teign Suite has recently been extended and there is also a large sponsors' suite which can accommodate up to 250. However, if you wish to organise a substantial party, do telephone the course to check on availability. An alternative if these rooms are unavailable is to have a marquee in Tattersalls. It is clear however that the course really relies on the passing racegoer and they will be pleased to hear that picnics can be enjoyed at the racecourse—a charge of £1.50 is made for cars parked alongside the rails. If self-catering sounds too much like hard work, then there is the new Terrace Restaurant which overlooks the winning post, along with a self-service carvery and more modest snacks in the bars. Any prior enquiries with regard to catering should be made to the racecourse or alternatively, addressed to the racecourse's caterers Partyfare Ltd. (01626) 331285 or (01404) 43035. Although children are admitted free, there are no special play areas for them. There are three public telephones and disabled people have the benefit of a viewing ramp and a lift in the Grandstand and the Teign Suite.

For those racing fans looking for a long weekend in the country, this is a fabulous answer. The racecourse is extremely welcoming and the standard of racing is not bad. There are also many splendid hostelries nearby in which to spend your ill-gotten gains.

Local Favourites

In Newton Abbot, the **Queens Hotel** (01626) 363133 welcomes visitors before and after racing, as does the excellent **Langstone Cliff Hotel** (01626) 865155. A reasonably priced alternative is the **Lamora Guest House** (01626) 65627. There is also the **Passage House Hotel** (01626) 55515—modern but extremely welcoming—and the **Two Mile Oak** (01803) 812411—really filling bar snacks. One such pub in Kingsteignton is the excellent **Old Rydon Inn** (01626) 54626. Another king this time in Kingskerswell, **Pitt House** (01803) 873374 is a good restaurant in a 15th century thatched dower house.

If you have the chance, visit Dartmouth, where the **Carved Angel** (01803) 832465 is the finest restaurant in the area. Another excellent port of call in this delightful naval town is the **Royal Castle** (01803) 833033. All along the coast one finds nooks and crannies to explore and eventually one arrives at the larger resorts of Paignton, Torbay and Torquay. In Staverton both **Kingston House** (01803) 762235 and the **Sea Trout** (01803) 762274 are worth visiting.

There are all manner of activities to be found in Torquay and having played golf, fished or even after a trip to the races one place to visit is **Remys** (01803) 292359, ideal for dinner. Further round the coast one comes to Teignmouth and the extremely welcoming **Bay Hotel** (01626) 774123. No less excellent is **Thomas Luny House** (01626) 772976, an award-winning, yet relatively inexpensive guesthouse. For people not wishing to visit the coast there are a number of excellent and secluded places to sample. A quiet country inn in which to spend a night is the **Rock Inn** (01364) 661305 in Haytor Vale. In nearby Haytor, the **Bel Alp** (01364) 661217 is an extremely welcoming country house hotel to consider, as is the excellent **Leusdon Lodge** (01364) 631304 in Poundsgate. In Ashburton, the **Holne Chase Hotel** (01364) 631471 is a superb place to stay and it also has a fine restaurant.

There are seven public houses by the name of **Church House** within a small radius. One you should certainly visit is located in Rattery (01364) 642220—a welcoming place for a drink and substantial bar snacks. Another is in **Torbryan** (01803) 812372—typically cosy. Nearer to Newton Abbot is Woodland and the superb **Rising Sun**. The **Hare and Hounds** (01626) 873119 at Kingskerswell has a good carvery the **Barn Owl** (01803) 872130—is extremely friendly and has bedrooms—the **Chasers Arms** (01626) 873119 at Stokeinteignhead is also recommended.

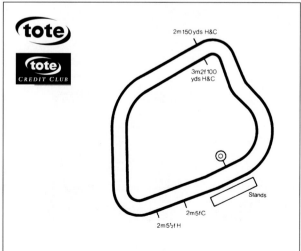

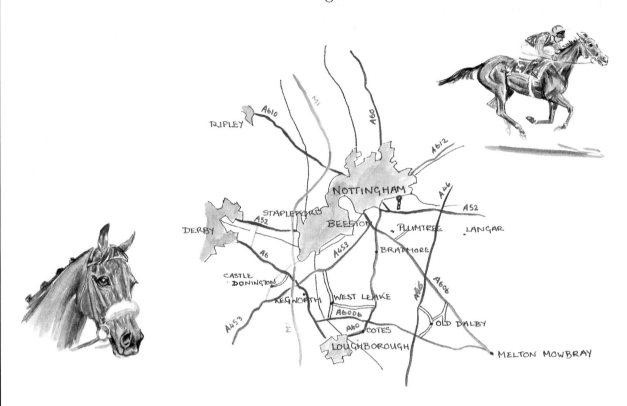

Artist: **Claire Eva Burton** **WALKING OUT** *Courtesy of:* **The Artist**

Nottingham is run by the **Racecourse Manager, Sally Westcott**, ably assisted by **Secretary**, **Ann Whelbourne** and **Events & Leisure co-ordinator, Nina Daly** (the friendliest and best looking team in the Midlands—so they tell us!) **Clerk of the Course** is **Major Charles Moore**. The team can be contacted at **Nottingham Racecourse, Colwick Park, Colwick Road, Nottingham NG2 4BE. Tel (01159) 580620. Fax (01159) 584515.**

The course lies east of the city off the B686 Colwick road. The M1 offers good going but does suffer from the odd tailback. Southbound travellers should exit at junction 25 and follow the A52 to pick up the A6011 at West Bridgford. From there follow the brown tourist signs and the Park & Ride racecourse signs. The A46 from Leicester is an alternative although renowned for one-paced lorries. From the A46, follow the A606 and the A612. The nearest railway station is in the city, two miles from the course (trains leave London from St Pancras). Buses (Nos 20 and 21) leave the city centre every 15 minutes. If you do take the wheels, you will be pleased to hear that all parking is free. Helicopters may land in the centre of the course by prior arrangement with the management.

Nottingham used to be a dual purpose course, but a couple of years ago switched to flat racing only. Even so Annual Members get to enjoy about 24 fixtures from the end of March to the beginning of November. The themed summer evenings of free entertainment have proved to be very popular—demonstrating that when racecourses do offer an extra something it certainly pays off.

In 1999, entrance to the Members Enclosure in the Centenary Stand was £15, the Grandstand in Tattersalls £10 and the Silver Ring £5. Annual Membership costs £145 or £260 for a married couple, including parking and use of the Centenary Stand and Enclosure. A Junior badge for those 16-24 years old costs £80. All annual badges entitle the bearer to a free racecard as well as discounts on admission for their guests, a real incentive to join that should be taken up by other courses. Nottingham also offers discounts for those who pay for their annual membership early. Children under 16 are admitted free if accompanied by an adult.

The Grandstand has also been refurbished. Recent innovations include a new Sheriff of Nottingham bar, a Pizzahut and the Champagne and Seafood bar. The private boxes have capacities of between ten and fifty people. Packages are available to include badges, bar, Bucks Fizz and a meal—contact the racecourse for further information. There is space for a marquee which will take up to 600 guests. The restaurant has been moved to the top floor of the Grandstand and has the best view in the house. It is advisable to book—particularly for window seats! The caterers, Letheby and Christopher can be contacted via the racecourse office (0115) 9580620. If you are going to Nottingham for the first time, please note that a dress code is in effect in the Members and patrons are requested not to wear denim, T-shirts or shorts (ties and polo neck shirts preferred).

Nottingham also provides more than adequate extra facilities. Children have an adventure playground in addition to the playground in the Silver Ring. Disabled people have a viewing stand and a lift in the Centenary Stand. Pay telephones abound although no extra credit is available through the high street banks. This may prove a problem if you get carried away in the off-track betting shops located in Tattersalls and the Silver Ring or in the Tote betting shop. Nottingham's management have a great enthusiasm for the sport. We wish them all well in 2000

Local Favourites

The better hotels in the city are essentially extremely modern affairs. The new **Holiday Inn** (0115) 950 0600 is close to the course and does mean you can avoid the city centre, although all the city facilities are accessible. The **Forte Crest** (0115) 947 0131 is a 13-storey hotel which boasts panoramic views of the city. Alternatively, the **Stakis Nottingham** (0115) 941 9561 should not be ignored. The **Nottingham Moat House** (0115) 941 4444 is another up to date hotel. Outside the city, one hotel geared to the businessman's requirements is the **Forte Post House** (0115) 939 7800 which has good facilities and is extremely convenient for the M1 (junction 25). **Le Tetard** (0115) 959 8253 is French and is convenient for the racecourse (a three mile drive). Other restaurants to consider include the excellent **Sonny's** (0115) 947 3041, and **Higoi** (0115) 942 3379 an excellent Japanese restaurant. **Saagar** (0115) 963 2014 is a particularly good Indian restaurant and **Harts Restaurant** (0115) 9110666 is definitely worth investigation.

Outside the town, one place definitely to visit is the outstanding public house in Old Dalby, the **Crown** (01664) 823134. If you're a real ale fan then this is the pub for you and the pub food in this gorgeous converted farmhouse is excellent. Highly recommended by those at the racecourse is the **Peacock** at Redmile Belvoir. The **Martins Arms** in Colston Bassett (01949) 81361 also warrants attention—good food and accomodation here. There is also a restaurant in which you can dine in the evenings. Although it is a bit of a trek, **Stapleford Park** (01572) 84522 just outside Melton Mowbray is excellent. Although expensive, this 16th century marvel is worth every penny for a luxurious stay and good food. The **Priest House** (01232) 810649 has a delightful setting and is handy for the M1. In Plumtree, **Perkins** (0115) 937 3695 offers a tempting menu off the blackboard and this makes for an ideal post-racing spot. Another quiet pub in which to reflect on the day to come, or just gone by, is the **Star** at West Leake. The **Victoria** at Beeston will appeal to real ale aficionados. The **Village Hotel and Leisure Club** (0115) 946 4472 is also one to note as is **Risley Hall** (0115) 939 9000 an appealing hotel. The **White House** has a fine setting, overlooking the waters of the River Soar and the **White Lady** (01623) 797447 in Newstead Abbey is a restaurant worth paying a visit. In Castle Donington, the **Cross Keys** (01332) 812214 has good food and a cosy atmosphere. Finally, the **Royal Horseshoes** in Waltham-on-the-Wolds is a pleasant village pub with above average accommodation—ideal for lovers of England's countryside.

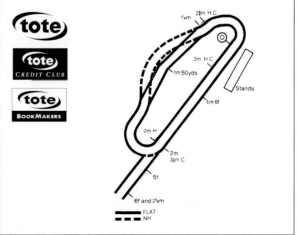

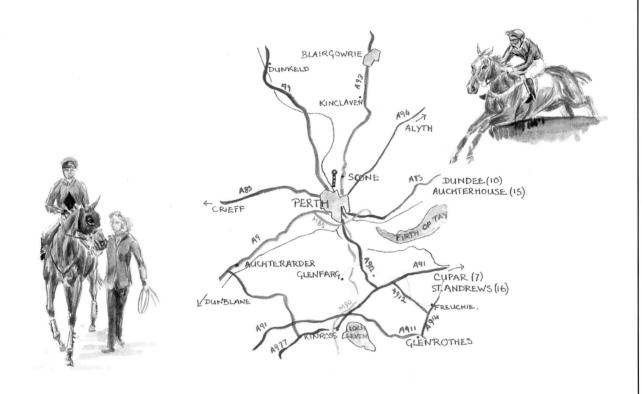

Artist: **Margaret Barrett SAFELY OVER** *Courtesy of:* **The Artist**

Murrayshall Country House Hotel and Golf Course

The Murrayshall Country House Hotel and Golf Course is only four miles from Perth, set in 300 acres of parkland. The hotel has a traditional country house style and the bedrooms offer en suite facilities, direct dial telephones and televisions with magnificent views overlooking the golf course to the Grampian Mountains.

Guests dine in the Old Masters Restaurant, which offers a wide selection of dishes with the emphasis on quality Scottish fare. Adjacent to the hotel is the clubhouse, which provides informal dining throughout the day

The 6420 yard, 18 hole, par 73 course is interspersed with magnificent specimen trees lining the fairways, water hazards and white sanded bunkers to offer a challenge to all golfers. Buggies and sets of clubs are available for hire. There are various types of membership available to the course including a competitively priced country membership to golfers residing more than 50miles/80kms from Murrayshall golf course. Alan Reid, the resident professional, is pleased to give tuition from half an hour to a week's course. Should the weather be inclement, tuition is given in the indoor golf facility. Golf breaks and golf schools are available throughout the year.

Other sporting activities include tennis, croquet and bowls. However, situated only a few miles from the famous salmon waters in the River Tay, even closer to Perth racecourse only one mile from the hotel, Murrayshall is uniquely placed to make it an attractive venue for whatever might bring you to this area of Scotland.

Private dining and conference facilities are available in both the hotel and clubhouse. Conference organisers, requiring the best of service for their senior delegates, will find Murrayshall the ideal conference haven.

Murrayshall is the ideal venue to entertain guests, whether it be golf related or a meal before or after the races. Corporate golf packages are offered at all three courses with the opportunity to place your company name and logo on a tee and to reserve the course for your company golf day. Golf societies and green fee players are welcome. A second golf course is well on its way to completion, with play anticipated early in the millennium.

Murrayshall Country House Hotel and Golf Course
Scone
Perthshire
PH2 7PH
Tel: (01738) 551171
Fax: (01738) 552595
Pro shop: (01738) 552784

This friendly course is run by **Sam Morshead** as **General Manager** and **Clerk of the Course** while **Lucy Whitaker** is **Secretary** and **Treasurer**. They can be found at **Perth Racecourse, Scone Palace Park, Perth PH2 6BB. Tel (01738) 551597 Fax (01738) 553021 web site: www.perth. races.co.uk**

Although Perth is Britain's most northerly racecourse, some 450 miles from London, it is fairly accessible from all quarters of the country. When you reach Perth by car watch out for new Tourist Board signs for Scone Palace which will conveniently take you to the racecourse itself. Edinburgh is 44 miles away and the M90 can be taken from Edinburgh via the Forth Bridge, making your way through the Ochil Hills and past Loch Leven—a wonderful drive. The A9 struggles through the beautiful Perthshire countryside via Aviemore, Blair Atholl, Pitlochry and Blairgowrie. Even the train picks out numerous beauty spots as it shunts north from Edinburgh and the distant Kings Cross in London, and there is a free bus service to the course from the Perth town centre. Helicopters may be landed by prior arrangement while aircraft should be landed at Scone aerodrome some two miles away. Car parking at the racecourse is plentiful and free.

The wooded parkland of Scone Palace is the setting for this superbly picturesque course. The fixture list is well designed and all the meetings are run over two or three days. The sponsorship at the course is particularly good and this, coupled with the general popularity of the course, ensures some good fields. Meetings take place in late April, mid May and early June, mid August and September, with an evening meeting in July, although these fixtures have yet to be confirmed. The main race of the year is the £12,000 added three mile chase at the Festival Meeting in April, sponsored by The Press & Journal. Visitors to Perth can also take in trotting races at various times of the year, including a new fixture in July.

The rates for the various enclosures are as follows: Members £14, £8 for the Paddock Enclosure, with pensioners and students at £4, and a mere £2 for the Course Enclosure. The Annual Membership subscription for 1999 was set at £85 for a single badge with a £145 charge for a double badge and £45 for a Junior Membership. There are discounts of £2 per person for clans of 15 strong or more which applies to Tattersalls only. This enclosure has been enlarged to allow people to get nearer the last fence and hurdle and an additional uncovered viewing area has been put up in the same area. All enclosures have excellent views of the course and its sweeping wooded turns. However, if you're one of those people who hate to be parted from your car then centre course parking is an option at a price of £5 good value for picnic lovers

The Grandstand is delightfully compact and allows for a superb atmosphere as the well backed favourite strides by. Private boxes which will accommodate between 20 and 30 people can be arranged with the General Manager, with full catering facilities to fit the required budget. There is now an excellent stand for corporate hospitality and private parties which can cater for parties from 16 to 50, all with private viewing facilities. There are restaurants in all the enclosures and the course caterers are Wheatsheaf Catering Ltd. There are telephones at the course and viewing ramps for the disabled. Special facilities for children are now provided during the August holiday fixture.

A new owners and trainers bar was recently added as well as a new parade ring with winner's enclosure. The old saddling boxes have been renovated to create three new hospitality boxes and new saddling boxes and pre-parade ring have been built. Improved facilities in the centre of the course now offer snack & bar facilities & an improved Tote area. Perth may be Britain's most northerly

track but it is also one of the country's most attractive—it's no small wonder that Perth has been voted the best small course in the North four times in the past eight years.

Local Favourites

In Perth, the **Hunting Tower** (01738) 583771 is a comfortable place in which to stay. Excellent value accommodation is plentiful in Perth with **Clark Kimberley** (01738) 637406 and the **Clunie Guest House** (01738) 623625 providing comfort and style. **Number Thirty Three** (01738) 633771 in George Street is a seafood restaurant to note **Let's Eat** (01738) 643377 is also good. The **Stakis Perth** (01738) 628281 is extremely well run and worthy of attention. Kingfauns Castle (01738) 620777 a renowned 17th century castle is also first class. An hotel exceptionally close to the racecourse is **Murrayshall House** (01738) 551171 in New Scone. The hotel offers a fine restaurant and a championship golf course and comes thoroughly recommended. An alternative idea is to visit Auchterhouse where the **Old Mansion House** (01382) 320366 provides an outstanding hotel-restaurant double. People making use of the A94 should note Alyth and here, the **Lands of Loyal Hotel** (01828) 633151 is a pleasant and reasonably priced country house hotel in which to stay. Eastwards, one finds Blairgowrie, home of a wonderful golf course, Rosemount. South of the town in Kinclaven by Stanley, the **Ballathie House** (01250) 885268 has another gorgeous Tayside setting. Another outstanding hotel to consider is **Dalmunzie House** (01250) 885224, family run and welcoming—cottages are also available in the grounds for those who prefer the more independent life.

Another majestic place is, of course, **Gleneagles Hotel** (0764) 662231. Not only are there superb golf courses but the hotel exudes class—a first rate establishment in every way. More modest but still friendly accomodation can be found at the **Glenfarg Hotel** (01577) 830241. En route to England, try Cleish near Kinross, where **Nivingston House** (01577) 850216 offers an inviting restaurant and some comfortable accommodation. We should also alert you to two outstanding establishments, one at Dunblane, the other at Dunkeld. **Cromlix House** (01786) 822125 is superb and the restaurant is one of Scotland's finest. **Kinnaird House** (01796) 482440 is another hotel and restaurant that oozes class and is a great place to celebrate if the right horse wins—note the excellent game fishing here. Another hotel to please game fishermen is **Dunkeld House Hotel** (01350) 727771 a delightful riverside setting for this welcoming establishment. Just outside Perth **Dupplin Castle** (01738) 623224 is family run, extremely welcoming and thoroughly relaxing. Ideal after a tight finish in the last.

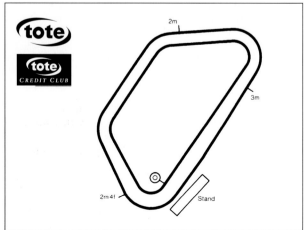

MUD, SWEAT AND TEARS
by Margaret Barrett   15" x 18"

ALDANITI IN RETIREMENT
by Claire Eva Burton   19" x 22"

ALL OUT
by Constance Halford-Thompson   15" x 20"

LAMMTARRA/PENTIRE KING - KING GEORGE VI
& QUEEN ELIZABETH DIAMOND STAKES, ASCOT
by Mike Heslop   17³/⁴" x 21³/⁴"

OUT OF THE STALLS
by Constance
Halford-Thompson
12" × 16"

ON THE BEACH,
LAYTOWN
by Constance
Halford-Thompson
12" × 16"

DANCING BRAVE - PRIX DE L'ARC DE TRIOMPHE
by Mike Heslop   14" x 25" or 7" x 12"

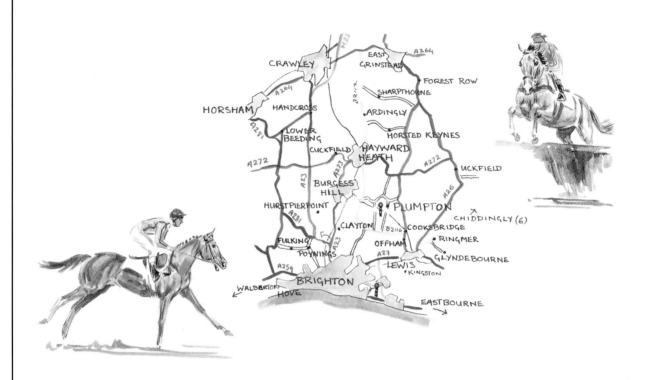

Artist: **Malcolm Coward BOTTOMS UP, PLUMPTON** _Courtesy of:_ **Sally Mitchell Fine Arts**

Plumpton is a well run friendly racecourse within easy striking distance of London. **Grant Knowles** is **Chief Executive** of the racecourse, **Mrs Lorna Bromley-Martin** is **Manager** and **Clerk of the Course** is **David McHarg** they can be contacted at the racecourse office on **(01273) 890383. Fax: (01273) 891557.**

Plumpton lies approximately 50 miles from London, midway between Haywards Heath and Lewes. The M23 is the best route south but after this, the motorist is left with various A and B roads. The A23, the A273 and the B2112 seem the likely routes to punt on. From Brighton and the south coast, the A27 Lewes road coupled with the A273 should oblige. The course lies in the village of Plumpton Green. The quaint name of this village reflects its unspoilt character but the quiet is occasionally broken by the train. This is good news for racegoers though, as the station lies beside the course. The best idea is to catch the Victoria-Hastings train to Plumpton Station. There is also a free Bus Service from Brighton to Plumpton on racedays. It you can't spare the time to train it, helicopters are able to land at the racecourse. For parking, there is a charge no unless you venture into the centre of the course with a picnic in mind, in which case, it will cost £6 per person. 2000 should follow the same pattern as last year with 16 days racing and, as with many of the smaller National Hunt courses, the Easter meeting proves to be the most popular.

The prices for entry into Plumpton's Members Enclosure are £14 and children under 15 are allowed in free of charge. Adults are required to pay £10. A similar arrangement exists in the Course Enclosure where adults pay £6. If you wish to join the Members at Plumpton on an annual basis, then the cost is £125. You will also be entitled to 18 reciprocal days of equestrian sport at other racecourses. Further news to report is that parties of 20 or more receive a 20 per cent discount in any of the three enclosures.

For people wishing to do some entertaining, Plumpton racecourse may have the answer. Bookings for Private Boxes for groups 10-40 guests are offered and should be made through the Racecourse. Box rental is from £100 per meeting. Additional rooms accommodating up to 70 guests are also available and marquee sites are ideally located for entertainment of larger parties. For all catering requirements contact Appetance, which has recently taken over this function, (01273) 401777.

Snacks are available throughout the various enclosures. The Members restaurant and bar, and the downstairs Member's Paddock Bar have been enlarged and refurbished. The racecourse can provide packages in the restaurant for parties of 6 or more who do not wish to hire private boxes. There are bars in all the enclosures and a speciality seafood bar in Tatts. Snacks are available throughout the various enclosures. Special facilities to keep children occupied when they get tired of watching the racing, are available at the New Year, Easter and Countryside Raceday Meetings.

This delightful course, does provide good entertainment and we are delighted to hear of its continuing improvements which have recently included spending a quarter of a million pounds to upgrade the grandstand facilities in all areas. If you have not visited Plumpton before, we would warmly recommend a midweek winter afternoon where good racing in a pleasant atmosphere is assured.

Local Favourites

We start at a pinnacle of excellence, some way north of Plumpton—**Gravetye Manor** (01342) 810567 in Gravetye, south of East Grinstead. Another top hotel can be found at Cuckfield, **Ockendon Manor** (01444) 416111—the building is 16th century and the traditional open fires and panelling add immense charm to the excellent facilities. The restaurant is also particularly well thought of. Ashdown Forest has some delightful scenery and an excellent base from which to explore is the **Chequers Inn** (01342) 824394 at Forest Row. In Lower Beeding, **South Lodge** (01403) 891711 is an attractive restaurant and boasts some excellent accommodation within. For lovers of luxury, a final recommendation here is for **Horsted Place** (01825) 750581 near Uckfield, where both the rooms and the restaurant are of a standard seldom equalled.

Much further south, one arrives in the extremely pleasant Sussex town of Lewes. Here one finds an hotel engulfed by a roaming creeper—**Shelleys** (01273) 472361. There are a number of restaurants in Lewes. **Pailin** (01273) 473906 is a fine one where imaginative cooking ensures delightful eating. Staying in this part of the world need not cost a fortune and for the avid bargain hunters **Millers** (01273) 475631 should fit the bill. In Ditchling the **Bull** (01273) 843147 is a pleasant coaching inn. While restaurants come and go, pubs generally stand their ground. In Fulking, the **Shepherd and Dog** is a pleasant small country pub and the bar snacks here are excellent. Closer to the racecourse at Clayton, the **Jack and Jill** is also a friendly place while the **Rainbow Arms** in Cooksbridge is welcoming and provides good bar snacks too. Another pub with a good restaurant is aptly named the **Stewards Enquiry** on the Lewes Road near Ringmer. The **Highlands** in Uckfield is another establishment patronised by those in search of good fare. Not too far away we find Chiddingly's the **Six Bells**—most appealing with old beams and excellent snacks as well as some good beers. In Horsted Keynes, try the **Green Man** or the excellent **Gardners Arms** at Ardingly, more excellent snacks in an ancient and traditional free house. Another fairly convenient stop could be made at the **Hare and Hounds**, a pleasant village pub east of Uckfield. Racegoers who like country pubs with charm, should try **Juggs** in Kingston. Rustic to the core, it is a country pub for a country course. Finally, a selection of pubs in Plumpton Green that come recommended by those who run the course - the aptly named **Winning Post**, **The Fountain** and **The Plough**. In Plumpton itself the **Half Moon** also comes highly recommended. Just a few to consider when planning your racing in 2000.

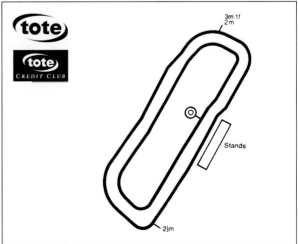

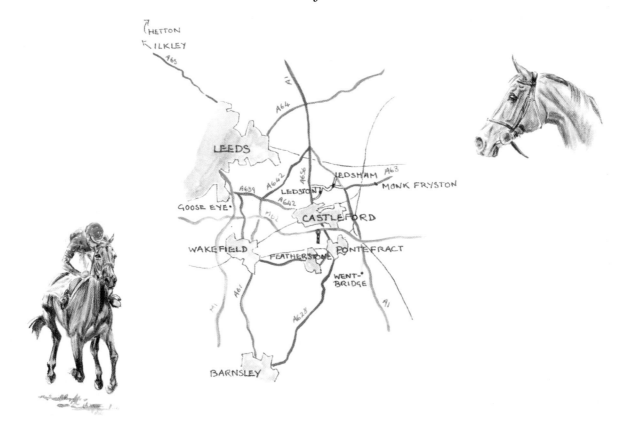

Artist: **Margaret Barrett** **TURNING FOR HOME** *Courtesy of:* **The Artist**

A lot of hard work goes into making Pontefract one of the most popular racecourses in the north of England. The man in charge of this most progressive of courses is **Norman Gundill**, who acts as **Clerk, Manager** and **Secretary**. He can be contacted at **The Racecourse, Pontefract Park, Pontefract. Tel (01977) 702210** (racedays only) or at **33 Ropergate, Pontefract WF8 1LE. Tel (01977) 703224 Fax (01977) 600577.**

The course is marvellously situated for motorway access, the entrance being only half a mile from junction 32 of the M62 making it an excellent location for racegoers from almost all areas of the country. Leeds lies nine miles west of Pontefract and the A1 and M1 and M18 are all within ten miles of the course. Although there are plenty of busy rail stations nearby, Doncaster, York and Leeds, Pontefract is not on a main line station so this is probably a course where one should take the car. There are vast car parking areas and all parking is free, other than the Special Reserve Park, where a charge of £10 is levied. Buses are an option too, with those from Pontefract and Leeds passing the gates. If you are in a particular hurry, there are ample open playing fields in the park in which to place one's helicopter. You must check with the Secretary first though, just in case some other activity is taking place.

A few years ago the Paddock section of the main stand was extended and a new Dalby Stand was built, greatly adding to the amenities at the course and there is now a new Tote facility which will serve the Third Ring. The course was granted an additional evening meeting in June and a Sunday fixture in August. Charges for 1999 were £14 for a daily membership, £9 for entrance to the Paddock, £4 for the Silver Ring and £2.50 for the Third Ring. The best value, however, is the Third Ring car park which cost £5 per car and includes up to four people. If you wish to become an Annual Member the adult single badge is priced at £105, whilst a husband and wife team can be members for the very reasonable sum of £140. The prices for 2000 will probably stay the same.

Annual Members are also entitled to reciprocal meetings at Thirsk, Doncaster, Haydock Park, Beverley, Newcastle, Market Rasen, Nottingham and Catterick. The racecourse executive is also to be applauded for reciprocal meetings at a variety of Yorkshire County Cricket Club venues including Headingley and Sheffield. The course also offers special discounts for parties in all racecourse enclosures. Contact the Secretary for further details.

For those wishing to entertain guests at Pontefract, although the Club Chalet has been made into a bar for Owners and Trainers and is no longer available for private parties, the Private Room in the Main Stand looks directly out over the course and larger parties can be accommodated in the Entertainment Suite. The private boxes in the Dalby Stand certainly appear good value. The stand was built on the site of the old Club entrance and Champagne Bar. Each box seats up to 20 and the stand itself faces down the finishing straight, overlooks the horsewalk and has views over the Parade Ring—a superb place at which to make the most of a day's racing. Charges vary so it is best to contact the racecourse for details. Pontefract would certainly be a tremendous place to have a company summer party with a difference. Catering arrangements should be made directly with the racecourse caterers, Craven Gilpin & Sons (0113) 2876387.

Snack bars can be found throughout the course and more substantial food can be found in the Club and Paddock restaurants. Finally, should you wish to have a picnic, the place to go is the Third Ring car park on the stands side. Both the stands serving the Silver Ring and the Third Ring are being refurbished. There is a special playground for the youngsters in the Third Ring and if under 16 they will be admitted free when accompanied by an adult.

A fully supervised crèche operates in the Third Ring at holiday meetings at Easter and August and at evening meetings. Another good reason to go racing at this friendly, well run racecourse.

Local Favourites

Pontefract is ideally placed for venturing further north, and one place that should be visited is Ilkley—a little distant but well worth the trek. Here, **Rombalds** (01943) 603201 is a really excellent place to stay—home comforts and a warm Yorkshire welcome are the order of the day. What's more, if you happen to wake up a little hungry on Sunday morning after an evening at Pontefract, fear not, their Edwardian breakfast is an absolute monster and should keep the largest of wolves from the door. Ilkley is cluttered with some delightful antique shops. The **Box Tree** (01943) 608484 is a celebrated restaurant to note. The **Grove** (01943) 600298 is also well thought of. Closer to the course Leeds has a few good fancies (see Wetherby).

Returning to more local spots, one should consider some places in which to have an ale or two. In Ledsham, the **Chequers** is an enormously popular free house, resplendent with oak beams and open fires. In Ledston's Main Street, one finds an equine establishment, the **White Horse** and another warm welcome and fire, so I understand. The **Greyhound** in Saxton is also a pleasing Yorkshire hostelry. In Wentbridge, the **Wentbridge House Hotel** (01977) 620444 is a glorious, early 18th century hotel, very cosy and well appointed, standing in 15 acres of grounds. The restaurant here is well thought of, a fine place to visit prior to the racecourse and perfect for a post race celebration. Another historic and worthy entry to the Pontefract shortlist is found at Monk Fryston. Here, **Monk Fryston Hall** (01977) 682369 has pleasant interiors and formal gardens as well as a more modern wing. **Rogerthorpe Manor Country House Hotel** in nearby Badsworth (01977) 643839 comes personally recommended by the racecourse management making it a fine place to stay when visiting Pontefract in 2000.

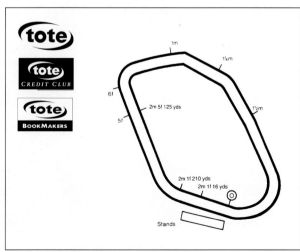

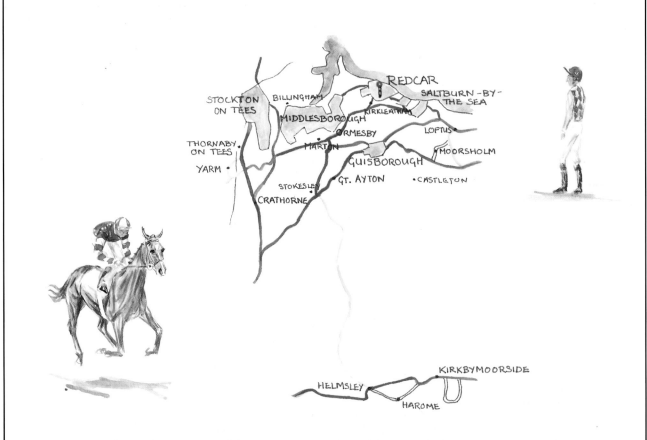

Artist: **Terence Gilbert** **THE FINISH** *Courtesy of:* **The Artist**

The team in charge at Redcar is headed by the Chairman, **Lord Zetland**, ably assisted by **Mr J E Gundill, Clerk of the Course and General Manager**. They can be contacted at **Redcar Racecourse, Redcar, Cleveland TS10 2BY. Tel (01642) 484068 Fax (01642) 488272.** International Racecourse Management are also part of the impressive executive structure. Together they form as fine a team as you will find in racing and continuing improvements at the racecourse are evidence of this.

Redcar racecourse is located in the south of this coastal town to the north east of the Yorkshire Moors. Redcar is accessible by road from the A19 dual carriageway, which passes within 15 minutes of the racecourse (via the Parkway). The A19 links to the south with the A1 at Dishforth and to the north at Newcastle. Travellers from the east will find the A67 and the A66 routes the most direct into Redcar and the racecourse. The nearest railway station is in the town itself, a distance of approximately half a mile from the track—a ten minute walk at the most! A fast train service runs from Kings Cross to Darlington where you can catch the local train to Redcar or a 268 or 269 bus. The bus station is a mere 150 yard hike from the Grandstand—perfect. There are ample free parking facilities with three major areas for cars and coaches. People using light aircraft should ring Mr Towers on (01642) 485419. There is a landing strip 660 metres long. Full details are available from Mr Towers, but beware the 250 volt powerlines to the east! Helicopters may land on the course with prior warning.

The principal racing days here include the Spring Bank Holiday Monday with other days in June, July, August and September. Two of the feature races are the Zetland Gold Cup, which will be worth some £20,000 in prize money, and also the £100,000 Comcast Teesside Two Year Old Trophy which is the focal point of Redcar's racing calendar.

Annual Membership in 1999 was priced at £98 and £40 for Juniors (under 25). The charge for Joint Membership. was £145. Annual Membership includes a car pass for each meeting plus the use of a private room, bar, catering and Tote kiosk. The use of a private bar is an excellent concept and one which all the racecourses should adopt for their annual patrons. The daily admissions for the Members, Tattersalls and the Course were priced at £14, £9 and £3 respectively. OAP's receive discounted admission in Tattersalls of £4.50 and only £1.50 for the Course enclosure. The racecourse offers a discount to parties of 12 or more, reducing the daily prices to £10 for the Club, £5 for Tattersalls and £2 for the Course and one free ticket is included with pre-booked groups of 12 tickets. The stand facilities are excellent and the colourful flower beds form a cheerful feature—all further indications of the management's eagerness to please.

The course will be happy to provide information with regard to boxes, conference suites and rooms for smaller gatherings. The Paddock Rooms have added a new dimension to Redcar's facilities as a fully self-contained entertainment centre with magnificent spectating facilities and suites to cater for between 35 and 140. A major refurbishment has been carried out during the past few years, completely renovating the facilities which now include the Crow's Nest viewing restaurant with full table service, while the Voltigeur restaurant has a carvery. The Classic Suite provides great corporate hospitality and caters for up to 120 guests. The four luxurious executive boxes cater for 8-12 guests (Silver Service) or 15 + if Buffet-style menu. Last year a new Winning Enclosure bar was added as well as a food hall for Tatts patrons. For those whose punting instincts are stronger than their hunger or thirst, the new state-of-the-art Tote Betting shop will serve admirably. Catering is handled by Romfords (01642) 478024 or (01434) 688864. Please contact John Toner the Catering Manager.

Children are admitted free if under the age of 16 and accompanied and there is a playground provided. Other facilities include a viewing ramp for the disabled opposite the winning post, and lavatories for the disabled in all enclosures. Although there are no special banking facilities, public telephones are available for any necessary credit punts and there is a Tote betting shop. Go and visit and try one of the Tote's new bets in 2000.

Local Favourites

The north east of England may not enjoy the most illustrious of reputations elsewhere, but in this case ignorance is not bliss. Few who venture this far north are in any hurry to leave. In Crathorne, near Yarm, there is an extremely fine hotel the **Crathorne Hall Hotel** (01642) 700398. The hotel enjoys a splendid setting and it is thoroughly welcoming—a good choice. In Yarm itself, **Santoro** (01642) 781305 is a good Italian restaurant to note. At Staddle Bridge, **McCoys at the Tontine** (01609) 882671 is a great name for a truly delightful hotel run by the McCoy brothers with a genuine 1930s feel. In Stockton-on-Tees, the **Swallow Hotel** (01642) 679721 boasts extremely comfortable accommodation and is high on the list of visiting business people. **Romanby Court** (01609) 774918 is a fine restaurant to consider in Northallerton, **Solberge Hall** (01609) 779191 is also good.

If the bustle of the city centre hotels are not to your liking then you may care to try the **Grinkle Park Hotel** in Loftus (01287) 640515—the parkland setting of this Victorian hotel is especially attractive. Alternatively, why not sample the luxurious **Ayton Hall** (01642) 723595 in Great Ayton. **Manor House Farm** (01642) 722384 is somewhat smaller and can be found at Ingleby Greenhow. Farther afield in Goathland, the **Mallyan Spout Hotel** (01947) 86206 is recommended. The **Endeavour** in Staithes (01947) 840825 is a really splendid restaurant.

There are several pubs to note in the area and one such establishment is the **Ship** at Saltburn-by-the-Sea, splendid seafood, snacks and good views—well worth a trip out. Farther west in Egglescliffe, the **Blue Bell** (01642) 780358 has good food as well as fine views of the River Tees. A little further afield the **Horse Shoe** at Egton Bridge (01947) 895245 has a lovely setting and good value bedrooms a similar description can be applied to the **Duke of Wellington** (01287) 660351 in Danby. A peaceful atmosphere in which to peruse your Racing Post and consider the day ahead at Redcar races.

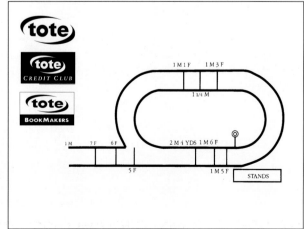

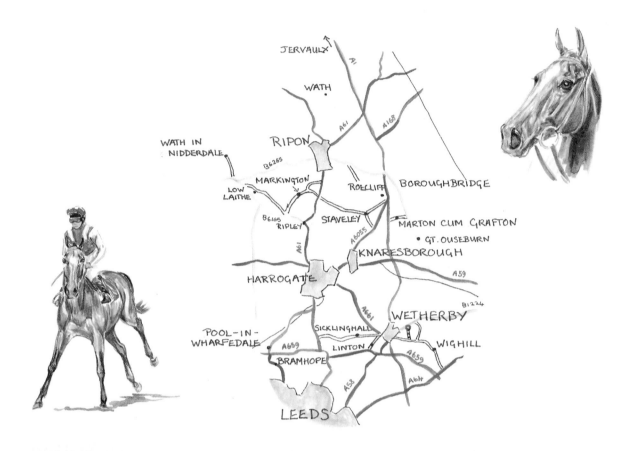

Artist: **Philip Toon COOL IN THE SHADE** *Courtesy of:* **The Artist**

The authorities are headed by **Michael Hutchinson** who acts as **Managing Director** and is assisted by **Clerk of the Course, James Hutchinson.** They can be contacted at 77 North Street, Ripon, North Yorkshire HG4 1DS. Tel (01765) 602156 Fax (01765) 690018.

The most obvious way to get to Ripon is by car for there is no train station at the town itself and while trains do stop at Harrogate, the nearest major station is at York which is some 23 miles away. If you do wish to travel by train then the King's Cross line is the one to board. London itself lies 200 miles away and the best way of reaching the racecourse from the south is to use the A1/A1(M). The course is two miles east of Ripon, off the B6265 which in turn is just four miles from the A1. The A61 from Leeds and Harrogate is a useful road from the south and this, together with the A19, will assist racegoers from the north east. Similar access is provided by the A61 from Thirsk for those travelling from the east. A new bypass to the east of the city takes you directly to the course. There are ample parking areas at the racecourse and this is provided free. If people are hurrying to the course then helicopters are a welcome option provided you give prior warning.

The spring and summer months play host to Ripon's race meetings and August is particularly crowded with excellent fixtures. The William Hill Great St Wilfrid Handicap (£25,000) is the feature race whilst many a good entry is attracted by the Champion Two Year Old Trophy (£20,000). Lovers of summer sports who enrol as Members of Ripon will also be offered a taste of another splendid summer game—cricket. Annual Members are given nine days' complimentary Yorkshire cricket, as well as reciprocal meetings at Newcastle, Haydock, Doncaster, Redcar, Catterick, Market Rasen, Hexham and Pontefract. Membership for husband and wife is £135, a single badge £90 and a junior (under 21) is required to pay a £60 subscription. If you are able to justify only the occasional visit to Ripon then daily badges cost £14 in the Club, £9 in Tattersalls, and £4 and £3 in the Silver Ring and Course Enclosures. Children under 16 are admitted free as long as they are accompanied.

Various group discounts are available for Tattersalls and the Silver Ring. Starting with parties of 20 or more and becoming more generous as the numbers increase. A 50 per cent discount is given to parties which can scramble together 250 people. I would have thought. If you are looking for an afternoon with slightly more than the average entry badge allows, then a range of boxes is available for hire, catering for between 25 and 100 people. If you require precise details, contact the course as they have an excellent printed brochure. These offer good value but don't forget to sort out the catering at the same time. For bigger parties a marquee area is available in the Paddock but there is not too much room and if you are organising a bigger event, there is also a location available in the car park adjacent to the Paddock. Taking a car and four passengers into the course enclosure for £10 offers excellent value.

There are restaurants and snack bars in all enclosures—parts of the Members' and Tattersalls stands have been rebuilt, increasing and improving the facilities available—while new railings around the Parade Ring create a smart appearance and give added protection for both horses and people. As an added attraction, music lovers will enjoy a variety of music from Ripon's award-winning re-creation of a Victorian bandstand. Ripon was the first course to have a children's playground and there are now two—one on either side of the course—marvellous. Other details to note are that there are telephones in the Paddock, Silver Ring and Course enclosures. Disabled racegoers are well catered for in all rings with reserved car parking. There are William Hill operated betting shops in all Rings. Those

of you who have not visited Ripon should give it a try. It is fondly called the 'Garden Racecourse' and is one of the most pleasing in the country.

Local Favourites

Ripon has much to offer to the sightseer—notably Fountains Abbey, Ripon Cathedral, Newby Hall and the recently re-opened canal. Ripon's leading hotel the **Ripon Spa** (01765) 602172 is a particularly racing orientated abode, while the **Unicorn** (01765) 602202 is a traditional coaching inn. Less glamorous, but quite agreeable accommodation can also be had at the **Crescent Lodge Guest House** (01765) 602331. One pub within sight of the course **The Blackamoor Inn** comes highly recommended. The **Old Deanery** (01765) 603518 is a charming restaurant with rooms which is particularly well fancied.

In Markington the **Hob Green Hotel** (01423) 770031 is another extremely restful place to stay with award winning gardens and excellent food. Great character and some good accommodation can be found in the **Sportsman's Arms** (01423) 711306 in Wath-in-Nidderdale. If you love the country, stay here—it's a charming setting and the food is also first class as is the **Yorke Arms** (01423) 755243 at Ramsgill. The **Rose Manor Hotel** (01423) 322245 is also well thought of and can be found in Boroughbridge.

Harrogate will also make a good base while you visit Yorkshire. An 18th century building with an extremely attractive setting is a fair description of the splendid **Studley Hotel** (01423) 560425 where a good restaurant is complemented by comfortable accommodation. **Rudding Park** (01423) 871350 will appeal to golfers as well as racegoers. The value of staying in Harrogate is that firstly one can leave one's non-racing partner in a delightful town in which to browse and secondly, in the evening one has a number of restaurants to visit. The **Drum and Monkey** (01423) 502650 is good, downstairs—a bustling bar and superb food, upstairs a more formal and extremely popular dining room. **The Bistro** (01423) 530708 is also good. Racing devotees may wish to visit **Grundy's** (01423) 502610.

For people who have to rush home the same day then a few options before you set sail. In Staveley, the **Royal Oak** (01423) 340267 is a welcoming country pub with good food while in Roecliffe, the **Crown** (01423) 322578 is another great little pub. Other public houses handy for the A1 include the **Olde Punch Bowl** in Marton cum Grafton and the **Ship at Aldborough**—note the Roman connection here. The **Sawley Arms** in Sawley is highly recommended for meals. A final tip before we leave this area—**The George** at Wormald Green (01765) 677214, is sure to impress if price is no object. Racing at Ripon can be competitive and will need a clear head. A trip in 2000 is recommended.

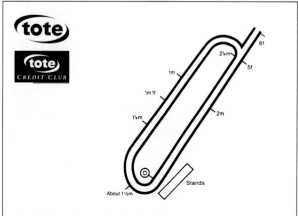

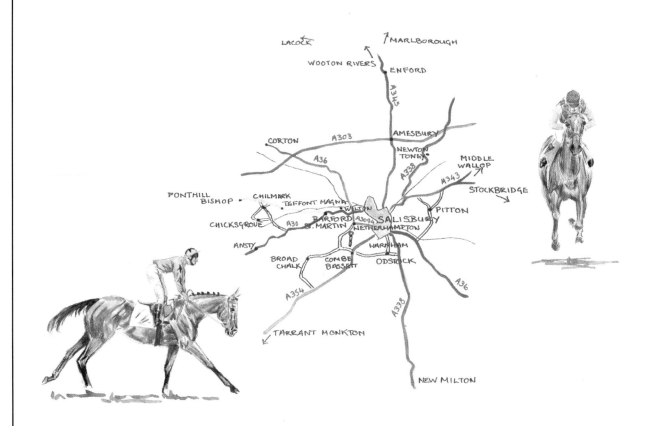

Artist: **Brian Halton SETTLE** *Courtesy of:* **The Artist**

Salisbury

Salisbury is an enchanting racecourse and keen racegoers should definitely make the effort to attend a meeting here in 2000. **Ian Renton** runs Salisbury as the **Clerk of the Course**. He can be contacted at **Salisbury Racecourse, Netherhampton, Wiltshire SP2 8PN** or on **(01722) 326461/327327 Fax (01722) 412710.**

The racecourse is located three and a half miles south west of Salisbury on the A3094. The best plan is to aim for the town and from there you should follow the signs to the racecourse. The A360 is the best route from the north. For people heading from the east or the west of the country the A30 is ideal. Other modes of transport to be considered are the train/bus double. The first leg is the Waterloo-Salisbury line which should be coupled with a courtesy bus from Salisbury station to the racecourse. If you wish to use the helicopter then there is no problem—as long as you telephone the management in advance. There are excellent car parking facilities at the course which are provided free of charge.

In 2000, racing will likely follow the same format as in 1999 with the major meeting again being the Bibury Meeting which takes place in late June. The feature race on the card is the Champagne Stakes worth £15,000. Other major races of the season are the Upavon Fillies Stakes (£25,000) in August and the Dick Poole Stakes (£12,000) in September.

There are two evening meetings scheduled for July and there is entertainment for the children and jazz bands and barbecues add a certain spice to some competitive racing. Additionally, the Sunday meeting in May is well worth a visit when plenty of entertainment is laid on for all the family to accompany an excellent programme of racing.

Admission prices may increase slightly in 2000 but last year the visitor was asked £14 for the Members, £10 for Tattersalls and £5 for the Course Enclosure. Children are admitted free, if accompanied. If you wish to become an Annual Member the rate is £105. However, in addition you receive a car pass and eleven reciprocal meetings plus, of course, the prestige of belonging to the oldest known racing club still in existence — the Bibury.

If you wish to organise a party at Salisbury, and it's a special place to have one—discounts are available, subject to numbers on advance bookings. Private hospitality boxes located above the Members Bar and the new Festival Stand accommodate between 12 and 40 guests. These are available for daily hire from £600 per day or on an annual basis. Daily sublets can be arranged, depending on the day and the box required. However, it is always worth contacting the racecourse for availability or cancellations. The best idea however, may be to organise a marquee or chalet located adjacent to the parade ring and the winning post catering for up to 300 guests. Salisbury runs its own Bibury Club Catering Company and provides an excellent food and service to the recently refurbished Members Restaurant where advance booking is essential. There is also a snack bar located in the Bibury Suite if you fancy something less substantial and a seafood bar in the refurbished Paddock Bar. On the drinking front, Members can enjoy the Wessex Bar, while in Tattersalls, a temporary Pavilion Bar is erected to cater for the larger crowds in July and August. Disabled people are given the opportunity to enjoy racing by virtue of a raised viewing area—situated in the Members Enclosure. A Tote betting shop is located in Tattersalls and telephones are available. An evening or afternoon at Salisbury is thoroughly recommended.

Local Favourites

Hampshire, Dorset and Wiltshire are home to an enticing array of country pubs. Here is a quick listing of some of the various contenders: the **Compasses** (01722) 714318 in Lower Chicksgrove has bar snacks and a traditional atmosphere as well as a separate restaurant and cosy rooms if required. Another pub-restaurant ideal for informal post-race nosh is the **Black Dog** (01722) 716344 in Chilmark. The **Black Horse** (01722) 716251 in Teffont Magna has super food and pleasing accommodation. The same can be said of a critter—the **Fox Inn** (01258) 880328, a lovely village pub. In Broad Chalke, the **Queen's Head** (01722) 780344 is a good stayer and in another gorgeous village, Fonthill Bishop, the **King's Arms** is a picturesque alternative, while the **Victoria and Albert** in Netherhampton is very convenient so too is the **Barford Inn** at Barford St Martin (01722) 742242. The list goes on and on. If you love the country and it's traditionally copious cuisine, then this is an area for you. Three local tips worth following are the **Rose and Crown** at Harnham, the **Pembroke Arms** at Wilton and **Cricket Field Cottage** (01722) 322595. All three also offer good accommodation. We then come across a couple of tools. Before you take offence, relax—merely a reference to two other excellent pubs in the vicinity, the **Malet Arms** in Newton Toney, and the **Silver Plough** (01722) 712266 in Pitton, a tremendous hostelry with a restaurant. A good pub to stay in is the **Barford** (01722) 742242—good value and good food.

Then there's Salisbury. A charming city and the county town of Wiltshire. The rivers Avon, Bourne, Wylye and Nadder converge here. Many people visit the area to see the cathedral or shop in the market and the town is a busy and thriving focal point. The **Rose and Crown** (01722) 327908 has a lovely setting on the banks of the River Avon, overlooking the cathedral. The **Old Bell Inn** (01722) 327958 also has pleasing bedrooms and two lovely four posters and the bar is a civilised meeting place. The **White Hart** (01722) 327476 has great character and is an ideal choice before racing at the Bibury Club. **Milford Hall** (01722) 417411 is also reported to be of an excellent standard. If you are in search of a pub then the **Haunch of Venison** (01722) 322024 exudes character and provides good food while the Tudor **King's Arms** (01722) 327629 offers good value accommodation. The **Coach and Horses** (01722) 336254 also offers good food. Outside the town, a really super pub to note is the **Fox and Goose** at Coombe Bissett—well worth a post-race pint.

Some distance from Salisbury, but a definite must if you have time, is the **Sign of the Angel** (01249) 730230 at Lacock—also a possibility for Newbury. Marlborough offers the splendid **Ivy House Hotel** (01672) 515333 which is thoroughly recommended. Closer to the racecourse, try **Howard's House Hotel** (01722) 716392—a real gem of a place—an ideal port of call for those of you wishing to break the journey before racing at Salisbury.

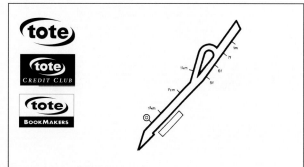

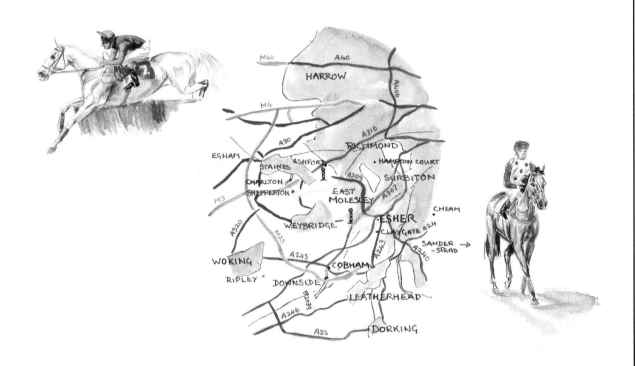

Artist: **Katy Sodeau OUT OF THE STALLS** _Courtesy of:_ **The Artist**

Sandown Park

At Sandown, **Steve Brice** is the **General Manager** while **Andrew Cooper** is the **Group Racing Manager** for United Racecourses Ltd, and **Tim Darby** is **Marketing and Sponsorship Manager Tel (01372) 461253.** If you wish to contact them, write to **Sandown Park Racecourse, Esher, Surrey KT10 9AJ. Tel (01372) 463072 Fax (01372) 465205.Web site: www.sandown.co.uk** There is also a bookings hotline on **(01372) 470047.**

The racecourse is a mere 15 miles from the centre of London in the suburb of Esher. The best route from the capital is to take the A3 out of central London itself. The A308 and the A309 are trunk roads that run nearby, and the racecourse itself lies off the A307, the Portsmouth Road. Racegoers from London are strongly recommended to use the Esher—Waterloo / Clapham Junction line as it passes the course. If you live closer to the course, buses from Kingston, Guildford and Staines all go to Esher and stop in the High Street. Assuming that you are in a car, you will find free parking off the Portsmouth Road. Parking in the Members car park carries a charge of £2. If time is of the essence you can take a helicopter and land on the golf course in the centre of the track—but please check beforehand. Golf is of course suspended on racedays.

Fixtures for 2000 are expected to include sixteen flat meetings (four of which are evening meetings), ten National Hunt fixtures, and the famous mixed meeting on Whitbread Gold Cup Day, when the combination of the Thresher Classic Trial and the Whitbread produces arguably the most exciting day's racing of the year. Other highlights at Sandown are the Sunderlands Imperial Cup, the Agfa Diamond Chase and the Coral-Eclipse Stakes on the flat—the first major clash of the generations each summer.

Classic Days in 1999 warranted charges of £26 (Club) £16 (Club Junior) £15 (Grandstand) and £6 (Park). On Premium Days, the charges were a bit lower—£17, £14, £12 and £5. On feature days, the Club is £16 and the Grandstand is £10 with Juniors charged at £12 and the Park at £5. If you book ahead for Classic and Premium Days you can save some money on all of these rates. Annual Membership now runs from October to September, and is around £190 per year, £75 for Juniors. You can also get a Jump Membership only at £85 or Flat only for £125. Finally, if it is your intention to organise a party to Sandown then contact the course for the full range of discounts or add-ons available.

The 36 boxes at Sandown are let on an annual basis. However, you may be lucky enough to sublet one of these and should phone the Club Secretary to see what is available. Numerous private rooms are also available to rent and marquee sites can be organised. The caterers here are Ring & Brymer who can be contacted on (01372) 465292. The Members Restaurant, located at the top of the Members Grandstand, will set you back approximately £30 for lunch and you are advised to book. As well as the Tack and Saddle restaurant in the Grandstand, costing approximately £6.50 per head, there are all manner of snack bars at the course but these can be rather pricey. The Country Bar is now open for exclusive use by Annual Members, Owners and Trainers. You may prefer to take your own picnic to enjoy in the car parks. Unless, of course, you are an owner and can enjoy the Winning Owners Room near the Winners Enclosure where winning owners can watch a video replay of their race. It is often said that sponsorship and entertaining go hand in hand. Sandown has some excellent ways of entertaining guests and during the warmer weather it has a Summer Pavilion next to the pre-parade rings and winners enclosures that offers some excellent packages for groups of 20 or more guests from £95 plus VAT per head upwards. The tariff includes members badge, wine, a three course meal, racecards etc. for each guest. A great way to spend a summer afternoon or evening.

The course improvements continue and over the past year both the weighing room and the owners and trainers bar have been renovated and refurbished. A Tote betting shop has been installed for both Tatts and Members.

There is now a family picnic area in the Park Enclosure. Children under 16 are admitted free to the course and are well catered for at Sandown with a large playground. A crèche has now been opened providing first class facilities free for young children. Similarly, facilities for the disabled here are excellent with specially equipped toilets, viewing areas, reserved parking and access ramps to all areas.

Sandown also has an excellent record in producing a really high standard of racing across its fixture list. Owners report it to be one of the most accommodating in the country as do trainers. With punters and patrons having similarly positive beliefs it is little wonder that Sandown is considered by many to be their favourite racecourse. We wish them well in the year 2000, and beyond.

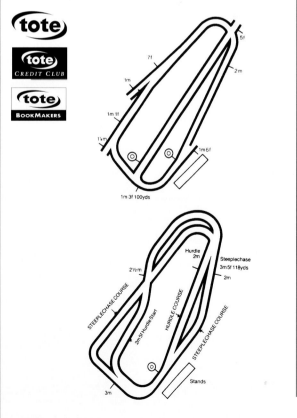

Artist: **John Atkins** *SANDOWN PARK* *Courtesy of:* **The Artist**

Because of Sandown's proximity to London, many race-goers will inevitably be heading back to the capital after a day at the track so it is difficult to know where to start a selection of hotels and restaurants. For those who want luxury and have the money to spend, **Blakes Hotel** 0171 370 6701 in South Kensington is quite superb as is the renowned **Browns Hotel** 0171 493 6020. That bastion of old-fashioned English values, **Claridge's** 071 629 8860 on Brook Street needs no introduction - its discreet luxury and elegance are quite unsurpassed. Park Lane delivers a number of excellent hotels. The **Dorchester** 0171 629 8888 has recently been totally refurbished and is crying out for a pre-race inspection. The **Grosvenor House** 0171 499 6363 is another impressive hotel and a star performer for the Forte stable. The **Inn on The Park** 0171 499 0888 and the **Hyatt Carlton Tower** 0171 235 1234 are two other thoroughbreds with outstanding restaurants as well. If the above are slightly out of the range of the impoverished racegoer, then it goes without saying that London provides a veritable multitude of accommodation at vastly varying rates. One highly recommended establishment that combines comfort and value is the **Aston Court Hotel** 0171 602 9954.

So far, the emphasis has been on central London. A bit farther south on Wimbledon Common, **Cannizaro House** 0181 879 1464 is a delight, a true country house overlooking the common and superbly appointed throughout. Staying south of the river, **Prima Donna** 0171 223 9737 in Battersea is a hot favourite—delicious Italian food and very good value. **Mi Piache** (01372) 462200

and **Le Petit Pierrot** at Claygate are both newcomers to the Sandown field but they're convenient and good if you are seeking a port of call.

What of those who prefer to stay in the Esher area to sample the local delights? The **Dining Room** (01932) 231686 at Hersham serves good English food, whilst the **Hilton National** (01932) 864471 in nearby Cobham has excellent facilities such as saunas and whirlpool baths. If you are lucky enough to fly to Sandown by helicopter, then you will be pleased to know that your chopper is also welcome here. Elsewhere, in Coatham the **Woodlands Park Hotel** (01372) 843933 is an improving type and an excellent choice for visitors to Sandown. Slightly farther afield, in Weybridge, the **Warbeck House Hotel** (01932) 848764 is unpretentious but recommended. The **Oatlands Park Hotel** (01932) 847242 is a strong local fancy and a recent upgrading makes it a handy favourite. **Casa Romana** (01932) 843470 is an excellent Italian to note. **Good Earth** (01372) 462489 is extremely handy and first rate Chinese restaurant. Less convenient but outstanding cuisine can also be found at **Michels**, Ripley (01483) 334777—excellent.

Finally, Sandown, Kempton and Epsom are not only joined by their association with United Racecourses, but also by very close proximity to one another. So, if you are still fishing for more ideas and suggestions of where to eat or stay, then either the Kempton or Epsom section should provide all you require. One place that comes highly recommended by the racecourse management and handy for all three is the **Petersham Hotel** in Richmond 0181 940 7471. The restaurant here is also really first class.

Artist: **John Atkins** *SANDOWN PARK, PULLING UP* *Courtesy of:* **The Artist**

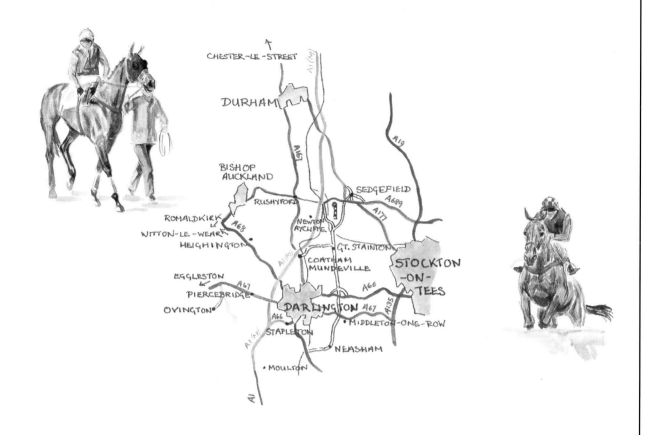

Artist: **Klaus Philipp STEEPLECHASER** *Courtesy of:* **Private Collection**

The team in charge here are **Chairman Bob Bowden, Clerk of the Course,** and **Manager** and **Secretary, Alan Brown,** who can be contacted at **The Bungalow, Sedgefield Racecourse, Sedgefield, Stockton on Tees TS21 2HW Tel (racedays only) (01740) 620366 Office (01740) 621925 Fax (01740) 620663.**

The racecourse is approachable from Middlesbrough and the east via the A177, while the A1(M) makes the racecourse easily accessible for both northbound and southbound travellers, just follow the brown tourist signs to the course. For racegoers from the larger conurbations to the southwest the M62 and the A1(M) provide good routes. Despite its proximity to the Great North Road, the track has a remote and quiet setting. Major train routes run to the centre of Darlington some 250 miles from London. The closest rail stations are at Stockton-on-Tees (nine miles away), Durham (twelve miles) and Darlington itself. There is ample free parking for a variety of vehicles, although there is a charge of £2 in the Paddock car park. Helicopters are also able to land at Sedgefield, but do please call in advance.

Sedgefield is the only course in County Durham and prides itself on being known as 'The Friendly Course'. There were 21 national hunt fixtures on offer in 1999 and the fixture list has remained relatively unchanged. The course's major race each year is the Durham National Handicap Steeplechase and it should be noted that the management here have managed to attract excellent sponsorship support to boost the prizes.

The course has only two enclosures: a combined Paddock and Tattersalls area which is reasonably priced at £9 (OAPs £5) and the Course Enclosure which is equally good value at £3. The course also offers special party rates with a 50 per cent discount for groups of 40 or more in the Paddock. Children under 16 are admitted free in both enclosures.

During recent years the racecourse management have spent over a million pounds on improvements to the track, stabling and public amenities. A new weighing room, incorporating two entertainment suites with viewing balconies overlooking the parade ring and winners enclosure have been added as well as a renovated public bar. A new pavilion has recently been built to house a bar, snack bar, a restaurant and private boxes with new Tote facilities. There are now ten private boxes, the six additional ones situated in the new pavilion. All have excellent views of the winning post. Two sponsors suites are available for hire, the first seats up to 100 while the smaller one seats up to 40. The caterers are Ramside Event Catering who can be contacted on 0191 236 4148. Good value lunches are available at Sedgefield in the Pavilion Restaurant which seats 100. There are various snack bars to keep the hunger pangs at bay as well as two restaurants, offering both à la carte and table d'hôte dining.

There are two special Family Evenings which is splendid to report. This type of entertainment is excellent and if recent research is to be believed, this is the area with the most growth potential. The disabled racegoer has special ramps to ensure a pleasant day. An on-course betting office is in existence as well as telephones, although no banking facilities are available. Sedgefield is well supported by the local community and visitors from further afield are encouraged to visit this unspoilt, well run racecourse which has been significantly refurbished in recent years. A visit in 2000 should certainly be put in the diary.

Local Favourites

Sedgefield is surrounded by a number of good hotels and a visit in 1999 is well recommended. **Blackwell Grange** (01325) 380888 in Darlington is also one to note. An excellent Italian restaurant is **Sardis** (01325) 461222– which, given the quality, is well priced. Heading north we find **Headlam Hall** (01325) 730238–a worthy selection–whilst the **Dog** (01325) 312152 is a possibility for a pre-race pint. **Redworth Hall Hotel & Country Club** (01388) 772442 is a fine hotel–a good restaurant here as well. **Ramside Hall** 0191 3865282 outside Durham is also handy. A good golf course for those who enjoy this sport.

Stapleton offers the **Stakis White Horse Hotel** (01325) 382121–not grand but comfortable and convenient. For an excellent post-race nosebag try the **Black Bull** (01604) 377289 in Moulton. It's a mile and a half off the A1 at Scotch Corner and is one of the most celebrated fish restaurants in the country. In Rushyford, three miles from the course, one finds the **Eden Arms Hotel** (01388) 720541 which receives promising reports from locals in the know. On the doorstep of the racecourse itself, the **Dun Cow** (01740) 620894 will provide for your every reasonable need! The **George** at Piercebridge (01325) 374576 has a magnificent setting and offers good food and some accommodation.

Over in the city of Durham the cathedral is awe-inspiring and the castle is also worth a look. If you are going to stay here, then the better hotels include the stylish **Royal County** 0191 3866821 which overlooks the River Wear and the **Three Tuns** 0191 386 4326. If you like a good restaurant try **Bistro 21** in Aykley Heads 0191 384 4354 it's a real gem. In Coatham Mundeville, a 15 minute drive from Sedgefield between Darlington and Newton Aycliffe, one finds a hot favourite–**Hall Garth** (01325) 300400, a well appointed 16th century mansion–thoroughly recommended.

There are two places nearer the course that should also be considered in your each-way plans. Firstly, **Hardwick Hall** (01740) 620253, which lies one mile west of the town making it most convenient for early morning race enthusiasts. Secondly, the **Nags Head** (01740) 620234, an extremely friendly pub which offers good bar snacks as well as having a separate restaurant. A good idea for a pre-race rendezvous when travelling the turf in 2000.

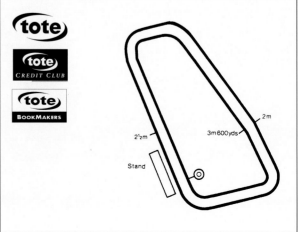

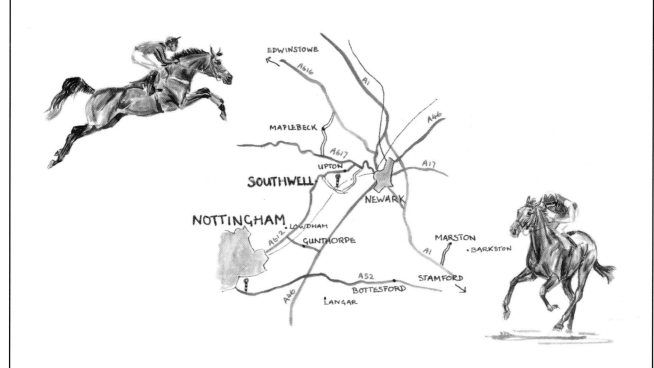

Artist: **Katy Sodeau CIRCLING BEFORE THE START** _Courtesy of:_ **The Artist**

The Clerk of the Course at Southwell is **Michael Prosser**, the Operations Manager is **Amanda Boby**, the **Commercial Manager** is **Pat Mitchell**, and the **Estate Manager** is **David Williams**. They can be contacted at the **Southwell Racecourse, Rolleston, Newark NG25 OTS. Tel (01636) 814481. Fax (01636) 812271.**

The racecourse itself has a splendidly scenic setting. A Midlands track, it is situated just outside the Nottinghamshire village of Rolleston some five miles from Newark and within access of various motorway routes. Westminster Abbey is some 138 miles away and the A1 is the most direct route to follow. Northbound travellers should exit for the racecourse on the A6065 and then pursue the A617. The A46, which runs from east to west, serves racegoers from those points of the compass. The A617 should be used by travellers from the north west and is convenient owing largely to its connection with the M1, junction 29. Drivers should also note the new Newark bypass. If you do not wish to travel by car, then the train is a cert. In fact, Rolleston's station is one of the most convenient racecourse stations in the land. Nottingham is on London's St Pancras line and from here one can catch a train to nearby Rolleston. Some of the Mansfield/Newark buses also stop in Rolleston a quarter of a mile from the course. As one would expect with such a rural track, there are plenty of parking areas in the fields around which are free. Helicopters may land in the centre of the course, subject to prior agreement.

As a result of its all-weather track, Southwell has experienced a whole new lease of life. The 2000 fixture list will follow a broadly similar pattern to 1999. Admission to the course is £12 for Daily Members and £7 for Tattersalls. OAP's may get in to Tatts for £5 if they are members of the Diamond Club into which there is a £250 admission charge. The cost of Annual Membership at Southwell is £160 for a single and £270 for a Married Couple. Membership includes parking, reciprocal meetings and the use of the Queen Mother's Restaurant, Paddock viewing balcony and Members Bar and Restaurant. The racecourse offers attractive discounts to Tattersalls according to the size of your party—contact the racecourse management for details. For groups of 30–50 there is a £1 discount rising to £1.50 for groups of 50 or more. These discounts are restricted to Tattersalls only.

This year will see the completion of new Corporate Hospitality suites at Southwell, which will be able to accommodate parties of up to 50 people. Each will overlook the track and adjoin the Members Suite. The present members area will be extended substantially to take care of the course's growing membership and those wishing to dine in the Queen Mother restaurant. When it is complete, the Members Suite will be able to host up to 450 people.

Other details to be noted when considering a day's outing at Southwell—children under 16 are admitted free if they are accompanied by an adult. If the racing does not grip them then they will be delighted to hear that there is a supervised play area available at a small cost of £1 per child. There are two telephones in the Tote hall and one in the Members Bar and Weighing Room. Facilities for the disabled are good. Both floors are purpose built with lavatories, a lift and viewing platform. There is a Tote and Ladbrokes betting shop in the Grandstand too.

This is a developing racecourse with a constant eye to the future. It boasts a small hotel with an 18 hole golf course and all manner of other facilities. The development of the golf course emphasises well the endeavour to offer racecourses as a facility over and above the racecourse itself. There are also American-style training barns. With a constant eye ahead, RAM Racecourses Ltd are reconditioning this essentially rural track. They are experts in the art and we wish them well. All-weather racing does a huge amount for the sport—congratulations to all involved.

Local Favourites

The **Saracen's Head Hotel** (01636) 812701 is the ideal starting point for visitors to Southwell racecourse. The inn dates from the 16th century and its Stuart heritage is displayed in many paintings. Southwell also boasts **Upton Fields House** (01636) 812303 an excellent bed & breakfast establishment. Somewhat further afield, the **George** (01780) 755171 at Stamford is a magnificent old coaching inn whilst the **Cavendish** (01246) 582311 occupies a superb setting in the grounds of Chatsworth and has a fine restaurant with venison a speciality. In Stamford, a super old market town, note the **Lord Burghley**—a lively pub renowned for its fine ales. Other places to stay include the **Bull and Swan Inn** (01780) 63558 and the **Crown Hotel** (01780) 63136—both are marvellous old inns and make for a pleasant place to stay. For those heading south, the **Ram Jam Inn** (01780) 410776 on the A1 at Stretton is convenient and well recommended as a good stopping place. The **Black Swan** (016360 626474, is a really good restaurant in Beckingham. The **Square & Compass** in Normanton on Trent is a good pub to remember, as is the handy **Red Lion** in Thurgaton.

The **French Horn** at Upton, is certainly worth visiting for its good value, quality pub food and is especially convenient for Rolleston and the racecourse. In Maplebeck, a little further north, the **Beehive** village pub is worth a visit despite or perhaps because it is a little out of the way in the Nottinghamshire countryside. Travelling in the same direction, the medieval village of Laxton offers the hospitable **Moorgate Farmhouse** (01777) 870274 and the **Dovecote** is a friendly place to visit. In Marston, the **Thorold Arms**, convenient for A1 travellers and for **Marston Hall**, offers a particularly good drop of ale and nice bar meals. In Bottesford, due north of Belvoir Castle, one finds an excellent and intimate restaurant—the **Peacock** at Redmile (01949) 842554. Other than Belvoir Castle itself, Newstead Abbey is a sight worth seeing, home of the poet, the sixth Lord Byron, housing numerous personal articles; the gardens too are ideal for a diversion for the less than enthusiastic racing partner. Golfers might care to note the **De Vere Belton Woods** (01476) 593200—a large hotel with good leisure facilities. **Harry's Place** (01476) 61780 at Great Gonerby is top of the handicap in the restaurant stakes—first class. Four miles further north you find **Barkston House** (01400) 50555 in Barkston, a charming restaurant with rooms. South of Southwell at Lowdham, the **Springfield Inn** (01602) 663387 is a comfortable place in which to stay, as is **Langar Hall** (01949) 60559 in Langar whilst Southwell's **Racecourse Hotel** (01636) 814481 is excellent value. The **Full Moon Inn**, just one mile from the racecourse is also a newcomer of note. Finally, we recommend a local favourite; the **Old Forge** at Southwell (01636) 812809. Bed and Breakfast may be had at **Racecourse Farm** (01636) 812176, a five minute walk from the course.

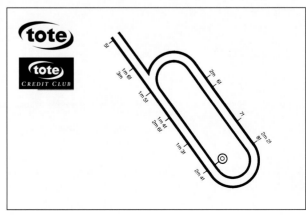

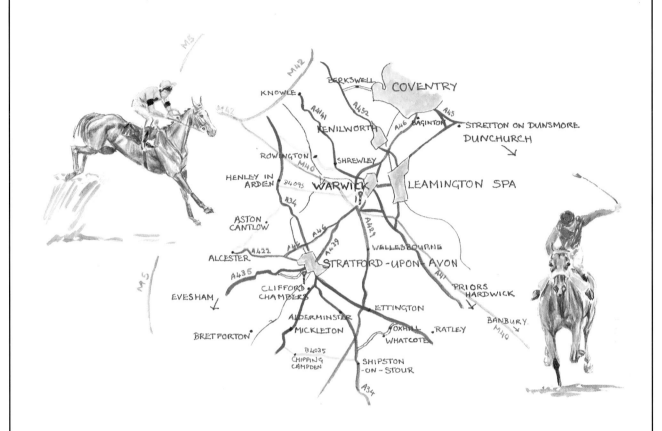

Artist: **Malcolm Coward** **RIDING A FINISH** *Courtesy of:* **Sally Mitchell Fine Arts**

Originally built in 1820 as two fine Georgian houses, complete with stabling and large gardens, Dukes has recently been totally refurbished with 22 bedrooms, including suites and four posters for the romantically inclined. All have televisions with satellite channels, radios, direct dial telephones and tea and coffee making facilities.

Ideally situated in the centre of Stratford-upon-Avon, this elegant hotel, furnished with many antiques, offers a 'Country House in Town' atmosphere within two minutes walk of Shakespeare's birthplace and only five minutes away from the Royal Shakespeare Theatre. It is the only privately owned and operated listed town house hotel in the centre and has ample free parking for residents and guests.

The Harlequin restaurant features a range of à la carte dishes complemented by a selection of reasonably priced, interesting wines from around the world. Guests with a smaller appetite will find the Harlequinade menu appealing, served in the bar, lounge or by room service. As a special service for those attending the theatre, the hotel offers a pre-theatre dinner from 6.15 in the evening.

What better way to round off a day at Stratford, Warwick or Worcester races than to enjoy a quiet meal, a bottle of excellent wine, an entertaining evening at the theatre and finally to relax in the elegant comfort of one of Dukes' rooms. Truly a hotel that lives up to its motto, "We are small enough to care and big enough to cope".

Dukes Hotel
Payton Street,
Stratford-upon-Avon
Warwickshire CV37 6UA
Tel: (01789) 269300
Fax: (01789) 414700

Racecourse Manager is **Mr Stephen Lambert** and the Company Secretary is **Miss K Self** at Stratford He can be contacted via **The Racecourse. Luddington Road, Stratford upon Avon. CV37 9SE. Tel (01789) 267949 /269411 Fax (01789) 415850.**

Stratford is fairly easy to reach from all directions and the racecourse lies one mile south west of the town. Access is via the M40 (Warwick turn off) from the north. From other directions, the M5, M42 and M6 are all within a half hour's drive of the course. The new Stratford bypass is handy and there are AA signs to the racecourse to further assist on racedays. If you wish to travel by train from London then you should aim for Stratford-upon-Avon from Euston, changing at Coventry, or Paddington changing at Leamington Spa. There is no bus directly from the station to the course but buses from the town heading to Evesham do pass the entrance to Luddington Road. There is ample parking at Stratford with a large free car park. A charge of £2 is made for cars parking in the main car park in the centre of the course from which you can access the new exit route from the racecourse. Members park separately. There are also good facilities for coaches but limited scope for helicopters so please arrange with the racecourse in advance.

In 1999 there were 14 fixtures, including the popular Monday in March which coincides with the Cheltenham festival, drawing a good crowd. and a Sunday meeting in July. The major fixture remains the Horse and Hound Cup Final Championship Hunters Steeplechase which is now a two day festival. In 1999, Annual Membership badges cost £95 with an extra £7 required for an annual car park badge. Daily Membership is now £14. Entrance to Tattersalls is £10, whereas the Course Enclosure costs £4. If you are planning a party, 15 is the minimum required for a 20 per cent reduction. For further details, contact the Manager. Children under 16 are welcomed at no charge.

There is a new hospitality room at Stratford and the course does have plenty of facilities in the way of boxes, conference areas and function rooms. The Avon Suite is specifically designed for corporate hospitality, catering for up to 90 people. Requests for these facilities should be directed to the racecourse management. The outside caterers are Jenkinson Caterers Ltd who can be contacted on (01785) 252247. The course has several bars which have recently been refurbished and provide snacks. The Paddock Suite Restaurant has also undergone a £350,000 refurbishment and is available for bookings.

The new grandstand provides comfortable and improved facilities. Members now have a champagne/ seafood bar, tea room, Tote and William Hill betting shop, while Tatts patrons benefit from a new snack bar, Tote, betting shop and bar. There is also a large box on the second floor for corporate entertainment. There are some amenities for disabled racegoers for whom a small stand is provided, with excellent viewing. Telephones are located in the Members Enclosure and Tattersalls but there is no bank at the course so bring plenty of readies with you.

Stratford racecourse is a good track. The M40 extension makes the trip far speedier for many visitors and this will hopefully boost attendances. There are all manner of reasons for going racing: a day in the fresh air, a rendezvous with friends, a tilt at the ring or, if you are lucky, to watch your own horse run. Stratford does not profess to being Britain's foremost racecourse but it provides good racing in a convenient location and a visit should be considered in 2000.

Local Favourites

The first production of *A Midsummer Night's Dream* apparently took place in the grounds of **Alveston Manor** (01789) 204581. The house retains much of its Elizabethan charm and is a relaxing place to stay. A Georgian hotel convenient for the theatre is **Stratford House** (01789) 268288, less expensive and with an excellent restaurant. On the Warwick road the **Welcombe Hotel** (01789) 295252 is also well thought of, boasting 18 holes of golf, some delightful rooms and a first class restaurant. Pride of place goes to **Ettington Park** (01789) 450123 in nearby Alderminster. The hotel is magnificent, the bedrooms are charmingly furnished and the bars and library comfortable and relaxing. In Ettington itself, the **Chase Hotel** (01789) 740000 is good value with an excellent restaurant. Among the wealth of guesthouses that form an equally important part of Stratford's accommodation industry, **Broad Marston Manor** (01789) 720252 is recommended. Another hotel of acclaim outside Stratford-upon-Avon—the **Billesley Manor** (01789) 400888, is a fine gabled manor house. Those seeking fine fare might consider **Liaison** (01789) 293400 or **The Opposition** (01789) 269980. The **Boatside** (01789) 297733 has a pleasant riverside setting.

People who prefer a day out without an overnight stay might wish to sample any one of a number of pubs. In Wellesbourne, the **King's Head** (01789) 840206 is good for lunch and **Charlecotte Park**, a superb Elizabethan mansion, lies close by and can be viewed between April and October. The **Charlecote Pheasant** (01789) 279954 is a good hotel to visit. The **Butcher's Arms** at Priors Hardwick, more of a restaurant than a pub, is handy for the A41 while the A34 reveals the **White Hart** (01789) 450205 at Newbold-on-Stour, an excellent place to have a bar snack. In Oxhill, the **Peacock** is an extremely hospitable village pub as is the **Royal Oak** in Whatcote. Traditionalists will enjoy the **King's Head** at Aston Cantlow, another tremendously atmospheric pub. In Wilmcote, the **Swan House** is also splendid with an excellent and varied menu. If you are keen to enjoy the Cotswolds after the Stratford steeds then a reasonably priced and extremely relaxing hotel to visit is the **Three Ways** (01386) 438429 at Mickleton—the restaurant is also quietly civilised with a fine wine list. In Chipping Campden, two establishments worthy of note are the **Cotswold House Hotel** (01386) 840330 and its restaurant and the **Noel Arms** (01386) 840317. Finally, close by at Charingworth, **Charingworth Manor** (01386) 78555 provides accommodation and service of the highest standard, while the **Houndshill** (01789) 740267 is a pleasant inn on the A422 and an ideal place to stay.

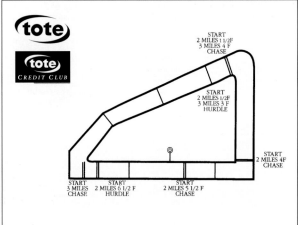

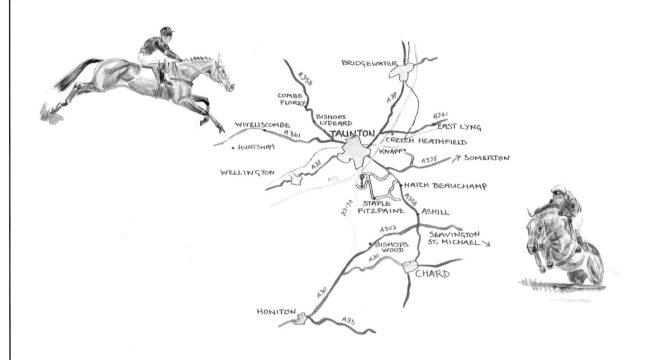

Artist: **David Trundley** **TAUNTON EVENING MEETING** *Courtesy of:* **The Artist**

Michael Trickey, the well known West Country point-to-point trainer and hunter judge, who regularly judges at the Dublin and Great Yorkshire shows, is **Clerk of the Course**. He and **John Hills**, the **Manager** and **Secretary**, can both be contacted via the course at **Orchard Portman, Taunton, Somerset TA3 7BL. Tel (01823) 337172 Fax (01823) 325881.** Few racecourse managers are so genuinely enthusiastic about the task in hand, and we warmly recommend a visit if you are exploring the south west in 2000.

Taunton is 100 minutes from London on a fast train with a direct service from Plymouth and has good connections from the North and Midlands. The course is situated close to the M5, 50 minutes south of the M4 intersection, while the A303 is fast achieving near motorway status as a major trunk route giving access from the south coast. Why not travel the day before racing and spend the night in a local hostelry? Buy your day badge and a plentiful supply of Tote vouchers in advance from the racecourse secretary and you won't need to worry about living it up overnight in the Cider County. Our punter could also settle comfortably into a Pullman seat on the Paddington train secure in the knowledge that his Day badge will be £12, Paddock £9 or Course £5. Cars are free—unless they go onto the centre of the course as the base for a family picnic or portable grandstand, in which case have £3 handy.

Those who know Taunton well are delighted by the new pre-Parade Ring and Winners Enclosure which has been returned to the Parade Ring. Together they give the dedicated punter a much improved view of the horses before and after the race.

When the weather is wet and the wind keen, the Saddle Room on the ground floor of the Paddock Stand is an ideal place to have tea, coffee and a snack while you put your feet up and study the form. Catering is now 'in-house' at Taunton and very popular it is too! You can choose from the 'Racegoers Special' - a two or three-course quick service lunch in the Orchard Restaurant, or you can really indulge yourself and book a table in the restaurant with a birds-eye view of the course. The latter will cost you £38 for an all day table with a three course lunch, afternoon tea, complimentary racecard and tea and coffee service throughout the day. Admission is also included at a special discounted rate. These tables are popular though, so please book early. There is also a first-class Owners and Trainers Bar which is situated next to the Parade Ring and enjoys a fine view of the course.

You may enjoy your day at Taunton so much that you decide to become an Annual Member. 2000 prices are likely to be £80 for a single membership and £135 double for a Gentleman and Lady. This will give you 13 days racing at Taunton plus another 14 at other courses around the country including Newbury, Cheltenham, Chepstow and Wincanton.

The course betting shop is run by Peter Jolliffe. This and the Tote betting shops are in Tattersalls, together with two public telephones for credit punters. The course has reserved a prime viewing area next to the restaurant for the disabled, and all the public parts of the course help accommodate their needs. Manager John Hills is a man who clearly loves his racing—if you love yours, take a trip to Taunton and you won't be disappointed.

Local Favourites
In the town itself, the **Castle Hotel** (01823) 272671 on Castle Green is excellent in every way. One mile outside the town at Bishop's Hull lies the outstanding (and outstandingly reasonable) **Meryan House Hotel** (01823) 337445. Also south of the town is **Rumwell Manor Hotel** (01823) 461902 a quietly elegant hotel set in five acres of parkland. The city centre is changing nearly every day but restaurants are a little thin on the ground although **Porters Wine Bar** (01823) 256688 is an enjoyable establishment. Some of the many pubs in the area are obviously good places to meet for a post-race beverage. In Staple Fitzpaine, close to the racecourse, the **Greyhound** (01823) 480227 is a splendid little pub serving an excellent pint and good bar snacks. It also has an adjoining restaurant, a fine place for post-race dinner. The **Volunteer** at Seavington St Michael is a good place both for its cooking and for that extraordinary stuff, Scrumpy. Another good value food pub is the **Square and Compass** (01823) 480467 in Ashill. The **Rose and Crown** at East Lyng is also good. Breaking momentarily from the pub scene, it is well worth seeking out **Farthings Country House Hotel** (01823) 480664 at Hatch Beauchamps—an attractive Georgian house convenient for the racecourse. **Nightingales** (01823) 480806 is a well thought of restaurant to consider here. The **Mount Somerset** (01823) 44250 is also well worth a pre race inspection.

Many people racing at Taunton are locals just out for a quick day's sport. If, however, you have made a bit of an effort to go to Taunton races, then one great place to reward yourself is the **Kingfishers Catch** (01823) 432394 at Bishops Lydeard on the A358 (more a restaurant than a pub) en route to the splendid Dunster Castle. A hotel which affords great comfort is **Langley House** (01984) 623318, near Wiveliscombe on the A361. With sofas, an array of fresh flowers and some splendid views, one really feels the closeness of the countryside. For an informal stay and personal attention, this cannot be beaten—an excellent restaurant here as well. We finish with two splendid pubs. The **Rising Sun** (01823) 490436 in the very appropriately named Knapp especially for those who enjoy fish and the **Rose and Crown** (01823) 490296 at Stoke St Gregory—an outstanding establishment and very welcoming (some good value rooms here - ask for the cottage rooms). Further north in Nether Stowey lies the **Apple Tree Hotel** (01278) 733238—highly recommended. Take a trip this year to the south west—it's a delightful part of the country.

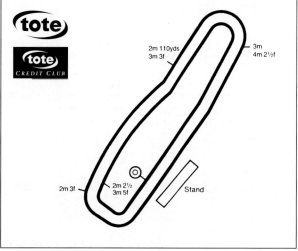

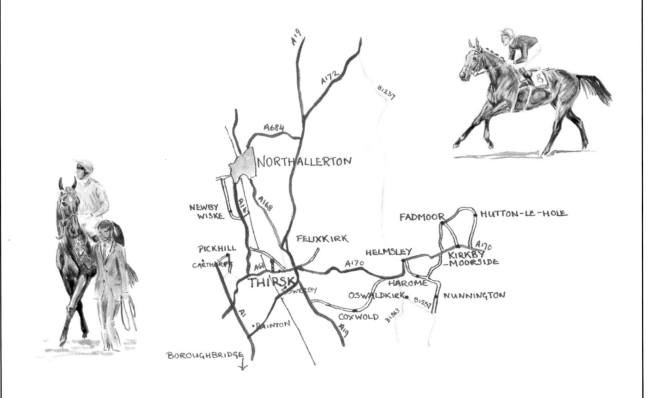

Artist: **Peter Smith COMING IN AFTER THE LAST RACE, EVENING** *Courtesy of:* **Frost & Reed**

The Worsley Arms Hotel is an attractive stone built Georgian inn in the heart of Hovingham, near York, with a history stretching back to Roman times. The hotel was built in 1841 by Sir William Worsley, the first Baronet. Today the hotel still belongs to the Worsley family and is privately operated by Euan and Debbi Rodger. Hovingham Hall, the family house which stands on the edge of the village was designed around 1760 by Thomas Worsley, and is now the home of Sir Marcus Worsley, the fifth Baronet. His sister, Her Royal Highness the Duchess of Kent was born there.

This country Inn of renown, named Yorkshire Hotel of the Year 1997/8, has the welcoming and restful atmosphere of a pleasant country house. The spacious sitting rooms are ideal havens for morning coffee, full afternoon tea, or an aperitif.

Food is undoubtedly a highlight. The chef, Andrew Jones, with a wealth of local produce on the doorstep, aims to combine the best of traditional and modern cooking with presentation that reflects an individual style. His food can be enjoyed in the Wyvern Restaurant or in the more informal Cricketers Bistro. In recognition of the quality of the food, the AA has, for a third year running, awarded the hotel two AA Rosettes.

The bedrooms, each with private bathroom, are individually and tastefully decorated, providing every comfort and modern facility.

The village is on the edge of a designated Area of Outstanding Natural Beauty; national parks are on the doorstep, the nearby Yorkshire Dales and the North York Moors. The area is rich in romantic and historic sites—the ruined abbeys of Rievaulx and Fountains, the castles of Helmsley and Pickering, the stately homes of Castle Howard, Duncombe Park and, of course, Hovingham Hall. Leisure pursuits abound as the hotel is ideally placed for quality racing, golfing (the championship courses of Ganton and Fulford are within half an hours drive, shooting and walking.

The Worsley Arms Hotel
Hovingham
York YO6 4LA
Tel: (01653) 628234
Fax: (01653) 628130
E mail: worsleyarm@aol.co.uk

Mr Christopher Tetley acts as Clerk of the Course, Manager and Secretary and can be contacted at Thirsk Racecourse, Station Road, Thirsk, North Yorkshire YO7 1Ql. Tel (01845) 522276 Fax (01845) 525353.

The racecourse is situated just off the A61 west of Thirsk. The best route for travellers from the south is to use the A1/A1M northbound and then follow the A61, or the A19 if journeying from York. Southbound drivers should also use the A1, or alternatively the A61 or A19. If travelling from the east, the A170 is convenient whilst eastbound journeyers should take the M62 and the A1 north. There is ample car parking to be found on arriving. If you wish to travel by train, the Kings Cross line is pretty swift and Thirsk station is a mere six furlongs away from the station, although you will need to change en route. Buses to Thirsk will take you to within a quick canter of the track but there are no special race buses. One other point that should be noted is that there are facilities for helicopters if you're lucky enough to have one. In the past one frequently heard of jockeys missing races due to delays on the A1. The road is clearer now but make sure you set off in good time just to be sure.

With so many weekend fixtures, the Thirsk racegoer is thoroughly spoilt. The 2000 Guineas Trial is the oldest Classic trial in the country. The Thirsk Hunt Cup day is also good value. There were some thirteen racing days held during 1999 with the meetings in April, May and August perennially the most popular.

There are three enclosures at Thirsk: the Members, Tattersalls and the Family Ring. In 1999, prices were £14, £9 and £3. Party bookings are encouraged and various arrangements and discounts can be agreed with the course. This largely depends on your ability to gather troops to the fray. Basically, the more the merrier. However, these party terms do not apply to the Members Enclosure. In 1999, Membership cost £90, whilst Associate Membership cost £150—this apparently means a man, plus another member of the family—family is not defined! Annual Members are also entitled to a 10 per cent discount in selected local restaurants. Juniors are welcomed and the Annual Membership subscription is good value at £40. Your membership also entitles you to nine reciprocal meetings and eleven days courtesy of Yorkshire Cricket Club—what a bargain! Cars can be parked beside the course in the Family Ring on all days.

The racecourse rests at the foot of the Hambleton Hills and has an excellent setting, subject naturally to the weather. There are several snack bars around the course and a more substantial restaurant can be found in the Members Stand. The Grimthorpe Hall in Tattersalls, combines bars, a tea bar, fast food outlets and Tote facilities. Bookings for lunch should be made through Craven Gilpin & Sons in Leeds (0113) 287 6387. Bars in both the Members and Tattersalls have also been improved. If you wish to have a picnic then the racecourse welcomes this and if you want to order a viewing box this can also be arranged—there are a choice of five and they can hold from ten to twenty people. For large functions there is an ideal place near the Paddock for a marquee and a new function room for Members overlooking the lawns and Parade Ring will open in April 2000. This will cater for two parties of 50, one of 100 or individual tables which can be reserved for the full day. Again, arrangements and bookings can be made through the racecourse. This is a friendly racecourse in a beautiful part of England—well worth a visit.

Local Favourites

In Thirsk itself, the **Golden Fleece** (01845) 523108 is a convenient place to stay. The hotel is an old coaching inn and it faces onto a cobbled market square. Just outside the town is the small but cosy **Sheppard's** (01845) 523655. Climbing into the Hambleton Hills one arrives at Helmsley. Here, there are a number of good hotels, pubs and another scenic market place. This is an ideal base for exploring the nearby Dales and two sights that should definitely be seen are the ruins of Rievaulx and Byland Abbey. The **Black Swan** (01439) 770466 is extremely comfortable with a fine restaurant. A similar accolade befits the **Feathers** (01439) 770275.

Another good spot is the **Fauconberg Arms** in Coxwold, a first class pub popular locally (always a good sign) with some good bedrooms. In Harome the **Pheasant** (01439) 771241, a pleasant hotel, provides good accommodation in relaxing surroundings and **The Star Inn** (01439) is also excellent. In Kirkbymoorside, the **George & Dragon** (01751) 431637 excellent for a bar snack and some cosy bedrooms make it an ideal place to stay.

The **Plough** (01751) 731515 in Fadmoor is first class. Other good restaurants can be found near Northallerton. In nearby Staddle Bridge, an outstanding restaurant is **McCoys** (01609) 882671. An evening here will be one to remember. In Pickhill, the appropriately named **Nags Head** (01845) 567391 is a favourite—good food and some pleasant accommodation. The **Bay Horse** in Rainton and the **Fox and Hounds** in Carthorpe are also very popular. Another interesting alternative is the excellent **Solberge Hall** (01609) 779191 in Newby Wiske, a really appealing place with delightful views of the moors. A little further afield, but extremely conveniently situated for the A1 is the **Crown Hotel** (01423) 322328 in Boroughbridge. Those who enjoy a really first class inn should sample the delights of the **Worsley Arms Hotel** at Hovingham (01653) 628234—an excellent establishment.

Other selections in this excellent field—all within five miles of the course—include the **Crab and Lobster** (01845) 577286 at Asenby—extremely popular and rightly so—make sure you get there early. The **Carpenters Arms** (01845) 537369 at Felixkirk and the **Whitestonecliffe Inn** (01845) 597271, in Sutton under Whitestonecliffe are also good. Slightly further afield, in Kilburn, is the **Forresters Arms** (01347) 868386. Kilburn is the home of the famous 'Mouse Man' furniture maker. Finally, we come to the **George and Dragon**, Melmerby, (01765) 640303. This is a small inn located between Thirsk and Ripon—ideally placed for two of Yorkshire's excellent racetracks.

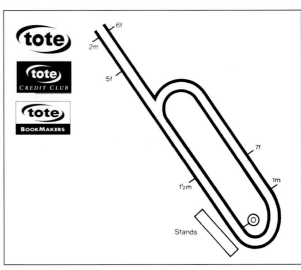

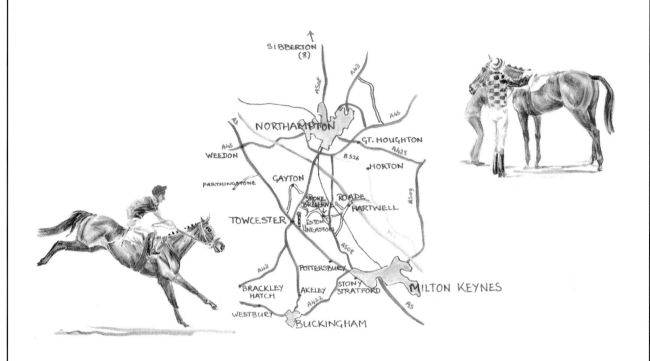

Artist: **K G Parker-Barratt LOOSE HORSE LEADS BY A NOSE** *Courtesy of:* **The Artist**

Lord Hesketh leads the Towcester team as Chief Executive, and Hugo Bevan is Clerk of the Course. Contact can be made by writing to Towcester Racecourse, Easton Neston, Towcester, Northants NN12 7HS. Tel (01327) 353414 Fax (01327) 358534.

The racecourse itself is situated one mile south east of the town of Towcester which lies at the intersection of the A43 and the A5. Although the course itself has a tranquil setting, the M1 is only a few miles away. People travelling from both the north and south should get on to the M1 and exit at junction 15a. The A43 towards Oxford should be followed for some six miles until the junction with the A5. From the town centre, follow the signs for the racecourse.

The major train routes leave Euston and racegoers are advised to go either to Milton Keynes or Northampton. The former is some eleven miles away and the latter nine. Bus services run from Northampton but only as far as Towcester, half a mile short of the racecourse. A better bet would be to take a helicopter, but make arrangements with the racecourse staff beforehand. There is ample free parking space which is ideal for picnics and there is a roped off area for Members parking.

In 1999 there was a total of 16 fixtures, including one Sunday meeting. The bank holiday meetings at Easter and in early May are always popular—6000 racegoers wisely decided to spend last Easter Monday at Towcester and evening meetings also bring out the locals in droves. The course provides lots of entertainment for evening, Easter and bank holiday meetings and this is obviously paying dividends.

Day badges will be £13 for the Members, £9 for Tattersalls and £5 for the Course Enclosure. People lucky enough to justify getting the most out of an Annual Membership will pay £125 single or £115 each double (no junior rates).

The £1 million redevelopment of the Grace Stand includes a 150 seater restaurant and six private boxes with lifts to all floors for the disabled. If you are wishing to take a party racing then do contact the racecourse for discounts which are given on group bookings of 20 or more. If you prefer more exclusive comfort then the Members Lawn has a newly erected Paddock Pavilion, which can cater for groups from 20 to 250. The Empress of Austria suite can cater for up to 30, while for smaller groups there is the Old Press Box or the Stewards Tower. Alternatively you could have a marquee beside the Grace Stand or hire one of the range of corporate hospitality boxes.

The racecourse has the standard telephone and betting facilities in Tattersalls but there are no banking facilities available. Towcester has much to commend it, not least its marvellous setting. It is surely one of the most charming country courses in Britain. It is no surprise that many rate this unassuming course as one of the country's most appealing. A visit for 2000 is an absolute priority.

Local Favourites

If you should wish to make a weekend trip to Towcester then the following hotels are to be noted. In Northampton, the Northampton Moat House (01604) 739988 is good. Another to remember is the Swallow Hotel (01604) 768700. The hotel is modern in design but luxurious and the leisure facilities are good. The Racecourse has links with the Stakis Northampton Hotel (01604) 700666 and the Saracen's Head (01327) 350414 in Towcester itself and if you mention you are visiting for the races you can get a special rate. Also, opposite the racecourse is The Folly which has recently been re-furbished and offers quality food.

The Farthingstone Hotel, Golf & Leisure Centre (01327) 361291 is well placed for the racecourse and is very comfortable. The Plough (01327) 350738, on the road out of Towcester, is well worth a post-race quickie and the Brave Old Oak is also worth your attention. In Stoke Bruerne a canal-side stop-off reveals the Boat Inn (01604) 862428. The pub itself has a fairly modern interior but the welcome is genuine as is the restaurant—a sound each-way chance. Bruerne's Lock (01604) 863654 with its canalside setting is also reported to be good.

Only six miles from Towcester lies Roade. The aptly named Roadehouse Restaurant (01604) 863372 has a pleasant situation in the village which is only two miles from junction 15 of the motorway. There are rooms here as well. In Horton, the French Partridge (01604) 870033 is an outstanding restaurant. After a cold afternoon's racing, there could be nothing better than sitting down to some quite superb game—a really first class idea. The Vine House Restaurant (01327) 811267 at Paulerspury also offers excellent cooking and some pleasing bedrooms, definitely one for the Towcester visitor. In Weedon, the Crossroads (01327) 340354 is convenient for the M1, junction 16, and is also extremely pleasant. (Breakfasts and coffees are served to non-residents). There are a number of pubs which have appeal: in Akeley, the Bull and Butcher (01280) 860257 is friendly and offers superb steaks, in Brackley Hatch, the Green Man may be inspected, whilst Potterspury offers the Old Talbot. North of Towcester, the Red Lion (01604) 770223 at East Haddon offers good bar food, good beer and some pleasant accommodation. For those keen on having an outstanding weekend, two somewhat distant thoughts. Hartwell House (01296) 747444 is the first—seeing is believing—a classic country house hotel located near Aylesbury. Alternatively, Woburn is a pleasant town where Woburn Abbey warrants a look, whilst other places to visit include the Bedford Arms (01525) 290441, an elegant inn and Paris House (01525) 290692—a marvellous restaurant with racing connections. Finally, The Bell is a pleasant place to enjoy a pint and bar snack.

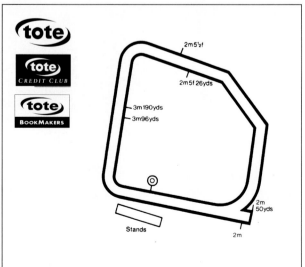

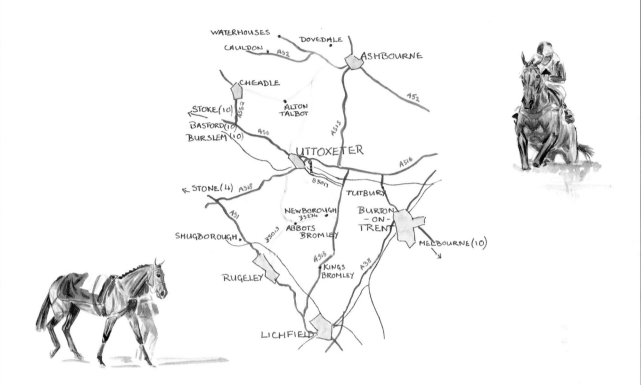

Artist: **Peter Smith** **FIRST HURDLE - THE BACKSTRAIGHT** *Courtesy of:* **Frost & Reed**

At Uttoxeter, **Rod Street** is the **General Manager** and his seconds-in-command are **Louise Aspinall and James Morley**. **Clerk of the Course** remains the redoubtable **David McAllister**. **Lynda Fletcher** is **Club Secretary** whilst **Lisa Harrobin** takes care of **Advance Bookings**. Uttoxeter also has another extremely valuable asset in their 'hands on' **Chairman, Stan Clarke CBE**. All may be contacted at **The Racecourse, Wood Lane, Uttoxeter, Staffordshire ST14 8BD. Tel (01889) 562561 Fax (01889) 562786**.

Uttoxeter is conveniently situated in the heart of the Midlands, equidistant between Stoke-on-Trent and Derby, just off the new A50, which has made the course even more accessible, London is 135 miles away to the south east. The course is a short hop from the town centre, just off the B5017 and is clearly signposted from the A50, A515. From the north or south of the country, the M6 is the motorway to aim for. Exit at junction 14 and then use the Stafford ring road. The new M40/M42 link is also a possibility if you do not wish to tackle the M1/M6 combination. All parking at the course is free and there is plenty available.

For those who prefer to travel by train, Uttoxeter Railway Station is right next door—you can walk off the platform straight onto the racecourse. Frequent Intercity services from Birmingham, Glasgow, Liverpool and Manchester run to Derby and Stoke-on-Trent, both of which run regular connecting trains to Uttoxeter. A direct service also operates from Crewe. By air, helicopters may land (by prior arrangement with the management) at the course itself, whilst light aircraft may use Tatenhill Airfield at Needwood, 7 miles from the racecourse. Telephone Tatenhill Aviation on (01283) 575283.

Uttoxeter enjoys an attendance of up to 15,000 on busy days and is surely a shining example of what can be achieved in all-round excellence at the races. Uttoxeter has been named "Best Regional Racecourse" for nine out of ten years, as well as the most "Owner Friendly". Prize money will be over £1,000,000 and this has played a large part in attracting better horses for competitive jump racing. Uttoxeter now has two pattern races and the BBC covers the February and March meetings—another worthy tribute, along with Channel 4 coverage in January, May and December.

Admission prices at Uttoxeter for 2000 are £15 for the Members Enclosure, £10 for Tattersalls and £5 for the Centre course (a great place to picnic or bring your own barbecue, with a point-to-point atmosphere). On Midlands National day in March, Club and Tattersall prices rise to £25 and £15 respectively for the £150,000 added event. There are discounts for pensioners and under 16s are admitted free when accompanied by an adult. Annual Membership is excellent value at £160 for a single badge or £240 for a double badge. Juniors pay just £75. As well as 21 days at Uttoxeter, membership includes 20 reciprocal fixtures at other courses. Also included are all fixtures at Uttoxeter's sister courses, Newcastle and Brighton, as well as Fairyhouse, which all adds up to a staggering 100 days! Outstanding racing value for the enthusiast.

Uttoxeter is an ideal place for corporate hospitality and the immaculate facilities at the progressive racecourse provide a setting in which companies can entertain in either a formal or informal manner. 65 rooms and boxes are available for parties of between 10 and 1000 guests. The latest addition to the hospitality facilities is the new Staffordshire stand.

The Members restaurant, the Platinum Suite, has been recently refurbished to the highest standards and tables may be reserved in advance and retained throughout the meeting. There is also a brand new Members Bistro—Woodrows—which is further evidence of the constant improvements at this excellent course. Tables may also be reserved in Hoops Champagne and Seafood bar adjacent to the Paddock.

At major meetings and on bank holidays, youngsters can enjoy a funfair and quad bikes—an excellent way to distract the kids. There are three public telephone boxes and reserved parking on the rails for disabled racegoers as well as a viewing platform and loos.

This is a thoroughly well-run and friendly racecourse offering fine facilities—a visit in 2000 should be a high priority.

Local Favourites
South of Stoke, in Stone, the **Crown** (01785) 813535 is an 18th century coaching inn set in lovely gardens which offers a pleasant restaurant. **Granvilles** (01785) 816658 is also a wine bar and restaurant to consider. Note **Callow Hall** (01335) 343403—a tranquil retreat. There are many pubs hidden away in these parts and invariably they have superb views. A place worth taking some trouble to find is the **Old Beams** (01538) 308254 at Waterhouses. This is a tremendous restaurant which has character and charm as well as some excellent food and pleasant bedrooms—thoroughly recommended.

In Uttoxeter itself, the **White Hart** (01889) 562437 is an historic coaching inn and the bar here makes a good place to meet if you are planning to see friends before the races. Another good inn is **Ye Olde Dog and Partridge** (01283) 813030 in Tutbury. The building dates from the 15th century and the bars here are typical of this kind of inn, welcoming and refreshing. The **Mill House** (01283) 813634 is a delightful alternative to consider. Perhaps an even more enchanting place to stay can be found in Rolleston-on-Dove. Here, the **Brookhouse Inn** (01283) 814188 has charming bars, a good restaurant and extremely pleasing bedrooms. Another superb hotel and restaurant double can be found close to here; the **Dovecliffe Hall** (01283) 531818 at Stretton. If you are seeking somewhere relatively inexpensive try the **Crown** (01283) 840227 in Abbots Bromley. **The Beeches**, in Doveridge (01889) 590288 is an excellent farmhouse-style establishment offering cosy accommodation and superb meals. Finally, the **Blacksmiths Arms** (01889) 562178 in Marchington offers innovative and realistically priced cuisine in rustic country-pub surroundings and is a favourite with the management of this first rate racecourse.

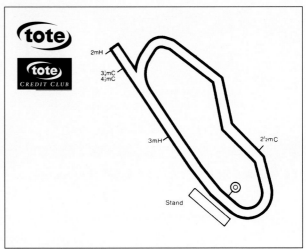

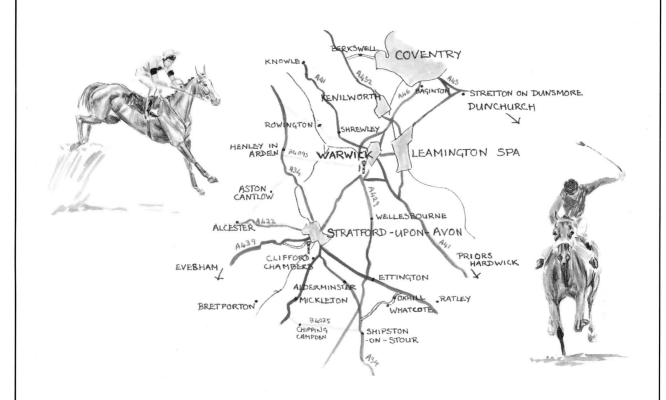

Artist: **Malcolm Coward COMING IN AT WARWICK** *Courtesy of:* **Sally Mitchell Fine Arts**

Reputedly the oldest moated manor house in England, New Hall is now a country house hotel of unrivalled style and presence. Personally run by Ian and Caroline Parkes it has been awarded 4 Red Stars by the AA, 2 AA Rosettes for food and was the AA Inspectors' Hotel of the Year for England in 1994. Among other accolades it also holds the highest RAC award, the Blue Ribbon for seven years.

Guests dine in the 16th century oak-panelled restaurant, where the award-winning chef creates superb cuisine which is unmistakeably English but exhibits flair and imagination. The comprehensive wine list, selected personally by Ian Parkes, contains the best of the old world but also features some superb newcomers.

Part of the restaurant lends itself to semi-private dining, while the Oak Room provides private dining for up to eight people. Boardroom facilities are also available in the Garden Room, the Sir Alfred Owen Room and the Chadwick Room, while the Great Chamber provides an inspiring setting for meetings of up to 50 guests.

Set in twenty six acres of private garden and surrounded by a lily-filled moat, the hotel provides extensive leisure facilities—a croquet lawn, archery, putting, an all-weather tennis court and its own 9 hole par 3 golf course. Keen golfers will be delighted by New Hall's close proximity to The Belfry's championship courses. The hotel can arrange golf here for its guests as well as at Moor Hall and Little Aston. Other championship courses in the immediate vicinity include Forest of Arden, Copt Heath and Fulford Heath. Truly a golfer's paradise.

New Hall is seven miles from the centre of Birmingham. Warwick, Coventry, Lichfield and Stratford upon Avon are all within easy reach. A veritable haven for the golfer and non-golfer alike.

New Hall
Walmley Road
Royal Sutton Coldfield B76 1QX
Tel: 0121 378 2442
Fax: 0121 378 4637

Hugo Bevan, Clerk of the Course and Christian Leech, Racecourse Manager can be contacted at Warwick Racecourse, Hampton Street, Warwick CV34 6HN. Tel (01926) 491553. Fax (01926) 403223. Adam Waterworth is Raceday Clerk of the Course.

Warwick racecourse lies close to the junction of the A46 and the A41 and is convenient for the M1, M5 and M6, a mere eight miles from Stratford (which should be avoided in the summer) and 20 miles from Birmingham—following the M6–M42 (junction 2), thence on the A41. The A46 via Leamington Spa from the north and via Stratford from the south is most convenient. Travellers from the south and west might join the A46 from the A422, (Anne Hathaway's cottage marks the appropriate junction). Road travellers should also note the new M40 link as junction 15 is only two miles from the racecourse making it extremely handy for Londoners and those from the south east.

The somewhat difficult train journey from London has been improved and there is now an hourly service direct from London to Warwick and Leamington. The station is a 20 minute walk from the racecourse. There is free parking for 3000 cars and there is also parking in the Members car park, but you will be charged £5 as a non-member for the privilege. Coaches are also welcome here with space for 100 altogether. Helicopters may land in the centre of the track at Warwick by arrangement but as for light aircraft, they are somewhat unwelcomingly sent to Coventry.

Racing in 1999 included 12 days of flat racing plus a dozen National Hunt meetings, as well as one mixed fixture in March, one of the few on this side of the Irish Sea. Annual Membership rates for 1999 were £120 for a full badge and £75 for a National Hunt badge. Juniors (16 to 24) are charged £50 but please also note an extra £10 is asked for a car park badge if required. A Half Yearly Membership may be purchased from June 1st at a cost of £60. In addition to racing at Warwick, full Members are entitled to reciprocal arrangements at ten other courses. Each member is also given two vouchers which admit guests to the Club during the year. The Daily Club badge in 1999 was £15, Tattersalls (Grandstand and Paddock) £10 and £5 for the Course Enclosure. Warwick is undertaking a £3 million refurbishment of the Members and Tattersalls grandstands, to include greater viewing dining and betting facilities, and during that time the two enclosures will be combined with an admission charge of £9 up until July 2000 when new price details will be announced. Accompanied children under 16 are admitted free. Discounts on a sliding scale are given for parties of 20 or more in Tattersalls, if booked in advance.

Boxes in the Paddock Suite are available on a daily basis and enjoy spectacular views as well as from the balcony over the Paddock and racecourse. The elegant Castle Suite accommodates 60 for lunch or dinner and 80 for a buffet meal whilst the Chandler Suite, situated on the ground floor of the Members Enclosure, has a private viewing stand. The suite may be divided into three rooms if required. The Spartan Missile Room is opposite the winning post offering entertaining views of the betting ring too. There are snack bars in all enclosures and two restaurants: the Paddock Bar and recently refurbished Members Bar. Booking is advisable on major racedays and can be done by telephoning the course caterers, Amadeus on 0121 767 2543. The Council Room in Tatts has also been refurbished and more upgrading is planned over the next few years. An exclusive Owners and Trainers room is also available.

A crèche is provided for all Saturday fixtures and bank holiday fixtures. Disabled people are accommodated by means of a raised stand, ramps and lavatories in the Members Enclosure. There are no banks on site at Warwick so come prepared as there is a betting shop in Tattersalls and the Course Enclosure (open Saturdays and bank holidays only).

While it is fair to say that no Midlands course is a major sporting venue, several provide excellent entertainment. Furthermore, Members here can enjoy a variety of racing at under £5 a head and to my mind that represents very good value.

Local Favourites

If you are staying nearby, a number of hotels stand out. A well thought of hotel is the Hilton National (01926) 499555, most convenient for the A46 and the M40. By contrast, the Old Fourpenny Shop (01926) 491360 is small but appealing. The Glebe (01926) 624218 in Barford has good leisure facilities—an interesting option. We have also had a tip from one of Britain's foremost jockeys—the Woodhouse Hotel in Princethorpe (01926) 632131. Walton Hall (01789) 842424 is also a very good local hotel with a good restaurant, and we're told by a reliable source that Henrietta's (01926) 642212 in Kineton is excellent. Another popular local watering hole is the Racehorse in Stratford Road. Kenilworth has two fancied restaurants Simpsons (01926) 864567 and the Restaurant Bosquet (01926) 852463, while Charlecote offers the Charlecote Pheasant (01789) 470333—a pleasant hotel for a weekend away. Another original establishment, the Case is Altered in Five Ways is delightful (no youngsters though). However, children are welcomed at another fine establishment, the Bulls Head at Wootton Wanen.

Further north in Henley-in-Arden a friendly place to stay is the Ashleigh House (01564) 792315, an Edwardian country house with views over the Warwickshire countryside. In Sutton Coldfield, New Hall 0121 378 2442 offers a stylish haven in the oldest moated manor house in England. Alternatively try the Stakis Birmingham Metropole 0121 780 4242 or, as a contrast, splendid Tudor Yew Trees—superb character and a very high standard. The bedrooms are cheerful and the bars are an extremely good place to meet before dining in the Oakwood Restaurant. Perhaps the most outstanding place to visit in the area is Mallory Court (01926) 330214. Situated in Bishops Tachbrook, south of Leamington Spa, this is a picture of elegance. Bedrooms are sumptuous, while the restaurant provides exquisite French cooking. In the Parade of Leamington Spa itself, one finds a more modest, but no less welcoming hotel, the Regent (01926) 427231, a restaurant here of note as well. We trust one of the above appeals whilst visiting Warwick in 2000.

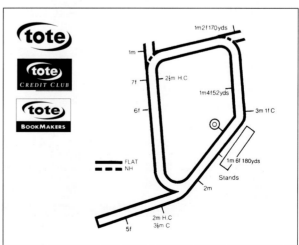

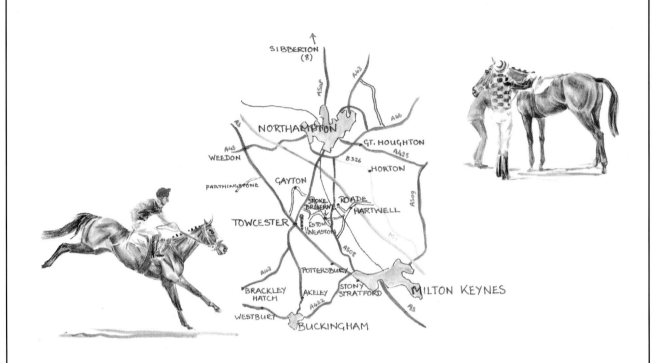

Artist: **Klaus Philipp** **AFTER THE RACE** *Courtesy of:* **The Artist**

Wetherby

Wetherby is an extremely popular racecourse and there is no doubt this is a well run course, as most of the Yorkshire tracks are. It has an informal atmosphere but provides an excellent standard of racing. **Christopher Tetley** is **Clerk of the Course, James Sanderson** is the **Manager** and **Melissa Green** is in charge of **Sales & Marketing.** They can be contacted through **Wetherby Steeplechase Committee Ltd., The Racecourse, York Road, Wetherby, West Yorkshire LS22 5EJ. Tel (01937) 582035. Fax (01937) 580565.**

The course is one of the most accessible in the country, being close to the A1 and thereby providing an excellent route for both north and southbound vehicles. Wetherby is 200 miles from London and close to Leeds, Harrogate and York. York is about 13 miles from the racecourse and buses run there from outside the railway station. The B1224 is the most direct route from York. The M62 runs from the west of the country and it connects with the A1 at junction 33, ten miles south of Wetherby. There is a railway station in Harrogate about nine miles away and a bus station in Wetherby which is one and a half miles from the course. Leeds, twelve miles distant, connecting to the bus is probably a better bet. Car parking is ample and is provided free of charge.

Fifteen fixtures are due to be scheduled next season, including one Sunday meeting in November. A number of local Yorkshire trainers send good horses to Wetherby and a generally high standard of racing can be expected. The crowd is both vocal and knowledgeable and this generates a superb atmosphere coupled with the traditionally hearty voices of a Yorkshire crowd—always entertaining for southerners!

Annual Membership is good value at £130. Joint Membership for married couples is also well priced at £210, but there is a two year waiting list. Daily Membership rates are £15, Tattersalls £9 rising to £16 and £15 respectively, on high days and the popular Course Enclosure is £3, reduced to £1.50 for pensioners. Cars are admitted to the centre of course for £12 (including up to 4 adults). Children under 16 are admitted free if accompanied by an adult.

In 1995 the new Saddling-up Enclosure, Weighing Room and Administration Complex was built at a cost of £375,000. In January 1999, construction began on The Wetherby Millennium Stand, an impressive new Members' Grandstand, complete with 10 magnificent boxes, to be operational from 29th October 1999. At a cost of £4.15 million this development offers state-of-the-art facilities and surroundings such as 3 new bars, a restaurant with a Parade Ring view and raised viewing for 500. Other facilities include a children's playground in the Course Enclosure, and viewing facilities close to the winning post for disabled people. There is no racecourse bank but there are public telephones and a betting shop which is located in the Paddock Enclosure.

All in all, Wetherby is a friendly racecourse. It is one of the top jumping tracks in the north and the only one of the nine Yorkshire courses devoted entirely to National Hunt racing. Although probably still not for everyone, summer jumping seems to be catching on with many trainers and owners keeping their top of the ground horses for racing at this time of the year. We can't think of a better place to hold one than Wetherby. Provided the ground was not too firm and the entries held up it would be sure to attract an immense crowd. Whatever the going or weather, I can always recommend a day at Wetherby where racing over the sticks is at its best. Be sure to visit in 2000.

Local Favourites

In West Yorkshire, there are relatively few hotels but several pubs. However, Leeds makes up for the lack of hotels elsewhere and a selection includes the **Hilton National** (0113) 244 2000, which is modern and comfortable. A more traditional, 1930s hotel is the **Queen's** (0113) 243 1323 in the city square. There are many good restaurants in Leeds but one with a definite pedigree is **Sang Sang** (0113) 246 8664. **42 The Calls** (0113) 244 0099 is a marvellously novel and good value weekend haunt to consider if in these parts. It also demonstrates what can be done with derelict buildings. Furthermore, **Brasserie Forty Four** (0113) 234 3232 is an excellent place in which to enjoy dinner and **Pool Court at 42** (0113) 244 4242 makes this a trio of excellence to challenge any. A winner in the last at nearby Wetherby and dinner in any of these would satisfy the most discerning of punters. An alternative, however, is **Oulton Hall** (0113) 282 1000, a classy performer with good leisure facilities from the DeVere stable. Other good restaurants include **Rascasse** (0113) 244 6611 and **Leodis** (0113) 242 1010 both with excellent fayre and settings.

If you can escape the city, then run to Harewood where the best known landmark in the village is Harewood House. Open from April to October, the gardens, collections of Chippendale furniture and superb English works of art are all fascinating. Here the **Harewood Arms** (0113) 288 6566 is ideally placed and reasonable. Good public houses nearby are the **Windmill** in Linton and the **White Swan** (01937) 832217 at Wighill, a marvellous country boozer with a fine collection of racing prints—a pleasant restaurant as well. Whilst we are in the vicinity of Linton, **Wood Hall** (01937) 587271 is quite outstanding. This is a converted Georgian manor which has excellent amenities. **Linton Springs** is also well regarded. A good guest house is **Prospect House** (01937) 582428—offering a pleasant welcome to the weary (or exuberant) traveller. **David Wooleys** (01943) 864002 is a good restaurant to consider.

There are two hotels convenient for the racecourse, The **Bridge Inn** at Walshford (01937) 580115 and the **Jarvis Wetherby Hotel** (01937) 583881.

Much of the countryside in Yorkshire is full of mystery, none more haunting than that surrounding the former home of Emily and Charlotte Bronte. A pub that dates back to well before the birth of the sisters can be found at Bardsey, the **Bingley Arms**, a mere four miles from Wetherby—the perfect place to celebrate an historic win at the races.

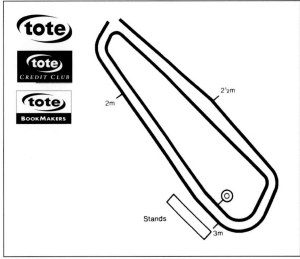

The Lamb Inn at Hindon, a fine 17th century Inn, is situated in the picturesque of Hindon, a Wiltshire village between Shaftesbury and Salisbury. It is noted for its friendly welcome and traditional atmosphere.

The oldest part of the building boasts a distinguished history as an historic Coaching Inn supplying fresh horses for traffic travelling between London and the West Country. Each of the fourteen attractively decorated en suite bedrooms is equipped with television and telephone. The Lamb is open all year round and can cater for meetings, conferences and weddings.

The restaurant always prides itself in the preparation of the finest local vegetable and game produce. Fresh seafood is supplied daily en-route to London from the various Cornish ports. The bar with its welcoming log fires and relaxing ambience tempts visitors with a variety of fine local and guest cask-conditioned ales. There is an imaginative and extensive bar menu,

offering both hot and cold food at lunch time and in the evening.

John Croft and Cara Scott continue the tradition of previous patrons of the Lamb in their enthusiastic involvement in both the Flat and National Hunt racing scenes. The Lamb at Hindon, is conveniently placed for both Wincanton and Salisbury racecourses with Taunton and Bath being slightly further afield. In addition other outdoor activities, including riding, hunting, shooting and fishing are all easily arranged and there are several fine golf courses in the local area.

Being located in the gate way to the West Country you have an abundance of places to visit including the New Forest, Stonehenge, Longleat Safari Park, Thruxton Race Track, and the towns of Salisbury, Warminster and Wincanton, so whatever the reason for your visit you will find The Lamb Inn the ideal venue.

The Lamb Inn
Hindon
Sailsbury
Wiltshire
SP3 6DP
Tel: (01747) 820573
Fax: (01747) 820605

Artist: **Philip Toon** **BETWEEN THE SHOWERS** *Courtesy of:* **The Artist**

Artist: **Heather St Clair Davis BUSY MORNING** *Courtesy of:* **Frost & Reed**

The Unicorn Inn

This popular and friendly 270 year old village inn is situated in the village of Bayford only one and a half miles (or 12 furlongs) from the racecourse at Wincanton. A former coaching inn on the old Exeter - London route (the old A303), the Unicorn has kept many of its original features including flagstoned floors, beams, open fireplaces and a hidden well. Michael and Carrie Sims extend a warm welcome to all racegoers.

Michael and Carrie themselves own an early retired racehorse, and on racedays you will find the inn extremely busy with owners and punters swapping stories and jokes in a great atmosphere. There is an impressive selection behind the bar - with real ales including local and guest beers, along with a list of fine wines from around the world.

The inn has been sympathetically modernised and has en-suite accommodation. You will find that, while everything has been done to enhance your comfort, nothing has been done which detracts from the beauty of the building and its fabulous location. Highly regarded lunches and evening meals are served using best quality local produce. Secure car parking is available and courtesy transport to the racecourse is provided for overnight guests.

Aside from the racecourse, other places to visit nearby include Stourhead House and Gardens, Alfred's Tower, King Arthur's Fort, Haynes Motor Museum, Yeovilton Air Museum, Glastonbury Tor, Clarkes Village and Stonehenge.

For a relaxed visit to the races it would be difficult to find anywhere so welcoming and atmospheric.

The Unicorn Inn
Bayford
Wincanton
Somerset BA9 9NL
Tel: (01963) 32324

The Unicorn Inn

Wincanton is a very worthwhile establishment to visit and win or lose you will surely enjoy a good day out. **Ian Renton, Clerk of the Course**, and **Madeleine Bridger, Assistant Manager/Marketing Executive** have the enviable task of running this most popular of jumping courses. They can be contacted at **The Racecourse, Wincanton, Somerset BA9 8BJ. Tel (01963) 32344. Fax (01963) 34668.**

The course itself lies just off the A303 bypass, on the B3081 and like many racecourses on racedays is signposted by AA signposts and local directional signs. If you are travelling from London some 110 miles away, then the M4 and the M3 both trek in that westward direction. Equally satisfactory is the old A4. Wincanton itself lies on the A303. Travellers north and south should note the A357 and the A37 respectively. A public bus service winds its way to Wincanton, but the nearest railway stations are at Templecombe on the Waterloo line seven miles away, where a free coach service will meet the London Waterloo train, or at Castle Cary on the Paddington route. There is a taxi service from both stations but taxis at the latter need to be ordered in advance. Large car parks are available and there is no charge for parking. Finally, helicopters may land in the centre of the course by prior arrangement.

On your arrival there will inevitably be some fairly competitive racing. The Boxing Day meeting, including the Mid Season Chase and the Lord Stalbridge Gold Cup is the most popular. Other leading races include the Jim Ford Challenge Cup and the Axminster 100 Kingwell Hurdle in late February and the Tanglefoot Elite Hurdle and Badger Chase in November. These races often attract excellent horses and local trainers use them as 'prep' events for more prestigious races later in the year.

In the 1999/00 season visits to Wincanton will cost £15 for Members, £10 for Tatts and £5 for the Course Enclosure. The price of an Annual Members Badge is £110, with a £5 discount if you join before the end of November. A car pass is also thrown in which gives you preferential parking plus ten reciprocal days racing at various tracks around the country including Ascot, Salisbury, Newbury, Taunton, Exeter, Bath, Sandown, Cheltenham and Doncaster. For those aged between 17 and 22 Junior Annual Membership is available at £60 and the Junior Club costs £8, although this is not available on Boxing Day. If one wishes to gather a group of friends together then a 15-20 per cent discount applies for parties in excess of ten and if you are taking a really substantial number then further discounts can be arranged. Bigger parties of 30 to 120 may wish to make use of the private rooms available. Companies or individuals wishing to take advantage of these facilities should contact the racecourse.

You may well be surprised at the excellent value you can receive entertaining at the races. The course has seven boxes which are let either daily or annually. Sited on the top floor they offer splendid views of the course. Another plan for a party at the races is to arrange for your own marquee—an area near the parade ring is ideal. If you like the idea of lunching whilst you fill out your bets, then the Members Restaurant overlooks the Paddock and should serve you well—bookings can be made through the course office. The three course lunch will cost about £18. The Stalbridge Bar and the Tattersalls Bar have both been refurbished and there is a new Tote Members betting shop. The racecourse caterers are Parkers Catering at Milborne Port (01963) 250368. Alternatively, there are the snack bars and a picnic area in the Course Enclosure. Car parking on the course costs £5 plus £5 for each occupant. This is a great way to get the best out of racing, particularly for newcomers to the sport.

Under 16s are admitted free with children's entertainment and a crèche available at the Easter Monday and October Sunday meetings. There are plenty of telephones and excellent disabled viewing in the Hatherleigh Stand. Special discounts can be made in advance for disabled people on written application to the course. Wincanton offers exciting and competitive racing with welcoming staff who will ensure you have a happy and, hopefully, a successful day at the races.

Local Favourites

Wincanton is a first rate jumping track to visit and the following establishments may help stave off a winter chill after a day at the races. An excellent pub to try is the **Unicorn Inn** (01963) 32324 in Bayford, which has a pleasant atmosphere, good bar snacks and a number of bedrooms. In Hindon, one finds the **Lamb** (01747) 89573 with some good bar food and comfortable accommodation. As the road diverges one has the choice of Warminster or Mere. In Mere you should visit the **Old Ship** (01747) 860258 which has a pleasant bar with appetizing snacks. The town also houses the highly recommended **Chetcombe House Hotel** (01747) 860219 and the **Talbot Hotel** (01747) 860427. In Warminster you have an excellent proposition in the form of **Bishopstrow House** (01985) 212312, an outstanding Georgian mansion. The hotel is a delight and the restaurant is excellent. In Shepton Mallet, **Blostin's** (01749) 343648 enjoys an extremely good following, while **Bowlish House** (01749) 342022 is much recommended for a pleasant evening after a successful day at Wincanton races. Some accommodation here and also at **Brottens Lodge** (01749) 880352—a first rate restaurant. At Evercreech the **Pecking Mill** (01749) 830336 offers good food and some bedrooms. Nearer to Wincanton, several places should be mentioned. Bruton offers **Truffles** (01749) 812255, a restaurant of note. Two **Bulls** now, one in Brewham, the other in Hardway—good bar food here. And nearby Stourton proves a worthy diversion with a Palladian mansion and superb gardens. The **Spread Eagle** (01747) 840587 is the local to note and it has some accommodation if required. In Bourtons, neighbouring Wincanton, the **Hunters Lodge Inn** is popular with racegoers. Wincanton itself offers the charming and good value **Lower Church Farm** (01963) 32307, while in Holbrook, the **Holbrook House** (01963) 32377 is an ideal place to stay. Not quite so convenient but appealing is **Bonds** (01963) 350464 in Castle Cary, which has delightful bedrooms and a fine restaurant. The **George** (01963) 350761 in the market place is also good. South of Wincanton in the village of Barwick, **Little Barwick House** (01935) 23902 is most accommodating and offers an outstanding dinner, the specialities being fish and game. Nearby, a handy pub for the A30 is the **Queen's Head** (01963) 250314, at Milborne Port, which has excellent value accommodation and some good bar snacks. Our final thought for racegoers considering a visit to Wincanton is the outstanding **Charlton House** (01749) 342008 a superb Georgian house which reveals an outstanding hotel and restaurant double.

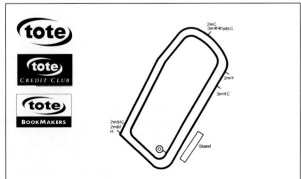

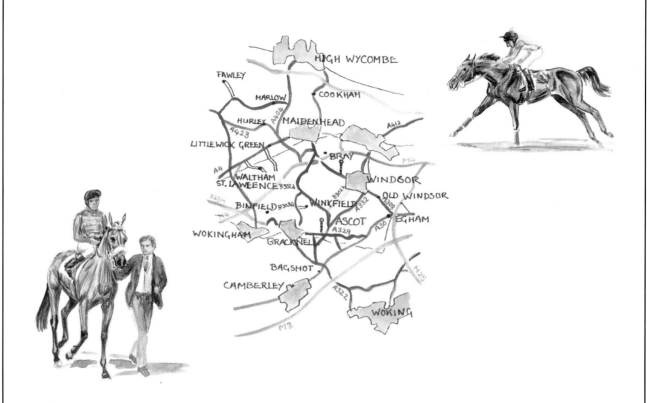

Artist: **Klaus Philipp** **AFTER THE RACE** *Courtesy of:* **The Artist**

Windsor

Windsor is a busy racecourse, renowned for its mid-summer evening races. The **Clerk of the Course** at Windsor is **Fraser Garritty** and he can be reached on **(01753) 865234.** The **Racecourse Manager, Sally Dingle** can be contacted at the racecourse office, **Royal Windsor Races, The Racecourse, Windsor, Berkshire SL4 5JJ. Tel (01753) 865234/864726 Fax (01753) 830156.**

The racecourse is on the A308 between Windsor and Maidenhead. West and eastbound traffic on the M4 should leave the motorway at junction 6. The M3 traffic from the south should leave the motorway at interchange 3 and follow the A332 to Windsor. Travellers from the north and the east will find a combination of the M25, M4 and the A308 the best route. For those who might prefer a slight change from the normal mode of transportation, why not travel by river bus. The summer shuttle boat service operates from Barry Avenue Promenade close to Windsor Bridge in the town centre and takes racegoers to the racecourse jetty, close to the Paddock. The journey takes about ten minutes and there is a bar on board. For further information contact French Brothers (01753) 862933/851900. There are frequent rail services from Waterloo and Paddington to Windsor and Eton (Riverside) and Windsor and Eton (Central) respectively, both two miles away. The Green Line bus terminus is one mile from the course. The car parking facilities cost £1, £1.50 and £2 and coaches just £5. On another plane, helicopter landing facilities are available but permission should be sought in advance.

In 1999 Windsor restricted itself to Flat racing-a pity but it seems this is in the best interests of the course. Most racing here is run on Monday evenings with an August bank holiday and Saturday evening meeting as well. These occasions are enormously popular with owners and this assures good support from some of the country's leading stables which in turn guarantees huge crowds. A simple formula and a great success! These evenings often precede the year's major flat meetings and serve as an excellent aperitif for the week's principal attractions. What better way to spend a summer evening? However, the traffic out of London is usually so congested that an early start is strongly advised.

In 1999 Annual Membership Badges for Royal Windsor Race Club were priced at £140 each. Daily badges are £15 for the Club, £10 for the Tattersalls and Paddock Enclosure and £4 for the Silver Ring. The course encourages advance bookings for the Tattersalls Stand and Paddock, for which a 25% discount is offered for parties of 20 or more. A similar deal is available for the Silver Ring where the discount is £1. The executive also encourages the reservation of the Churchill Suite and private boxes in the Royal Windsor Grandstand and Paddock Pavilion, overlooking the finishing straight. Lunch and dinner can be reserved by contacting the course caterers, Letheby & Christopher (01753) 832552. The potential for company and business entertainment is particularly interesting when one considers the evening meetings. Corporate hospitality is organised by the racecourse office. It is also worth noting that children under 16 are admitted free and there are public telephones available but no banks are in attendance as yet. Disabled people are well looked after with a special viewing stand and reserved paddock viewing. Admission for wheelchair users is free of charge, which is excellent.

All in all Windsor has great appeal. The new Royal Windsor Stand, housing the Castle Restaurant and viewing boxes is an excellent addition. We hope that the investment is richly rewarded in the years to come.

Local Favourites

If you do wish to stay in the area then a hotel that is worthy of recommendation is **Fredrick's** (01628) 635934 on Shoppenhangers Road—the bedrooms are comfortable and the restaurant excellent. The menu changes frequently and one is treated to some splendidly imaginative cooking. A similarly outstanding hotel and restaurant double is to be found along the Windsor road—it is an absolute pearl and its name is **Oakley Court** (01628) 74141. All manner of facilities are complemented by excellent service, gracious surroundings and beautiful grounds. The restaurant, the **Oak Leaf Room** is another great pleasure. For people who do not wish such extravagance then **Sir Christopher Wren's House Hotel** (01753) 861354 is excellent—the **Stroks Restaurant** has a splendid setting and is definitely one to sample. A further example of good fare and good value service is **Melrose House** (01753) 865328.

In Eton, on the High Street to be precise, the **Christopher Hotel** (01753) 852359 has comfortable bedrooms and a palatable selection of real ales. This is also a good base for exploring the antique shops of Eton if this happens to be to your liking. The **Eton Wine Bar** (01753) 854921 is also very good. Returning to Windsor, a number of suggestions arise. There are several excellent establishments that nestle beneath the magnificent castle, the **Castle** (01753) 851011 being a particularly notable example. Another well known landmark in Marlow is the **Compleat Angler** (01628) 484444. Its setting on the Thames is renowned as one of the most superb spots. The **Valaisan** restaurant is also outstanding and visitors can enjoy marvellous views of the river. In Taplow a superb hotel is **Taplow House** (01628) 670056—excellent comfort and once again an elegant formal restaurant-the **Tulip Tree**. Lovers of truly excellent cooking should consider **L'Ortolan** (01189) 883783 in Shinfield, its excellent. Similarly The **Waterside Inn** (01628) 620691 is, on its day, up there with the best - some pleasant rooms here as well. Also consider **Cliveden** (01628) 668561 an incredible hotel and restaurant for those who came up trumps with a good win.

People looking for a less formal evening meal should consider the **Walnut Tree** in Farly, and in Cookham the **Royal Exchange** is also well worth a trip. Also in Cookham, the **Bel and Dragon** in the High Street is good—there is a fine restaurant to be found here. Elsewhere in Cookham lovers of oriental cuisine should seek out the **Peking Inn** (01628) 520900—where booking is advisable. **The Inn on the Green** in Cookham Dean is also to be noted. The **Long Barn** in Cippenham, also offers good food and great character. In Dorney, the **Palmer Arms** (01628) 666612 is also excellent serving really tremendous bar meals.

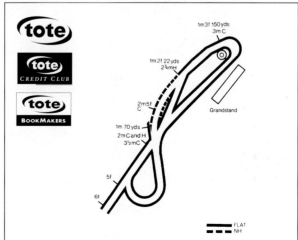

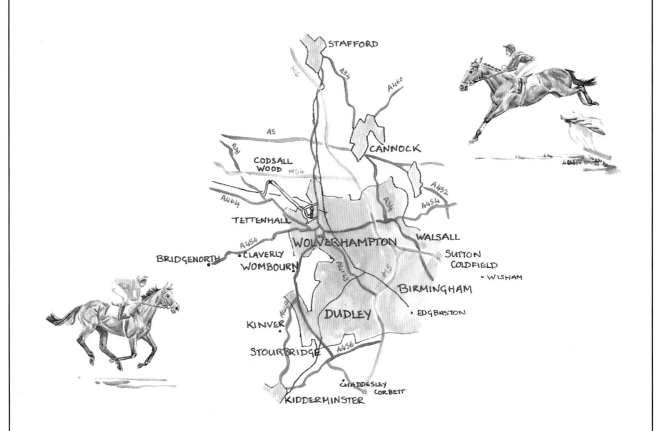

Artist: **John Lewis Fitzgerald** **FINAL FURLONG** *Courtesy of:* **Solomon & Whitehead**

Racing has been revolutionised at Wolverhampton. The complex now calls itself Dunstall Park Centre, and enquiries should be addressed to the **Clerk of the Course Michael Prosser** at **Dunstall Park Centre, Gorsebrook Road, Wolverhampton WV6 0PE Tel (01902) 421421 Fax (01902) 421621.**

The course lies some 16 miles north west of Birmingham, close to Tettenhall, and the area is well served by motorways. Lancastrians should follow the M6 to junction 12 and thereafter the A449. Racegoers from the south west should pursue the M5 to the M6 and on to the M54 to junction 2 followed by the A449, whilst Welshmen should aim for Wellington and the M54. London racegoers will find the M1 and the M6 most useful. The course is approximately 130 miles distant. The nearest railway station is in Wolverhampton—take the train from Euston and then grab a taxi for the five minute journey to the course. There is a bus station in the town centre and buses run to the course. Free parking is provided for cars with 2000 spaces and plenty of room for coaches. Helicopters can land at the course but please contact the racecourse management in advance.

Fixtures for 2000 should continue at a similar pattern to previous years, with around 50 meetings. As the only floodlit racecourse in Great Britain, regular Saturday evening racing makes for a superb night out, and there is a continuing growth of restaurants and style of dining to cater for the increasing popularity. 1998 saw the successful return of a summer evening jumping fixture - no floodlights needed! Full Annual Membership of the Club Enclosure at £150 is excellent value. Access to the Club Enclosure is for Annual Subscribers, day members, owners, trainers, executive box holders and invited guests. The 400 seater tiered viewing restaurant offers panoramic views of the racetrack for all racegoers with a courier betting service available at each table. Admission to the racecourse is £8 and on selected dates £10 for all areas other than the Club Enclosure which is £15 and on selected dates £20. Pensioners may apply to join the Diamond Club at the really good value price of £2.50, which allows a discount of £2 off either Tattersalls or Member's enclosures. For Saturday evening meetings there is a choice of four restaurants which all offer various deals including your entry, racecard, three course meal and dancing until midnight. In 1999 prices started at £21.50 in the Ringside, £32.90 for the tiered Zongalero Viewing Restaurant, £34.50 in Lesters and £39.50 in the Member's Restaurant. Some special themed evenings are planned, and entrance prices may vary accordingly, so please check in advance. Discounts are also offered for parties of over 40 on Tattersalls entrance, while there are two free places available in the Ringside Restaurant for parties with up to or over 41 guests.

The eight private boxes accommodate parties of 16–64 seated and up to 80 for buffets and are let on a daily basis. Larger function suites are also available for corporate and private hire. Packages are tailored to include hire of box, a four course silver service meal, access to the Owners and Members lounge, admission charge and car parking. A courier betting service is also available on request. The popular Fashion Festival is run in conjunction with the prestigious Weatherby Dash sprint in August. Contact the course for a fixture booklet with a list of themes.

Wolverhampton is an amazing achievement. Some £15.7 million has been invested to create an all-weather track, turf course, floodlights, a new Grandstand, boxes and a 400 seater restaurant on the top floor. Not to mention a 54 bedroomed Holiday Inn Hotel.

Local Favourites

The most obvious recommendation is the **Holiday Inn Garden Court Hotel** at Dunstall Park (01902) 713313. The 54 rooms are all en suite with TV, telephone, tea and coffee making facilities. Accommodation starts at £84 per night b&b for two and is specially tailored for the punter, being linked to the main grandstand and with the Racing Channel and SiS in every bedroom. The hotel also boasts a relaxing bar and bistro, and disabled facilities—a fitness room is available for use by hotel guests. The **Mount** (01902) 752055 is also well worth a pre or post race inspection

One of the best known leisure centres in the country is situated at Wishaw: the **Belfry** (01675) 470301—a whole host of pursuits can be enjoyed here aside from golf. The hotel's restaurants promise nouvelle cuisine as well as English fare. Alternatively, you may wish to visit the **Moor Hall Hotel**, Sutton Coldfield (01213) 083751 which also has strong associations with the nearby golf course and is a most welcoming place to stay. Another Hall also can be found at Sutton Coldfield, **New Hall** 0121 378 2442. This is an outstanding establishment with an inspiring setting and a fine restaurant—just two good reasons for staying here. If any or all of the above are full then another good place to try is the **Standbridge Hotel** (01213) 543007.

In Birmingham, one finds some very large hotels. The **Hyatt Regency** 0121 643 1234 is extremely good and has a distinguished restaurant—Number 282. Similarly, the **Holiday Inn** 0121 631 2000 offers excellent leisure facilities. If you get a yen for Chinese food, the **Queens Cantonese** restaurant (01902) 713399 in Queen Street, Wolverhampton comes highly recommended. For a taste of something different the same applies to a local pub with Tex Mex food, the **Bentlands Pub** (01902) 843654 which is in Suckling Green Lane, Codsall, Wolverhampton or the **Barley Mow** who specialise in Yorkies.

Chaddesley Corbett also offers an establishment of distinction in **Brockencote Hall** (01562) 777876. The house, restaurant and grounds are all worth a pre-race inspection: combined they make up a great favourite. Finally, on the hotel front, another sporting hotel with great appeal is **Patshall Park** (01902) 700100, where the accent is on an excellent golf course. To complete our section on a rather bizarre note, visit the **Crooked House** (01384) 238583 an unusual establishment with good food. The **Mill House** 0121 459 5800 in Kings Norton is small but exceptional. One final trip to consider is to Worfield and the **Old Vicarage** (01746) 716497—a delightful setting and good food.

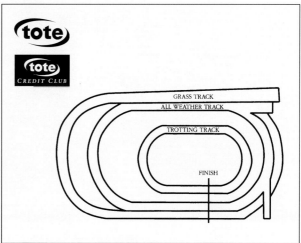

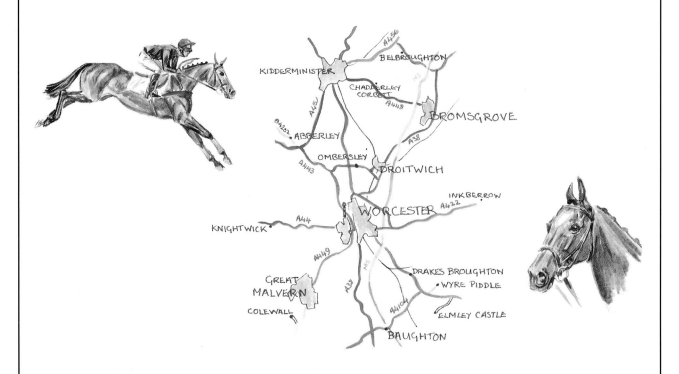

Artist: **Heather St Clair Davis DUEL** *Courtesy of:* **Frost & Reed**

The people in charge of the course at Worcester are John Baker, the **Manager**, and Hugo Bevan, the **Clerk of the Course**. Administration and corporate hospitality are the preserve of **Christine Draper**. The course address is: **Grandstand Road, Worcester WR1 3EJ. Tel (01905) 25364. Fax (01905) 617563.** The telephone number for racedays only is **(01905) 21338**

To reach the racecourse, which lies some 120 miles west of London and 20 miles from Birmingham, one might use any one of the following routes. From the west, the M5 (junction 6) and thence the A449 and the A38 provide a winning combination. The course itself rests between Broadheath and Herwick. The A58 from Birmingham provides a smooth route for racegoers from the West Midlands. The M5 (junction 7) is another route which benefits from the A38. From the Cotswolds, the A44 is a pleasant trek—the A443 is a help here. People who consider this to be the age of the train, can use it via the Paddington line. Get off at Worcester Foregate St. If the proverbial flying horse is preferred to the so-called iron horse, then phone the manager in advance who will inform you where to land your chopper. Car parking is free, except for picnic parking where a £3 charge is made.

The 2000 season enjoys a fixture list similar to that of 1999, with five summer fixtures and some excellent evening meetings. There are several Wednesday afternoon fixtures, of great appeal to the farming community who are so much the backbone of the National Hunt game. A wet and windy Wednesday at Worcester may not immediately appeal but even when the elements prove uncooperative a day out can prove well worthwhile. Annual Membership is now available but please check with the racecourse for rates. Members Daily Badges in 1999 were priced at £13.50, entrance to Tattersalls £10.50 and the Silver Ring £5.50. OAPs are entitled to Centre Course tickets at £2.75. Something also worth noting is a discount for parties of twelve or more when prices of £10.40, £8 and £4.40 are available for Members, Tattersalls and the Centre Course respectively. You should book in advance to obtain these prices and you may pay by credit card. Badges can be purchased from the Manager's office but must be paid for at least seven days in advance.

What sounds great fun are the riverboats moored behind the grandstand for parties from 30 and 200. The Worcester management team are clearly refusing to give in to the ravages of the Severn, and are instead harnessing its beauty for their own ends. For landlubbers there are the usual boxes and a superb sponsors' room capable of holding up to 120 people. Punters please note that the Croft Suite also has a restaurant for which reservations can be made, on (01905) 25970. A marquee has now been erected on a permanent basis next to the Paddock and this can accommodate an extra 60 hospitality guests. It is clear that there is plenty of scope for all sorts of additional entertainment and this is reflected in the fact that the racecourse has the support of numerous sponsors.

Other advantages of coming to Worcester are that children are admitted free before their 16th birthday. In addition, there are children's facilities during the summer. Disabled people have special viewing facilities and there is a lift to the Members restaurant. Telephones can be found adjacent to the grandstand where the course betting shop is also located. Make no mistake, this is a delightful racetrack—its facilities are good and a day's racing here is to be thoroughly recommended.

Local Favourites

The ancient cathedral city of Worcester, which is delightfully peaceful, also has some excellent antique shops and a variety of hotels and restaurants should you be anticipating a large gamble coming off. The **Giffard Hotel** (01905) 726262, overlooking the cathedrals precincts, is modern while **Brown's** (01905) 26263 is a splendidly converted corn mill, ideal for lunch and dinner and situated beside the cricket ground. Returning Cathedral-wards, a thirsty fellow should find the **Farriers Arms,** a traditional public house. A converted glove factory makes for another noteworthy hotel, with good accommodation and a fine restaurant, called **Fownes** (01905) 613151. **Il Pescatore** (01905) 21444 is a good Italian restaurant to look out for.

Outside the city itself, amid the fruit trees and the whiff of hops, one finds a feast of delights, starting with the racecourse. In Colwall, the **Colwall Park Hotel** (01684) 40206 stands in front of the old National Hunt course and is a tremendous place to stay. The hotel offers English cooking and the Edwardian dining room is backed up by an extensive bar menu. Some lovely places can be found in and around Great Malvern. In Malvern Wells, the **Croque-en-Bouche** (016845) 65612 is one of the country's finest dining places. Alternatively, visit the **Cottage in the Wood Hotel** (016845) 73487. A really wonderful place to stay, it also has a highly regarded restaurant which is open to non-residents. One commendable hotel in Malvern is the **Foley Arms** (01684) 73397, a charming Georgian edifice in which to slumber. Another great place to stay with a good restaurant is the **Elms Hotel** (01299) 896666 in Abberley. Where next? Try Bromsgrove and **Grafton Manor** (01527) 579007 where tradition and luxury combine to make yours a delightful stay. Less glamourous but still comfortable is the **Phepson Guest House** (01905) 69205 in Himbleton. Whilst in Droitwich Spa, the **Chateau Impney** (01905) 774411 is yet another good idea for those of you seeking refined stabling when visiting these parts.

In Wyre Piddle, the **Anchor** (01386) 552799 is a grand pub cum restaurant. The **Talbot** (01886) 821235 at Knightwick is also a tremendous inn with good value accommodation. Followers of the Archers might care to make a pilgrimage to the **Old Bull**, Inkberrow whilst those looking for some good pub food should visit the **Bear and Ragged Staff** (01886) 833399 in Bransford or The **Bell** at Pensax (01299) 896677. And don't forget Ombersley, where the **Kings Arms** (01905) 620315, the **Crown and Sandys Arms** (01905) 620252 provide good food and warm hospitality. A fitting double for visitors to Worcester racecourse.

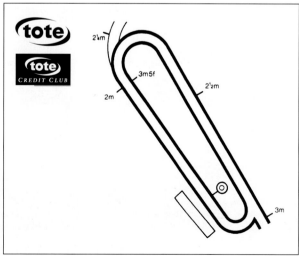

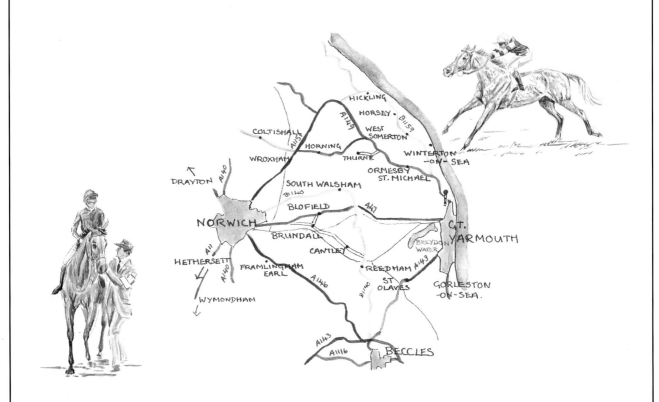

Artist: **Philip Toon SUNSHINE & SHADOWS** *Courtesy of:* **The Artist**

Those in charge at Yarmouth are **David Henson** who is **Clerk of the Course** and **David Thompson** as **Racecourse Manager**. They can be contacted at **The Racecourse, Jellicoe Road, Great Yarmouth NR30 4AU. Tel (01493) 842527. Fax (01493) 843254.**

The journey to Yarmouth by road has now been made much faster by the opening of the southern bypass around Norwich and by the many new sections of dual carriageway on the A11 and A47. From London, the following treble is advised—the M11, A11 and A47. The A12 via Colchester, Ipswich and Lowestoft however, will certainly prove a more stimulating option. Were you to make a seafront promenade the night before, please note that a bus runs regularly from the seafront to the racecourse. Furthermore, the local bus routes run from each of the town's holiday centres. The nearest railway station is in Yarmouth itself and although no bus runs directly from here, the track is only a leisurely 30 minute walk away but is also only 5 minutes away from the main road where the bus runs. London racegoers should use the Liverpool Street line. Back on the roads, the A47 via Norwich serves the racegoer travelling from the north and west of the country. There is plenty of room for car parking, for which there is a £1 charge. Limited space is reserved for coaches if pre-booked with the course management.

Average attendance here is around 3000 and meetings in 2000 will hopefully follow the same pattern as last year with 17 fixtures including four evenings and one Sunday, the highlight being the three day September meeting. The great Mtoto won his first race here and some superb two year olds make the short trip from Newmarket for their racecourse debut. If you only want the odd day's racing here a daily membership is the ticket and £13 is the asking price. If you wish to be closer to the bookmakers then Tattersalls is the answer and this cost £9 in 1999. Alternatively, the Silver/Family Enclosure will cost you £5 for the day. An Annual Members' badge cost £130 in 1999 and the racecourse now also does a joint annual membership for £215. Membership includes a car park sticker and reciprocal meetings at Huntingdon, Fakenham and Nottingham. Discounts are also available, a party of 20 or more being admitted at a reduced rate into Tattersalls.

The racecourse is eager to combine business with leisure and there are four hospitality boxes and a large new marquee ideal for corporate entertainment. The boxes can be hired on a per person basis with prices starting from £15; catering costs are additional. All the boxes are fitted with closed circuit television screens and are located in the centre of the course. Should you wish to arrange a private room or even a marquee, then contact South Norfolk Caterers. Smaller and more discreet festivities can be organised through the Club restaurant, while the more rushed may get snacks from numerous points around the track. Those under 16 years are admitted free if accompanied by an adult. Indeed, Yarmouth are focusing their attention on families. There are playgrounds, sideshows, a bouncy castle, train rides and extra sideshows arranged for evening and Sunday fixtures. One point you should remember is that there is no bank, so have enough readies to hand. If you wish to bet at the on-course betting shops, you'll find them in Tattersalls and the Silver Ring. There are facilities for disabled people in all enclosures. British resorts are increasingly having to compete with exotic holiday spots abroad. They need to offer the visitor a good time. One such offering is a day at the races and in this respect the local Yarmouth community are well served. We wish them a bumper season in 2000.

Local Favourites

A traditional seaside hotel is the **Imperial** (01493) 851113, an ideal meeting place prior to the races. A strong local recommendation comes for the **Furzedown** (01493) 844138—another popular haunt of racegoers. Two local favourites noted by the racecourse management include the **Burlington** (01493) 844568 and the **Star** (01493) 842294. They are certainly worth a pre-race inspection, The **Imperial** (01493) 851113 is also well thought of. Two fine restaurants are **Friends Bistro** (01493) 852538 and **Seafood Restaurant** (01493) 856009 on the North Quay. The latter is fairly pricey but is a great favourite of the Newmarket trainers. In Gorleston-on-Sea the **Pier Hotel** (01493) 662631 has spectacular views along the river, harbour-mouth and across the glorious sandy beach out to sea—ideal when visiting Great Yarmouth. East of the town, in South Walsham, one finds a very English mansion, **South Walsham Hall and Country Club** (01603) 270378. The hotel is beautifully situated for the Norfolk Broads. A short journey away, but well worth it all the same is Framlingham Pigot, where the **Old Feathers** (01508) 62445 is a restaurant in which great culinary delights are found—try the fresh seafood, while in nearby Gorleston The **Cliff Hotel** (01493) 662179 is also good.

Norwich itself is a delightful city, over 1000 years old. The better hotels are **Sprowston Manor** (01603) 410871, **Dunston Hall** (01508) 470444 (good leisure facilities here) and the **Maids Head Hotel** (01603) 761111, a 13th century building ideally situated near the cathedral. If you enjoy good fish then **Greens Seafood** (01603) 623733 is excellent, while splendid Italian cuisine can be found at **Marco's** (01603) 624044. Norwich is something of a gastronomers paradise. Other restaurants for consideration include the best in the field **Adlards** (01603) 633522 and **Brasteds** (01603) 625949—handy for the impressive cathedral and castle. Three stayers of merit outside the town include the **Petersfield** (01692) 630745 at Horning, the **Kingfisher** (01692) 581974 at Stalham and **Church Farm Hotel and Country Club** (01493) 780251 at Burgh Castle. If you are wishing to journey further westwards then try the **Park Farm** (01603) 810264 in Hethersett. Good facilities and restaurant make this a most appealing place to stay. A number of good boozers can be found either on the coast or amongst the Norfolk Broads. Lovers of real ale should try the **Fur and Feather** (01603) 720003 at Woodbastwick, it is excellent. In Hickling, the **Pleasure Boat Inn** (01493) 393378 has a charming waterside setting as has the **Eels Foot** in Ormesby St Michael—both of these serve good food. In appropriately named Horsey, the **Nelson's Head** is a pleasant coastal pub, while at Winterton-on-Sea, the **Fisherman's Return** (01493) 393305 has some comfortable bedrooms and also does good bar food—ideal for escaping the throngs when racing at Yarmouth.

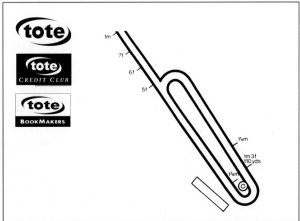

The hotel is the result of the tasteful blending of two beautiful William IV detached houses. The Mount Royale is owned and run by Richard and Christine Oxtoby and their son Stuart and daughter Sarah. Stuart has recently taken over as Managing Director. The Oxtoby's have spent a good deal of effort on restoring the former glory of these buildings and their efforts have been well rewarded.

Any traveller having an interest in English history must surely rate the fascinating city of York at least alongside London. The capital of the north and second city of the realm, it began its long and fascinating life around AD71 as a fortress to protect the Roman 9th legion. The marauding Vikings gave the city its name, derived from Jorvik or Yorvik. This period of history has been magnificently captured in the Jorvik Viking Centre, one of the most entertaining museums in the country.

The minster or cathedral is the largest medieval structure in Britain. There has been a minster on the site since the 7th century. The present one is the fourth and was started about 1220, taking 250 years to complete. The city is still protected by ancient city walls, guarded by defensive bastions, working portcullis and barbican at the Walmgate bar.

Wander around the Micklegate bar, where traitors' severed heads were displayed or visit the National Rail Museum.

Staying in York involves mixing with some of the most fascinating sights in the world. Relaxing afterwards in the intimate cocktail bar of the Mount Royale, or enjoying a delicious meal in the restaurant overlooking the delightful garden, enhances the whole experience. Enjoying the gracious beauty of the hotel, the style and antiquity of much of the furnishings, or slipping into the secluded heated swimming pool is the perfect way to pamper the body as well as the mind.

The hotel is ideal for the small conference or private party, and is only a short drive from the rolling Yorkshire Dales. The perfect base, offering peace and tranquillity in the heart of this wonderful city.

Mount Royale Hotel
The Mount
York, YO24 1GU
Tel: (01904) 628856
Fax: (01904) 611171
e mail: reservations@mountroyale.co.uk
web site: www.mountroyale.co.uk

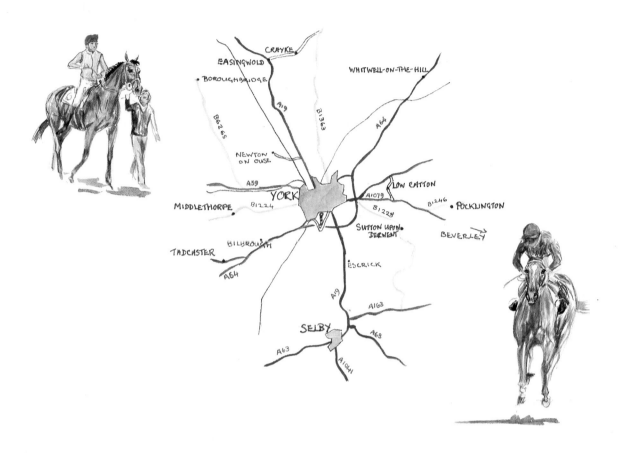

Artist: **Neil Cawthorne** **YORK RACECOURSE** *Courtesy of:* **The Artist**

York is an extremely complete racecourse. It may not host the thrills and spills of the winter game but its calendar of spring and summer fare is sumptuous. In 1997 York received our award for Racecourse of the Year—they did not let us down and received a similar accolade from the Racegoers Club. This is a racecourse where the newcomer to the sport as well as the more seasoned campaigner will surely be satisfied. In an age of competing leisure time York not only waves a worthy flag for racing but for sport in general. It is to be applauded for this excellent work.

The man in charge here is the extremely capable **John Smith** who acts as **Clerk, Manager** and **Secretary**. He can be contacted at **The Racecourse, York YO2 1EX. Tel (01904) 620911 Fax (01904) 611071.**

The course is located a mile outside the centre of the beautiful cathedral city which lies some 200 miles from London. York railway station is a mile from the racecourse and is on the Kings Cross line (London to York in as little as 106 minutes). There are frequent buses to complete the journey to the track, only five minutes ride away. A combination of the A64 and the A1036 is the answer for visitors from south, east and west, while from the north, the A19 and York Ring Road help you avoid the busy city centre. There are numerous car parks which are well organised and free. One way of avoiding the traffic is to come by helicopter and land at the course—I don't suppose you will find a long queue in the skies over York. Landing facilities for light aircraft also exist close to the course, at Rufforth. Full details are available from the racecourse office.

Particularly valuable races include the Grosvenor Casinos Dante Stakes, the Tattersalls Musidora Stakes and the Merewood Yorkshire Cup run in May—the platform for racing of the highest calibre including two Classic trials. In August, the Ebor Festival includes some of the most impressive racing of the year with the Aston Upthorpe Yorkshire Oaks and the Scottish Equitable Gimcrack. The overriding popularity and good feeling of the summer meeting is superb but less crowded fixtures can be enjoyed in June, July, September and October. In all, the course offers a total of 15 days racing with over £25 million in prize money.

Daily charges for 2000 have yet to be finalised but for the August meeting in 1999 were £35, £17, £6 and £4 for the Members, Tattersalls, Silver Ring and Course Enclosures, respectively. On other days Members were charged £18, with Tatts at £10 but there were small extra charges in the County Stand and Tattersalls for the May Meeting and Saturday fixtures where the Silver Ring is £5 and the Course Enclosure is £3. There is a generous saving on three day badges for the May, August and October meetings and further details of these are available from the racecourse—'phenomenal value' I'm assured! A new 24 hour credit card hotline for badge orders over £30 has been set up on (0345) 585642. Senior citizens are given discounts in the Silver Ring and Course enclosures—an excellent policy. There is a waiting list for Senior County Stand annual membership, but for those fortunate enough to obtain it, there are reciprocal arrangements included with daily membership at Haydock, Newcastle, Doncaster and Chester and with Yorkshire County Cricket Club! Party organisers should also note that the racecourse offers concessions for all meetings except the August Festival and Saturday fixtures.

With the Knavesmire Stand and the remodelling of existing facilities, York is almost unrivalled in the choice of quality facilities for private entertaining. Subject to availability, quality 'dining with viewing' suites are available for parties of between 4 and 400. The Dante Suite (200 guests); Knavesmire Boxes (20, 40 and 50 guests) and Melrose Boxes (16, 30 and 40) are outstanding. A complete gamut of

restaurants and bars features the famous Gimcrack Room and the 'dine with view' Ebor Restaurant (advance booking only) in the new stand where the all-in admission, gourmet luncheon and Grandstand viewing seat package offers real value. Enquiries should be addressed to Craven and Gilpin at the racecourse, (01904) 638971. The Silver Ring and the Course Enclosure have numerous places to feed and sup. John Smith is keen to attract families to race meetings and there is a free 'colts and fillies' crèche in operation at meetings held during the school holidays.

Incidentally, champagne enthusiasts should note that the York racecourse offers a different brand on sale at each meeting at a bargain price. Prices start from below £20 - only Ascot sells more champagne than York.

There is no doubt that York is one of the most successful and best run racecourses in the country. It is thoughtfully managed and immensely popular. Witness the shop facilities, information service and disabled facilities. The racecourse has managed to combine the new stands with the more traditional features really well. The course really tries to take care of the owners and trainers who provide the product too and they now have a new club of their own on the first floor of the Melrose Stand. Visitors should try to see the museum (4th floor, main grandstand) which superbly illustrates the rich history of the Knavesmire turf. The Knavesmire has a glorious past but it also has a sparkling future. The August Festival is one of the most popular in the calendar. Some say that the north is starved of top class racing—those who proclaim this have surely never visited York. To miss the August Festival is surely to miss one of the highlights of the sporting summer, and it must be remembered that there are a number of less expensive enclosures.

Comfort and enjoyment of the facilities by the racegoing public is one thing, but their safety and security should never be compromised. While beautiful to behold, the race horse can be a volatile and dangerous creature. Record crowds at York have brought home to its management the potentially dangerous situation of the location of its winner's enclosure. To be sure the little lawn in front of the weighing room created its own unique atmosphere, but to get there, horses and jockeys had to weave their way through the crowds after the race - not an ideal situation! Admirably, York now has a new and much safer winner's enclosure at the stands end of the parade ring. Although this meant demolishing the raised viewing area around the parade ring, many more people can now see the winning connections and it's a much safer situation for all. Several other racecourses, notably Newcastle, have repositioned their winner's enclosures and it is a move to be lauded.

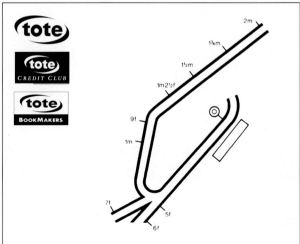

Y ork City has so much to offer—the racecourse, the castle, the minster and its many quaint streets which now house some super shops. The Shambles is perhaps the best known of these—a delightful warren with tiny lanes running into each other. More recent additions to the city include the Yorkshire Museum, the Jorvik Viking Museum and the National Railway Museum. For racing fanatics looking for a suitable place to 'ditch' loved ones whilst at the course, York is without doubt the most complete choice.

The city's hotels really capture the imagination. However, in order to make the most of the visit, rooms should be booked well in advance. The city's leading establishment is **Middlethorpe Hall** (01904) 641241 which is set in superb grounds and overlooks the racecourse and has an excellent restaurant. Another first class hotel is found within two beautifully kept William IV houses, the **Mount Royale** (01904) 628856. One of the highlights here is the charming dining room which overlooks beautiful gardens. This hotel is a real favourite and is strongly recommended. Another listed building is the excellent **Judges Lodging** (01904) 638733—superbly stylish—and do visit the 18th century wine cellars which now house an exquisite cocktail bar. For a prime position opposite the Minster, the **Dean Court Hotel** (01904) 625082 is the one to opt for—very comfortable too. The city straddles the Ouse and a most modern hotel which overlooks the river is the **Viking Moat House** (01904) 659822. Two further additions to the Yorkshire stable are the huge and modern **Forte Post House Hotel** (01904) 707921 and the **Grange**

Hotel (01904) 644744 in Clifton. The latter boasts an excellent restaurant within its Regency walls. Its newly refurbished seafood restaurant has a racing 'cyclorama' which has to be seen. A view of the Tote-Ebor start can be gained from the **Swallow Hotel** (01904) 701000. Also in York is the **Royal York** (01904) 653681 a gigantic but elegant edifice right next to the station. Another good bet is the **Newington Hotel** (01904) 625173 which overlooks the two mile start and also sponsors its own race. **4 South Parade** (01904) 628229 offers excellent accommodation but sadly does not have a restaurant.

York has something to offer every taste and pocket, and those planning a flutter well beyond their means may wish to save a little on their accommodation. If so, they should try the still excellent but relatively modestly priced **Hudsons Hotel** (01904) 621267, the **Town House** (01904) 636171 or the equally relaxing **Grasmead House Hotel** (01904) 629996.

Restaurants in York are not as strong as the hotels but pay special attention to **Barbers Restaurant** (01904) 627929, an established vegetarian restaurant. An excellent venue for a pre-race brunch or post-race tea is the famous **Bettys** in the centre of York—renowned for its truly moreish cream cakes. Two other distinguished restaurants are **Melton's** (01904) 634341 and **19 Grape Lane** (01904) 636366 which offers outstanding English cooking.

York is unsurprisingly riddled with pubs. The **Black Swan** (01904) 625236 on Peaseholme Green offers a lively atmosphere and some good value bedrooms. For a riverside setting try the **Kings Arms**. There are a

Dean Court

In its unrivalled position in the shadow of York Minster, the Dean Court offers you the best in comfort, fine food and personal service. The majority of rooms have been refurbished recently including newly created deluxe and superior rooms, each of which has a feature bed, an excellent bathroom and many little extras.

You may wish for a chauffeur driven limousine or champagne hamper for your day at the races (although hampers are not permitted in the racecourse enclosure). These arrangements can be made by the hotel's professional staff all of whom will ensure your visit to York races is a memorable one—perhaps a racing certainty!

Dean Court Hotel
Duncombe Place
York
YO1 2EF
Tel: (01904) 625082
Fax: (01904) 620305
e mail: deancourt@btconnect.com
website: www.deancourt-york.co.uk

number of pubs beside the Ouse which appeal and for a more central location try the **York Arms** in Petergate. Real ale lovers will enjoy the **Tap and Spile** in Petersgate, while shoppers can enjoy some refreshment in the **Olde Starre** in Stonegate. **Aldwark Manor** (01347) 838146 at Alne near Easingwold is well worth considering for those wishing to stay outside York itself. Further north at Helmsley, the **Feversham Arms** (01439) 770766 offers elegant accommodation and excellent lunches. A trip to Malton can never go amiss, after all this is one of Britain's major racing towns. There are numerous pubs of note here, the **Kings Head** is especially of note and the **Green Man** (01653) 600370 is a good place to stay. The **Talbot** (01653) 694031 and **Greenacres County** (01653) 693623 are also well worth shortlisting. If passing through Hovingham, meanwhile, do not overlook the **Worsley Arms Hotel** (01653) 628234, another great favourite, and secluded Nunnington contains the well known **Ryedale Lodge**. (01439) 748246. Little more than a brisk gallop away at Low Catton, lies the comfortable **Derwent Lodge** (01759) 371468. A pub to note here is the inappropriately named **Gold Cup** (01759) 371354. The **St Vincent Arms** in Sutton Upon Derwent is a good boozer and the **Three Hares** (01937) 832128 in Bilborough is also

one to note—excellent food here—a strong fancy. The **Ship Inn** (01904) 905609 at Acaster Malbis has good food and good value accommodation. Finally, the **Dawnay Arms** (01347) 848345 is a recommended stayer after the last.

The **Crown** (01423) 322328 at Boroughbridge is another racing favourite, and rightly so, drawing racegoers from all the Yorkshire courses. **Fairfield Manor** (01904) 670222, is also well positioned for the many who choose to visit the Knavesmire. Heading off towards Beverley, an inn of great character is the **Feathers**, Pocklington (01759) 303155 — an ideal choice if your trip is on a more restricted budget. The **Londesborough Arms** in Market Weighton (01430) 872214 is another extremely welcoming establishment to add to the shortlist. A first class racing haunt which offers a friendly welcome and good food is the **Bay Horse** (01423) 770230 at Burnt Yates—a bit of a drive but well worth the effort. Another is the **Boars Head** (01423) 771888—a particularly smart establishment. There are many people who visit York for the races but it has many other attractions, so do try to book in advance. A combination of racing at York, coupled with a stay in delightful York City itself or the neighbouring countryside is as ever warmly recommended.

Studley Hotel

This relaxing hotel offers everything that a guest needs for a comfortable, hassle-free stay. From the moment you step into reception you will appreciate the friendly welcome and delightful surroundings, perhaps enjoying a quiet drink at the residents' bar or relaxing in the comfortable lounge.

The hotel offers tastefully decorated and comfortable lounges and a choice of two bars. There are 36 en suite bedrooms all enjoying the most comprehensive facilities, including direct dial telephone, colour tv, satellite tv, tea and coffee-making facilities.

To satisfy the best of appetites, Le Breton offers French and seasonal dishes, and has both an extensive à la carte menu and, in the evening, an impressive table d'hôte menu. The 'Studley Special' for breakfast will leave any guest prepared for the day ahead.

The 3 Star Studley Hotel has been awarded an AA Rosette for food and is commended by the English Tourist Board with 4 crowns. One of the most attractively situated hotels in Harrogate this venue provides the ideal location for the discerning visitor. Just 30 minutes from York, Leeds, the M1 and M62, and 20 minutes from the A1 puts Studley Hotel on the doorstep of many of Yorkshire's greatest sights - Fountains Abbey, Harewood House, Ripley Castle and horse racing at Ripon, Wetherby, Thirsk and York.

Studley Hotel
Swan Road
Harrogate
North Yorkshire
HG1 2SE
Tel: (01423) 560425
Fax: (01423) 530967

Travelling
the
Turf

in
Ireland

Your horse is in the lead, racing with your colours, under a name you chose.

And all for less than £20 per week.*

When you share the cost of keeping a horse in training as a member of a syndicate, you can get closer to the action than ever before. In a syndicate of ten members, each member can expect to spend less than £20 per week for the year.

Providing information on syndicate membership is just one of the services we offer at Irish Thoroughbred Marketing.

We are an industry/government-funded organisation and can provide impartial advice on everything from choosing a horse to engaging an agent or trainer.

So go on. Get a piece of the action.

For more information, call us on 1850 30 11 11.

*Price does not include initial purchase of horse.

IRISH THOROUGHBRED MARKETING

Leopardstown Racecourse, Foxrock, Dublin 18
www.itm.ie

Travelling the Turf in Ireland - Introduction
By Ian Carnaby

A day at the races? In Ireland, it amounts to rather more than that. Not quite a pilgrimage, perhaps, but certainly a glorious escape. That is why a single day won't quite do, because the evenings are just as enjoyable as the afternoons. There comes a point where unbridled optimism takes over. In Ireland, we horse players shall all be rich tomorrow.

The story is told of the London businessman who went to the Punchestown Festival and left his mobile phone on when sitting down to lunch in the Pavilion. He fielded calls for a while, even making notes on the menu, but gave up when the names of various dark horses in the bumper made a nonsense of his other commercial decisions.

Incidentally, a good Irish bumper, or Flat race for National Hunt-bred horses, can be educational in several ways. The best performers may well be snapped up by powerful English stables with a view to turning them into champions. And then there are the jockeys or, more correctly, the 'amateur riders'. Seven pound claimers, many of them, 'with just a bit of experience in the point-to-point field, you know'. Then the betting starts, and it soon becomes abundantly clear that those with the inside information are not too worried about the man on top, after all. When he proceeds to give a very fair impersonation of Lester Piggott winning the 1972 Derby on Roberto, the rest of us are in on the secret, too.

The Irish will move heaven and earth to ensure their guests have a good time, but there is room for shrewdness amid the banter. And that is just as well because the bookmakers, spinning their boards around on the rails (not permitted in England) and advertising their prices to two jostling sets of punters, work to very attractive margins. In case anyone is under any illusions, the country is not short of astute businessmen. It's true in the world of commerce - witness the vibrant economy - and it's undoubtedly true on the racecourse. Racing here is more fun than anywhere else in the world, but when engaging in battle with the old enemy, never doubt that you need your wits about you.

Happily, there is no shortage of good advice. It proliferates at the great festivals at Punchestown and Galway, on big racedays at the Curragh, and especially at Clonmel, where all-night poker sessions fill most of the hours before the horses are due to line up again. Whether the casual visitor will still have the wherewithal to profit from the steady stream of information coming his way is another matter, of course.

The newcomer to Ireland is sometimes surprised to discover how many people his host actually knows. There is much mingling and, even when an Irishman professes no great interest in horse racing himself, it generally transpires that he has a cousin, an aunt or a brother with a horse running that very day. Apparently, it has 'just a bit of a chance, nothing more than that, you know'.

The sport brings people together in an almost magical way - of J. P. Donleavy, William Trevor or, more recently, Jamie Reid - whose novel Home on the Range contains a wonderfully evocative description of horses galloping on the beach at Sligo.

It has never been easier to make the necessary arrangements, so go racing in Ireland and be a part of it all. See how close the big names pass by on the way to the start at Punchestown, and note how informal big race days are at the Curragh, even though literally millions of pounds may be at stake. Marvel at the Easter Monday crowds at Fairyhouse on Jameson Irish Grand National Day, spilling all over the place as if let loose at some vast country fair. Or enjoy a quiet lunch in Dublin before making your way to an evening meeting at Bellewstown, where the final flight of hurdles is so close to the line that they might just as well call the first horse to jump over safely, the winner. No one would complain if they did.

Make the journey soon. Stop settling for the quiet smile of satisfaction, which sometimes accompanies 'weighed in!' Opt instead for the whoop of sheer joy which goes with 'Winner All Right! Winner All Right!' Travelling the Turf in Ireland is one of the most relaxing, enjoyable tours a racing man can make. And there is no time like the present.

Artist: **Jay Kirkman HORSE & LAD**
Courtesy of: **Jonathon Cooper, Park Walk Gallery**

National Hunt

Saturday 8th January	Ladbroke Hurdle - (Leopardstown)
Sunday 23rd January	A.I.G. Europe Champion Hurdle - (Leopardstown)
Thursday 27th January	Cuisine de France Thyestes Chase - (Gowran Park)
Sunday 6th February	Hennessy Cognac Gold Cup Chase - (Leopardstown)
Monday 24th April	Jameson Irish Grand National - (Fairyhouse)
Tuesday 25th April	Power Gold Cup - (Fairyhouse)
Tuesday 2nd May	BMW Chase - (Punchestown)
Tuesday 2nd May	Country Pride Champion Novice Hurdle - (Punchestown)
Wednesday 3rd May	Heineken Gold Cup - (Punchestown)
Wednesday 3rd May	Stanley Cooker Champion Novice Hurdle - (Punchestown)
Thursday 4th May	I.A.W.S. Champion 4 Year Old Hurdle - (Punchestown)
Thursday 4th May	Ballymore Properties Champion Stayers Hurdle - (Punchestown)
Thursday 4th May	Triple Print Novice Chase - (Punchestown)
Friday 5th May	Shell Champion Hurdle - (Punchestown)
Friday 5th May	David Austin Memorial Handicap Chase - (Punchestown)
Wednesday 2nd August	Compaq Galway Plate Handicap Chase - (Galway)
Thursday 3rd August	Guinness Galway Handicap Hurdle - (Galway)
Wednesday 20th September	Guinness Kerry National Chase - (Listowel)
Sunday 3rd December	Avonmore/Waterford Hatton's Grace Hurdle - (Fairyhouse)
Sunday 3rd December	Chiquita Drinmore Novice Steeplechase - (Fairyhouse)
Sunday 3rd December	Avonmore/Waterford Hatton's Royal Bond Novice Steeplechase - (Fairyhouse)
Sunday 10th December	John Durkan Memorial Chase - (Punchestown)
Tuesday 26th December	Denny Gold Medal Chase - (Leopardstown)
Wednesday 27th December	Paddy Power Handicap Chase - (Leopardstown)
Thursday 28th December	Ericsson Chase - (Leopardstown)

Flat

Saturday 27th May	Hibernia Foods Irish 2,000 Guineas - (Curragh)
Sunday 28th May	Entenmann's Irish 1,000 Guineas - (Curragh)
Sunday 2nd July	Budweiser Irish Derby - (Curragh)
Sunday 16th July	Kildangan Stud Irish Oaks - (Curragh)
Sunday 13th August	Heinz 57 Phoenix Stakes - (Leopardstown)
Sunday 3rd September	Moyglare Stud Stakes - (Curragh)
Saturday 9th September	Esat Digifone Irish Champion Stakes - (Leopardstown) (part of the Emirates World Racing Champion Series)
Saturday 16th September	Jefferson Smurfit Memorial Irish St Leger - (Curragh)
Sunday 17th September	Aga Khan Studs National Stakes - (Curragh)

Travelling the Turf in Ireland - Fixtures 2000

JANUARY

1st Saturday	Tramore, Co. Waterford
2nd Sunday	Naas, Co. Kildare
3rd Monday	Cork, Co. Cork
3rd Monday	Fairyhouse, Co. Meath
5th Wednesday	Punchestown, Co. Kildare
6th Thursday	Thurles, Co. Tipperary
8th Saturday	Leopardstown, Co. Dublin
9th Sunday	Navan, Co. Meath
13th Thursday	Tramore, Co. Waterford
15th Saturday	Naas, Co. Kildare
16th Sunday	Fairyhouse, Co. Meath
19th Wednesday	Down Royal, Co. Down
22nd Saturday	Punchestown, Co. Kildare
23rd Sunday	Leopardstown, Co. Dublin
27th Thursday	Gowran Park, Co. Kilkenny
29th Saturday	Fairyhouse, Co. Meath
30th Sunday	Naas, Co. Kildare

FEBRUARY

3rd Thursday	Clonmel, Co. Tipperary
5th Saturday	Naas, Co. Kildare
6th Sunday	Leopardstown, Co. Dublin
10th Thursday	Thurles, Co. Tipperary
12th Saturday	Punchestown, Co. Kildare
13th Sunday	Punchestown, Co. Kildare
17th Thursday	Clonmel, Co. Tipperary
19th Saturday	Gowran Park, Co. Kilkenny
20th Sunday	Navan, Co. Meath
24th Thursday	Thurles, Co. Tipperary
26th Saturday	Naas, Co. Kildare
27th Sunday	Fairyhouse, Co. Meath

MARCH

1st Wednesday	Downpatrick, Co. Down
4th Saturday	Tramore, Co. Waterford
5th Sunday	Leopardstown, Co. Dublin
9th Thursday	Thurles, Co. Tipperary
11th Saturday	Navan, Co. Meath
12th Sunday	Naas, Co. Kildare
17th Friday	Down Royal, Co. Down
17th Friday	Wexford, Co. Wexford
18th Saturday	Gowran Park, Co. Kilkenny
19th Sunday	Leopardstown, Co. Dublin
22nd Wednesday	Downpatrick, Co. Down
23rd Thursday	Clonmel, Co. Tipperary
25th Saturday	Navan, Co. Meath
26th Sunday	Curragh, Co. Kildare
30th Thursday	Tipperary, Co. Tipperary

APRIL

1st Saturday	Down Royal, Co. Down
1st Saturday	Gowran Park, Co. Kilkenny
2nd Sunday	Cork, Co. Cork
2nd Sunday	Fairyhouse, Co. Meath
8th Saturday	Wexford, Co. Wexford
9th Sunday	Curragh, Co. Kildare
13th Thursday	Clonmel, Co. Tipperary
14th Friday	Listowel, Co. Kerry
15th Saturday	Listowel, Co. Kerry
16th Sunday	Listowel, Co. Kerry
16th Sunday	Leopardstown, Co. Dublin
22nd Saturday	Cork, Co. Cork
23rd Sunday	Fairyhouse, Co. Meath
23rd Sunday	Cork, Co. Cork
24th Monday	Cork, Co. Cork
24th Monday	Fairyhouse, Co. Meath
25th Tuesday	Fairyhouse, Co. Meath
27th Thursday	Ballinrobe, Co. Mayo
29th Saturday	Navan, Co. Meath
30th Sunday	Navan, Co. Meath

MAY

1st Monday	Curragh, Co. Kildare
1st Monday	Down Royal, Co. Down
2nd Tuesday	Punchestown, Co. Kildare
3rd Wednesday	Punchestown, Co. Kildare
4th Thursday	Punchestown, Co. Kildare
5th Friday	Punchestown, Co. Kildare
7th Sunday	Gowran Park, Co. Kilkenny
8th Monday	Cork, Co. Cork (E)
10th Wednesday	Sligo, Co. Sligo (E)
11th Thursday	Tipperary, Co. Tipperary (E)
12th Friday	Dundalk, Co. Louth (E)
13th Saturday	Fairyhouse, Co. Meath
14th Sunday	Leopardstown, Co. Dublin
14th Sunday	Killarney, Co. Kerry
15th Monday	Killarney, Co. Kerry (E)
16th Tuesday	Killarney, Co. Kerry
17th Wednesday	Gowran Park, Co. Kilkenny (E)
19th Friday	Cork, Co. Cork (E)
19th Friday	Downpatrick, Co. Down (E)
20th Saturday	Downpatrick, Co. Down
21st Sunday	Clonmel, Co. Tipperary
21st Sunday	Navan, Co. Meath
22nd Monday	Roscommon, Co. Roscommon (E)
24th Wednesday	Leopardstown, Co. Dublin (E)
25th Thursday	Clonmel, Co. Tipperary (E)
26th Friday	Down Royal, Co. Down (E)
27th Saturday	Curragh, Co. Kildare
28th Sunday	Curragh, Co. Kildare
29th Monday	Kilbeggan, Co. Westmeath (E)
30th Tuesday	Laytown, Co. Louth
31st Wednesday	Fairyhouse, Co. Meath (E)

JUNE

1st Thursday	Tipperary, Co. Tipperary (E)
2nd Friday	Dundalk, Co. Louth (E)
2nd Friday	Wexford, Co. Wexford (E)
3rd Saturday	Naas, Co. Kildare
4th Sunday	Naas, Co. Kildare
4th Sunday	Sligo, Co. Sligo
5th Monday	Leopardstown, Co. Dublin
5th Monday	Tralee, Co. Kerry
6th Tuesday	Tralee, Co. Kerry
7th Wednesday	Gowran Park, Co. Kilkenny (E)
9th Friday	Cork, Co. Cork (E)
10th Saturday	Curragh, Co. Kildare
11th Sunday	Navan, Co. Meath
12th Monday	Ballinrobe, Co. Mayo (E)
13th Tuesday	Ballinrobe, Co. Mayo (E)
14th Wednesday	Leopardstown, Co. Dublin (E)
15th Thursday	Tipperary, Co. Tipperary (E)
16th Friday	Wexford, Co. Wexford (E)
17th Saturday	Navan, Co. Meath
18th Sunday	Roscommon, Co. Roscommon
19th Monday	Roscommon, Co. Roscommon (E)
21st Wednesday	Clonmel, Co. Tipperary (E)
23rd Friday	Dundalk, Co. Louth (E)
24th Saturday	Cork, Co. Cork
25th Sunday	Gowran Park, Co. Kilkenny
26th Monday	Kilbeggan, Co. Westmeath (E)
27th Tuesday	Tramore, Co. Wexford (E)
28th Wednesday	Leopardstown, Co. Dublin (E)
30th Friday	Curragh, Co. Kildare (E)

JULY

1st Saturday	Curragh, Co. Kildare
2nd Sunday	Curragh, Co. Kildare
3rd Monday	Sligo, Co. Sligo (E)
4th Tuesday	Cork, Co. Cork (E)
5th Wednesday	Bellewstown, Co. Meath (E)
6th Thursday	Bellewstown, Co. Meath (E)
7th Friday	Bellewstown, Co. Meath (E)
8th Saturday	Leopardstown, Co. Dublin
10th Monday	Roscommon, Co. Roscommon (E)
12th Wednesday	Dundalk, Co. Louth (E)
13th Thursday	Down Royal, Co. Down
14th Friday	Down Royal, Co. Down (E)
14th Friday	Wexford, Co. Wexford (E)
15th Saturday	Wexford, Co. Wexford

211

16th Sunday	Curragh, Co. Kildare
17th Monday	Killarney, Co. Kerry (E)
18th Tuesday	Killarney, Co. Kerry
19th Wednesday	Killarney, Co. Kerry (E)
19th Wednesday	Leopardstown, Co. Dublin (E)
20th Thursday	Killarney, Co. Kerry
21st Friday	Kilbeggan, Co. Westmeath (E)
22nd Saturday	Leopardstown, Co. Dublin
23rd Sunday	Tipperary, Co. Tipperary
24th Monday	Ballinrobe, Co. Mayo (E)
25th Tuesday	Ballinrobe, Co. Mayo (E)
26th Wednesday	Naas, Co. Kildare (E)
27th Thursday	Tipperary, Co. Tipperary (E)
28th Friday	Dundalk, Co. Louth (E)
29th Saturday	Curragh, Co. Kildare
31st Monday	Galway, Co. Galway (E)

AUGUST

1st Tuesday	Galway, Co. Galway (E)
2nd Wednesday	Galway, Co. Galway
3rd Thursday	Galway, Co. Galway
4th Friday	Galway, Co. Galway (E)
5th Saturday	Galway, Co. Galway
6th Sunday	Galway, Co. Galway
7th Monday	Naas, Co. Kildare
7th Monday	Cork, Co. Cork
8th Tuesday	Roscommon, Co. Roscommon (E)
9th Wednesday	Fairyhouse, Co. Meath (E)
9th Wednesday	Sligo, Co. Sligo (E)
10th Thursday	Sligo, Co. Sligo
11th Friday	Kilbeggan, Co. Westmeath (E)
12th Saturday	Wexford, Co. Wexford
13th Sunday	Leopardstown, Co. Dublin
13th Sunday	Tramore, Co. Waterford
14th Monday	Tramore, Co. Waterford (E)
15th Tuesday	Dundalk, Co. Louth
15th Tuesday	Tramore, Co. Waterford (E)
16th Wednesday	Tramore, Co. Waterford
17th Thursday	Tipperary, Co. Tipperary (E)
18th Friday	Cork, Co. Cork (E)
19th Saturday	Fairyhouse, Co. Meath
20th Sunday	Curragh, Co. Kildare
21st Monday	Roscommon, Co. Roscommon (E)
22nd Tuesday	Tralee, Co. Kerry
23rd Wednesday	Tralee, Co. Kerry
24th Thursday	Tralee, Co. Kerry
25th Friday	Tralee, Co. Kerry (E)
25th Friday	Kilbeggan, Co. Westmeath (E)
26th Saturday	Tralee, Co. Kerry
26th Saturday	Curragh, Co. Kildare
27th Sunday	Tralee, Co. Kerry
28th Monday	Downpatrick, Co. Down
29th Tuesday	Sligo, Co. Sligo
31st Thursday	Gowran Park, Co. Kilkenny

SEPTEMBER

1st Friday	Dundalk, Co. Louth
2nd Saturday	Cork, Co. Cork
3rd Sunday	Curragh, Co. Kildare
3rd Sunday	Ballinrobe, Co. Mayo
4th Monday	Galway, Co. Galway
5th Tuesday	Galway, Co. Galway
6th Wednesday	Galway, Co. Galway
7th Thursday	Clonmel, Co. Tipperary
8th Friday	Kilbeggan, Co. Westmeath
9th Saturday	Leopardstown, Co. Dublin
11th Monday	Roscommon, Co. Roscommon
13th Wednesday	Fairyhouse, Co. Meath
14th Thursday	Gowran Park, Co. Kilkenny
15th Friday	Downpatrick, Co. Down
16th Saturday	Curragh, Co. Kildare
17th Sunday	Curragh, Co. Kildare
18th Monday	Listowel, Co. Kerry
19th Tuesday	Listowel, Co. Kerry
20th Wednesday	Listowel, Co. Kerry

21st Thursday	Listowel, Co. Kerry
22nd Friday	Listowel, Co. Kerry
23rd Saturday	Listowel, Co. Kerry
25th Monday	Ballinrobe, Co. Mayo
30th Saturday	Curragh, Co. Kildare
30th Saturday	Down Royal, Co. Down

OCTOBER

1st Sunday	Tipperary, Co. Tipperary
4th Wednesday	Fairyhouse, Co. Meath
5th Thursday	Thurles, Co. Tipperary
6th Friday	Downpatrick, Co. Down
7th Saturday	Cork, Co. Cork
7th Saturday	Navan, Co. Meath
8th Sunday	Punchestown, Co. Kildare
9th Monday	Roscommon, Co. Roscommon
12th Thursday	Gowran Park, Co. Kilkenny
13th Friday	Gowran Park, Co. Kilkenny
14th Saturday	Gowran Park, Co. Kilkenny
15th Sunday	Curragh, Co. Kildare
15th Sunday	Cork, Co. Cork
18th Wednesday	Navan, Co. Meath
19th Thursday	Punchestown, Co. Kildare
21st Saturday	Tipperary, Co. Tipperary
22nd Sunday	Naas, Co. Kildare
25th Wednesday	Tipperary, Co. Tipperary
26th Thursday	Thurles, Co. Tipperary
27th Friday	Fairyhouse, Co. Meath
28th Saturday	Leopardstown, Co. Dublin
29th Sunday	Wexford, Co. Wexford
29th Sunday	Galway, Co. Galway
30th Monday	Galway, Co. Galway
30th Monday	Leopardstown, Co. Dublin

NOVEMBER

1st Wednesday	Clonmel, Co. Tipperary
2nd Thursday	Curragh, Co. Kildare
4th Saturday	Navan, Co. Meath
5th Sunday	Punchestown, Co. Kildare
9th Thursday	Clonmel, Co. Tipperary
10th Friday	Down Royal, Co. Down
11th Saturday	Down Royal, Co. Down
11th Saturday	Naas, Co. Kildare
12th Sunday	Leopardstown, Co. Dublin
12th Sunday	Cork, Co. Cork
16th Thursday	Thurles, Co. Tipperary
18th Saturday	Punchestown, Co. Kildare
19th Sunday	Navan, Co. Meath
23rd Thursday	Tramore, Co. Waterford
25th Saturday	Naas, Co. Kildare
26th Sunday	Clonmel, Co. Tipperary
29th Wednesday	Downpatrick, Co. Down
30th Thursday	Thurles, Co. Tipperary

DECEMBER

2nd Saturday	Fairyhouse, Co. Meath
3rd Sunday	Fairyhouse, Co. Meath
3rd Sunday	Cork, Co. Cork
8th Friday	Clonmel, Co. Tipperary
9th Saturday	Navan, Co. Meath
10th Sunday	Punchestown, Co. Kildare
13th Wednesday	Fairyhouse, Co. Meath
16th Saturday	Navan, Co. Meath
17th Sunday	Thurles, Co. Tipperary
26th Tuesday	Leopardstown, Co. Dublin
26th Tuesday	Down Royal, Co. Down
26th Tuesday	Cork, Co. Cork
27th Wednesday	Leopardstown, Co. Dublin
27th Wednesday	Clonmel, Co. Tipperary
28th Thursday	Leopardstown, Co. Dublin
29th Friday	Leopardstown, Co. Dublin
31st Sunday	Punchestown, Co. Kildare

(E) - denotes evening meeting.
Dates of fixtures may be subject to alteration.

Sligo

Down Royal

Downpatrick

Dundalk

Ballinrobe

Roscommon

Navan

Laytown

Bellewstown

Galway

Kilbeggan

Fairyhouse

Curragh

Leopardstown

Naas

Punchestown

Limerick

Thurles

Listowel

Tipperary

Gowran Park

Tralee

Clonmel

Killarney

Cork

Tramore

Wexford

Ballinrobe

Contact: **Mr Norman Molloy, Manager, Ballinrobe Race Committee, Ballinrobe, Co Mayo Tel: 00 353 92 41219 John Flannery, Clerk of the Course, Tel: 00 353 87 289 5974 Racedays: Tel: 00 353 92 41052 Fax: 00 353 92 41406.**

Ballinrobe has a very old tradition of racing in various forms with meetings recorded in 1774 and steeplechases included in the 1834 meeting. The present course was purchased in 1921.

Possessing a slightly elevated track, Ballinrobe boasts an exceptional view of the whole course. General facilities updated in 1998.

Location
One mile from Ballinrobe Town N84.

Refreshment Facilities
Bars and restaurants

Local Hotels
Ashford Castle, Tel: 00 353 92 46003, internationally renowned 5 star Castle; Ryans Tel: 00 353 92 46243 and Donaghers, Cong

Local Restaurants
Flannerys, Ballinrobe, in top 100 pubs; Red Door, Ballinrobe; Echoes, Cong, among the 100 best restaurants in Ireland.

Places of Interest/Activities
Angling in 60,000 acres of brown trout fishing, golf - 18 hole championship course. Is also a major area for items of historical and archeological interest.

Bellewstown

Contact: **Mr Kevin Coleman the Secretary/Manager, 9 Palace Street, Drogheda, Co Louth, Tel: 00 353 41 9842111, Fax: 00 353 41 9837566.** Racecourse address **Bellewstown Racecourse, Bellewstown, Co Meath, Tel: (Racedays only) 00 353 41 9823301 Fax: 00 353 41 9823644.**

Bellewstown racecourse, on the Hill of Crockafotha in Co Meath, is beautifully situated in a rural setting with magnificent views of the Mountains of Mourne to the north and the Irish sea to the east.

Bellewstown is an annual three day meeting which takes place in the first week of July. The races have always been associated with the smell of freshly mown hay and the taste of strawberries and cream. We do not know exactly when racing started in Bellewstown, but the first record of races appears in the August edition of the Dublin Gazette and the Weekly Courier in 1726.

George Tandy a former Mayor of Drogheda and brother of the famous Napper Tandy persuaded King George III to sponsor a race at Bellewstown in 1780. The race was called His Majesty's Plate and was valued at £100.

All the English monarchs continued to sponsor a race at Bellewstown until 1980, when Queen Elizabeth II decided to discontinue the race. However, the Queen continues to sponsor a race at the Curragh called the Royal Whip.

Location
The racecourse is 23 miles north of Dublin, off the main Dublin/Belfast road and seven miles south of Drogheda.

Public Transport
There is a special bus service from Dublin (Busarus) Tel: Bus Eireann 00 353 1 836 6111 for departure time. Buses also run from Drogheda.

Other Facilities
There is a free area beside the track which includes a carnival for children.

Local Hotels
Neptune Beach Hotel Tel: 00 353 41 982 7107, Bettystown; Old Mill Hotel and Glen Side Hotel, Julianstown; Rosnaree Park Hotel, Westcourt Hotel Tel: 00 353 41 983 0965 and Boyne Valley Hotel Tel: 00 353 41 9837737, Drogheda; Conyngham Arms Hotel Tel: 00 353 41 24155, Slane; Ashbourne House Hotel, Ashbourne. Contact the Irish Tourist Board Tel: 0171 493 3201 for an accommodation list.

Local Restaurants
Bacchus at the Coast Guard, Bettystown; Black Bull Inn, Buttergate and Monasterboice Inn (all Drogheda); Forge, Collon, Co Meath.

Places of Interest/Activities
The racecourse is close to the historic sites of Tara, Slane, Newgrange, Dowth and Knowth and the beautiful Boyne Valley. There are several 18 hole golf courses nearby.

Artist: **Alison Wilson STUDY OF A RACEHORSE**
Courtesy of: **The Artist**

Bettystown in Co. Meath is attracting much interest these days with the development of the new deluxe Neptune Beach Hotel and Leisure Club. The hotel has the most spectacular setting on the beautiful sandy beach at Bettystown.

All 38 spacious and luxurious en-suite bedrooms, most of which will command breathtaking views of the sea, are complete with trouser press, ironing facilities, hair dryer, satellite television and direct dial telephone.

The large comfortable foyer with its glowing log fire and relaxing leather furniture provides a warm and welcoming atmosphere for all guests. Morning and afternoon tea is served in the foyer and a relaxing drink can be enjoyed in the Victorian style Neptune Bar.

The elegant restaurant 'Le Pressage', is the ideal setting for a business luncheon or an intimate dinner. The cuisine is always of the highest standard with fine food and superb wines to suit all tastes. After dinner guests can also enjoy a cocktail in the stylish Seaview Lounge.

The Neptune Beach is the perfect venue for conferences and banquets of any size from small business meetings to exhibitions or seminars for up to 200 people. The main conference/banqueting room boasts spectacular sea views and is equipped with the most up to date audio visual equipment.

The leisure club provides the very best in health and fitness equipment, with a spectacular 20 metre swimming pool, jacuzzi, steam room and a hi-tech fitness suite.

The Hotel is ideally located just 30 minutes north of Dublin Airport and 5 miles from Drogheda. The Neptune Beach is a golfer's delight with three championship courses in the surrounding area, while the racing fraternity will be perfectly placed for the courses at Fairyhouse, Bellewstown, Dundalk, Laytown and Navan.

Neptune Beach Hotel & Leisure Club
Bettystown
Co. Meath
Tel: 00 353 41 982 7107
Fax: 00 353 41 982 7412
e mail: info@neptunebeach.ie
web site: www.neptunebeach.ie

Clonmel

Contact: **Mr J L Desmond, Manager, Clonmel Racecourse, Davis Road, Clonmel, Co Tipperary, Tel: 00 353 52 22611/22032 Fax: 00 353 52 26446 Racedays: 00 353 52 25719 Fax: 00 353 52 25719.**

Clonmel, an historic town, lies at the foot of the Comeragh Mountains and is situated in the valley of the beautiful River Suir. To the north east lies Slievenamon.

Clonmel racecourse (Powerstown Park) is located in a picturesque setting north of the town. Racing, which had been open and free to spectators for over a hundred years at Clonmel, was enclosed in 1913 by Villiers Morton Jackson and became the commercially run Powerstown Park racecourse.

Morton Jackson also roped in the bookies to a distinct area of the course, banned gaming sideshows, brought in detectives and police to deter pickpockets and provided entry to a roofless grandstand accommodating 1500 at a charge of two shillings a head!

Since then Clonmel has grown and developed and today it is not uncommon to have in excess of 120 horses running at any one meeting. Extensive refurbishment has been carried out at Clonmel Racecourse during 1998. A new grandstand including a Bar and catering complex has been constructed. Along with a new computerised turnstile entrance, the weighroom/jockeys room has also been extensively upgraded and refurbished.

Location
Clonmel racecourse (Powerstown Park) is situated within two miles of the town centre, off the Waterford-Clonmel road. It is 100 miles from Dublin, 30 miles from Waterford, 24 miles from Tipperary and 12 miles from Cahir.

Refreshment Facilities
Self service restaurant, snack bars and bars

Local Hotels
Hotel Minella Tel: 00 353 52 22388, Clonmel Arms Hotel Tel: 00 353 52 21233 and Hearns Hotel Tel: 00 353 52 21611

Local Restaurants
Include La Scala, Emerald Garden (Chinese), Jasmine Court (Chinese), Mulcahys and Sean Tierney's Bar & Restaurant.

Places of Interest/Activities
Cahir Castle, Rock of Cashel, Kilkenny Castle and Mitchelstown's Caves, together with scenic drives also Golf and Pony trekking.

Cork

Contact: **Mr Michael Lane Executive Director/ Secretary, at Cork Racecourse (Mallow) Limited Killarney Road, Mallow, Co Cork Tel: 00 353 22 50207 Fax: 00 353 22 50213.**

There is a long tradition of horse racing in the region. The first ever steeplechase took place in 1752 between the church steeples of Buttervant and Donerail, just a few miles from Mallow. In 1777, six consecutive days of racing were on offer in the Mallow area, "all to be run according to the King's Plate articles".

With the demise of Cork Park in 1917, the need for a new racecourse in Ireland's largest county was apparent. Mallow, formed at the instigation of and under the control of Lieutenant Colonel F F MacCabe, commenced racing in 1924.

The racecourse re-opened at Easter 1997, following a £7 million refurbishment backed by the Irish Horseracing Authority, the Irish Government and local private and industry sponsorship.

Location
The racecourse is situated one mile from Mallow town on the Mallow-Killarney road (N72). Racegoers travelling from Cork and Limerick (N20) should go under the railway bridge at the roundabout. Patrons coming from Dublin and Waterford (N73 and N72) should take the town park bypass to reach the roundabout.

Public Transport
Mallow is well served by bus and rail. Most trains from Dublin (Heuston Station) to Cork stop at Mallow. Tel: Irish Rail (larnrod Eireann) 00 353 1 836 6222 for train timetable. Taxi service from Mallow Station to the racecourse.

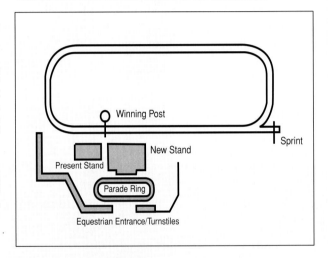

Refreshment Facilities
Corporate restaurant (pre booked) , self service restaurant, snack bar

Local Hotels
Hiberian Hotel Tel: 00 353 22 21588, Central Hotel Tel: 00 353 22 21527, Longueville House Tel: 00 353 22 47156 and Springfort Hall Tel: 00 353 22 21278, Mallow; Assolas House Tel: 00 353 29 50015 in Kanturk

Local Restaurants
The Roundabout Inn & Restaurant, The Black Lamb and Kepplers in Mallow

Places of Interest/Activities
Mallow Castle and herd of white deer in Mallow; Doneraile Park in Doneraile; Blarney Castle in Blarney; also fishing, golf and pony trekking.

Artist: **Heather St Clair Davis A STUDY OF PEACE**
Courtesy of: **Frost & Reed**

A beautiful, former Quaker Mansion, Hotel Minella is an impressive stately home presiding over a stretch of the rippling River Suir. Tasteful modernisation blends into the background of the original 1863 building which commands nine acres of lovingly maintained grounds. All in all, a rare example of a hotel able to combine the comforts of the 20th century with the dignity and elegance of a bygone age which time, and three major wars, have tossed aside. Opened in 1962 by Mr & Mrs Nallen the Minella is now run by the second generation of Nallens John & Elizabeth.

Clonmel itself -Cluain Meala- the Medow of Honey, has aptly been described as the 'sportsman's paradise'. Long associated with many great names it is a renowned horse and greyhound breeding area. Few countries offer as much for a serious golfer with courses ranging from park land pleasure of Thurles to the justly famous and demanding hills of Clonmel - a mere two miles from the hotel. Both of these are 18 hole, par 71 courses. The hotel is happy to arrange an all inclusive mini-holiday to ensure a more relaxed day.

For the racing enthusiast, this premier county is ideal. The Clonmel racecourse is just two miles from the Minella and less than an hour's drive away are the courses of Gowran, Tipperary, Wexford, Tramore, & Cork. For a diversion from these temptations why not try your hand at swimming, boating and canoeing on the Suir, mountain climbing in the Comeragh mountains and the beautiful Knockmealdown range. Club Minella, our exclusive 5 star Health & Leisure Complex, opened in June 1999. Awaiting you is a 20 metre pool, jacuzzi, outdoor Canadian hot tub, aerobics room, sauna, gymnasium, outdoor tennis court, putting green as well as cruising on our pleasure boats on the Suir.

With the wealth of beautiful countryside in the area, you could take a walk or step up the pace a little by going pony trekking in the Nire Valley.

The Minella offers a warm and friendly welcome at the end of a whirling day. Enjoy a quiet drink in the cocktail bar, overlooking the lawns and the banks of the Suir, and then move to the oak-panelled dining room to sample some of the Minella dishes. Enjoy traditional Irish cuisine at its best: prime roast beef, grilled steaks and fresh fish, all complemented by a fine selection of wines.

The 70 bedrooms offer the perfect end to a perfect day. All have an en-suite bathrooms, colour televisions, direct dial telephone, hairdryer and alarm clock radio. Eight executive suites have private jacuzzi or private steam room all offer a stunning morning view over the river or Comeragh Mountains.

The Minella Stables are just 5 miles from the Hotel & Mr Nallen Senior will be delighted to offer guided tours of the stables and famous "minella" horses at any time.

A home away from home . . . the Nallen Family await your visit.

Hotel Minella
Clonmel
Co Tipperary Ireland
Tel: (00 353 52) 22388/24381 Fax: (00 353 52) 24381
web site:www.tipp.ie/hotel-minella.htm
e mail: hotelminella@tinet.ie

The Stand House Hotel is the ideal location whether you are taking a trip to the races, having a relaxing break or an active holiday.

The hotel, which is only 30 minutes from Dublin in the heart of the Curragh, offers excellent accommodation, entertainment and leisure facilities.

With 63 luxurious en-suite bedrooms, complete with direct dial telephone, trouser press, hair dryer and satellite television, and an acclaimed restaurant featuring top-class international cuisine, there is no doubt that a stay at the Stand House Hotel will be a luxurious one.

Should you wish to mix business with pleasure you will be attracted to our corporate racing deals. We can tailor packages to meet the needs and budget of the specific client, ensuring that you get exactly what you're looking for.

With a total of eight conference rooms catering for any number from 3 to 800, the Stand House Hotel is the perfect venue for weddings, banquets or for any special occasions. All the rooms reflect the elegance and atmosphere of the original 18th century building.

The Stand House Hotel is surrounded by a number of great attractions. As well as the following race courses: The Curragh, Naas, Leopardstown, Punchestown, there are the golf courses: Cill Dara, The Curragh, Naas, K Club, Castle Warden, and Kilkea. There is car racing at Mondello Park, while the National Stud and the scene of the hit movie Braveheart are also located nearby.

For the last word in comfort all guests have use of the luxurious leisure centre with its 20 metre deck level swimming pool, sauna, steam room, Jacuzzi and fully equipped gymnasium. Guests may also relax in the Beauty Salon and L'Oreal Hair Salon (extra charge.

The Stand House Hotel
Leisure and Conference Centre
The Curragh
County Kildare
Tel: 00 353 45 436177
Fax: 00 353 45 436180
e mail: standhse@indigo.ie

Contact: **Mr Brian Kavanagh, Manager** at **Curragh Racecourse, The Curragh, Co Kildare Tel: 00 353 45 441205 Fax: 00 353 45 441442**

E mail: info@curragh.ie
Web site: http://www.curragh.ie

In a country where breeding classic racehorses is almost as widespread as the green grass on which they thrive, the Home of the Classics is the Curragh racecourse. The ancient Gaelic name Curragh actually means racecourse and in the very earliest Irish manuscripts, the Curragh figured as a place of sport for Celtic Kings and their people.

The 17th century saw the Curragh become a sporting resort of the chief governors and administrators of Ireland. Every summer Dublin Castle was almost deserted as the lord lieutenant and his entourage came to Kildare to watch or compete in the racing at the Curragh. The number of King's Plates varied over the two centuries from 1700, but the vast majority of them were contested on the Curragh. Not surprisingly therefore the Curragh became the social centre and administrative headquarters of racing in Ireland over that time.

Artist: **Peter Curling LUSH SUMMER**
Courtesy of: **The Artist**

At the end of the 18th century, the Curragh had become permanently fringed by the lodges and stables of the most prominent owners, breeders and trainers in the country. These lodges and stables in name and even in fabric have survived in the hands of an equally illustrious racing community today. The first Irish Derby took place at the Curragh in 1866—this famous Classic has a legendary reputation for bringing out the best in horses and riders. It also ranks as Ireland's premier sporting and social event.

Today, as the headquarters of thoroughbred racing in Ireland, the Curragh caters for all five classic races in the country, as well as fourteen other prestigious meetings during the Irish racing calendar.

Location
The Curragh racecourse is situated 29 miles south west of Dublin on the main Dublin-Cork-Limerick road. It is nine miles from Naas and two miles from Newbridge.

Public Transport
By rail you can buy a combined admission and return ticket at Dublin (Heuston Station) for £14, for all Saturday and Sunday meetings. To check train schedules contact Larnrod Eireann on 00 353 1 836 6222. A special bus leaves Busaras, Store Street, Dublin 1, for the Curragh on racedays and departs the racecourse after the last race. For further information on departure times contact Bus Eireann 00 353

1 836 6111. Special coaches can be hired for group outings, for further details contact 00 353 45 879007.

Admission Rates
For regular meetings in 1999 prices were as follows: Saturdays £8, Sundays £10, Classic and Group One meetings £12. Prices for 2000 Irish Derby Festival Weekend are as follows Friday meeting £10, Saturday £12 and Sunday in the West End Enclosure £15, Reserved Enclosure £35. Senior citizens and students have a 50% concession except for Irish Derby Day. Children under 14 who must be accompanied by an adult are admitted free to all meetings except again for Irish Derby Day when the charge is £4 Grandstand and £8 reserved enclosure. For seating and balcony access reservations call the racecourse.

Annual badge prices which admit to all meetings are adults £115, senior citizens £60 and under 25's £60. A portion of the main stand is reserved for annual badge holders. Badge holders also have access to the Members Bar and free parking in car park 'B'.

Corporate Hospitality
Private suites and hospitality rooms are available to cater for 10-160 people. All-in hospitality packages include: top level badge, racecard, reserved seat, pre-lunch reception, four course lunch with wine, complimentary bar, afternoon tea. Contact the Marketing Manager at the racecourse on 00 353 45 441205.

Refreshment Facilities
The Horseshoe Restaurant at the Curragh is open from noon on racedays. To reserve tables for lunch and afternoon tea call 00 353 1 626 1466. Within the Tote Hall there is a self service area with hot meals and snacks served from noon onwards. There are five bars. The Curragh View Bar and Horseshoe Bar on the first floor have clear views of the course and the finishing post. The Curragh View Bar also serves hot and cold food from a deli and baguette bar. The Vintage Crop Bar is located under the West Stand next to the bookmakers ring, The Railway Bar is in the Tote Hall and the Paddock Bar is on the reserved upper balcony.

Other Facilities
A PA system relays full race commentary to all areas of the course. There is a closed circuit TV in all public areas and results of UK races are displayed beside the weigh room.

For children a crèche and outdoor playground are provided at the west end of the stand. In both these areas children are supervised by qualified nursing and child care staff. On Irish Derby Day both the crèche and playground are closed.

Artist: **Peter Curling WINTER RATIONS**
Courtesy of: **The Artist**

Local Hotels

Keadeen Hotel Tel: 00 353 45 431666 in Newbridge; Stand House Hotel Tel: 00 353 45 436177, Curragh Lodge Hotel Tel: 00 353 45 522144, Kildare; Kilkea Castle Tel: 00 353 45 503 45156, Castledermot; Ardenode Hotel Tel: 00 353 45 864198, Ballymore Eustace; Tulfarris House Tel: 00 353 45 867555, Blessington; Barberstown Castle Tel: 00 353 1 628 8157, Kildare Hotel and Country Club Tel: 00 353 1 601 7200, Straffan; Red Cow Morans Hotel Tel: 00 353 1 45 93650, Dublin.

Local Restaurants

Lumville House, Red House Inn and Togher's Roadhouse, all in Newbridge; Silken Thomas in Kildare; The Hideout, Berney's, McTernan's, Kilcullen and Poulaphouca House, all in Ballymore Eustace. Contact the Irish Tourist Board Tel: 0171 493 3201 for a full accommodation list.

Places of Interest/Activities

Irish National Stud; Japanese Gardens in Kildare; Castletown House in Celbridge; Lakeside Leisure Centre in Blessington; also golf, fishing, hunting, horse riding.

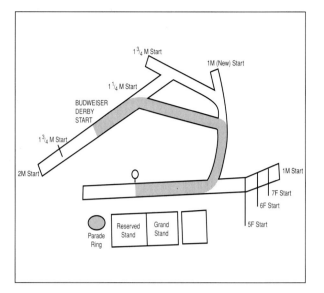

Artist: **Heather St Clair Davis** **IN THE VALLEY** *Courtesy of:* **Frost & Reed**

Set in the heart of County Kildare, Barberstown Castle is an internationally known, historic country house hotel. Built in the 13th century, the castle is situated only 30 minutes drive from both Dublin Airport and the bustling city centre, making it an ideal location for the city or the beautiful countryside.

The castle has been elegantly refurbished and decorated in glowing colours to provide the highest standards in comfort. With 22 en-suite bedrooms, all have been decorated in an individual style and dedicated to the ordinary and extraordinary people who have lived within its walls, inviting public rooms including the original castle keep, the warmth of the drawing room and the cocktail bar, you'll find your stay pleasant and enjoyable.

Since 1991 the restaurant at Barberstown, renowned for its creative food has consistently received the RAC Restaurant award and Rosettes from the AA. A fine selection of freshly prepared local food is available on both a la carte or table d'hote menus.

Golf can be arranged at the Kildare Country Club as well as at several championship standard courses nearby. Expert equestrian tuition, hunting, shooting and all other country pursuits are available in the area.

For the racing fraternity, meetings take place at the nearby courses of Punchestown (5 miles from Castle) with the festival meet every April, The Curragh (10 miles) with all the classics, Leopardstown (20 miles), Fairyhouse (12 miles), Naas (5 miles) and Navan (13 miles). Along with the various racecourses you will find the Tattersalls Sales in Fairyhouse, Goffs Bloodstock sales in Kill, the Equine Centre and the National Stud - all are close by. In the heart of both flat and National Hunt racing country, Barberstown Castle is the ultimate venue for the racing enthusiast.

Barberstown Castle
Straffan
Co. Kildare
Tel: (00 353) 1 628 8157
Fax: (00 353) 1 627 7027
e mail: castleir@iol.ie

Down Royal

Contact: **Mr Michael Todd,** at **Down Royal Racecourse, Maze, Lisburn, Co Down BT27 5BW Tel: 01846 621256 Fax: 01846 621433**

The history of Down Royal goes back over 300 years to the reign of James II. Created by Royal Charter in 1685, The Down Royal Corporation of Horse Breeders was tasked with "Encouraging the Breed in the County of Down". Undoubtedly the most famous horse to race at Down Royal was the "Byerly Turk" one of the three foundation stallions of the Stud Book.

Down Royal Racecourse will host the Northern Ireland Festival of Racing in 1999 a two day N.H. Meeting in November.

Location
Down Royal Racecourse is situated 2 ½ miles from Lisburn and 10 miles south of Belfast. It is adjacent to the A1 which is the main Belfast/Dublin route. The Racecourse is twenty minutes from Belfast International Airport and thirty minutes from Belfast City Airport.

Corporate Hospitality
Corporate hospitality packages are available for all race meetings.

Refreshment Facilities
The Racecourse has a modern Grandstand with a capacity for 2500 people and incorporates the following public amenities: Large Island Bar, Fast Food Counters, Carvery Counter, Tote Hall, Seating and Tables, Toilets, Close Circuit T.V., Viewing Windows overlooking Parade Ring

Local Hotels
Beechlawn Hotel Tel: (01232) 612974, Dunmurry; White Gables Hotel, Hillsborough; Ballymac Hotel Tel: (01846) 684313, Stoneyford, Lisburn

Local Restaurants
The Racecourse Inn, Maze, Lisburn; The Hillside Restaurant, Hillsborough (Egon Ronay Recommended); The Plough, Hillsborough (Egon Ronay Recommended); The Tidi Doffer, Ravernet, Lisburn (Winner of the British Airways Award for best hostelry).

Places of Interest/Activities
Irish Linen Centre/Lisburn Museum, Lisburn (Award winning attraction). Tourist Information available - (01846) 660038. Hillsborough - a beautiful Georgian village with many speciality shops, pubs and restaurants.

Downpatrick

Contact: **Mr Iain Duff, Doonhamer, 71 Lismore Road, Downpatrick, Co Down Tel: 01396 841125 Fax: 01396 842227. c/o Ballydugan Road, Downpatrick, Co Down, Racedays: 01396 612054 Fax: 01396 615923.**

The first race meeting to be held at Downpatrick was over 300 years ago - 1685. Racing has continued to take place with few breaks since, and on the present course for the last 200 years which is situated one mile away from the centre of this historic town.

A tight, undulating, track of 1 ¼ miles, many top National Hunt horses have started their careers at Downpatrick including the dual National winner Rhyme n' Reason, Cheltenham winners Rathgorman, Tourist Attraction and Sparky Gayle.

Downpatrick is possibly the friendliest course in Ireland with a strong local following. It has a supporters club which was formed in the early '70s and has raised substantial sums since its inception. Notably, Downpatrick is one of the four racecourses where all races are sponsored.

Local Hotels
Burrendale Hotel and Country Club, Newcastle Tel: (01396) 722599

Artist: **Heather St Clair Davis** **WATCH OUT FOR THE LOOSE HORSE** *Courtesy of:* **Frost & Reed**

Dundalk

Contact: **Mr Norman Colfer, Manager,** at **Paddock Lodge, Ratoath, Co Meath, Tel: 00 353 1 825 6618.** The racecourse address is **Dundalk Racecourse, Dowdallshill, Dundalk, Co Louth, Tel/Fax: (Racedays only) 00 353 42 34800**

Dundalk is derived originally from the Great Fortress, now called the Moat of Castletown, which was the residence of Cuchullin, the legendary hero and chief of the Red Branch Knights in the first century. This 'Dun-deal-gan' was the fortress of Delga, a Firbolg chief who had originally built it. The racecourse, founded in the early part of this century is in a lovely setting at the foot of the Cooley mountains and beside Carlingford Lough.

Location
Dundalk is located 52 miles North of Dublin. The racecourse is situated one and a half miles from the town centre, off the Newry Road.

Corporate Hospitality
Hospitality room available to cater for 40-120 people. There are a wide variety of structured sponsorship packages to cater for all budgets.

Refreshment Facilities
Self service restaurant, snack bars and bars.

Local Hotels
Derryhale Hotel Tel: 00 353 42 9335471, Imperial Hotel Tel: 00 353 42 9332241 and Fairways Hotel Tel: 00 353 42 9321500 in Dundalk, Ballymascanlon Hotel Tel: 00 353 42 9371124 in Ballymascanlon; Carrickdale Hotel Tel: 00 353 42 9371397 in Ravensdale.

Artist: **Peter Curling A WINTER SCENE**
Courtesy of: **The Artist**

Carrickdale Hotel & Leisure Complex and The Canal Court Hotel

Situated 5 miles north of Dundalk Racecourse on the main Dublin-Belfast road, the Carrickdale Hotel offers a warm welcome to all its guests.

There are 100 en suite bedrooms including executive suites all with direct dial telephone, hairdryer, satellite television and tea/coffee making facilities.

Our leisure complex offers you the ultimate in relaxation with a swimming pool, jacuzzi, steamroom and fully fitted gym.

The lively lounge bar offers midweek entertainment with a friendly atmosphere and professional service.

The hotel restaurant has a variety of menus available to suit all budgets, with the emphasis on fine food. Our chefs use only the best local produce to create a wide selection of national and international dishes.

So whether it's business or pleasure that you're after, be sure to call us at the Carrickdale Hotel.

Carrickdale Hotel and Leisure Complex
Carrickcarnon
Ravensdale
Dundalk
Co Louth
Ireland
Tel: 00 353 42 9371397
Fax: 00 353 42 9371740

The Canal Court Hotel has been built to the highest standards but with the emphasis on old fashioned quality. With the first class leisure facilties you will be hard pressed to find a more complete venue. Downpatrick, Down Royal and Dundalk race courses are all within easy reach. From the minute you walk through the doors into the front lobby you will know you've made the right choice.

Canal Court Hotel
Merchants Quay Newry
Tel: (01693) 251234
Fax: (01693) 251177

Contact: Dick Sheil, Chief Executive at **Fairyhouse Racecourse**, Ratoath, Co. Meath, Tel: 00 353 1 8256167 Fax: 00 353 1 8256051.**Email: fairyhse@indigo.ie, Web site: http//indigo.ie/fairyhse/**

Fairyhouse is the home of Ireland's premier National Hunt race, the Jameson Irish Grand National, which is run every year on Easter Monday. In 2000 it will be on the second day of our popular Easter festival which will run from April 23rd to 25th.

The first meeting held in Fairyhouse was in 1848 when the Ward Union Hunt held their point-to-point at this venue. From these small beginnings Fairyhouse quickly established itself as one of Ireland's premier racecourses. In 1870 the Irish Grand National was run and the winner was 'Sir Robert Peel'. The Grand National quickly became Ireland's most valuable and prestigious steeplechase and each success has its own rich tale, none more amazing that the win in 1929 of a six year old mare 'Alike', owned and ridden by 5'4" Frank Wise who was missing three fingers and who rode with a wooden leg.

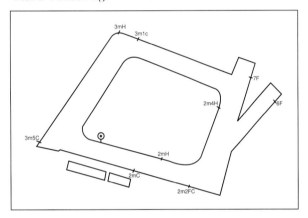

Artist: **Roy Miller THE BEACH**
Courtesy of: **The Artist**

Fairyhouse has a fully supervised and equipped crèche for children aged up to 9 years of age, with both indoor and outdoor play areas.

The racecourse opens its superb new grandstand and the refurbished Jameson Stand in November 1999. These new facilities will offer increased comfort to the racegoer. The new development includes new grandstand, weighroom building, Tote hall, betting shop, bars, restaurants, private suites and corporate hospitality rooms.

Throughout the year these Corporate facilities are available for numbers from 10 to 400. All suites and function rooms will have Tote, CCTV and either silver service or buffet style dining.

Local Hotels
The Newgrange Hotel Tel: 00 353 46 74100, Navan, The Great Southern Hotel Tel: 00 353 1 844 6000 and the Red Cow Morans Tel: 00 353 1 45 93650 are just some of the many hotels within a short distance from the racecourse. Contact the Irish Tourist Board Tel: 0171 493 3201 for a full accommodation list.

Refreshment Facilities
New Grandstand silver service restaurant, self service restaurants, seafood bar, fast food outlets and a choice of six bars.

Local Restaurants
Ryan's Steak House and Chez Francis Restaurant in Ratoath; Mill House in Clonee; The County Club in Dunshaughlin

Places of Interest/Activities
The racecourse is close to the historic sites of Tara, Slane and Newgrange as well as the beautiful Boyne Valley. Fishing and golf are available nearby.

Fairyhouse has always been one of the finest and fairest racecourses and continues to attract the leading horses both on the flat and over jumps. Arkle, Desert Orchid, Flying Bolt, Captain Christy, Prince Regent, Persian War, L'Escargot, and more recently Istabraq, See More Business and Bobbyjo are just some of the legendary greats that have graced the almost 2 mile circuit.

The racecourse is located 12 miles north west of Dublin, just off the N2 or the N3. The racecourse is within half an hours drive from Dublin Airport and City Centre, and is easily accessible via the Westlink motorway and Blanchardstown bypass. Bus Eireann provides a special bus service from Busaras for racemeetings. Tel: 00 353 1 8366111.

In 2000 Fairyhouse will host 18 days racing with the feature being our three day Easter Festival featuring the Irish Grand National, the Powers Handicap Hurdle and the Powers Gold Cup. The pre-Christmas festival (Dec 2nd - 3rd), features three Grade 1 races and is now firmly established as Ireland's first major National Hunt fixture of each new season. Fairyhouse also races on New Year's Bank Holiday (Jan 3rd).

Fairyhouse has an exclusive membership package which includes admission to all racemeetings, private member's room looking onto the racetrack with an exclusive members' area in the stand and members' car park. Fairyhouse is linked with two English racecourses, namely Uttoxeter and Newcastle. This enables members from each of the aforementioned courses complimentary admission to all meetings throughout the year.

Four star Red Cow Moran's Hotel combines classic elegance with modern design. A magnificent staircase sweeping from the marble lobby welcomes guests to this hotel of character and distinction. All the hotel's 123 executive bedrooms are fully air conditioned with teletext TV, voicemail phones, trouser press and tea/coffee making facilities. Eight luxuriously appointed suites ensure that Red Cow Moran's Hotel can cater for the most prestigious and discerning guests.

Strategically located only 15 minutes from the airport and ten minutes from Dublin city centre, Red Cow Moran's Hotel is ideal for those going raceing. The Curragh, Punchestown, Naas, Leopardstown and Fairyhouse courses are all within convenient driving distance of this deluxe hotel. The hotel offers extensive free parking for guests.

The Winter Garden Restaurant, with warm wood, airy conservatory and modern lighting, offers imaginative Irish cuisine with an array of international dishes and an extensive wine list. Guests may also choose to sample the traditional ambience of the renowned Red Cow Inn, a 200 year old pub situated with the hotel's grounds which has a choice of two restaurants, the Carvery and the Carriage.

After a thrilling day at the races what better way to unwind than with a drink in one of the four bars within the complex including the spacious and tranquil surroundings of the hotel's residents bar. For those who want to continue on into the night the Red Cow Inn also offers Club Diva, one of Dublin's premier nightspots within the hotel's grounds.

For corporate entertainment the hotel has extensive banqueting and conference facilities for up to 700 delegates as well as private syndicate and boardrooms for smaller parties.

Red Cow Moran's Hotel
Naas Road
Dublin 22
Ireland
Tel: 00 353 1 45 93650
Fax: 00 353 1 45 91588

Ardilaun House Hotel
Conference Centre & Leisure Club

Ardilaun House or Glenarde House as it was originally known was built around 1840 as a Town House for the Pearse Family who were Distillers and had large estates in South Galway.

Many of the Pearse family hold a place in local history. Augusta became Lady Gregory, was co-founder of the Abbey Theatre. Burton was founder of the Galway Blazers and a well-known racehorse trainer whose best horse was probably The Tetrach. Henry S. Pearse, who also resided at what is now Ardilaun House Hotel, was one of the stewards of the first Galway race meeting in Ballybrit in August 1869, and his horse won the first race on that day.

In 1922, the distillery closed and soon afterwards the Glenarde House and Estate was sold to Mr. Patrick Boland of the Biscuit Family. In 1961, the property with 5 acres was acquired by Mr. & Mrs. Patrick D. Ryan (Former Chairman of the Galway Race Committee) and its conversion into a hotel commenced - the hotel opened on St. Patrick's Day 1962.

1999 saw major investment and up-grading of the hotel and its facilities. A state of the art leisure centre was created, complete with a deck level swimming pool, jacuzzi, sauna, steam room, gym, aerobics room and a health and therapy suite and billiard room.

Golf, tennis, pitch & putt, the beach and the city centre are all within five minutes drive of the hotel.

Renovations also took place in the public areas and conference centre, with the addition of a designated board-room. The hotel relaunched itself as the Ardilaun House Hotel, Conference Centre & Leisure Club.

The Ardilaun is now a 90 bedroom, 4 star hotel, with five acres of grounds and gardens, offering superb facilities and comforts for the racegoer.

Special rates are available to readers of *"Travelling the Turf in Ireland"* for the September and October Meetings.

Brochures on request.

ARDILAUN HOUSE

Ardilaun House Hotel
Taylors Hill
Galway
Co. Galway
Tel: 00 353 91 521433
Fax: 00 353 91 521546
e mail: ardilaun@iol.ie
web site: www.ardilaunhousehotel.ie

Galway

Contact: **Mr John Moloney, Manager** at **Galway Racecourse, Ballybrit, Co Galway Tel: 00 353 91 753 870 Fax: 00 353 91 752 592, Web site: http://www.iol.ie/galway-races, E-mail: galway @iol.ie**

Records of organised race meetings in Co Galway go back to the middle of the 18th century and, according to local tradition, steeplechase races were run annually at Kiltulla, east of Ballybrit, for many years prior to 1868. In 1868, due to flooding of the course, they were transferred to Bushfield, beyond Oranmore. These, we are told, were the forerunners of the Galway races.

Sources record that there was an attendance of around 40,000 on the opening day at Ballybrit on Tuesday, 17th August 1869, and that 35,000 people turned up on the second day of the meeting. It is reported that the park in Eyre Square was used as a camping site to accommodate the huge crowds that arrived for the occasion. The first meeting was an overwhelming success and the Galway Races have gone from strength to strength ever since. The Galway Plate is one of the most important steeplechases in Ireland. The new Millennium Stand with its viewing terrace for 8,000 people and a second floor seating balcony for 2,000 people also features a wide range of amenities. The 1999 summer festival meeting became the first festival in Ireland to run for a full week - where new records for both attendances and betting were set.

Location
Galway is 136 miles from Dublin. The racecourse is situated four miles outside the city centre off the Galway-Tuam road. Directions to the course from the city are clearly marked with AA signs.

Public Transport
Regular train service to Galway from Dublin (Heuston Station). Tel: Irish Rail (Iarnrod Eireann) 00 353 1 836 6222 for train timetables. Special continuous bus service from Galway city centre during racing.

Admission Rates
Admission for the festival in July will be £10. September, October festival admission £6. For further information contact Galway Racecourse Tel: 00 353 91 753870.

Corporate Hospitality
Throughout the festival week the programme of National Hunt and flat racing including the famous Galway Hurdle and Galway Plate guarantees exciting racing for seven days. The Galway races 'Hospitality Village' offers a choice of packages in the Blazers Pavilion (ideal for groups of 6 or more) or Blazers Private Suite (for groups of 40 or more). Marquees are erected for the Summer/Autumn Festival, providing hospitality suites for all entertaining guests. There is also a new panoramic restaurant on the top level of the new millennium stand which caters for 200 people.

Refreshment Facilities
Self service carvery restaurant, seafood wine bar, snack bars and bars within the Millennium Stand.

Other Facilities
Children's crèche

Local Hotels
Ardilaun House Hotel Tel: 00 353 91 521433, Corrib Great Southern Hotel Tel: 00 353 91 755281; Galway Ryan Hotel Tel: 00 353 91 753181, Oranmore Lodge Tel: 00 353 91 794400 and Connemara Coast Hotel Tel: 00 353 91 592108, Galway; and Ashford Castle Tel: 00 353 92 46003, Cong.

Local Restaurants
Park House and Eyre House in Galway; Twelve Pins, Donnelly's and Ty ar Mor in Barna; Drimcong House in Moycullen

Places of Interest/Activities
Walking tours of Galway, Connemara, Burren, Co Clare, Coole Park, Gort and the Aran Islands; also golf, fishing and pony trekking

Gowran Park

Contact: **Mr Tom Carroll, Manager** at **Gowran Park Race Company Limited Gowran, Co. Kilkenny Tel: 00 353 56 26225 Fax: 00 353 56 26173.**

Since the first race meeting was held in June 1914, the course has become recognised as one of the best trial courses for both steeplechasing and flat racing in the islands. Levmoss, who pulled off the unique double of the Ascot Gold Cup and the Prix de L'Arc de Triomphe, first won on the flat at Gowran. Arkle, Nicholas Silver and Foinavon all ran at Gowran before going on to greater success overseas. recently, Danoli and Doran's Pride have raced against each other at the brand new October Kilkenny Racing Festival.

The Cuisine de France Thyestes Chase (January) is the big event of the calendar, the first major steeplechase in the year. The Red Mills trial Hurdle (February) has become one of the classic Cheltenham Trials, and if Cheltenham week has not satisfied your taste for racing, the Tetratema Cup, which has been run since 1918, takes place on the Saturday after the big English meeting. In May the flat racing kicks off with The Glanbia Classic trial over the bank holiday weekend, and in June the Victor McCalmont Memorial Stakes and the McEnery Cup are run. The ever popular mid-June Jack Duggan Handicap Hurdle keeps the national hunt fans happy. In September, the Denny Cordell Lavarack Memorial Race draws an eclectic crowd from the music, film and fashion industries worldwide to celebrate the Memorial Race of the music producer behind Tom Petty, Bob Marley and the Cranberries, mid-October is the Kilkenny Racing Festival, a 3-day event run concurrent with a Carnival in Kilkenny City.

Location
The racecourse is approximately 1/4 of a mile outside Gowran village on the Dublin-Waterford road. Gowran is 8 miles from Kilkenny, 80 miles from Dublin, 15 miles from Carlow and 5 miles from Thomastown.

Public Transport
Bus Eireann provides a special bus service from Dublin (Busaras) for most race meetings. Tel: 00 353 1 836 6111 to

Artist: **Roy Miller THE GALLOPS**
Courtesy of: **The Artist**

check times of departure. Also Rapid Express Tel. 00 353 51 872 149 and Tom Duffy (special raceday coaches from Dublin) Tel. 00 353 1 832 8169

Corporate Hospitality

The Helen Sheane suite caters for 30 - 100 people; the cocktail bar caters for 20 - 40 people; hard standing 'pads' are also available for siting of marquees.

Refreshment Facilities

Self service restaurant, snack bar and bars

Local Hotels

Club House Hotel Tel: 00 353 56 21994 and Hotel Kilkenny Tel: 00 353 56 62000, Kilkenny; Mount Juliet Hotel Tel: 00 353 56 73000, Kilkenny River Court Hotel, Thomastown; Kilkea Castle Tel: 00 353 503 45156, Castledermot, Dinn Ri in Carlow.

Local Restaurants

Laugton House and Kyteler's Inn in Kilkenny; Lord Bagenal in Leighlinbridge; The Long Man of Kilfane in Kilfane

Places of Interest/Activities

Kilkenny Castle, St Canice's Cathedral, Rothe House, Castle Yard, all in Kilkenny; also fishing, horse riding and golf, shopping and plenty of festivals.

Kilbeggan

Contact: **Mr Patrick J Dunican, Manager at Kilbeggan Racecourse, Kilbeggan, Co Westmeath Tel: 00 353 506 32176 Fax: 00 353 506 32125**

Kilbeggan Races is a truly Irish occasion. The quiet midlands town is transformed on race evenings into a festival of social and sporting pleasure, drawing admirers from every corner of Ireland. You can meet friends, circulate freely; you can eat drink or cheer without restriction, you can bring the family or whoever, where for your few pounds the odds are much better than a lottery ticket, and where you can boast afterwards it was sheer skill that made you pick the winner.

If you are bright, witty and rich you will enjoy Kilbeggan Races and if you are not, you will enjoy it just the same.

Westmeath C.C. sponsor a feature hurdle race in May. The Lean Midlands National is a July high light and Bank of Ireland sponsor a major hurdle race during the season, also Max Premium Dog Food sponsor a Handicap Steeplechase in September, attracting hundreds to the racing the Irish love best, National Hunt. The only racecourse in Ireland which all races are over jumps under National Hunt Rules.

The friendship and atmosphere gives Kilbeggan the edge over other events. The neighbourly attitude makes it even easier for visitors to join in and savour the excitement of real racing enjoyment.

In the heart of Ireland a unique course with a natural setting, both easy on the eye and ideal for viewing.

The development of Kilbeggan Racecourse is a great credit to the local community which is reflected in the increasing numbers of visitors who attend - it really is worth a visit.

Location

Kilbeggan is situated on the cross roads of Ireland and the racecourse is 1 mile from the town centre. It is 13 miles from Mullingar, 20 miles from Athlone, 8 miles from Tullamore, 56 miles from Dublin, 131 miles from Cork and 198 miles from Belfast.

Public Transport

Bus service from Dublin (Busaras) Tel 00 353 1 8366111 for time of departure. Taxis from town centre to racecourse.

Corporate Hospitality

Superb tented village area on the hill overlooking the entire racetrack and also adjacent to the parade ring and main tote and which has facilities to cater for groups from 100 people to 2,000 people. The Balcony Suite, in the new pavilion and hospitality room is also able to cater for 30-250 people.

Refreshment Facilities

Self service restaurant, snack bars and bar.

Local Hotels/Restaurants

Bridge House Hotel Tel: 00 353 506 22000, Tullamore. Bloomfield House Hotel Tel: 00 353 44 40894, and the Greville Arms Hotel Tel: 00 353 44 48563, Mullingar.

Places of Interest/Activities

Locke's Distillery, Museum, Belvedere House and Gardens, Mullingar (Genesis) Tullynolly Castle, Birr Castle and gardens also numerous golf courses and lakes for both course and fly fishing.

Killarney

Contact: **Mr Michael Doyle, Manager at Killarney Race Co Ltd, Racecourse, Killarney, Co Kerry Tel: 00 353 64 31125 Fax: 00 353 64 31860**

Renowned in verse, song, literature and paintings, the lakes of Killarney together with the background mountains give the racecourse one of the most natural settings in Ireland.

Race meetings were held frequently in Killarney on two different racecourses between the years 1827 and 1901. In 1936, after a lapse of 35 years, racing was resumed at the present racecourse. Killarney's celebrated four day Summer Festival commenced in 1947. The races are run along the bank of the River Flesk on ground where the Fianna (Celtic Warriors) roamed over 2000 years ago.

Throughout the years a host of famous people and international celebrities have enjoyed their visit to Killarney races, particularly the Summer Festival meeting.

Location

Killarney racecourse is half a mile from Killarney town centre, off the Kenmare road. Cork Airport, 50 miles; Farranfore Airport, nine miles.

Public Transport

Regular train service from Dublin (Heuston Station). Tel: Irish Rail (Iarnrod Eireann) 00 353 1 836 6222 for train timetables. Regular bus service from Dublin (Busaras). Tel Bus Eireann 00 353 1 836 6111 for times of departures.

Corporate Hospitality

Hospitality rooms available to cater for 20-100 people

Refreshment Facilities

Self service, restaurant, bars and snacks

Local Hotels/Restaurants

There are numerous hotels, guesthouses, B&Bs and self-catering units in Southern Kerry. There are also over 100 restaurants, many of which are to be found in the Good Food Guides. Contact the Irish Tourist Board Tel: 0171 493 3201 for a full accommodation list.

Places of Interest/Activities
Muckross House and Abbey, Killarney National Park, Ross Castle, Gap of Dunloe and Torc Waterfall. There is a 9 hole golf course within the racecourse. Also golf (eight major courses in South Kerry), pitch & putt, pony trekking, swimming, fishing, boating, mountaineering and magnificent beaches within 20 miles

Laytown

Contact: **Mr Kevin Coleman,** the **Secretary/Manager,** at **9 Palace Street, Drogheda, Co Louth, Tel: 00 353 41 9842111, Fax: 00 353 41 987566.**

Local folklore has it that it was the parish priest who, in 1876, organised the first race meeting on Laytown's three miles of golden strand. Held intermittently since then, it was not until 1901 that local landowner, Paddy Delaney, established the meeting as we know it today. Nothing, not even two World Wars, has stopped it taking place since then.

Laytown races have not changed very much through the years, but they are unique because they are the only grandstand races held in Europe which have the approval of the governing bodies. The enclosure consists of a three acre field, elevated above the beach. Steps which have been built up into the face of the sand dunes and these form the Grandstand. Marquees are erected on the day before the races and these are used to provide a weigh room, bars and snack bars.

On Race-Day, the strand is closed from early morning and work on the course then commences. By the time the first race is ready to start the tide has gone out, and racing can begin.

Location
Laytown is a small seaside resort on the east coast of Ireland, 29 miles north of Dublin. To reach the course, turn off the N1 Dublin-Belfast road at Julianstown.

Public Transport
Regular train services from Drogheda and Dublin (Connolly Station). Special bus service from Drogheda. Tel: 00 353 1 836 6111 Irish Rail (Iarnrod Eireann) for train timetable.

Refreshment Facilities
Snack bars and bars provided in the marquees

Local Hotels
Neptune Beach Hotel Tel: 00 353 41 9827107, Bettystown; Old Mill Hotel, Julianstown; Rosnaree Park Hotel, West Court Hotel Tel: 00 353 41 983 0965 and Boyne Valley Hotel Tel: 00 353 41 9837737, Drogheda; Conyngham Arms Hotel Tel: 00 353 41 9884444, Slane; Ashbourne House Hote, Ashbourne

Local Restaurants
Bacchus at the Coast Guard, Bettystown; Monasterboice Inn, Drogheda; Forge-Collon Anchor, Mornington

Artist: **_Peter Smith_ RUNNING THE SANDBAR** _Courtesy of:_ **_Frost & Reed_**

Contact: **General Manager, John White** and **Racing Manager, Tom Burke** for specific information on racing fixtures or updates on the state of the "going" at; **Leopardstown Racecourse, Foxrock, Dublin 18, Tel: 00 353 1 2893607, Fax: 00 353 1 2892634, E-mail: info@leopardstown.com, Website: www.leopardstown.com**, Office hours are 9.30am - 5.30pm Monday to Friday and from 8am on each race day.

Leopardstown Racecourse is the only remaining racecourse in the greater Dublin area. It is set in superb surroundings, nestled in the foothills of the Dublin mountains, over looking Dublin bay, six miles due south of the Dublin city centre. Access to the racecourse is via the M50 - coming from the north, west and south-west of the city, the N11 southbound from the city centre and the N11 northbound from Co. Wicklow. For major events AA road signage is provided. We advise those planning to visit the racecourse to leave ample time for the journey as traffic can be congested approaching the track. There are free parking facilities at the racecourse for approximately 6000 cars and a designated area for coach parking.

The racecourse operates throughout the year with a total of 23 meetings culminating with the hugely successful post Christmas 4-day National Hunt Festival.

The racing calendar in Leopardstown can broadly speaking be broken down into 9 National Hunt meetings and 14 Flat meetings. The National Hunt Season opens with the 4 day Christmas festival, 26-29 December and closes with our post Cheltenham meeting in March. The flat season runs from April to November with the key meetings in this period including the Heinz 57 Phoenix Stakes and the Esat Digifone Champion Stakes, a race which is now part of the Emirates World Series Racing Championship.

Racing at Leopardstown has become a popular and effective vehicle for corporate sponsors. All of our major national hunt and flat meetings have sponsors, many long-standing and others recently becoming involved in race sponsorship. The Hennessy Gold Cup, The AIG Europe Champion Hurdle, The Ladbroke Hurdle, The Derrinstown Stud Derby Trial, The Heinz 57 Phoenix Stakes, The Golden Pages Handicap and The ESAT Digifone Champion Stakes, are some of Leopardstown's most prestigious races. In December The Ericsson Chase, The Paddy Power Handicap Chase and The Denny Gold Medal Novice Chase are all integral parts of the four day post Christmas Festival. On O'Callaghan Day in November the entire card is sponsored by the Hotel Group as is the case with Bord Gais Day in October. Ladies' Day is held in May 1999, a meeting sponsored annually by The Doyle Hotel Group, long time supporters of Leopardstown.

Leopardstown Racecourse on its 171 acre site has, in recent years, been the focus of a major upgrade and renovation programme. Many of the facilities have been completely upgraded in recent years and this upgrading is continuing in other areas. The "Members Bar" which overlooks both the parade ring and the racetrack has become an integral part of the course and caters for our 1000+ Annual Members. The Box Holders' Bar with its minimalistic interior and prime viewing of the parade ring continues to serve the needs of

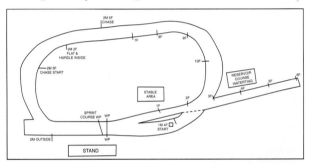

Artist: **Peter Smith THREE ABREAST** *Courtesy of:* **Frost & Reed**

the 300+ boxholders. In the Grandstand, Madigans Bar with its stripped pine floors and high tables now buzzes on race days with our younger patrons. Jodam is always a firm favourite with racegoers, while Fillies Cafe Bar, with its "delicious dishes and liquid delights" is open all day Monday to Sunday, on racedays and non-racedays.

Leopardstown has 27 private suites many of which are rented at on an annual basis. A number are retained for daily bookings and they can accommodate up to 24 people. Catering at Leopardstown is provided by Fitzers Catering under the name of "Leopardstown Hospitality". A wide ranging choice of menus are available from finger buffets to full à la carte. Each suite is equipped with a private bar and Tote facilities are within close proximity.

Our Silken Glider Restaurant on the first floor is always busy on race days where patrons can enjoy a silver service meal. The restaurant accommodates approximately 300 people and advanced booking is always advisable. Bookings can be made with Fitzers at Leopardstown on Tel: 00 353 1 2893691 Fax: 00 353 1 2893659 E-mail: leopardstown@fitzers.ie Monday - Friday 9.30am - 5.00pm. The Paddock Food Hall, serving up hot snacks and quick meals throughout the day is located in the Tote Hall area on the ground floor and the traditional "steak sandwiches" are available throughout the building in various locations.

A number of corporate rooms are available for hire including the Centenary and Levmoss Rooms together accommodating approximately 250 people. The Leopardstown Pavilion, one of the three elements which incorporate the Baileys Centre, overlooks the final fence with a stunning vista of the entire racetrack. This new facility shows off Leopardstown to its full potential and has proved hugely popular with corporate groups since its opening in April 1999. This glass fronted Pavilion boasts an entirely flexible space on 2 floors accommodating groups from 50 up to 1000 on the two floors in an open plan scenario.

The Baileys Centre is a £15 million development incorporating three seperate areas - the Leopardstown Pavilion, the Kilkenny Shop and ICON - a unique food and drink experience created by Baileys.

Our close neighbour, Westwood - Dublin's most popular

health and fitness centre, plays host to a state of the art creche and children's play area. Sitting in the middle of the racecourse is Leopardstown's 18 hole Golf Course which also incorporates a 48 bay floodlit driving range

Leopardstown Racecourse, Foxrock, Dublin 18-23 days racing per year, state of the art pavilion, corporate facilities, Dublin's best health and fitness centre-Fitzone, child's play area, an 18 hole golfcourse, 9 bars and a night club.

Public transport
On racedays from the city centre, Busarus (the Central Bus Station) leaves 1.5 hours before racing - for more information contact 00 353 1 703 44 20 Website : www.dublinbus.ie On the return to the city, buses leave the racecourse 15 minutes after the last race. Additional buses 46, 46a, 63, 84 and 86 from town.

Local Hotels
Montrose Hotel and Stillorgan Park Hotel Tel: 00 353 1 288 1621, Stillorgan; Fitzpatrick Castle Hotel Tel: 00 353 1 284 0700, Killiney; Dublin offers many hotels including Berkeley Court Hotel Tel: 00 353 1 660 1711, Shelbourne Hotel Tel: 00 353 1 676 6471, Burlington Hotel Tel: 00 353 660 5222, Davenport Hotel Tel: 00 353 1 607 3500, Jury's Hotel Tel: 00 353 1 660 5000, Mont Clare Hotel Tel: 00 353 1 607 3800 and Red Cow Morans Hotel Tel: 00 353 145 93650

Local Restaurants
Leopardstown Inn in Leopardstown; Lavins Thatched Restaurant and Beaufield Mews in Stillorgan; The Goat Grill in Goatstown; Lamb Doyle's in Sandyford; Palmers Golden Ball, in Kilternan.

Places of Interest
Leopardstown racecourse is only 15 minutes from Dublin which provides a myriad of attractions for visitors - galleries, museums, theatres, cinemas, churches, catherderals and shops, as well as Dublin Zoo in Phoenix Park, the largest enclosed public park in Europe. The course itself offers a wide range of activities on non-racedays. These include an 18 hole golf course, driving range, squash and indoor tennis. Tel: 00 353 1 289 5341 for information on golf and 00 353 1 289 5665 in relation to squash and tennis.

We can with certainty say that we have something for everyone!

Artist: **Klaus Philipp** **FINAL FURLONG** _Courtesy of:_ **The Artist**

Limerick

A new racecourse is currently under construction at Greenmount, Patrickswell, Limerick, for further information contact: **Ms Colette Henchy, Manager** at **Limerick Racecourse, Greenpark, South Circular Road, Limerick Tel: 00 353 61 229 377 Fax: 00 353 61 227 644.**

Local Hotels
Limerick Inn Tel: 00 353 61 326666 and Castletroy Park Hotel Tel: 00 353 61 335566 in Limerick; Clare Inn, and Dromoland Castle Tel: 00 353 61 368144 in Newmarket-on-Fergus; Adare Manor Tel: 00 353 61 396566, and Dunraven Arms Tel: 00 353 61 396633 in Adare; Fitzpatrick's Bunratty Hotel Tel: 00 353 61 361177 in Bunratty; the Great Southern Hotel Tel: 00 353 61 471122 in Shannon. Contact the Irish Tourist Board Tel: 0171 493 3201 for a full accommodation list.

Local Restaurants
Matt The Thresher, Little Italy and Punch's Pub & Restaurant, Limerick; Durty Nelly's, Bunratty; The Gooser, Killaloe

Places of Interest/Activities
King John's Castle in Limerick; Bunratty Castle & Folk Park in Bunratty; the Burren and Cliffs of Moher in Co Clare; also golf, fishing, hunting and shooting.

Listowel

Contact: **Mr Brendan Daly** is the **Secretary, c/o William Street, Listowel, Co Kerry, Tel/Fax: 00 353 68 21144**

Racing commenced at Listowel in 1858. The races were held previously at Ballyeagh, near Ballybunion, but due to faction fighting they had to be moved and Listowel was chosen as the new venue. Due to the popularity of races, known originally as the North Kerry Hunt Steeplechase, the meeting was extended from the original one day event until it became a six day fixture in 1992.

Listowel Races is one of Ireland's oldest and most successful racing festivals and is held in the last week of September. In addition there is a 3 day weekend race meeting in April.

Location
Listowel is 16 miles from Tralee and 50 miles from Limerick. The course is situated five minutes from the town centre.

Artist: **Refna Hamey COLOURS**
Courtesy of: **The Artist**

Public Transport
Regular train services from Dublin (Heuston Station) to Tralee and Limerick. Tel: 00 353 1 836 6222 Irish Rail (Iarnrod Eireann) for train timetables. Special bus services are provided daily from Tralee and Limerick railway stations to Listowel during the festival meeting.

Corporate Hospitality Rooms
Hospitality room available to cater for 40-100 people. In April of this year the new grandstand complex officially opened which offers great facilities for all racegoers.

Refreshment Facilities
Dining room, self service restaurant, snack bars, fast food outlets and bars.

Local Hotels
Listowel Arms Hotel Tel: 00 353 68 21500, Listowel; Cliff House Hotel Tel: 00 353 68 27777, Golf Hotel and The Marine Links Hotel Tel: 00 353 68 27139, Ballybunion. Contact the Irish Tourist Board Tel: 0171 493 3201 for a full accommodation list.

Local Restaurants
Three Mermaids, Horseshoe Bar, Elite Grill Room, Quirkes and Mamma Mia - all in Listowel.

Places of Interest/Activities
Town Park and Listowel Castle in Listowel, a local festival is held to coincide with the races providing nightly entertainment in the town; also golf and fishing.

Artist: **Refna Hamey JUMPERS DREAM**
Courtesy of: **The Artist**

Naas

Contact: **Mrs Margaret McGuinness, Manager** at **Naas Race Company Plc, Tipper Road, Naas, Co Kildare, Tel: 00 353 45 897391 Fax: 00 353 45 879486**

Naas racecourse is located on the main dual carriageway on route N7 southbound. Dublin is just 20 miles away. It is just 35 minutes drive from the Airport and an hours drive from the Ferryports.

Naas is a Grade 1 National Hunt Track and a Grade 11 Flat track, the stiff uphill finish is a true test for Cheltenham bound contenders.

The new £2 million stand complex includes restaurants, bars, corporate suites, indoor tote betting, and an S.P. shop. Patrons will be able to book tables for lunch in the new restaurant which is overlooking the racecourse and with tote betting at this level you need never leave your table. The betting ring has been improved and lowered to facilitate viewing from the stands and a new surface put in. Patrons wishing to have a bet with the bookmakers have easy access from the restaurant to the ring. Phase two will include upgrading of the stable yard and all other buildings.

Admission rates are adults £7/£8, students and senior citizens £3.50/£4. Free car and bus park.

Special Bus Eireann Service for race meetings from Dublin (Busaras) Tel: 00 353 1 8366 111 for time of departure. Arrow trains (Irish Rail 00 353 1 836 6222) run from Monday to Saturday from Heuston station to Sallins. From there a feeder bus will take you to Naas.

Local Hotels
The Ambassador Hotel Tel: 00 353 45 877064, Kill. Lawlors Hotel, Naas. Court Hotel, Naas. Town House Hotel, Naas. Harbour View Hotel, Naas. Hotel Keadeen Tel: 00 353 45 431666, Newbridge. Kildare Hotel and Country Club Tel: 00 353 1 601 7200, Straffan and Setanta House Hotel, Celbridge.

Local Restaurants
Manor Inn, Butt Mullins, Johnstown Inn, and Joe Olives

Places of Interest
Irish National Stud. Japanese Gardens in Kildare. Fishing, golf, hunting and pony trekking.

Navan

Contact: **Tom Burke Racing Manager c/o, Navan Racecourse, Proudstown, Navan, Co. Meath. Tel: 00 353 46 21350, Fax: 00 353 46 27964**

1999 was an exciting year for Navan Racecourse when it completed the first phase of its development and investment plan. The Proudstown Racecourse situated 2 miles from Navan town, 30 miles due north of Dublin City on the N3, had an extremely successful year with attendances and sponsorship all on the increase.

The Racecourse will play host to 15 meetings in 2000 between October and June - an increase of 3 on 1999. Its main meeting is the Golden Pages Troytown Chase in November, named after the famous Aintree Grand National winner who was bred close by. The track is well respected by owners and trainers who often prep their horses here prior to the Cheltenham Festival. Often the horses who win

at Navan, go on to perform well in major races in the UK. Navan's recent £2 million development has provided new bars, a large self-service restaurant and new corporate facilities overlooking the racetrack. These new facilities which opened at the end of 1998 have been welcomed by Navan's loyal patrons who come again and again to this friendly welcoming track. Admission to the racecourse varies between 6 to 38. Day membership is also available. There is on course catering ranging from snack bars to full dining facilities. Corporate tables and private function rooms can be booked by arrangement. Restaurant and bar facilities are open seven days a week.

In addition to its racecourse, Navan has a fantastic 18 hole Golf Course with 9 holes lying alongside the track and the newer 9 being within the track itself. The thriving Golf Course brings new people to the racetrack throughout the year and membership is currently available - please contact the Administration Office at 00 353 46 21350 for more details. A Golf Driving Range is also in operation.

Public Transport
Buses from Dublin depart from Busaras from 7.30am (9.00am on Sundays) and leave at approximately 1 hour intervals, arriving at the Mercy Convent in Navan approximately 1.5 miles from the racecourse. Full details from Bus Eireann at 00 353 1 8366111 Website - www.buseireann.ie

Local Hotels
Navan now has a number of excellent hotels, namely the Newgrange Hotel Tel: 00 353 46 23119, the Ardboyne Hotel Tel: 00 353 46 73732 and the Beechmount House Hotel Tel: 00 353 46 21553, within the town offering excellent accommodation opportunities. The offices of Meath Tourism are based in the town Tel: 00 353 46 73426 and they would be happy to provide advice on accommodation bookings.

Local Restaurants
Being located close to Dublin, Navan has benefited from some exciting developments in the town. There are many excellent pubs and restaurants. The popular restaurants include Hudson's Bistro Tel: 00 353 46 29231, the Loft Tel: 00 353 46 71755 and the China Garden Tel: 00 353 46 23938.

Places of Interest
Other local attractions include the Passage Tomb of Newgrange (only 10 miles from the racecourse). Older than the Pyramids of Egypt, the tomb is over 5,000 years old and is one of the most famous megalithic monuments in Western Europe. Nestled in the Meath Valley is of course the River Boyne, which lends itself to many senic walks and fishing opportunities. The famous Battle of the Boyne took place in 1690, and its site is now a popular tourist attraction.

Artist: **Alison Wilson** ***GOING DOWN TO THE START*** *Courtesy of:* **The Artist**

The management at **Punchestown** is headed by **Chief Executive Charles Murless** who together with his capable team is contactable at the race course office. **Tel: 00 353 45 897704 Fax: 00 353 45 897319.** The address is **Punchestown Racecourse, Naas, Co Kildare.**

As everyone already knows, Ireland is renowned for its unique and friendly atmosphere. No place is this seen to better effect than at Punchestown where even banks and schools are closed without question or complaint to enable everyone to participate in the festivities that take place each year! Peerless Punchestown as it is often referred to, conjures up something special in the minds of all who have been fortunate enough to attend and sample the unique atmosphere that has made it famous. It has been a huge success story with growth beyond the stone walls and big banks which were used at the first meeting held in 1854 over two days to what is today, one of the premier National Hunt venues in the British Isles. Fences and hurdles were first introduced in the early 1860s but nearly 150 years on, Punchestown still maintains its famous bank course which is seen at its best in late April when it is raced over twice in three days for the Ernst & Young Certified Hunters Steeplechase for the Ladies Perpetual Cup and the Quinns of Baltinglass Steeplechase for the La Touche Cup. These races are truly unique to Punchestown and provide a great challenge for horse and rider as well as a wonderful spectacle for all National Hunt enthusiasts.

The racecourse has recently undergone a £15m re-development, which has seen it transformed into a state of the art complex capable of catering for the huge crowds, which are now attracted each year. It boasts top class restaurant facilities in the panoramic, glass-fronted restaurant overlooking the racecourse, the de Robeck restaurant together with a self-service restaurant, seafood

bar, and champagne bar as well as numerous snack food outlets throughout the grandstand. These are supported by the various hospitality marquees which are always packed to capacity and have a special atmosphere all of their own.

Punchestown has become a major attraction for overseas visitors, especially from the UK, who come in their thousands to sample the unique Irish atmosphere and 'craic' during the National Hunt Festival which takes place in late April or early May each year. This is one of the principal National Hunt events of the season including The BMW Steeplechase, The Heineken Gold Cup, the LAWS Champion

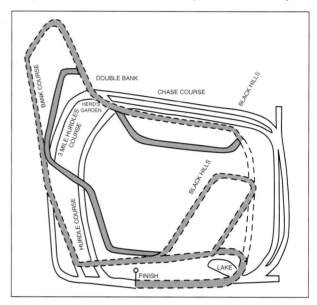

Four Year Old Hurdle and the Shell Champion Hurdle. Together with a top class supporting card, this meeting attracts a plethora of the very best equine talent from all corners of the British Isles.

The racecourse is easily accessible and is only 30 minutes from Dublin City centre travelling via the N7 to Naas which is only 3 miles from Punchestown. During the three day National Hunt Festival a special bus service is available from the Central Bus Station (Busarus), Store Street, Dublin 1 Tel: 000 353 1-836 6111. Punchestown is well sign posted with well laid-out car parking facilities to ensure the ever increasing attendances are continually satisfied and sufficiently well catered for. The racecourse has a landing facility suitable for helicopters, however the office must be notified prior to your intended arrival.

Racegoers will be able to enjoy 15 racedays in 2000, including the four-day National Hunt Festival (2nd-5th May). Rates of admission vary throughout the year starting from £7 to £15 for entry to the Grandstand Enclosure and £23 for access to the Reserved Enclosure. Prices are naturally at the higher end of the scale for the National Hunt Festival but discounts are available for advance and group bookings by contacting the ticket office at the racecourse. Senior citizens and children are also allowed entry at reduced admission rates on the day. Car parking is free, however to avoid any possible delays it is advised to arrive early. Annual membership is £105 which provides access to the members car park and Reserved Enclosure for all racedays representing great value for the regular racegoer. Disabled racegoers are well catered for with a reserved car park close to the entrance. The racecourse is completely wheelchair friendly with reserved areas overlooking the parade ring and racecourse and lifts provide access to all levels of the grandstand.

Location
Punchestown racecourse is approximately three miles from Naas on the Naas-Ballymore Eustace Road. It is just 45 minutes (23 miles) from Dublin (Route N7) just over an hour's drive from Dublin Airport and Dun Laoghaire and two hours from Rosslare.

Corporate Hospitality
Corporate hospitality packages are available in the tented village at the Spring National Hunt Festival. For further information contact Corporate Sport & Leisure 00 353 1 676 6650 or Punchestown Racecourse 00 353 45 897704.

Refreshment Facilities
Dining room/self service restaurant, snack bars, bars, and a reserved dining room facility is available at the Spring Festival.

Local Hotels
Hotel Keadeen Tel: 00 353 45 431666, Newbridge; Moyglare Manor in Maynooth; Rathsallagh House Tel: 00 353 45 403112, Dunlavin; Ambassador Hotel Tel: 00 353 45 877064, Kill; Naas Court Hotel, Harbour View Hotel and Gregory Hotel, all in Naas; Kildare Hotel and Country Club Tel: 00 353 1 601 7200 in Straffan; Curryhills House and Country Club in Prosperous. Contact the Irish Tourist Board Tel: 0171 493 3201 for a full accommodation list.

Local Restaurants
Lawlors and Butt Mullins, Naas; Silken Thomas, Kildare; Johnstown Inn, Johnstown; Ballymore Inn, Ballymore

Places of Interest/Activities
Irish National Stud; Japanese Gardens in Kildare; Castletown House in Celbridge; Russborough House, Lakeside Leisure Centre in Blessington; also fishing, pony trekking and golf.

Artist: **Jonathon Trowell BUSINESS AS USUAL** _Courtesy of:_ **Osborne Studio Gallery**

Roscommon

Contact: **Mr Michael Finneran, Manager** at **Roscommon Racecourse, Racecourse Road, Roscommon Tel: 00 353 903 63494 Fax: 00 353 903 63608 Racedays Tel: 00 353 903 26231 Fax: 00 353 903 26231.**

Roscommon racecourse is steeped in National Hunt tradition. The first ever recorded race meeting took place in 1837 and was organised by the British military which then had a base in the town. Racing proper began in 1885 and has continued ever since, with the exception of a 12 year period from 1936 to 1948.

Location
The racecourse is situated one mile from Roscommon on the Castlebar Road. Roscommon is 90 miles from Dublin, 47 miles from Galway, 20 miles from Athlone and 50 miles from Sligo.

Public Transport
Regular train services from Dublin (Heuston Station) to Roscommon. Tel: Irish Rail (Iarnrod Eireann) 00 353 1 836 6222 for train timetable. Taxi service from Roscommon Station to the racecourse.

Corporate Hospitality
Hospitality rooms available to cater for 20-100 people.

Refreshment Facilities
Dining room, self service restaurant, snack bar, tea room, bars.

Local Hotels
Abbey Hotel Tel: 00 353 903 26240 and Royal Hotel Tel: 00 353 79 62016 in Roscommon.

Local Restaurants
Gleeson's and Westdeli in Roscommon.

Places of Interest/Activities
Lough Key Forest Park in Lough Key; County Heritage and Genealogical Centre in Strokestown; burial place of the kings of Ireland and Connacht in Rathcroghan; Arigna scenic drive; also boating, fishing, wind-surfing in Hudson Bay; Munsboro Equestrian Centre; River Shannon Cruises.

Sligo

Contact: **Mr Brian Kennedy, Manager** at **Ballymote, Co Sligo, Tel: 00 353 71 83342 Fax: 00 353 71 83342 Racedays Tel: 00 353 71 62484.**

Sligo town, in the heart of Yeats country, boasts one of the most scenic racecourses in the country. William Butler Yeats regarded Sligo as the Land of Heart's Desire. On either side of Sligo town stand the giant sentinels—Benbulben and Knocknarea. Round about are all the other places immortalised in Yeats' poetry—Hazelwood, Inisfree, Lisadell, Slish Wood, Dooney, Drumcliffe, etc.

Racing at Sligo has been taking place for over 180 years, being founded at the time when racing enjoyed great prosperity in the country. Indeed so great was the proliferation of race meetings over the period 1805 to 1815 that the organising committee of the Sligo Races decided that its 1814 meeting "will commence in August so as to give the racehorses time to travel to Bellewstown, Maze, Derry and Monaghan, and to come to Sligo".

The programme at all meetings is comprised of National Hunt and flat races.

Corporate Hospitality
The Cleveragh Room available to cater for 60 to 100 people.

Location
The racecourse is situated at Cleveragh, half a mile from the town centre, just off the Dublin-Sligo Road. Strandhill Airport is six miles away and Knock Airport is 35 miles.

Public Transport
Regular train service to Sligo from Dublin (Connolly Station).Tel: Irish Rail (Iarnrod Eireann) 00 353 1 836 6222 for train timetable. Taxi service from train station to the racecourse. Also served by Bus Eireann from Dublin (Busaras) Tel: 00 353 1 836 6111 for departure times.

Refreshment Facilities
Bar, restaurant, snack bar.

Local Hotels
Sligo Park Hotel Tel: 00 353 71 60291, Silver Swan Hotel and Southern Hotel Tel: 00 353 71 62101 in Sligo; Ballincar House Hotel Tel: 00 353 71 45361 and Yeats Country Hotel Tel: 00 353 71 77211 in Rosses Point

Places of Interest/Activities
Within a five mile radius of Sligo town are the contrasting beaches of Rosses Point and Strandhill; also golf at Strandhill, Tubbercurry and Ballymore Golf Clubs, surfing, angling and horse riding also at Strandhill

Thurles

Contact: **Mr Pierce Molony** at the **Racecourse, Thurles, Co Tipperary Tel: 00 353 504 22253 Fax: 00 353 504 24565 Racedays Tel: 00 353 504 23272 Fax: 00 353 504 23245. E mail: thurles@iol.ie**

Thurles, situated in the sporting county of Tipperary, is celebrated as the centre of the Gaelic Athletic Association. It is also the heart of the famous Scarteen hunting county.

Earliest records show a three day meeting in June 1732. In October 1760, there was a six day meeting .

The February meeting is renowned as a major trial for the forthcoming National Hunt Festival meetings at Cheltenham, Fairyhouse and Punchestown.

Location
The racecourse is situated one mile west of Thurles town, five miles west of the main Cork-Dublin Road. Thurles is 10 miles north of Cashel, 30 miles west of Kilkenny, 40 miles east of Limerick, 60 miles north of Cork and 60 miles south of Athlone.

Public Transport
Regular train service from Dublin (Heuston Station) and Cork. Tel: Irish Rail (Iarnrod Eireann) 00 353 1 836 6222 for train timetables. Free minibus service to racecourse.

Corporate Hospitality
Hospitality room available to cater for 50-100 people

Refreshment Facilities
Self service restaurant, bars, tea room

Local Hotels
Hayes Hotel Tel: 00 353 504 22122 and Anner Hotel Tel: 00 353 504 21799, Thurles; Cashel Palace Hotel Tel: 00 353 62 62707, Cashel; Dundrum House Hotel Tel: 00 353 62 71116, Dundrum; Horse & Jockey Inn

Local Restaurants

Park Avenue House and Inch House both in Thurles; Chez Hans and Legends in Cashel

Places of Interest/Activities

Rock of Cashel; Holycross Abbey; Devil's Bit Mountain; also hunting, local equestrian centres and an excellent 18-hole golf course in Thurles

Tipperary

Contact: **Manager** at **Tipperary Racecourse Limerick Junction, Co Tipperary, Tel: 00 353 62 51357 Fax: 00 353 62 51303**

The first recorded meeting of Tipperary Races at Barronstown Course was Monday, 27 March 1848. In 1871/72, the races were abandoned due to smallpox, but were revived in 1881. In the early days of Barronstown (the predecessor to Limerick Junction racecourse) there was only one bookmaker, who also had a roulette table.

The first races at Limerick Junction took place in September 1916 promoted by Mr T Gardiner Wallis by the celebrated racing personality and his trainer Senator J J Parkinson and colleagues Stephen Grehan and Charles Moore.

A major incentive to the commencement of Limerick Junction was the promise of a special railway siding from the Great Southern and Western Railway Company.

The name was changed from Limerick Junction to Tipperary Racecourse for a meeting on 8 May 1986.

Location

Situated off the main Tipperary-Limerick road, the racecourse is two miles from Tipperary, 24 miles from Limerick, 40 miles from Shannon Airport, 64 miles from Cork and 112 miles from Dublin.

Public Transport

Regular train services from Dublin (Heuston Station) and Cork to Limerick Junction Station, which is within easy walking distance of the track. Tel: Irish Rail (Iarnrod Eireann) 00 353 1 836 6222 for train timetables. Mini Bus service on certain racedays from Tipperary Town to the racecourse, phone racecourse for details.

Admission Rates

Adult entry to the racecourse is £7 and £3.50 for senior citizens and students and group discounts are available.

Corporate Hospitality

Hospitality rooms available to cater for 20-100 people

Refreshment Facilities

Dining room, snack bars

Local Hotels

The Ballykisteen Golf and Country Club opposite the racecourse has restaurant and bar facilities. There's also the Royal Hotel Tel: 00 353 62 33244, Tipperary; Aherlow House Hotel Tel: 00 353 52 56153, Glen of Aherlow; Dundrum House Hotel, Dundrum; Cashel Palace Hotel Tel: 00 353 62 62707, Cashel

Local Restaurants

Tipperary Town has a diversity of restaurants ranging from traditional to Chinese. Donovans (O'Brien Street) is excellent for lunch and hosts Irish music. Others include the Brown Trout (Bridge Street), Chaser O' Brien (Pallas Green) and Chez Hans (Cashel)

Places of Interest/Activities

Rock of Cashel; Cahir Castle; Mitchelstown Caves; scenic Glen of Aherlow; also golf, fishing, hunting and shooting

Tralee

Contact: **Mr Patrick Crean, Secretary** at **Tralee Racecourse, Ballybeggan Park, c/o The Spa, Tralee, Co Kerry , Tel: 00 353 66 7136148 Fax: 00 353 66 7128007 Tel: (Racedays only) 00 353 66 7126188 Fax: 00 353 66 7126090.**

Racing is recorded in Tralee as far back as 1767, when a week-long meeting was held, the results of which are recorded in the Turf Club.

Great pride was taken in these meetings as is indicated by the organisers of the August 1805 meeting when they observed "The thanks of the meeting was unanimously given to the Steward for his uniform politeness and attention and his daily punctuality in paying the plates." Various venues in the locality were used until the present site, in Ballybeggan Park, was first opened to racing in 1889.

The park was formerly a deer park, and the stone for the surrounding limestone wall was quarried out of the land in the infield area of the course. The estate was formerly the property of Daniel O'Connell, The Liberator, in whose honour the Liberator Handicap is run annually.

The Tralee August meeting is the centrepiece of the International Rose of Tralee Festival. The festival sparkle spreads to the course for six days of great racing—this is a unique experience and is not to be missed. The two day June bank holiday meeting is an ideal way to get into the summer with traditional Kerry hospitality and scenery.

Location

Tralee racecourse is one and a half miles from the town centre, off the Tralee-Killarney road.

Public Transport

Regular train service from Dublin (Heuston Station). Tel Irish Rail (Iarnrod Eireann) 00 353 1 836 6222 for train timetable. Tralee railway station is approximately 1 mile from the racecourse. A special bus service from the railway station to the racecourse is provided on racedays.

Corporate Hospitality

Hospitality suite available to cater for 60-120 people

Refreshment Facilities

Dining room, snack bars and a new fast food outlet

Local Hotels

Abbey Gate Hotel Tel: 00 353 66 7129888, Brandon Hotel, Tel: 00 353 66 7123333 the Earl of Desmond, the Grand Hotel Tel: 00 353 66 7121499, Imperial Hotel, Ballygarry House Hotel, Meadowlands Hotel, Jenny Johnson Hotel and Tralee Court Hotel Tel: 00 353 66 7121877—all in Tralee. Contact the Irish Tourist Board Tel: 0171 493 3201 for a full accommodation list.

Local Restaurants

Aisling Geal, Numero Uno and the Oyster Tavern in Tralee; The Tankard in Fenit; Nick's in Killorglin

Places of Interest/Activities

A nine hole golf course at the racecourse opened in June 1997. The town also boasts the highly acclaimed high-tech county museum, a refurbished working windmill, an aquadome, the Geraldine Experience, Tralee Steam Railway, Siamsa Tire, and the National Folk Theatre

Tralee is the gateway to the Dingle Peninsula and the starting point for the Ring of Kerry. There are also magnificent beaches nearby at Banna and Inch; an 18 hole golf course designed by Arnold Palmer at Barrow; and sea angling at Fenit.

Tramore

Contact: **Michael Murphy, Roseville, New Ross, Co. Wexford, Tel: 00 353 51 421681 Fax: 00 353 51 421830** or to contact the racecourse direct: **Tramore Racecourse, Tramore, Co Waterford, Tel: (Racedays only) 00 353 51 381425 Fax: 00 353 51 390928.**

From 1806, racing was taking place at Tramore in what was known as 'the Black Strand'. It was right beside the sea and, before the First World War, had succumbed to the waves.

In 1914, Martin Murphy commenced racing again on his own property where all meetings still take place today. Those race meetings, held under the aegis of the Red Cross, were continued by Mr Murphy until his death in 1920.

In that year a new company made up of the renowned Senator J J Parkinson, Francis Murphy and Thomas Fleming took over control.

For many years the Fleming family were synonymous with Tramore Racecourse. In 1997 a new race company was formed, headed by Peter Queally. The improvements which have been carried out on the track have received very favourable comments from both trainers and jockeys. The facilities for the racegoers have also been upgraded. Tramore Festival in August ranks among one of the most popular meetings of the summer.

Location
The racecourse is situated eight miles from Waterford city on the main Tramore road and one mile inland from Tramore town centre. Waterford Airport is nine miles from Tramore.

Public Transport
Regular train service from Dublin (Heuston Station) to Waterford. Tel: Irish Rail (Iranrod Eireann) 00 353 1 836 6222 for train timetables. Local bus service to the track.

Corporate Hospitality
Hospitality room available to cater for 20-100 people

Refreshment Facilities
Self service restaurant and bars.

Local Hotels
Jurys Hotel, Tower Hotel and Granville Hotel in Waterford; Majestic Hotel and Grand Hotel in Tramore; Waterford Castle in Ballinakill. Contact the Irish Tourist Board Tel: 0171 493 3201 Fax: 0171 493 9065 for a full accommodation list.

Local Restaurants
The Esquire in Tramore; The Ship in Dunmore East

Places of Interest/Activities
Celt World Theme Park, Funfair and Amusements in Tramore; Waterford crystal factory in Waterford; also golf and fishing.

Wexford

Contact: **Michael Murphy, Roseville, New Ross, Co. Wexford, Tel: 00 353 51 421681 Fax: 00 353 51 421830 Racedays Tel: 00 353 53 42307 Fax: 00 353 53 43702.**

Steeped in tradition and deriving its name from its Viking heritage, Wexford has always been foremost in the breeding of horses in Ireland. Jumping is particularly associated with Wexford and many of Wexford's native sons as well as her horses have achieved outstanding National Hunt success.

The earliest records of racing here took place on reclaimed boglands in the 1870s. By 1902, however, this had ceased and racing commenced again on the present course in 1951.

The course is only 15 miles from the major sea port of Rosslare.

Location
Wexford racecourse is situated just outside the town off the Dublin-Rosslare bypass, 15 miles from Rosslare ferry port.

Public Transport
Regular Dublin-Rosslare train service. Tel Irish Rail (Iarnrod Eireann) 00 353 1 836 6222 for train timetables. Good taxi service from Wexford train station to the racecourse.

Corporate Hospitality
Hospitality rooms available to cater for 15-100 people

Refreshment Facilities
Self service restaurant, snack bar and bars

Local Hotels
Talbot Hotel, Wexford Lodge Hotel, Whites Hotel and Whitford House Hotel in Wexford; Tuski House Hotel and Hotel Rosslare in Rosslare; Ferrycarrig Hotel in Ferrycarrig

Local Restaurants
The Granary, Lobster Pot, Oyster Restaurant and Tim's Tavern—all in Wexford

Places of Interest/Activities
Wexford Wildlife Reserve in Wexford; Irish National Heritage Park in Ferrycarrig; Johnstown Castle Park in Johnstown; John F Kennedy Arboretum in New Ross; also golf and fishing.

For further information contact:
Irish Horseracing Authority,
Marketing & Promotions Department,
Leopardstown Racecourse,
Foxrock,
Dublin 18,
Ireland

Betty O'Connell
(Promotions/Tourism Manager)
Tel: 00 353 1 8351965
Fax: 00 353 1 8351964

Shirley Finnegan
(Administrator)
Tel: 00 353 1 2892888
Fax: 00 353 1 2898412
E mail: Info@irishracing.iba.ie
Web page: www.iba.ie/ibarace

For a full list of accommodation contact the
Irish Tourist Board,
150 New Bond Street,
London,
W1Y 0AQ
Tel: 0171-493-3201
Fax: 0171-493-9065

Great Horses for Great Courses

Ireland, a country famous for its thoroughbred horses, offers visitors an ideal opportunity to sample the unique atmosphere of thoroughbred horse racing. With 27 racecourses located throughout the island, you can be assured that wherever you are in the country, a race meeting will not be too far away.

The Curragh plays host to all five Irish Classics: the 1,000 and 2,000 Guineas at the end of May, the Derby on the first Sunday in July, the Oaks in mid July and the St Leger in mid September. The vast expanses of the Curragh are unrivalled anywhere else in Europe, providing a true and fair test of a thoroughbred racehorse.

Budweiser Irish Derby day at the Curragh has become one of the highlights of the Irish social calendar. Usually staged in glorious sunshine at the height of summer, the talent in the enclosures is matched only by the talent on the racecourse as English and French Derby heroes lock together in combat for the Classic crown of Europe.

Leopardstown, nestling at the foot of the Dublin mountains just eight kilometres from Dublin city centre, provides a picturesque stage for top quality Flat and National Hunt (jump) racing. The Group One Heinz 57 Stakes in August sees the fastest juveniles in Ireland and Britain hurtle down the famous six-furlong straight that dissects the round course. The Irish Champion Stakes, part of the Emirates World Racing Championship Series in September pits the best middle-distance performers of all ages in Europe against each other in its quest to discover the supreme champion.

Nowhere in the world is National Hunt racing more cherished than in Ireland, and the cocktail of agility, speed and stamina that are the ingredients of a successful National Hunt horse are nowhere more in evidence than at the Leopardstown Christmas Festival meeting, which begins on St. Stephen's Day and provides four days of the best quality jump racing of the year.

Fairyhouse at Easter and Punchestown in the first week of May this year, complete the triad of Festival meetings for the National Hunt purist. The Irish National - the richest steeplechase on the calendar - is traditionally staged at Fairyhouse on Easter Monday. The four-day Punchestown Festival is steeped in quality, as the British National Hunt champions come over to tackle the Irish on their home soil. The perennial winners at Punchestown are invariably the racegoers.

Ireland's summer festival programme - where racing is the centrepiece of festivals of music, merriment and general 'craic' - is spearheaded by the Galway Festival during the last week in July. Like pilgrims they flock from the four corners of the world to the west coast of Ireland to experience the uniqueness that is Galway. The stone walls, the music, the three-card-trick man, the barren land, the dance - they all conspire to create an atmosphere that is wholly impossible to describe to the uninitiated. One could be forgiven for thinking that the action on the racecourse was a mere side-show. For any person with even a peripheral interest in racing, a visit to Galway is absolutely imperative.

The Festivals at Killarney in July, Tralee in August and Listowel in September provide an ideal opportunity for racegoers to take in the breathtaking landscape of County Kerry in the south-west. The holiday atmosphere at the racetrack permeates each of these scenic towns for the week as tourists, racegoers and even jockeys and trainers join in the 'craic' while unwinding after racing.

The seaside resort of Tramore stages a four day Festival in mid-August. Timed as it is to coincide with what is traditionally the warmest period of the Irish summer, its proximity to the sea provides visitors with the opportunity to partake in a range of water sports. The town of Tramore truly comes alive during race week, with bars and restaurants swinging into action, and a plethora of daytime activities providing entertainment for the whole family.

At the end of September, the Irish racing roadshow returns to Co Kerry for the Listowel Festival, featuring the Kerry National, at a time of year when many of the better National Hunt horses return to action after their summer break.

The beauty of Irish racecourses is their individuality. Every course boasts its own unique qualities. Horseracing is at the very heart of what we do in Ireland. Where horses come first.

Artist: **Heather St Clair Davis SHE'LL GIVE YOU WINGS, SIR** *Courtesy of:* **Frost & Reed**

Point-to-Point in Ireland

For many years now the best Irish thoroughbred National Hunt horse is eagerly sought overseas, but to nowhere is it as consistently and regularly exported than to Great Britain. This trend, which has proved most profitable and beneficial to buyer and seller over the years, shows no signs of tapering off and indeed if one looks at the facts and figures, it seems to be very much on the increase. Whilst the Irish-bred has long been exported to England to the point-to-point fraternity, it is in the area of Park racing where the most growth has occurred in the past 10-12 years. Whilst the older type of animal has long graced the English point-to-point field, it is the success of the better Irish animal, particularly the one from the point-to-point academy, which has hit the headlines in recent years.

The last two Gold Cup winners - **Mr Mulligan and Cool Dawn** - were ex point-to-point performers, while the Aintree Grand National has been captured by the Martin Pipe trained ex-Irish **Miinnehoma**. Other top recruits to the ranks in the past five years include this year's Whitbread Gold Cup victor **Call It a Day**, Welsh National winner **Belmont King**, Grand National runner up **Suny Bay**, in addition to such top class winners as **Ask Tom, Island Chief, Gales Cavalier, Unguided Missile, General Crack, Wandering Light** and **Yes Man** to name but a few.

It would be difficult to find better value at any sporting fixture than that which is found at the some 80 plus point-to-point meetings which take place throughout Ireland from the first day of January up to the last weekend in May. On the Northern Ireland scene, a day's racing will cost the racing enthusiast about a tenner, which covers admission to the course and a racecard with detailed and ample information - ample enough to ensure that the punter's ongoing battle with the 'Auld Enemy' is more than an exercise in 'hit and miss'. In the South, admission is either £3 per head or £5 a Car, whilst a comprehensive racecard only costs a pound. Most meets in the South are usually run on a Sunday, with a few on Saturdays and similarly a couple in mid-week, although competition from Park Sunday racing appears to be about to hit an all time high. The traditional day for competing in the North of Ireland is Saturday with a few mid-week dates. At present the number of horses competing in the point-to-point field continues to rise steadily and the 1998 season saw a record

number of some 2,480 hopefuls coming before the starter. As with most sports events run during the winter months, one is inclined to be somewhat at the mercy of the elements, but the point-to-point brigade are invariably a hardy bunch. There are some seventy five courses sprinkled throughout the country with about five or six utilising the inside of courses in Park venues such as Dundalk and Listowel. In addition there are four venues which stage more than one point-to-point fixture during the season. Also there are 2 two day Festivals held here with the East Antrims running a two-day fixture in Loughanmore and the season usually winds up with the South Unions availing of the last weekend in May staging another popular Saturday/Sunday double header. Indeed the latter has tried with some success to make this an annual International fixture with a few races open to U.K. runners, making this a pleasant and somewhat laid back gathering - with the emphasis on fun and craic!

However, if one expects this apparent low-key attitude to permeate through the rest of the season, then one is in for a big surprise, as nothing could be further from the truth.

Though the sport basically purports to be amateur, very little from the organisation, the running and the competitive attitude leads one to believe that it is anything other than professional in the main.

The standard of rider, and in particular the leading ones, is of a particularly high standard and one only has to mention the names of Adrian Maguire, Norman Williamson and Timmy Murphy who have joined the professional ranks subsequently, to highlight the standard which the sport has achieved in regards to jockeyship.

For overseas National Hunt and point-to-point enthusiasts, visitors could easily ensure that they take in either a Saturday or Sunday point-to-point, in addition to a weekend Park fixture (there are many excellent National Hunt meets at this time of year) and in the process sample both sides of the racing spectrum. One thing is for sure however, whether it is wearing the wet gear at an inclement point-to-point in the Pigeons or at the more comfortable surroundings of Leopardstown, you are sure to enjoy the atmosphere and racing that is unique to an Irish National Hunt meeting.

Artist: **Refna Hamey** *THEY GAVE THEIR ALL* *Courtesy of:* **Artist**

On the road southwest from Limerick, you come across what is probably the prettiest village in Ireland. This is Adare - straddling the River Maigue, picturesque with sturdy cottages, deep-set windows and mellow thatch. Here too is the Dunraven Arms Hotel, one of Ireland's premier hotels, carefully restored and renovated in keeping with the old-style village, which is something of a visitor attraction in itself. The Dunraven Arms welcomes you to not only spacious and tastefully refurbished bedrooms (with TV and direct dial telephone) but to the highly-rated award-winning Maigue Restaurant which offers exceptional cuisine and a very good cellar. The newly opened leisure centre comprises a 17m swimming pool, Therapy clinic, Steam room, and Computerised Gym Studio. The river itself affords good salmon and trout fishing and for equestrian enthusiasts, the Dunraven Arms caters famously for riding and fox hunting. For golfers, there's the beautiful 18-hole Adare Golf Course (designed by Robert Jones)

and Adare Manor Golf Club. Lahinch and Ballybunion Championship Golf Courses are within driving distance. Shannon Airport is just a short 25 minute drive away. Our highly professional staff guarantee to make your stay a memorable one!

For racing enthusiasts, Limerick, Mallow, Listowel, Tralee and Killarney racecourses are all within half an hour to 45 minutes of the hotel. Hunting holidays are a speciality, with the County Limerick Foxhounds, Limerick Harriers, Scarteen-Black & Tans, Tipperary Foxhounds and Galway Blazers on the doorstep.

AA Three Rosettes, Gilbey's Gold Medal Award, Egon Ronay, RAC Hospitality, Service & Comfort Award, Mouton Cadet Award, Bord Fàilte Awards of Excellence.

"Dunraven Arms, the best hotel in Ireland" David Nicholson, Racing Post '98.

Dunraven Arms Hotel
Adare
Co. Limerick
Tel: 00 353 61 396633
Fax: 00 353 61 396541
E-mail: dunraven@iol.ie

Artist: **Terence Gilbert LAYTOWN RACES** *Courtesy of:* **The Artist**

AINTREE
Tel: 0151 523 2600 Fax: 0151 530 1512
CONTACT: Dickon White, Marketing Manager

BOXES/HOSPITALITY: By arrangement; **MARQUEE:** Tented village with restaurant facilities; **FUNCTION/CONFERENCE FACILITIES:** Available non-racedays; longest 9 hole golf course in UK; weddings in Queen Mother Stand; **CATERING:** Letheby & Christopher (01242) 523203; **DISCOUNTS & PACKAGES:** Contact for details; **RACE SPONSORSHIP:** From £2500 at May & November meetings

ASCOT
Tel: (01344) 876060
CONTACT: Kate Gold, Business Development Manager

BOXES/HOSPITALITY: 285 private boxes available for fixed fee or part of catering & entrance package; **MARQUEE:** Available all summer meetings to accommodate 20-300 guests; **FUNCTION/CONFERENCE FACILITIES:** Available all year; Ascot Pavilion accommodates 1200 for dinner; exhibition hall and numerous suites; special private tours arranged; **CATERING:** Full service up to 1200; **DISCOUNTS & PACKAGES:** Available at all meetings, contact for details; **RACE SPONSORSHIP:** Available for televised and non-televised races

AYR
Tel: (01292) 264179 Fax: (01292) 610140
CONTACT: Carol Moore, Corporate & Sponsorship Manager

BOXES/HOSPITALITY: 30 of various sizes; **MARQUEE:** Available at major meetings; **FUNCTION/CONFERENCE FACILITIES:** Contact for details; disabled access; **CATERING:** Strachan Kerr (01292) 264179; **DISCOUNTS & PACKAGES:** 20% for groups in grandstand booked and paid in advance; special lunch and grandstand package for groups of 10 or more at £70 + VAT pp; **RACE SPONSORSHIP:** Contact Graeme Speirs, Marketing Executive

BANGOR-ON-DEE
Tel: (01978) 780323 Fax: (01978) 780985
CONTACT: Jeannie Chantler

MARQUEE/HOSPITALITY: Sites opposite Parade Ring to accommodate parties up to 200; no site fee; **FUNCTION/CONFERENCE FACILITIES:** Dee Suite for 50-100 guests, with television and Tote; Maelor Room for up to 20 with television; **CATERING:** Hughes of Welshpool (01938) 553366; **DISCOUNTS & PACKAGES:** Contact for details; **RACE SPONSORSHIP:** Flexible approach; contact for details

BATH
Tel: (01295) 688030 Fax: (01295) 688211
CONTACT: Sylvia Wilcox

BOXES/HOSPITALITY: Daily private boxes to accommodate groups of 20 or more from £300 + VAT; Lansdown Room in Paddock area for up to 100, hire charge £150 + VAT; Paddock Room up to 40 guests, £100 + VAT; **MARQUEE:** Sites adjacent to the Paddock area, prices upon request from the racecourse; **FUNCTION/CONFERENCE FACILITIES:** Facilities available for meetings, conferences etc. on non-racedays; **CATERING:** Letheby & Christopher (01242) 523203; **DISCOUNTS & PACKAGES:** Discounts for groups of 20 plus in Tattersalls if booked 14 days in advance; **RACE SPONSORSHIP:** Full package available tailored to budget and marketing aims; contact for details

BEVERLEY
Tel: (01482) 867488 or 882645 Fax: (01482) 863892
CONTACT: Mrs Jane Johnson

BOXES/HOSPITALITY/MARQUEE: 3 entertaining boxes in the main grandstand can be taken as one for large parties; on the second floor there are 5 boxes one of which accommodates parties of up to 50 guests; **FUNCTION/CONFERENCE FACILITIES:** Contact for details; **CATERING:** Craven Gilpin (0113) 287 6387; **DISCOUNTS & PACKAGES:** Contact for details; **RACE SPONSORSHIP:** Contact for details

BRIGHTON
Tel: (01273) 603580 Fax: (01273) 673267
CONTACT: Phil Bell, Commerical Manager

BOXES/HOSPITALITY/MARQUEE: For 10 - 150 guests in a variety of rooms/luxury marquees; **FUNCTION/CONFERENCE FACILITIES:** Contact for details; **CATERING:** Alexanders 0171 357 7304; **DISCOUNTS & PACKAGES:** Hospitality packages at £60, £70 and £80 + VAT pp **RACE SPONSORSHIP:** From £500

CARLISLE
Tel: (01228) 522973
CONTACT: Ann Bliss, Administration Director & Secretary

BOXES/HOSPITALITY/MARQUEE: Contact for details; **FUNCTION/CONFERENCE FACILITIES:** Contact for details; **CATERING:** Romfords (01434) 688864; **DISCOUNTS & PACKAGES:** 20% plus free ticket to Club and Tattersalls for groups of 10 or more, 25% for groups of 45+, prepaid gift voucher Gold packages £30 pp; **RACE SPONSORSHIP:** Packages from £500 - contact for details

CARTMEL
Tel: (01539) 536340 Fax: (01539) 536004
or
Tel: 0151 523 2600 Fax: 0151 522 2920
CONTACT: Andrew Tulloch, General Manager

MARQUEE: Available on a daily basis to accommodate 30-200 guests; picturesque setting makes racecourse ideal venue for entertaining; **CATERING:** Romfords (01434) 688864; **DISCOUNTS & PACKAGES:** 20% discount for parties of 5 or more, with badges purchased one month in advance; **RACE SPONSORSHIP:** Contact General Manager for sponsorship and hospitality details

CATTERICK
Tel: (01748) 811478 Fax:(01748) 811082
CONTACT: Lorna Paterson, Sales & Marketing Manager

BOXES/HOSPITALITY: Private luncheon suite (20-40 Guests) at £150 + VAT or Paddock Suite (40-80 Guests) at £200 + VAT; **MARQUEE:** Quotations on request; **FUNCTION/ CONFERENCE FACILITIES:** See main racecourse entry; disabled access; also holds biggest Sunday market in the North East of England; **CATERING:** Craven Gilpin & Son (0113) 287 6387; **DISCOUNTS & PACKAGES:** £2 off Tattersalls and one free pass for parties of 10 or more; **RACE SPONSORSHIP:** Packages tailor-made to suit your specific requirements wherever possible, contact Sales & Marketing Manager for details

CHELTENHAM
Tel: (01242) 513014 Fax: (01242) 224227
CONTACT: Rosemary Hammond, Racecourse Secretary

BOXES/HOSPITALITY: For 12-24 guests on daily basis except for Festival at £250-£500; £528 per 12 guests with badge and lunch in April & October; **MARQUEE:** Festival—from £780 per day for 24 guests; temporary boxes from £365 for 32 guests; **FUNCTION/CONFERENCE FACILITIES:** No availability during Festival; functions from £10 per person subject to minimum number; also see main racecourse entry; **CATERING:** Letheby & Christopher (01242) 523203; **DISCOUNTS & PACKAGES:** Group discounts available at all meetings; packages to suit requirements, including behind the scenes tours and talks by jockeys; Panoramic restaurant from £49 per person including badge, lunch and tea—spectacular view overlooking the course for tables of 4 to 12 guests—all prices subject to VAT; **RACE SPONSORSHIP:** From £2000. Contact Mr Peter McNeil, Commercial Manager

CHEPSTOW
Tel: (01291) 622260 Fax: (01291) 627061
web site: http://www.chepstow-racecourse.co.uk
e mail: enquiries@chepstow-racecourse.co.uk
CONTACT: Rodger Farrant, Clerk of the Course
or Peter Horleston, Company Secretary

BOXES/HOSPITALITY: Chepstow, set in an area of outstanding natural beauty, if proud of its 39 Private Boxes and 9 Hospitality Suites - all commanding an excellent view across the Racecourse. These facilities can cater for 20-200 people, the Members Restaurant has tables for 2-12 people; **MARQUEE:** Two marquee sites are available on Racedays - one is strategically situated close to the Winning Post, while the other can create the perfect garden party atmosphere; **FUNCTION/ CONFERENCE FACILITIES:** Non-racing activities can easily be accommodated and are very welcome to Chepstow. The Lysaght Suite can seat 150 theatre style as can the Wyndcliffe Suite. Weddings, private parties, dinner dances etc are a speciality. Ample free parking. Daily delegate rates start from £24.50; **CATERING:** Letheby & Christopher (01242) 523203 or (01291) 625189 (Racedays only); **DISCOUNTS & PACKAGES:** Discounts apply for pre-booked parties of 20 or more in both Members and Tattersalls, all inclusive packages are available on request; **RACE SPONSORSHIP:** National Hunt and Flat Racing, some race days offering television coverage, packages can be arranged to suit budget and marketing needs - contact the racecourse for details

CHESTER
Tel: (01244) 323170 Fax: 01244) 344971
CONTACT: Lucy Moreau, Marketing Manager

BOXES/HOSPITALITY: 23 all normally sold, but some sub-lets available; contact for details; **MARQUEE:** Tented village at May meeting, private ground-level hospitality suites for 40 guests each in the Paddock at every meeting, marquees to accommodate up to 500 guests; **FUNCTION/CONFERENCE FACILITIES:** On non-racedays space available; contact for detailed brochure; **CATERING:** Letheby & Christopher (01273) 275552; **DISCOUNTS & PACKAGES:** Discounts and packages by prior arrangement, contact for details; **RACE SPONSORSHIP:** Available for all meetings

DONCASTER
Tel: (01302) 320066 Fax: (01302) 323271
CONTACT: Tim Betteridge, Executive Sales & Marketing

BOXES/HOSPITALITY: St Leger Stand boxes for 12-24 guests; Royal Box holds 40-60; Arena Scene boxes available for the St Leger Festival for 24 guests; various hospitality packages available; **MARQUEE:** Large number available for parties of 20 or more guests in Paddock area and near winning post; **FUNCTION/CONFERENCE FACILITIES:** Suites include Classic for 60 guests; Yorkshire for 30-60 and Ormonde 30; St Leger Banqueting Suite & Conservatory accommodate 100-220 and 40-60 for full hospitality; **CATERING:** Metro (01302) 349740; **DISCOUNTS & PACKAGES:** Contact for details; **RACE SPONSORSHIP:** All packages are tailor made to suite sponsors objectives and budgets, televised races available

EPSOM
Tel: (01372) 470047 Fax: (01372) 470427
CONTACT: Hector Nunn or Lucy Roberts

BOXES/HOSPITALITY: Epsom has a wide range of boxes, suites and restaurants for private hospitality; **MARQUEE:** Contact for details; **FUNCTION/CONFERENCE FACILITIES:** Contact for details; **CATERING:** Contact for details; **DISCOUNTS & PACKAGES:** For groups of 12 or more there are discounts on Grandstand tickets, you can receive a discount of between £2 and £4 per person depending on meeting, as long as your booking is received 7 clear days in advance; **RACE SPONSORSHIP:** Contact for details

EXETER
Tel: (01392) 832599 Fax: (01392) 833454
CONTACT: Mrs Charlotte Faulkner, Club Secretary

BOXES/HOSPITALITY: Contact for details; **FUNCTION/ CONFERENCE FACILITIES:** Contact Mrs Faulkner for details (01392) 832599; **CATERING:** Catering Division (01392) 832599; **DISCOUNTS & PACKAGES:** Contact Mrs Faulkner for details; **RACE SPONSORSHIP:** Contact GK Billson, General Manager

FAKENHAM
Tel: (01328) 862388 Fax: (01328) 855908
CONTACT: David Hunter, Racecourse Manager

BOXES: None available; **MARQUEE:** Various sizes by arrangement with caterers; **FUNCTION/CONFERENCE FACILITIES:** One suite to accommodate up to 120 guests; **CATERING:** Event Caterers (01603) 219991; **DISCOUNTS & PACKAGES:** 10% discount for groups of 10-19; 20% for 20-29; 30% for 30-39; **RACE SPONSORSHIP:** Terms negotiable to suit individual needs

FOLKESTONE
Tel: (01342) 834800 Fax: (01342) 835874
CONTACT: Claudia Fisher, Sales & Marketing Director

BOXES/MARQUEE: Corporate hospitality boxes from £35 + VAT per head; new restaurant overlooking course; **FUNCTION/CONFERENCE FACILITIES:** All facilities available for use on non-racedays; **CATERING:** Letheby & Christopher (01273) 814566; **DISCOUNTS & PACKAGES:** Contact for details; **RACE SPONSORSHIP:** From £500

FONTWELL PARK
Tel: (01243) 543335
CONTACT: Geoff Stickels, Clerk of the Course

BOXES/MARQUEE: Contact the racecourse for details; **FUNCTION/CONFERENCE FACILITIES:** All facilities available for use on non-racedays; **CATERING:** Letheby & Christopher (01273) 814566; **DISCOUNTS & PACKAGES:** Contact the racecourse for details; **RACE SPONSORSHIP:** From £500

GOODWOOD
Tel: (01243) 755022 Fax: (01243) 755025
CONTACT: Emma Everest, Hospitality Sales Manager

BOXES/HOSPITALITY: 65 available, increasing to 85 for Festival; **MARQUEE:** By arrangement; **FUNCTION/CONFERENCE FACILITIES:** Available for conferences, dinner dances and weddings (licensed for civil ceremonies); **CATERING:** Payne & Gunter Tel: (01243) 775350; **DISCOUNTS & PACKAGES:** Packages all-inclusive with flexible catering arrangements; discounts for parties of 20 plus and 40 plus; **RACE SPONSORSHIP:** Contact the racecourse for details

HAMILTON PARK
Tel: (01698) 283806 Fax: (01698) 286621
CONTACT: Hazel Dudgeon, Chief Executive

BOXES/HOSPITALITY: Sizes range from parties of 12-100 guests; **MARQUEE:** Central location on winning post providing garden party atmosphere between races; **FUNCTION/CONFERENCE FACILITIES:** Fully sound-proofed with break-out rooms; facilities for private parties, weddings, and exhibitions; **CATERING:** Peppermill Catering (01698) 429310; **DISCOUNTS & PACKAGES:** Advance purchase discounts depending on size of group; flexible approach to tailored packages for specific needs; call for further details; **RACE SPONSORSHIP:** Various options available; discounts available when combined with corporate hospitality

HAYDOCK PARK
Tel: (01942) 725963 Fax: (01942) 270879
Web site: http://www.demm.co.uk/racenews/haydock
CONTACT: Richard Thomas, Managing Director

BOXES/HOSPITALITY: The Tommy Whittle Stand offers boxes with a view over the racecourse for up to 20 guests; boxes for up to 40 guests are also available; the Park Suite can cater for groups of between 50 and 200; the Park Suite restaurant has tables for 2-24; the Lancaster Suite restaurant in the County Enclosure has tables for 2-24; **MARQUEE:** the Pagoda Pavilion offers marquees in the Parade Ring or in the centre of the course which are available during summer meetings; **CONFERENCE FACILITIES:** Non-race day facilities can cater for any type of meeting or conference from groups of between 10 and 5000 people; the same facilities can also be used for weddings, private parties, etc. exhibition facilities are available in the Carling or Caffrey rooms in the Makerfield Stand; 10 acres of hard standing; daily delegate packages available from £23.50 + VAT per person; **CATERING:** Letheby & Christopher (01273) 814566; **DISCOUNTS & PACKAGES:** Badge discounts for pre-booked parties of 25 or more in Tattersalls & Newton enclosures; all-inclusive hospitality packages from £48-93.50 per person; **RACE SPONSORSHIP:** Flat & National Hunt regular or televised races available—contact the racecourse for details

HEREFORD
Tel: (01981) 250436 Fax: (01981) 250192
CONTACT: Miss A J Trigg

BOXES/HOSPITALITY: Five available on a daily basis; **MARQUEE:** Space available in Tattersalls and Club enclosures; **FUNCTION/CONFERENCE FACILITIES:** Club enclosure, bars and restaurant complex available for conferences, meetings, weddings, etc., contact caterers for details; disabled access; **CATERING:** Hughes of Welshpool (01938) 553366; **DISCOUNTS & PACKAGES:** Contact the racecourse for brochure; **RACE SPONSORSHIP:** Variety of packages available, contact for details

HEXHAM
Tel: (01434) 606881 Fax: (01434) 605814
CONTACT: Charles Enderby, Clerk of the Course or
Mrs. Linda Clements on (01434) 609643

BOXES/HOSPITALITY: 3 available in new Ramshaw Stand with superb views; **MARQUEE:** Available for large parties; **FUNCTION/CONFERENCE FACILITIES:** Henderson Room function suite available on non-racedays for seminars, conferences, weddings, parties, etc.; new Ramshaw Members stand opened in 1998 with large function suite; **CATERING:** Romfords (01434) 688864; **DISCOUNTS & PACKAGES:** 20% discount for large parties; **RACE SPONSORSHIP:** The course has a flexible approach to sponsorship and tries to meet the sponsor's needs.

HUNTINGDON
Tel: (01480) 454610 or 453373 Fax: (01480) 455275
CONTACT: Margaret Hillison (raceday events)
Julian Martin (non raceday)

BOXES/HOSPITALITY: 6 boxes overlooking the course each accommodate 24 guests; new trackside chalets host up to 75; prices from £500; special rates for owners subject to availability; **FUNCTION/CONFERENCE FACILITIES:** All facilities available for conferences, seminars on non-racedays; daily delegate rates on request; **CATERING:** Letheby & Christopher (01638) 662750; **DISCOUNTS & PACKAGES:** 20% discount for groups of 15 plus; all inclusive packages from £48 per person; **RACE SPONSORSHIP:** Contact the racecourse for details

HUNTINGDON

If you are looking for the perfect opportunity to entertain in style and promote your company, then Huntingdon racecourse provides the ultimate racing experience. Ideally located near the A14 and A1, only 3/4 of an hour from London, Huntingdon racecourse can provide great National Hunt racing, a unique conference and corporate hospitality venue as well as an ideal sponsorship opportunity.

Opened for the meeting on August 30th, 1999, the recently refurbished Members Grandstand has created a new 170 seat restaurant which will be available for both raceday and non-raceday activities as well as a refurbished first floor and ground floor bar. Also available are 6 corporate boxes and 6 trackside chalets. All these facilities have a view of the racecourse. If you or your organisation would like to reserve the facilities that we have available here at the racecourse for functions such as meetings, private parties, seminars and wedding receptions, then please contact the racecourse office (01480) 453373.

KELSO
Tel: (01668) 281611 Fax: (01668) 281113
CONTACT: Richard Landale, Manager

BOXES/HOSPITALITY: 14 hosting from 10-70 guests each, most for groups of 25-35; from £100-£450; **MARQUEE:** For groups from 50-100, but can accommodate up to 900; contact for quotes; **FUNCTION/CONFERENCE FACILITIES:** All suites and marquee facilities available on non-racedays with catering facilities by arrangement; disabled access; **CATERING:** Millhouse Marketing (01890) 750227; Peter Allan (01668) 281184; **DISCOUNTS & PACKAGES:** £2 discount per ticket to parties booking and paying in advance; **RACE SPONSORSHIP:** From £750

KEMPTON PARK
Tel: (01372) 463072
CONTACT: Central Racing Department

CORPORATE HOSPITALITY: Contact Hector Nunns on the above phone number; **CATERING:** Ring & Brymer (01932) 780124; **RACE SPONSORSHIP:** Contact Tim Darby

LEICESTER
Tel: (0116) 271 6515 or (01604) 30757 Fax: (01604) 30758
Contact: Maria Szebor

BOXES/HOSPITALITY: Hospitality complex overlooking the course offers boxes to accommodate 12-20 guests, or double boxes for 30-40, each with television and Tote facilities; **MARQUEE:** Available by arrangement; **FUNCTION/CONFERENCE FACILITIES:** Barleythorpe Room holds 50 guests for buffet, 30 for full dining; Fernie Room for 30/buffet, 20 full dining; **CATERING:** Drewetts Countrywide Caterers (01788) 544171; **DISCOUNTS & PACKAGES:** Contact the racecourse for details; **RACE SPONSORSHIP:** Contact the racecourse for details

LINGFIELD PARK
Tel: (01342) 834800 Fax: (01342) 832833
CONTACT: Claudia Fisher, Marketing Director

BOXES/HOSPITALITY/MARQUEE: Contact the racecourse for details; **FUNCTION/CONFERENCE FACILITIES:** All facilities available on non-racedays; **CATERING:** In-house catering; **DISCOUNTS & PACKAGES:** Contact the racecourse for details; **RACE SPONSORSHIP:** From £500 turf or all-weather course

LUDLOW
Tel: (01981) 250052,
Tel racedays: (01584) 856221
Fax: (01981) 250192
Fax racedays: (01584) 856217
CONTACT: Bob Davies, Clerk, Secretary & Manager

BOXES/HOSPITALITY: Private rooms to accommodate up to 30 guests with television and private bar facilities; **MARQUEE:** Excellent sites to accommodate any size, well situated for viewing; **FUNCTION/CONFERENCE FACILITIES:** Clive Pavilion is largest in the area, hosting up to 500 for meals; caters for trade and antique fairs, exhibitions; contact caterers for details; disabled access; **CATERING:** Hughes of Welshpool (01938) 553366; **DISCOUNTS & PACKAGES:** Discounts for groups of 12 plus; special all-inclusive raceday packages for £40 per person including Members badge, luncheon in room or marquee; **RACE SPONSORSHIP:** Available in a range of flexible packages, contact for details

MARKET RASEN
Tel: (01673) 843434 Fax: (01673) 844532
CONTACT: Miss Pip Adams Racecourse Manager

BOXES/HOSPITALITY: Daily & Annual available; **MARQUEE:** By arrangement; **FUNCTION/CONFERENCE FACILITIES:** Brocklesby Suite for 100-300 guests; County Room for 10-100 guests; individual consultancy rooms for 2-20 guests; **CATERING:** Craven Gilpin & Son (0113) 287 6387; **DISCOUNTS & PACKAGES:** Groups 15 or more offered discounts on badges; **RACE SPONSORSHIP:** Contact the course for details

MUSSELBURGH
Tel: 0131 665 2859 Fax: (0131) 653 2083
CONTACT: Bill Farnsworth, General Manager/Clerk

BOXES/HOSPITALITY: Individual boxes on the upper floor fro groups of up to 24, with a larger room on ground floor to accommodate up to 150. All facilities overlook the winning post and views of the finishing straight; **MARQUEE:** Various sites and facilities available, contact for details; **FUNCTION/CONFERENCE FACILITIES:** Facilities available all year for non race day activities with catering if required; **CATERING:** Contact Bill Farnsworth; **DISCOUNTS & PACKAGES:** Packages, 20% in Grandstand and 10% Club Stand for groups of 10 or more, booked and paid for in advance. Racegoers package available contact for details; **RACE SPONSORSHIP:** Contact for details

NEWBURY
Tel: (01635) 40015 Fax: (01635) 528354
CONTACT: Anne Halteh, Corporate Sales Manager

BOXES/HOSPITALITY: Berkshire Stand boxes accommodate 20 guests each, may be combined for larger parties of 80-90; Paddock Pavilions take up to 1000 with full catering, television, Tote available; **MARQUEE:** By arrangement; **FUNCTION/ CONFERENCE FACILITIES:** Available on non-racedays, arrangements made through the caterers; **CATERING:** Ring & Brymer (01635) 521081; **DISCOUNTS & PACKAGES:** 20% discount for groups of 12 or more in Tattersalls and Silver Ring if booked in advance; 50% discount in Members for ages 18-21; packages available, contact for detailed brochure; **RACE SPONSORSHIP:** Available for both televised and non-televised races

NEWCASTLE
Tel: 0191 236 2020 Fax: 0191 236 7761
CONTACT: Malcolm Winters, General Manager
BOXES/HOSPITALITY: Range of boxes/marquees to suit various sized groups; all-inclusive packages available from £50-70, £65-85 for Northumberland Plate meeting in June; **MARQUEE:** Contact for details; **FUNCTION/CONFERENCE FACILITIES:** Range of suites available to accommodate 12-80 guests available on non-racedays for meetings, conferences, etc.; **CATERING:** Ramside Event Catering 0191 236 2020; **DISCOUNTS & PACKAGES:** Contact for details; **RACE SPONSORSHIP:** Packages available from £1000; Sky televised races for flat and NH season

NEWMARKET
Tel: (01638) 663482, Fax: (01638) 663044
Rowley Mile (01638) 662762
July Course (01638) 662752
CONTACT: Corporate Hospitality & Events Department

BOXES/HOSPITALITY: Contact for details; **MARQUEE:** Full range available from £865-£2150; **FUNCTION/CONFERENCE FACILITIES:** Range of facilities available non-racedays for meetings, conferences, seminars, exhibitions, dinner dances and weddings; accommodation for 12-500 guests; **CATERING:** Letheby & Christopher (01242) 523203; **DISCOUNTS & PACKAGES:** Individual inclusive packages from £65-£225 per person; 20% discount for groups if booked 14 days in advance; **RACE SPONSORSHIP:** Contact the racecourse for details

NEWTON ABBOT
Tel: (01626) 353235 Fax: (01626) 336972
CONTACT: Pat Masterson, Manager

BOXES/HOSPITALITY: 11 private boxes available for hire some of which are available for daily hire. The Teign Suite is also available and can accommodate up to 250 guests; **MARQUEE:** Can be arranged for the Tattersalls; **FUNCTION/CONFERENCE FACILITIES:** Contact for details; **CATERING:** Partyfare Ltd (01626) 331285 or (01404) 42502; **DISCOUNTS & PACKAGES:** Contact for details; **RACE SPONSORSHIP:** Contact for details

NOTTINGHAM
Tel: (0115) 958 0620 Fax: (0115) 958 4515
CONTACT: Sally Westcott, Racecourse Manager

BOXES/HOSPITALITY: Annual lease package £5000 + VAT (24 meetings); part-time lease package £1320 (6 meetings); daily box lets for 10-70 guests from £275-600 + VAT; **MARQUEE:** Range of sites and facilities available, contact for details; **FUNCTION/CONFERENCE FACILITIES:** Contact Anne Whelbourne or Sally Westcott; **DISCOUNTS & PACKAGES:** Discounts for groups of 10 or more in Members and Tattersalls/Grandstand; packages available from £53 + VAT; **RACE SPONSORSHIP:** All-inclusive VIP sponsorship packages for 10 people from £1400 + VAT

PERTH
Tel: (01738) 551597 Fax: (01738) 553021
CONTACT: Sam Morshead, General Manager

BOXES/HOSPITALITY: 11 boxes for private parties of 14-20 guests, 1 box for 60 guests; **MARQUEE:** Facilities are always available to cater for larger parties, contact the racecourse for further details; **FUNCTION/CONFERENCE FACILITIES:** All available on non race days for seminars, exhibitions, dinner dances and weddings. You name it, they can do it; **CATERING:** Ring & Brymer 0131 331 2120; **DISCOUNTS & PACKAGES:** Groups of 15 or more are offered discounts on badges; **RACE SPONSORSHIP:** The best oppor tunities, over 60 indvidual companies support Perth racecourse

PLUMPTON
Tel: (01273) 890383 Fax: (01273) 891557
CONTACT: Lorna Bromley-Martin, Manager

BOXES/HOSPITALITY/MARQUEE: Private boxes for 10-40 guests from £100; additional rooms accommodating up to 70 guests; marquees available for larger parties; **FUNCTION/CONFERENCE FACILITIES:** All facilities available for use on non-racedays; **CATERING:** contact Appetance (01273) 401777; **DISCOUNTS & PACKAGES:** 20% for 20 or more; **RACE SPONSORSHIP:** From £600

PONTEFRACT
Tel: (01977) 703224 or
(01977) 702210 racedays only
CONTACT: Norman Gundill, Clerk, Manager & Secretary

BOXES/HOSPITALITY: 8 Dalby Stand private boxes offer views of the finishing straight and Parade Ring to accommodate 20-24 people each or larger groups up to 80 when joined; private room with box for 25-30; entertainment suite private building for groups of 30-150; **MARQUEE:** Chalet marquee units overlooking the Parade Ring for 30-50 guests; **FUNCTION/ CONFERENCE FACILITIES:** Facilities available on non-racedays for conferences, seminars, exhibitions, dinners, dances, weddings, etc.; **CATERING:** Craven Gilpin (0113) 287 6387; **DISCOUNTS & PACKAGES:** Varying discounts for groups from 10-200 plus in all enclosures; **RACE SPONSORSHIP:** Contact for details

REDCAR
Tel: (01642) 484068 Fax: (01642) 488272
CONTACT: J E Gundill, General Manager

SUITES/HOSPITALITY: Sizes vary for parties of 35-140; **MARQUEE:** Various sizes available; **FUNCTION/CONFERENCE**

FACILITIES: 3 suites to accommodate 15-110 guests; **CATERING:** Blue Ribbon Cuisine (01642) 478024; **DISCOUNTS & PACKAGES:** Contact for details; **RACE SPONSORSHIP:** Contact for details

RIPON
Tel: (01765) 602156 Fax: (01765) 690018
CONTACT: J M Hutchinson, Clerk of the Course

BOXES/HOSPITALITY: 8 Rowels boxes with viewing balcony for groups of 25-100 from £11 per person; private chalet next to Parade Ring for up to 35 guests, £140; Claro Room near Bandstand for up to 50 guests, £200, for all facilities add Club Enclosure admission at £10.50 + VAT pp; **MARQUEE:** Sites near to Parade Ring to suit party from £10.75 + VAT per person; contact caterers for details; **FUNCTION/CONFERENCE FACILITIES:** Range of facilities for all types of uses on non-racedays. Contact Managing Director for details; **CATERING:** Craven Gilpin (0113) 287 6387; **DISCOUNTS & PACKAGES:** Group discounts; packages to suit needs, contact for details; **RACE SPONSORSHIP:** Races available from £500-5000

SALISBURY
Tel: (01722) 326461 or 327327
CONTACT: Ann Holland, Racecourse Secretary

BOXES/HOSPITALITY: Private hospitality boxes available for groups of 12 to 40 guests; daily hire from £600; **MARQUEE:** (Or Chalet) located adjacent to the winning post and parade ring for up to 300 guests; **FUNCTION/CONFERENCE FACILITIES:** Contact for details; **CATERING/DISCOUNTS & PACKAGES:** Contact for details; **RACE SPONSORSHIP:** From £750 per race, contact the racecourse for further details

SANDOWN
Tel: (01372) 463072 Fax: (01372) 465205
Bookings Hotline: (01372) 470047
CONTACT: Hector Nunn or Alison Rowan

BOXES/HOSPITALITY: 36 boxes let on an annual basis, for sub letting availability contact the racecourse; **MARQUEE:** Sites can be organised, contact for details; **FUNCTION/CONFERENCE FACILITIES:** Numerous private rooms are available to rent; **CATERING:** Ring & Brymer (01372) 465292; **DISCOUNTS & PACKAGES/RACE SPONSORSHIP:** Contact for details

SEDGEFIELD
Tel: (01740) 621925 Fax: (01740) 620663
CONTACT: Alan Brown, Manager and Clare Robinson, Secretary
BOXES/HOSPITALITY: 11 boxes available per meeting; recommend booking at least two months in advance to reserve; **MARQUEE:** Sites available to accommodate groups of 50-300; **FUNCTION/CONFERENCE FACILITIES:** Two function suites available; **CATERING:** Ramside 0191 236 4148—variety of menus; **DISCOUNTS & PACKAGES:** Rates available on application; **RACE SPONSORSHIP:** From £750 per race

SOUTHWELL
Tel: (01636) 814481 Fax: (01636) 812271
CONTACT: Pat Mitchell, Commercial Manager

BOXES/HOSPITALITY: Corporate hospitality boxes for up to 24 guests; £42.50 + VAT per person; **MARQUEE:** Available May-September for parties 40-200 from £30 + VAT per person; **FUNCTION/CONFERENCE FACILITIES:** Available to suit all requirements, including conferences, exhibitions, trade shows, wedding receptions, fairs, music concerts, etc; also operates nearby hotel; disabled access; **CATERING:** Available for all functions; **DISCOUNTS & PACKAGES:** By arrangement, contact for details; **RACE SPONSORSHIP:** From £250 per race

STRATFORD
Tel: (01789) 267949 or 269411 Fax: (01789) 415850
CONTACT: Alison Gale, Manager and Secretary

BOXES/HOSPITALITY: Contact the racecourse for details; **FUNCTION/CONFERENCE FACILITIES:** Function rooms available non-racedays for meetings, exhibitions, dinner parties, weddings, etc.; **CATERING:** Contact for details; **DISCOUNTS & PACKAGES:** Prices from £55.00 + VAT; **RACE SPONSORSHIP:** Contact for details

TAUNTON
Tel: (01823) 337172 Fax: (01823) 325881
CONTACT: John Hills, Manager and Secretary

BOXES/HOSPITALITY: Private and Corporate Boxes and Suites available for groups from 12-80. Book early; **MARQUEE:** By arrangement; **FUNCTION/CONFERENCE FACILITIES:** Available to suit all requirements including exhibitions, wedding receptions (civil wedding licence), and private dinner parties; **CATERING:** In house: The Orchard Restaurant, Manager - Troy Hill (01823) 325035; **DISCOUNTS & PACKAGES:** Discounts for parties of 20 or more; contact for further details; **RACE SPONSORSHIP:** Races available from £750

THIRSK
Tel: (01845) 522276 Fax: (01845) 525353
CONTACT: Christopher Tetley, Clerk of the Course
BOXES/HOSPITALITY: For 10-20 guests overlooking the winning post; **MARQUEE:** Sites on lawns; **FUNCTION/CONFERENCE FACILITIES:** Facilities available non-racedays, contact for details; **CATERING:** Craven Gilpin (0113) 287 6387; **DISCOUNTS & PACKAGES:** For groups of 20 plus; **RACE SPONSORSHIP:** Contact for details

TOWCESTER
Tel: (01327) 353414 Fax: (01327) 358534
CONTACT: Lords Hesketh, Chief Executive

BOXES/HOSPITALITY: Private boxes in the new Grace Stand available on a three year lease; additional boxes available on a daily basis; private rooms & suites for 12-300 guests ; **MARQUEE:** Sites available on the Parade Ring lawn; **FUNCTION/ CONFERENCE FACILITIES:** Newly completed Grace Stand available for business meetings, corporate entertainment or large special events **CATERING:** Letheby & Christopher; **DISCOUNTS & PACKAGES:** Group discounts available in all enclosures; combined corporate hospitality & sponsorship packages available; **RACE SPONSORSHIP:** Named races available from £1000 + VAT

Set in beautiful parkland, Towcester is one of the most scenic racecourses in Britain and offers the ideal venue for relaxed corporate entertaining or virtually any occasion.

The recently completed Grace Stand is under starters orders to bring the Heart of England's businesses galloping into the Millennium. The elegant building, with its Chinese lanterns and panoramic views offers a unique setting, unique business opportunities and a unique package of corporate entertainment and special events.

There are facilities for day conferences, training seminars, product launches and promotions, incentive rewards, business meetings, corporate entertaining, activity days for companies, gala dinners and outdoor events big and small.

The setting is amongst the best you will find, in the beautiful parkland estate of Easton Neston, within easy access from the A5, just a mile to the south east of Towcester and on the M1 close to Northampton and Milton Keynes.

UTTOXETER
Tel: (01889) 562561 Fax:(01889) 882786
CONTACT: Louise Aspinall, Commercial Executive

BOXES/HOSPITALITY: 65 available on a daily and annual lease; Paddock or Course view; **MARQUEE:** Luxury marquees available for 50-1000 guests; **FUNCTION/CONFERENCE FACILITIES:** All kinds of functions catered for from product launches, conferences and seminars to training courses, theme nights and weddings; suites available to accommodate from 15-500 guests; **CATERING:** Available for up to 1000 guests; **DISCOUNTS & PACKAGES:** Discounts for groups; packages from £60 per person + VAT; **RACE SPONSORSHIP:** From £1000 + VAT; Channel 4 and BBC televised meetings

WARWICK
Tel: (01926) 491553 Fax: (01926) 403223
CONTACT: Lisa Rowe, Racecourse Manager

BOXES/HOSPITALITY: Private boxes overlooking Parade Ring and Course available from £110; suites for parties of 10-80; **MARQUEE:** Contact the racecourse for details; **FUNCTION/CONFERENCE FACILITIES:** Full range of function suites available, contact the racecourse for details; **CATERING:** Amadeus 0121 767 2543; **DISCOUNTS & PACKAGES:** Group discounts for parties from 15-80 plus; **RACE SPONSORSHIP:** Packages from £1800; Channel 4 televised meetings

WETHERBY
Tel: (01937) 582035 Fax: (01937) 580565
CONTACT: Christopher Tetley, Manager/Clerk of the Course

BOXES/HOSPITALITY: 4 Chalets at £100 + VAT each per day plus bar/catering; **MARQUEE:** Contact for details; **FUNCTION/CONFERENCE FACILITIES:** Contact Alison Dalby, Secretary for details; **CATERING:** Contact for details; **DISCOUNTS & PACKAGES:** Contact for details; **RACE SPONSORSHIP:** Contact for details

WINCANTON
Tel: (01963) 32344 Fax: (01963) 34668
CONTACT: Madeleine Bridger

BOXES/HOSPITALITY: Boxes with spectacular views of the course available; boxes and suites for 12-96 guests; **MARQUEE:** Contact the racecourse for availability; **FUNCTION/CONFERENCE FACILITIES:** Contact the racecourse for availability; **CATERING:** Contact the racecourse for availability; **DISCOUNTS & PACKAGES:** Prepaid Club & Tattersalls enclosure discounts—15% for groups of 10-19, 20% for 20 or more; **RACE SPONSORSHIP:** From £2,000. Contact for further details.

WINDSOR
Tel: (01753) 865234 or 864726 Fax: (01753) 830156
CONTACT: Mrs S A Dingle, Racecourse Manager

BOXES/HOSPITALITY: Overlooking course with private balcony; **MARQUEE:** On paddock lawn; **FUNCTION/ CONFERENCE FACILITIES:** Facilities for conferences, training, fun-days, exhibitions; **CATERING:** Letheby & Christopher (01753) 832552; Castle Restaurant overlooks the course—dining and racing package available from £48 per person; luxury hampers for al fresco dining; **DISCOUNTS & PACKAGES:** 25% discount for groups of 20 or more in Tattersalls & Silver Ring; **RACE SPONSORSHIP:** From £2500, includes private suite, badges, etc.

WOLVERHAMPTON (DUNSTALL PARK)
Tel: (01902) 421421 Fax: (01902) 716626
CONTACT: Michael Prosser, Clerk of the Course

BOXES/HOSPITALITY: 8 tastefully decorated with private balcony, television, access to betting facilities; **FUNCTION/ CONFERENCE FACILITIES:** wide range of facilities for groups up to 700 inside; 22 acres external grounds; hotel adjacent to course with full facilities; disabled access; use on non-racedays for weddings, meetings, conferences, exhibitions, trade shows, circuses and other entertainment; **CATERING:** 2 companies offering quality cuisine at competitive prices; **DISCOUNTS & PACKAGES:** 40 plus entry £7 per person plus free tickets; **RACE SPONSORSHIP:** Contact Lesley Gross at the racecourse

WORCESTER
Tel: (01905) 25364 or 21338 Fax: (01905) 617563
CONTACT: Christine Draper

BOXES/HOSPITALITY: 3 Paddock-side boxes available each to accommodate 12 guests; can be opened together to accommodate 36; **MARQUEE:** Available on various sites; **FUNCTION/ CONFERENCE FACILITIES:** Severn Suite on top floor of grandstand holds 120 for dinner with excellent viewing of racecourse; **CATERING:** Plyvine Ltd (01905) 25970; **DISCOUNTS &**

PACKAGES: 10% discount with advance booking; 20% discount for parties of 12 or more; box for 12, including badges, catering and sponsored race from £1050 + VAT; **RACE SPONSORSHIP:** From £500 - £12,000

YARMOUTH
Tel: (01493) 842527 Fax: (01493) 843254
CONTACT: David Thompson, Manager

BOXES/HOSPITALITY: Available for 20-200 guests; Marquee: Arranged to suit party; **FUNCTION/CONFERENCE FACILITIES:** See main entry; fêtes, car boot sales, wedding parties, etc. by arrangement; **CATERING:** South Norfolk Caterers (01603) 219991; **DISCOUNTS & PACKAGES:** 15% discount for 20 plus with advance booking; **RACE SPONSORSHIP:** £500-£1000 plus VAT depending on race dates

YORK
Tel: (01904) 620911 Fax: (01904) 611071
CONTACT: Philip Smedley

BOXES/HOSPITALITY: 11 Knavesmire boxes and several older boxes to accommodate 10-70 guests available for day rental; Dante Suite and private stand for up to 200 guests; annual Melrose boxes subject to availability—contact for details; **MARQUEE:** Tented village pavilions available May-September to host up to 40 guests each; larger marquee for August-October can also be arranged; **FUNCTION/CONFERENCE FACILITIES:** Excellent facilities available all year on non-race days to accommodate up to 1000 people for conferences and exhibitions; flexible arrangements; racecourse, exhibition, conference & banqueting centre to provide the venue for the World of Racing Exhibition & Show, May 29-31 1998; **CATERING:** Full catering facilities by Craven Gilpin (01904) 638971; **DISCOUNTS & PACKAGES:** Discounts for parties of 12 or more in Tattersalls, Grandstand and Silver Ring for all meetings except August Ebor meeting; Hospitality Club and Ebor Restaurant all-inclusive dining packages; **RACE SPONSORSHIP:** Contact David Grouse, over 80% of races sponsored but some opportunities available: non-televised races from £3500 + VAT to £70,000 + VAT for televised Group 1 race

Artist: **Terence Gilbert** *BOTTOMS UP Courtesy of:* **The Artist**

*A*s we reach the millennium, never before has it been easier to hop on a jet and experience the thrills and colour of racing in another country. The babble of the crowd and the punting currency may seem foreign at first, but once your horse comes down the stretch to win in a photo finish, you will feel just as much at home at Sha Tin as Sandown.

For this edition of Travelling the Turf we've added some Racing Jaunts for your punting pleasure. After all, there's no reason why you shouldn't be able to enjoy a day at the races, even if your holiday takes you to the tropical beaches of the Caribbean or skiing in the Swiss Alps.

Now, with the launch of the Emirates World Series, top horses, jockeys, trainers and owners are taking to the skies in search of one of the turf's new holy grails. A new, hopefully true, world champion horse will be crowned after a series of races as diverse as the Dubai World Cup, the King George and Queen Elizabeth Diamond Stakes, the Breeders Cup and the Japan Cup, and several more in between.

Travelling the Turf has always encouraged racegoers to go in search of green pastures beyond their own horizon and find a comfortable bed for the night after sampling some of the best of local fare. Now you can do it on the other side of the world! Wherever you might go, we hope our guide to world racing gives you the winning edge.

Artist: **Hubert De Watrigant** **THE SPIRIT OF RACING** *Courtesy of:* **Osborne Studio Gallery**

Wellington Cup	January	**Trentham, New Zealand**
Barbados Gold Cup	March	**Garrison Savannah, Barbados**
Dubai World Cup	Saturday March	**Nad Al Sheba, Dubai**
Australian Derby	April	**Randwick, Australia**
Derby Italiano	May	**Rome, Italy**
Poule D'Essai des Poulains	May	**Longchamp, France**
Poule D'Essai des Pouliches	May	**Longchamp, France**
Kentucky Derby	May	**Churchill Downs, USA**
Preakness Stakes	May	**Pimlico, USA**
Belmont Stakes	June	**Belmont Park, USA**
Prix du Jockey Club	June	**Chantilly, France**
Prix de Diane	June	**Chantilly, France**
Japanese Derby	June	**Tokyo, Japan**
Deutsches Derby	July	**Hamburg, Germany**
Prix du Jacques Le Marois	August	**Deauville, France**
Prix Morny	August	**Deauville, France**
Travers Stakes	August	**Deauville, France**
Prix du Moulin	September	**Longchamp, Paris**
Prix de La Salamandre	September	**Longchamp, Paris**
Prix Vermaille	September	**Longchamp, Paris**
Grosser PreisVon Baden	September	**Baden Baden, Germany**
Prix du Cadran	October	**Longchamp, Paris**
Prix de L'Arc de Triomphe	October	**Longchamp, Paris**
Velka Pardubicka	October	**Pardubice, Czech Republic**
Canadian International	October	**Woodbine, Toronto**
Cox Plate	October	**Flemington, Melbourne**
Melbourne Cup	November	**Flemington, Melbourne**
Japan Cup	November	**Tokyo Racecourse**
Breeders Cup	November	**Gulfstream Park, Florida, USA**
Hong Kong International Races	December	**Sha Tin, Hong Kong**
New Zealand Derby	December	**Ellerslie, New Zealand**

Artist: **Paul Hart DANCING BRAVE** *Courtesy of:* **The Artist**

While most of our Racing Around the World concerns seeing the great events in the international racing calendar, there are other times and places during the year when you might want to get away for a quick sporting fix in a somewhat unusual locale. No one would pretend that places such as Barbados, the Czech Republic or Switzerland are worth visiting solely for the quality of horses, jockeys or trainers, but as racing occasions they are all first class places to visit at the right time of the year. True racing people have taken them to their heart and celebrate them in style.

BARBADOS GOLD CUP

While steeplechase fans will be in their element come January, many of the flat world's leading owners and trainers look to sunnier climes for a bit of rest and relaxation. Nowhere has been as popular with the sun worshippers than Barbados in recent years because that warm Barbadian welcome mixed with a few rum punches is the perfect antidote to the winter blues. The sun, sea and sand might be perfect, but the icing on this cake comes with a bit of racing thrown in as well. Given that the timing is right, you might even be able to take in a cricket test match.

Barbados is the place where Sir Michael Stoute got his start in the training business and the local race track also has a familiar ring about it too - Garrison Savannah - the same name of the horse that won the Cheltenham Gold Cup for Jenny Pitman in 1991! You'll find the course just a couple of miles outside the capital of Bridgetown and

it has been the home of horse racing here since 1845 when British officers raced their horses on what was then the parade ground. Things are a bit more organised now with three racing seasons a year, from January to March, May to August, and October to December organised by the Barbados Turf Club, St Michael, Barbados, West Indies. Tel: (246) 426 3980, Fax: (246) 429 3591, e mail: barturf@sunbeach.net web site: barbadosturfclub.com. Mr Robert Bourque is the President and Debra P Hughes is Secretary.

The track is a six furlong, oval grass strip with races from five to 11 furlongs. The most important races in the calendar are the '5000' run in February, the Sandy Lane Gold Cup and the Banks Guineas in March, the United Barbados Derby in August and the Heineken Stakes on Boxing Day. Although this is the serious information for the dedicated fan, the emphasis at all meetings is on family entertainment and you can enjoy a picnic under the shade of the tall trees ringing the course and sample some Barbadian cuisine in the form of pudding and souse, rice and stew or fried fish and fish cakes. All of this can be washed down with a Planter's Punch, the main ingredient of which is the local rum.

The more serious punter can enjoy the view of racing from either the Grand Stand, Field Stand, Sir John Chandler Stand, or if you can wangle an invitation, one of the corporate boxes overlooking the paddock bend. Admission to the Grand Stand will set you back $10 BDS or about $5 US on normal race days, which rises to $20 BDS on Gold Cup day. The Club House charge is $25 BDS and $50 on Cup day.

As its economy depends more on importing tourists

Artist: **Hubert De Watrigant ROUGE TOQUE BLANCHE** *Courtesy of:* **Osborne Studio Gallery**

than exporting sugar and rum these days, as you would imagine there are a wide range of places to hitch your hammock on this tropical isle. Many are on the south and west coast, the 'Caribbean' side of the island where the white sand gives way to calm blue waters. Here you will find the Almond Beach Club & Spa at Vauxhall, St James (246 432 7840), a low key group of pastel buildings set amidst palms right on the beach. It has all the facilities and three pools, but families with children under 16 will have to look elsewhere. Any age, however, will be welcomed at its sister hotel the Almond Beach Village near Speightstown, St Peter (246 422 4900) which has equally fine accommodation. Club Rockley at Worthing (246 435 7880) is set in 70 acres of tropical gardens, has seven swimming pools and a nine hole golf course; a free shuttle bus will take you to the hotel's beach side bar and restaurant. If you don't mind a bit of self catering, you could try the Rainbow Reef at St Lawrence Gap (246 428 5110). It's apartments are right on the beach and there's also a pool and nine hole golf course. One of Barbados' landmark hotels is the famous Sam Lord's Castle (246 423 7350) at St Philip on the south-east coast which has a large complex of rooms, pools and tennis courts around the castle. A few other choices which are definitely in the luxury category, are that watering hole of the rich and famous, the Sandy Lane Hotel, as well as the Colony Club, Royal Pavilion and Treasure Beach, all of which are in St James on Barbados' 'platinum' east coast.

VELKA PARDUBICKA (Czech Republic)

It's known as the "European Grand National" and the sight of a large field of jumpers negotiating the 31 obstacles which include stone walls, banks, hedges and a monster known as the Taxis fence, that are strung out along the twists and turns of this four and a quarter mile race is a truly thrilling experience. Thanks to international television coverage and the sporting participation of a regular flow of horses, trainers and jockeys from Britain, Ireland and France during the past few years, the event has grown in stature to a 'must do' for the ardent jump racing enthusiast.

You can swill as much of the local Pilsner brew as you wish in the pleasant confines of the quaint old town of Pardubice itself before taking in the Czech St Leger on the Saturday and if your stamina matches that of the horses, return the next day for the Velka Pardubicka itself. The best connections to get there are probably through the delightful city of Prague, just an hour to the west.

Held each October, 1999 marked the 125th running of the Velka Pardubicka and interestingly it was a British professional jockey, L Sayers who won the very first race in 1874 on Fantome. Another well-known rider in his day who rode in the Velka was Count Karel Kinsky; he is the only Czech to have also won the Grand National at Aintree in 1883. That should be good enough to win any pub quiz!

The course operates its own betting system, like the Tote in Britain or the Pari Mutual in France or North America, here known as the SCARS Tip. Better do your homework before you go, because there are some pretty complicated each way bets on offer, as well as one where you can bet that the favourite will be beaten! The minimum stake is 50 crowns, or about £1, but the maximum pay out on any single bet is 10,000 crowns or £200, so don't dream in lottery figures about your winnings. Admission to the course ranges from £4 in

one of the open air stands, to £60 in private boxes with catering. Racing here also takes place in May, which features a British Day at the end of the month, June, August and September.

The capital of the Czech Republic, Prague is a lively city to visit and one that has become extremely popular with visitors from the west since the Iron Curtain came crashing down a decade ago. Here you will find a wide range of hotels and restaurants from which to choose, as well as many pubs and bars where you can sample the famous Pils.

Closer to the racecourse itself, take a few hours and visit Pardubice Castle, a renaissance castle and Museum near the old Pernstyn square in the old part of Pardubice. Just a few miles outside the town is the Kuneticka Hora, a Gothic castle from the 15th century. A bit further away, about 12 miles west of Pardubice, real horse people will find Kladruby nad Labem - the original six hundred year-old stables established in 1579 for breeding the famous Kladrubian white horses; another must see is Slatinany Castle with its Museum of the Horse. It's located in a large old park with walks through the forest about 10 miles south from Pardubice

Some of the hotels recommended by locals in Pardubice include: the 160 room Hotel Labe, which has its own large restaurant and casino; the smaller Clubhotel Harmony, Belehradska, 00420- 40- 6435020; the Hotel Zlata Tika on Trossova, 00420-40-6613478; the 17 room S.M.G. Sporthotel, Sukovo 00420-40-512082 which has a sauna and spa facilities; Hotel u Andela Zamecka 00420-40-514028; the 50 room Hotel Bohemia Masarykovo , in Chrudim 00420-455- 620351; or the larger 200-room Hotel Cernigov Riegrovo, 00420-49-5814111, e-mail: cernigov@hk.anet.cz, http://www.cernigov.cz which has its own night club, restaurant and casino right on the premises. If you are getting a bit hungry after the races try U Nouzu, Hradite na Pmsku 22, restaurant, with its terrace and wine cellar, about 3 miles north of Pardubice towards Kuneticka Hora, 040 45005; or right in the old part of Pardubice near the castle on Zamecka 24 is Na Kovarne with its restaurant, pub and terrace, 040 514028.

ST MORITZ (Switzerland)

Swiss racing might sound like a contradiction in a land better known for skiing and fondue, but each year mother nature completely freezes over the lake at St Moritz and the good burghers of the town stage a racing spectacular on ice! The sight of horses and jockeys flying across the white packed snow against an Alpine backdrop is truly a unique experience, and the hospitality adds a new dimension to apres racing.

Of course you'll have to be here in January and February to take in the action and hope that a sudden thaw doesn't halt the proceedings! This is one of the few places in the world where you can go skiing in the morning and racing in the afternoon. Surprisingly, the quality of the racing is probably a far cry better than that on show at Lingfield at the same time of the year, and the horses adapt remarkably well to the conditions under foot. Several top jockeys from other countries are also usually on hand and the meetings have a winter carnival air about them. Some jump races over hurdles are also usually put on to keep fans of racing over the sticks happy.

The Swiss practically invented good hotel keeping so you won't be pressed to find some excellent accommodation. It's best to book early though, as St

Moritz is a traditional watering hole for the rich and famous at this time of the year and of course skiing is the name of the true winter game. Although it's usually not cheap, and nothing is in Switzerland, there is a good choice of hotels, apartments and guest houses in St Moritz itself. Some favourites include: Badrutts Palace Hotel, a luxurious resort with old world hospitality overlooking the lake, (41 81837 1000); also overlooking the lake and mountains is the recently renovated Carlton Hotel (41 81832 1141); the excellent Kulm Hotel (41 81832 1151) on Via Veglia which has welcomed guests since 1856 and also has a fine view of the lake; or the elegant five star Park Hotels Waldhaus (41 81928 4848) which features art nouveau fireplaces and is set in its own 60 acre private park.

If accommodation is booked up here, you could also try another ski resort, Davos which is not too far away, or the very toney Klosters. The nearest big city and major international airport is to be found in Zurich, which also offers a wide choice of accommodation and is quite interesting in its own right; here the family-run Baur au Lac Hotel (220 5020) on Talstrasse combines luxury with old-world elegance, while just outside the city the Dolder Grand Hotel (251 6321) on Kurhausstrasse is a fairy-tale castle set in the woods with pretty views over the Zurichsee. Right in the centre of the city you could also try the Savoy Baur En Ville (215 2525) on Am Paradeplatz, Zurich's oldest hotel, or the cosy elegance of the Widder (224 2526), a converted row of townhouses on Rennweg.

CAROLINA & COLONIAL CUP
(South Carolina)

When 50,000 jump racing fans assemble each spring at Springdale Race Course near Camden, South Carolina for the Carolina Cup, it's probably the world's biggest point to point. Timber fences, some five feet high, are the name of the game and it has become such an event that people come from hundreds, if not thousands, of miles to enjoy a massive tail-gate party while they witness the thrills and spills of some of the best steeplechasers in North America. Grab your picnic hamper, pack the beer in ice and you can be a good ol' boy or girl for the day.

You'll probably fly in to the South Carolina state capital of Columbia, which is just a half hour's drive from Camden on Interstate Highway 20, or you could take the more leisurely and historic US Route 1.

Springdale Race Course is part of a 600-acre training facility that was given by Marion duPont Scott to the State of South Carolina. The Carolina Cup is part of a six-race card and dates back to 1930; the formula of steeplechasing over a long galloping course with stiff timber fences has been brought to Britain in the last few years in the form of the Marlborough Cup, which, like its American counter-part, is beginning to attract huge crowds.

The Carolina Cup is held at the end of March, while in the autumn at the end of November, the Colonial Cup is also held on the same course. A $100,000 steeplechase, it has produced some good winners such as Lonesome Glory who went on to win at Cheltenham, and usually attracts some good horses from the UK. The whole day has a fairground atmosphere with

terrier trials, a market, classic cars, rides and special exhibitions. To find out more, contact their web site at www.carolina-cup.org. General admission for the Colonial Cup is $10-15, with general parking at $5 or $50 for preferred parking which includes two tickets. Reserved parking in the infield is $75, which also includes two tickets, or $125 for Front Row Paddock Side. $300 will get you a six-seater box in the Grandstand and covers all admission and parking, while $400 will get you the same deal with lunch included. While you're in the area you should also pay a visit to the Carolina Cup Racing Museum, which has interactive exhibits and memorabilia relating to the history of steeplechasing in North America.

Part of the Confederate old south, South Carolina has a lot going for it to entertain and amuse the visitor. If you want more information on where to see or what to do from your armchair, just log into the excellent web site at www.travelsc.com. Camden itself is in the state's 'Olde English District', which perhaps not surprisingly has counties such as Lancaster and York! Here you can find a room for the night at the Colony Inn on US 1 (803 432 5508), the Knights Inn on DeKalb St and US 1 (803 432 2453) or the Plantation Motel on Jefferson Davis Highway (803 432 2300). There are lots of other smaller guests houses and b & bs to choose from. Columbia is the nearest main city and also has lots of hotels and restaurants. South Carolina's coast is not to be missed and we strongly suggest a visit to historic Charleston which dates back to 1670 and has lots of Civil War connections, as well as Georgetown, and the seaside beach resorts of Myrtle Beach and Hilton Head Island.

Artist: **Hubert De Watrigant JOCKEYS** _Courtesy of:_
Osborne Studio Gallery

Racing in France

Long before Le Chunnel was completed, making it easier than ever to hop across the channel for a day or weekend at the races in France, thousands of British racing fans have swarmed to Paris' Longchamp for the Arc weekend in early October, or drifted lazily to Deauville in the summer for some sea air with their sport.

Artist: **Harry Matthews LADY WITH UMBRELLA LONGCHAMP** *Courtesy of:* **The Artist**

Now the traffic travels in both directions, and on any given Saturday in the UK you will be able to see top French jockeys such as the bubbly Olivier Peslier compete head to head with his Italian/English counterpart Frankie Dettori. On Sunday in France, the location might have changed but the action often repeats itself, adding a fascinating elan to the racing action. The entente cordiale stretches to several of each country's top trainers and there are few Group races run in France without a representative from the Henry Cecil or Peter Chapple-Hyam yards, or alternatively, with horses sent from France by Criquette Head or Andre Fabre to try and take the top prizes in British flat racing. And it continues year-round through the winter in the National Hunt game, with Martin Pipe taking his cheque book to pick up a top class hurdler at Auteuil or Francois Doumen bringing top French steeplechasers to English shores to try and win yet another top prize.

The common denominator in all this cross channel activity is often the owners who have significant strings of horses with trainers in both countries. The Aga Khan, Sheikh Mohammed, Sheikh Hamdan and the Maktoum family have long led the way, not to mention Khalid Abdullah, and others such as Daniel Wildenstein, the Niarchos family of France and Britain's Robert Sangster who have also encouraged the two-way traffic by taking a sporting chance with their top steeds.

Despite some problems in recent years which saw the closure of one course at Evry, French racing has taken some positive steps in the last few years to improve the viability of the sport, and has never been keener to welcome the visiting racegoer from abroad. Taking into account the very high class racing on offer and the first class facilities for the visitor, racing in France is good value.What's more you can load up your car with some first class Bordeaux and Brie for the trip home. What are you waiting for?

The organising body for much of thoroughbred racing is France-Galop and they can provide details on the courses and fixtures. Drop them a line at France-Galop, 46 place Abel Gance, 92655 Boulogne, France. Tel: 1 49 10 2030. Fax: 1 47 61 9332. If you are into the Internet, they also have a web site at WWW.paristurf.tm.fr.

There are a number of British companies which run regular trips to French racecourses such as Longchamp, Chantilly and Deauville. They enjoy the benefit of being able to block book whole sections of the course for their clients to enjoy private facilities at big events such as the Arc weekend. In October literally thousands take up the offer and the British presence can often dominate proceedings at Longchamp. If you wish to let someone else make all the arrangements you could contact Horse Racing Abroad, 24 Sussex Road, Haywards Heath, West Sussex RH16 4EA. Tel: (01444) 441661. Fax: (01444) 416 169. A typical two-day Arc weekend by either Eurostar train or air, with a hotel room, course admission transfers and some extras, runs to about £220. This company are experts in arranging racing trips around the globe and Paris is their most popular venue.

LONGCHAMP

The surrounding Bois de Boulogne gives Longchamp a country feel and it is sometimes hard to remember that you are close to the centre of Paris. Reflecting its pre-eminence as the course of France's capital city, Longchamp is the course for many of the most important races in the country's racing calendar. From the French Guineas for colts and fillies in the spring, to the end of season European championship that is the Prix de L'Arc de Triomphe, Longchamp is the home of French racing at its best.

M. Grandchamp is the Clerk of the Course at Longchamp and he can be contacted at Hippodrome de Longchamp, Route des Tribunes, Bois de Boulogne, 75016 Paris. Tel: 1 44 30 7500. Fax: 1 44 30 7599.

To get to the course, you can either take the number 244N Bus (Pte Maillot) or hop on the free shuttle bus provided by the racecourse from the Porte d'Auteuil. If the Metro is your choice, take the direction Porte d'Auteuil-Longchamp. Once you have reached the racecourse, compared with most major British courses it is relatively inexpensive to get in. There is one large public enclosure which covers the entire course and it costs FF 25 (about £2.50) to attend for a mid-week meeting and FF 40 (£4) for weekend fixtures or bank holidays. About FF 50 is asked for some of the biggest fixtures of the year such as the Arc de Triomphe. Even better still, those 18 years old or younger get in for nothing, while if you are 18-25 years old or over 60 years young, the price of admission is reduced by half. There is also a large public enclosure in the centre of the course, which is free to everyone!

There will be additional costs if you wish to reserve a seat in one of the restaurants, which you can do by telephoning ahead on 1 42 88 9138 or 1 44 30 7590. For those who enjoy the luxury of a private box, you can arrange one by contacting Myriam Richard, Tel: 1 49 10 2287.

In the new millennium, Longchamp will see no fewer than 32 racing fixtures. Prime amongst these will be Arc day itself on the first Sunday in October, with a fine supporting card that also includes the Abbaye sprint over five furlongs, a race that often goes to an English invader. Get there a day earlier and you can watch one of the best stayers' races of the year, the Prix du Cadran which has attracted some of Britain's best long distance specialists. Leading up to the Arc, in early September are a number of Arc trials that try to establish some form for the big race itself. They are fascinating contests in themselves and well worth going to see live. If you do go on the first Sunday in September, you will be able to watch the Prix du Moulin de Longchamp, the race named after the windmill that provides a unique land mark at the far bend. Come to Longchamp in the spring and you will be able to take in the first of the French classics for colts in the form of the Dubai Poules d'Essai des Poulains and its counterpart for fillies, the Essai des Pouliches. A couple of weeks earlier, and one of the first Group races in the calendar awaits you in the form of the Prix Ganay.

Longchamp is a right handed track of 2,400 metres (about a mile and a half) who's principal characteristic is the sweeping bend before the finishing straight. So there is in effect, a turn for home into a 'false straight', and then another turn for home in the run to the finish line itself. Just to add some interest there are actually two finishing lines, so don't tear up your ticket on the tierce until the race is well and truly over! The outside course is bisected by a straight course upon which the famous Prix de l'Abbaye sprint is held over five furlongs.

Artist: **Jonathan Trowell CHANTILLY**
Courtesy of: **Osborne Studio Gallery**

Paris Local Favourites

What can be said of Paris that has not already been said? No doubt if you are a racing fan, you will be coming either in the Spring or the Autumn when the major races at Longchamp take place, and it is also a time when this vibrant city is at its finest. The Arc de Triomphe, Champs Elysees and Eiffel Tower are Paris' most famous landmarks but the way to really feel Paris is to walk amongst some of the smaller streets in either Montmartre, Le Marais or the Quartier Latin, the famous left bank on the other side of the Isle de Notre Dame. For anyone surfacing from the Metro for a very first view of Paris, it should be taken at night from the Trocadero overlooking the Seine and the Tour Eiffel. Hopefully the fountains will be playing under coloured floodlights to ensure a magic moment any visitor to this city of lovers will never forget.

There are an incredible number of excellent restaurants in Paris, and hotels by the bucket full, so recommending just a few is tricky. Naturally, a lot depends on your budget. If time is tight and money no object then try The Crillon (1 44 711500), The Bristol (1 53 43 4300) or the Hotel Vernet (1 44 31 9800), all outstanding hotels with restaurants of superb quality. The Parc (1 44 05 6666) is also excellent and conveniently situated, as is the St-James Paris (1 44 05 8181). Finally, if you are into art nouveau try Alain Ducasse (1 47 27 1227) - a real jewel!

CHANTILLY

With its connections to French royalty going back centuries, Chantilly is perhaps the most elegant of French racecourses and home to some of the country's, and Europe's, leading Group races for three year-olds such as the United Arab Emirates Prix du Jockey Club (French Derby) for colts, and the Prix de Diane Hermes (French Oaks) for fillies. A dramatic backdrop is provided by the magnificent 18th century chateau and the Grandes Ecuries, the stables which housed the steeds of nobility in days gone by.

Chantilly also has added interest as the locale is also one of the top training centres in France, and home to the operations of such notables as Andre Fabre, Criquette Head or the English transplant John Hammond - the French Newmarket, one could say, but vive la difference!

M. Francois Cop is the Clerk of the Course at Chantilly and M. Yves de Chevigny is Director of the Training Centre. If you wish to get in touch with them write to Hippodrome des Princes de Conde, Route du Pesage, 60500 Chantilly. Tel: 3 44 62 4100. Fax: 3 44 57 3489.

Chantilly is situated about 30 miles north of Paris and is easily accessible from the capital. It also handy for Charles de Gaulle airport if you are flying in directly. If you are driving from the direction of Paris, take the A1 autoroute and exit at Survilliers. Alternatively, you could take the trains which run directly to Chantilly from Paris' Gare du Nord station. There are also trains which make other stops along the way and it might be best to check before you set off with the SNCF, Tel: 3 42 80 0303.

Despite the architectural opulence of the surroundings at Chantilly, like most French racecourses, it is quite cheap to get in. The public enclosure in the centre of the course is absolutely free, while general admission to the remainder of the course and grandstand area costs a mere FF 25 (about £2.50) during the week, or FF 40 (£4) on Sundays and bank holidays. Children and teenagers

Artist: **Hubert de Watrigant LE ROND DE PRESENTATION** *Courtesy of:* **Osborne Studio Gallery**

under 18 are free and those 18-25 years old and over 60s enjoy a fifty per cent reduction on the normal price. If you wish to book a seat or table in the restaurant, call ahead on Tel. 3 44 58 9001.

Chantilly holds 22 days of racing spread from the end of April until the third week of September. This is quite a comeback, as it was just a few years ago that this wonderful venue was cut back to only six days racing because of financial constraints - such was the sad state of French racing then. Thankfully now its all systems go and you could get off to an early start with a visit on a Sunday in May to see the running of the Prix Hocquart. The main action of the year of course takes place in June with the running of the French Derby and Oaks on consecutive Sundays. Other fixtures are scattered throughout May, June, July and September, but most often on weekdays.

Chantilly is a sweeping, right handed course of 2,000 metres (about a mile and a quarter) and provides a true test of ability.

Chantilly Local Favourites

As an overall place to pay a visit in the area just outside Paris, Chantilly ranks right up at the top along with such other marvellous venues as Fontainbleau or Versailles. It is connections with the horse though, that make it a must for those with an interest in racing and you should really make a point of visiting the highly-regarded Musee Vivant du Cheval (the Museum of the Living Horse). Other notable places to visit nearby include the Abbaye de Chaalis at Hermenonville, the town of Senlis, and of course the Musee Condee and the park and Chateau de Chantille itself.

If you wish to find a bed for the night in a place that maintains the aristocratic theme of Chantilly, try the Chateau Mont Royal (Tel: 3 44 54 5050) a charming chateau hotel that was built at the turn of the century as a hunting lodge and sits in its own forest about six miles outside Chantilly. It has an excellent restaurant and the hotel will very kindly arrange golf, riding or fishing for you nearby. Another highly rated hostelry is the Golf Hotel Blue Green de Chantilly (3 44 58 4777) a good place for an extended stay if you like to try a round on the fairways. Although perhaps not quite as luxurious as these choices, either of the Hotel du Parc (3 44 58 2000), close to the centre of the town, or the baronial Chateau de Montvillargenne Hotel situated in the midst of a pretty forest, will not see you stuck for a bed for a night. For fine dining, one restaurant to put into the notebook is the Chateau de la Tour (3 44 62 3838). Other first class restaurants include the Tour d'Apremont (3 44 25 6111) and Verbois (3 44 24 0622) on the route de Creil.

If you wish to get more information on what to do while you are in the Chantilly area, contact the local tourist office on, Tel: 3 44 57 08 58.

DEAUVILLE

Everyone loves to go to the seaside for the summer and with Deauville you can paddle your feet in the sea in the morning, gorge yourself on fine cuisine and wines at lunch, play the ponies in the afternoon and then try to double your winnings at the casino all night. Though not as ancient as say Chantilly, Deauville is not without its connections to royalty as racing here was first started here in 1864 by the Duc de Morny, the Emperor's younger brother and after whom one of the major races of the year, the Prix Morny is named.

M. Deshayes is the Clerk of the Course at Deauville and if you wish to contact him you can at Hippodrome de Deauville-La Touques, 45 avenue Hocquart de Turtot, 14800 Deauville, France. Tel: 2 31 14 2000. Fax: 2 31 14 2007.

To get to Deauville from Paris where you might begin your journey when in France, you could drive there taking the A 13 Autoroute that goes from Paris to Caen. By train, you would start your journey at the Gare St Lazare, getting off at Deauville Station. Of course you could also fly there directly if you had your own plane and then you would head for the airport at St Gatien. For landing information, Tel: 2 31 65 1717. Alternatively, mariners may enjoy a trip on the ferry which docks at Le Havre, fairly close to your destination.

The surroundings and hotels in Deauville might be on the luxurious side, but like most French courses, it won't cost you very much to get into the course. FF 25 (£2.50) is the price of general admission during the week and it goes up to FF 35 (£3.50) on Sundays and bank holidays. Those under 18 and over 60 are free, while the 18-25 year-olds get in for half price. Of course a private box would be more and if you would like to arrange one, call ahead to Myriam Richard on Tel: 1 49 10 2287. Deauville has three fine restaurants, La Toque, Les Jardins du Paddock and Les Haras, and if you would like to book a table call Tel: 2 31 14 3114

Racing at Deauville takes place from the middle of July to the end of August, and again for an all too brief couple of days in October. The main action takes place though in August when all of Paris has deserted its streets to find a place for the annual vacation. Racing is put on just about every Saturday and Sunday during the month and the big day is the Sunday when the Group 1 Prix Morny is staged, one of the top races for two year olds in France. In the past this race has been won by such stars as Machiavellian, Arazi and Hector Protector and almost always throws down vital clues to the future classics.

Another top class race is the Prix Jacques le Marois for older horses. Perhaps you too could find a future star here if you go to the Agence Francaise Yearling Sales which are held each August in Deauville. If all this doesn't satisfy your appetite for looking at horses, you could always take in a polo match!

In 2000, this right-handed course of about 2,000 metres (a mile and a quarter) will host 19 fixtures, the bulk of which are in August, the month when many take place on both Saturday or Sundays of 'le weekend'.

Deauville Local Favourites

Being an elegant sea-side resort that has always attracted the well-heeled Parisian, it is not surprising that

Deauville boasts a good complement of excellent hotels. After you've spent some time on the beach, perhaps bought a yacht at the sales, did some shopping at designer boutiques and gambled the day and night away at the course and casino, you might consider bedding down at any one of the following recommended hostelries: the Hotel du Golf (Tel: 2 31 14 2400) is a rambling Tudor chateau that has been recently renovated and enjoys splendid views of the River Seine as it meets the sea, true to its name, you can also get in a round of golf on the hotel's own course; the Golf's sister hotel, the Royal (2 31 98 66 22) is also run by the Lucien Barriere group, enjoys sea views and is handy for the centre of town and the Casino; others you could try are the Mercure (2 31 98 6633), the L'Amiraute (2 31 88 6262) and the Hotel Yacht Club (2 31 87 3000) overlooking the quay side near the town centre, or L'Augeval (2 31 81 1318). You don't have to be Greek to stay at the Helios Hotel (2 31 14 4646), but you might take home your winnings to the Hotel Le Trophee (2 31 88 4586). Deauville accommodation tends to get fully booked up when the racing is on during the summer, so it's best to reserve ahead if you can.

Artist: **Martin Williams** **DEAUVILLE, LA TOUQUES**
Courtesy of: **The Artist**

There is a delightful atmosphere in Deauville and there are numerous restaurants - many are very relaxed and dinner just seems to go on and on. Try Ciro's (2 31 14 3131) or the appropriately named Yearling (2 31 88 3337) which is well regarded. At nearby Touques the Village (2 31 88 0177) is good, as is Aux Landiers (2 31 88 0039) - a real gem in which to plan your winning bets in real peace.

If the pace is a bit hectic in Deauville, you might take a break and do a bit of a tour to nearby Trouville, the delightful Honfleur, with yet even more outstanding restaurants, or Caen both of which offer some interesting sight-seeing and some museums worth a visit. If your horse has won or money is no object come what may, try the Ferme St-Simeon (2 31 89 2361), a spectacular restaurant. If you can't get enough of the equine action in Deauville, you might pay a visit to the nearby course at Clairefontaine which usually offers a mixed card of both flat and jump racing.

If you need any advice on some of the many attractions that Deauville has to offer, contact the Office du Tourisme on Tel: 2 31 14 4000.

Racing in Germany

After some years in the doldrums, racing in Germany has made a real come-from-behind finish in the nineties and now is one of the top places in Europe to go for some quality racing. Since unification a few years ago, Berlin's historic Hoppegarten has been brought back into the illustrious fold of German racecourses, a list which also includes Hamburg, the home of the

German Derby held each year on the first Sunday of July; Cologne, where the German 2,000 Guineas is staged and one of the country's leading training centres; as well as other major tracks at Munich, Hanover, Bremen, Dortmund, Dusseldorf and Frankfurt which provide a variety of top notch flat and jump racing.

With their high prize money, German Pattern races have become major targets for top European owners and trainers since they were opened up to foreign competition in recent years and there are few Group races which will not see a runner from the John Dunlop or Clive Brittain stables, and probably ridden by a Dettori or Fallon if they take place on a Sunday! The Maktoum family of Dubai set up a training operation there in the 1990s and although relatively modest compared with their operations in France and England, this also adds to the international flavour and the class of racing. Germany has long had some top trainers of its own in the form of Andrew Schutz based at Cologne, and Andreas Wohler in Bremen, Peter Schiergen is also an outstanding traner to follow and with the right breeding stock they are now going overseas to take on the world at meetings such as the Breeders Cup - and with the success many British trainers would envy. German bloodstock continues to improve and it will be interesting to see what will be achieved in the coming years.

By most yardsticks, top amongst German racecourses for racing, hospitality, scenery and a generally great time comes Baden Baden, a real jem of a place on the edge of the Black Forest.

BADEN BADEN

Baden Baden is one of Germany's most popular and prettiest of courses, with a long history of racing going back to 1858. Back in Victorian times it was visited by those who came originally to take the waters at the town's spa, but is now really a year-round resort. Nestled between the Black Forest and the Rhine, it's a delightful place to escape to no matter what the time of year, but for the racing fan, it is the spring and late summer/autumn when Baden Baden's two main racing festivals take place that make a visit to the town particularly appealing. The racecourse is considered by many to be the country's number one course: Germany's answer to Ascot in a beautiful parkland setting.

The course is run by the private Internationaler Club, which has about 130 members, and for which Dr Frank Joyeux is the General Manager, Peter Banzhaf the Racing Director and Bodo Heitz the Clerk of the Course. They can be contacted at Internationaler Club e.V., Lichtentaler Allee 8, 76530 Baden Baden, Germany. Tel: 07221 21120. Fax: 07221 211222. On racedays you can reach them at the course on Tel: 07221 211216.

If you are driving there the quickest way is to take the A5 Autobahn which links Basel in Switzerland with Karlsruhe and take the exit signed Baden Baden-Iffezheim and you will find the course about 8 miles north west of the town, next to the village of Iffezheim. If you are travelling by train, head for the Baden Baden-Oos station and board the special buses laid on for racedays which will take you the last five miles to the course. Otherwise, a taxi will cost you only about DM 20 (£7). If you are lucky enough to come by private aeroplane, you should land at the new airport at Sollingen which is only about 20 minutes away. For those taking commercial flights, Strasbourg is the nearest airport with regularly scheduled flights and it is about a half hours drive away. Foreign owners and trainers are treated particularly well here and if you let the officials know in advance, they'll line you up with a badge and even make arrangements to collect you from the airport or railway station.

Artist: **Klaus Philipp** *BADEN-BADEN* *Courtesy of:* **The Artist**

Less elevated visitors though won't find the tariff too high to spend a day at the races, with general admission only DM 10 (about £3). If you want a reserved seat it will cost you a bit more, with prices ranging up to DM 70 (£23), depending upon where you sit. There are six days of racing during each of the two annual meetings and you can buy badges which cover the entire meeting: for example, a six-day badge for the Schwarzwald Terrace restaurant, with its fine views of the course from the top level of the stands, would set you back about DM 230 (£75) or DM 180 (£60) for the Wein Terrace restaurant just below it. Box seats come in at about the DM 200 (£70) level for all six days, or about DM 50 (£17) on a daily basis. Children are allowed in to the course for a modest DM 4 (a little over £1) and they will find various things to entertain them during their visit, including a children's playground. There is also a baby care room which is free.

Although the whole course and setting really is first class, Baden Baden lets you enjoy your racing anyway you like it, from the casual pleasure of a beer and bratwurst on a park bench next to the track, to a fine meal in the more formal surroundings of a private box. You could start the day with an early morning breakfast on the Clubhouse Terrace and watch the horses work out on the course and come back later for a big lunch in the Black Forest Terrace with a view of the real racing action in the afternoon.

Although Baden Baden is probably best known for its flat racing, the course also holds jump racing over hurdles and fences. In fact, there are no fewer than five different courses here, including the Old Course, New Course and Straight Course, which have a total of two miles of excellent turf racecourse between them, with a two furlong final straight. The Steeplechase Course is two miles and three furlongs around, with sixteen fences with a short, steep hill known as the Kapellenberg, while the Hurdles Course is a tighter one with a quarter mile circumference and completely flat.

There are usually nine races a day on each of the twelve days of racing held at Baden Baden of different classes and distances. Included in these are no fewer than ten European pattern Group races, so the standard of racing is really quite high. Highlight of the spring meeting is the Group 2 Baden Airpark-Grosser Preis der Wirtschaft. In late summer and early Autumn, the Mercedes-Benz Grosser Preis von Baden is a Group 1 contest that has been won by some outstanding horses.

Putting a bet on your selection on the Tote here will be familiar to most punters, with win, place, Forecast and Tricast wagering from a minimum stake of DM 2.50 (just under a pound). If your German is good enough, the racing paper "Sport-Welt" will help you with your selection. For those used to racing in Britain, Ireland or Australia, there are also on-course bookmakers who will take your bet. If you aren't in the stands when the stalls fly open, there are over 100 TV monitors to help you follow the race. Don't worry if you get to the course without having changed your pounds or francs into local currency as there is a foreign exchange and cheque cashing service at the on-course Deutsche Bank branch.

With some of the finest racing in Europe at the highest level, a visit to Baden Baden is a must for every racing enthusiast. Like the spa town, the racecourse prides itself on looking after its guests!

Baden Baden Local Favourites

If you are visiting Baden Baden for the races, you will be fortunate to be staying in a place that has some of the finest hotels and service in the world, with over a century of catering for just about anyone's personal whim. Spa towns tend to pamper their guests and this is one of the ultimate places to be pampered. You could take the waters before or after racing, play a round of golf at one of the resorts many courses or if you are on a roll with a few winners, try your luck at the world famous casino in the Kurhaus.

The Caracalla-Therme and the Friedrichsbad are the two best known bathing spots where a garden of earthly delights awaits those wishing to take the cure before taking in a more cultural experience at the theatre or concert. Right in Baden Baden, the Lichtentaler Allee and historic old town is filled with elegant boutiques and shops just waiting to relieve you of your winnings from the course or casino.

Baden Baden is right on the doorstep of the region's wine growing district, the Rebland, which has some of the finest wines in Germany as well as some extremely good eating places in addition to some glorious scenery. A day touring around here, or a short hop over the Rhine to neighbouring Alsace would be sure to prompt a trip to the gym when you return home.

In the very top rank of hotels here, there is the famous Brenner's Park Hotel (07221 9000) which is firmly in the luxury category as is excellent nearby hotel on the out skirts of Baden Baden (07226/55601). Also top class is Monch's Posthotel (07083 7440) in nearby Bad Herrenalb. First class accommodation can be found in either the Europaischer Hof Hotel (07221 23561) or the Badischer Hof hotels, both run by the quality Steigenberger hotel chain which also provides on-course catering services at Baden Baden. If you fancy a stay in the heart of the Black Forest, try the Hotel Bareiss (07442 470) near Baiersbronn-Mitteltal - it's a complete resort with all kinds of sports facilities. Here you wont be too far away from the fabulous Restaurant Schwarzwaldstube (07442 4920) with its classic fine French cuisine. One thing you should really do before leaving home though is to book ahead, as racing at Baden Baden has had a resurgence in popularity in recent years and you might be disappointed if you don't have a reservation at the hotel of your choice.

Artist: **Klaus Philipp ABARY IN LONGCHAMP**
Courtesy of: **The Artist**

Racing in Canada

WOODBINE

When it was built in the 1950s, the sprawling complex that is Woodbine Racetrack lay in peaceful countryside amid farms to the north west of the city of Toronto. Now this booming city of almost three million people has all but swallowed it up and as you sit in the grandstand the roar of jet engines overhead signals the approach to the busy international airport close by, bringing visitors from around the world.

Artist: **Jonathan Trowell THE FAVOURITE**
Courtesy of: **Osborne Studio Gallery**

Woodbine is a first rate, modern complex that, while filled with punters only a few times a year for major races such as the Queen's Plate in late June and the Canadian International in October, offers an excellent day at the races at a very reasonable cost - in fact admission to the course itself is free!

Run by the Ontario Jockey Club, the key people at Woodbine are David Willmot, President and CEO, John Whitsun who is Vice President of Thoroughbred Racing and Chris Evans, Racing Secretary and Handicapper. They can be contacted at Woodbine Racetrack, PO Box 156, Rexdale, Ontario, Canada, M9W 5L2. Tel: (416) 675 6110. Fax: (416) 213 2126. Web stie: ojc.com/attrack/woodbine.html. The Web site is an excellent way to visit Woodbine, if you can't get there in person.

The course is very easy to drive to by car. Just a few minutes from Toronto International Airport, take Bellfield Road to Carlingview Drive if you wish to avoid the traffic and enter via the backstretch or follow Highway 409 to Highway 27 and the main entrance. Allow about a half hour or more to cover the 15 miles from downtown Toronto, taking the Queen Elizabeth Way west to Highway 427 right to the track. Valet parking is also available at a small charge at the Clubhouse entrance. Alternatively you could take Toronto's efficient subway system and hop in a taxi or connect with the free Racetrack buses which leave from Kipling Station just under an hour before the first race to the main entrance and returning after the last race. Seating is on a first-come, first served basis. If you need any assistance with directions, give the course a ring on (416) 675-RACE.

Thoroughbred racing takes place at Woodbine from the end of March through to the first week in December, although there is Harness Racing here seven months of the year. There are usually ten races a day of varying calibre and distances, mostly on the dirt track but some held on the turf course. There are big stakes races held on Saturdays, Sundays and holidays throughout the year, with the Queen's Plate for Canadian bred three year olds, the first leg of the Canadian Triple Crown in late June providing the highlight of the summer season and the EP Taylor Stakes and Canadian International with a guaranteed purse of Can$1.5 million attracting some of the best turf horses from around the world in mid October. In 1996 Woodbine played host to the Breeders Cup and trainers and jockeys all seemed to agree that the track's new mile and a half turf course provided one of the fairest tests to equine ability in North America. Woodbine also operates a simulcasting system with other racetracks in North America beaming in live racing on TV from other courses, complete with pari-mutuel betting.

Admission to the large Grandstand and course itself is free, but there are admission charges to access various bars, restaurants and other facilities. There are also thousands of free seats in the Grandstand on several levels offering excellent views of all parts of the track. Some sections have reserved seating at a small charge on big race days. A race programme costs $2.50 and contains past performances plus a brief form guide; for the purist handicapper, a copy of the Daily Racing Form is also a must. The minimum bet on the pari-mutuel is $2 Canadian (about $1.50 US), so you don't have to bring loads of cash to enjoy yourself.

At the top end of the scale is the Woodbine Club, an exclusive member-only private club whose panelled lounges and bars offer luxurious accommodation. If you are just visiting Toronto for a few days it might be worth your while to find a member who can take you as a guest. If you get lucky and cash in a big daily double, you might want to stump up the $1,000 for your own membership!

Woodbine has a number of restaurants and bars to

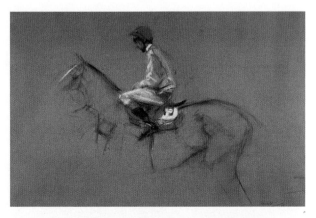

Artist: **Jonathan Trowell LEADING OUT**
Courtesy of: **Osborne Studio Gallery**

Artist: **Barrie Linklater THE FINAL CHALLENGE**
Courtesy of: **The Artist**

choose from but reservations are advised for busy weekends and holiday meetings, Tel 888-675 7223. Favourites on the second floor is a new dining room with panoramic views and overlooks the finish line. Each table has its own TV monitor showing track odds and racing. On the third floor Clubhouse level is Champions, a bar and delicatessen counter serving soup and sandwiches, which has an outdoor patio and casual dining. No reservations required here but there is a $5 admission surcharge. On the first floor, the Finish Line bar also offers light snacks; the Oaks Lounge on the second level and the Walking Ring patio on the first floor offer serious liquid refreshment possibilities and a view of the saddling paddock. At the east end of the grandstand are three other bars, Willows, Silks Lounge and the Winners Circle, which will also wet your whistle, but have no views of the track. The grandstand complex also contains a food court with a wide choice of snack and fast food outlets, the hot roast beef sandwiches at the carvery are a safe bet.

Having fully satisfied your appetite, why not spend a while visiting the Canadian Horse Racing Hall of Fame on the ground floor of the grandstand. In addition to celebrating such equine heroes as Northern Dancer and the great 'Big Red' Secretariat, who had his last race at Woodbine, winning as he pleased by more than 6 lengths, you can explore the rich history of the turf in Canada.

If you have a day to spare while visiting Toronto, it would be a shame to miss out seeing Niagara Falls, about an hour and a half drive west. Stop at historic Niagara on the Lake, which holds the annual Shaw Festival each summer, for a bite to eat. Just a few miles past the falls itself is Fort Erie, which holds racing from June through September from Saturday to Tuesday each week. The 'Fort' is an older course that has a real country feel to it and weekends attract large crowds from Buffalo, New York, just across the river.

Toronto Local Favourites
Toronto is well worth a visit in itself, with a multitude of first class hotels and a fabulous range of restaurants that reflect the city's multi-ethnic population. In fact, there are more restaurants per capita in Toronto than any other city in the world! You might never leave the airport strip of hotels and eateries, but you would be missing much if you did not try and stay downtown. It's a clean, safe walking city with lots of shopping, sites and nightlife, so why not enjoy it to the maximum? The Yorkville area in mid-town Toronto is an excellent bet with hotels such as the classic Park Plaza (416 924 5471) on Avenue Road with its fifties roof garden bar. The Four Seasons Hotel (416 964 0411) opposite offers all the luxury that chain usually provides. For a fun night out and a lot of local colour try the Brunswick Tavern on Bloor Street West, a favourite watering hole. Dip south on Spadina Avenue and you are in Chinatown. The Pink Pearl on Dundas Street is only one of many excellent restaurants here, or for a bit of jazz and some delicatessen delights drop into Grossman's Tavern on Spadina. A fun place to dine and a local landmark is Ed's Warehouse, handy for taking in a musical at the Royal Alex Theatre next door.

There are many hotels right downtown and a safe bet is the Royal York Hotel (416 368 2511) opposite Union Station or for a bit of turn of the century elegance try the King Edward Hotel (416 863 3131) on King Street, handy for shopping in the vast Eaton Centre or exploring the nightlife. Toronto is right on Lake Ontario and the Harbourfront area hops night and day. Stay at the Radisson Hotel (416 203 3333) right on the water and take a ferry to the Toronto Islands for a bit of green quiet and the best view of the city skyline. See the sites from the top of the CN Tower or take in a baseball game in the covered Sky Dome at its foot. Toronto and Woodbine are a winning daily double.

Artist: **Katie O'Sullivan FINAL ADJUSTMENTS** *Courtesy of:* **Osborne Studio Gallery**

Racing in New York

The three principle thoroughbred racetracks of Belmont and Aqueduct near New York City and Saratoga in upstate New York are run by the New York Racing Association Inc., PO Box 90, Jamaica, New York, 11417. Tel: (718) 641 4700. E Mail: nyra@nyra.com. They also have an excellent website giving details of all three tracks, updates on big race entries and general news; well worth a visit at nyracing.com/contact.html.

BELMONT PARK

Anyway you look at it, Belmont, like New York City itself, is a big place. The main grandstand which was built as part of a major refit in the late 1960s is awesomely large and stretches most of the finishing straight. On big race days such as the Belmont Stakes they can fit in upwards of 90,000 people and at least 33,000 of those will not have any trouble getting a seat. By North American standards the course itself is also pretty impressive with a mile and a half dirt track, while the Widener turf course in just over a mile and a quarter. Of all racetracks in America Belmont is probably the one best suited to the running style of British and European horses, so visitors from across the Atlantic might have an even chance of making a few bob if they spot any imported runners here.

Belmont is on Long Island and to get there from Manhattan take the Queens Midtown Tunnel to the Long Island Expressway, east to Cross Island Parkway and south to Exit 26-D. From Connecticut take any route to the Throgs Neck Bridge to the Cross Island Parkway, or from New Jersey you can use the George Washington Bridge from the north or from the south the Interstate bridge to the Staten Island Expressway and the Verazzano Bridge. From Manhattan you could also take the 8th Avenue subway to connecting buses at 169th or 179th streets, or by rail via the Long Island Railroad from Penn Station to make connections at Jamaica.

Once you've reached the track it will cost a mere $2 to park the car, or an additional $2 for preferred parking closer to the entrance. A courtesy shuttle bus will take you to the admission entrance. If you're feeling really quite lazy it's worth paying an extra $4 for valet parking. There is special parking available for both the grandstand and clubhouse. Admission to the Grandstand is only $2, but it's probably worth spending another $2 to get into the Clubhouse, then you can go anywhere you like. Children under 12 are free.

Racing is held at Belmont over long stretches in the spring and summer and again in the autumn and, apart from the month of August when everyone moves to Saratoga, alternates with Aqueduct. So if you're visiting New York City at any time other than August, you can get some local action. No racing is usually held on Mondays (except bank holidays) and Tuesdays, as well as the occasional Wednesday on a bank holiday week. Watch out for Palm Sunday and Easter Sunday though, as they are both 'dark', as is Yom Kippur.

There are big races just about every weekend, but one to catch in April would be the Wood Memorial, a Kentucky Derby trial for three year-olds, followed by the highlight of the season, the Belmont Stakes in June which forms the third leg of the American triple crown. It's by far the biggest day of the year with a supporting card of excellent Group 1,2 and 3 races. The crowds pack in and the course looks at its glorious best. Of course Belmont has held the Breeders Cup and will very probably do so again sometime soon, however the regular autumn programme has its own rewards with the Man O'War and the Woodward weight-for-age stakes providing excellent quality racing in September followed by the Jockey Club Gold Cup in October and its fine supporting card of Group races.

Belmont is big, but even on the biggest races days there seems to be acres of space in the cavernous Grandstand and getting something to eat or drink is little problem. The Clubhouse has several restaurants including the glass-enclosed Garden Terrace Dining Room on the fourth floor with its great view of the track. There is a $2 seating charge, a $10 minimum order and you are required to wear a sports jacket or suit. The Paddock

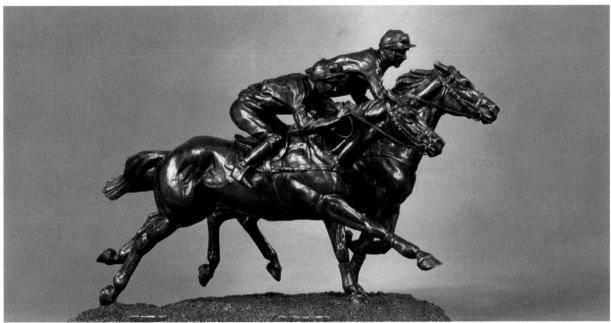

Artist: **Gill Parker** **CAPTAIN LEO & LUCKS LADY DIANE** *Courtesy of:* **Lord & Lady Baden Powell**

Dining Room on the second floor overlooks the pad-dock (naturally!), while the Belmont Cafe on the first floor offers lighter fare and also offers breakfast for those who like to get up early and watch the horses go through their morning paces. On weekends its best to reserve, so call ahead on (516) 488 1740. There's also a food court with a choice of fast food snacks and the backyard picnic area for you to bring your own picnic. There are bars throughout the complex on all levels, some as long as your mother- in- law's last visit!

If you happen to be in New York City during the winter, from December to early March and are desper-ate for some action, you could spend an afternoon at Aqueduct. which is not that far from Manhattan in Jamaica (Long Island that is!). It's probably easiest to go by subway - take the 'A' train to the Old Aqueduct sta-tion and pick up a free bus to the track. The big "A" will always be a favourite with some Noo Yawkers, but it's really a bit like the all-weather at Lingfield on a cold, wet January day. Come to think of it, you should be where anyone else with a bit sense in the Big Apple has already gone - to Florida!

New York City Local Favourites
For New York City, you've really got to be in the heart of the action, and that means mid-town Manhattan. Shopping at Saks, Bergdorff-Goodman or Brooks Brothers on Fifth Avenue, taking in a concert at Carnegie Hall or seeing a show at Radio City Music Hall, it's all right here. Put a bit of breathing space between you and the skyscrapers by taking a stroll through Central Park (by day, please!) and drop down to Greenwich Village or SOHO at night for some great din-ing, drinking and music. The flagship of Manhattan hotels is of course the Plaza Hotel (212 546 5493) at Central Park South and Fifth Avenue, made famous by scores of movies - remember Lisa Minelli and Dudley Moore in "Arthur"? If you find the tariff for the night a bit steep, try lunch in the Palm Court instead or sample a few oysters Rockefeller in the Oyster Bar downstairs.

Sunday lunch could take you to the Tavern on the Green in Central Park; it's a rambling, way-over-the-top

sort of place but lots of fun. A visit to Rockefeller Plaza is a must and the cafe overlooking the skating rink in the late autumn and winter is a great place to people watch over lunch. In the evening dine and dance in art deco style in the magnificent Rainbow Room - a great way to blow your winnings. Late night hunger pangs can be satisfied at one of the many delis around town; try Wolfs Famous Delicatessen on Sixth Avenue where the wafer thin roast beef is piled high on rye. Wherever you stay in New York, go out in the morning to one of the many local diners for breakfast where a couple of dollars will get you eggs sunny side up or easy over with your bottomless cup of coffee. New York offers an incredible choice when it comes to hotel of every size and description. Wouldn't it be better to stay in a place that offers some character with a convenient location for some Edwardian elegance and connections to the New York literati try the Algonquin (212 840 6800) on West 44th street. The Carlisle (212 744 1600) on Madison Avenue is a real gem and only one block fron Central Park. Although it has a mere 60 rooms The Lowell (212 838 1400) on East 63rd Street has working fireplaces to enjoy in its bedrooms and art deco elegance. For a great afternoon tea and fine views over Central Park go to The Pierre (212 838 8000) on famous Fifth Avenue.

SARATOGA

The song might say "I like New York in June", but you will love Saratoga in August. That's the month that this sleepy Victorian spa town in upstate New York is transformed into the racing centre of North America. Virtually the whole of the Big Apple is transported three hundred miles north to escape the swelter of the city in summer, joined by many racing professionals and enthusiasts from around the world attracted by the quality of racing, sporting art exhibitions and summer yearling sales. There has been racing at Saratoga since 1863 and the racetrack just like the town itself oozes Victorian charm.

Saratoga is just under an hour's drive north of Albany in upper New York state and is easily reached from

Artist: **Heather St Clair Davis** FINAL BEND, SARATOGA *Courtesy of:* **Frost & Reed**

New York City or western New York using the New York Thruway to Exit 24 at Albany, then the Northway (87) to Exit 14 and Route 9P to just outside the track entrance. From Vermont or New Hampshire take Route 40 to Schuyerville and Route 29 to Saratoga. When you arrive, $5 will get you trackside parking but it's only $2 in the main parking areas where many pack a picnic and barbecue and have a tail-gate party.

A great way to start the day is to have breakfast on the Clubhouse porch and watch the early morning workouts. Admission is free and breakfast is served between 7:00 and 9:30 am every racing day. Expert commentators describe the training sessions; afterwards you can hop on a tram for a free tour of the barn area or catch the Paddock show and starting gate demonstration.

Artist: **Roy Miller LONG SHADOWS**
Courtesy of: **The Artist**

A holiday atmosphere pervades Saratoga, with lots of people bringing their fold up chairs and coolers into the track to sit among the tall pine trees, listening to the strains of a Dixieland band while watching the betting shows and races on TV monitors slung from the trees. It costs only $2 to get into the track, or $4 for the Clubhouse with children under 12 admitted free. To be sure of a seat overlooking the course it's best to reserve one in advance - $6 in the Clubhouse and $4 for the Grandstand. Write before July 1st to Saratoga Reserved Seats, PO Box 030257, Elmont, NY USA 11003 Tel: (718) 641 4700. A few Grandstand seats do go on sale each morning at the track entrance from 8:00 am, or you can buy them the night before at the Holiday Inn in the centre of Saratoga.

Any day at Saratoga is a great day, even though it's just as hard as any other place to pick a winner. Racing starts at the end of July and runs through to the Labour Day bank holiday which is the first Monday in September - six days a week (Tuesday's are 'dark' days).

The quality of the racing is excellent with a top handicap or group race almost every day. Highlights of the meeting include the Group 1 Whitney Handicap and Sword Dancer Invitation Handicap and the Travers Stakes for three year olds over a mile and a quarter run towards the end of August. Thrown in here and there are also some steeplechases, just to make things even more interesting if you're a jumping fan at heart! If you have an hour or so to spare before racing, a visit to the racing museum near the main entrance is also a good bet.

Saratoga offers a wide choice of fast food outlets and you can get just about anything you want from steaks to grits and ice cream. There are also several restaurants and bars from which to choose including the Turf Terrace, Club Terrace, Carousel Restaurant and Lounge, Paddock Tent and At The Rail Pavilion most of which should be reserved in advance and carry seating charges. Call Service America (718) 529 8700 before July 20 or (518) 587 5070 during the race meeting.

Saratoga may be very laid back, but America does insist on a little formality with its racing and Gentlemen are expected to wear suits or sports jackets in certain areas such as Box Seats, the Turf Terrace and the At The Rail Pavilion. Show up here in shorts or jeans (even designer labels) and you will be turned away! The rest of the course is a lot more relaxed, but you're supposed to keep on your shoes and shirts at all times - that goes for the ladies too!

Saratoga Local Favourites
Saratoga Springs is extremely busy during the entire month of August when the racing community descends en masse, many people staying in the same place every year. If you want to stay right in town then it is advisable to book as early as possible - up to a year before you visit! One top notch hostelry right in Saratoga is the Ramada Renaissance (518 584 4000). With demand so high for accommodation, it's not surprising that the prices are also high compared with other places not that far away. After taking in a day's racing you could do a neat escape for the night to the cool mountains in neighbouring Vermont. There are lots of great inns here, especially around Woodstock, but the Rutland Inn is a real gem in the sleepy town of the same name and it's just under an hour away. There are also many hotels in New York's state capital of Albany, just a half hour south, as well as small towns such as Ithica, the home of Cornell University in the Finger Lakes region. A visit here could also include a trip to a winery to sample some of the local tipple - some of it surprisingly good.

Racing in Florida

When the temperature dips on the late Autumn sensible North American racing folk pack their binoculars and forward their Daily Racing Form to the sunny climes of the sunshine state of Florida. Decades before Godolphin decided to experiment by wintering their horses in the Arabian Gulf, American trainers and owners moved their horses here and raced them under the waving palms. Racing in Florida is centred around the Miami area and the two tracks which host the main winter season are Hialeah and Gulfstream Park. If you do end up near Miami at other times of the year, you could also catch some thoroughbred action at Calder, just south west of the city, where racing is held from the end of May.

HIALEAH PARK

Built in the 1920s when Miami first took off as a winter tourist destination with Northerners wishing to escape the snow and winter, Hialeah has bags of atmosphere. The complex of buildings was built in mock 16th-century French Mediterranean style, with lots of arches and red tiled roofs. They are surrounded by lush tropical gardens and, fringed by palm trees, the course itself contains a lake with a resident flock of flamingos which usually explodes into flight when the starting gates burst open, signalling the start of a race. Hialeah in the 1950s saw such greats as Eddie Arcaro riding Nashua and Bold Ruler to victory, followed by one Willie Shoemaker on board Northern Dancer and Buckpasser a few years later - the very stuff of legend.

The course is located at 2200 East 4th Avenue, Hialeah, Florida, USA 33011. Tel: (305) 885 8000. Michael Mackey is General Manager, while Stephen Brunetti is Director of Racing. There is lots of regularly updated information on Hialeah's web site: www.hialeahpark.com.

Hialeah is only 5 minutes north of Miami International Airport and is easily reached via highway I-95 by car. On weekends you can take a bus from Miami Beach, or any day from Broward or Palm Beach use Metro Rail right to the door, which also gives you free admission and a free ride home! Parking costs from $1 in the general grandstand to $4 for valet parking at the Clubhouse.

Admission is only $2 to the Grandstand, $4 to the Clubhouse. If you go during the week, it's half price and on opening and closing day, it's free! At other times, save those tickets to Panther, Marlin and Heat games as well as many movie ticket stubs as they also give you free admission. Programmes are only $1, or $2 if you want the full simulcast card to bet on televised races from other tracks, including the Dubai World Cup and the Kentucky Derby.

Racing is held at Hialeah almost every day over a two month period from the middle of March to the third week in May with a nine race card during the week, ten races on weekends and eleven on big stakes days. Thursdays after the first week in April are usually 'dark'. Highlights of the meeting are the Widener Handicap at the end of March, the Kentucky Derby trial Flamingo Stakes for three-year olds in early April, won by such racing greats as Chief's Crown and Seattle Slew, and the Turf Cup a few weeks later. There's a special breakfast at Hialeah on Flamingo day which is the biggest day of the year.

Artist: **Roy Miller THE WINNER COMES IN LAST**
Courtesy of: **The Artist**

If you're wondering who those people are in the private boxes, well they've rented them for the whole season, paying anywhere from $200 to $600 to entertain their friends and guests. If you strike it lucky on the Superfecta, why not splash out and join the Turf Club at $350 single or $600 double and enjoy your cocktails in the stylish surroundings of its private bar and restaurant. Otherwise there are lots of bars, cafes, restaurants and fast food outlets to satisfy your thirst or appetite throughout the Grandstand or Clubhouse. If you need any information on how to place your bet, a taxi or hotel, or directions, check with any of the Customer Service Centres. The course also provides a variety of children's entertainment as well, including a video game room, carousel and bouncy castle as well as puppet shows and pony rides on certain days.

With the Florida sun blazing down and just a gentle breeze to keep the palms in motion, there's no doubt that racing at Hialeah is excellent value for money.

GULFSTREAM PARK

While it may not have the charm or character of Hialeah, there is some seriously good racing at Gulfstream and it holds the prime time of Florida racing when the weather is at its worst in the rest of North America. Its lush, tropical setting also makes Gulfstream one of the world's most beautiful courses and it offers a variety of entertainments and a great day out in the sunshine for the serious or casual racegoer.

Gulfstream is run by Takeshi Doden, Chairman of the Board, and Douglas Donn, President and CEO and is located in Hallandale, between Fort Lauderdale and Miami and it's very handy for both places using the I-95, US 1 and Hallandale Beach Boulevard. You could use either Miami International or Ft Lauderdale/Hollywood International airports to reach your destination.

Be sure to mark that date in your calendar now! Gulfstream Park will be holding the 1999 Breeders' Cup Championship on Saturday November 6. It will be the third time the track has hosted one of the biggest and richest events in the racing calendar, watched by millions of people around the world. Although British and European horses did not have much luck here in 1989 or 1992, presumably because of the heat, who could forget Sunday Silence and Easy Goer battling it out in the Classic in 1989 or AP Indy winning the same race and the Horse of the Year title in 1992? Write to Gulfstream Park, 901 South Federal Highway, Hallandale, Florida, USA 33009 requesting ticket information. Tel: (954) 454 7000. Fax: (954) 454 7827. E mail: marketing@gulfstreampark.com. Gulfstream's web site also has a registration page: www.gulfstreampark.com/breedersform.html.

The Breeders Cup day apart, Gulfstream holds its major meeting of the year from early January to the middle of March. There is racing every day except Tuesdays and post time is 1:00 p.m. Admission to the Grandstand is $3 or $5 for the Clubhouse. Both include a free programme and parking. As many trainers use the Florida racing season as a prep for the US Triple Crown for three year olds, the highlight of season at Gulfstream is the Grade 1 Florida Derby held in the middle of March. It carries a purse in excess of $750,000 and usually attracts some top members of the classic generation. There are three gourmet dining rooms to satisfy your hunger, two in the Clubhouse and one in the Turf Club, all with terraced seating for a view of the track. There is also a large, air-conditioned (of course!) cafeteria in the Grandstand as well as no fewer than 21 other restaurants and snack bars here and 14 bars.

Florida Favourites

There's no shortage of places to stay, eat or drink in South Florida, after all it has been the favourite sun destination for North Americans for almost a century now. First time visitors might be surprised at the amount of Spanish that is spoken everywhere, but it gives Miami its unique flavour as the major gateway to Central and South America and provides the Latino punch in the pina colada. Two great centres of interest are the Art Deco revival area of Miami Beach and the laid-back delights of Key West, and hundred and odd miles to the south. Both are sure bets for accommodation, food, drink and fun people-watching.

the Tagmeme Trail through the Everglades to the west coast and collect some sea shells on Signable Island. Of course if the kids are along on the trip you won't be able to leave the sunshine state without a stop off at Disney World in Orlando. Actually, big kids seem to like it too!

Racing in Kentucky

Kentucky is the spiritual home of racing in America. This is Bluegrass Country and perhaps the most important breeding place for top notch thoroughbreds on the continent. The annual Keeneland Sales attract

Artist: **Peter Curling MORNING CHAT** *Courtesy of:* **The Artist**

Handy for either Hialeah or Gulfstream are several top notch hostelries including the Turnberry Isle Resort (305) 932 6200 on West Country Club Drive and just 10 minutes from the track, the Sheraton Bal Harbour (305) 865 7511 on Collins Avenue about 20 minutes away in Bal Harbor, and the Marriott Harbor Beach (954) 525 4000 and Pier 66 Hyatt Regency (954) 525 6666 both in Fort Lauderdale a half hour away. Closer to the track, in fact only five minutes away and a bit less expensive, is the Hollywood Beach Clarion Hotel (954) 459 1900 on South Ocean Drive. The nice people there also give discounts to people connected with racing. There are many top notch restaurants in the Miami area and just a few that come highly recommended are: Manero's on East Hallandale Beach Boulevard (954) 456 1000; Chef Allen's (305) 935 2900 on NE 29th Avenue in North Miami Beach, Las Brisas (954) 923 1500 on Surf Road in Hollywood or Joe's Stone Crabs (305) 673 0365 on Buskin Set in Miami Beach. If you need any advice on where to stay or what to do close to the racing action you could contact either the Greater Miami Convention & Visitors Bureau Tel: (305) 539 3000 or that of Fort Lauderdale (954) 765 4466.

Florida really does have everything for the visitor - sun, sand and lots to see. If you have time to spare, take

horse people with fat wallets from all over the world and yearlings sold here go on to fame and glory in most parts of the globe. Of course the racing is top notch here, but just to tour around the countryside following mile after mile of white fencing around the stud farms is the experience of a lifetime for those who love horses and racing, a feeling similar to those found around Newmarket or in much of Ireland.

CHURCHILL DOWNS

There are five racetracks in Kentucky but the daddy of them all is Churchill Downs, home of the Kentucky Derby, held on the first Saturday in May and the first leg of the US triple crown for three year-olds. Around one hundred and forty thousand people pack the Downs on Derby Day and as the first strains of My Old Kentucky Home waft over the crowd as the horses come out to parade for the big race spirits and emotions run high. This is mint julep time, when everyone can be a Kentucky Colonel for the day. Louisville lies on the banks of the Ohio River and is about an hour's flying time from Chicago, just under two hours from New York and about four from Los Angeles and is served by many different airlines so there isn't much problem getting there.

The world famous twin spires of Churchill Downs can be found at 700 Central Avenue, Louisville, Kentucky, USA 40208. Tel: (502) 636 4400. Fax: (502) 636 4430. Web site: kentuckyderby.com. Jeff Smith is President of the company that runs the track while Don Richardson is Vice President of Racing. The track first opened in 1875 and has one of the longest and most illustrious histories in the annals of the American turf and the Derby has been held here every year since.

The Kentucky Derby is actually a week long affair, with many other activities going on. For early risers there's 'Dawn at the Downs' where you can breakfast track-side each day and watch the contenders and other horses go through their morning workouts. There are special Jockeys autograph sessions, the 'Festival in the Field' concerts with rock bands, handicapping contests and seminars and backstretch tours, just to mention a few. Away from the track, all of Louisville gets into the swing with hot air balloon races, one of the largest firework displays on the continent and a steamboat race down the Ohio River - all part of the Kentucky Derby Festival.

Like most tracks in North America, admission to Churchill Downs on most racing days won't break the bank, but on Derby and Oaks days general admission rises to $30 and $15 respectively. If you wish to sit down anywhere it's best to reserve a seat ahead of time - contact the course for details; prices range from $42 for a seat in the First Floor Grandstand Bleachers on Derby Day to $4,400 for an eight seater box in the Clubhouse. On Oaks day there are 12,000 bleacher seats available free in the infield on a first-come, first-served basis. A great tradition of the Oaks and Derby days is the tailgate party which sees 80,000 people enjoying their barbecues and beer in the forty acres of the infield. The main grandstand area has many bars and restaurants for those non-tailgaters and a mint julep on Derby day will cost you about $5, but that's not bad because you get to keep the souvenir glass!

Of course the Kentucky Derby week is the highlight of the year at Churchill Downs, but the track stages many more days racing in both the Spring and the Autumn. The Spring meeting covers about 48 days racing, from the end of April until the end of June. Race days are normally Wednesday through Sunday, all week during Derby Week, and with a few Mondays and Tuesdays thrown in. The Autumn meeting has 24 days

racing held daily except Mondays and runs for the month of November. Post time is normally 3:00 pm on weekdays in the Spring and 1:00 on weekends and holidays but one Kentucky Derby and Oaks days the first race is moved up to 11:30 am. The Autumn meeting has a daily 1:00 pm start, except on Thanksgiving (the third Thursday in November) and closing weekend when it is brought forward to 11:30 am. No excuses now to miss the daily double!

In the Spring, the annual 'Run for the Roses' is just the icing on the cake of a whole week of great racing here which kicks off the Saturday of the week before with the Derby Trial stakes, the last prep race for the big event itself and runs through the Kentucky Oaks for three year old fillies on Derby eve Friday. Each of these and other graded races are championships in their own right. If all of this flat racing is a bit much for those who prefer the jumps, take heart and stick around for Churchill Downs annual Steeplechase Racing day on Sunday at the end of June. Three jump races are part of a ten race card including the $100,000 Grade 1 Hard Scuffle Steeplechase.

Kentucky has several other racetracks which host racing at other times of the year. Keeneland at Lexington of course also holds the annual summer yearling sales in July and is the centre for breeding; you could spend days or weeks visiting famous stud farms such as Gainesway, Shadwell Stud, Darby Dan Farm, Calumet Farm, the Kentucky Horse Center or Spendthrift Farm. Tours can often be arranged if you enquire ahead of time.

Artist: **Asad Kuri Montana VERY ALERT**
Courtesy of: **The Artist**

Kentucky Local Favourites

Getting around Louisville can be an experience in itself. For something different, why not hop on a horse drawn carriage for a tour by Kentucky Carriage (802) 944 6065 or by horse drawn trams by Louisville Horse Trams (502) 581 0100. There are lots of choices of places to stay in Louisville. The Aleksander House B&B on First Street (502) 637 4985 might be the cosy spot for the November racing at Churchill Downs as it features open fireplaces, gourmet breakfasts and four poster beds in an old Victorian house. The Camberley Brown Hotel on West Broadway (502) 583 1234 is much larger with 300 four-star rooms. Another Victorian house hotel is the Columbine Inn (502) 635 5000 on South Third Street, where you can sit on the porch overlooking their gardens. The Inn at The Park on South Fourth Street (502) 637 6930 also offers Victorian elegance with your B&B.

Within walking distance right downtown are a host of eateries. You could go for a pizza and beer with some live entertainment at Bearno's by the Bridge on West Main Street (502) 584 7437 or if seafood is your choice try Joe's Crab Shack on River Road (502) 568 1171 which is loud, lively and a lot of fun. A bit more up-market is the Bristol Bar & Grille at Riverfront Plaza (502) 562 0158 serving American and international cuisine; slightly more relaxed and reasonable is Deke's Marketplace Grill on West Market Street (502) 584 8337. Right on the river you can dine aboard the Star of Louisville at West River Road (502) 581 7827 or on the decks of Towboat Annies River Cafe (502) 589 2010 with its great view of the Ohio River.

If you'd like to take home a souvenir of your visit to Kentucky, why not stop off at The Festival Gallery on Fourth Avenue in Louisville (502) 581 1986 which stocks a wide range of racing art on the Derby and its heroes. Another place to relive some memories and pick up some memorabilia is the Kentucky Derby Museum (502) 637 1111 which has three floors of exhibits on thoroughbred racing and the Derby itself, as well as a gift shop.

If you need any information on where to stay or what to do, contact the Louisville Convention & Visitors Bureau, 400 South First Street, Louisville, Kentucky, USA 40202. Tel:(502) 584 2121 or visit their web site at www.louisville-visitors.com.

Artist: **Asad Kuri Montana A VIEW FROM A BAD STARTER** *Courtesy of:* **Mr Mark Hardiman**

Racing in California

Southern California's normally benign climate makes racing a year 'round pleasure. Don't worry about earthquakes or the El Nino effect, here in lotus land some of North America's top trainers such as D Wayne Lukas ply their trade, sometimes venturing farther afield to pluck top prize money. Actually it's surprising that they actually leave at all given the level of racing right at home. This is a spot to go racing under the palms in first class comfort before you head off to Malibu for some surfing, tour the big movie companies lots, see the original Disneyworld, shop on Rodeo Drive or cruise down Sunset Strip. California's got it all, and more! This State actually has nine racecourses and if you were visiting San Francisco for example it would be a shame not to not to put on a few exactors at Golden Gate Fields, or do the daily double at Del Mar in San Diego. The two top bets though are Hollywood Park and Santa Anita in the Los Angeles area.

Artist: **Asad Kuri Montana IN THE SAND** *Courtesy of:* **The Artist**

SANTA ANITA

Racing at Santa Anita goes back to 1907 but it was in 1933 that the present course was built and, while many changes have been made over the years, it still maintains its classic Art Deco design and park-like setting.

Santa Anita Park covers 320 acres and is situated in the suburb of Arcadia, about 14 miles north east of downtown Los Angeles and 30 miles from LA International Airport. Any one of a number of freeways will connect to the Interstate 210 Freeway to take you there by car; exit at Baldwin and turn right. When you arrive there is a choice of three parking areas: General Parking is $3, Preferred (a bit closer to the track) is $5, or you can have someone else park your car for $8 for Valet Parking.

You can contact the track at Los Angeles Turf Club, PO Box 808, Arcadia, California, USA 91066-0808. Tel: (626) 7223. Fax: (626) 574 9860. E mail: sainfo@santaanita.com. Web stie: santaanita.com. William Baker is the Chairman and CEO of the Los Angeles Turf Club, while Thomas Robbins is VP and Director of Racing.

Two race meetings are held here each year. The Oak Tree meeting runs for six to seven weeks in October and November, with about 32 days of racing. The longer winter/spring meeting traditionally opens just after Christmas and runs through mid-April. The Grade 1 Santa Anita Derby is California's 'Spring Classic' for three year-olds and is a major stepping stone to the Kentucky Derby. It is held on the first Saturday in April, exactly a month before the Derby, and many winners such as Triple Crown hero Affirmed have gone on to win the Run for the Roses after success in California. Other top races are the Santa Monica Handicap for older fillies and mares, also a Grade 1 race run at the end of January, the half million dollar Strub Stakes in early February, the San Luis Obispo Handicap over a mile and a half on the turf for four year olds and up in mid February and the $1 million Santa Anita Handicap over a mile and a quarter in early March. Santa Anita hosted the Breeders' Cup in 1984 and 1993 and will probably do so again, a testimonial to this excellent venue.

There are three levels, and prices, of admission to Santa Anita. A $5 General Admission allows you to wander around the Grandstand with its excellent views of the track and finishing line, the Infield with its picnic grounds and playground for the kids, the Paddock Room which is the ground floor of the grandstand with lots of betting, food and beverage facilities as well as the Paddock Gardens around the parade ring. The Club

House will set you back $8.50 and also has excellent facilities including dining tables overlooking the first turn on the track after the finish line. At the upper end of the scale at $10 on weekdays and $15 on weekends and holidays, the Turf Club is quite luxurious if a bit more formal, with reserved seats at the finish line and fine dining while you put on your bets. Reserved Club House and Grandstand seats are available only at busy weekends and holidays. If you go into the Grandstand and wish to upgrade to other areas you can do so by going to the Reserved Ticket Booth and Terrace Gate for the Club House or the Turf Club. Children under 17 are allowed in free if accompanied by an adult, as are those over 65 on certain special days. Box seats holding four to six people are also available for hire and most include a private television set. If you would like to reserve one, call (626) 574 6400.

There are a number of dining rooms and terraces, snack stands and bars located throughout the park. Dining facilities with full-service menus are located in the Club House and Turf Club. The Terrace Food Court, near the main grandstand entrance, feature a variety of self-service food. In the infield at the centre of the track, the Wine Shed offers deli-style food, beer and wines.

Santa Anita runs a number of programmes for people who like racing, including a 'Clocker's Corner' where you can watch the early morning workouts and have a bit of breakfast as well as handicapping classes with experts who will share their wisdom in picking winners. They are all free of charge. In fact if you need any information about anything at the track, check with the Patron Service Desks that are located throughout the grandstand.

HOLLYWOOD PARK

You certainly don't have to be a movie star to visit Hollywood Park, but you might just bump into a few while you are there. The course has been nicknamed "The track of Lakes and Flowers" and you will see why when you step inside. It has a beautifully picturesque setting and a spectacular view of the hills surrounding Hollywood. The movie star connection is in fact a very real one as the Hollywood Turf Club was founded by Jack L Warner of Warner Brothers films in 1938 and its original shareholders included Walt Disney, Bing Crosby and Sam Goldwyn. Always one step ahead of the pack, Hollywood boasts a number of 'firsts' including the introduction of the film patrol camera for use by the stewards in 1941, the first Sunday racing in 1973 and now the first racetrack to have its own casino.

Hollywood Park is to be found just three miles east of Los Angeles International Airport at the intersection of Century Boulevard and Prairie Avenue. Take the 105 or 405 Freeways to get there. If you need to contact the course, write to PO Box 369, Inglewood, California, USA 90306-0369, otherwise the street address is 1050 South Prairie Avenue, Inglewood, California USA 90301-4197. Tel: (310) 419 1500. Fax: (310) 419 8022. A virtual visit to their Web site can be arranged at www.hollywood-park.com. The men in charge at this excellent venue are Eual Wyatt Jr who is General Manager and Martin Panza, Racing Secretary.

Hollywood gives you a choice of three different places to watch the racing, dine or have a drink. General admission to the Grandstand and parade ring is only $6, while you could pay $9.50 to step up into the Clubhouse. For those wishing a little bit more luxury, try the Turf Club which carries a $25 admission charge.

Parking is all free no matter where you go and you get a free programme on entry. If you arrive by foot or bus, they knock $1.50 off these prices. Anyone under 30 years old gets in on Friday nights for only $1 and if you're over 62 you can attend on Wednesdays and Thursdays for a $3 discount. If you bring the kids, they are free of charge under 17 years and there is lots to keep them occupied with a playground and carousel at the North Park. Once you're inside, Hollywood offers a choice of over 30,000 seats in the grandstand and clubhouse, with another 3,000 in the Turf Club. There is also a wide variety of place to eat and drink, from a hot dog and beer to a four course meal in the Winners Circle dining room in the Clubhouse.

Hollywood has seen some notable stars of the equine variety over the years including the great Citation, the perennially tough John Henry and champion Affirmed who became racing's first $2 million winner in 1979 with a victory in the Hollywood Gold Cup. This was also the course that hosted the very first Breeders Cup meeting in 1984, the first of three held here, when 65,000 people jammed the place and bet almost $12 million! Hollywood completed a $100 million expansion in 1994 which included a golf and sports centre and the Hollywood Casino where you can play poker, black jack or bingo as well as bet on the simulcast races from as far away as Hong Kong - 24 hours a day of gambling pleasure.

There are two seasons of racing at Hollywood Park, from the end of April to July and November through December. Daily post times are 1:00 pm except Friday when racing moves to the evening with the first race at 7:00 pm. The big race of the spring and summer meeting is the $1 million Hollywood Gold Cup staged at the end

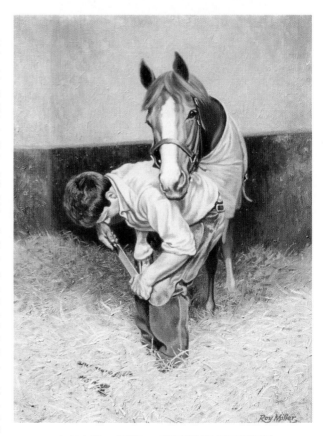

Artist: **Roy Miller MUTUAL RESPECT**
Courtesy of: **The Artist**

of June with a fine supporting card. Some legendary horses have won the Gold Cup over the years, including the great Cigar, Round Table, Swaps, Citation and Sea Biscuit. In the Autumn there is a three day Turf Festival held over the Thanksgiving Weekend that features six group races on the grass and attracts turf stars from across North America and Europe - a sure winner. There are lots of stars in Hollywood, but Hollywood Park has to be one of the biggest and brightest!

Southern California Local Favourites
There are so many things to see and do in southern California, you could spend a lifetime here - small wonder so many people move here for the good life. Hollywood Park is only ten minutes from the beach and 20 minutes from Beverly Hills and there are thousands of hotel rooms close at hand. Despite the traffic jams on the freeways, you really do need a car here to get around. Handy for either racetrack, the Beverly Wilshire Hotel (310) 275 5200 on Wilshire Boulevard in Beverly Hills offers the ultimate in luxury and star spotting possibilities. Also firmly in the top bracket are the Beverly Hills Hotel (310) 276 2251 also on Wilshire and the Radisson Plaza (310) 546 7511 in Manhattan Beach. A bit further away from Los Angeles, you could try the Ritz-Carlton (310) 823 1700 on Admiralty Way in Marina Del Ray. If you wanted to save a bit of money to play the ponies, try the budget priced Embassy Suites Hotel (310) 215 1000 on Airport Boulevard in LA or Motel 6 (310) 419 1234 on West Century. If you need any assistance with local information or hotels, there is a tourist information bureau in Los Angeles Airport

There is a wide choice of hotels that are all handy for a trip to Santa Anita, including the Doubletree Hotel (626) 792 2727, Ritz-Carlton Huntingdon Hotel(626) 568 3900 or Hilton Hotel (626) 577 1000, which are all in Pasadena. In Arcadia where the track is located you could stay at the Embassy Suites (626) 445 8525, the Hampton Inn (626) 574 5600 or the Santa Anita Inn (626) 446 5211. Arcadia also has a good choice of restaurants. You could try Anthony's for Italian food (626) 446 3171, go to Peppers (626) 446 5529 or the Arroyo (626) 821 2021 for Mexican specialties. If you like steak and seafood (known here as 'Surf and Turf') drop in to The Derby (626) 447 2430. A taste of the orient can be found at Tokyo Wako for Japanese (626) 351 8963 or the Panda Inn for Chinese in Pasadena (626) 793 7300. For more information about the Santa Anita area, call the Pasadena Convention and Visitors Bureau on (626) 795 9311.

If shopping is your game, you can do it 'til you drop and rub shoulders with the movie stars on Rodeo Drive in Beverly Hills. The Farmer's Market on West 3rd Street in Hollywood is also lots of fun and probably a lot less expensive, as is the Olivera Street area downtown with its Mexican-style marketplace with lots of shops, artisans and restaurants. Little Tokyo, the largest Japanese area in the USA is not far away on First and San Pedro Streets as is Chinatown, north of Sunset Boulevard between Almeda and Hill streets. While you're here you should make a pilgrimage and wish upon a star at Disneyland (714) 999 4565, stroll along the Hollywood Walk of Fame on Hollywood Boulevard and Vine Streets or take the tour at Universal Studios (818) 622 3801. If you've got time, hop on down to San Diego and play a few horses at Del Mar or cross the desert to Las Vegas for unlimited action, day and night.

Artist: **Susan Crawford PILSUDSKI** *Courtesy of:* **Rosenstiel's**

Racing in Australia

The Australian horse race that everyone in the world seems knows best is the Melbourne Cup. Held at the beginning of November at Flemington Racecourse in the city that gives its name to the prize, the Cup is the event that caps a month long series of races and brings the entire country to a halt for the day. In antipodean terms it's Royal Ascot, The Derby and Kentucky's Run for the Roses all rolled into one big blast of fun.

From an international perspective, it is also a race that more and more trainers and horses are taking a tilt at from far afield. At face value, the conditions for foreign contenders are horrendous - a long and tiring trip probably half way around the world to a different hemisphere, and then you face a two mile handicap probably carrying near top weight against a field of twenty or so top locals who have been primed to their best condition for weeks. But an Irish horse lifted the prize a few years ago and the names of Vintage Crop and Dermot Weld will forever be etched in Australian racing history.

For the foreign visitor the equine action leading to the Cup begins a month earlier at Caulfield with the 1,000 Guineas and Caulfield Cup, moves to Moonee Valley for the WS Cox Plate and continues at Flemington for the Victoria Derby. All of these races are major local events that bring out the Aussie punters in droves and provide a holiday atmosphere to some pretty topnotch racing action.

There are about twenty major racecourses in this sports loving nation and they are spread from Tasmania to the Northern Territory and across to Western Australia. The foreign punter though can find many a day's pleasure in those located in and around Sydney and in Melbourne, which has four courses including Flemington, Caulfield, Sandown and Moonee Valley, where they hold night racing under the lights.

The thoroughbred racing season stretches year round in Australia , with action both over the sticks and on the flat. The major flat races that will catch the visitor's eye though take place between the middle of August and the end of May, which is summer 'Down Under'. As the breeding season also flip-flops with the Northern Hemisphere there is also a growing business in shipping stallions from Europe and North America to the land of Oz to do double hemisphere duty. There are many stud farms around the major Australian racing and training centres and they are well worth a day out in themselves. If you want more information on the breeding side or stud farms, contact Mr Daryl Sherer, Thoroughbred Breeders Australia, 571 Queensberry Street, North Melbourne, 3051, Victoria Tel (+613) 9326 3966 Fax (+613) 9326 3866

To get into the mood before you go racing in Australia, try to dig out the video of the film that was made about the Aussie wonder horse, Phar Lap. He won just about everything worth winning in Australia, including the Melbourne Cup in 1930 under record top weight, before being shipped to the USA where his career ended somewhat tragically.

FLEMINGTON RACECOURSE

Flemington is situated about four miles west of the state of Victoria's capital city of Melbourne next to the Maribyrnong River. It is easily accessible from the city by car or tram and on race days by special trains or by boat along the river. The train arrives upsides the back of the main stands; if you're driving use Entrance A on the opposite side at the junction of the Smithfield and Ballarat roads to enter the large free parking area in the centre of the course; trainers and their horseboxes, and the disabled can use Entrance B, which takes them right next to the stand to the "Birdcage". This is the stabling area where horses are installed before racing and it got its name because it's here that Gentlemen racegoers used to show off their 'birds' or lady friends. You don't have to take your bird these days and it is open to the public.

Artist: **Harry Matthews WHIP CRACK**
Courtesy of: **The Artist**

The track is run by the Victoria Racing Club whose Chief Executive is Brian Beattie and they can be reached at 400 Epsom Road, Flemington, Australia, 3031. Tel: (03) 9258 4666. Fax: (03) 9258 4605. If you need to get in touch with the track itself call (03) 9371 7171. They also have a helpful website at WWW.vrc.net. au

Flemington has been the home of the Melbourne Cup since it was first run in 1861 and the race has been run each year here since on the first Tuesday in November. The main course itself is a wide, sweeping ellipse of about a mile and a half in circumference and is used for both flat and hurdle races. There is also a steeplechase course, with all brush fences, used for jump racing. Although it can hold up to 100,000 people (and does on Cup day!) it's a pretty course with a country feel to it. The Henry Cecils of this world and other rose fanciers can take note that it has one of the largest rose gardens in Australia which are carefully tended to show their best come the date of the Melbourne Cup. The best viewing of the course is from the Hill Stand opposite the winning post, which has four levels and has the full facilities for betting both with the bookmakers, the Tote, as well as restaurants, bars and snack bars. The newer Prince of Wales Stand next to it was opened by Prince Charles in 1985. There are also on-course shops selling souvenirs, clothes, books and videos, so you have no excuses not to bring something back for a friend.

Australia is one of the few places in the world outside Britain and Ireland that has private bookmakers on course and you can either bet with them or the Tote. The bookies here have already entered the computer age though, using electronic boards to record the bets. They also take bets by phone from off-course punters.

Although getting into the course on regular race days only costs a few dollars, understandably, admission prices do go up a bit when it comes to the big days of racing at Flemington for the four day Melbourne Cup Carnival which features the Cup itself, the Derby and the Oaks. Admission on Cup day with a reserved seat in the Lawn Stand will set you back A$82 (about £34), while admission alone is about A$25 (£10.50). The course offers various package deals which include reserved seats on each of the big race days and a four day package of admission and a reserved seat in the covered Hill Stand will cost you A$197 (£82) for example. The Hill Stand also has two top notch restaurants, The Panorama and The Skyline, but you will have to fork out about A$925 (£385) for a Panorama/Skyline 4-day package (Single days N/A).

Artist: **Hubert de Watrigant LE PARAPLUIE**
Courtesy of: **The Osborne Studio Gallery**

Melbourne Cup day brings out all kinds of people to the racetrack and offers lots of fun and entertainment, a lot like Australia and its people themselves. It's both the formal recognition of a champion in the making and a great excuse to squeeze a few tinnies, put a shrimp on the barby and let your hair down, so no matter how conservatively or crazily you dress to go there, you will be sure to have a good time. Just be sure to say G'day to your neighbour!

Melbourne Favourites
Despite the high rise buildings which first catch the eye, Melbourne still retains much of its Victorian architecture and this gives the city a pleasant, old fashioned feel at street level. You can 'go walk about' here as there are lots of pedestrian malls with interesting shopping and a wide variety of restaurants and bars. The Sovereign Hill area of the city is a place where you can go to relive the city's gold rush days. If you are a real sports fan, be sure to visit the Melbourne Cricket Ground, which is Australia's biggest sports stadium and can hold 100,000 spectators. It was built for the 1956 Olympics which

were held here and also contains a fascinating Cricket Museum. Not far away from Melbourne is the Yarra Valley which is famous the world over for its vineyards and wineries, some of which you can visit to sample the tipple before its exported. For those who'd like to see the local wildlife a bit closer, take a trip to Philip Island where you can cuddle a Koala, try to catch a Kangaroo or just watch the seals or penguins at play.

To find a bed for the night in Melbourne, you could try either the Grand Southern Cross Hotel (03 9653 0221) or The Sofitel Melbourne (03 9653 0000). Accomadation is also available at the popular Crown Towers Hotel (+613) 9292 8888 which is part of the Casino. Other possibilities are The Windsor (03 9653 0653) or the Hotel Como (03 9824 0400) in South Yarra. If you want to step out of an evening and sample some local brew, try the Victoria Hotel in Albert Park, the Palace Hotel, a favourite local hang-out, or the Fawkner Club which has an open-air courtyard. Restaurants abound in this city, with a wide choice of different types of cuisine. The Melbourne Oyster Bar (03 6702745) on King Street will do for seafood lovers, or they could try The Last Aussie Fishcaf (03 6991942) on Park Street in South Melbourne. For a taste of the orient try the Bamboo House (03 6621565) or the Flower Drum (03 66325313) which are both on Little Bourke Street.

Racing in Japan

If racing in Hong Kong seems all about large amounts of money changing hands, in Japan its more yen than most people can count. Huge crowds generate equally huge betting turnover and that in turn makes for exceptional prize money. The average prize money on offer for each race at top courses like Tokyo rings up well in excess of £100,000. If you were a foreign owner this might seem like the veritable pot of gold, but racing in Japan has long been closed to foreign horses except for a few Group races such as the Japan Cup. There are moves afoot however to open up racing to horses from other countries and this should add some interest for the visiting punter in the future. Japanese breeders have spent the rich pickings at the courses buying some expensive horse flesh for many years and you can go and visit studs such as Shadai Farm.

Japan has ten racecourses run by the Japan Racing Association spread around the country, including two Tokyo Racecourse and Nakayama which are near the capital. Racing takes place largely around the weekends from mid-March to mid-June and again from October to the end of the year when the international flavour is added in the form of the Japan Cup. There are also another thirty or so racecourses that are run by local authorities which offer various levels of thoroughbred racing in settings that range from large urban centres to small country courses.

TOKYO RACECOURSE

Tokyo Racecourse, or Fuchu as it's known to local punters, is the Newmarket of Japanese racing. Originally built in 1933, it has been updated and expanded ever since, most recently in 1993, to a commodious complex that attracts equally huge crowds of people when racing is held on Saturdays and Sundays during the season. The course actually lies in the Forest of Fuchu from which it derives its local name and from the stands you get a superb view of the famous Mount Fuji and you will be able to enjoy the racing in complete comfort either live or captured on huge television screens around the park. It's here that they hold the Japanese Derby for local three year-olds in the spring and cap it all off in the autumn with the International Japan Cup which sees horses from all over the world going for glory under their equally famous jockeys.

Mr. Akihito Sato is the General Manager of Tokyo Racecourse. Tel: 423 63 3141. Fax: 423 40 7070. You can visit the Japan Racing Association website, which has information on all the courses they run on www.jait.jrao.ne.jp which will give you the English language version.

To get to the racecourse it's probably best to take the metro underground train. Fuchu-keibaseimonmae Station on the Keio Line which departs from Shinjuku Station has a concourse that directly connects with the racecourse. It takes about thirty minutes to get there from Shinjuku. Alternatively, Fuchi-Honmachi Station also has a direct overhead passageway leading into the track's West Gate.

Basic admission to the course is only Y200 (about £1) which gives you access to all areas of the course except the reserved enclosure. Y500 (£2.50) gives you a reserved seat in the E area, while prices from Y1,500 (£7.50) (C area) to Y3,500 (£17) (S area) will provide you with admission and a reserved seat in various areas of the reserved enclosure. Some of the S reserved seats on the fifth and six floors are in pairs for couples (sounds cosy) and have a built-in TV monitor. The Grandstand can hold a staggering 200,000 people, just to put some scale on things and what's really amazing is that they actually have room to move around, see the horses and place their bets. It's called Memorial 60 as it was completed to commemorate the 60th anniversary of Tokyo Racecourse in 1993 and extended to stretch 460 metres or almost three furlongs - practically the entire length of the home stretch. Small wonder that this is the largest grandstand in the world! The course itself has four tracks. The turf track is the biggest at about a mile and a half around and inside are a dirt track, a steeplechase course (jump fans take note) and a training track. State-of-the-art might be an over-used expression these days but the facilities for fans here really qualify. Two giant

Turf Vision screens give you an excellent view of the action down the backstretch and the run to the finish line from any part of the grandstand. There is a large amphitheatre around the paddock so you can check on the condition of the horses before the race. Some of them wear some pretty strange looking headgear, but don't be put off! The winner's circle is a large area directly in front of the grandstand.

There are no fewer than 1,100 closed circuit TV monitors scattered throughout the racecourse and these provide information on the horse's weight (not a bad idea), pari-mutuel odds and dividends, as well as paddock views of the horses and the racing itself. In the first floor of the basement is a Video Hall with a giant screen. The course has its own video and book store called the PR Corner as well as an FM radio station just for racegoers on track. Try a bit of sushi in the Fast Food Plaza downstairs in the basement or for something a bit more formal there is the Restaurant New Tokyo on the third floor or the Restaurant Hotel Okura on the sixth floor.

No doubt you might come to Fuchu for the Japan Cup in November as it usually attracts a top notch field of international stars with their owners, trainers and jockeys. Under the guidance of Sir Michael Stoute in 1997 Pilsudski capped an incredible season by doing the Breeder's Cup -Japan Cup double, a truly remarkable achievement for a British horse. The top races of the spring season are the Yushun Himba (Japanese Oaks) for home bred three year old fillies, the Tokyo Yushun (Japanese Derby) for local colts and the NHK Mile Cup which is also open to foreign bred horses. Other Grade 1 races which also attract invited international horses are the Yasuda Kinen over a mile for older horses and the Emperor's Cup for three year olds and up. For National Hunt fans, there is at least one jump race included in the programmes for both spring and autumn, but you'd have to go to Nakayama to see the Japanese version of the Grand National!

While your here be sure to visit the JRA Racing Museum at the racecourse. It has some incredible hands-on displays where you can experience what it's like to be a jockey riding in a race and shows depicting the

Artist: **Katy Sodeau** *HEAD TO HEAD* *Courtesy of:* ***The Artist***

world's great races. Go into the Epsom Promenade where they have a 1/50 scale walk-through of Epsom Racecourse, Tokyo's sister course, where British punters can check out a bit of old Blighty. There's lots of things for children of all ages to do here as well, with pony and carriage rides in the infield as well as a miniature railway to take you around. If all this becomes a bit much and you need a bit of peace and quiet to study the form or contemplate zen and the art of motorcycle maintenance, sneak away to the Japanese Garden in the woods behind the paddock.

Tokyo Favourites

There's no shortage of things to see and do in sprawling Tokyo. The Ginza is this city's famous shopping area and most famous landmark for visitors and its busy both day and night. You might want to leave your cheque book or credit card at home though as many of the imported goods are more expensive here than at home. No wonder Japanese tourists do some hard shopping when they are out of the country on holiday.

Artist: **Peter Smith EBB TIDE**
Courtesy of: **Frost & Reed**

Still you could just go into some of the big Japanese department stores and enjoy being greeted by the staff with a bow when you enter or take the elevator - that doesn't happen in too many places anywhere else, but it certainly does in Japan! No trip to Japan would be complete without sampling some of the local fare and there are sushi bars dotted around everywhere. If you are daring try a bit of the Fugu. It's a puffer fish and if the chef has left in just a bit of the liver, you won't see the next sunrise! Perhaps a safer bet and often more palatable to western tastes is tepanyaki cooking where your party sits around a horse-shoe table sipping sake while the chef grills prawns or Kobe beef in front of you. Too much sake and the karaoke will no doubt beckon!

Not too far away from the racecourse, there are a number of superior hotels in Shinjuku, all catering to western tastes, including the Hotel Century Hyatt Tokyo (3 3349 0111), the Hotel Park Hyatt Tokyo (3 5322 1234), the Tokyo Hilton (3 3344 5111) and the Keio Plaza InterContinental Tokyo (3 3344 0111). Of course these are just a few of the many possible places to stay and if you wanted something a little bit closer to the Tea House of the August Moon, take a trip outside Tokyo to the countryside and you will have little problem finding a place to leave your shoes at the door. While eminently worthwhile, visiting Japan is certainly not cheap and let's hope you have a few winners at the races to help replenish your wallet!

Racing in Hong Kong

Perhaps it is the counterfoil to their otherwise industrious and conservative natures, but the people of Hong Kong love a punt on the horses and this makes racing, and betting, a big business in this former British colony. Of course it was the Brits who exported their rules and

regulations for the Sport of Kings back in the early nineteenth century and thoroughbred racing is organised here by the Hong Kong Jockey Club whose Chief Executive is Lawrence T. Wong. You can contact them at 1 Sports Road, Happy Valley, Hong Kong. Tel: (852) 2966 8111. Fax: (852) 2577 9036. E mail: jcinfo@hkjc.org.hk. Web site: www.hongkongjockeyclub.com

Some might say sadly not 'Royal' any more, but even though the Union Flag was lowered a few years ago, it's business as usual under the new regime and it will probably see thoroughbred racing spread rapidly throughout China during the coming years. Racing means money, money, money and here the profits from racing not only generate a thriving sport, but are used to support run social services and good causes which directly benefit the local population, including hospitals, clinics, schools, parks and swimming pools. The Jockey Club operates the Tote as well as the local lottery and generates a surplus after taxation of about HK$2 billion per season.. Racing here though is also a lot of fun and the quality of racing is excellent, with many trainers, horses and jockey's coming from around the world to capture some big prize money.

Hong Kong has two racecourses in Sha Tin and Happy Valley and between them 78 race meetings will be held in the 1999/2000 racing season between early September and late June. Meetings are held most Saturdays and Wednesdays and some Sundays, each attracting an average crowd of 38,500 racegoers oncourse who stake several million betting tickets a race meeting. Betting turnover here is the highest in the world per person and added up to a massive HK$81.billion last season. The highlight of the year and probably of most interest to visitors are the Hong Kong International Races which attract leading horses, trainers and jockeys from all over the world.

SHA TIN RACECOURSE

Sha Tin is the modern showpiece of Hong Kong racing, having been built on reclaimed land and opened in 1978. It's here during the first half of December that the big races are held around the course's large sweeping oval. The big date of the year here is the Hong Kong International Races which include the Hong Kong Cup (G1), Hong Kong Mile (G2), Hong Kong Vase (G2) and Hong Kong Sprint (L). Horses competing in these races come from Australia, Europe, New Zealand, Malaysia & Singapore as well as North America, Japan and the United Arab Emirates, so you might be excused if you don't get the form right at first try. Accompanying the race meeting is also a top international sale of thoroughbreds which attracts buyers from almost as far afield. Other highlights of the year include the Hong Kong Derby run in March, the Hong Kong Gold Cup in March and the Queen Elizabeth II Cup held in the middle of May.

Hong Kong prize money is well endowed by the high tote turnover and some of the world's top jockeys are invited to come here to compete for a season or two on a regular basis, while others fly in for the big races.

Located in Hong Kong's New Territories, you can get to Sha Tin from the centre of town very easily by bus, train or taxi. Once there it will cost you HK$10 (about £1 or US$1.60) to get into the course or HK$50 (£5) to get into the Members' Enclosure. If you are a visitor to Hong Kong, take your passport with you if you wish to buy admission to the Members' at the main gate.

Sha Tin hosts a total of about 45 race meetings throughout the season, split between day and night racing. Most are run over the main turf course, but others take place on the all-weather track and a few are mixed all-weather and turf. A nine-race card in the afternoon starts at 1:30 pm, while for a ten-race fixture the first race is moved back to 1:00 pm. Night meetings begin at 6:30 pm and take place on Saturday or Sundays.

Inside the course, which can hold up to 85,000 people, there are lots of restaurants and fast-food stalls to choose from. There are two huge grandstands where you won't have any problem finding a seat, as well as the Club Building overlooking the winning line with a view straight down the finishing straight. A huge colour TV screen also helps the view from ground level. Grandstand 2 connects directly with the railway station, while Grandstand 1 has the parade ring to its rear. There is also a special visitors box for tourists to use, as well as a number of private boxes.

HAPPY VALLEY

Despite its verdant, almost pastoral, name, Happy Valley's situation makes Longchamp or Belmont Park seem way out in the middle of the country. The course is right in the centre of the city, surrounded by tall buildings and making it an absolutely unique urban amphitheatre of equine action. Some have claimed the land on which Happy Valley is situated is the world's most expensive piece of real estate and it would be hard to disagree judging by the buildings which frame it.

Happy Valley is so close to the centre of Hong Kong that you could just as easily walk there as take a bus, subway train or taxi. Admission follows the same pattern here as Sha Tin at HK$10 (about £1 or US$1.60) to get into the course or HK$50 to get into the Members' Enclosure. Don't forget to take your passport with you to buy admission to the Members' at the main gate. The course also has the usual array of wining and dining possibilities in restaurants and fast food stalls, as well as a visitors' box for tourists. There is a high-rise complex of stands overlooking the straight and the finish line and with a large colour TV screen in the middle of the infield, you won't miss a thing at this relatively tight track. Make sure you back a jockey who knows his way around!

Happy Valley holds about 30 meetings a year, also split between day and night racing and all on the turf. A nine-race card in the afternoon commences at 1:30 pm, while for a ten-race fixture the first race is moved back to 1:00 pm. Night meetings begin at 6:30 pm on Wednesdays and sometimes the odd Tuesday, and an hour later if held on a Saturday.

The course also contains the fascinating Hong Kong Racing Museum situated next to the Happy Valley stand which is well worth a visit if you can spare the time.

For those more interested in flexing their credit cards than racing, the Causeway Bay shopping and entertainment complex is just a five minute walk from the course.

Hong Kong Favourites

There is so much choice in Hong Kong, you could easily spend weeks here and still not find your shopping list exhausted. Anything made to measure, from shirts to suits, are an absolute bargain compared with prices anywhere else and once they've got your measurements you can re-order from anywhere in the world (provided your shape stays the same!). If you want a suit try William Cheng (2739 7888) - outstanding value and they can make them in three days! There are hundreds of restaurants to choose from and a lot of the better ones are housed in the plethora of first class hotels that can be found in Hong Kong.

The Excelsior (2837 6840) situated in the harbour front in Causeway Bay is an excellent choice with numerous restaurants. Have a drink in Tutts on the 34th floor for a view that will take your breath away. Another choice is the Mandarin Oriental (2522 0111) for more fine dining, breathtaking views and true elegance. You could also try the Hong Kong Renaissance (2375 1133) or the Hotel Nikko (2739 1111). Closer to Sha Tin, the Regal Riverside Hotel and the Royal Park Hotel also come highly recommended. There is also a large shopping mall in Sha Tin about a five minute ride from the racecourse.

The pace of Hong Kong is extremely frenetic. Visit the Banking Centre and if you can, go up the Peak in a tram - there's a fantastic harbour view and find the little bar and restaurant which nestles here - it's an absolute beauty. When arranging a visit to Hong Kong , talk to the major airlines - they offer some tremendous fly and stay deals at some really first class hotels. The flag may have changed in Hong Kong but so much still remains the same - it is a city that is thoroughly recommended.

Artist: **Terence Gilbert DUBAI WORLD CUP**
Courtesy of: **The Artist**

Imagine a green oasis in the middle of the desert, imagine also the finest selection of the world's thoroughbreds, imagine also a watering hole of genuine excellence - well this is racing in Dubai. The richest race in the world, the US $4 million Dubai World Cup, may attract your immediate attention, but in racing terms it is just the tip of the iceberg in this land of oil, sheikhs and stallions. Although everything in Dubai might look shiny, new and modern on the surface, it really just masks the long history of racing in this part of the world. It is, after all, where the modern day thoroughbred originated and where the power behind one of the most successful thoroughbred operations in the world lie today in the form of the rulers of Dubai, the Maktoum family, led by its head Sheikh Mohammed.

It may be rather ironic that when British aristocracy went shopping for horses to be bred for racing in the eighteenth century they ended up in this part of the world and the sires they brought home formed the original stock from which all thoroughbreds racing today are descended. Now, fuelled by the wealth of black gold, Arab sheikhs and princes comb the world for the best horses money can buy and bringing some of them home to breed and race.

During the past decade, Dubai has sprung up almost magically to be one of the top tourist destinations in the world, and now it's also a place where the visitor can enjoy some excellent racing during the winter months. The most important factors contributing to this have been the formation of the Godolphin Stable by Sheikh Mohammed which now sees some of the world's best horses returning here for a bit of rest and recreation each winter, the building of Nad al Sheba as the country's showpiece track, and the institution of the world's richest race, the US$4 million Dubai World Cup to tempt foreign owners and trainers to bring their champions here to win the big prize.

Racing in the United Arab Emirates is run by the Emirates Racing Association and you can contact them at Suite 203, City Tower 1, PO Box 1178, Dubai. Tel: (9714) 313311. Fax: (9714) 313322. Michael Osborne is the Chief Executive. Perhaps reflecting their keen interests in horses and racing the UAE actually has five racecourses, Nad al Sheba, Jebel Ali, Abu Dhabi, Sharjah, and the Ghantoot Racing and Polo Club and they all run have fixtures run on various days of the week during the winter season run under the auspices of the Emirates Racing Association. If the action at these five doesn't quite satisfy your appetite, you could always take in a bit of camel racing which is held a stone's throw from Nad al Sheba at the Dubai Camel Racetrack - it's an amazing sport!

NAD AL SHEBA

A patch of scrubby desert on the edge on the edge of the town of Zabeel just a decade ago, Nad al Sheba now glistens in the sun as a green jewel for equestrian sport. Of course it has taken enormous amounts of money to build this fine complex, but it is now reaping dividends as a new centre of world class racing and, lured as ever by rich prize money, owners and trainers from around the world now bring their best stock to race each March, joined by some of the best international jockeys. Where the best go, the rest usually follow and Dubai is now firmly on the map as a place where the lover of horse racing is pencilling in his next trip.

Although he might be one of the richest men in the world, Sheikh Mohammed is very much a hands-on

Artist: **Klaus Philipp FINISH**
Courtesy of: **The Artist**

horseman and he has applied the same approach to building and running Nad al Sheba. Since the first race was run here in 1992, there have been many improvements and additions that make the expression 'state of the art' an understatement.

Nad al Sheba is run by the Dubai Racing Club and you can contact them at Suite 203, City Tower 1, Sheikh Zayed Road, PO Box 1178, Dubai, United Arab Emirates. Tel: (9714) 329888. Fax: (9714) 329777. Ali Khamis Al Jafleh is the Chairman and Kevin Greely the Racing Secretary.

You could probably spot this oasis from a satellite orbiting the earth, but to be a little more precise the racecourse is located about three miles south east of the city of Dubai and if you are driving there it is signposted on the Dubai to Abu Dhabi Road at the Metropolitan Hotel junction or from the roundabout close to the Dubai Polo Club and Country Club. When you get there you can park your car for nothing in the general area; if you already have a badge there is a special area reserved for you at the rear of the grandstand.

General admission to the course is free and this allows you to go just about anywhere. You also get a complimentary programme and form guide! However you will probably wish to go into the Club House area as well and you can buy a day badge for DHs 70 (about £12 or $19) at the entrance to it. Club House admission also gives you access to the Dubai Golf and Racing Clubs' members box on the second floor of the grandstand with its great view of the course. There are a total of 4,000 seats for spectators in the grandstand so you shouldn't have too much problem finding a seat. There is a wide variety of food and drinks in the Club House, as well as the Spike Bar and Links Steakhouse restaurant where you can dine surrounded by cowboy memorabilia. There are also some 14 private boxes for hire; the availability of these might be somewhat limited as they are sold primarily to the corporate market, but it might be worth enquiring with the course if you wish to entertain a group of people.

In the public enclosure you can dress casually, but those in the Club House or private boxes are encouraged to don 'smart casual' attire. Of course Dubai being an Arab country, women are expected to dress 'modestly', which means the extremities should be appropriately covered. The course has a Ladies Day during the racing season and it's an event when the smartest clothing is pulled out of the wardrobe.

The high rolling punter will have a bit of difficulty getting a bet on here as gambling per see is not allowed under Islamic law. However, to give everyone a sporting chance at winning something, there is a free 'competition' to win big cash prizes. A Pick 6 (selected winners of all six races) competition is held every race meeting and carries a prize fund of DHs 40,000 (£7,000 or $11,000). There are also other prizes for picking the forecast in the Fifth race, as well as a Big 5 Jackpot where you have to name the first five horses home in correct finishing order. In the third and fourth races there is a Daily Double, although here you are invited to select the first three finishers in correct order to claim the loot. You may not be able to battle with the bookies or tap into the tote in Dubai, but you might just come away with some extra cash and one thing's for sure, as it's free to enter you won't lose your shirt!

There are usually six or seven races per fixture and as it would be unwise for man or beast to exert themselves in the heat of the desert sun, racing is held at night under the lights when things cool down a bit. Post time for the first race is at 7:00 pm, except during Ramadan in January when it moves to 9:00 pm. Four of Dubai's trainers use Nad al Sheba as their training base and they usually work out the horses between 6:00-9:00 am each morning. You can have breakfast at the track in the morning and watch them go through their paces.

Racing at Nad al Sheba is staged from the beginning of November until the third week in April on Sundays and Thursdays. The only exception to the usual fixture arrangements is the Dubai World Cup meeting itself which is held on a Saturday at the end of March. Although it has only been run four times since its inception in 1996, the World Cup has established itself as a major Group 1 fixture in the international racing calendar and, in addition to the 30,000 spectators on-course, it is beamed to millions around the world who watch eagerly on television. Tense anticipation and exciting finishes have been the order of the day so far. The first running of this mile and a quarter race on the sand saw the legendary Cigar extend a long winning streak and win narrowly under jockey Jerry Bailey. The second year saw the Sir Michael Stoute trained Singspiel stay on up the stretch to capture the prize for Sheikh Mohammed at his home track, while the third thrilling finish was provided by winner Silver Charm who beat Swain by the width of a nostril. These will be tough acts to follow, and it will be worthwhile going there to see it in person.

The World Cup is supported on the same card by the mile and a quarter Dubai Duty Free, which although it serves as a consolation race for horses not qualified for the World Cup itself, would be the feature race on any other card with US$ 500,000 in prize money to be won. Horses from Britain and Europe may always be at a bit of a disadvantage when running on dirt, but the way some of them have adapted gives hope for the future. If you want to see how the Sheikh Mohammed maroon and white silks or his Godolphin blue fare over the winter season this is the place to go. The added attraction of a host of world class jockeys in action is another great bonus.

For more information on the Dubai World Cup, write to Suite 213, City Tower 1, PO Box 1178, Dubai, United Arab Emirates. Tel: (9714) 322277. Fax: (9714) 322288. E mail: dubaiwcp@emirates.net.ae. Web site: www.dubai worldcup.com.

Dubai Favourites

Although the racing might be the sport that lures you to this part of the world, as many thousands of people have already found out, it is now one of the top destinations in the world for an all round winter holiday with some almost-guaranteed great weather. The second running of the Dubai World Cup may have been a wash-out but it only serves to prove the general rule that in Dubai the sun always shines. This means that you can partake of any other sport at your leisure including sailing or windsurfing, golf on several different courses, polo, or treks into the desert on all-terrain vehicles or by camel! With many people coming here to work from all over the world, Dubai has quite a cosmopolitan flavour and the choice of restaurants, from Mexican or Lebanese to Indian and Italian, as well as bars and nightlife is also pretty impressive.

If you have taken the children with you, or feel a bit young at heart yourself, you could visit the new Wonderland theme park on the edge of Dubai Creek. Not too far away, but worth a visit is Sharjah with its Arabic souk or marketplace where you can shop for antiques, jewellery or oriental rugs.

There should be little problem finding accommodation here as there is a wide range of choice and location, almost all of it to high international-class standards. Some to note in the luxury category would be the Hatta Fort Hotel ((085 23211), the Hilton Beach Club (9714 445333) or the Metropolitan Hotel (9714 440000) which is closest to the racecourse itself. The Jumeriah Beach (9714 480000) as its name suggests is close to the seaside. A little less luxurious perhaps and at a lower tariff, you could try the Imperial Suites Hotel (9714 515100), Astoria Hotel (9714 534300) or the Palm Beach Hotel (9714 525550). Anywhere you choose, you are likely to come to the conclusion that Dubai is a future winner for a holiday.

Artist: **Harry Matthews CAPE VERDI**
Courtesy of: **The Artist**

Point-to-Pointing in Britain

Artist: *Heather St Clair Davis* BRUSH FENCE, WINDSOR WOODS, GREAT MEADOW
Courtesy of: Frost & Reed

There is literally no better way to get to the 'grass roots' of racing than to park your car in a muddy field and soak up the unique atmosphere of the Point-to-Point world. During the season, which runs from January to June, hundreds of thousands of people do just that and enjoy a countryside day out for the whole family at a price that won't break the budget.

Most hunts charge between £10 and £20 per car load of people no matter whether you arrive in a Land Rover or a Mini, but others have begun to charge by the head, say £5 or so and children are usually free. Here there are no officials or artificial barriers to tell you where to stand according to the price of your badge because the great thing about Point-to-Points is that everyone can go anywhere they like, save the refreshments marquee of the local sponsor or the loos of the opposite sex! Although, you never know, invitations to those might be forthcoming after a few warming libations break down what few barriers there are.

Although there are sure to be lots of opportunities to sample the hospitality and home-made cooking of the local Hunt that stages the event, be sure to pack a picnic in the boot and whatever your favourite tipple may be, to share with friends. A pound or two will get you a programme, complete with form guide, and there will be lots of bookies to pit your wits against to try to win your tenner back.

As all the riders are amateurs of varying levels of ability, shapes and sizes, it might be a good idea to check out the human form in the parade ring as well as the equine conformation as it's generally unwise to back a horse, no matter how fit and well turned out, if it is ridden by a fourteen stone plus owner who looks as though he should take up Sumo wrestling instead.

But let's have three cheers for these eager amateurs who take their steeds over the many fences of a three or four mile race, often in the worst of weather conditions with little hope of much reward, barring a nice bit of silverware and a modest cheque that hardly covers the cost of the petrol to get the horsebox there in the first place. The infectious love of the sport is what drives them on, and the support and encouragement of their family and friends who turn up in droves to cheer them on. Where else can anyone get a World Cup winning ovation just for completing the course!

There's serious business though lurking amongst all the fun. Today there are about as many Point-to-Point horses in training as National Hunt horses and many successful young Point-to-Point horses go on to race well under Rules and can prove just as valuable in the horse buying and selling business. Ireland has a whole industry that breeds and brings along young horses, many of which end up crossing the Irish Sea for large amounts of money. A well conformed Strong Gale five

Artist: **Heather St Clair Davis** COUNTRY MEET *Courtesy of:* **Frost & Reed**

year old with a maiden win in Irish Points can be worth its weight in gold, such is the rising level of competition in the British Pointing world.

The rule says that horses must be fairly hunted a certain number of times during the fox hunting season to qualify for Point-to-Point races. Although it is hard to imagine some of these gleaming steeds spending hours chasing hounds and foxes across the moor, the conditions for qualification at least impose some sort of order about who races against whom. The annual day of Point-to-Point racing tops up the coffers of the Hunt that organises it and keeps subscriptions at a reasonable level for most members. Also, as the Countryside Alliance has pertinently pointed out in its defence of mounted hunting, if there were no fox or stag hunting, there would be no Point-to-Points.

Most Point-to-Points have at least six races, but if entries are large some may be split into several divisions and it is not uncommon to find a ten race card on offer. The trick for the organisers then is to get them all run before the winter twilight dissolves into night. In some cases the first race may be brought forward half an hour so it is best to check the local newspaper for details closer to the date. All the sporting papers and many dailies carry the latest details of meetings. The printed programme will give you details on each type of race, whether it is for maidens (horses which have never won a race), confined, restricted, or Opens for Ladies or Gentlemen, or both.

For the Point-to-Point community, the highlight of the season often takes place at Cheltenham, Sandown, Stratford, or Aintree where the best horses and riders take each other on over the 'big fences' in Hunter Chase races. Certainly, the Foxhunter's at both Cheltenham and Aintree offer the supreme tests and it takes a very good horse indeed to win one of these, but the Horse and Hound Cup at Stratford can offer just as much of a challenge.

Perhaps, these big occasions excepted, half of the fun at most Point-to-Points is the friendly country carnival atmosphere and the chance to meet many local people if you are visiting unfamiliar places around the country. They are great places to find out what is going on, the best pubs and places to stay. Of course it helps to have even the most tenuous connection with hunting or racing, but please don't go on about 'ferret racing' as Flat racing is sometimes referred to. To most of these people there is only one kind of racing and that means going over four feet of packed birch. Nevertheless, a warm welcome usually awaits you at the bar run by volunteers from the local Hunt and if you buy someone a drink you'll probably have made a friend for life.

If you are with the family, make sure everyone is prepared for the worst of British weather. If things get really foul, a retreat to the car will help maintain family sanity and if you have arrived early enough to pick a good viewing spot you might just stay there and not miss much of the action anyway. A good rule of thumb to ensure the best parking spot is to arrive at least one hour before the first race and park next to any vehicle that looks like it might have been there since the last Point-to-Point!

There are roughly 120 Point-to-Point courses in England, Scotland and Wales, or put another way, about twice as many as the Flat and National Hunt courses in Britain so there are lots to choose from when going Pointing. Although there are a few, such as those at Hexham, Fakenham, Wolverhampton, Market Rasen and Wetherby, that have been constructed inside the National Hunt course and enjoy use of their facilities,

the vast majority are put up on farmers' fields. They generally offer little in the way of permanent weather-proof amenities, but as the tents and marquees spring up magically on raceday, the course leaps to life like a Bedouin encampment. The viewing can vary with the proximity or absence of a convenient hillside on which to park the car, but they are often situated in some of the best scenery Britain has to offer. Some courses are used several times a season. Almost all meetings now take place on Saturdays, bank holidays and on Sundays, which are extremely popular, so there is little excuse not to pack your field glasses, thermos, sausage rolls and a bottle of tipple and set out in good time to enjoy the fun from mid-January to June.

Let's have a tour of the Point-to-Point courses in England, Scotland and Wales and you can see just how close some of this fun takes place to your town or how close to a meeting you may be if you plan to take a trip to visit 'foreign' parts. We have organised our trip around the country according to the Point-to-Point Association's own areas.

For further information you should contact the Point-to-Point Secretary for a particular area. As these sometimes change from year to year, a current list may be obtained through the Point-to-Point Secretaries Association. There are also commercial telephone lines which are listed in the sporting newspapers and which charge a prevailing 0891 rate (usually 39p per minute). These give weekly updates on fixtures, the state of the going, meeting times, race details and directions and they are an excellent way of obtaining the latest information.

DEVON & CORNWALL

Bishops Court near **Ottery St. Mary** is a Devon course that offers superb viewing. This relatively flat, tight course is located one mile south west of the town, off the B3174. The East Devon hold a meeting here at the beginning of March.

The scenic old **Buckfastleigh** racecourse a few miles west of Torquay off the A38 is the setting for the fixtures of the South Pool Harriers in late February and the Dart Vale and Haldon Harriers a month later in March.

Those planning to visit **Lifton** in Devon, the scene for the Tetcott Foxhounds meeting in early May and the South Tetcott Foxhounds raceday a few weeks later, will not be at all disappointed with the very good viewing of this relatively recent addition to the south western circuit. For both horse and rider the course is undulating and quite sharp. It is located three miles north of Launceston, two miles off the A30.

Bratton Down, ten miles north of South Molton off the B3226, is also the scene of some exciting late season action beginning in late April with the meeting of the Tiverton Staghounds. In May the Dulverton West Foxhounds hold their racing here, with the Exmoor Foxhounds finishing the season off in the balmy early summer of June. Point-to-Point racing has been held on this gently undulating course for several generations and the extended uphill finish can produce some exciting climaxes. Viewing is best from the centre of the course and between the races you can enjoy excellent views of Exmoor.

A course of even longer standing is **Kilworthy**, which first held Point-to-Point racing when the Great War was a recent memory. Located one mile north of Tavistock and the same distance west of the A386, this is a predominantly flat, galloping course that tests the stamina of horses and the eyesight of spectators, so please remember to pack your field glasses in order to follow your selection at the farthest point of the course. On the home stretch, though there are few problems in discerning winners and losers as there is good viewing of the long straight to the finish. Mark this venue down in your diary for the end of March when the Lamerton Foxhounds hold their meeting. Also near Tavistock is **Cherry Brook** where the Spooner's and West Dartmoor hold their annual fixture in early April.

Artist: ***David Trundley FLETE PARK*** Courtesy of: ***The Artist***

Good viewing can also be found at **Hockworthy**, six miles west of Wellington between the M5 and the A361. This undulating course with its uphill finish is home to the usual mid-week fixture of the Tiverton Foxhounds halfway through April.

Those setting off from Plymouth might keep in mind another popular Devon location in **Flete Park**, once the home of the great National Hunt amateur jockey, Lord Mildmay and after whom the second most famous course at Aintree is named. Proceed two miles north of Modbury, and about ten miles east of Plymouth, north of the A379 you will find this demanding course which suits horses that can stay the distance. April is the time that the Dartmoor Foxhounds hold their meeting here, while the Modbury Harriers host a fixture in early May. The course offers reasonably good viewing.

A few miles south of Exeter brings you to the **Black Forest Lodge** course near Kenton off the A380 where the Silverton Foxhounds offer a fine day out with entertainments for children as well as bars, hot food and trade stands. Their fixture usually takes place in early January, followed by the Mid Devon which have a Sunday fixture in mid-February. The spring sunshine of the early May bank holiday sees the Stevenstone Foxhounds put on their races at the Devonshire course of **Vauterhill**, nine miles south of Barnstaple, off the B3217.

The Point-to-Point course at **Bishopsleigh** located nine miles north east of Crediton, east of the A377, has

had some of its viewing problems sorted out over the years and now has good viewing on offer. The redesigned layout has also taken out some of the qualities that made it a stern test of a horse's stamina. The Easter Bank Holiday Monday is the date that the Eggesford Foxhounds usually hold their annual meeting.

Umberleigh's lone meeting of the Torrington Farmers' Foxhounds in June sadly ends what is now a full almost six month Point-to-Point season. Perhaps because they will have to wait another six months to begin another season is the reason so many people turn up to view the action on this tight, up and down hill course which may be found five miles south east of Barnstaple, adjacent to the A377. It is best to move around in the middle of the course not to keep warm as is the case earlier in the season, but to make the best of seeing both the horses and the panoramic view.

Cornwall may not have the wide choice of courses that Devon enjoys, but there are probably enough to keep a tin miner happy. Certainly **Great Trethew** offers the spectator more than adequate viewing of the majority of this hilly, testing course with its climb to the finish. It may be found three miles south east of Liskeard and one mile south of the A38. The second week in February is the time to make the meeting of the East Cornwall Foxhounds, while the South Cornwall Foxhounds usually hold their meeting in early March.

Another fixture to note at the end of February is that of the East Cornwall at **Lemalla**, six miles south west of Launceston, south of the A30. Unfortunately the viewing isn't very good at this sharp, undulating course.

A couple of hunts including the North Cornwall Foxhounds enjoy meeting at the popular Royal Showground site at **Wadebridge**, Cornwall, one mile west of the town and adjacent to the A39. This event normally takes place in early February. The course itself is a bit twisting and slightly undulating and has

Artist: ***David Trundley DAY'S END, UMBERLEIGH***
Courtesy of: ***The Artist***

fair viewing. The showground facilities are also used by the Western Foxhounds who hold their meeting about mid-March. The Four Burrow Foxhounds put on a popular bank holiday fixture at Easter, on a new course at Trebudannon near St Columb, Cornwall. The viewing is excellent on this left-handed circuit and the course has the distinction of being the most southwesterly location in Britain. You can find it about five miles from the A30 on the Newquay road.

Mounsey Hill Gate is in neither Cornwall nor Devon, but this Somerset course is the annual venue for the Dulverton East Foxhounds annual meeting in the pleasant climes of late May. The course is situated four miles north of Dulverton adjacent to the B3223. It is extremely tight with sharp bends and offers adequate viewing.

THE WEST COUNTRY

The West Country has a long established tradition of racing horses over obstacles and so it is not surprising to find a wide and interesting variety of Point-to-Point courses to choose from. The Point-to-Point Association's Taunton area actually covers the four counties of Somerset, Avon, Dorset and Wiltshire so be sure to fill up the petrol tank before setting off in the motor.

Larkhill in Wiltshire has long been one of the premier venues for racing in this part of the world and the level of competition at many of the meetings here is of the highest calibre. The course was built about 50 years ago and is owned by the Army, which explains why so many of its meetings have military connections. It is situated about three miles north west of Amesbury, west of the A345, and just a short drive from Salisbury. For those starved of action since the previous season, Larkhill is the place to head as the Army meeting is usually held in mid January—please note the late morning start. A few weeks later you could return to take in the Royal Artillery, and a fortnight or so after that the United Services Hunt meeting. The Staff College and RMA Draghounds also hold their meeting here in early March, followed by the New Forest Buckhounds at the end of March and the South and West Wilts Hunt at the end of April. The winter meetings can bring some testing, windy weather conditions to bear down on the spectator, but the going conditions on this galloping course are usually good, no matter what the weather. Although you may seem a little distant from the action the viewing is good and there are some permanent facilities in which to find some shelter.

Moving south towards Bournemouth and Poole we find the Dorset course of **Badbury Rings**, adjacent to the B3082 and about five miles south east of Blandford. This is a National Trust beauty spot and so the scenery is more than a match for the racing. Viewing is excellent at this sweeping, rectangular course which usually enjoys the benefit of good going no matter what the early season weather may bring. The racing gets underway here in February with the meeting put on by the Hursley Hambledon Hunt. In March the Wilton usually host their meeting followed by the Portman in April.

Staying in the same county we find **Little Windsor**, home to the Cattistock meeting which is usually held at the beginning of April. The course can be found four miles south of Crewkerne and two miles west of the A3066. A second fixture is also held here a few weeks earlier in mid-March by the Seavington Hunt.

The apple cider country of Somerset has a number of popular Point-to-Point courses within its boundaries.

Holnicote, located alongside the A39, three miles west of Minehead and two miles east of Porlock, is one to be noted for its picturesque setting, something that might be overlooked by the horses as they slog through the sometimes heavy going. Spectators might as well admire the scenery for the little they can see of the horses, as there are few places from which to follow the race at this flat, sharp course. The weather is usually fine enough to spread the picnic blanket on the grass if you decide to go to the Devon & Somerset Staghounds meeting in May, or the Minehead Harriers & West Somerset fixture a week or so later.

Kingston St Mary is a relatively recent addition to the Somerset Point-to-Point scene. The course, situated at Fennington Farm three miles north of Taunton and east of the A358, has reasonable viewing of a twisting circuit that leads horse and jockey up and down hills on a virtually constant series of bends. The Taunton Vale host their meeting here on Easter Monday. A hunt that formerly used this venue, the West Somerset Vale, now hold their April meeting at **Cothelstone** which nestles in the Quantocks a few miles north west of Taunton, off the A358. Two other hunts, the Quantock Staghounds and the Weston & Banwell Harriers, also hold fixtures here usually in March and May. A single fixture is held at **Cotley Farm**, two miles south of Chard, Somerset, and the length of the Epsom Derby off the A30. There is very good viewing of the races put on by the Cotley Hunt at their Bank Holiday Monday meeting in early May. This is a galloping, undulating course which suits horses that can go the distance and sometimes throws up a big priced winner. The Blackmore and Sparkford Vale host their annual meeting in early April at **Charlton Horethorne**, six miles south west of Wincanton off the B3145.

Early season action takes place in February when the South Dorset Hunt host their annual racing get together at **Milborne St Andrew** in Dorset, four miles east of Puddletown and south of the A354. Dorset seems to have a surfeit of places with names that bring back memories of childhood innocence, but there is nothing puerile about the racing here on this flat, galloping course which has reasonably good viewing.

Although located in Devon, **Stafford Cross** is the scene of the action for the annual meeting of the Axe Vale Harriers, whose Point-to-Point fixture in April is part of the Taunton circuit. The course is located three miles west of Seaton, adjacent to the A3052 and has been going for over 50 years. With its pretty setting, everyone should enjoy a visit here although those whose interests lie more particularly with the racing action might be disappointed with the lack of opportunity to view it. It's a flat, relatively easy course which produces some quickly run events.

THE SOUTH EAST

Inmates of the nation's capital don't have to wait until the hop-picking season to escape to the Kentish countryside as the Point-to-Point season gets underway on the South East circuit in early February.

Charing, about five miles north west of Ashford off the A20, is the scene of a couple of early season fixtures. Those packing their hampers won't have to travel too far from their cars to enjoy some good viewing of the South East Hunt's club meeting at the end of Feburary or the Mid Surrey Farmers Draghounds fixture a few weeks earlier. The Ashford Valley Hunt hold their races around early April on this well drained undulating course that suits stayers. Viewing is best from inside the course.

Also in Kent is **Detling**, three miles north east of Maidstone and north of the A249, home to the West Street Tickham Hunt fixture, usually in March. The course is easily approached by the M2 and the M20 and the good viewing from the centre of the course makes it worth a visit. The racing surface is virtually flat, so it is best to put your money on a horse that likes a good gallop and is able to stay on through the slight uphill finish

Good viewing is also found at **Aldington**, six miles south east of Ashford and south of the A20 where the East Kent Hunt holds a meet on Easter Monday. This is another undulating course which will put a horse's staying ability to the test if some rain has got into the ground.

Yet another Kent venue is at **Penshurst**, four miles south west of Tonbridge and west of the B2188. Alas, although you will have ample room to park your car, actually seeing the race will be a bit problematic as the viewing is not so good here. But in the hunting world the show always goes on, no matter what the obstacles, and the meets of two hunts, the West Kent and the Old Surrey & Burstow, are to be found here each April. If the weather is nice you might consider getting a crowd together and renting a Derby open-top double decker bus to provide your own vantage point—the hire charge could be more than offset by the admission charge for one vehicle and with a driver you could really have a party to remember! There are usually large crowds to keep you company at this sharp, undulating course with its testing uphill finish.

No doubt the regular Point-to-Point racegoers in the Surrey stockbroker belt can afford several double decker buses to enjoy the fun at the Surrey Union meet at **Peper Harrow**. This lies three miles west of Goldalming, six miles south west of Guildford and west of the A8. Quite poor viewing again here, so the buses will be needed to allow decent views of the horses going round and round this flat, sharp course with its continual bends. The merry-go-round image for horse and rider may be apt, as this meet often attracts those more interested in party pursuits than in racing. The fine May bank holiday weather certainly does bring them out.

Just over the county boundary in Sussex are three courses that will perhaps appeal more to the serious Point-to-Point enthusiast, as all have good or even very good viewing. The Chiddingfold, Leconfield & Cowdray sounds like three hunts rolled into one, and if the number of people attending their annual fixture in March is anything to go by they certainly have a large crowd of supporters. Literally thousands flock to **Parham**, three miles south east of Pulborough adjacent to the A283, to see racing at this flat, galloping course which suits horses that can stay a distance. Another fixture at this popular venue is that put on by the Crawley & Horsham Hunt later in March.

Another Sussex course with very good viewing is to be found at **Heathfield**, one mile east of the town, adjacent to the A265. Here, amidst some beautiful countryside, the Southdown & Eridge hold two annual meetings, usually in late March and on Easter Monday. The course is a real test for horse and jockey as they attempt to negotiate the sometimes tight, twisting bends before the long climb to the finish. This course very definitely suits stayers.

Bexhill is a new addition to the Point to Point scene at this end of England Be sure to check the annual Point-to-Point calendar about the end of April so you won't miss the East Sussex & Romney Marsh Hunt fixture held here. The course is situated one-half mile north of the town at Buckholt Farm, Sidley just off the A269.

EAST ANGLIA

Although East Anglia is sometimes referred to as a forgotten bit of England, whoever coined the phrase certainly did not go to many Point-to-Point meetings! In the geography of the organising body, the Point-to-Point Association, this circuit actually covers courses in Cambridgeshire, Essex, Suffolk, Hertfordshire and Norfolk. With an abundance of courses and racing of the highest calibre, it is certainly not forgotten by racing enthusiasts. The season here runs from January to mid May.

One of the first off the mark are the Cambridgeshire Harriers who hold their meeting in January at **Cottenham**, five miles north of Cambridge, east of the B1049. There is very good viewing here from the bank and particularly from a grandstand, which attests to the fact that this was once an old National Hunt course. The racing surface is virtually flat and usually attracts very good quality fields. This is a very popular course and most fixtures are well attended. The Cambridge University Draghounds meet here in February, followed by the Fitzwilliam in March and the Cambridge University United Hunts Club in May.

Higham, seven miles north east of Colchester and west of the A12 is the venue for the Waveney Harriers' seasonal fixture in January. Not surprisingly, for this part of the country, the course is flat and suits horses that like to go into an early lead. With no hills from which to gain a vantage point the viewing is only fair and most find the centre of the course the best place from which to see. The season continues here with the North Norfolk Harriers in March. The Easton Harriers in March and the Essex & Suffolk in April.

A March fixture is to be found at **Ampton** in Suffolk, four miles north of Bury St Edmunds near the A134 where the Dunston Harriers hold races on this sharp, undulating course which suits stayers. The Suffolk Foxhounds also host their meeting here - usually in February.

Many swear that Cambridgeshire can feel the coldest place in Britain when the wind whips in from the Russian steppes so it is best to warm yourself both inside and out if you plan to visit the late January meeting of the Cambridgeshire Hunt at **Horseheath**, three miles east of Linton and adjacent to the A604. The viewing is quite good and the crowds can be large at this galloping course which suits stayers. As the season goes on the weather should warm up for the Point-to-Points of the Thurlow in late February and the Puckeridge in March.

Although it may not win any prizes for beauty, the Essex course at **Marks Tey** does have the advantage of being conveniently situated adjacent to the A12, five miles west of Colchester, one of Britain's oldest recorded towns. There is a bank here that offers good viewing of most of the course for those attending the Essex Farmers & Union meeting in February. The going is likely to be punishing at this time of the year, which adds to the test of stamina on this galloping course with its uphill finish. Things may be a bit easier underfoot later on when the Essex Farmers hold a return meeting at Easter. The East Essex also host a meeting here, usually in April.

Staying in Essex, there is also a meeting of the Hunt which is named after the county and which holds its

Point-to-Point at **High Easter**, off the A1060, nine miles north west of Chelmsford, usually around Easter. This venue is a relatively new addition but is quite an easy galloping course with good viewing.

Northaw in Hertfordshire holds the honour of being one of the closest Point-to-Point courses to London, if that bit of trivia may be claimed as a mark of distinction. No doubt, when racing was restarted here in the 1960s after a forty year hiatus it didn't feel as close as it does now. If you are venturing from the capital you will find it two miles north east of Potters Bar, off the B156. The course is gently undulating and the sometimes deep going in wet weather can prove a test for stayers. Developments at the course a few years ago improved the viewing of the races but the interests of the large crowds seem to be focused as much on imbibing as on the punting. The Enfield Chase Hunt usually meet here on the early May bank holiday.

About the same time of year, you could venture a bit further afield to attend the West Norfolk Foxhounds meeting which is held on its own course inside the National Hunt course at **Fakenham**, two miles south west of the town. There is excellent viewing here with all the benefits of the refreshment facilities and stands that a permanent racecourse has to offer. The course itself runs inside and out of the National Hunt course and may be a bit tight for some horses

SOUTH MIDLANDS AND SANDHURST

Those in the conurbations of Birmingham, Coventry and the Black Country find themselves conveniently close to some of the most competitive Point-to-Point racing Britain has to offer. For the touring visitor there are the added attractions of Oxford and Shakespeare country, and for those whose literary interests centre more on studying equine form than sonnets there is the added bonus of several National Hunt racecourses. This includes **Stratford**, which annually holds the Cup Final for Point-to-Point horse and rider, the prestigious Horse and Hound Champion Hunters' Steeplechase.

A delightful evening can be spent in the bucolic environs of Warwickshire if you plan to go to the meeting of the Warwickshire Hunt at **Ashorne**, four miles south of Warwick via the A41 and M40. The bank holiday in May should reasonably guarantee some fine weather at this leafy course which has very good viewing. The meet usually attracts some good horses from many other areas to provide competitive racing on a circuit that is slightly undulating with an uphill finish. One to be recommended.

One of the major meetings of the year is staged at the relatively new venue of **Barbary Castle** in Wiltshire, four miles south of Swindon and close to Wroughton, by the Point-to-Point Owners' and Riders' Club. There is excellent viewing at this galloping course and the

Artist: **Heather St Clair Davis** **TIMBER RACING** *Courtesy of:* **Frost & Reed**

Artist: **David Trundley HEYTHROP POINT** *Courtesy of:* **The Artist**

too busy trying to set new personal bests in a different kind of competition—drinking! (This does tend to be a boozy day out). Other, perhaps more sober chances to visit later in the season include April for the Bicester-with-Waddon Chase fixture, May for the Vale of Aylesbury followed by the Berks & Bucks Draghounds later in the month.

Older Oxonions may find themselves drawn to the toney atmosphere of the Heythrop Hunt's April mid-week meeting at **Heythrop**, which is on the A361 just two miles north east of Chipping Norton. Here there is good viewing of a long, gently undulating course that suits horses who lead from the front. For those who prefer to bypass the upwardly mobile set, another hunt meeting held at Heythrop is the Farmers' Bloodhounds scheduled for mid February.

fixture is a great way to kick off the season in January. You could return in March for the meetings put on by the Avon Vale Hunt or the Tedworth a few weeks later.

Tweseldown in Hampshire is the setting for a number of major Point-to-Point fixtures. The course is located three miles west of Aldershot, off the A325 and six miles from the M3. There are some excellent permanent facilities here, including a clubhouse—reminders of the fact that this was once a National Hunt course that was later taken over by the Army to hold its own races. The Army connection is now past, but two hunts hold their fixtures here including the Thames Valley Combined Hunts which open the season in January, followed by the Tweseldown Club in mid-February. As might be expected, the stand provides an excellent view of the finishing line but those who like to see the running of the entire race are better off moving about the hill in the middle of this undulating triangular course.

Another Hampshire course to visit lies at **Hackwood Park**, two miles south east of Basingstoke and east of the A339. Here you can see the Vine & Craven meet on Easter Monday and the Hampshire Hunt meeting a bit earlier in March. You might be better standing close to one of the jumps near the finish at this course as there are few places that offer a satisfactory vantage point. For competitors, however, negotiating this sharp, flat circuit offers a fair test of a horse's running and jumping abilities.

The Buckinghamshire course of **Kimble**, five miles south of Aylesbury on the B4009, is the home of the Vale of Aylesbury Hunt. Its fixture generally takes place over the Easter weekend. It is a flat course and is very popular. Offering good viewing, especially for those who arrive early.

You don't need a degree to attend the Oxford University Hunt Club meet in early February at **Kingston Blount** off the B4009, two miles north of the M40 at junction 6. There is good viewing from an incline above the finish of this up-hill-and-down-dale course. Undergraduates may not notice this as they may well be

Another meeting that draws the crowds is the Old Berkshire Easter Bank Holiday meeting at **Lockinge**, two miles south east of Wantage, adjacent to the B4494. Here the gradients are more pronounced than at Heythrop but there is a very short run-in after the last has been jumped. There is excellent viewing here.

Other courses in this vicinity include **Mollington**, five miles north of Banbury and adjacent to the A423. This galloping course with an uphill finish has excellent viewing and is home to the meeting of the Grafton in March and another meeting of the Bicester-with-Waddon Chase earlier that month. The South Midlands Area Hunt Club meet which is usually staged about the end of April.

Artist: **David Trundley MOLLINGTON** *Courtesy of:* **The Artist**

Gloucestershire holds the **Siddington** Point-to-Point course, two miles south east of Cirencester, west of the A419. This is a long-established location for racing and even though quite level it is a good test of stamina. Viewing is generally good for all the race—bar the finish, oddly enough. The Vale of White Horse meeting is usually held at about the end of March. A recent addition to the Point-to-Point scene in this part of the country is the new course at **Paxford**, situated between

Moreton-in-Marsh and Chipping Camden. Members of the North Cotswold Hunt host their annual fixture here on Easter Monday, one of the busiest weekends of the season.

Over in Northamptonshire the Oakley Hunt hosts its March meeting at **Newton Bromswold**, three miles south east of Rushden and east of the A6. The viewing is very good here and the undulating galloping course usually attracts a fair number of competitors.

Artist: **Refna Hamey THEY GAVE THEIR ALL**
Courtesy of: **The Artist**

MIDLANDS

The National Hunt course at **Market Rasen** is a popular venue for Point-to-Pointing in the Midlands. The course is built inside the racecourse and situated one mile east of the Lincolnshire town of the same name. This sharp, undulating course offers excellent viewing from the stands and all the refreshment facilities anyone could ask for. It is home to the meetings of the Lincolnshire United Hunts Club in early February, and the Burton a few weeks later

Thorpe Lodge, four miles south west of Newark on Trent, Nottinghamshire and near the A46, hosts the South Notts Hunt on Easter Monday. There is excellent viewing from a slope overlooking the finishing straight at this predominantly flat course that is a reasonable bet for both horse and rider.

Brocklesbury Park is conveniently located near the A18 just ten miles west of Grimsby and adjacent to the B1210. Here, the Brocklesbury hold their race meeting on this flat, parkland course usually at the end of February, followed by the South Wold in March. Viewing is good and the course has a slight uphill finish.

Another National Hunt course to hold popular fixtures is **Southwell**, one mile south west of the town, near the A6097. Here, the Blankney in March and the Grove & Rufford in late April set up their temporary racing homes and fences are placed inside the main course. As you might imagine, viewing is excellent from the stands of this sharp, flat course. Nearby, the much overlooked Southwell Cathedral is well worth a visit and you are not too far away from Nottingham and some of the oldest pubs in England.

Some of the busiest action in the Point-to-Point calendar takes place at the **Garthorpe** course in Leicestershire. It is situated about five miles east of Melton Mowbray, world famous for its pork pies, and adjacent to the B676. This is home to some of the best known fox hunts in the land, including the Belvoir which holds its meeting on a Sunday in late March, as

does the Cottesmore a few weeks before, the Quorn which meets in April and the Melton Hunt Club which has a late May fixture. The viewing is very good from almost anywhere around the course which is fairly flat.

Dingley in Northants, set off the A427, three miles east of Market Harborough is also the venue of a busy schedule of racing. Here the Harborough Hunt Club stage an end of season fixture in late May. The Woodland Pytchley in April and the Fernie in early May also hold their Point-to-Point fixtures here. The hillside parking provides a natural grandstand for excellent viewing and all the facilities are conveniently located close at hand. The course is virtually flat with a tight bend just before the uphill finish that can make the difference between winning and losing for many a horse and pilot.

Northants is also home to **Guilsborough**, ten miles north of Northampton, adjacent to the A50. This flat course with its sharp bends offers just fair viewing for the Pytchley fixture in April.

Yet another Midlands area course is found at **Clifton on Dunsmore** in Warwickshire. The Atherstone Hunt holds its meeting here in April and the course is located off the A5, just three miles east of Rugby. There is very good viewing of this galloping course which was built on the site of the old Rugby racecourse, providing a bit of nostalgia for those with long memories.

Artist: **Refna Hamey LOOSE TAILS & TIDY TAIL**
Courtesy of: **The Artist**

WEST MIDLANDS

Members of hunts with cash to buy the good horses usually produce some excellent Point-to-Point racing and no exception is the smart Beaufort Hunt which holds its meeting, usually in March, at **Didmarton**, off the A433, six miles south west of Tetbury in Gloucestershire. The fixture is well organised and the top of the range lines of four wheel chariots taking members and supporters there is a good testimonial to the health of their bank accounts! For those more interested in four legs than wheels, the viewing is very good at this undulating course with its downhill finish.

Staying in this area which hosts other classics of equine competition, Cheltenham and Badminton, we find the course at **Andoversford**, conveniently situated six miles south east of the home of National Hunt racing at the junction of the A40 and A436. Here the Cotswold Hunt have the benefit of longer days to hold their April fixture. Viewing may be described as fair for the undulating course with its uphill finish.

Maisemore Park by contrast has very good viewing for

the two meetings held here by the Ledbury, usually in early April, followed by the Cotswold Vale Farmers a few weeks later. The course is to be found two miles north west of Gloucester adjacent to the A417. It's a flat, reasonably sharp course with a short run-in to the finish.

A well frequented venue is to be found at **Chaddesley Corbett** in Hereford and Worcester, adjacent to the A448 and six miles west of Bromsgrove. Here the Harkaway Club host their meeting in February, followed later in the season by the Worcester Hunt and the **Albrighton Woodland** in late May. The usually fine weather brings out the crowds to these popular meetings and there are often big fields offering challenging punting. Although the viewing is excellent at this galloping course, it's best to arrive well in time to secure a good parking spot.

Artist: **Alison Wilson ALBRIGHTON** *Courtesy of:* **The Artist**

In March, **Upton-upon-Severn** is the setting for the meeting of the North Ledbury Hunt. The course also hosts the Croome and West Warwicks in April and is located five miles north of Tewkesbury, west of the A38. There are many good spots from which to view the racing either from the hill overlooking the finish or from the centre of the course. This is a flat, galloping course that suits stayers.

Another testing course is **Upper Sapey**, the venue for the March meeting of the Clifton on Teme Hunt. It is located six miles north of Bromyard and adjacent to the B4203. Being in Hereford and Worcester it's not surprisingly a hilly, undulating course with viewing that can be described as reasonable depending upon where you might be standing.

Back in Gloucestershire is **Woodford**, a mere fifteen miles north east of Bristol adjacent to the A38 and five miles from junction 14 of the M5. The Berkeley Foxhounds meeting is usually held here towards the end of April. The course is flat, built on a water meadow, and although spectators have the benefit of a hill from which to view, both horse and rider tend to disappear from view for a part of the race, making it hard to follow the one you have put your money on.

WELSH BORDER

Closer to the Welsh Borders in perhaps the most scenic part of Hereford & Worcester country is a

glorious Point-to-Point area of its own. You shouldn't really need an excuse to visit this delightful part of rural Britain, but if there is a local Point-to-Point being held so much the better.

For the brave at heart one of the earlier meets in the season is the North Herefordshire Hunt fixture at **Whitwick** a few miles east of Hereford near the A438.

It is just a short hop over to **Garnons**, seven miles west of Hereford, north of the A438, to visit the March racing fixtures of the Ross Harriers and the South Herefordshire Hunt. Like most in this area, Garnons is a pretty setting and there are generally good views of all parts of this undulating course.

Just over in Shropshire is **Bitterley**, home to the April fixture of the Ludlow Foxhounds. The course is situated north of the A4117, four miles north east of this picturesque and historic market town. You shouldn't need more of an excuse to visit than exploring Ludlow before or after racing, but the viewing is good on this virtually flat, sharp course with its slight incline towards the finish.

Not far away from Ludlow, ten miles west to be precise, is **Brampton Bryan** near the A4113 where the United Pack and the Teme Valley hold their April race meetings. The longer daylight hours towards the end of April allow the Teme Valley to hold their fixture as an evening meeting so even the latest sleepers have little excuse for not attending! Racing has been held on this course for many a year now and although the viewing is just fair, the scenery more than makes up for it. The course is flat and suits horses that like to go on at a good gallop.

In early May, the Radnor & West Herefordshire hold their meeting at **Cursneh Hill**, off the A44, one mile west of Leominster. A bank provides good viewing for this sharp, undulating course and the weather is usually kind to spectators, although not always to the horses as the ground can dry out to be very firm indeed.

Although you may be tempted by more literary pursuits when visiting the used book capital of the world in pretty Hay-on-Wye, why not get a bit of fresh air at the Point-to-Point fixture usually held in May at **Bredwardine**. This course is located seven miles east of the town near the B4352 and is the racing home of the romantically named Golden Valley Hunt. The flat, galloping course offers good viewing from your car on the hillside parking area and is set amidst some magnificent scenery. So put down that Dickens and go for it!

SOUTH AND WEST WALES

There is a long and busy season in the Welsh Point-to-Point world, running from February through to the end of May. Although it might help if you know a few words in Welsh, racing and punting are like music, something else Wales is famous for, and transcends language barriers.

The early season action often gets underway at **Erw Lon**, Dyfed, in West Wales, situated about ten miles north of Carmarthen near the B4459. Like most February fixtures, the Vale of Clettwr races begin early, about noon and it's best to wrap up in a few layers of clothing to accommodate the uncertain weather. The course itself unfortunately does not have very good viewing for spectators but moving around will at least keep you warm. The jockeys and horses are probably a bit better off on this flat, galloping course. Other fixtures held here are those of Carmarthenshire Hunt in March and of the Llandeilo Farmers later in the season in May.

Another West Wales course is found at **Lydstep**, three miles south west of Tenby off the A4139. Here there is excellent viewing of the the Pembrokeshire in late March, and the South Pembrokeshire on Easter Monday. This is a sharp, gently undulating course and the going is usually pretty kind to horses. As is generally the rule in Wales, the scenery here is quite beautiful, which no doubt also accounts for the course's popularity with visitors.

Popular evening meetings are held on the Welsh circuit late in the season at **Bassaleg** in Gwent. The course is conveniently located near the A468 a few miles north west of the M4, junction 28. Here the Ystrad Taf Fechan and the Tredegar Farmers are hosts in May.

The Brecon and Talybont usually have an early March fixture at **Llanfrynach**, off the B4558 and three miles south east of Brecon. A natural bank provides good viewing of this flat, twisting course which generally has testing conditions under foot and hoof.

A couple of fixtures are usually held each year at the Gwent course at **Howick**, two miles west of Chepstow near the B4235. The Llangibby get theirs underway in March, with the Curre following up in April. There is lots of room for parking the car at this popular venue and the viewing is good for most of the race, bar the most important place for the punter—the finishing line! Socialising holds better prospects as you are likely to find a warm welcome. The triangular layout suits horses which prefer a galloping course but are able to handle a sharp bend.

Other Welsh fixtures to be noted include the Tivyside meeting in February at **Pantyderi**, Dyfed, seven miles north east of Newcastle Emlyn and adjacent to the B4332. This is quite a recent addition to the Point-to-Point scene. The course is predominantly flat and there is good viewing. The Banwen Miners Foxhounds also host a fixture on the early May Bank Holiday Monday.

At **Llanvapley** in Gwent the Monmouthshire Hunt hold their annual March fixture. There is excellent viewing of the entire course, which is to be found four miles east of Abergavenny off the B4223. The scenery is pretty and the racing circuit itself is flat and twisting.

The Glamorgan Hunt meets for racing each year in April at the South Glamorgan course of **St Hilary**, two miles east of Cowbridge, south of the A48. Although horses and riders do tend to dissolve a bit into the distance here and it is best not to forget your field glasses, a hill provides a good view of all the action on this flat, sharp course.

Two fixtures are held at **Bonvilston** in South Glamorgan, west of Cardiff near the A48: the Pentyrch hold theirs about mid-April, while the Gelligaer Farmers wait until the weather warms up in May.

A relatively new course at Laleston is the home of the Llangeinor Hunt, which holds its meet here in late April. The Mid Glamorgan venue is signposted from the A4106, off the A48 and located about 2 miles west of Bridgend.

The Mendip Farmers have also found a new home for their end of March Fixture at **Ston Easton,** located just off the A37. This undulating, right-handed track offers views covering the entire course.

NORTH WESTERN

At **Whittington**, off the B6254 and two miles south of Kirkby Lonsdale, the Vale of Lune Harriers host their annual fixture, usually in early April. The viewing is excellent on this testing course and you won't lose much time moving from the refreshment facilities to place your bet with the bookies. Later in the month, the Holcombe Harriers hold their meeting at the same course.

Moving south, **Eyton-on-Severn** is the popular venue for a trio of Point-to-Point fixtures during the season. The Tanatside Hunt kicks off the action in March, and thereafter the South Shropshire in April and finally the North Shropshire Hunt in the merry month of May. This Shropshire course is located six miles south east of Shrewsbury, near the B4380. It's a big, basically galloping flat course next to the river Severn and offers the visitor good viewing from a hill. There is usually lots of entertainment for the whole family with a country carnival atmosphere.

In North Staffordshire, the Hunt of the same name holds its annual event in April at **Sandon**, four miles east of Stone off the A51, preceded by the Meynell & South Staffordshire Hunt which holds its meet in March. There is usually a large turnout of horses and riders to contest the races, offering quite a challenge to those more interested in punting than the scenery. For those trying to follow their selection in races with large fields, there is excellent viewing from an embankment, which may partly account for the course's popularity.

Back in Shropshire is **Weston Park**, six miles east of Telford south of the A5 and home to the February Point-to-Point meeting of the West Shropshire Draghounds, as well as hosting the Albrighton Foxhounds in May. It is a sharp, flat course built on old parkland and the viewing is best from the inside near the winning post. Not far away is the Ironbridge Gorge on the edge of Telford, so allow a little extra time for a visit.

Moving just over the county boundary in Cheshire, there are a number of Point-to-Point courses well worth attending. **Eaton Hall** is just four miles south of the historic city of Chester itself, just off the A483. Here, the Sir Watkins Williams-Wynn hold their meeting around March, preceded by the Flint & Denbigh in early March. Facilities for visiting families are good with lots of entertainment. It is a flat course with reasonable viewing which can be restricted if there is a large crowd. Car parking is on the tarmac of an old airfield runway.

The Cheshire meet around March at **Alpraham**, off the A51, three miles south east of Tarporley. Viewing is best from the centre of this course, which is mostly flat and suits stayers, especially when there has been a bit of rain.

The Cheshire Forest meet at **Tabley**, two miles west of Knutsford, five minutes from junction 19 of the M6. This meet, in the heart of the Manchester stockbroker belt, usually takes place in early April on the Sunday after the Grand National at Aintree. The perfect double for those with stamina to spare!

At **Flagg Moor**, the High Peak Harriers hold their mid-week meet in April. This Derbyshire course is situated near the A515, six miles south east of Buxton and its exposed location as the highest point to point course in Britain can prove quite a test for spectator and competitor alike in bad weather. It is well worth the effort though to stand on the bank and watch the horses take on this testing course with its uphill finish.

Perhaps we shouldn't be surprised at a Point-to-Point meeting taking place in what is more city than country, but who else but the progressive management at **Wolverhampton** racecourse would actually do it? They now have a full hand of virtually every type of horseracing conceivable, with flat racing on both turf and all-weather courses. The excellent facilities, located one mile north of the town off the A449, might just make you want to leave your Barbour and wellies in the car for the Wheatland Hunt meeting in balmy May. Parking in the centre of the course ensures at least some chance of a picnic atmosphere, but those who seek shelter could always do lunch in the 'panoramic' restaurant !

YORKSHIRE

Although they are actually located in the Cleveland Hills and County Durham, a number of Point-to-Points worthy of note share the area fixture lists with Point-to-Points of the Yorkshire circuit. Probably because of their proximity, many of the horses running here also find their way to racing fixtures in the North and Scotland. The Zetland and Old Raby Hunts share the facilities of **Witton Castle**, just off the A68, three miles west of Bishop Auckland. This flat, tight course is on a water meadow of the River Wear and circumnavigates a small lake and it is lots of fun watching the fishermen landing their catch while horses thunder past. The course has been known to lose its fences to winter floods carrying them down the river, but it's quite a sheltered spot and viewing is excellent from the hill rising from the valley. Racing takes place usually in February and the May bank holiday.

Mordon is easily found for those travelling north or south just near the A1(M) and a few miles south of Sedgefield Racecourse and home to the South Durham Hunt which usually hosts its annual fixture here in early March. It is pretty flat apart from a small rise at the far end which leaves jockeys and riders silhouetted against the sky before they turn the corner for home. The Hurworth Hunt holds its Point-to-Point fixture at the end of March at **Hutton Rudby**, about four miles west of Stokesley near the A19.

A new course has been built at **Stainton** which is only one mile south of Middlesbrough off the A19. Here the Cleveland Hunt holds its meeting in early April. A course on the edge of an industrial city, but if you look south you could be in the deepest countryside.

Another venue close to the A1 is to be found at the **Wetherby** National Hunt course. Here, the Badsworth and Bramham Moor Hunts hold their fixtures, in February and March. Pointing at a National Hunt course may not be the purist's cup of tea but the facilities are excellent and there is the benefit of viewing from the grandstand.

A tough test of stamina is brought to bear at the **Whitwell-on-the-Hill** course which is six miles south west of Malton, adjacent to the A64. The Middleton Hunt meets here, usually in April. They have worked hard to improve this galloping course over the years and the viewing is excellent. This is a great place from which to explore some of the local sights, including places such as Castle Howard and the North Yorkshire moors.

A little to the north, the Sinnington Hunt usually stage their meet in February at **Duncombe Park**, situated one mile south west of the picturesque village of Helmsley and set just off the Thirsk to Scarborough A170 road. Viewing is recommended from the centre of this undulating course with its long, uphill finish.

Also close by is **Easingwold**, where the York and Ainsty Hunt holds its annual meeting, usually in April, followed by the Bilsdale Hunt in May. The course is handy for York, with its famous Minster, the Shambles for shopping and town walls to walk along. The A19 will take you there and the course is 14 miles north west of the city itself. This almost flat course suits horses of limited stamina and the viewing is fairly good, with just part of the far side of the course out of sight.

The Bedale & West of Yore Hunt holds its racing at **Hornby Castle**, three miles south of Catterick and a few miles west of the A1. The meet usually takes place in April. This course suits stayers but the viewing is reputed to be not very good so don't say you haven't been warned!

The same does not hold for the exposed **Charm Park** at Wykeham, adjacent to the A170 and five miles south west of Scarborough. Viewing of the Derwent Hunt meeting in March and the Staintondale on the Easter Monday is excellent, but you are advised to wrap up warmly particularly if the weather is coming in from the North Sea. The course itself is flat and galloping and is a fair test for both horse and rider.

Just five miles northwest of Beverley, and west of the B1248, is **Dalton Park** where the Holderness Hunt holds its annual fixture, usually in March. The viewing is fairly good on this basically flat course which usually provides a test of stamina given the prevailing soft going at that time of year. Spectators are also advised to take a pair of wellies.

Although in Lancashire, **Gisburn** is the scene for the Pendle Forest & Craven Hunt's annual Point-to-Point meeting, usually held about the beginning of May. The course is located one mile south west of the town, off the A59. Although the course itself has a few qualities to recommend it for horse and rider, viewing is not very good and it can be difficult to actually get the car in and out of the course.

NORTHERN

Corbridge or 'Downhills' as it is known locally, is home to the fixtures of the Tynedale, Braes of Derwent and Border Hunts. Located just three miles north of this picturesque village with its Roman connections, the course slopes down into the broad Tyne Valley and offers excellent viewing as well as some superb scenery. Take the A68 from North or South, turning east about one mile along the B6318. This is the original road bisecting the country and built largely on the remains of Hadrian's Wall, so there's lots of local history to soak up too. Fixtures are usually held in March April and May.

The Haydon Hunt moved their fixture from Corbridge to **Hexham** racecourse a few years ago and built a new course inside the existing National Hunt track. They have literally weathered the storms of adversity and now have a course that tests the endurance of animal and rider to the limit. Spectators can soak up the magnificent views, while enjoying the permanent refreshment facilities of the National Hunt course. Some purists might think this is going a bit soft, but getting inside between races can be a relief from the location's notoriously fickle weather, no matter what the season. The course is situated just south of the town on Yarridge Heights and the fixture is usually now scheduled for late May, hopefully ensuring good going.

Tranwell, the home of the Morpeth Hunt Point-to-Point on Easter Monday, is situated on a rather exposed former aerodrome site, just off the B6524, a few miles from the market town of Morpeth and not far north of Newcastle upon Tyne. Viewing from a small rise in the middle of the course is fair, but the fixture is quite popular with Northumberland folk and urban Geordies alike. Take something warm to wear if the weather is coming in from the north east. The turf here is beautiful old grass that is kind to equine and human feet alike, so why not get out and walk the course before racing.

Just three miles east of Alnwick, seat of the Duke of Northumberland and just off the B1399 is **Ratheugh Farm** and the Point-to-Point course built on ducal land for use by the Percy, West Percy & Milvain, College Valley and North Northumberland Hunts. With three fixtures there is ample opportunity to sample the superb views stretching across the Northumberland plain to the North Sea while having a grandstand view of every fence jumped. Parking is on quite a steep slope just below the crest of an architectural folly mounted hill so have your handbrake tested beforehand and hold onto your drinks! Fixtures take place in January, February and April.

The historic border town of Kelso (A699) is always a delight to visit and the **Friars Haugh** Point-to-Point course is just a stone's throw across the Tweed from its market square, and is overlooked to the north by the Duke of Roxburghe's imposing yet romantic Floors Castle. The course is basically flat and galloping but there is a short, sharp climb halfway round that tests the mettle of the front runner. This is home to the Berwickshire, Jedforest and Duke of Buccleuch Hunt fixtures. Meetings are usually scheduled for February, and March.

It is only a short drive from Kelso to **Mosshouses**, four miles north of Melrose just west of the A68. This is a testing, galloping course which suits stayers. Home to the Lauderdale Hunt, the course is one of the highest in Britain and can lay on some fickle Border weather so you are best advised to take some waterproof clothing, even though the meet is usually held in May. Those beating a retreat to the car will not be disappointed though as viewing is very good indeed and on a fine day there's no real match for the scenery.

The **Lanark** course is one mile east of the town off the A73 on the site of the old Lanark racecourse. It replaced the old venue at Bogside racecourse for the Lanarkshire and Renfrewshire and Eglinton Hunts. Fixtures are usually held in February and March.

In deepest Fifeshire is **Balcormo Mains** which has the honour of being the most northerly Point-to-Point course in Britain, located three miles north east of Leven off the A915. This is home to the Fife Foxhounds and viewing is good on this undulating, galloping course which suits stayers who are good jumpers as well. Everyone's best advice seems to be to get there early to ensure the best vantage point from your car as the weather can be bracing. As you're not far from Perth's beautiful National Hunt course, why not do a bit of a recce of the town and see if you'd like to bide a wee while. Racing is usually held in April.

Back closer to the English border is **Lockerbie** Point-to-Point course situated two miles south west of the town near the A709. It would be a pity if you were hurtling along the newly upgraded A74 to or from Glasgow and neglected to visit this course's Sunday fixture put on by the Dumfriesshire in April. A small hill behind the parade ring helps the viewing on this basically square flat course with its tight bends. It may be worth your while to linger a bit in order to visit the town of Dumfries with its Rabbie Burns connections.

Cumbria and the English Lakeland country host two Point-to-Points. At **Dalston**, five miles south of Carlisle off the B5299, the Cumberland Farmers Foxhounds hold their annual fixture on an almost completely flat course. Viewing is excellent from a short, steep hill sloping down to the meadow. There is a country show atmosphere at this very popular event and the usually large fields in the maiden events produce some exciting racing, The meeting is held in March.

Further west of Carlisle on the A586 is a relatively new course at **Aspatria** where the Cumberland Hunt hold their annual meeting. It is a fine, compact course on two gently sloping fields with good viewing from the parking area. Apart from one short rise it is almost all downhill, producing some exciting finishes from the last fence to the winning post. Walk the course for views of the hills of English Lakeland to the south and the broad estuary of the Solway Firth to the North. The Cumberland meet is usually held in May.

*Artist: **Heather St Clair Davis** EASY WINNER Courtesy of: **Frost & Reed***

Under Starters Orders

Artist: **Heather St Clair Davis** *AT THE WATER* *Courtesy of:* **Frost & Reed**

The sheer spectacle and colour of seeing racehorses and jockeys close up, the bustling activity that surrounds the betting, the lively excitement of the race itself, the sociability of a day out in the open air with family, friends or business associates, and the opportunity to win yourself a few pounds—you can't beat being there, which is why nearly five million people go racing each year.

Like most things the more you know about what's going on, the more fun you'll get from a day at the races, and here we hope to increase your enjoyment by supplying some basic information about racegoing.

There are fifty-nine racecourses in Britain, staging two codes of horse racing, flat racing and jump racing, both of which take place all year round. Sixteen courses race only on the flat, twenty-four only over jumps, and nineteen under both codes, including racing on artificial surfaces at three All Weather tracks.

Flat Racing reaches its peak in the summer and autumn and features the five Classics: 2000 Guineas, 1000 Guineas (Newmarket), Oaks, Derby (Epsom) and St Leger (Doncaster) as well as a number of major meetings such as Royal Ascot featuring some of the world's most valuable thoroughbreds. However, cheering home one of the leading jockeys such as Frankie Dettori or Kieren Fallon at any of the many other flat meetings staged around the country can be equally exciting, particularly if they are riding your fancy!

Jump Racing, over steeplechase fences or hurdles, starts quietly during the summer months and reaches its climax with the Cheltenham National Hunt Festival in March and the Grand National at Aintree a few weeks later. Though on a different scale the smaller racecourses offer a distinct charm all of their own with many of them staging meetings that have a very strong local feel.

The variety of horse racing on offer in Britain is unparalleled anywhere in the world and the fifty-nine racecourses, each with its own particular character and atmosphere, offer a wide range of experiences and cater for all tastes and all pockets.

Every day's racing is a refreshing and exciting occasion, and a great horse or a famous race can transform the day into one of those magical occasions when you are grateful simply to be able to say, 'I was there.' And there's always the chance that you may go away richer than when you arrived.

What to wear and what to take

Do not be put off by images of top hats and exotic headgear at Royal Ascot: these days morning dress is required only in the Royal Enclosure at that meeting and in the Queen's Stand at Epsom on Derby Day. But at many courses there is a dress code for the Members' Enclosure which, for example, may require a man to wear a jacket and tie. Indeed, for some people dressing up is all part of the fun of going racing. If in doubt, do not hesitate to telephone the course for guidance.

The key to dressing for the races is not so much style as comfort: there's no point in looking terribly fashionable if you're freezing cold as the sun goes down. To enjoy a day's racing to the full may require a good deal of walking around, so give particular thought to your footwear.

You will probably want to take with you a newspaper for a list of the runners and expert guidance (possibly the trade paper, the Racing Post, which provides in-depth information), a pen or pencil to note your selections, and enough money to get you through the day! Some courses have banks which will cash you a cheque, and you can purchase Tote betting vouchers at any course by cheque or credit card.

If you take a camera you must disarm the flash, as flash photography can upset the horses (which will in turn upset many of your fellow racegoers). You will not normally be allowed to take food and drink (including alcohol) into the enclosures (unless picnicking in a Course Enclosure), but you will find a wide selection on sale inside. Catering varies dramatically from the sandwich/snack bar to full lunch facilities in more formal dining areas usually found in the Members' Enclosure.

Getting there and getting in

Most racecourses are well served by public transport, and some have railway stations within a very short walk. For drivers, many courses provide free parking (major meetings are sometimes an exception) and some have an area in a Course Enclosure where you can take your car and picnic while watching the racing. This offers first class value for those who just want a day out in the fresh air but the view of the finish is more often than not somewhat distant.

Bear in mind that race traffic approaching the big meetings can be heavy, so always allow yourself extra time on the major days: much better to arrive too early and spend half an hour in the bar studying the form (or studying other racegoers) than sit fuming in a jam while the second race is being run!

In any case, aim to arrive about an hour before the first race, to give yourself time to get to know the layout of the track and its facilities. Walking on the course itself, when allowed, is often fun and informative and you will be given plenty of warning to get back to safety before the horses start thundering down on you!

The 'action' will commence about half an hour before the advertised time of the first race, when the runners will be taken into the pre-parade ring or nearby boxes to be saddled up. For anyone new to the sport do try to find these boxes or the pre-parade ring - you often see horses at their most majestic and the bustle as trainer, lad and owner assess their charges is a fascinating sight.

Which enclosure to choose

Most racecourses are divided into several enclosures and you can pay for admission on the day.

Top of the range is the **Members'** or **Club Enclosure**, for the use of annual members of that course (like season ticket holders at a soccer ground) but usually available to non-members for a daily charge.

The cost varies depending on the course and the nature of the occasion—the average is around £12 to £15, but perhaps double that on the day of a very big race. For big meetings you can often book in advance (and for some it is wise to do so, you could receive a discount if booking before a certain date).

The Members' Enclosure—admittance to which is by a small cardboard badge which you should keep displayed—has the best viewing and the best facilities, and your badge allows you to take advantage of all the facilities in other enclosures, usually called **Tattersalls** or **Grandstand** and **Paddock** (and popularly known as 'Tatts'). Here, for an entrance charge in the region of £8 to £10 (higher at major meetings), you will have access to the parade ring and winner's enclosure (where the horses can be seen at close quarters) as well as a good view of the track and extensive catering, drinking and betting facilities. The presence of the bookies gives Tatts—usually the largest enclosure on the course—its characteristic hubbub and atmosphere. On the rail which divides Tatts from Members are to be found the 'rails bookmakers', who bet—mostly on credit—with some of the heavy hitters among the punting fraternity. If you are fascinated by the financial side of racing but would only bet in small sums, loiter here for a while - some of the figures will make your head spin!

The **Silver Ring** or **Course Enclosure** is the cheapest (around £3 to £5), at most courses having no access to the parade ring and winner's enclosure, but with betting and catering facilities. Cars are allowed in the Course Enclosure at some racecourses and picnicking is a very popular pastime.

The exact nature of the enclosures may differ from course to course and from meeting to meeting—for instance, some courses merge enclosures on particular days: if you need guidance telephone in advance. Children up to the age of sixteen are admitted free to most racecourses if accompanied by an adult (there are age restrictions in the Members Enclosure at some courses.) In general, facilities for small children have improved immensely over the last few years, with a crèche available on some courses and entertainments, such as bouncy castles, much in evidence on many Saturday, Sunday and Bank Holiday meetings. When compared with most other sporting or leisure pursuits racing stands almost alone in this and as a result provides really good value family entertainment.

At the other end of the age range, many courses offer concessions to senior citizens.

A day at the races is the ideal social occasion for clubs and other groups, and most courses offer party rates with a generous discount: for details contact the individual course, or Racecourse Communications on 01344 625912.

Understanding Your Racecard

Your basic tool for a successful and informed day at the races is the racecard, your programme for the day, available around the racecourse for a small charge. Do not buy a racecard from anyone other than official sellers. A man who wanders up to you in the car park and offers to sell you one will have 'marked your card' with tips, and will expect to be paid well over face value for his insights!

The amount of information in the racecard varies from course to course, but wherever you are racing you will find it an invaluable aid to your day.

At the head of each race listed in the racecard will be details for that event, including the prize money on offer, and it may be helpful to know the different

Artist: **Mike Heslop CHIEF SINGER - GOODWOOD**
Courtesy of: **The Artist**

categories of race:

In a **Conditions Race** (or **Weight-For-Age**) the horses carry specified weights according to such factors as age, sex, whether they have won before or the nature of the races they have won.

A **Handicap** is a contest in which the weight each horse is to carry is individually allotted by the official handicapper according to past performance, the theoretical object being to equalise the chances of all horses in the race. There are many other considerations, apart from the weight your horse must carry, not least

the going and the distance. A **Nursery** is a handicap for two-year-olds. A **Rated Stakes** on the flat or a **Limited Handicap** in jump racing is one in which the range of weights is kept narrow: this encourages the participation of high-class horses, who will not have to make large weight concessions to other runners.

Directly after a **Selling Race** the winner is offered at public auction—a highly interesting and often entertaining sight for racegoers.

Other types of race—such as **Claiming Race**, **Auction Race** or **Median Auction Race**—will often be explained in the individual race conditions printed in the card.

Over the jumps there are further variations, including:

Novices' Race hurdle or steeplechase, for horses which have not won a hurdle or chase respectively before 1st May of the previous season.

National Hunt Flat Race, popularly known as a 'bumper', in which prospective jumping horses race without the inconvenience of having to jump fences or hurdles;

Hunter Chases are for horses which have been regularly hunted and have graduated from Point to Point Racing.

Planning your agenda for the day

Most days at the races develop a rhythm which will probably consist of looking at the runners in the parade ring, choosing your fancy and going off to have a bet, watching the race from the stand or another vantage point, then going down to the winner's enclosure to watch the placed horses come back in. Then off to the parade ring again to assess the next race. Races are usually run half an hour—or a little longer—apart.Naturally, depending on the success of your horses you may choose to break this cycle with a well

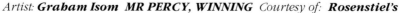

Artist: **Graham Isom MR PERCY, WINNING** *Courtesy of:* **Rosenstiel's**

earned visit to the bar.

The parade ring is one of the main features of any racecourse, and the people you see in the middle are owners, trainers, racecourse officials and stewards of the meeting. Five to ten minutes before the 'off time' the jockeys will appear, and shortly afterwards they will mount their horses and set off to the starting point of the race.

But it is fun to vary that rhythm. Try not to watch every race from the same position, however good it might be. Go down to the rails for a race or two and experience the thrill of a close finish—hooves pounding, whips cracking, jockeys pushing their mounts forward. Try to get to the start of a race—especially a flat race started from stalls, to witness at close hand the loading and the explosive moment when the gates crash open and the runners spring into their stride. At a jumping meeting, stand by a fence or hurdle as the field comes over to get the true flavour and spectacle of the sport.

Before the race, look at the runners in the pre-parade ring, where they will be led round before being saddled and taken off into the parade ring proper. Here you will get valuable clues about the well-being and attitude of the runners.

After the race, the winner and either two or three placed horses return to the winner's enclosure to be greeted by their trainers and usually by their delighted owners. The presentation of trophies and the auction of the winner (after a selling race) take place here.

Choosing your fancy

It is a common misconception that betting is an essential part of going racing. It is not, and racing enthusiasts can have a highly enjoyable day revelling in the atmosphere and spectacle without betting at all.

But most racegoers like at least to dabble in betting, however, and will have to decide which horse to bet on. Make the most of inspecting the horses in the paddock —this will provide the best clues and allow an advantage even the television cameras cannot always share.

A baffling amount of information in newspapers and form summaries in the racecard is available to illuminate —or confuse!—as you make your choice, but don't be shy of going back to the most basic starting point of all: looking at the horse.

In the paddock and going down

There is ample time, both in the pre-parade and parade ring, to indulge in 'paddock inspection' of each runner. Beyond general admiration for the magnificent sight of a well-turned out thoroughbred, what should you look for?

With horses, as with humans, beauty is in the eye of the beholder, and fitness in a horse is relatively easy to spot. Generally, the encouraging signs in a horse before the race are a coat with a good sheen to it, an intelligent and alert countenance, high head carriage with big ears pointing slightly inwards, a well-muscled body and a springy step.

A horse which is well muscled may be said to 'carry plenty of condition', whereas one with a lean and ribby look will have 'run up light'.

Be cautious of a horse sweating up but not necessarily dismissive, as some horses run better when they are on edge. Sweating around the eyes and ears is not a good sign.

Consider how the horse walks. An easy, loose stride is ideal, and a little jig-jogging suggests that he is on good

terms with himself whereas the horse that will not be led round calmly is nervous and wasting valuable energy.

Take account of the equipment the horse is wearing. Blinkers—a hood fitted over the horse's head to prevent backward vision focuses his concentration on what is going on ahead, and can transform the performance of a horse with a shoddy attention span. Pay particular attention to a horse who is wearing blinkers for the first time . . . as many experts suggest this is when the blinkers are at their most useful. A visor is similar to blinkers, but has a slit in each eye-shield to allow some lateral vision. It is commonly thought that the fitting of blinkers or a visor suggests an ungenuine horse, but this is not necessarily the case, so do not be put off if all the other factors appear to be in his favour.

Try to watch each horse cantering down to the start, and have a good look at his action. If he strides out well, in an easy, flowing motion, he is comfortable on the ground, whereas if he moves to post scratchily he is not happy with the surface—and is likely to be even more unhappy at galloping speed.

But the most beautiful and sweetly moving horse in the world is not much of a betting proposition if he cannot run fast enough, so at some point you need to get to grips with the basics of that mass of information which, once interpreted correctly, should yield the winner—form.

Form and what to look for

Form is simply information about a horse's past performances, and by amassing data from each past performance about the going, the course, weight carried, style of running, jockey, time the race took to run, distance of the race, distances between the horses at the finish, and so on, and then relating that information to the same information about every other runner in the race, the form student can supposedly work out which horse is most likely to win.

The study of every last nicety of form is highly complicated and hardly necessary for other than the most serious and dedicated punter, but you can grasp the basics by considering these broad headings:

Distance of the Race: Most horses have an ideal range of distances over which they run, and a horse running significantly out of that range may not do himself justice, through lack of stamina or lack of speed.

Going: The 'going' is the state of the ground—ranging from hard to heavy—and many horses run better on one particular surface than on others. It is not necessarily the case that the firm-ground specialist will never win on the soft, but the firm will suit him better. They say a good horse should be able to run on any ground.

Class: Form is relative, and running fifth in the Derby would be better-class form than winning a very minor race. Is the horse you fancy going up or down in class?

Time: Although horses do not race against the clock, the time of a race can be highly significant when measured against the standard for course and distance.

Course: The old theory of 'horses for courses'—that is, that some horses perform particularly well at certain courses—is borne out again and again; if a horse has won before at the course and the terrain suits him, then this can be an important indicator of his chance. This may often be because a track goes from left to right instead of the other way round which sometimes suits certain horses' style of racing.

Trainer and Jockey: Have they been among the

Artist: **John Atkins NECK & NECK**
Courtesy of: **The Artist**

winners recently, and are they in form? A trainer out of form may indicate sickness in the yard, while a jockey going through a purple patch can be guaranteed to have that extra ring of confidence which could make the difference between victory and defeat.

Weight: Has the horse a chance at the weights—that is, the weight it has to carry in relation to the weights carried by its rivals?

But if all this study of form is just too complicated, why not fall back on the age-old system of choosing your fancy by its name?

Backing your fancy

Having made your choice, how do you put your money on your selection?

Getting On: There are three ways of having a bet on a racecourse:
- on the Tote
- with a bookmaker
- in the racecourse betting shop

The **Tote**—whose selling points (identified by the Tote logo and by staff in red uniforms) are to be found in every enclosure, including Members'—operates on a pool basis, whereby all the money bet in a particular pool is shared out among the winners, once a standard percentage has been deducted. This percentage covers the Tote's operating costs and is also used to support racing in numerous ways. As a result if you're going to lose money it helps racing if you lost it with the Tote!

Artist: **John Atkins PADDOCK DETAIL, LEG UP**
Courtesy of: **The Artist**

That's the principle. The practice is very simple. You go up to one of the counters or kiosks, state the number (not the name) of the horse you wish to back, the nature and amount of the bet, and hand over your stake. You will be given a ticket which, if successful, you take back to any counter to exchange for your winnings (including stake). For Jackpot, Placepot, Quadpot, Trifecta and Multibet wagers you fill in a card and take that to the counter. Full instructions are on the back of the card.

The big difference between betting on the Tote and with a bookmaker is that at the moment of making your bet with the Tote you cannot know for sure what your return will be should your bet win, since the final amount in the pool (and thus the amount to be divided) cannot be known until the race has started and the pool has been closed. Television screens near the Tote counters will give an indication of the current odds of each horse, and by that means you will have a very good idea of the return that you can expect.

Principal bets with the Tote

Win: You bet on the horse to win the race.
Place: You bet on the horse to be placed first or second in races of five, six or seven runners; first, second or third in races of eight runners or more; first, second, third or fourth in handicaps of sixteen runners or more.
Each-Way: This bet on the Tote, as with a bookmaker, is two bets win and place.
Dual Forecast: In races of three or more runners, pick two horses to finish first and second (in either order).
Trifecta: Aim to select 1-2-3 in correct order. Operates on designated Trifecta.

[The Tote is the only way to bet for place only. Other methods ask you to bet each-way]

Artist: **John Atkins LOADING UP**
Courtesy of: **The Artist**

Jackpot: You pick the winners of the first six races at the designated Jackpot meeting.
Placepot: You pick horses to be placed in each of the first six races (or to win any race with fewer than five runners).
Quadpot: You pick a horse to be placed in each of the final four legs of the Placepot.
Multibet: Multiple bets—doubles, trebles, and so on. All Multibet selections must run at the same meeting.

The minimum bets on the Tote are as follows:
Win Only £2
Place Only £2
Each-way £2

So a '£2 each way' bet costs £4 because you're betting win and place. However, a £1 each-way bet is available in all Silver Ring and Course enclosures, and in other enclosures at some of the smaller courses. **Dual Forecast** £2: If you're selecting three or more horses the minimum unit stake goes down to £1. The cost of a £1

Dual Forecast works out like this: **3 horses £3, 4 horses £6, 5 horses £10**—and so on to the total number of runners.

Tote Trifecta, Jackpot, Placepot, Quadpot and **Multibet: £1**. However, permutations are accepted down to a minimum unit stake of 10 pence. For instance, two selections per race in a Placepot to a 10p unit costs £6.40 2x2x2x2x2x2=64 (@ 10p).

Artist: **Terence Gilbert CHELTENHAM 99**
Courtesy of: **The Artist**

The Tote dividend (or 'Tote return') is declared after the race—at the end of the day in the case of Jackpot, Placepot and Quadpot—to a £1 unit, including the stake. So if the winning Tote return is given as £9, that includes the stake of £1 and is the odds equivalent of 8-1.

A Tote Course-to-Course service is also available. This allows you to bet at any Tote point on races at both the 'home' course and any other track where racing is taking place at the same time.

Remember:
- with Tote betting, you will not know the exact amount of your winnings until after the race
- state the course, race number, stake and type of bet
- state the racecard number of the horse, not his name
- check the ticket before the race as mistakes cannot be rectified after the start
- you can collect your winnings at any Tote counter or kiosk
- if you forget to cash in a winning ticket, send it to the address on the back and you will receive a cheque by post

The Bookmakers
Betting with bookies, who are to be found in the Tattersalls/Grandstand and Paddock and Silver Ring/Course Enclosure, is very simple, but it's as well to be aware of the basic distinction between a bet to win and an each-way bet, which some, but not all, bookmakers will take.

A bet **To Win** means just that: if your horse wins, you do; it if doesn't, you don't; and if it dead-heats, you receive half what you would have received for an outright win.

An **Each-Way** bet is actually two separate bets. One to win, one for the horse to be placed (that is, to finish in the first two in races of five or more runners, the first three in races of eight or more runners, the first four in a handicap

of sixteen or more runners). Since an each-way bet is two bets, you hand over twice the unit stake: a bet of £1 each way costs £2. The odds for a place are normally one fifth the win odds—the bookmaker will advertise the fraction on his board, but some bookies offer one quarter the odds in handicaps.

So how do you make that bet? Go into the betting ring and shop around by looking at the boards on which the different bookmakers will be displaying the odds of each horse. Each bookmaker will advertise the minimum stake he will accept and his maximum payout, and you will soon find one happy to take even a very small bet. The boards usually display a minimum bet and type of bet the bookie with accept.

Say you want to have £5 to win on Dead Cert . . . most bookmakers have him marked up at 6-1, but one has him at 7-1, which seems to you to be a good price. Go up to that bookie and ask for 'a fiver to win on Dead Cert'. The bookmaker will call out to his clerk, poised with a ledger, '£35 to £5 Dead Cert', and will then announce the number on a small coloured card which he will give you.

This is your receipt for the transaction, and many punters like to make a note of the bet on the back of the card. Whether Dead Cert's officially returned Starting Price (SP) is longer or shorter than 7-1, your bet is made at that price—so by taking longer odds than SP you can 'beat the book'. Starting Price is the price at which the horse is returned in the betting shops. The great fun of this is finding a bookie who offers your horse at a more generous price.

When Dead Cert scoots home in front (as he certainly will!), return to the same bookmaker as soon as the course announcer has declared 'weighed in' to indicate

Artist: **Terence Gilbert DERBY 99**
Courtesy of: **The Artist**

that the result is confirmed, and you will receive £40—seven times five for your fiver at 7-1, plus your original stake back.

Among the many advantages of betting on-course with a bookmaker are that there is no betting tax to be paid as there is with off-course betting.

Remember:
- with the bookmaker always shop around and aim to 'beat the book' by backing a horse at longer odds than its official SP
- state the name of the horse, not the number
- always listen to the bet called by the bookmaker to

his clerk to ensure that he has understood you correctly
• always keep your card as a receipt
• never throw away what you might consider a losing bet until the 'weighed in' signal has been given
• no betting tax is levied on bets made at the racecourse.

Artist: **Katy Sodeau** *OUT IN THE COUNTRY*
Courtesy of: **The Artist**

The Racecourse Betting Shop

Betting in a racecourse betting shop is very similar to betting in any High Street shop. You can have a variety of bets including combination bets such as doubles and trebles at much smaller stakes than a bookmaker would appreciate. You can also bet at the day's other meetings. As in a High Street betting shop, you fill in a slip and hand it over together with your stake. The slip is receipted and you are given a duplicate, which you return to the counter for paying out should you be successful. Winnings are calculated at the Starting Price. A deduction—usually 6 per cent—is made from returns, this sum going towards racecourse improvements.

Remember:
• in the racecourse betting shop you can bet in smaller amounts than with a bookmaker
• the betting shop is the place to go for combination bets or wagers at the day's other meetings
• you'll pay a small deduction on any winnings
• in the shops run by high street bookmakers the bets can be collected in the high street shops.

In summary, betting is great fun but there are a few golden rules: never bet more than you can afford to lose, don't chase your losses and don't believe everything you hear—most of it is rubbish!

What to look for in the race

How you 'read' the race depends a great deal on whether or not you have a financial stake in its outcome. If you've backed one of the runners, you're likely to be keeping an eye on him all the way through the race, which may cause you to miss significant moves elsewhere in the field. On the other hand, that moment when you see your horse is starting his winning run adds exquisite spice to your day at the races!

One of the most telling factors in any race is pace. If the horses go too slowly early on, then speed up for a sprint finish, the form may turn out to be suspect, whereas a 'truly run' race, with the field going a good gallop all the way, is more reliable. A sprint race (five or six furlongs on the Flat) is likely to be run flat out from the start, while in a long-distance race the runners tend to gradually pick up speed in the later stages.

Look for horses coming 'off the pace' to make a challenge as the race heats up, and try to spot those who are running on towards the end of the race: even if they do not win this time, that can be encouraging for future prospects.

To be able to glean information about the future prospects of horses is one of the most fascinating aspects of watching a race live, and before long you'll be able to recognise the tell-tale signs for when you come racing again.

Needless to say racing is one sport which hugely benefits from your taking binoculars and, if you don't have your own, they are often available for daily hire at the racecourse.

Artist: **Katy Sodeau** *IN FRONT OF THE CROWDS*
Courtesy of: **The Artist**

A racing phrase book

Do not be put off by some of the strange terms you may hear on the racetrack. Like any traveller in a foreign country, the novice racegoer will soon pick up a smattering of the language, and then rapidly become fluent. The following might help those racegoers keen to enhance their language skills.

Accumulator - two or more selections in different races: winnings from one are placed on the next

Allowance is the weight concession the horse is given to compensate for its rider's inexperience

All Weather - flat racing which takes place on an artificial surface (All Weather tracks are found at Lingfield Park, Southwell and Wolverhampton - Dunstall Park).

Amateur (rider) on racecards, their names are prefixed by Mr, Mrs, Captain, etc. to indicate their amateur status

Ante-Post betting (usually on the most important races) days, weeks and even months before the race is due to take place

Apprentice - a young jockey tied by annually renewed contract to a licensed trainer while he or she is learning the business of race-riding. The amateur is given a weight allowance determined by the number of winners he or she has ridden.

Backward describes a horse which needs time to mature

Claimer a type of race in which horses can be claimed by others for a price; a claiming jockey is an apprentice

Clerk of the Course official in charge of all aspects of running the actual raceday

Colours the racing silks worn by the jockeys

Colt - a male, ungelded horse up to four years old

Conditional Jockey - the jumping equivalent of an apprentice

Connections - the owner(s) and trainer of a racehorse

Course Specialist - horse which tends to run well at a particular track

Dam - mother of a horse

Distance - the length of a race: 5 furlongs is the minimum and the 4½ miles of the Grand National the longest. Also, the margin by which a horse wins or is beaten by the horse in front: this ranges from a 'short head' to 'by a distance' (more than 30 lengths) a 'length' is measured from the horse's nose to the start of its tail

Distance, The - an unmarked point 240 yards from the winning post (thus 'below the distance' means closer home than that point)

Draw - for flat racing only, describes a horse's position in the starting stalls, drawn randomly the day before

Evens or Even Money - when your stake exactly equals your winnings—thus £5 at evens wins a further £5

Filly - female horse up to four years old

Foal - horse of either sex from the time of its birth until 1 January the following year

Furlong - 220 yards (one eighth of a mile)

Gelding - castrated horse

Going - the description of conditions underfoot on the racecourse. Official Jockey Club going reports progress as follows ' Heavy—soft—good to soft—good—good to firm—firm—hard

Green - (of a horse) inexperienced

Hand - unit of four inches in which a horse's height is measured, at the shoulder

Jolly - betting parlance for the favourite in a race—the horse with the shortest odds

Judge - the official responsible for declaring the finishing order of a race and the distances between the runners

Juvenile - two-year-old horse

Maiden - horse which has not won a race

Mare - female horse five years and over

Monkey - betting parlance for £500

Objection - complaint by one jockey against another regarding breach of rules during a race

Odds On - where the winnings are less than the stake (which is of course returned to you): thus a winning £2 bet at 2 to 1 on wins you £1

Off the Bit/Off the Bridle - describes a horse being pushed along by his jockey, losing contact with the bit in his mouth

On the Bit/On the Bridle - describes a horse going well within himself, still having a grip on the bit

Open Ditch - steeplechase fence with an artificial ditch on the take-off side

Over the Top - where a horse is said to have gone if he has passed his peak for the season

Pace - 'up with the pace' means close to the leaders; 'off the pace' means some way behind the leaders

Paddock - area of the racecourse incorporating the pre-parade ring, parade ring and winners enclosure

Pattern - the elite races, divided in Flat racing into Groups One, Two, Three and Listed, and in jumping into Grades One, Two and Three

Penalty - weight added to the allotted handicap weight of a horse which has won since the weights

were originally published

Photo Finish - electronic photographic device which determines minimal distances in a close finish

Plate - shoe worn by a horse for racing

Plater - horse which usually runs in selling races (selling 'plates')

Pony - betting parlance for £25

Rule 4 - betting rule covering deductions made from winning bets if a horse is withdrawn after the betting market has been formed but before the 'Under Starter's Orders' signal, the amount deducted depends on the price of the withdrawn horse

Run Free - describes a horse going too fast, usually early in the race, to allow it to settle

Schooled - trained to jump

Scope - the potential for physical development in a horse

Short Runner - a horse who barely stays, or doesn't stay, the minimum distance—five furlongs on the flat, two miles over jumps

Sire - father of a horse

Spread a Plate - when a racing plate or horseshoe becomes detached from an animal's hoof, this sometimes causes a delay while the horse is re-shod

Springer/Steamer - a horse which shortens dramatically in the betting

SP/Starting Price - the official price of a horse at which bets are settled in the betting shops

Stewards - the panel of men and women—usually a total of four—who are responsible for seeing that the Rules of Racing are adhered to.

Stewards' Enquiry - enquiry by the stewards into the running of a race

Tic-Tac - the bookmaker's method of relaying odds information on the racecourse, by means of hand signals

Under Starters Orders or **Under Orders** occurs when the race is off; an announcement that the horses are 'Under Starter's Orders—they're off' is made as the horses leave the stalls (or start in jump races): if a horse is withdrawn by the starter all bets are refunded

Walkover - a 'race' with only one runner

Weigh In/Weigh Out - weighing of jockey before and after a race to ensure that the correct weight has been carried! The announcement 'weighed in' signals that the result is official, and all bets can be settled

Yankee - a combination bet involving four selections in different races: six doubles, four trebles and one four-horse accumulator—eleven bets

Yearling - a horse of either sex from 1 January to 31 December of the year following its birth

Further information

For further information about going racing: fixtures, admission prices, group discounts, annual membership - please contact the individual courses or Racecourse Communications Limited, Winkfield Road, Ascot, Berkshire SL5 7HX tel: (01344) 625912; fax (01344) 627233. Racecourse Communications is a subsidiary of the Racecourse Association, the trade organisation representing the 59 racecourses in Great Britain.

Racing in Art
& Featured Artists

Artist: **Graham Isom** **ONE MAN** Courtesy of: **Rosenstiel's**

Sporting art is a peculiarly British field and, of all the areas of sporting art, none can match the equestrian world for the sheer range and quality of artwork produced. For over 350 years, British artists have been delighting followers of the turf with their attempts to portray on canvas the passion of the racecourse, the gallops and the stable yard and, even though racing in the twenty-first century has become a truly global pastime, it is still a field in which British artists lead the world.

Racing art thrives as an artistic theme because the sport provides all the attributes necessary for a really great picture. The power of the horses, the shimmer of the silks, the drama of the chase, the teeming of the crowds and the scent of victory all combine to bring to a good racing picture an unsurpassable sense of beauty and atmosphere.

Great artists from around the world have been inspired by the colour and intensity of equestrian life, including Degas, Manet and Dufy. Yet there can be no doubt that racing art in its current format owes more to its British founding fathers, and particularly to the inspirational quartet of Stubbs, Munnings and Herring Senior and Junior, than to anyone else. The story of racing art is very much the story of racing in Britain.

Francis Barlow, who thrived in the seventeenth century, is acknowledged to be the first great English sporting artist. Often called 'The Father of British Sporting Art', he was fortunate to flourish during the reign of Charles II, whose love of the turf promoted the increasing popularity of horseracing and the establishment of the national headquarters of racing at Newmarket.

The new sport was further boosted by the arrival in England at the turn of the eighteenth century of the Darley Arabian, the Godolphin Arabian and the Byerley Turk, the three great Arab stallions from which all thoroughbreds in the world can now be traced. With these strong new bloodlines, a succession of great horses to grab the attention of the public (as seen in John Beer's tribute "Fathers of the Turf") and the fact that Queen Anne and King George I continued to patronise Newmarket, racing rapidly became a sophisticated industry supported both by the established aristocracy and by the new rich.

Artist: **J Beer FATHERS OF THE TURF**
Courtesy of: **Rosenstiel's**

In its early format, racing was thus truly the 'Sport of Kings' and perhaps its very exclusivity was responsible for the proliferation of remarkable racing art in the eighteenth century. Patronised by monarchs and aristocrats, the links between wealth, power and the racecourse stimulated the demand for equestrian art of the finest quality. The walls of a gentleman's home were as likely to be covered with pictures of his great horses as they were of his wife and family and the thriving eighteenth century economy created an enormous new market of wealthy horse-lovers who were prepared to invest their profits in art.

Perhaps the greatest sporting artist of all flourished under this amiable eighteenth century regime. George Stubbs (1724-1806) made his name through his remarkable capacity to portray the anatomy, muscle structure and movement of the horse, a talent which he acquired after extensive travels to study the work of Renaissance Masters in Italy and his own learned researches in what he called his 'equine pathological laboratory' where dead horses were suspended from the ceiling for dissection. The result of his labours was perhaps the greatest book in racing literature, "The Anatomy of the Horse", which was published in 1766 and which changed the world of equestrian art for ever with its emphasis on precise anatomical detail.

Stubbs's enormous talents were soon recognised and he began a series of classic pictures for great patrons, mainly featuring relaxed friezes of mares and foals, hunters at grass and thoroughbreds out in the paddocks with their jockeys or stable lads.

Artist: **Stubbs ROSALETTA**
Courtesy of: **Rosenstiel's**

From the classic early portraits of great thoroughbreds by Stubbs and contemporaries like John Wootton and the Sartorius family, equestrian art was developed in the nineteenth century by artists keen also to capture wider perspectives of the sport. Although the traditional horse portrait continued to thrive, the bustle of the course, the shimmer of the jockeys, the hum of the spectators and the straining sinews of the race itself became the theme of many of the great equestrian artists of the early nineteenth century, including Ben Marshall, John Ferneley Sr, Henry Alken Sr and John Frederick Herring Sr.

Artist: **J F Herring Senior DONCASTER GOLD CUP 1838** *Courtesy of:* **Rosenstiel's**

Artist: **Henry Alken** *Engraved by:* **Thomas Sutherland EPSOM RUNNING** *Courtesy of:* **Rosenstiel's**

In the nineteenth century, engraved reproductions of great paintings also became increasingly popular since, in a time of economic strength, they allowed those who were newly well-off but who could not afford an original painting to hang a superb reproduction on their wall instead. A very high percentage of the market for engravings was centred particularly upon sporting and racing art and the trade in images of celebrated horses and the great races in which they ran grew to huge proportions at the enthusiastic demand of race-goers from all parts of society.

The introduction of the railway in Victorian times not only freed trainers from their local tracks and allowed them to take their great horses to meetings all around the country but also led to an increase in racecourse attendance, with the result that 'a day at the races' became as much a social event as a sporting one. Victorian artists like Isaac Cullin picked up on this trend with their studies of racecourse life in which the elegance of the surroundings and the eminent personalities of the time almost become more important than the horses.

Artist: **Isaac Cullin TATTERSALL'S**
Courtesy of: **Rosenstiel's**

Another major breakthrough in the world of racing art which occurred in the Victorian era was the publication in America in 1878 of photographs by Edward Muybridge which proved that racehorses never ran in

Artist: **Sir Alfred Munnings UNDER STARTER'S ORDERS** Courtesy of: **Rosenstiel's**

the famous 'rocking horse' style which had been a feature of all racing art up until that date. The rocking horse pose depicted by generations of artists showed the horse's front legs splayed forwards and back legs splayed backwards at the same time and can be seen clearly in JF Herring Sr's "The Doncaster Gold Cup of 1838". There was general amazement at Muybridge's discovery that horses never in fact ran in this way and his research, quickly taken up by prominent artists like Edgar Degas, changed the appearance of racing art forever.

The colossal impact of the Impressionists on the general art world at the turn of the twentieth century was not acknowledged by many equestrian artists, who continued to paint within the traditional conventions. There were some exceptions, including Sir John Lavery's equestrian work, but the real flowering of twentieth century racing art did not occur until Sir Alfred Munnings burst onto the scene, with his Impressionist emphasis on light and colour. The enormous success of Munnings's career is perhaps reflected in the fact that he was elected President of the Royal Academy in 1944, which was a considerable achievement not only because he came from a relatively humble background but also because the Academy had long been ambivalent towards those working in the unfashionable world of sporting art.

Munnings's work has influenced many of the equestrian artists of the late twentieth century. His best racecourse paintings were a riotous assembly of vigorous colours, vibrant jockeys' silks, atmospheric skies and straining horses and they transmit a discernible sense of the tension and thrill enjoyed by all true lovers of the turf.

And now, at the turn of a new century, we are fortunate to live in an age both in which racing art is valued and in which racing artists are thriving. The remarkable standards achieved by acclaimed contemporary equestrian artists like Susan Crawford, Claire Eva Burton, Graham Isom, Jay Kirkman and Peter Curling are reflected in the enormous demand for their original paintings, limited editions and fine art prints.

Susan Crawford's "We Three Kings", her much-loved tribute to Arkle, Red Rum and Desert Orchid, is now one of the world's best-selling prints of all time; an amazing achievement for a painter in what is essentially a niche market.

Artist: **Susan Crawford WE THREE KINGS**
Courtesy of: **Rosenstiel's**

Similarly, Peter Curling's magnificent limited edition print, entitled Istabraq, sold out within months of its publication in 1998 and raised an unbelievable £100,000 for leukaemia research in the process. Istabraq was signed by a great quartet from the racing world, including the horse's owner, JP McManus; his young trainer, Aidan O'Brien; his jockey, Charlie Swan and the artist, Peter Curling, and the addition of relevant celebrity signatures is a growing trend in the modern marketplace for racing art.

of this trend has been the enormous success of the pair of jockeys by the acclaimed equestrian artist, Jay Kirkman, which were published in the labour-intensive and hand-made limited edition silk-screen format earlier this year. Innovative, atmospheric and unique, "Jockey in Blue" and "Jockey in Gold" represent all that is best about racing art as we turn into the next century.

Artist: **Peter Curling ISTABRAQ** *Courtesy of:* **Rosenstiel's**

The print market for equestrian images continues to boom and this can only be a tribute both to the quality of the artists working in the field and to the continued support of racing owners and patrons who ensure that our leading racing artists are supplied with commissions stretching long into the future.

We are, however, witnessing a diversification in the market for racing art as so many of the big store groups are now selling framed pictures. In response, the best of the high street galleries are looking for ways to distinguish themselves and stand out from the crowd, which has led them into a general move towards more unusual and expensive art. An excellent example

Racing art has now been with us for over 300 years and its prospects have never looked more rosy. From the classic pictures of Stubbs and Herring to the more contemporary feel of the limited editions on offer from modern masters, there is truly something for anyone with a fascination for this Sport of Kings.

David Roe
Felix Rosenstiel's
Widow & Son

Artist: **Jay Kirkman JOCKEY IN BLUE**
Courtesy of: **Rosenstiel's**

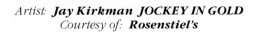

Artist: **Jay Kirkman JOCKEY IN GOLD**
Courtesy of: **Rosenstiel's**

ROBERT AINSWORTH

Robert Ainsworth was interested in art and drawing from an early age, in fact he first exhibited his work at the age of 12.

He now concentrates his artistic skills on painting equestrian, sporting and wildlife scenes. He exhibits in London and at regional game fairs and shows, painting in watercolour, acrylic and pastels.

DOROTHY AIRTH

After growing up in the Vale of York where there were plenty of horses to study, Dorothy Airth studied at York Art School. By dint of covering the exam papers with drawings of horses Dorothy received her Illustration Diploma with notable marks and went on to spend a year at Newcastle under Roger de Grey.

After moving to Lancashire, Dorothy was able to keep horses for the first time and this, together with the fine skies and landscapes, encouraged her to try her hand at racing scenes as well as undertaking commissions for portraits of horses.

Dorothy also paints and exhibits small oil paintings and country scenes in pastels. In addition to horses she also paints portraits of dogs and other animals. Commission prices on application.

JOHN ATKINS

John Atkins is a painter and sculptor of animals and sporting subjects but specialises in horses and racing. His works in oils, water colour and acrylic are in many private collections in the United Kingdom and abroad.

He prefers to work direct from life as far as possible, painting and drawing at meetings, finding inspiration in the colour, movement and atmosphere of the racing scene. Commission prices on application.

MARGARET BARRETT

Born in a house overlooking the Derby course at Epsom, Margaret Barrett cannot remember a time when she did not draw and paint horses. She holds a degree in Fine Art and her paintings have since been exhibited in London, Tokyo and New York. She won the Society of Equestrian Artists prize for best Oil Painting in an exhibition held at Christies. Her work is published as limited edition prints and also appears as book illustrations.

Her work shows a lifetime's love of horses and the countryside, but her speciality is in racing scenes. She responds to the power and grace of these magnificent animals by capturing a sense of movement that can almost be heard as well as seen!

Margaret accepts commissions for people, horses and racing scenes. Prices on application.

CLAIRE EVA BURTON

Claire Eva Burton has always been interested in horses and racing. She began by sketching horses at local point-to-points and this led to full-time study at Medway College of Art. On leaving college, Claire worked for trainers Mick Haines and Tommy Gosling at Epsom but after a nasty fall she decided to study horses from the ground. She attends many race meetings where she sketches scenes and later completes the paintings in her studio.

Claire has held many exhibitions in London and is kept busy with commissions, including one for 12 pictures to decorate the Queen Mother's Box at Cheltenham. Claire's work is extremely popular and many limited editions of her work have been published. Please see our print section for further details. Commission prices on application.

ROSEMARY COATES

Rosemary studied at the Ruskin School of Fine Art and Drawing in Oxford having been brought up in the heart of Berkshire where she spent her time with horses. Rosemary has worked on commissions for over ten years and specialises in equestrian field sports.

Her pictures sell in the USA and through sporting shops and the racecourses as well as through the National Horse Racing Museum in Newmarket. Commission prices on application.

PETER CURLING

Peter Curling was born in Waterford in Ireland in 1955, he ws educated in England and Florence and now lives permanently in Ireland.

He has been fascinated by horses since his earliest childhood and began to sketch and paint at his local stables whilst he was still at school. He later lived for a time in Newmarket, riding out with the eminent trainer Michael Stoute. Peter Curling rode his own horse, Caddy, to Victory at Limerick Junction in 1985.

His originals are now exhibited all over the world.

TERENCE GILBERT

Terence Gilbert's equestrian and sporting paintings are highly sought after. His knowledge of anatomy and draughtsmanship, together with his eye for colour and painting techniques have ensured that he is represented in collections all over the world.

Terence's career began as a freelance illustrator working for advertising campaigns, film companies, international magazines and leading publishers. In 1975, Terence exhibited paintings in the United States. This was so successful that he was given the opportunity to devote his time to fine art.

Through his London gallery connections, he has an enviable history of commissions including Ronald Reagan and Charlton Heston. Recent recognition has come from Buckingham Palace through a painting of Terence's being presented by Prince Charles to the Crown Prince of Saudi Arabia. Limited Edition Prints of his polo paintings are available on application.

BRIAN HALTON

Brian Halton is a sporting artist who teaches painting and sculpture to A level students. His main interest lies in racing and he has been painting commissions for some twenty years.

Brian spends much of his time working on commissions of all sporting themes such as greyhound racing, tennis, golf, football, cricket and boxing as well as all aspects of racing. Commissions include Sir Stanley Matthews, Denis Law, George Best, Nigel Benn and Prince Naseem.

He and his wife run a small gallery that has a strong equestrian theme and includes work by other artists. Commission prices on application.

REFNA HAMEY

Refna is no stranger to horses, a keen observer of all equine sports and a natural draughtswoman, her paintings show innate composition skills, firmness of touch and vitality of colour.

She is immensely capable of showing the moods and movements of her subjects and they are depicted from a great variety of angles.

Refna studied at Cambridge and Kingston Schools of Art. She trotted off to Newmarket regularly to paint from life. It was the painting of Mill Reef, which started the success story. This led to more commissions: Observe, Celtic Shot, Saxon Farm and Kibah Tictoc, to name a few.

Refna has had work accepted by the Royal Academy. Her most recent exhibition was at the Tryon and Swann Gallery.

PAUL HART

Paul Hart studied illustration at Medway College of Art and Design learning mainly figure work in a variety of mediums. After leaving college I worked as a freelance illustrator carrying out commissions for companies such as IPC magazines, Longmans Educational Books and Readers Digest.

His first equestrian paintings were of shire horses at ploughing matches and he has had some of them reproduced as greeting cards by Medici and Gordon Fraser. Since then he has concentrated mainly on horse racing subjects starting with a commission of Desert Orchid and more recently a commission for Sir Mark Prescott. Some examples of his work have been reproduced as limited edition prints.

MICHAEL HESLOP

Michael Heslop is one of the foremost sports artists in the world, having studied at Somerset College of Art and Design for four years, followed by a final year at Brighton College of Art and Design.

He has exhibited and won awards in England, America, Spain, Sweden, Switzerland and Australia, and is collected by many of the world's leading professional sportsmen and women. His career spans a period of some twenty-five years.

His commitment and intense love of the subject stems from his active participation in many sports, both as a competitor and a coach.

His work is meticulously researched and composed and is based on a sound technique and an interest in detail and atmosphere.

He now lives and works from Topsham, a picturesque village in Devon, having returned from a successful eighteen months as resident artist in Sweden. Michael now concentrates on sporting subject commissions and limited edition prints.

ELIZABETH HOWIE MCCRINDLE

Born in a country village in Ayrshire, Elizabeth has spent all her life painting and loving horses. After twenty four years in the textile industry she now works as a full time artist.

The bulk of her work consists of commissions but she has exhibited successfully in galleries throughout Scotland and south of the border.

Her paintings can be found in private collections throughout the UK, Northern Ireland, USA, Mexico, Canada, Germany, Zimbabwe and New Zealand. Prices start at £200 for a head study and £500 for a full study.

JACQUIE JONES

Jacquie Jones' responsive and enlightened style is a result of the incredible passion and confidence with which she paints, employing unnerving strokes of colour and joy in a variety of mediums. Her works range from the serene and tranquil, as seen in 'Salukis and Hawks', to the raw, energetic power of 'Racing Vigour'.

Jacquie's work is very much influenced by all cultures associated with the horse, especially that of the Arab world. The freedom that the horse enables man to enjoy is the primary focus of Jacquie's style and it is this freedom that she paints.

Alongside her special interest in racing and the racehorse, Jacquie portrays every aspect of the equine world, through equestrian sports into Arabian images, horse portraiture, hunting, eventing and dressage scenes. In addition Jacquie paints other countryside pursuits and is much influenced by her love of working dogs. This variety of subjects keeps her energy and artistic diversity at the highest possible level.

Jacquie is a Friend of the Equestrian Artists Society of England. She has illustrated three books, Racing Dreams, Ponies and Dreams and Badger Creek. Jacquie has previously exhibited in Newmarket and the United Arab Emirates. In 1997, Jacquie was appointed the first ever artist in residence to the National Horseracing Museum in Newmarket.

The main theme running through Jacquie's work is energy, movement, colour, joy and an intangible spirit.

DENNIS KIRTLEY

Dennis Kirtley, born in Sunderland, is entirely self-taught. Throughout his life he has nursed a passion for horses, in particular the English thoroughbred and his drawings and paintings of the noble animal are scattered worldwide. His patrons from the racing world are numerous and include the late Prince Aly Khan and the late Sir Victor Sassoon.

His subjects range from Derby winners Crepello and St Paddy in the fifties and sixties to champions Known Fact, Be my Guest and the brilliant Golden Fleece in more recent times. Dennis has exhibited at numerous galleries and in 1977 published a limited edition print entitled Lester showing the champion jockey surrounded by many of his greatest winners. Prices on application.

ELIZABETH KITSON

Elizabeth Kitson rode and taught riding from an early age, horses being a major part of her life. Later she started painting seriously, starting with military actions, then specialising in portraits of people and animals, particularly horses and dogs, in oils and pastels - always getting a good likeness - action, movement and light being her special interest. She works mainly for commission.

She has exhibited in London and the provinces. Commissions have included the 'Battle of Waterloo' which is now a limited edition print. Her pictures have sold in many different countries. She is a member of Society of Equestrian Artists and runs their Devon Art Workshop. She is also a member of the Society of the Armed Forces Art Society and the Army Art Society.

ASAD KURI MONTANA

Asad's interest in horses began at an early age when drawing cowboys and Indians. Since studying fine art in London, he has exhibited at the RHH summer exhibitions, and other galleries in Dubai and Canada, and he now teaches equestrian art in Salisbury.

His view is that painting horses is easy but capturing the movement and characteristics of each individual horse is the key point in equestrian art.

He attends some of the major horse shows and trials, but his main passion in life is British racing with all its beauty, colour, fullness and ups and downs.

Over the years he has painted for many breeders, owners and trainers in the UK, Dubai and Canada. Commission prices and other details are available on application.

JANE LAZENBY

Jane was born in Barnsley in 1969, and grew up horse mad, getting her first pony on her 13th birthday. She still competes in a variety of disciplines on her homebred mare.

She studied fine art at Newcastle, graduating in 1992, and was one of nine UK finalists to have their work chosen for exhibition in New York.

Jane spends the majority of her time working on commissions, specialising in equestrian portraits and scenes. She has exhibited in London with the Society of Equestrian Artists, and throughout Yorkshire.

She has work in private collections in New Zealand, Australia, the USA and across the UK. Commission prices on application.

BARRIE LINKLATER

Barrie Linklater specialises in equine and human portrait work and a broad range of equestrian paintings, particularly racing scenes.

He has spent his entire working life with pencil and brush, first as an illustrator in England then four years in Australia, returning to London to build a reputation for portrait and equestrian painting in the classical style, with commissions for HRH The Duke of Edinburgh, Sheik Ahmed-al-Maktoum, Lady Beaverbrook, York Race Committee and others. Twelve of his paintings now hang in the Royal Collection, and others in the USA, Canada, Holland, the Far East, Dubai and Australia. He has exhibited widely and is a long standing member of the Society of Equestrian Artists

HARRY MATTHEWS

Harry Matthews was born on Merseyside, the son of a corner shop bookie and is consequently a racing fanatic. A self-taught portrait painter and professional illustrator, his many qualifications include a fine art honours degree in print-making and colour theory.

A prize-winning artist he has exhibited at the Royal Academy, the Westminster Gallery and Mall Galleries, Goodwood House, Newmarket Racing Museum and many others worldwide. His work now hangs in the collections of royalty, well known international celebrities and most notably, other artists.

Acclaimed for his exceptional figure work, Harry has no set style but being a natural gambler will always seek to experiment. Commission prices on application.

ROY MILLER

ASEA, AAEA (American Academy of Equine Art) is one of the world's foremost equestrian artists, Roy Miller does not himself know why he developed his artistic speciality. He has said that he only knows that he has drawn and painted horses since a boy. "What I do know", he says, "is that initially my fascination was with the colours of the jockeys silks rather than the horses themselves. The old paddock was a bit dreary, but once the jockeys appeared it was transformed."

A native of Manchester, Roy Miller began work as a commercial artist at the age of 14. In the evenings he studied at the Regional College of Art in Manchester. In 1961 he moved to London and worked as a freelance illustrator. He has had many exhibitions including the R A

Summer Exhibition in 1961, but the turning point in his career came when, in 1972, he visited a racecourse. Within three years his talents for equestrian painting were recognised and acclaimed and he became a full-time equestrian artist.

The Queen is among those who have a Miller in their private collection and he has painted for owners, trainers and breeders worldwide. He has also been commissioned to design and paint the originals for the Lester Piggott gates at Epsom racecourse. Roy Miller has also successfully published many limited edition prints. Please see our print section for further details. Commission prices on application

KRISTINE NASON

Kristine Nason is an English artist whose talent has been passed down through generations of her family. Always entranced by the beauty of horses, she began accepting commissions for equestrian paintings by the age of fourteen.

In 1992, following a career in fine art publishing and design in which she forged a name for herself as an accomplished artist with work in collections all over the world, Kristine decided to concentrate once again on painting equestrian subjects.

She is rapidly building a reputation in this field for her sensitive interpretation of character, and skill in depicting the complicated anatomy of the horse. She also accepts commissions for portraits of people and dogs. Prices on application.

WILLIAM NEWTON

In 1987 following eight years as a professional National Hunt jockey, William Newton returned to his first passion of sculpture. Much of his work, and one of his greatest strengths, is in the portrait sculpture of animals, in particular horses.

Besides having taken part in numerous mixed exhibitions he has held two successful one man shows (1995 and 1997) both at Jonathan Cooper's Park Walk Gallery, London SW; the next being scheduled for June 2000.

He was responsible for sculpting the prestigious trophies for both the 1998 and 1999 Vodafone Derby and Oaks - Epsom Downs.

GILL PARKER

Gill cast her first bronze in 1983. An early association with the Sladmore Gallery led to her first one woman exhibition in November 1984. Successful exhibitions around

Britain and the United States followed, as have two more solo shows with the Sladmore Gallery.

A member of the Society of Equestrian Artists, Gill won the President's Medal at their annual show in 1993. Entirely self-taught, she has kept horses for many years and has an appreciation and knowledge of all aspects of the equestrian world. Gill has completed commissions of some of the greatest horses in the racing and eventing world including Dancing Brave, Rainbow Quest and Mrs Moss. Limited edition bronzes are available, commission prices on application.

K G PARKER-BARRATT

This artist started drawing at a very early age. Fascinated by the movement of a horse, he always enjoyed drawing and painting horses. He had no formal art education and was completely self taught. In his teens he started to take an interest in the life and works of Sir Alfred Munnings and has done extensive studies on this artist. Most of his work is done in acrylic and oils.

Two years ago he moved to Penzance, Cornwall. In the short time he has lived there he has taken an interest in the local race meetings and he is now in the process of completing two paintings of St Buryan races and the Penzance Mounts Bay race meetings.

KLAUS PHILIPP

After the war, Klaus Philipp returned to the farm from which he had been evacuated and spent the majority of his time looking after the horses and competing in many competitions successfully. He used to sketch the horses on the farm and paint commissions for friends to supplement his earnings.

Klaus later joined the mounted police where he became Captain in charge of a troop of 30 horses. He continued to paint and found that his love and feel for the horse helped him to portray the animal naturally. He left the police force in 1980 and became a full-time artist. His work is highly regarded and is found in many private collections all over the world. Commission prices on application.

PHILIPPA PORLEY

Philippa started riding and competing in the show ring from the age of two, thus beginning a lifelong interest in all equestrian disciplines. After gaining an honours degree in 1995, she decided to paint full time, with commissions now sold as far afield as Australia and America.

Philippa enjoys working with both pastels and oils and specialises in fine detail and true likenesses. The artist has painted British and Olympic team members in dressage, Showjumping and Eventing, Horse of the Year Show showing champions, and leading National Hunt horses Cool Dawn, French Holly and Addington Boy. Philippa loves the challenge of capturing each individual character. Commission prices on application.

MICHAEL ROBSON

Michael was born in Beverley in 1957, a stone's throw from the racecourse. He has been drawing and painting animals from an early age and has specialised in horses and racing scenes since turning professional in 1989. Michael spends a great deal of time working on commissions and will undertake any equestrian scene. Commission prices on application.

DIANE SARGEANT

Diane Sargeant's interest in horses began at an early age. A great love and respect of the horse was developed whilst working with them. She carried this passion with her and now, as an entirely self-taught artist, gains inspiration for her paintings by attending race meetings and point-to-points.

Diane enjoys working in a variety of media and, although her love for the horse provides the main impetus for her work, she also portrays many other subjects, including wildlife, for which she has won awards.

Her work is exhibited regularly in and around Leicestershire, and is held in high regard in private collections both abroad and in the UK. Commission prices on request.

PETER SMITH

Peter Smith was born in 1949 and has always been fascinated by horses. Having studied at the Carlisle and Glasgow Colleges of Art, he now lives near Ayr racecourse where he makes the preliminary sketches on which he bases his paintings. Originally influenced by Stubbs and Munnings, Peter's work now has a strength and directness that is completely his own. His mastery of colour and his unique ability to capture on canvas the speed and movement of steeplechase racing is his hallmark.

Frost and Reed have exhibited Peter Smith's paintings for some years in the United States and, as a

result, he has a large clientele there. Commission prices on application.

KATY SODEAU

Katy is a self-taught artist in her thirties. She originally trained and worked in architecture but became hooked on painting horses when she lived in Newmarket in the 1980s. Katy is still fascinated by the challenge of portraying the speed and excitement of horseracing in her painting.

Katy has now been working as a professional artist for four years. She has had successful solo shows in a variety of venues around East Anglia and has exhibited at the Society of Equestrian Artists. Katy has her own web site at www.katy.ndirect.co.uk

BRIAN STANLEY

Brian Stanley is a self-taught artist specialising in painting horses. He has undertaken many commissions including the famous Lloyds black horse. He exhibits locally and also in London and the Cotswolds. His paintings have sold in North America and throughout Europe and the United Kingdom.

He has won two blue ribbon awards at the Three Spires Art Show in Truro and has exhibited at the Society of Equestrian Artists. Commissions undertaken.

HEATHER ST CLAIR DAVIS

Born in the Cotswold Hills, Heather was brought up amid horses and art and, after graduating from Art College in Cheltenham, she moved to the United States, where she now lives on a farm in Vermont. Over the years she has established a distinguished reputation as a leading contemporary equine artist. Heather's outstanding ability as a painter of landscape and her professional knowledge of horses are fundamental to her success. She returns to England for her subjects: hunting scenes, racehorses exercising, the excitement of steeplechasing or flat racing, horses hacking home after a morning ride or quietly grazing in a sweeping Gloucestershire landscape. Her work is inspired, original and rewarding to own. Heather is a founder member of the American Academy of Equine Artists.

PHILIP TOON

An entirely self-taught artist who has been painting professionally for about seven years. His main interests lie with racehorses and racing scenes.

He has exhibited his work at Newbury and Warwick racecourses

and many galleries up and down the country. Philip undertakes many private commissions: mainly equine, but he also covers many other subjects. Commissions are undertaken and prices are available on request.

JONATHAN TROWELL

Was born in Durham in 1938. He studied at the Sunderland College of Art and won a scholarship to the Royal Academy Schools. He received the Landseer Silver Medal for Painting, the Bronze Medal for drawing and the Sir James Knott Travelling Scholarship which enabled him to work in Spain and North Africa.

He has exhibited at the Royal Academy Summer Exhibition, the Royal Society of Portrait Painters, Young Contemporaries and the Fine Art Society. His work features in many private and public collections including those of HRH The Prince of Wales, Culham College, Oxford—Newnham College, Cambridge—The Royal College of Art, the Imperial College, The Bank of Japan, BP, de Beers and CIBA-Geigy.

DAVID TRUNDLEY

David Trundley, born in 1949, was bred in Cambridgeshire. He grew up a keen sportsman reaching county standard at football, cricket, squash and athletics. Later, he moved to Taunton from where he paints racehorses with a passion. Most of his spare time is spent at racecourses gathering material for his paintings and the result is a delightful enthusiasm shining through his charming pictures.

David paints mostly in acrylic and adopts a fresh, impressionistic approach to his work. He exhibits at the Tryon Gallery, London. Commission prices on application.

MARTIN WILLIAMS

After gaining a BA(Hons) degree in graphic design, Martin Williams worked in the creative departments of several major advertising agencies in London.

Since painting his first equestrian subject 'by pure chance' ten years ago, his fine art career has developed rapidly. His work is now in the collections of many leading owners, trainers and jockeys around the world and he has been paid the ultimate compliment of having his work purchased by fellow artists and sculptors.

Martin's increasing reputation is based on an impressive use of colour and the ability to capture light, mood and atmosphere in a range of media. Although specialising in racing subjects, he is also an accomplished landscape and portrait painter.

Martin has recently exhibited in Tokyo but his work can be seen on a more regular basis at Equus in Newmarket and at the Osborne Studio Gallery in London. Commission prices on application.

ALISON RUTH WILSON

Alison studied Fine Art at the Slade School in London and then spent several years working in the theatre as a Scenic Artist. A commitment to the survival of the practice of Life Drawing as a discipline led her into teaching as a specialist lecturer. She continued to do this part time for a number of years until deciding to concentrate entirely on her own work.

The precise structural drawing and exacting technical standards which characterise her work make her particularly in demand for portrait commissions. She works primarily in oils, but also in pencil, pastel and silverpoint. Private commissions can be undertaken.

SUE WINGATE

Sue Wingate studied at three art colleges over a 7 year period and obtained an MA at the end of a three year course at the Royal College of Art.

Initially concentrating on large landscapes, Sue widened her subject matter in 1980 to include animal studies of all kinds and especially subjects from the equine world.

Sue has undertaken some prestigious commissions, including paint-

ings of horses such as Teenoso and Secreto (both Derby winners), Chief Singer, Never So Bold, Dancing Brave, Desert Orchid, Kalaglow, By the Way etc. In September 1990 Sue had a large exhibition in the Museum and Art Gallery, Doncaster. The painting entitled 'The Spirit Of The St Leger' was specially commissioned as a centrepiece and now forms part of the museum's permanent collection. Examples of Sue's work can be found in private collections all over the world.

Sue is a director of her own business called Field Galleries which markets reproductions of her paintings on quality greetings cards and prints. Please see our print section for further details. Commission prices on application.

Artist: **K G Parker Barratt A FALLER** _Courtesy of:_ **The Artist**

GLORIOUS GOODWOOD
by Harry Matthews   16" x 22"

POST HASTE
by Johnny Jonas   16" x 22"

NO RECALL
by John King   12" x 15"

AFTER THE RACE THAT NEVER WAS
by John King   9" x 12"

GLORIOUS GOODWOOD
by Sue Wingate   19" x 14"

RARIN TO GO
by Sue Wingate   19" x 14"

HEAD ON
by Jonathan Trowell   17" x 21"

THE FINAL BEND
by Constance Halford-Thompson   15" x 20"

WARREN HILL   20″ × 26″

THE DEVIL'S DYKE   20″ × 26″

ALL TO PLAY FOR   18” x 13”

THE HIGH STREET   20″ × 26″

THE JULY COURSE   20″ × 26″

GLORIOUS GOODWOOD 1901
by Terence Gilbert   15½" x 23½

SCENES OF NEWMARKET
by D. Trundley   24″ × 30″

STUDIES OF CHELTENHAM
by D. Trundley   24″ × 30″

GENEROUS
by Roy Miller   20" x 20"

ARKLE
by Roy Miller   15¼" x 17"

SHERGAR
by Roy Miller   12½" x 12½"

THE NATIONAL THAT NEVER WAS
by A J Dent   21" x 14"

STORMIN HOME
by A J Dent   21" x 14"

A CLASSIC FINISH (Silver
Patriarch and Benny the Dip)
by Sue Wingate   19" x 14"

VIKING FLAGSHIP
by Claire Eva Burton   18" x 25"

THE SPIRIT OF THE ST LEGER
by Sue Wingate   19" x 14"

THERE GOES YOUR SHIRT!
by Gilbert Holiday   11¼" x 19¼"

A POINT TO POINT
by Gilbert Holiday   14¾" x 17¾"

AT THE END OF THE RAINBOW
by Gilbert Holiday   12¼" x 19¼"

RETURNING TO PADDOCK
by Gilbert Holiday   12½" x 19¼"

GERANIUM WITH LILAC CAP
by Jonathan Trowell   17" x 20"

LAMMTARRA
by Roy Miller   17¹/₂" x 17"

INTO THE LEAD
by Margaret Barrett 12" x 10"

CHAMPIONS
by Roy Miller   15¹/₄" x 18¹/₄"

SHEER DELIGHT
by Margaret Barrett   9" x 12"

CHANTILLY
by Jonathan Trowell   20" x 16"

THE FINISH
by Mark Churms   12" x 8"

WEST TIP
by Mark Churms   8¹/₂" x 11¹/₂"

NORTHERN DANCER
by Ingo Koblischek   16" x 20"

SHERGAR
by Ingo Koblischek   16" x 20"

NIJINSKY
by Ingo Koblischek   16" x 20"

Print Order Form

Print	Artist	Size	Price incl.VAT	Edition Size	Qty.	Cost
Following prints are found on page 57						
We Three Kings	Susan Crawford	14" x 25"	£ 42.00	Open		
We Three Kings	Susan Crawford	7" x 12"	£ 17.00	Open		
The Snow Tunnel	Roy Miller	19" x 14"	£ 64.50	475		
Desert Orchid	Claire Burton	17" x 15"	£ 26.00	Open		
Sudden Blizzard	Roy Miller	12½" x 13"	£ 47.00	475		
Evergreen Champions	Roy Miller	17½" x 22"	£ 84.50	550		
Following prints are found on page 155						
Mud Sweat and Tears	Margaret Barrett	15" x 18"	£ 59.00	850		
Aldaniti In Retirement	Claire Burton	19" x 22"	£ 66.00	600		
All Out	C. Halford-Thompson	15" x 20"	£ 76.00	500		
Lammtarra/Pentire King	Mike Heslop	17¾" x 21¾"	£ 88.00	500		
Out of the Stalls	C. Halford-Thompson	12" x 16"	£ 45.00	500		
On The Beach, Laytown	C. Halford-Thompson	12" x 16"	£ 45.00	500		
Dancing Brave	Mike Heslop	13" x 24½"	£ 99.00	500		
Following prints are found on page 310						
Glorious Goodwood	Harry Matthews	16" x 22"	£ 55.00	500		
Post Haste	Johnny Jonas	16" x 22"	£ 55.00	500		
No Recall	John King	12" x 15"	£ 47.50	850		
After The Race That Never Was	John King	9" x 12"	£ 47.50	850		
Glorious Goodwood	Sue Wingate	19" x 14"	£ 75.00	500		
Rarin' to Go	Sue Wingate	19" x 14"	£ 75.00	500		
Following prints are found on page 311						
Head On	Jonathan Trowell	17" x 21"	£ 65.00	325		
The Final Bend	C. Halford-Thompson	15' x 20"	£ 65.00	500		
Warren Hill	Neil Cawthorne	20" x 26"	£ 65.00	850		
The Devil's Dyke	Neil Cawthorne	20" x 26"	£ 65.00	850		
All to Play For	Margaret Barrett	18" x 13"	£ 45.00	250		
Glorious Goodwood 1901	Terence Gilbert	15½" x 23½"	£ 58.00	500		
The High Street	Neil Cawthorne	20" x 26"	£ 65.00	850		
The July Course	Neil Cawthorne	20" x 26"	£ 65.00	850		
Scenes of Newmarket	D. Trundley	24" x 30"	£ 61.00	500		
Studies of Cheltenham	D. Trundley	24" x 30"	£ 61.00	500		
Following prints are found on page 312						
Generous	Roy Miller	20" x 20"	£ 85.00	550		
Arkle	Roy Miller	15¼" x 17"	£ 78.00	850		
Shergar	Roy Miller	12½" x 12½"	£ 40.00	850		
The National That Never Was	A J Dent	21" x 14"	£ 65.00	480		
Stormin' Home	A J Dent	21" x 14"	£ 69.00	480		
A Classic Finish	Sue Wingate	19" x 14"	£ 80.00	500		
Viking Flagship	Claire Eva Burton	18" x 25"	£ 82.50	495		
Spirit of the St Leger	Sue Wingate	29" x 19½"	£ 75.00	575		
There Goes Your Shirt	Gilbert Holiday	11¼" x 19¼"	£ 65.00	500		
At the End of the Rainbow	Gilbert Holiday	12½" x 19¼"	£ 65.00	500		
				Sub-total		

Prints illustrated on pages 57, 155, 310, 311, 312 and 313.

Print	Artist	Size	Price incl. VAT	Edition Size	Qty	Cost
A Point to Point	Gilbert Holiday	14¾" x 17¾"	£ 65.00	500		
Returning to Paddock	Gilbert Holiday	12½" x 19¼"	£ 65.00	500		
Following prints are found on page 313						
Geranium with Lilac Cap	Jonathan Trowell	17" x 20"	£ 76.50	350		
Lammtarra	Roy Miller	17" x 17½"	£ 76.50	450		
Into the Lead	Margaret Barrett	12" x 10"	£ 41.50	850		
Champions	Roy Miller	15¼" x 18¼"	£ 68.50	500		
Sheer Delight	Margaret Barrett	9" x 12"	£ 35.50	850		
Chantilly	Jonathan Trowell	20" x 16"	£ 88.50	275		
The Finish	Mark Churms	12" x 8"	£ 25.00	1000		
West Tip	Mark Churms	8½" x 11½"	on application	1000		
Northern Dancer	Ingo Koblischek	20" x 16"	£ 99.00	400		
Shergar	Ingo Koblischek	20" x 16"	£ 99.00	1000		
Nijinsky	Ingo Koblischek	20" x 16"	£ 99.00	500		
The Racecourses of Britain	Rosemary Coates	16" x 20"	£ 25.00	Open		
Point-to-Pointing in Britain	Rosemary Coates	16" x 20"	£ 25.00	Open		
Postage & Packing						**£5.00**
					Total	

All prints are individually signed. limited edition unless otherwise stated.

I enclose a cheque for the sum of £_____ payable to Kensington West Productions Ltd.

Please debit my Access / Visa / Amex / Diners card by the sum of £_____

No. ☐☐☐☐☐☐☐☐☐☐☐☐☐☐☐☐

Name _____

Address _____

_____**Tel. No** _____

All orders should be sent to:
Kensington West Productions Ltd, 5 Cattle Market, Hexham, Northumberland, NE46 1NJ
Alternatively telephone your order on (01434) 609933

_____ *Book Order Form* _____

Title	Hardback	Qty.	Softback	Qty.
The Spirit of Racing	£16.99			
The Tote Guide to Horse Racing	£ 6.99		£ 4.99	
Following the Fairways 12th edition	£18.99		£14.99	
Fishing Forays 4th edition	£17.99			
The Spirit of Football	£14.99			
Ports of Call	£18.99		£14.99	
The Spirit of Cricket	£16.99			
The Spirit of Rugby	£16.99			
Icons of Sport	£16.99			

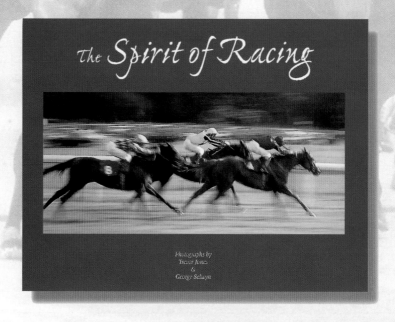

New Telephone Code Details

Telephone Number Changes April 22nd 2000

From 22nd April 2000 you will no longer be able to dial certain codes for some areas in England and all codes in Northern Ireland. Codes in London, Cardiff, Coventry, Portsmouth, Southampton and Northern Ireland will begin with 02, while all local numbers will become eight-digit. You can use the new codes now so it's probably a good idea to get used to the changes before April.

London

The dialling code for the whole of London will be (020), folllowed by an eight-digit local number. For example
(0171) 123 4567 will become (020) 7123 4567
(0181) 123 4567 will become (020) 8123 4567

Cardiff

The dialling code will be (029), followed by an eight-digit local number, so (01222) 123456 will become (029) 2012 3456

Coventry

The dialling code will be (024), followed by an eight-digit local number, starting with 76, so (01203) 123456 will become (024) 7612 3456

Portsmouth

The dialling code will be (023), followed by an eight-digit local number, starting with 92, so (01705) 123456 will become (023) 9212 3456

Southampton

The dialling code will be (023), followed by an eight-digit local number, starting with 80, so (01703) 123456 will become (023) 8012 3456

Northern Ireland

The dialling code for Northern Ireland will be (028), followed by an eight-digit local number. For example
(01232) 123456 will become (028) 9012 3456
(012477) 123456 will become (028) 4271 2345

Artist: **Heather St Clair Davis EVENING IN THE RAIN** *Courtesy of:* **Frost & Reed**

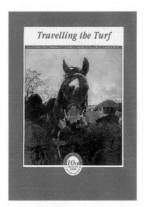

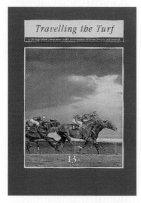

Artist: **Peter Curling A WINTER SCENE** *Courtesy of:* **The Artist**